Strategic management and organisational dynamics

PEARSON

We work with leading authors to develop the strongest educational materials in business and management bringing cutting-edge thinking and best learning practice to a global market.

Under a range of well-known imprints, including Financial Times Prentice Hall, we craft high-quality print and electronic publications which help readers to understand and apply their content, whether studying or at work.

To find out more about the complete range of our publishing, please visit us on the World Wide Web at: www.pearsoned.co.uk.

Strategic management and organisational dynamics

The challenge of complexity to ways of thinking about organisations

Sixth Edition

Ralph D. Stacey

**Financial Times
Prentice Hall**
is an imprint of

Harlow, England • London • New York • Boston • San Francisco • Toronto
Sydney • Tokyo • Singapore • Hong Kong • Seoul • Taipei • New Delhi
Cape Town • Madrid • Mexico City • Amsterdam • Munich • Paris • Milan

Pearson Education Limited
Edinburgh Gate
Harlow
Essex CM20 2JE
England

and Associated Companies throughout the world

Visit us on the World Wide Web at:
www.pearsoned.co.uk

First published under the Pitman Publishing imprint 1993
Second edition published 1996
Third edition published 2000
Fourth edition published 2003
Fifth edition published 2007
Sixth edition published 2011

ISBN 978-0-273-72559-6

British Library Cataloguing-in-Publication Data
A catalogue record for this book is available from the British Library

Library of Congress Cataloging-in-Publication Data
Stacey, Ralph D.
  Strategic management and organisational dynamics : the challenge of complexity to ways of thinking about organisations / Ralph D. Stacey. – 6th ed.
    p. cm.
  ISBN 978-0-273-72559-6 (pbk.)
  1. Strategic planning. 2. Organizational behavior. I. Title.
  HD30.28.S663 2011
  658.4′012–dc22

2010029934

10 9 8 7 6 5 4
15 14 13

Typeset in 10/12.5pt Sabon by 35
Printed by Ashford Colour Press Ltd., Gosport

To the memory of my mother Auriel

Brief contents

List of boxes   xv
List of tables   xvi
Preface   xvii

1   Strategic management in perspective: a step in the professionalisation
    of management   2

2   Thinking about strategy and organisational change: the implicit
    assumptions distinguishing one theory from another   26

Part 1   Systemic ways of thinking about strategy and organisational dynamics

3   The origins of systems thinking in the Age of Reason   46

4   Thinking in terms of strategic choice: cybernetic systems,
    cognitivist and humanistic psychology   64

5   Thinking in terms of organisational learning and knowledge
    creation: systems dynamics, cognitivist, humanistic and
    constructivist psychology   98

6   Thinking in terms of organisational psychodynamics: open systems
    and psychoanalytic perspectives   126

7   Thinking about strategy process from a systemic perspective:
    using a process to control a process   148

8   A review of systemic ways of thinking about strategy and
    organisational dynamics: key challenges for alternative
    ways of thinking   172

9   Extending and challenging the dominant discourse on organisations:
    thinking about participation and practice   198

Part 2   The challenge of complexity to ways of thinking

10   The complexity sciences: the sciences of uncertainty   234

11   Systemic applications of complexity sciences to organisations:
restating the dominant discourse   262

Part 3   Complex responsive processes as a way of thinking about strategy and organisational dynamics

12   Responsive processes thinking: the interplay of intentions   296

13   The emergence of organisational strategy in local communicative
interaction: complex responsive processes of conversation   328

14   The link between the local communicative interaction of strategising
and the population-wide patterns of strategy   350

15   The emergence of organisational strategy in local communicative
interaction: complex responsive processes of ideology and
power relating   374

16   Different modes of articulating patterns of interaction emerging
across organisations: strategy narratives and models   398

17   Complex responsive processes of strategising: acting locally on
the basis of global goals, visions, expectations and intentions for
the 'whole' organisation over the 'long-term future'   434

18   Complex responsive processes: implications for thinking about
organisational dynamics and strategy   464

References   496

Index   521

Contents

List of boxes		xv
List of tables		xvi
Preface		xvii

1 Strategic management in perspective: a step in the professionalisation of management — 2

1.1	Introduction	2
1.2	The origins of modern concepts of strategic management: the new role of leader	6
1.3	Ways of thinking: stable global structures and fluid local interactions	15
1.4	Outline of the book	20
	Further reading	25
	Questions to aid further reflection	25

2 Thinking about strategy and organisational change: the implicit assumptions distinguishing one theory from another — 26

2.1	Introduction	26
2.2	The phenomena of interest: dynamic human organisations	27
2.3	Making sense of the phenomena: realism, relativism and idealism	31
2.4	Four questions to ask in comparing theories of organisational strategy and change	36
	Further reading	38
	Questions to aid further reflection	38

Part 1 Systemic ways of thinking about strategy and organisational dynamics

3 The origins of systems thinking in the Age of Reason — 46

3.1	Introduction	47
3.2	The Scientific Revolution and rational objectivity	48
3.3	The eighteenth-century German philosopher Immanuel Kant: natural systems and autonomous individuals	50

3.4   Systems thinking in the twentieth century: the notion of
        human systems   54
3.5   Thinking about organisations and their management: science
        and systems thinking   56
3.6   How systems thinking deals with the four questions   60
3.7   Summary   61
        Further reading   61
        Questions to aid further reflection   62

4   Thinking in terms of strategic choice: cybernetic systems,
    cognitivist and humanistic psychology   64

4.1   Introduction   65
4.2   Cybernetic systems: importing the engineer's idea of self-regulation
        and control into understanding human activity   66
4.3   Formulating and implementing long-term strategic plans   72
4.4   Cognitivist and humanistic psychology: the rational and the
        emotional individual   80
4.5   Leadership and the role of groups   84
4.6   Key debates   85
4.7   How strategic choice theory deals with the four key questions   89
4.8   Summary   94
        Further reading   96
        Questions to aid further reflection   96

5   Thinking in terms of organisational learning and knowledge
    creation: systems dynamics, cognitivist, humanistic and
    constructivist psychology   98

5.1   Introduction   99
5.2   Systems dynamics: nonlinearity and positive feedback   100
5.3   Personal mastery and mental models: cognitivist psychology   103
5.4   Building a shared vision and team learning: humanistic psychology   110
5.5   The impact of vested interests on organisational learning   114
5.6   Knowledge management: cognitivist and constructivist psychology   116
5.7   Key debates   118
5.8   How learning organisation theory deals with the four key questions   120
5.9   Summary   123
        Further reading   124
        Questions to aid further reflection   124

6   Thinking in terms of organisational psychodynamics: open systems
    and psychoanalytic perspectives   126

6.1   Introduction   127
6.2   Open systems theory   127
6.3   Psychoanalysis and unconscious processes   130
6.4   Open systems and unconscious processes   135

6.5   Leaders and groups   138
6.6   How open systems/psychoanalytic perspectives deal with the
       four key questions   141
6.7   Summary   145
       Further reading   146
       Questions to aid further reflection   146

7   Thinking about strategy process from a systemic perspective:
    using a process to control a process   148

7.1   Introduction   149
7.2   Rational process and its critics: bounded rationality   149
7.3   Rational process and its critics: trial-and-error action   152
7.4   A contingency view of process   156
7.5   Institutions, routines and cognitive frames   157
7.6   Process and time   159
7.7   Strategy process: a review   161
7.8   The activity-based view   162
7.9   The systemic way of thinking about process and practice   166
7.10   Summary   170
       Further reading   171
       Questions to aid further reflection   171

8   A review of systemic ways of thinking about strategy and
    organisational dynamics: key challenges for alternative
    ways of thinking   172

8.1   Introduction   173
8.2   The claim that there is a science of organisation and management 174
8.3   The polarisation of intention and emergence   184
8.4   The belief that organisations are systems in the world or in the mind 187
8.5   Conflict and diversity   191
8.6   Summary and key questions to be dealt with in Parts 2 and 3
       of this book   195
       Further reading   196
       Questions to aid further reflection   196

9   Extending and challenging the dominant discourse on
    organisations: thinking about participation and practice   198

9.1   Introduction   199
9.2   Second-order systems thinking   201
9.3   Social constructionist approaches   212
9.4   Communities of practice   217
9.5   Unpredictability and strategy without design   220
9.6   Critical management studies / labour process theory   223
9.7   Summary   224
       Further reading   224
       Questions to aid further reflection   225

Part 2   The challenge of complexity to ways of thinking

10   The complexity sciences: the sciences of uncertainty   234

   10.1   Introduction   235
   10.2   Mathematical chaos theory   237
   10.3   The theory of dissipative structures   240
   10.4   Complex adaptive systems   244
   10.5   Different interpretations of complexity   253
   10.6   Summary   259
         Further reading   260
         Questions to aid further reflection   260

11   Systemic applications of complexity sciences to organisations: restating the dominant discourse   262

   11.1   Introduction   262
   11.2   Modelling industries as complex systems   263
   11.3   Understanding organisations as complex systems   271
   11.4   How systemic applications of complexity sciences deal with the four key questions   284
   11.5   Summary   286
         Further reading   287
         Questions to aid further reflection   287

Part 3   Complex responsive processes as a way of thinking about strategy and organisational dynamics

12   Responsive processes thinking: the interplay of intentions   296

   12.1   Introduction   297
   12.2   Responsive processes thinking   299
   12.3   Chaos, complexity and analogy   310
   12.4   Time and responsive processes   318
   12.5   The differences between systemic process and responsive processes thinking   320
   12.6   Summary   323
         Further reading   326
         Questions to aid further reflection   326

13   The emergence of organisational strategy in local communicative interaction: complex responsive processes of conversation   328

   13.1   Introduction   330
   13.2   Human communication and the conversation of gestures: the social act   331

13.3   Ordinary conversation in organisations   337
13.4   The dynamics of conversation   344
13.5   Leaders and the activities of strategising   346
13.6   Summary   347
       Further reading   348
       Questions to aid further reflection   348

14   The link between the local communicative interaction of
     strategising and the population-wide patterns of strategy   350

14.1   Introduction   351
14.2   Human communication and the conversation of gestures:
       processes of generalising and particularising   354
14.3   The relationship between local interaction and population-wide
       patterns   361
14.4   The roles of the most powerful   369
14.5   Summary   371
       Further reading   372
       Questions to aid further reflection   372

15   The emergence of organisational strategy in local communicative
     interaction: complex responsive processes of ideology and
     power relating   374

15.1   Introduction   375
15.2   Cult values   376
15.3   Desires, values and norms   378
15.4   Ethics and leadership   384
15.5   Power, ideology and the dynamics of inclusion–exclusion   387
15.6   Complex responsive processes perspectives on decision-making   394
15.7   Summary   396
       Further reading   397
       Questions to aid further reflection   397

16   Different modes of articulating patterns of interaction emerging
     across organisations: strategy narratives and models   398

16.1   Introduction   399
16.2   The emergence of themes in the narrative patterning of ordinary,
       everyday conversation   403
16.3   Narrative patterning of experience and preoccupation in the game 411
16.4   Reflecting on experience: the role of narrative and storytelling 415
16.5   Reflecting on experience: the role of second-order abstracting   418
16.6   Reasoning, measuring, forecasting and modelling in strategic
       management   422
16.7   Summary   432
       Further reading   432
       Questions to aid further reflection   432

17   Complex responsive processes of strategising: acting locally on the
basis of global goals, visions, expectations and intentions for
the 'whole' organisation over the 'long-term future'   434

   17.1   Introduction   435
   17.2   Strategic choice theory as second-order abstraction   437
   17.3   The learning organisation as second-order abstraction   453
   17.4   Institutions and legitimate structures of authority   456
   17.5   Strategy as identity narrative   459
   17.6   Summary   461
          Further reading   461
          Questions to aid further reflection   461

18   Complex responsive processes: implications for thinking about
organisational dynamics and strategy   464

   18.1   Introduction   464
   18.2   Key features of the complex responsive processes perspective   465
   18.3   How the theory of complex responsive processes answers the
          four key questions   468
   18.4   Refocusing attention: strategy and change   475
   18.5   Refocusing attention: control, performance and improvement   483
   18.6   Refocusing attention: research   486
   18.7   Rethinking the roles of leaders and managers   491
   18.8   Summary   494
          Further reading   494
          Questions to aid further reflection   495

   References   496

   Index   521

Supporting resources

Visit **www.pearsoned.co.uk/stacey** to find valuable online resources

For instructors
- Teaching notes

For more information please contact your local Pearson Education sales
representative or visit **www.pearsoned.co.uk/stacey**

List of boxes

Box 3.1   Key concepts in Kantian thinking   54

Box 4.1   Cybernetics: main points on organisational dynamics   71

Box 4.2   Cognitivism: main points on human knowing and communicating   82

Box 4.3   Humanistic psychology: main points on human knowing and communicating   84

Box 5.1   Systems dynamics: main points on organisational dynamics   104

Box 5.2   Constructivist psychology: main points on human knowing   107

Box 6.1   General systems theory: main points on organisational dynamics   130

Box 6.2   Unconscious group processes: main points on organisational dynamics   135

Box 14.1   Key points about social objects   361

Box 18.1   Complex responsive processes: main points on organisational dynamics   469

List of tables

Table A.1   Classification of schools of strategy thinking   44

Table 12.1   Comparison of different ways of thinking about causality   301

Table 12.2   Human analogues of simulations of heterogeneous complex systems   319

Table 12.3   The differences between systemic process and responsive processes   324

Preface

When I was writing the Preface for the fifth edition of this book in March 2006, questions of credit crunch and major recession were not even on the horizon in the minds of most people. However, what I wrote then about the purpose of this book remains the same – indeed I think it has been quite dramatically reinforced by the unexpected developments of credit crunch and recession which have made it quite clear that leaders and managers do not have the power to choose the future of their organisations as the dominant discourse on strategy assumes. We need to reflect very seriously on how we think about strategic management rather than simply taking for granted the prescriptions presented in the dominant discourse and that is the purpose of this book.

This is a textbook of *ways of thinking* about organisations and their management, particularly strategic management. While most strategic management textbooks are concerned with presenting the key elements and prescriptions of strategic management to be found in the dominant discourse on the matter, this book is concerned with the implicit, taken-for-granted assumptions made in the ways of thinking expressed in that dominant discourse. The intention, then, is not to summarise what key strategic thinkers have written about generic strategies that managers should follow to secure competitive advantage and so produce superior organisational performance. Nor is the intention to convey received wisdom on how to design and implement conditions and processes conducive to effective organisational learning and knowledge management. The intention is, rather, to explore the ways of thinking reflected in the prescriptions for successful strategic content and process so as to highlight taken-for-granted assumptions. In order to do this, it is necessary to locate current thinking about strategy in the history of Western thought. The book raises and explores questions rather than presenting further explicit prescriptions. For example, why do we think that an organisation is a system, and what are the consequences of doing so? What view of human psychology is implicit in prescribing measures that managers should take to select the direction of an organisation's movement into the future? In a world in which the dominant prescriptions for strategic management are quite clearly not delivering what they are supposed to, I believe it is far more useful to reflect on how we are thinking, so that we may understand more about what we are doing rather than simply continuing to mindlessly apply the conventional wisdom.

This book, then, seeks to challenge thinking rather than simply to describe the current state of thinking about strategy and organisational dynamics. The challenge to current ways of thinking is presented in the contrasts that this book draws between systemic and responsive processes ways of thinking about strategy and organisational dynamics. While the systemic perspective is concerned with improvement and movement to a future destination, responsive process thinking is concerned with complex responsive processes of human relating in which strategies emerge. From this perspective, strategy is defined as the emergence of organisational and individual identities, so that the concern is with how organisations come to be what they are and how those identities will continue to evolve. From a responsive processes perspective, the questions of performance and improvement have to do with participation in processes of communicative interaction, power relating and the creation of knowledge and meaning. The challenge to ways of thinking presented in this book also comes in the form of insights from the complexity sciences. The book will explore the differences for organisational thinking between a way of interpreting these insights in systemic terms and a way of interpreting them in responsive process terms. The purpose of this book is to assist people to make sense of their own experience of life in organisations, to explore their own thinking, because how they think powerfully affects what they pay attention to, and so what they do. If we never challenge dominant modes of thinking, we end up trapped in modes of acting that may no longer be serving us all that well.

This central emphasis on ways of thinking has consequences for how this book is structured and presented. It does not focus just on what has come to be accepted as the academic discipline of strategic management, but also takes account of other organisational disciplines such as matters that would normally come under organisational behaviour. These distinctions between academic disciplines are rather artificial when it comes to making sense of what managers actually do. Also, the book reaches into the disciplines of psychology, sociology and philosophy in seeking to understand the ways of thinking reflected in the dominant discourse. There are no traditional case studies and few examples of how people have managed successfully. Case studies tend to be carefully structured accounts of someone else's organisational experience, usually written with some point in mind, which the reader is supposed to see. Examples of successful management practices are often introduced to subtly 'prove' that a particular prescription works. These devices are not consistent with the purpose of assisting readers to make sense of their own experience. Since this is a book about ways of thinking, the examples it provides are examples of ways of thinking. The main point, however, remains for readers to use the material in this book to make sense of their own experience.

The general structure of this sixth edition is the same as the fifth. There is a new introductory chapter in which I try to make clear why this is a book about thinking and why it does not present new prescriptions for success. Part 1 deals with the dominant discourse on strategic management as in the fifth edition, but I have added a new chapter which attempts to review where the dominant discourse has got to and what evidence there is for its prescriptions, concluding that there is no reliable scientific evidence supporting the prescriptions and yet it continues to be the dominant discourse. The chapter makes some suggestions as to why this is so. I have concluded Part 1 with a new chapter which incorporates material about second-order systems thinking and communities of practice from the previous edition and adds material mainly on social constructionist approaches and labour-process theory. I have done this because comments made by readers of the last edition, particularly Chris Rodgers, have made it clear that in trying to present a clear alternative to the dominant discourse based on complexity sciences and the work of Mead and Elias,

I have not recognised the extent to which second-order systems thinking, social constructionism, communities of practice and labour process theory do present radical alternatives to the dominant discourse with many of the same features as Part 3 presents in a theory of complex responsive processes. The final chapter of Part 1 is thus a recognition that the dominant discourse is being challenged in a number of ways which this book seeks to continue. Part 2 is once again concerned with the complexity sciences and how writers on organisations use them. I have incorporated some more recent work on organisational complexity, but reach the same conclusion: namely, that most of these writers simply re-present the dominant discourse. Part 3 continues to review the theory of complex responsive processes as a way of thinking about strategising. The last 3 chapters of this section have been substantially rewritten with Chapter 17 focusing particularly on what strategic management might mean from the perspective of complex responsive processes. I have removed the Reflective Management Narratives from the book because reviewers were not at all enthusiastic about them. Instead, the further reading at the end of the chapters refers to work that I could have used as reflective narratives.

I am grateful to users of previous editions who have made helpful comments and to my colleagues and other participants in the MA/Doctor of Management programme on organisational change at the University of Hertfordshire for the contribution they continue to make to how I find myself thinking.

Ralph Stacey
University of Hertfordshire
October 2010

Chapter 1

Strategic management in perspective
A step in the professionalisation of management

This chapter invites you to draw on your own experience to reflect on and consider the implications of:

- The history of the concepts and practices of strategic management.

- What difference it makes when one realises that the concern with strategic management is a recent phenomenon only some three decades old.

- The enormous emphasis that people place on tools and techniques and their insistent demand they be provided by academics and consultants.

- The role that business schools and consultants have played in the development of notions of strategic management.

- The reasons for continuing with outmoded ways of thinking about strategy, despite their lack of success, and the difficulty of taking up alternative ways of thinking.

This chapter is important because it presents the overall attitude taken toward the discipline of strategic management in this book. It explains why the book does not set out to provide prescriptions for strategic management. Instead it explains that this is a textbook of ways of thinking about strategic management, where the prescription is to take a reflective, reflexive approach to strategic management. The injunction is to think about what you are doing and why you are doing it as an antidote to mindlessly repeating outmoded theories.

1.1 Introduction

Over the past fifteen years I have received many comments from readers of the first five editions of *Strategic Management and Organisational Dynamics* which have given me some sense of what many readers expect to find in a textbook on strategic management. There seems to be a general expectation of a summary of the received body of accepted knowledge on strategic management which is already understood as that kind of management that is concerned with the 'big picture' over the 'long term' for the 'whole organisation'. Most seem to distinguish strategic management from other management activities which are concerned with the 'day-to-day', 'short term', 'tactical' conduct of specific organisational 'functions' and activities. What people usually mean when they talk about the long-term, big picture for a whole organisation is a clear view of the purpose of that organisation and the direction in which 'it' is intended to 'move', 'going forward into the future', so that its 'resources', 'capabilities' and 'competences' are 'optimally' 'aligned' to the sources of competitive advantage in its environment as 'the way' to achieve 'successful' performance. These activities of strategic management are normally taken to be the primary function of an organisation's 'leader', supported by his or her 'top leadership team' and it is widely thought that strategic purpose, direction and alignment should be expressed by the leader in an inspiring, easily understood statement of 'vision and mission'. When those lower down in an organisational hierarchy experience confusion and uncertainty, they frequently blame this on a failure of leadership, a lack of strategic direction on the part of the top management team, or at the very least a failure of communication down the hierarchy. What readers expect from a textbook on strategic management, therefore, is a set of 'tools and techniques' which can be 'applied' to an organisation to yield strategic 'successes' and avoid failures of leadership and communication. These tools and techniques should be backed by 'evidence' and illustrated by 'case studies' of major organisations which have achieved success through applying them – only then can they be accepted as persuasive.

If, however, instead of simply representing the predominantly accepted tools and techniques of strategic management, a textbook critiques or dismisses them, then there is a powerful expectation on the part of many readers that a useful textbook will propose new tools and techniques to replace them in the belief that, if managers do not have tools and techniques, they will simply have to muddle through in ways that are completely unacceptable in a modern world. The expectation is that a useful textbook will focus on what decision makers 'should' be doing to make decisions in certain kinds of problem situations in order to 'improve' their organisation's performance. Readers want to know what action they should take in order to successfully achieve the objectives they have selected or which have been set for them. They are looking for how to 'design' the management 'systems' which will deliver a more or less self-regulating form of 'control'. In short, as in other management development activities, readers of a textbook are looking for easily understandable 'takeaways' and 'deliverables'.

I have a strong sense, then, of a powerful, coherent set of expectations on the part of many readers, completely taken for granted as obvious common sense, concerning what they expect from a textbook on strategic management. In the previous paragraphs I have placed in inverted commas those notions that most people talking about strategic management simply take for granted as if their meanings were all perfectly obvious, needing little further explanation. However, I find it difficult to see the use of trying to present new prescriptions without exploring just what we mean when we make such take-for-granted assumptions. Furthermore, I find it difficult to match the continuing demand for simple tools with the major economic and political events of the past few years. It is hard to understand how anyone who has paid any attention to the events of global credit crunch and recession that we have all experienced since 2007 can continue to believe that there is a clear, reliable body of knowledge on strategic management containing prescriptive tools and techniques for its successful application. Surely the great majority of major international banks and other commercial organisations have not been successfully conducting strategic management over the past few years. If there really was such a body of knowledge then top executives in major corporations should have known how to practise strategic management to achieve success for each of their organisations. Since collapsing organisations mean that they clearly did not succeed, either there is no reliable body of strategic management knowledge or most leaders and top management teams must have been guilty of criminal neglect because they obviously did not use the prescriptions in the way that produces success over the past few years. Furthermore, we must surely question why massive investments by governments in Western Europe and North America in public sector services, now governed on the basis of private sector management tools and techniques, have yielded such disappointing improvements, if indeed they have yielded any significant improvement at all. If a set of tools and techniques for successful strategic management was actually available, governments must have been incredibly ignorant in not applying them so as to produce more acceptable levels of improvement.

It does not seem very rational to me to simply gloss over the major problematic events of the past few years and continue to take it for granted that there is a reputable body of knowledge on strategic management which provides prescriptive tools and techniques that do lead to success. The disquiet with received management wisdom in the light of recent history is compounded when we realise that, despite the claims that there is a science of organisation and management, there is no body of scientifically respectable evidence that the approaches, tools and techniques put forward in most textbooks do actually produce success (*see* Chapter 8 below). As soon as one accepts that the events of the past few years and the lack of scientific evidence cast doubt on the received wisdom on strategic management, the door opens to realising that 'change' and 'innovation' which most of us regard as positive, such as the development of the internet and the many uses to which it is being put, also cannot be explained by the taken-for-granted view of strategic management, because most of these 'creative' 'innovations' seem to have emerged without any global strategic intention or any organisation-wide learning process.

In view of such global experience and the lack of evidence, this book sets out quite explicitly and quite intentionally to contest the expectations which many readers bring to it. Starting with the first edition of this book, published in 1993, I have sought to question and counter the set of expectations I have described above for reasons similar to those presented above, but still there are those who criticise the book because it does not produce the expected tools and techniques. So, I need to state very clearly right at the beginning that this is not a textbook which simply summarises an accepted body of knowledge on strategic management but, instead, seeks to critique it; it is not a book which simply sets out alternative schools of strategic management for readers to choose between, but rather seeks to identify the taken-for-granted assumptions underlying each school; and it is certainly not a book which provides or supports tools and techniques for successful strategic management, but instead invites reflection on what the insistence on tools and techniques is all about. This is, therefore, *a textbook of the ways of thinking* that underlie the summaries of strategic management, the alternative schools of strategic management and the tools and techniques of strategic management. My primary concern is not simply with what strategic management is according to different schools and perspectives or with what they prescribe for success, but, much more important, with how we are thinking when we subscribe to particular definitions, schools and perspectives and accept particular tools and techniques. The key interest in this book is the taken-for-granted assumptions we make when we suggest a particular view on strategic management or recommend particular tools and techniques. The concern is not with the supposed tools and techniques of strategic management but with how we are thinking when we suggest such tools and techniques. Indeed, the concern is with what kinds of taken-for-granted assumptions we are making when we think that management in any form is about tools and techniques at all.

In *thinking about how we are thinking about strategic management* we inevitably find ourselves asking how we have come to think in the particular ways we have. In other words, the reflexive attitude underlying this textbook is essentially concerned with the history of thought. When did we start to think about strategy as the direction an organisation moves in? When and in what circumstances did we start to think of strategy as a key function of leadership having to do with visions? When and why did we develop the modern fixation on management tools and techniques? What this textbook does, then, is to review and summarise the *body of knowledge on ways of thinking about strategic management* and how this body of knowledge has evolved.

But why should we bother with the ways we have come to think? What is the benefit for busy executives whose primary concern is action? For me, the needs and the benefits are obvious and clear. Without reflecting on how and why we are thinking in the way we currently do we find ourselves mindlessly trapped in repeating the same ineffective actions. Already, after the collapse of investment capitalism in the 2007 to 2009 period, we see investment banks and management consultancies once more beginning to fuel waves of mergers and acquisitions as well as continuing to be rewarded with huge bonuses for employing the 'talent' for taking the kinds of risks which produced the collapse of the past few years. Despite the evident lack of success of major public sector improvement programmes in Western Europe, there is little evidence of a major re-think in modes of public sector governance. It is in order to escape being trapped in mindless action that this textbook focuses on the underdeveloped concern with thinking about organisations and their management.

For me, nothing could be more practical than a concern with how we are thinking and I can think of little more important for organisational improvement than having leaders and managers who can and do actually reflect upon what they are doing and why they are doing it. Surely if they adopt such a reflective, reflexive stance they will find themselves doing things differently in ways that neither they nor we can know in advance. If this book does finally point to a 'tool or technique' it is to the most powerful 'tool or technique' available to managers, indeed to any human being, and that is the self-conscious capacity to take a reflective, reflexive attitude towards what they are doing. In other words, the most powerful 'tool' any of us has is our ability to think about how we are thinking – if only we would use it more and not obscure it with a ready reliance on fashionable tools and techniques which often claim to be scientific even though there is no supporting evidence.

The other half of the main title of this book, *organisational dynamics*, signals my claim that an inquiry into thinking about strategic management needs to be placed in the context of what people in organisations *actually do*, rather than with the main pre-occupation of the strategic management literature which is with what managers are *supposed to do* but mostly do not seem to be actually doing. The term 'group dynamics' refers to the nature of interactions between people in a group and to the patterns of change these interactions produce over time in the behaviour of people in a group. Organisational dynamics has a meaning close to this – it refers to the nature of interactions between people in an organisation and to the changing patterns of behaviour these interactions produce over time, some aspects of which might be referred to as 'strategic'. In other words, the title of this book signals that it is concerned with *ways of thinking about* strategic management located in the context of thinking more widely about *what people actually think, feel and do in organisations*. And what we think, feel and do is always reflective of the communities we live in and their historically evolved ways of doing and thinking. Notions of strategic management are not simply there – they have emerged in a social history. So consider first what the origins of notions of strategic management are and then how we might characterise rather different ways of thinking about such a notion.

1.2 The origins of modern concepts of strategic management: the new role of leader

The origin of the English word *strategy* lies in the fourteenth-century importation of the French word *stratégie* derived from the Greek words *strategia* meaning 'office or command of a general', *strategos* meaning 'general', and *stratus* plus *agein* where the former means 'multitude, army, expedition' and the latter means 'to lead'. Strategy, therefore, originally denoted the art of a general and, indeed, writers on modern strategic management sometimes refer to its origins in the *Art of War* by the Chinese general, Sun Tzu, written some 2,500 years ago, and in *On War* by the Prussian general and military historian, von Clausewitz, written nearly 200 years ago. The claim is that the concept of strategy, understood to be a plan of action for deploying troops devised prior to battle, as opposed to *tactics* which refer to the actual manoeuvres on the battlefield, was borrowed from the military and adapted to business where strategy was understood as the bridge between policy or high-level goals and tactics or concrete actions. This location of the origins of strategy in a military setting fits well with the rather romantic view of leader as hero which has developed over the past few decades in the dominant discourse on organisations and their management. However, at least in the Byzantine Empire which existed for more than 1,000 years, the *strategos*, or general, had other important functions to do with governing the area under his control, particularly those of ensuring the conduct of the population census and the listing of wealth to provide the information essential for collecting taxes. In other words, the *strategos* was very much concerned with civil governance and policy. The word *policy* also entered the English language from the French word *policie* meaning 'civil administration', which in turn originated in the Greek *polis* meaning 'city state' and *politeia* meaning 'state administration'. From the fifteenth century onwards, 'policy' meant 'a way of management', or a 'plan of action', combining high-level goals, acceptable procedures, and courses of action, all meant to guide future decisions. I think it is more realistic to regard notions of strategy in modern organisations as expressions of more mundane, evolving modes of civil administration than of swashbuckling military deployments. The next question, then, is just when notions of business policy and strategy became evident in the discourse about the management of modern organisations, particularly business firms.

During the nineteenth century joint stock/limited liability corporations developed as legal forms, which made it much easier to raise finance for commercials ventures. Instead of having partners fully liable for all the losses an enterprise incurred, a joint stock company/limited liability corporation could raise finance from shareholders whose potential loss was limited to what they paid for their shares. This development meant that the owners (shareholders) of organisations and those who ran them (managers) became separate groups of people, in fact, different classes. As agents of the owners, managers were often criticised by shareholders when financial returns were below expectations, and when they tried to increase returns they were increasingly cast as villains by workers during frequent periods of industrial unrest. Khurana (2007) has carefully documented how this situation led to a quite intentional search in the USA for an identity on the part of the new managerial class, an identity which was to be secured by establishing a professional status linked to the prestigious disciplines of the natural sciences. Management was to be presented as a science, and a science of organisation was to be developed. Professions such as medicine and engineering were characterised by institutions which defined membership, established codes of ethics, encouraged research and professional development and often published professional journals. Professionals were educated at research-based universities. As part of the professionalisation of management, therefore, the first business school was set up at Wharton University in the USA in 1881 and this was followed by the founding of increasing numbers of university-based business schools in the ensuing decades. At much the same time, the need to hold managers legally accountable to shareholders resulted in legislation on public reporting of corporate activities and further legislation seeking to regulate the growth and financing of limited liability companies. These requirements for increasingly onerous reporting procedures created the need for financial and other surveys of companies, so creating a market for accounting/auditing firms, for engineering consultants and eventually management consultants. In addition to business schools, therefore, other aspects of the professionalisation of management were displayed in the development of professional membership institutions, professional educational organisations, and professional accounting, auditing and consulting bodies.

So, by the early years of the twentieth century, a managerial class, or in more modern terms a managerial community of practice (Wenger, 1998) had developed, particularly in the USA, which encompassed not simply hierarchies of managers running corporations but also management consultants and other advisers, as well as those concerned with the development of organisations and their managers, such as business school academics, wealthy capitalist philanthropists and government policy advisers.

Any community of practice engages in joint activities which develop a collective identity and they accomplish these identity-forming activities in ongoing conversation in which they negotiate what they are doing and how they are making sense of what they are doing with each other and with members of the wider society they are part of. It is in conversation that members of a community become who they are. The form of such conversation is thus of central importance because, in establishing what it is acceptable for people to talk about in a community, and how it is acceptable to talk, the conversational form, or discourse, establishes people's relative power positions and therefore who they are and what they do together. Every such community of practice is characterised by a dominant discourse, the most acceptable way to converse, which reflects power positions supported by ideologies. The dominant management discourse is reflected in how managers usually talk together about the nature of their managerial activity. It is also reflected in the kind of organisational research that attracts funding from research bodies, the kind of papers that prestigious research journals will publish, and the kind of courses taught at business schools, in the textbooks they use and in organisational training and development activities. However, evolving communities of practice are usually not simply monolithic power structures (as in fascism) with rigid ideologies brooking no dissension (as in cults). Most communities of practice are also characterised by some resistance to, or criticism of, the dominant discourse. A community of practice can change in the tension between the dominant discourse and the critique of it. Understanding a community of practice, therefore, requires understanding its forms of dominant discourse and the kind of dissension this gives rise to, the key debates characterising its conversation and how conflict generated by such debate is handled. The operation of the professional bodies of the management community described above provides an essential source of information on how the dominant discourse on organisations and their management has evolved. The most vocal of these professional bodies have probably been the business schools and management consultancies. The changes in business school curricula for educating managers and the changing composition of management consultancy work, therefore, provide an illuminating insight into the evolution of the dominant management discourse over the twentieth century.

By the 1920s business schools in the USA had developed three fairly distinct models of the curriculum for educating managers. First, some business schools delivered curricula devoted to training managers for jobs in specific industries – say, operations managers in steel manufacturing. Second, other business schools focused on business functions, providing courses on accounting, finance, business correspondence and sometimes history and some social sciences. Third, and this was particularly evident in the small group of elite business schools such as Wharton and Harvard, there was a focus on a science of administration for general managers, covering scientific management as in Taylorism, accounting, economics of the political, historical, institutional kind rather than the neo-classical analysis found in economics faculties, and training in the exercise of judgement rather than of routine procedures. In this third development there was an emphasis on the social purpose of business activity and on the presentation of managers as professionals whose purpose was the stewardship of society's resources. Such an identity as professional stewards of society's resources was a powerful counter to the accusations of workers that managers were their enemies and also a useful power shift in relation to shareholders. A list of courses in business school curricula of all types shows that over the 1920s and 1930s there were very few courses in business policy and none in strategy, strategic management, corporate planning, or even planning: economics was far less important than the social sciences and there was a strong interest in ethics (Khurana, 2007). Then, if we look at the kind of work that accounting and consulting firms were doing, we find that it was primarily to do with legal reporting requirements and the information required for this, studies of reporting structures and forms of organisation, and engineering and financial assessments for specific large investment projects. So, any notion of strategic management in organisations as we now understand it is a post-Second World War phenomenon, certainly not one stretching back to ancient Chinese, or even more recent Prussian, generals.

The Second World War was to have a major impact on the identity of managers – the management of organisations became a key aspect of winning a war that depended as much on the ability to organise the manufacture and transport of supplies as on the ability to direct military confrontations. During the war, therefore, governments found it necessary to take seriously the techniques of management and administration, and in the USA the government turned to the business schools to address the difficulties of administering a war economy, including the tasks of collecting statistics and other information and developing techniques for coordinated decision-making across many different organisations. This led to the development of techniques such as linear programming, systems analysis, computer simulations, network analysis, queuing theory and cost-accounting systems. There was progress in statistics and statistical sampling, as well as in survey methods and focus groups, under the pressures of assuring the quality of armaments. Engineers developed the theory of systems to provide forms of self-regulating control. A new and more rational conception of the managerial role using the modern techniques therefore developed during the war.

After the war, the managers who had acquired this kind of analytical expertise for the war effort were available in their thousands to work on social and economic reconstruction in business corporations and consulting firms, such as McKinsey, where they applied the new techniques to organisational problems. Management thus focused much more narrowly than before the war on the scientific manager who used models and analytical techniques and designed and manipulated systems. Management was equated with setting objectives, designing systems for meeting them, planning, forecasting and controlling. Managers were described as 'systems designers', 'information processors' and 'programmers' regulating the interface of the organisation and its environment in accordance with cybernetic systems theory. The rapid growth in corporate size and the rise of the conglomerate were characterised by a multiplicity of managers removed from the grass roots of the organisation's activities and they felt the need for models, maps and techniques that would enable them to exert control from a distance. This need for techniques of modelling, mapping and measuring to enable the taking of a generalised macro view from a distance in order to apply some degree of control had already been faced over a century before by tax collectors and other administrators of the business of the modern state. In a sense, post-war organisational managers were importing systemic practice from public administration while at the same time bringing more sophisticated models and techniques to both private and public administration.

In addition, in the USA the government provided education for returning soldiers, and this together with the need for more managers produced an explosive demand for places at business schools which were to train managers in the new techniques.

The American Association of Colleges and Schools of Business (AACSB) sought to improve the quality of business education, and philanthropic foundations, such as the Carnegie Foundation, the Ford Foundation and the Rockefeller Foundation funded business schools and so came to have an important impact on how they developed. These foundations wanted to raise the academic standards of the business schools by getting teachers at business schools to focus, in both their research and teaching activities, on techniques for solving real, complex problems using quantitative methods. Neo-classical micro-economic analysis now became more prominent than the social sciences because it provided analytical tools. The Ford Foundation was strongly of the view that there was now a science of management which would enable managers to make decisions solely on rational grounds using techniques such as decision analysis and game theory, making any appeal to intuition and judgement unnecessary. It was believed that this management science could be taught at business schools by a faculty without business experience but who were expert in decision-making techniques. Managers were regarded as technicians and the role of the faculty at the business schools was that of transferring to managers the decision-making and control techniques that they would need. The much changed conception of the management role brought with it a complete orientation toward profit. The ordinary manager's primary role was to perform the tasks required to maximise profits for shareholders. It was believed that the new management techniques could be applied in any organisation of any size so that experience in a particular industry was not necessary – expertise in decision-making and control was all that was needed. But at the top of the hierarchy there was a CEO who many have described, in this period, as a kind of industrial statesman who worked closely with outside bodies such as government ministers, politicians and regulatory authorities, while managers lower down in the hierarchy were simply technicians applying the techniques of decision-making and control that would maximise profits.

By the 1960s the AACSB was only accrediting standardised MBAs based on disciplines such as finance and quantitative analysis, including neo-classical micro-economics. Business schools began to experience a growing schism between faculty who lacked business experience and focused on research and techniques, and students who stressed their need for practical application. By the time we get to the late 1960s and early 1970s some business schools were trying to meet the need for integrating the various specialised courses they were teaching into an overall view of management and they did this by introducing capstone courses on business policy. In addition, in the 1960s specialist strategy consultants such as the Boston Consulting Group and Bain & Company grew rapidly (McKenna, 2006). By the 1970s independent management consultants had also become very important in government administration and advice. Consultants found a lucrative market in advising, first, universities, then religious institutions and then hospitals on their organisational structures and strategies. So, by the 1960s consultancies were involved in most kinds of organisation in giving advice on business policy, corporate planning and strategy and during this period management consultancy successfully established itself as a profession with its own institutions.

The period from the end of the Second World War to the economic crisis of the early 1970s was a period of more or less sustained company growth and economic prosperity and managers came to be thought of as professional problem solvers who employed a body of scientific knowledge to make rational decisions. This was the period in which, first, business policy and then corporate planning courses became more and more common in business schools – it came to be held that the crucial role of the CEO was that of defining corporate goals and creating strategy. The management consultancies developed the rapidly growing markets for advice on formulating and implementing corporate strategies, which increasingly included merger and acquisition activities. The concern with corporate strategy therefore generated enormous business for accounting and auditing firms, as well as investment bankers and management consultants; and of course this was all part of increasing activities to do with strategic planning in American corporations: it was estimated that by 1966 the majority of American manufacturing firms had some type of planning system (Brown *et al.* 1969) and much the same kind of result was produced by later studies of the situation in the mid-1970s (Haspeslagh, 1982; Kono, 1983; Fulmer and Rue, 1973). However, there were very few studies which examined the effects of strategic planning on corporate success (*see* Chapter 8 below). The few studies there were produced fragmentary and conflicting results (Rue and Fulmer, 1973). The story was much the same in Europe. In the UK the first business school, London Business School, was set up in 1964. A Long Range Planning Society was set up in London and the first issue of its journal, *Long Range Planning*, was published in 1968. In France the business School INSEAD was set up in 1957. In Switzerland IMI was founded in Geneva by Alcan Aluminium in 1946 and IMEDE was founded in Lausanne in 1957 by Nestlé. IMD was created in 1990 in a merger between IMI and IMEDE.

So, by the time we get to the early 1970s, corporate planning was very much a central part of the dominant discourse on management, but despite the claims this discourse made to a scientific status it could produce no reliable body of evidence to support the application of corporate planning techniques. This was the era, in both North America and Europe, of the growth of large corporate planning departments in commercial and industrial enterprises of any consequence. The growth of these departments, as well as the management consultancies, accounting firms, information technology advisers, investment banks and business schools created a huge demand for economists. I completed my studies in economics in the late 1960s and had the choice of planning-type jobs in the UK in Shell, Ford and British Steel, having discounted the possibility of applying to the World Bank or looking for a post in the USA. The future seemed rosy if you were an economist, particularly one educated, as I had been, at universities such as the London School of Economics which emphasised mathematics, statistics and econometric modelling. I took a job in 1970 forecasting steel demand at British Steel and then moved a short time later to the corporate planning department of a large international construction company, John Laing, which had been founded nearly a century before. I continued to work there until 1984 and then spent a year at an investment house in the City of London before taking up an academic career.

However, the apparently rosy picture for economists and their techniques was indeed short lived. In the early 1970s oil prices shot up and the world economy moved into significant decline, accompanied by alarming increases in inflation rates around the globe. The 1970s were difficult, turbulent years in both economic and political terms. The limits to our ability to forecast what would happen next became painfully obvious and the whole project of corporate, strategic planning was called into question. The Club of Rome established in 1968 called for limits to economic growth and this call became more influential in the 1970s. Large companies began to drastically reduce their corporate planning departments and the armies of economists had to find other forms of employment unless, as I did in continuing to work at John Laing, they managed to develop activities in existing corporate planning departments that other managers found useful.

By the end of the decade, the whole activity of corporate planning was coming in for major criticism, as indeed was the whole scientific, technical approach taught by business schools and installed by management consultants. Abernathy and Hayes (1980) of Harvard Business School wrote an influential article blaming the USA's lack of competitiveness against Japan on a highly rational, technique-oriented approach to management. This was followed by other influential books (for example, by management consultants Pascale and Athos, 1981) which compared management methods in the USA and Japan, finding the latter with its emphasis on wider discussion, teams and more inclusive decision-making far superior to American approaches based on rational tools and techniques applied in highly hierarchical ways. Then there was a very influential book, with much the same message, by the management consultants, Peters and Waterman (1982), which identified what they claimed from their research were the key practices of successful businesses which included an emphasis on culture, teams, leadership and visions. *Corporate planning* became a rather taboo term and instead people spoke of *strategic management*, now understood as an essential competence of visionary, inspirational leaders rather than a purely techniques-driven, rational activity. This shift was expressed in a still ongoing debate between rational planners and those who presented the notion of the learning organisation. In Chapter 8 below, I will mention a famous instance of this debate in an exchange between Ansoff and Mintzberg.

During the 1980s the field of strategy emerged as a particular form of management and a separate field of study not only in the private sector but in the public sector too as politicians preached and implemented what became known as the 'managerialist' form of corporate governance. The professional status of strategic planners is indicated by the founding of the Strategic Management Society at an initial meeting in London in 1981, with officers elected on a second conference held in Montreal in 1982, and a constitution approved at the third meeting in Paris in 1983. *The Strategic Management Journal (SMJ)* has, since its inception in 1980, been the official journal of the Strategic Management Society presented as an international institution although one heavily influenced by academics in the USA where its administration is located.

At much the same time, developments in the field of finance revolutionised teaching at elite business schools who now trained not general managers but professional investors and financial engineers for the investment banks, private equity and hedge funds, and management consultancies. Agency theory justified mergers and acquisitions and the leveraging of corporations with debt while minimising the importance of other stakeholders and dismissing any social function for managers. Managers had come to be regarded as the agents of shareholders, rather than any other stakeholders, who were to be controlled and rewarded through being provided with a part of an organisation's shareholding so that they would come to have the same motivation as shareholders. Business school lecturers, at least at the elite schools, increasingly had little contact with managers in industrial or service enterprises, becoming more and more concerned with strategy and finance. Business policy courses on MBAs became strategic-management modules strongly rooted in industrial economics.

By the time we get to the first decade of the twenty-first century, the pre-1970s notion that managers were fundamentally the stewards of society's resources and acted on behalf of all stakeholders gave way to a notion of managers as agents for shareholders whose prime function was to maximise shareholder value. This development of investment capitalism was reinforced by the elite business schools of the USA and Europe who focused on training investment bankers and management consultants, while the role of the lesser schools was reduced to preparing managers for the rational (mathematical) techniques required for their profit-maximising tasks. To compensate for the inadvertent downgrading of the professional role of managers by investment capitalism, business schools seized on a renewed purpose and identity which had become popular since the early 1990s under the name of *leadership*, and one of the most important leadership functions was thought to be strategy formulation and inspiring others to implement it. Now, of course, investment capitalism has been revealed to be deeply flawed, with the extended risk-taking of investment bankers, the near collapse and government bail-out of financial institutions, and the evolving recession and we do not know how central notions of management might evolve in response.

So, looking back over the past century, we find the earliest developments in the field of strategic management in the management consultancies where McKinsey (1932) perhaps caught the essence of the early concept of strategy, although he never used that word, when he talked about adjusting policies to meet changing conditions. After the War, the manager Barnard (1948) mentioned administrative strategy and this was picked up by Hardwick and Landuyt (1961). Another McKinsey consultant, Reilly (1955), talked about planning the strategy of a business. At the business schools Newman of Columbia Business School (1951) talked about the nature and importance of strategy; sociologist Selznick from Berkeley (1957) talked about the role of the leader to set objectives and define missions taking account of internal policy and external expectations; Moore (1959) conducted a sophisticated discussion of managerial strategies; Chandler (1962), historian from MIT, explored the relationship between organisational structure and organisational strategy; Gilmore and Brandenburg (1962) wrote about the anatomy of corporate planning; and Tilles (1963) from Harvard Business School discussed how to evaluate corporate strategies. Then 1965 saw the publication of *Corporate Strategy* by Ansoff, an engineer at Rand Corporation, and *Business Policy: Text and Cases* by Learned, Christensen, Andrews and Guth from Harvard Business School. After this, strategic management became a separate discipline for academics and consultants as a profession allying itself with economics and having its own professional societies and journals. Members of this new profession were also employed in corporate planning departments.

It is clear then that academics at a few of the elite business schools and consultants at the most prestigious management consultancies in the USA took the lead in developing the concept of corporate planning and strategic management after the Second World War. The 1960s saw explosive growth in ideas but the oil crisis of the early 1970s led to disillusionment through the 1970s, expressed, for example, by McKinsey consultants who called for a more consultative and inspirational approach (Peters and Waterman, 1982). Ever since there has been an ongoing debate about effectiveness and just what strategy means.

The above brief review of how the notion of strategic management came to occupy a central position in the dominant discourse on organisations and their management leads me to a number of conclusions relevant to embarking on a serious study of strategic management. These are as follows:

- Far from being an adaptation of ancient military wisdom to modern business corporations, the notion of strategic management as it is expressed in the current dominant discourse on organisations is a rather new one characteristic of only the last three decades, well within the career of anyone now on the verge of retirement. And it has changed significantly during three decades. For example, in the corporations I worked for during the 1970s no one used the language of strategic management as having to do with visions and missions. Of course the notion of strategic management has emerged in the long history of Western thought not just about organisations but about what it means to be a human agent and about society generally. In a textbook about ways of thinking, we will of course be concerned with this wider history of thought and the assumptions it brings with it which we now take for granted.

- Furthermore, there are rather clear sociological reasons for the emergence of the particular notions of strategic management to be found in the dominant discourse of the past three decades. Those reasons have to do with the ongoing search for a respected professional identity for the management class in response to the dubious success of rational techniques of analysis and corporate planning. The response has been a wider definition of strategic management to encompass culture, leadership and learning but without giving up the claim to scientific respectability upon which the professional identity of management is felt to depend. What is glossed over, however, is the lack of an evidence base to qualify as a science so that the claim to organisational and management science is largely an ideology which sustains particular power relations between managers and other groups in society.

- The dominant strategic management discourse does not, however, constitute a clear body of knowledge accepted by all. Instead, it is a set of highly contested concepts. If we are to get away from simply summarising the different sides in this argument and adopting a tolerant but ineffectual position in which we do not have to choose between them but can select a little of each; if we want to move away from being trapped in the repetitive thought patterns this leads to, then we have to explore what assumptions are being taken for granted in the debate and how we have come to make them. That is the purpose of this book: namely, to explore different ways of thinking and whether we need to reject some and uphold others or whether we can take a little of each depending on what we are confronting and what we want to achieve.

Since this is a textbook on ways of thinking about strategic management I want to move to a brief illustration of what I mean by the term 'ways of thinking' before finishing the chapter with an outline of the rest of the book.

1.3 Ways of thinking: stable global structures and fluid local interactions

I want to use the image on the cover of this book to point to what I think are two very different ways of seeing and thinking about a phenomenon, be it the image on the cover or a human organisation. The image on the cover is a close-up photograph of a tiny section of Caribbean coral reef off Roatan Island, Honduras. What you can readily see when you look at the picture as a whole, from a macro perspective as it were, is the structure of this tiny part of the reef which consists of the limestone skeletons of millions of dead coral polyps. One immediately obvious way for a modern person to see and think about this coral reef image is in terms of a stable structure. Thinking as a scientist who is objectively observing this structure it would be quite natural to hypothesise that the structure has been constructed according to some macro-principle or natural law: the pattern of the whole or global structure is determined by some deterministic global principle which can be expressed as a global mathematical equation so that the global structure or pattern is, in effect, the realisation or implementation of a macro-design. This would mean that changes in the structure are predictable and that it could only take a different form, a different global pattern, if the global laws, or design principles, governing it were to be changed. These notions of global laws, identifiable through the scientific method, producing stable, predictable global structural patterns constitute one clear way of seeing and thinking about the coral reef, a way which seems quite natural because it is perfectly consistent with traditional science.

However, one reading of the modern natural sciences of complexity offers a second way of seeing and thinking about the coral reef. This involves focusing attention not on the global macro-pattern of the reef but upon the component coral organisms from whose limestone skeletons the reef is constructed. A living coral polyp resembles a sea anemone, having a jelly-like sac attached at one end to a cup-shaped skeleton that it secretes around itself. It feeds from the other end by sweeping the sea water it dwells in with its tentacles, stunning microscopic prey which it then draws inside itself. Corals reproduce by releasing fertilised eggs which hatch to form larvae that settle on a suitable surface where they secrete their own skeletal cups, so growing into mature coral. Individual corals gather together in large colonies, interacting with each other and attaching themselves to the seabed, forming extensive reefs, usually in shallow, warm-water seas. Reefs grow upward as generations of corals die, leaving behind their skeletal cups which petrify as lime-stone, forming large, tree-like structures upon which the living coral and numerous other species dwell. Corals are extremely ancient animals, appearing in the fossil record in solitary form more than 400 million years ago, evolving into modern reef-building forms over the last 25 million years. Coral reefs can be thought of as unique complex systems forming the largest biological structures on earth, consisting of ecological communities evolving in indispensable symbiotic relationships with a type of brown algae. Each coral polyp component of a coral reef displays particular states, for example, the state of being alive and the state of being dead, which are dependent upon the numerous interactions between that coral polyp and others. This interdependence between the coral polyps makes it difficult to construct realistic models that match the natural level of complexity: the kind of global macro-model of the traditional scientific way of thinking described above simply does not incorporate the features which give a realistic picture of the ongoing development of coral reefs.

However, over the last 50 years or so a different approach to scientific modelling has been developed in what have come to be called the 'natural complexity sciences'. One model to be found in these sciences is called *cellular automata* where each component, such as a coral polyp, of a large system, such as a coral reef, is thought of as following simple rules of interaction with other components. These rules of local interaction are simulated on a computer and the global patterns, or structures, produced by these local interactions are observed. Such modelling, therefore, can be utilised to approach large-scale problems in which huge numbers of components (cells or agents) interact locally with each other to produce complex global 'wholes' in the complete absence of any global laws or global design principles: local interaction produces emergent global pattern without any 'direction' from a 'centre' in the form of global laws or designs that are to be realised or implemented. The complexity of species behaviour is shown to be generated by the simple, repeated local interactions of the base units (coral polyps) which produce emergent patterns that may survive over long periods of time. The models show that surprisingly complex behaviours can arise from the action of local processes that are not globally directed (Wolfram, 1986).

If we 'see' and think about the coral reef image on the cover of the book from this perspective, we focus our attention in a very different way to the first way of thinking described above. The major concern now is with the local interaction of living coral polyps, in other words, with micro-processes of interaction, rather than the macro-patterns of the reef's structure which at any one time is mainly the reflection of patterns of past deaths. When we focus on living local interaction, we see that any global 'structure' is not stable and given but takes the form of dynamic patterns of birth, growth and death so that the 'global' pattern is actually developing over long time periods in a live way: the pattern is emerging across a whole population of corals in the many local interactions between the corals. We notice that the 'global' pattern is not simply stable and regular, as in the build-up of dead corals, but actually, when account is also taken of the living corals, it is regularly irregular, a feature known in the complexity sciences as *fractal*, and hence unpredictable in detail. We realise that there are very interesting implications in the hypothesis that the coral reef grows not according to deterministic natural laws or design principles of a global nature, but according to the rules of local interaction between living corals which produce the pattern in which their skeletons are laid down to form the substructure of the reef. It is these ongoing local interactions between living corals, obscured in the traditional scientific perspective, which dynamically sustain the recognisable pattern of the whole coral reef, and different patterns can only arise if the local rules of interaction change. In other words, the global pattern cannot be changed by altering some global law or design, because there is none: a different pattern can only emerge across a whole population if the nature of the local interactions changes. These notions of local interaction producing unpredictably predictable, emergent, population-wide patterns in the complete absence of central design principles or global growth laws constitute a completely different way of seeing and thinking about the coral reef to the first one mentioned above, but it too qualifies as science, at least to those scientists taking a complexity approach.

I want to suggest that the image of the coral reef presents us with a metaphor for human organisations. We can also 'see' and think about human organisations in the two different ways identified above for 'seeing' and thinking about coral reefs. The dominant discourse on organisations corresponds to the first way of 'seeing' and thinking about coral reefs outlined above. Here leaders, managers and powerful coalitions of them are supposed to objectively observe their organisations and use the tools of rational analysis to select appropriate objectives, targets and strategic visions for their organisations and then to formulate strategies of macro-change, design organisational structures and procedures to implement actions to achieve the targets, objectives and visions of the strategies, as well as rational monitoring procedures to secure control over the movement of their organisations into the future. Powerful coalitions of managers are supposed to know what is happening through environmental scanning and internal resource analyses, on the basis of which they are supposed to choose the outcomes for their organisation, design the systems, including learning systems, which will enable them to be in control of the strategic direction of their organisation 'going forward' so that improvement and success are secured.

This way of thinking is highly abstract in that it takes us away from our direct experience of the micro-details of interaction between actual human beings, the organisational dynamics of the title of this book, and this abstraction is not in any way sensed as a problem; indeed, this approach is judged to be highly practical. From this scientific perspective, organisations change when powerful coalitions of leaders and managers change the strategic macro-designs, rules, procedures, structures and visions and then persuade others to rationally implement the overall strategies for changes. Strategy is ultimately a choice made by the most powerful, either on the basis of rational analysis or as aspects of learning processes. When thinking in this way, it makes unquestionable sense to ask what particular tools, techniques, competences, organisational structures, cultures, social networks, and so on, lead to success. It seems to be pure common sense to look for the best practices conducted in successful organisations as a guide to what we should be doing in our own organisation, establish benchmarks to judge our organisation's performance and ask for the evidence that any proposed approach to leadership and management actually works in practice. Judgements on proposals and views about organisations should be made in the light of examples of managers who have used them and succeeded. It is this mainstream way of thinking about organisations and their strategic management that will be explored in Part 1 of this book. We will be concerned primarily with the origin of such a way of thinking and with what assumptions it makes and takes for granted as the basis of its strategic prescriptions for what organisations *should* do.

What happens, however, if we 'see' and think about a human organisations in the second way of 'seeing' and thinking about a coral reef outlined above? The answer is that the focus of attention shifts from the long-term, big picture, strategic macro-level to the details of the micro-interactions taking place in the present between living beings such as coral polyps in the case of coral reefs and human persons in the case of organisations. Instead of abstracting from and covering over the micro-processes of organisational dynamics, such organisational dynamics become the route to understanding how organisations are being both sustained and changed at the same time and what part the activities of leading, managing and strategising play in this paradox of stability (continuity) and instability (change).

Drawing on the modern natural sciences of complexity as source domains for analogies with organisations, which is explained and explored in Part 2 of this book, the second way of thinking about organisations and their strategic management places the choices, designs and learning activities of people, including leaders, managers and powerful coalitions, in one organisation in the context of similar activities by people in other organisations. It becomes understood that both continuity and change in all organisations are emerging in the many, many local communicative, political and ideologically based choices of all members of all the interdependent organisations including the disproportionately influential choices of leaders and powerful coalitions of managers. What happens to an organisation is not simply the consequence of choices made by powerful people in that organisation. Instead, what happens to any one organisation is the consequence of the interplay between the many choices and actions of all involved across many connected, interdependent organisations. Instead of thinking of organisations as the realisation of a macro-design chosen by the most powerful members of that organisation, we come to understand organisations as perpetually constructed macro- or global patterns emerging in many, many local interactions. Continuity and change arise in local interactions, not simply in macro-plans. Strategies are thus no longer understood simply as the choices of the most powerful but as emergent patterns of action arising in the interplay of choices made by many different groups of people.

It is important to emphasise that this second mode of thinking turns the first mode of thinking on its head. According to the first mode of thinking, strategies are chosen by powerful managers and then implemented, while in the second strategies emerge in a way not simply determined by central choices but arising in the ongoing local interaction of many, many people where that interaction can be understood as the interplay of many different intentions and choices and strategies. The two modes of thinking contradict each other, and this means that we cannot say that mode one works in some situations while mode two is more appropriate in other situations – this attempt to have your cake and eat it simply blocks the radically different nature of mode-two thinking. If one mode of thinking resonates with, and makes sense of, our experience, then the other will not.

Taking the second, emergent view, therefore, obviously calls for a complete reconsideration of what we understand leadership, management and strategic management to be. It means asking what effect, if any, centrally made plans might be having on organisations and how that effect comes about only through local interaction. If this way of thinking resonates more fully with our actual experience of organisational life then it will not make much sense to talk about the application of a theory to practice in an organisation, or to ask for the general tools and techniques that this way of thinking produces for achieving success. Notions such as best practice, benchmarking and an evidence base for prescriptions for success all become highly problematic, indeed, often quite meaningless. It is this way of thinking that is explored in Part 3 of this book. If on reading this section you end up asking for examples of success flowing from thinking in this alternative way; if you claim that Part 3 is not practical and ask for how it might be applied and what tools and techniques it produces for managers, then I am afraid that we, writer and reader, have failed to communicate with each other, for you are asking questions from the first, traditional scientific, way of thinking about organisations which simply have no meaning if you are thinking in the second way. Thinking in the second way calls for more reflective, reflexive modes of acting creatively in unique contingent situations for which there are no generally applicable prescriptions. The consequence of making the shift from the first to the second modes of thinking is a move from asking what organisations *should* be like and how they *should* be managed to asking what they are actually like and how they are actually being managed. It is only on the basis of fresh insight into what we are actually doing, rather than some rational fantasy of what we should be doing, that we might find ourselves acting more appropriately in specific contingent situations.

Perhaps this conclusion leads you to ask why we need an alternative to the first, traditionally scientific, way of thinking about organisations, especially if that alternative leads to what look like impractical conclusions and removes the ground from underneath the whole idea of applications and decision-making tools and techniques. In my view, the pressing reason for why we do need an alternative way of thinking, no matter what the discomfort it produces, lies in some pretty fundamental problems created by mainstream thinking. As I write these words in early 2010, we are still dealing with the consequences of the 2007 to 2009 credit crunch and global recession. These events have made it clear that, despite all the rational, analytical techniques, environmental scanning and internal resource analyses; despite the visions, inspirations and charisms; despite the development of learning organisations and knowledge management systems; despite that fact that most top executives have been educated in business schools; despite all of this, managers, consultants, politicians and policy makers simply do not know what is currently going on, let alone what might happen as the consequence of their action and inaction. It is inconceivable to me that top executives in major banks in North America and Europe chose a future of collapse and subsequent resuscitation by state funding for their organisations. I cannot imagine that conservative bankers and right-wing politicians chose partial nationalisation of the banking system. The notion that the most powerful can choose what happens to their organisation is quite clearly now in tatters; but even more generally, the first, traditionally scientific, mode of thinking can only qualify as such if there is a robust evidence base for the prescriptions it makes for organisational success. Towards the end of Part 1 of this book (*see* Chapter 8), I will be pointing to how the literature on organisations and their management contains no such evidence base. We continue to claim publicly that we are applying theories and using the tools and techniques these produce to manage our organisations strategically in order to realise centrally chosen global states on the basis of science, while in fact we are simply acting on the basis of historically acceptable beliefs about management, if indeed we are not actually doing something quite different to what we claim publicly. The fact is that organisation and management sciences are not sciences at all but scientific emperors with no clothing. If we look at the history of the alliance of management and science we find that its raison d'être had little to do with the actual application of the scientific method to organisations and much more to do with the attempts of the new managerial class emerging in the nineteenth century to legitimise itself as a profession in the same way as scientists had done – to claim the legitimacy of science was to secure a powerful voice in human affairs and this is still the case today.

If what I have said is true, then why is there no sign of leaders and managers searching for, and moving to, a more useful way of thinking about their experience? I can find little sign of such a move as investment bankers rapidly revert to large bonus cultures and, aided by management consultants and ambitious CEOs, promote once more waves of merger and acquisition activity despite the lack of evidence that this produces long-term success. This points to why a major shift in thinking is a long way off, despite the inadequacy of current thinking. What blocks a shift in thinking is firstly ideological. Rational, planning, visioning, controlling approaches to organisations and societies all express an ideology of scientific rationalism and improvement on a large scale. Shifting to a different way of thinking means destroying an existing ideology and replacing it with a new set of beliefs, of a much more modest and humble nature and, since no one can engineer such a shift in ideology, it will have to emerge in many local interactions, if it does at all. Ideologies sustain patterns of power relations – they make current patterns of power relations feel natural. Any ideological shift therefore threatens existing patterns of power relations and so will inevitably be resisted and undermined. After all, what are leaders, CEOs, management consultants, investment bankers and politicians to do to justify their powerful positions and large financial rewards if the very basis on which they say they are acting is thrown into question, and how are business schools to sustain their professional positions if the bulk of what they teach is seriously flawed?

However, this is not some cynical commentary implying deception or stupidity on the part of the powerful, because the ideology is shared, and the current pattern of power relations is reflected, across the groups of the less powerful too, and for all of them these particular ideologies, patterns of power relations and ways of thinking are major aspects of their identities. No one can blithely and facilely contemplate the destruction of their very identity and so no one can easily move to a fundamentally different way of thinking. In inviting you to continue reading his book I am inviting you to challenge your own ideologies, power positions and ways of thinking while reflecting on what this implies for your identity. You will not change the world tomorrow by thinking differently, but you may find you have a more fruitful and interesting experience as a manager or as a teacher or adviser of managers. It is my experience that when people think differently they find themselves doing things differently, whether for the good or the bad. Engaging in the reflection and reflexive activity of challenging one's way of thinking is of major importance, well worth any discomfort and conflict it produces because few issues are more important than how our organisations are governed.

1.4 Outline of the book

This book is addressed to the community of practice constituted by people who manage organisations, those who consult to them, those who research and write about organisational activity and those who study all of this as part of gaining entry to, and developing the knowledge and skill required to participate in, the community of practice. Such participation requires the ability to engage in the community's dominant discourse. It is usual for textbooks to survey and summarise the dominant discourse and, in the case of the community of organisational practitioners, to present prescriptions for successful management together with some kind of evidence backing the prescriptions, usually in the form of case studies. Most strategy books focus attention, either explicitly or implicitly, on what managers are supposed to do to improve the performance of an organisation. The immediate concern is then with the scope of an organisation's activities, its future direction and how it secures competitive advantage. Many, probably most, textbooks on strategy simply present the major strand in the dominant discourse, together with its prescriptions, with little questioning, as if the underlying way of thinking was self-evident. Most of these textbooks, largely reflecting the origins of the major strand in the dominant discourse in economics, present a view of strategic management that is rational, formal and orderly. Some textbooks, however, do bring out the multifaceted nature of the dominant discourse and the sometimes conflicting strands of thinking reflected in that discourse. They clarify how early, rather simplistic, accounts of strategic management, largely drawn from economics, have been subjected to strenuous critique which presents much messier processes of strategic management involving politics, culture, acts of interpretation and expressions of emotion. To understand these messier aspects, this second category of textbook draws on ideas from psychology, sociology and philosophy as well as from economics.

This book is similar in some respects to this latter category in that it too points to the less rational, less orderly aspects of strategic management, also drawing on ideas from psychology, sociology and philosophy. This is signalled by the term 'organisational dynamics' in the title of the book. 'Dynamics' refers to patterns of movement over time, for example, whether the pattern of movement is regular or irregular. 'Organisational dynamics', therefore, refers to the patterns of movement over time in the interactions between the people who are the organisation, the community of practice. Such patterns could be described, for example, as regular patterns of dependence and conformity, or as irregular patterns of aggression and non-compliance. In the literature on organisations, organisational dynamics is often regarded as a discipline of its own, called 'organisational behaviour', for example, which is quite distinct from the discipline of strategic management, which is itself often distinguished from operational management. In coupling strategic management and organisational dynamics, the title signals that this book will not make what I regard as artificial splits between aspects of organisational activity that seem to me to be inseparable. It is people who practise management, whether strategic or otherwise, and it is therefore essential to understand the behaviour of people, the dynamics of their interactions, if one is to understand the practice of strategising.

However, while similar in some respects to the second category of strategic management textbooks mentioned above, this book also differs significantly from them, and this is signalled in the subtitle of the book. The subtitle refers to a 'challenge to ways of thinking about organisations' where that challenge is presented from a particular viewpoint, namely, 'complexity'. The term 'complexity' here refers to important insights coming from the natural complexity sciences to do with the intrinsic uncertainty and unpredictability of a great many natural phenomena, to the importance of diversity in the evolution of novel forms, and to the self-organising, emergent nature of that evolution. The insight is that novel, global, population-wide forms emerge unpredictably in self-organising, that is local, interaction, in the absence of any blueprint, programme or plan for the global, population-wide form. Since the major strand in the dominant discourse is based on assumptions to do with predictability and planning the development of the whole organisation, the insights from complexity clearly present a challenge. These insights, however, also challenge the critique of the rational, planning strand in the dominant discourse, because most of the critiques retain some notion of at least influencing the whole from some external position.

The purpose of this book, therefore, is to explore *ways of thinking* about organisations and their management. It seeks to identify the usually taken-for-granted, fundamental assumptions upon which particular ways of thinking are based. It further seeks to clarify how these assumptions lead to particular lines of argument that focus attention on organisational matters in particular ways. Taken-for-granted assumptions carry with them certain entailments that have an enormous impact on the kind of actions people in organisations take. The purpose of this book is *not* simply to summarise various strands of the dominant discourse and the criticisms that may be made of them or to indicate how the ensuing prescriptions have led to success or failure by presenting examples and case studies. Instead, the book provides brief summaries of the various strands in the dominant discourse only in the interests of bringing out what the implicit, taken-for-granted assumptions are. This book will also be locating various discourses about organisations in the wider traditions of Western thought, paying attention to how they have developed historically. Chapter 2 will set out a framework for analysing different ways of thinking – the taken-for-granted assumptions.

Part 1 of the book is an exploration of the dominant discourse. This dominant discourse is understood to include all perspectives on organisations that make the following assumptions. The first assumption is that organisations are, or are to be thought of 'as if' they were, systems. The second assumption is that these systems are external to the individuals forming them. Individuals are thought of as existing at one level, whereas organisational systems are thought of as existing at a higher level. The third assumption is that it is the individual who is primary – the autonomous individual. The dominant discourse is built on the foundations of cognitivist, constructivist, humanistic and psychoanalytic psychology where, for all of them, the individual is the primary unit of concern. Fourth, associated with this focus on the individual, is the notion of the organisation and the social as systems being constructed by the actions of individuals, with those constructions then acting back on individuals as a cause of their behaviour. The fifth assumption is that since they are external to and constructors of the organisational system, individuals can plan, design, or at the very least influence the movement of the system. Part 1 consists of Chapters 3 to 9.

Chapter 3 explores the origins and development of systems thinking and the notion of the autonomous rational individual in the thought of the German philosopher Immanuel Kant. These notions are the main pillars upon which are built the theories of organisational strategy covered in Part 1.

Chapter 4 is concerned with strategic choice theory, which prescribes formal, analytical procedures for formulating long-term strategies to produce successful performance and the design of administrative systems for their implementation. The chapter will explore how this theory is based fundamentally upon cybernetic systems theory and primarily cognitivist psychology.

Chapter 5 turns to alternative theories of how organisations evolve and change through processes of organisational learning. The theoretical foundations of these theories are to be found in an alternative theory of systems known as *systems dynamics* combined with cognitivist psychology, as in strategic choice theory, and also humanistic psychology.

Chapter 6 reviews a combination of yet another theory of systems, general or open systems theory and psychoanalytic perspectives on human action. This psycho-dynamic systems theory focuses attention on unconscious group processes and the way people defend themselves against anxiety, drawing attention to how these all create obstacles to rational task performance and learning.

Chapter 7 reviews the way in which those engaged in the dominant discourse have addressed the question of strategy process, that is, the matter of *how* strat-egising activities are conducted.

Chapter 8 reviews the evidence for the dominant discourse described in Chap-ters 3 to 7 and identifies key areas which call for an alternative way of thinking about strategic management and organisational dynamics.

Chapter 9 describes ways of thinking that have moved away from the dominant discourse to some extent by stressing participation, relationship, conversation, ideology, power and practice.

Part 2 of the book moves from the systems theories developed in the late 1940s and early 1950s to those developed more recently in what have come to be known as the *complexity sciences*. This Part looks at insights from the complexity sciences as a basis for an alternative way of thinking and points to how the potential for an alternative is missed when these ideas are taken up within the dominant discourse, avoiding any serious challenge to that discourse. This part consist of Chapters 10 and 11.

Chapter 10 describes the theories of chaos, dissipative structures and the agent-based models of complex adaptive systems.

Chapter 11 reviews a number of applications of chaos and complexity theory to organisations. I argue that most of these applications continue to be made within the systemic and cognitivist psychological perspective of the dominant discourse with the consequence of collapsing the potentially radical insights of these theories and the challenge to that dominant discourse. The result is the re-presentation of existing theories in new language.

Part 3 interprets the insights from the complexity sciences in a different way, moving away altogether from the notion of organisation as a system and from the focus on the individual. Instead, it draws on certain strands of thinking in sociology that stress human interdependence and regard individuals as thoroughly social selves that arise in human interaction. That interaction can be described as complex responsive processes of human relating. These responsive processes of interaction take the form of conversation, patterns of power relations and ideologically based choices. Furthermore, these continually iterated responsive processes occur as the living present, the present we live in, and are essentially local in nature. It is in such responsive local interaction that population-wide patterns emerge. Organisations are such population-wide patterns constituting collective identities. For example, the university where I work is the continual iteration of patterns of behaviour described as lectures, seminars, examinations, committee meetings and so on. Part 3 of the book responds to the challenge of complexity by reconceptualising an organisation as ongoing patterning in the interactions between people and denies that it constitutes a system or even that it is useful to think of an organisation 'as if' it were a system. No one can step outside the ongoing responsive processes of interaction and so no one can influence the emerging patterns from any external position. The only influence any of us can have is in our participating in the ongoing responsive process of relating to each other. This is not to take an ideological position in which relating is somehow good, because oppression, ethnic cleansing, racial abuse, murder and war are also iterated, ongoing, responsive processes of people relating to each other. The dominant discourse separates macro- (global or population-wide) and micro- (local) levels of existence or study, reflected in distinctions between the parts and the whole of a system and the separation of the individual and the group (organisation or society). The alternative presented in Part 3 takes the view that the macro is continually emerging in the micro as individuals simultaneously form, and are formed by, the social. This leads to a very different focus of attention with regard to organisational life and therefore has very different implications for action. Part 3 consist of Chapters 12 to 18.

Chapter 12 reviews the origins of responsive processes thinking in the thought of the German philosopher Georg Wilhelm Friedrich Hegel, and its further development in the work of the American pragmatist philosophers George Herbert Mead and John Dewey, and the processes sociologist Norbert Elias.

Chapters 13 to 16 review the theory of complex responsive processes as a perspective from which to understand strategy and organisational change. They develop an alternative psychological perspective in which relationship is the key to understanding human action, including organisations. This theory focuses on the self-organising and constructive nature of conversation, power relations and ideology in organisations.

Chapter 17 is concerned with how we might understand the impact of global strategies and policies from the perspective of complex responsive processes of interaction between people.

Chapter 18 examines how the theory of complex responsive processes might answer the four key questions posed earlier in this chapter and explores its implications for strategic management and organisational dynamics.

Each of the three part starts with a short introduction setting out the purpose of that part. Each part is divided into a number of chapters. It is usual nowadays to indicate at the start of chapters in a textbook what the learning outcomes are supposed to be for those reading the chapter. This practice reflects a particular theory of communication and learning that will be described in Chapter 13. According to this theory, meaning arises in an individual mind and is transmitted to another mind. If the idea is described with clarity and the transmission is successful, then the writer of a chapter can convey it to the reader who ought to be able to learn it. For reasons that I hope will become clear in Part 3, I do not find this a convincing theory of communication and instead ascribe to a view in which meaning arises in interaction between people, so that the meaning of what I write is located not in my words alone but in your response to them. It follows that I cannot know what the learning outcomes will be for you if you read a chapter.

So, instead of setting out learning outcomes, at the start of each chapter, I list the points about a particular way of thinking that I am trying to draw attention to and invite readers to draw on their own organisational experience to reflect upon these points. I try to indicate why I think the material in a particular chapter is important. Each chapter ends with a list of questions about the material in the chapter. These have not been designed as a kind of examination in which readers can check whether they have learned the material. Instead, the questions are intended as an aid to further reflection on the ways of thinking that have been discussed in the chapter.

It is also usual for a textbook to have a number of case studies that describe successful or unsuccessful managerial action. Readers are then supposed to analyse the case studies and draw conclusions about successful management practice. Since this book is about ways of thinking, some of which are incompatible with the case study method, I have not included any case studies or even examples that might convey the idea of 'right' management practices. Instead, the book provides further reading at the end of each chapter which includes references to reflective management narratives written by graduates from a doctoral programme I am involved with at the University of Hertfordshire. This is a part-time programme for organisational practitioners whose research is their work. The methodology they pursue is one that can be summarised as 'taking experience seriously'. What this involves is narrating some current organisational activity that the writer is involved in and reflecting upon, and making sense of, that activity in the light of traditions of thought. Their narratives therefore provide the reader with an opportunity to reflect upon, and perhaps discuss with others, just how a particular practitioner makes use of the ideas presented in Part 3 to make sense of what they are doing in organisations. In discussing these experiences readers may develop further their own thinking.

Further reading

A well-argued and carefully documented history of the development of management as a profession is provided by Khurana (2007). An instructive history of the evolution of management consulting can be found in McKenna (2006). It is worth reading both of these books to obtain a rounded view of how management and the study of organisations have evolved. They provide a basis for beginning to reflect upon what strategic management is, where it has come from and what kinds of social developments and intellectual assumptions it depends upon.

Questions to aid further reflection

1. Why do you think it has proved to be so difficult to provide evidence to support the dominant discourse's prescriptions for strategic management?
2. What is your own experience of what seems to work in managing organisations?
3. What roles have business schools and management consultants played in developing notions of strategic management?
4. Why do those concerned with organisations keep insisting on the provision of tools and techniques despite the lack of evidence that they work?
5. Why is it so difficult to take up alternative ways of thinking?

Chapter 2

Thinking about strategy and organisational change
The implicit assumptions distinguishing one theory from another

This chapter invites you to draw on your own experience to reflect on and consider the implications of:

- The fundamental concern of strategic management – the phenomena it seeks to deal with.

- Every practice of strategic management reflecting some theory.

- The taken-for-granted assumptions upon which each theory is built.

- How differences in these taken-for-granted assumptions lead to different theories.

- Different claims as to the nature of human knowing.

- Whether strategic management can qualify as an objective science or not.

The chapter is important because it sets out a basis for comparing the different ways of understanding and practising strategic management that have developed over the past few decades. This is the basis that will be used throughout the rest of the book.

2.1 Introduction

This book differs from most textbooks in that it quite explicitly advocates a particular way of thinking about organisations, and according to some reviewers this means that it is not a textbook at all. Whatever it is, this book is concerned with *ways of thinking about how organisations change over time*. It *explores explanations* of how organisations have become what they are, and how they will become whatever they will be in five, ten or however many years' time.

There are many different theories that seek to explain how organisations change, or fail to change, but none of them are universally accepted. Even those that dominate academic and management discourses provide only partial explanations of life in organisations. The purpose of this book is to examine what is similar in these competing theories, and how they differ. To put it another way, the purpose of this book is to explore different ways of making sense of one's experience of life in organisations. It is from my own experience that I describe, compare and comment on the various theories I will be presenting in the chapters that follow. My own experience inevitably colours how I describe those theories and what I have to say about them. In writing this book, therefore, I am revealing how I currently make sense of my experience of life in organisations and I am inviting you to consider whether this resonates in any way with your own experience.

The chapters that follow will briefly summarise various organisational theories, including their descriptions of, and prescriptions for, managing change. The aim will be to point to the assumptions made, and reasoning processes used, in these theories, matters that are often not made explicit by those presenting them. A distinction will be drawn between systemic and responsive processes ways of thinking about organisations and their strategies.

Two basic questions

What I am setting out to do in this book, then, is to review and compare different ways of explaining what strategy is, how it arises and how organisations change. There is no universally true explanation of how organisations evolve, only a number of increasingly contested accounts. If one is to avoid blindly following one of these accounts, mistakenly taking it to be the truth, then I think that it is necessary to stand back and ask two fundamental questions:

1. What are the phenomena that are being talked about when the terms 'strategy' and 'organisational change' are used?
2. How do human beings make sense of phenomena, including those that this book is concerned with, and in what traditions of thought is such sense-making located?

The second question is important because there are different explanations of how humans make sense of anything. The particular explanation one adopts directly affects the particular account one gives of any phenomena, including those to which the concepts of strategy and organisational change apply. The following section takes up the question to do with the phenomena of interest and the one after that considers different explanations of *how* we know anything.

2.2 The phenomena of interest: dynamic human organisations

Consider the general phenomena that strategy and organisational change are both concerned with in our experience. If I reflect upon my own experience of life in organisations, I am first of all aware that people in any organisation that I have ever worked for interact with people in other organisations in what I would think of as a population of organisations.

Populations of organisations

Over any time period, say one, five, ten years, in any geographic region, say Europe, thousands upon thousands of new organisations are set up, and within the same time frame many thousands are dissolved, mostly small ones but sometimes very large ones. In other words, in each period, there are large numbers of small organisational dissolutions and small numbers of large ones. Some organisations go on for a very long time: the Roman Catholic Church is more than 1,500 years old and a few commercial organisations have survived for more than a century. On average, however, the lifespan of commercial organisations in Western countries is about 40 years. In any time period, some organisations merge into others, while yet others split into separate organisations. Many acquire others and some sell parts of their organisation to others. Organisations supply each other with goods and services. Some exert regulatory power over others.

Over the years, surviving organisations change their structures and the composition of their activities and as they do so they threaten, or create opportunities for, others. Whole new industries appear as new technologies are developed, creating niches of new activities for both new and old organisations, while other industries disappear. Many organisations reduce their workforces in downsizing, de-layering activities. Many relocate their activities from one country to another. Some focus on one locality while others operate globally. From time to time, there are major changes in how organisations are governed. There are private and public, commercial and charitable, governmental and industrial organisations all interacting with each other in many different ways.

Dynamic phenomena

What is striking, I think, is just how much change is going on all the time but also, at the same time, how some organisations change very little. In other words, the phenomena of interest, namely populations of organisations, are highly dynamic ones. *Dynamics* means movement, and concern with the dynamics is concern with the patterns phenomena display as they evolve over time. Dynamic phenomena are ones that display patterns of change over time, and a study of dynamics is concerned with what generates these patterns and what properties of stability and instability, regularity and irregularity, predictability and unpredictability they display. One of the key features distinguishing one theory of strategy and organisational change from another is how they deal with the matter of dynamics. I will be pointing to this in the reviews of a number of theories in the chapters that follow.

It is striking how unstable the dynamics of populations of organisations are, on the one hand, but how stable they are, on the other. Or, to put it another way, what is striking is just how unpredictable are the moves made by organisations and yet how predictable they are. What I mean by this is that it is virtually certain that mergers and takeovers will take place and it is often clear in which industries this will happen. At the same time, it is often very surprising that one particular organisation should buy, or merge with, another. Members of an organisation, including its most senior managers, often experience such unpredictability and instability as anxiety provoking and stressful. Another striking point is how some organisations are merging with others, while yet others are splitting themselves into two or more parts. In other words, some are integrating while others are dividing.

Paradoxical phenomena

Populations of organisations change over time in ways that display both stability and instability at the same time, both predictability and unpredictability at the same time, both creation and destruction at the same time. What is one to make of it when the phenomena one is trying to understand, changes in populations of organisations, display such contradictory tendencies? Is this an apparent contradiction which arises for me simply because I do not understand the phenomena fully? Or is it a paradox, the genuine, simultaneous coexistence of two contradictory movements? How one answers these questions has important implications for the kind of theory of organisational change one develops. Some theories see only contradictions to be solved by further work, while others see paradox that can never be resolved. This position on paradox will be one of the features I will use to distinguish one theory of organisational change from another. I will return to this point later in this chapter and take it up again in subsequent chapters as I review a number of theories of organisational change.

Degrees of detail

Now, however, I think it is important to notice how I have been talking about organisations as 'whole' organisations interacting 'within' a whole population as if they were individual entities, which is a very common way of talking about organisations. In other words, the descriptions are at the macro level, that is, the level of the large, or the whole, rather than the small, or the entities that make up the whole, that is, the micro level. This too will be an important feature in the comparison between different theories of organisational change in the chapters that follow. Some theories focus on the macro level, some on the micro level and yet others on both, looking for how the micro and the macro might be linked.

More fundamental, however, is the matter of how one thinks about these 'levels'. In some theories, the micro and the macro are thought of as distinct levels of reality, each of which has its own distinctive properties as wholes. So, one level is the individual human being understood from some psychological perspective. The next level is the group having its own properties. The level above that may be the organisation consisting of groups of individuals to be understood in terms of organisational principles and above that are the levels of industry, economy and society. In these theories, then, organisational phenomena are wholes classified at different ontological levels. In other theories, however, the micro and the macro are not thought of as separate levels with distinctive properties. Instead, they are thought of as simply different degrees of examination. In these theories, individuals, groups and organisations are not wholes at different ontological levels but are simply aspects of the same processes of human interaction.

Moving now to the micro degree of examination, each organisation is itself a population of interacting groupings of individual people. In my experience, this interaction between members of an organisational population is characterised by political activity as people push for, or try to stop, particular activities. They may become angry with each other or feel betrayed. If you think of your experience of being promoted, having others promoted above you, or having the threat of downsizing hanging over you, you can see how emotions of some kind are inseparable from interactions between people within and between organisations. Another feature I will be pointing to, as I review a number of theories in the chapters that follow, is just how much account those theories take of the political activity and emotion involved in organisational evolution.

The phenomena of interest in this book have to do with life in organisations and this is not some interaction between abstract entities, but interactions between people that directly affect the meaning of their lives and their health. To gain some understanding of these interactions one has to participate in them and one's understanding will arise in one's own experience. From a macro perspective, it may well be possible to take the position of the objective observer who stands outside the phenomena of interest and offers explanations of their behaviour. However, explanation and understanding from the micro perspective relies much more on one's own personal experience. Here the explanation is offered from the position of a participant in organisational life. This is another distinguishing feature of the theories I will review, namely the extent to which the theory is offered from the position of the objective observer as opposed to the inquiring participant.

Interaction

Another important point to note about the phenomena that strategy and organisational change are concerned with is that they are all about interactions. For example, one kind of interaction takes place when one company buys another and another kind of interaction takes place when one company supplies another. From the perspective of an individual organisation, one kind of interaction takes place when a director resigns and another kind takes place when a director is handsomely rewarded. Furthermore, one interaction will inevitably touch off many more. When one pharmaceutical company merges with another, it changes the competitive balance for all of the others, making it highly likely that many of them will look for merger partners. This is because they are interconnected. Another very important feature distinguishing one theory of strategy and organisational change from another is the manner in which interaction and interconnection are understood.

Most theories think of interaction as constituting a network or a system. Individual minds might be thought of as a system consisting of, say, interacting concepts. A group may be thought of as a system consisting of, say, interacting individuals, while an organisation might then be thought of as a system consisting of interacting groups. An industry would then be thought of as a supra-system consisting of interacting organisations. When thought of in this way, interaction is always interaction between systems, producing yet another system, all of them nesting hierarchically in each other at different levels. Different theories of strategy and organisational change are built on different theories of the nature of a system. One of the main focuses of this book will be on different theories of systems and how these underpin different theories of organisational evolution. However, although most theories of strategy and organisational change are couched in systemic terms, there is an alternative. This is to think of interaction as responsive processes of direct communicating and power relating between human bodies. Such a perspective yields responsive processes theories of strategy and organisational change. This distinction between systemic and responsive process theories provides the principal way of distinguishing between different theories of strategy and organisational change. Parts 1 and 2 will review systemic theories and Part 3 will explore responsive processes theories.

In summary, then, the phenomena that this book is concerned with are continuously evolving populations of organisations where each organisation is itself an evolving population of groupings of individual people, each of whom is also evolving. In other words, we are concerned with dynamic patterns of interaction and interconnection. We can think about these patterns of interaction in terms of *systems* or in terms of *responsive processes*. We can take a macro or micro perspective and we can think of these as different ontological *levels* or simply as different *degrees of detail being examined*. We can notice the contradictions and we can adopt a *dualistic* way of thinking that resolves them or we can adopt a way of thinking that sees the contradictions as essential *paradoxes* that cannot be resolved. Finally, we can try to think from the position of the *objective observer* or from that of the *participative inquirer*. Which of all of these choices is made determines the kind of theory of strategy and organisational change one comes up with.

Having obtained some idea of the nature of the phenomena that strategy and organisational change are concerned with, consider now the second question posed at the end of Section 2.1, namely how to make sense of the phenomena.

2.3 Making sense of the phenomena: realism, relativism and idealism

The question of how we make sense of ourselves in our world is, of course, a very old one. One answer to that question is *realism*. From this perspective it is the nature of reality itself that determines the patterns we perceive and the meaning we make of our experience. The notion here is that there is a reality external to humans which exists before they try to interpret or explain it: that is, reality is pre-given. This means that the categories into which people classify specific instances are already there in the phenomenon they are trying to explain. A rose falls into the category 'roses' because there is a real difference between roses and other categories of flowers. An organisation falls into the category 'coal industry' because there is a real difference between organisations in this industry and those in the gas industry, say. If the categories exist in reality, then any other classification people might make would not produce an adequate explanation, a fact that they would discover when they tried to act in accordance with that explanation. Most natural scientists would probably adopt this position in relation to the natural phenomena that they try to explain. If one adopts this position, it is quite natural to suppose that a human being can stand outside the phenomena to be explained, taking the role of the objective observer who builds increasingly accurate explanations, or models, through experimentation. Mostly, realists do not see any inherent limitation on human ability to comprehend reality in its entirety. For them, it is only a matter of time before research progressively uncovers more and more of reality.

The opposite position to realism is *relativism* or *scepticism*, nowadays known as 'postmodernism'. Here the categories into which people classify their experiences are held to exist only in their minds, not out there in reality. Any explanations they come up with are, therefore, simply projections of their own minds. Those who hold this position maintain that there is no pre-given reality outside of humans. There is no reality, only the stories we tell each other and, according to those who take this position to the extreme, one story is as good as another.

Another position avoids the extremes of both realism and relativism / scepticism and this is *idealism*. Here, too, it is held that it is in the ways we think that the patterning of our experience arises. However, idealists do not believe that this means that our entire sense-making activity is purely relative. Chapters 3 and 12 will explore idealist ways of making sense in more detail. Chapter 3 will describe Kant's transcendental idealism, in which it is argued that humans inherit mental categories and understand their world in terms of them. Understanding is then not relative at all, but determined by pre-given categories in individual minds. Chapter 12 will briefly review Hegel's absolute or Romantic idealism according to which human understanding is a social process that avoids relativism.

There are also more recent views that might be understood as idealist. *Constructivists* (*see* Chapters 5 & 7) hold that, because of biological evolution, humans are capable of perceiving the world in one way but not others (Maturana and Varela, 1987). For example, the human visual apparatus receives light waves on three channels; it is trichromate. Some other animals have dichromate (two channels) or quatrochromate (four channels) vision. Each type of creature, therefore, sees the world of colour in a different way, in effect, through biological evolution, selecting aspects of reality for attention. It is impossible for one type of creature to see the world of colour that another type sees. Similarly, constructivists would point to limitations on human capacity to perceive reality imposed by the evolved nature of the human brain. By its very nature, the human brain selects aspects of reality to pay attention to. This position has something in common with realism in that it supposes a reality that exists outside of the human organism and is not simply the result of the mind's projection. Unlike realism, however, this is not an unproblematically pre-given reality but, rather, an individually constructed, enacted or selected reality.

Another position taken on the nature of the human capacity to explain experience is that of *social constructionism* (Gergen, 1985), which is a form of idealism. Some social constructionists adopt the sceptical position, holding that there is no reality out there, but others tend towards an idealist position in which social reality is socially constructed in language. Here, reality is not a pre-given world determining our explanation but, rather, our explanation is being socially constructed in our encounters with each other in the world. This form of social constructionism is similar to constructivism but with a very important difference. While constructivists focus upon the selective nature of the individual human being, social constructionists point to social interaction, particularly in conversation, as the selecting process. The constructionist position is this: every explanation people put forward of any phenomenon is a socially constructed account, not a straightforward description of reality. If this view is held, then it is impossible to adopt the role of the independent, objective observer when trying to explain any phenomenon. Instead, one can only come up with an explanation through participation in what one is trying to explain.

Social constructionists hold that it is impossible to take the position of objective observer and that those who claim to do so are simply ignoring the impact of their own participation or lack of it. This leads to the closely related notion of *reflexivity* (Steier, 1991). Reflexive entities are entities that bend back upon themselves. Humans are reflexive in the sense that any explanations they produce are the products of who they are, as determined by their histories. For example, I am trying, on these pages, to explain the different ways in which humans explain their experience. If I hold the reflexive position then I cannot claim any objectively given truth for my way of doing this. Instead, I have to recognise that the approach I am adopting is the product of who I am and how I think. This, in turn, is the distillation of my personal history of relating to other people over many years in the particular communities I have and do live in which also have histories. If I accept the argument about reflexivity, I can never claim to stand outside my own experience, outside the web of relationships that I am a part of, and take the role of objective observer. Instead, I have to take the role of inquiring participant (Reason, 1988). Furthermore, reflexivity is not simply an individual activity dependent on that individual person's history alone. This is because we are always members of a community that has a history and traditions of thought. Reflexivity, therefore, involves being aware of the impact on how one thinks of both one's personal history and the history and traditions of thought of one's community. It is for this reason that Chapters 3 and 12, particularly, give brief accounts of the central traditions in Western thought.

The individual and the group

The move to a Romantic idealist, reflexive, social constructionist position is very significant in terms of what is being assumed about the relationship between the individual and the group. Realist, transcendental idealist and constructivist positions are all presented in terms of the capacities and limitations of the autonomous human individual. The individual is taken to be prior and primary to the group and groups can then only be seen as consisting of individuals. On the other hand, some social constructionists see the group as prior and primary. Individuals are then the products of the group in some way. Other perspectives, mostly derived from Romantic idealism, are paradoxical in that neither the individual nor the group is primary. One forms and is formed by the other at the same time. This question of how to think about the individual and the group is central to the reviews of ways of thinking about strategy and organisational change explored in this book.

So, there are a number of different, contradictory ways of explaining how human beings come to know anything. Furthermore, there is no widespread agreement as to which of these explanations is 'true' or even most useful. The realist position probably commands most support amongst natural scientists and those social scientists, probably the majority, who seek the same status for their field as is accorded to the natural sciences. Social constructionists point to a significant difference between natural and social phenomena. Humans interpret natural phenomena, those phenomena do not interpret themselves. However, when it comes to human phenomena, we are dealing with ourselves, phenomena that are already interpreting themselves. Many constructionists hold, therefore, that while the traditional scientific approach might be applicable in the natural sciences it is not in the human sciences.

At this point, you might be wondering why I have apparently moved so far away from the central concern of this book, namely strategy and organisational dynamics. The reason is this: any view you take of the nature of strategy and change in organisations immediately implies a view on the nature of human knowing. If you think that an organisation's strategy is the choice made by its chief executive, following a rational process of formulation, then you are assuming a realist, transcendental idealist or perhaps constructivist position. You are implicitly assuming that the individual is primary, and that this individual takes the position of the objective observer of the organisation. Since this tends to be the dominant approach to explaining what strategy is, it is quite easy to take it for the truth. However, what I have been trying to show in the above paragraphs is that this would be a completely unwarranted assumption. Just how human beings know anything, and whether the individual or the group is primary, are hotly contested issues with no clear truth. Simply going along with today's dominant views on strategy, without questioning the foundations upon which they are built, amounts to shutting one's eyes to other possibilities which might make more sense of one's experience. For example, if one shifts perspective and considers that an organisation's strategy might emerge from conversational processes in which many participate, then one would be moving towards a social constructionist position and assuming that the group is primary or to some kind of absolute idealism where neither the individual nor the group is primary. Perhaps this might assist in making more sense of the experience of life in organisations.

Different theories of strategy and organisational change imply different ways of explaining how human beings know or do anything. If one wants to understand just what the differences are between one explanation of strategy and organisational change and another, then one needs, I believe, to understand what assumptions are implicitly being made about how humans know anything. The key aspect distinguishing explanations of human knowing is the way they treat the relationship between the individual and the group. In the rest of this book, I will be reviewing how various ways of understanding strategy and organisational change differ. I will be pointing to how some of the most important differences relate to the implicit assumptions made about human knowing and the relationship between the individual and the group.

I now want to move on to another extremely important aspect of how we make sense of the world and this has to do with the nature of causality.

The nature of causality

One way of thinking about the relationship between cause and effect in Western culture is linear and unidirectional. There is some variable Y whose behaviour is to be explained. It is regarded as dependent and other 'independent' variables, $X1, X2 \ldots XN$, are sought that are causing it. Linear relationships mean that *if* there is more of a cause *then* there will be proportionally more of the effect. This is the efficient, 'if . . . then' theory of causality.

For example, in organisations, a frequent explanation for success is that it is caused by a particular culture, a particular management style, or a particular control system. The more that culture, style or control system is applied, the more successful the organisation will be. Opposition parties always say that the government of the day has caused recession and inflation. More of the government's policies will, they say, lead to more recession and more inflation. All of this is what is meant by straightforward unidirectional, linear connections between cause and effect.

Many scientists, both social and natural, are increasingly realising that this view of the relationship between cause and effect is far too simplistic and leads to an inadequate understanding of behaviour. They hold that greater insight comes from thinking in terms of mutual or circular causality. The demand for a product does not depend simply on customer behaviour; it also depends upon what the producing firm does in terms of price and quality. In other words, the firm affects the customer who then affects the firm. Management style may cause success but success affects the style managers adopt. The government's policies may cause recession and inflation, but recession and inflation may also cause the policies they adopt.

When organisms and organisations are thought of as systems, complex forms of causality become evident to do with interconnection and interdependence, where everything affects everything else. In addition to the circular causality and interdependence of systems, there is also *nonlinearity*. This means that one variable can have a more than proportional effect upon another. Nonlinear systems then involve very complex connections between cause and effect. It may become unclear what cause and effect mean. The links between them may become distant in time and space and those links may even disappear for all practical purposes. If in these circumstances one proceeds as if simple linear links exist even if one does not know what they are, then one is likely to undertake actions that yield unintended and surprising results.

How one thinks about causality, then, will have an important impact on how one thinks about strategy and organisational change. This is a matter to which subsequent chapters will pay a great deal of attention.

Closely linked to the matter of causality is that of paradox. I have already said that how different theories deal with paradox is an important feature distinguishing them, so it is important to be clear about what paradox means.

The nature of paradox

There are a number of different ways in which we deal with the contradictions we encounter in our thinking. The first is to regard them as a *dichotomy*, which is a polarised opposition requiring an 'either . . . or' choice. For example, managers faced with the need to improve quality, requiring an increase in costs, may also be faced with the need to cut costs. If they think in terms of a dichotomy then they choose one or the other of these opposing alternatives. Or they could think of the choice facing them as a *dilemma*, which is a choice between two equally unattractive alternatives. Improving quality is unattractive because it increases costs, and cutting costs means destroying jobs, which is unattractive for humanitarian reasons. Dilemmas also present 'either . . . or' choices. Thirdly, a contradiction may be thought of in terms of a *dualism or a duality*. For example, managers may be faced with the need to customise their products to meet localised customer requirements, but they may also be faced with the need to standardise their products to meet global competition. If those managers think about this in dualistic terms then they might come up with the resolution or elimination of the contradiction through '*both* thinking globally *and* acting locally'. The mode of thinking in dualistic terms has a 'both . . . and' structure. Instead of choosing between one or the other, one keeps both but locates them in different spaces or times. So, in the above example, one pole of the contradiction is located in thinking and the other in acting. The 'either ... or' thinking of dichotomies and dilemmas and the 'both ... and' thinking of dualisms/dualities all satisfy a precept of Aristotelian logic, which requires the elimination of contradictions because they are a sign of faulty thinking.

Finally, one might think of a contradiction as a *paradox*. There are a number of different definitions of a paradox. First, it may mean an apparent contradiction, a state in which two apparently conflicting elements appear to be operating at the same time. Paradox in this sense can be removed or resolved by choosing one element above the other all the time or by reframing the problem to remove the apparent contradiction. There is little difference between paradox in this sense and dualism/dualities and this is the meaning of paradox that is usually taken up in the literature on systemic views of organisations.

However, paradox may mean a state in which two diametrically opposing forces/ideas are simultaneously present, neither of which can ever be resolved or eliminated. There is, therefore, no possibility of a choice between the opposing poles or of locating them in different spheres. Instead, what is required is a different kind of logic, such as the dialectical logic of Hegel (*see* Chapter 12). As it is used in this book, the word *paradox* means the presence together, at the same time, of self-contradictory, essentially conflicting ideas, none of which can be eliminated or resolved.

There are many examples of paradoxes in organisations. Each individual in an organisation has a paradoxical desire for freedom and the excitement that goes with chance and uncertainty, while at the same time fearing the unknown and wanting order and discipline. Businesses have to produce at the lowest cost, but they have to increase costs to provide quality. Organisations have to control what their employees do, but they have to give them freedom if they want to retain them and if they want them to deal with rapidly changing circumstances.

Many theories of organisation emphasise either/or choices. They prescribe either stability and success, or instability and failure. They usually do not recognise paradox as fundamental and, when they do, they prescribe some kind of harmonious, equilibrium balance between the choices. In this way the paradox is in effect eliminated; its existence is a nuisance that is not fundamental to success.

The way one perceives paradox says much about the way one understands organisational dynamics. The idea that, for success, paradoxes must be resolved, and that the tension they cause must be released, is part of the paradigm that equates success with the dynamics of stability, regularity and predictability. The notion that paradoxes can never be resolved, only lived with, leads to a view of organisational dynamics couched in terms of continuing tension-generating behaviour patterns that are both regular and irregular, both stable and unstable and both predictable and unpredictable, all at the same time, but which lead to creative novelty.

2.4 Four questions to ask in comparing theories of organisational strategy and change

In the previous sections of this chapter, I have been describing what I think the phenomena are that I am trying to explain when I talk about strategy and organisational change. Those phenomena are populations of organisations of various kinds and populations of people and groupings of people that make up each of those organisations. These populations of organisations and people are continuously interacting with each other in ever-changing but also repetitive ways. I have also been talking about how human beings come to know the phenomena of their worlds, including those of populations of organisations and people dynamically interacting with each other. In the course of describing the phenomena and how one might come to know them, I have listed a number of factors that I want to use to distinguish between various theories of strategy and organisational dynamics. These factors are:

- How the dynamics are understood.
- How paradox is handled in thought.
- What ontological states and what degree of descriptive detail are focused upon – macro or micro.
- What part emotion is seen to play.
- How the interactive/relational nature of the phenomena are conceptualised.
- How causality is understood.
- Whether the theory assumes a pre-given or a constructed reality.
- Whether the theory takes the methodological stance of the objective observer or the reflexive, participative enquirer.
- What theory of human knowing and behaving it assumes, particularly how it deals with the relationship between individuals and groups.

I now want to pull these factors together into four questions that I will put to each of the theories to be considered in the chapters that follow. The questions are:

1. How does the theory understand the nature of human interacting and relating? I will be considering whether the theory takes a systemic or a responsive processes perspective, and how each of these deals with dynamics and the nature of causality.

2. What theory of human psychology – that is, ways of knowing and behaving – does each theory of strategy and organisational change assume? I will be focusing particularly on how each psychological theory deals with the relationship between individual and group and the questions of emotion and power.

3. What methodology underlies each theory of strategy and organisational change? I will be asking whether the theory takes the position of objective observer of a pre-given reality or whether it takes the position of the reflexive, participative inquirer seeking to understand a constructed reality.

4. How does each theory of strategy and organisational change deal with the paradoxical nature of the population of organisations and groupings of people? I will be asking whether the theory sees opposing ideas as dichotomies, dilemmas, dualisms/dualities or paradoxes.

In the chapters that follow I am going to classify different explanations according to the answers they give to the above four questions. What I am trying to do is to tease out strands of thinking in order to expose assumptions and reasoning processes for comparison.

Further reading

If you wish to inquire more deeply into how that various views of individual and various ways of thinking have evolved you could read Taylor (2007).

Questions to aid further reflection

1. What are the phenomena that are being talked about when the terms 'strategy' and 'organisational change' are used?

2. How do we make sense of 'strategy' and 'organisational change' and in what traditions of thought is such sense making located?

3. What methodology is appropriate for understanding strategy and organisational change?

4. How do you think individual and group are related to each other?

5. What is your understanding of the concept of system?

Part 1

Systemic ways of thinking about strategy and organisational dynamics

The purpose of Part 1 is to explore the ways of thinking reflected in the dominant discourse about organisations and their management as well as the most prominent critiques of this discourse to be found in organisational and management literature. What the chapters that follow will be trying to do is tease out the taken-for-granted assumptions being made in the dominant discourse and the critiques of it.

Common to both the dominant discourse and most of its major critiques is the taken-for-granted assumption that organisations are systems. It is now usual, amongst both organisational practitioners and organisational researchers and writers, to talk about organisations as entities that actually exist outside human interaction. Human individuals with minds inside them are located at one level of existence, while organisations as things called 'systems' which actually exist are located at another level of existence. Human individuals are thought to create organisations as systems in their interaction with each other and these systems are then thought to act back on individuals as a cause of their behaviour. The dominant discourse, therefore, reifies organisations, sometimes regarding them as mechanistic things and sometimes claiming that they are living things, organisms, with purposes and intentions of their own. We have come, then, not only to reify organisations but to anthropomorphise them. It is widely assumed that individuals, as leaders and managers, can take the position of objective observer of such organisational systems and design them to achieve purposes ascribed to them or at least intervene in them and influence the direction they take. The dominant discourse thus reflects an implicit and powerful ideology to do with managerial control. Chapters 4, 5 and 6 will explore just how these taken-for-granted assumptions are expressed in the dominant theories of strategic choice, organisational learning and psychodynamic systems.

The prevailing assumption that organisations are actually existing things, whether mechanistic or organic, has not gone unchallenged. Chapter 9 will explore a particularly coherent critique presented within the tradition of second-order systems thinking by soft and critical systems thinkers. Writers in these traditions hold that organisations are not actual systems to be found in the real world. Instead, they argue that organisations are to be thought of 'as if' they are systems; indeed some of these writers hold that human thinking is innately systemic. This critique, therefore, represents an important movement in thought from a realist to an idealist approach in which organisations as systems are mental constructs. However, this does not amount to a movement away from the idea of system. An organisation is to be thought of 'as if' it is a system in order to structure organisational problems in the interest of finding more effective solutions. It continues to be taken for granted that organisational phenomena are at a different level to human individuals who can design, intervene, influence and solve systemic problems. However, here too there is a challenge to the dominant discourse and its ideology of managerial control. This flows from the recognition that individuals cannot simply be objective observers external to an organisational system, because they are also participants in it. This leads to an emphasis on participation, social interaction, politics, culture and ethics in what amounts to an ideology of improvement, emancipation, democracy and respect for the plurality of points of view. However, the fundamental assumptions to do with systems and the primacy of the individual remain intact in the critique mounted by second-order systems thinking.

Other critiques of the dominant discourse have also been presented and some of these will be considered in Chapter 8. One outstanding critique has been presented to the taken-for-granted assumption in the dominant discourse that managers are rational decision-makers. This critique has pointed to the considerable limitations placed on the possibility of rational decision making by the economic costs of gathering and analysing data, the information-processing capacity of the human brain, the influence of cognitive frames of reference on what people pay attention to, the interpretations people make of their situations, and the impact of emotion, fantasising and unconscious processes (*see* Chapter 6). Linked to this major critique are the descriptive studies of what managers actually do, which reveal how idealised an image the dominant discourse presents of managers as rational planners. This critique points to how messy actual decision-making is and how at least some major aspects of strategy simply emerge, which is understood as occurring by chance as opposed to intention. Then there are the relatively few studies of whether the prescriptions of the dominant discourse do actually achieve what they are supposed to. Taken together, these studies are inconclusive at best and tend to point to how ineffective the prescriptions of the dominant discourse prove to be. However, mostly these critiques again make the same fundamental assumptions as the dominant discourse to do with the systemic nature of organisations and the primacy of the individual, the latter being reflected even when social interaction is taken into account.

Another critique is also important, and this relates to the nature of organisational process. In a reaction to the focus on that content of strategies which will lead to successful performance, some writers have called for a focus on how strategy is formed: that is, on strategy process rather than strategy content. However, the process field continued to think about organisations as a whole, at the macro level, and took a macro view of the strategy process. Over the last few years there has been a reaction to the macro perspective, taking the form of a call for focusing attention on the micro level of what people actually do on an ordinary, daily basis when they strategise. This leads to a concern with conversations, ways of sense making, politics, emotion and identity. However, once again this critique mostly continues to be based on systemic thinking about organisations and individual-focused cognitivist, constructivist and humanistic psychologies.

Finally, this Part will consider social constructionist approaches which move away from the assumption of the autonomous individual to place all the emphasis on social interaction and critical management theory which has moved away from both the assumption of autonomous individual and from the notion of organisations as systems.

Given the taken-for-granted nature and fundamental importance of the idea of system and the concept of the individual in the dominant discourse, as well as the critiques of it, Chapter 3 will explore the origins and implications of these notions.

Chapters 4 and 5 then go on to briefly summarise the main elements of the dominant discourse on organisation and strategy with a view to identifying the fundamental underlying assumptions. In talking about the dominant discourse, I am not talking about a monolithic, uncontested way of thinking, but a number of often conflicting strands held together by the common underlying assumptions of the autonomous individual and the organisation as a system. There are various ways of classifying these strands. One common classification is to distinguish between those approaches to strategy that focus on content and those that focus on process (Chakravarthy and Doz, 1992). However, this distinction has been criticised because all theories focusing on content make at least some implicit assumptions about process, and vice versa. I will be looking specifically at the assumptions made about process in Chapters 8 and 12. An often-quoted classification of strategic schools of thought is that provided by Mintzberg *et al.* (1998) who make the following distinctions:

Prescriptive schools

- The *design school*, in which strategy is a deliberate process of conscious thought where responsibility rests with top management. The strategy seeks to match the internal capabilities of a firm with the opportunities proved by its external environment (Andrews, 1987; Chandler, 1962; Selznick, 1957).

- The *planning school*, where specialist strategic planners adopt formal, step-by-step techniques to do much the same as the design school (Ansoff, 1965).

- The *positioning school*, which is built on the design and planning schools but focuses on strategy content (Porter, 1980, 1985).

Descriptive schools

- The *entrepreneurial school*, in which strategy is seen as a visionary process carried out by leaders (Peters and Waterman, 1982).

- The *cognitive school* (Bogner and Thomas, 1993; Regner and Huff, 1993), which focuses on the mental and interpretive processes of strategisers.

- The *learning school*, where strategies emerge as people learn over time (Lindblom, 1959; Nelson and Winter, 1982; Quinn, 1980) as distinct from deliberate strategy (Mintzberg and Waters, 1985).

- The *power school*, which sees strategy as a political process (Pettigrew, 1977).

- The *cultural school*, which is concerned with the influence of culture on strategic stability (Peters and Waterman, 1982).

- The *environmental school*, which sees the environment as the active cause of strategy while the organisation is passive (Hannan and Freeman, 1989).

Synthesis

- The *configuration school*, which integrates the views of all the other schools in terms of configurations or in terms of transformations (Miller and Friesen, 1980; Mintzberg, 1983).

Table A.1 Classification of schools of strategy thinking

School	Strategic choice	Organisational learning
Mintzberg *et al.*	*Prescriptive schools:* design planning positioning	*Descriptive schools:* entrepreneurial cognitive learning power cultural
Whittington	classical	processualists systemic

Another writer, Whittington (2001), distinguishes amongst:

- The *classical approach*, which relies on the rational planning models.
- The *evolutionary approach*, which draws on the metaphor of biological evolution where change depends on chance and competition.
- The *processualists*, who emphasise the imperfect processes of forming strategies which, in practice, emerge from pragmatic processes of learning and compromise.
- The *systemic approach*, which regards strategy as linked to the cultures and power structures of the system in which it takes place.

In reviewing the dominant discourse in this part, I intend to adopt a simpler classification, distinguishing between those approaches that regard strategy as a more or less unproblematic choice and those that regard strategy as arising in some form of purposive organisational learning. The relationships between these classifications are roughly as set out in Table A.1. The school Mintzberg *et al.* (1998) call the 'environmental' school coincides more or less with what Whittington calls the 'evolutionary' approach. I have not included these under the heading of either strategic choice or organisational learning, because evolutionary approaches claim that what happens to an organisation happens mainly as a consequence of chance and competition. In making this claim they mount what is, perhaps, the major critique within the dominant discourse of the intentional, purposive basis of all the other theories. Not surprisingly, given their emphasis on chance and passivity, evolutionary approaches feature very rarely in the discussions of organisational practitioners, while the vocabulary of all the other schools is common parlance amongst them. I will refer in subsequent chapters to the evolutionary approaches in drawing attention to the critiques of the dominant discourse.

I will be arguing that all of the theories categorised in Table A.1 under the headings of both strategic choice and organisational learning, as well as the evolutionary critiques thereof, share two fundamental, taken-for-granted assumptions. First, they all think of organisations in terms of systems. Second, they are all based, implicitly or explicitly, on one or more of the individual-centred theories of human psychology, namely, cognitivism, constructivism, humanistic psychology or psychoanalysis. Chapter 4 will be concerned with the theory of strategic choice while Chapter 5 will explore the way of thinking reflected in theories of organisational learning. Chapter 6 will look at ways of thinking about obstacles to learning from a psychoanalytic perspective. Chapter 7 will then review the manner in which strategy process is dealt with in the dominant discourse. To end this Part, Chapter 8 will look at the evidence for the dominant discourse and identify the issues it has not succeeded in resolving and Chapter 9 will describes various ways of thinking that have been developed to deal with these unresolved issues: namely, second-order systems thinking, social constructionist approaches, communities of practice and critical management studies.

The purpose of Part 1 of the book, then, is to explore the ways of thinking underlying theories found in the dominant discourse. These chapters provide the basis for comparison with the perspective to be described in Part 3, which turns to ways of thinking that depart from both of the dominant discourse's underlying assumptions mentioned above. This way of thinking takes organisations to be ongoing processes of human interaction rather than systems, and views human psychology not in terms of the autonomous individual and consequent individual-centred psychologies, but in terms of people being fundamentally interdependent.

Chapter 3

The origins of systems thinking in the Age of Reason

This chapter invites you to draw on your own experience to reflect on and consider the implications of:

- How the idea of a system arose and what it consists of.

- The 'as if', hypothetical nature of original systems thinking and how this was lost in the later development of systems thinking.

- The notions of causality reflected in the idea of a system.

- The notion of the autonomous rational individual and the theory of causality that this implies.

- The dualistic 'both . . . and' structure of systems thinking.

- The caution against applying the notion of system to human action.

- The possibility of explaining novelty in terms of systems.

- How systems sciences, including theories of organisation, developed on the basis of systems thinking.

As subsequent chapters will show, the concept of system and the notion of the rational autonomous individual are both fundamental to the dominant discourse on organisations and their management. For the purpose of reflecting upon and becoming critically aware of the way of thinking reflected in this discourse, it is therefore of great importance to think about the origins of the concept of system and the notion of the autonomous rational individual and what their explanatory limitations might be. Taking a reflexive stance does not simply mean taking into account one's personal history and how this impacts on how one is arguing; it also means taking into account the history of the social traditions of thought in which one is embedded and how this impacts on what one is arguing. Awareness of the history of the concept of systems and autonomous individuals then becomes a key element in taking a critical position. Already in Kant's thought we can see how organisations have come to be thought of as systems external to individuals and how these rational individuals have come to be thought of as the designers of organisational systems, or at least interveners in them who can influence the direction of their movement. Part 3 of this book presents a fundamental challenge to both of these notions.

3.1 Introduction

Some time ago, I joined a task force of senior executives in a large international corporation. This task force had been appointed by the chief executive who was concerned about the strategic direction of the corporation. He felt that the corporation had become increasingly unable to cope with the rapid changes confronting it. It seemed to carry on operating as it always had done in a world that was now completely different. The chief executive believed that the organisation needed to change substantially from an inflexible bureaucracy into a nimble entrepreneurial organisation capable of developing new forms of competitive advantage. He also believed that this change would only take place if the people throughout the *whole* organisation changed the way they behaved and he was convinced that such behavioural change would only happen if the values driving behaviour were transformed. This was the task he set for the task force I joined: namely, identifying the new set of values required to transform the organisation and recommending the actions required to instil these new values into the organisation. This task force had been meeting for some time and when I joined them their frustration was evident. Despite sharing the chief executive's beliefs and despite their undoubtedly intelligent efforts, they had been unable to identify the required values, let alone how such values might be instilled in the *whole* corporation. Furthermore, they had no satisfactory way of explaining why they had not been able to carry out their task.

What struck me when I joined them was how they had not been questioning the way of thinking that led them to believe that they could change their whole corporation in the manner proposed. They were not exploring the assumptions they were making when they held this view. Instead, they were simply taking it for granted that it was possible to do what they had been asked to do. It seemed to me that they were implicitly thinking of their organisation as a whole, as a system, operating according to particular values. They thought that if they could identify these values and then change them, they could change the direction, the strategy, of the organisation. They seemed to be thinking about themselves as autonomous individuals who could objectively observe the organisational system and determine the values according to which it should operate and then ensure that it did in fact operate according to these values.

For me, the big question was whether it was possible to do what they were proposing to do and it was clear that they were not even asking themselves this question. Unless they could begin to reflect upon their way of thinking and its taken-for-granted assumptions, they would probably continue with their frustrating attempts to formulate and change values. To take the reflexive stance I am suggesting, it seems to me to be essential to understand how particular ways of thinking originated. Ways of thinking evolve – they have a history and understanding this history enables us to understand the nature of the assumptions we are making now as we approach important practical issues. It is for this very practical reason that this chapter introduces the subjects of strategy and change by turning to philosophy and the history of Western thought.

In order to understand the taken-for-granted assumptions made in theories of strategic management, therefore, it is helpful in a very practical way to understand something of the history of those theories within the wider history of Western thought. The chapters in this part of the book will be drawing attention to the manner in which all of the major theories of strategic management today depend upon systems thinking and take for granted the assumptions upon which that thinking is built. This chapter will explore the origins of systems thinking in Western philosophy, and to do this it is necessary to go back some four hundred years and consider how people in the West thought about themselves and the world they lived in, and how they thought about the way in which they came to know anything about themselves in the world they lived in.

In the Middle Ages people in the West thought that the world was created by God and they thought about themselves as creatures in nature and therefore also made by God, in fact in the image of God. The purpose of nature was to express the glory of God in following His eternal, timeless laws. These laws applied to human beings too but with one major difference: unlike other creatures, humans were believed to have souls enabling them to choose whether to obey the laws of God or not. Obedience led to rewards in the afterlife and disobedience led to eternal punishment. Knowledge of God's creation was through divine revelation so that humans knew what they knew because God had revealed it to them in the Scriptures. Knowing was a process of interpreting the eternal truth to be found in the Holy Scriptures. Individuals thought of themselves in terms of their place in the community rather than as separate individuals. There was no notion of an existential gap between individuals because who one was flowed from one's membership of a community and this was fixed by birth.

People thought in this way for hundreds of years, and then about four hundred years ago changes in social and political structures began a long process of weakening the Church and absolute monarchies, and this process was intertwined with changes in the way people thought. This gradual process of change in the way people thought has come to be known as the Scientific Revolution, leading to the Age of Reason.

3.2 The Scientific Revolution and rational objectivity

The Scientific Revolution was a movement of thought in which people came to hold that the eternal, timeless laws of nature could be understood not through revelation but through human reason. For example, Copernicus and others worked in the early sixteenth century, observing and measuring the movement of the planets and putting forward theories on the laws governing their movement. Galileo took this work up in the early seventeenth century, as did Newton and Leibniz later on in the seventeenth century. Also during this period, the philosophers Bacon and Descartes powerfully articulated the way in which people were coming to experience themselves as individuals with minds inside them. As Descartes put it, human minds are 'thinking things' and all we can be sure of is our own individual capacity to doubt. Everything is to be subjected to doubt and it is in this rational process of doubting that humans can come to know themselves and their world. By the end of the seventeenth century, then, the scientific method had been established, as had a highly individualistic way of thinking about ourselves.

Central to the scientific method is the individual scientist who objectively observes nature, formulates hypotheses about the laws governing it and then tests these laws against quantified data, so progressively moving towards a fuller and more accurate understanding of the laws. These laws were understood to take the form of universal, timeless, deterministic, linear 'if–then' causal links. For example, *if* twice as much force is applied to an object in a vacuum *then* it will move twice as far. The consequence of this Scientific Revolution, extending over more than a century, was that people in the West had come to experience themselves as autonomous individuals with a non-corporeal mind inside them, taking the form of internal worlds consisting of representations of the external world. This view of how people experienced themselves was concisely formulated in the philosophy of Leibniz. He saw individuals as windowless monads who internally represented external worlds, perceived both consciously and unconsciously, and related to each other across an existential gulf.

However, this way of thinking posed fundamental questions. First, the question arose as to how reasoning individuals were able to formulate hypotheses, involving the categorisation of phenomena in nature and the identification of relationships between them. For the realists, the answer lay in the nature of reality. There was no problem about knowing, because our bodies simply perceived reality as it was through the senses. For others, however, there was a problem about knowing that needed explanation. Descartes and Leibniz dealt with the problem by arguing that the mind contained innate ideas through which it recognised clear, distinct truths about the real external world. In other words, there is nothing problematic about knowing: external reality exists and we directly know it because we are born with minds having the capacity for knowing reality. However, Locke took a more sceptical position and argued that the mind had no innate ideas of reality but was initially a blank tablet waiting for experience to write upon it in the form of sensory impressions that represent external, material objects. The question then became how we could know that our mental representations correspond to reality.

Writing around the middle of the eighteenth century, Hume took a radically sceptical position and said that the mind imposes an order of its own on the sensations coming from the external real world, but that this order is simply an association of ideas, a habit of human imagination through which it assumes causal connections. There is nothing innate about knowing, and the causal connections we postulate are simply the accidents of repeated connections in the mind. Ideas result from connections in experience, not from an independent reality, and intelligibility reflects habits of mind, not the nature of reality. Hume claimed that there was no necessary order to our ideas other than the ways they were combined in our minds according to habit and the laws of association.

With this radically sceptical argument, Hume threw into doubt the Enlightenment idea that reason could unaided discover the order of the real world. As a result, the philosophy of Descartes, Leibniz and Locke no longer seemed to provide a firm foundation for science. Scepticism, with its conclusion about the relativity and unreliability of knowledge, threatened the very basis of science. This debate between the dogmatic rationalists, or realist scientists, and the radical sceptics about the nature of human knowledge is much the same as the more recent debate between modernist science and postmodernism. In both cases, science posits the existence of a unitary reality that can be reliably observed as truth, while radical scepticism/postmodernism points to the constructed, relative and plural nature of accounts of the world in which there is no truth, only many different 'stories' with, at the extreme, none necessarily better than any other.

Another fundamental question posed by the Scientific Revolution had to do with human freedom and choice. Since humans were part of nature, they had to be subject to its deterministic laws; but if they were, then it followed that they could not be free.

These two questions, one to do with the nature of human knowing and the other to do with the possibility of human choice, were taken up by the philosopher Kant. Systems thinking can be said to have originated in Kant's answers to these questions.

3.3 The eighteenth-century German philosopher Immanuel Kant: natural systems and autonomous individuals

Kant was impressed by the advances in human knowledge brought about by the scientific method, but he also recognised that it was not sufficient to simply postulate dogmatically that we know reality directly. He accepted that we know what we know through sensations coming from the real world and that the mind imposes some kind of order on these sense data so that we cannot know reality in a direct manner. He therefore postulated a dualism. On the one hand there was reality, which he called *noumenal*, and on the other hand there was the appearance of reality to us in the form of sensations, which he called *phenomenal*. He argued that we could never know reality in itself, the noumenal, but only the appearance of reality as sensation, the phenomenal. This bears some similarity to the position of the radical sceptics, but Kant departed from them when he held that our inability to know reality itself does not mean that all our knowledge is purely relative, simply the result of habits of association. Instead, the mind consists of innate categories which impose order on the phenomenal.

In this way he agreed with the radical sceptics in holding that we could not know reality directly but also agreed with the scientific realists in holding that there were innate ideas that imposed order on experience so that knowledge and truth were not simply relative. Examples of the innate categories of mind are time, space, causal links and what Kant called 'regulative ideas'. *Regulative ideas* are to be distinguished from *constitutive ideas*. A constitutive idea, or hypothesis, is a statement of what actually happens in reality. For example, if we say that an organisation actually is a system operating to fulfil some real purpose, then we are putting forward a constitutive idea. We are saying that the organisation really exists and it is really fulfilling some real purpose. However, if we put forward an hypothesis in which we are thinking about an organisation 'as if' it were a system operating 'as if' it had a purpose, then we are thinking in terms of regulative ideas. Obviously Kant would not talk about constitutive ideas, because he held that we could never know reality in itself. The activity of the scientist then becomes clear in Kant's scheme of things. The scientist has a mind consisting of categories of time, space, causal links and the capacity for forming 'as if' hypotheses, which enables him or her to formulate hypotheses about the appearances of reality and then test them.

Scientists, such as Newton and Leibniz, had understood nature in mechanistic terms and Kant was able to explain why this understanding was neither purely relative nor directly revealing of the reality of nature. He resolved the contradiction between realist and relative knowledge by taking aspects from each argument and holding them together in the 'both . . . and' way of a dualism. Knowledge of appearances was real and reliable while knowledge of reality itself was indeed impossible. In a sense *both* the scientific realists *and* the radical sceptics had a point and the *contradictions between them could be eliminated* by locating their conflicting explanations in different realms. This is typical of Kant's dualistic thinking in which paradoxes are eliminated, so satisfying the rule of Aristotelian logic according to which paradox, the simultaneous existence of two contradictory ideas, is a sign of faulty thinking. I want to stress this key aspect of Kantian thinking because it has become very widespread in the West. The ideas of figure and ground, of different lenses through which to understand the world, and different levels of existence such as the individual at one level and the organisation at another, are examples of this.

Kant, then, developed transcendental idealism as an alternative to realism, on the one hand, and to scepticism, on the other. His thinking can be labelled as 'idealism' because he held that we know reality through the capacities of the mind, and it is transcendental because the categories through which we know are already given outside our direct experience. In this way, Kant provided a sophisticated justification for the scientific method.

Self-organising systems

However, Kant went further than providing a philosophical justification of the mechanistic understanding of nature provided by scientists. He held that, while it was useful to understand inanimate nature in this way, it was not adequate for an understanding of living organisms. He suggested that organisms could be more usefully understood as *self-organising systems*, which are very different from mechanisms.

A mechanism consists of parts that form a functional unity. The parts derive their function as parts from the functioning of the whole. For example, a clock consists of a number of parts, such as cogs, dials and hands, and these are assembled into a clock, which has the function of recording the passing of time. The parts are only parts of the clock insofar as they are required for the functioning of the whole, the clock. Therefore, a finished notion of *the whole is required before the parts* can have any function and the *parts must be designed* and assembled to play their particular role, without which there cannot be the whole clock. Before the clock functions, the parts must be designed and before they can be designed, the notion of the clock must be formulated.

By contrast, the parts of a living organism are not first designed and then assembled into the unity of the organism. Rather, they arise as the result of interactions within the developing organism. For example, a plant has roots, stems, leaves and flowers that interact with each other to form the plant. The parts emerge, as parts, not by prior design but as a result of internal interactions within the plant itself in a self-generating, self-organising dynamic in a particular environmental context. The parts do not come before the whole but emerge in the interaction of spontaneously generated differences that give rise to the parts within the unity of the whole (Goodwin, 1994; Webster and Goodwin, 1996). The parts, however, have to be necessary for the production of the whole, otherwise they have no relevance as parts. The parts have to serve the whole; it is just that the whole is not designed first but comes into being with the parts. Organisms develop from a simple initial form, such as a fertilised egg, into a mature adult form, all as part of an inner coherence expressed in the dynamic unity of the parts. An organism thus expresses a nature with no purpose other than the unfolding of its own mature form. The organism's development unfolds what was already enfolded in it from the beginning.

Kant described this unfolding as 'purposive' because, although an organism is not goal oriented in the sense of moving towards an external result, it is thought of as moving to a mature form of itself. The development to the mature form, and the mature form itself, will have some unique features due to the particular context in which it develops, but the organism can only ever unfold the general form already enfolded in it. In talking about development being purposive, Kant introduced his notion of organism developing according to a 'regulative idea'. Since he held that we could not know reality, it followed that we could not say that an organism actually was following a particular idea. In other words, we cannot make the claim of a constitutive idea in relation to the organism. Instead, as observing scientists, we can claim that it is helpful to understand an organism 'as if' it were moving according to a particular purpose: namely, the regulative idea of realising a mature form of itself, that is, its true nature or true self.

For Kant, the parts of an organism exist because of, and in order to sustain, the whole as an emergent property (Kauffman, 1995). Organisms are self-producing and therefore self-organising wholes, where the whole is maintained by the parts and the whole orders the parts in such a way that it is maintained. In suggesting that we think in terms of systems, Kant was introducing a causality that was teleological and formative rather than the simple, linear, efficient (if–then) causality assumed in the mechanistic way of understanding nature. In systems terms, *causality is formative* in that it is in the self-organising interaction of the parts that those parts and the whole emerge. It is 'as if' the system, the whole, has a purpose, namely, to move towards a final state that is already given at its origin as a mature form of itself. In other words, nature is unfolding already enfolded forms and causality might be referred to as formative (Stacey *et al.*, 2000) in which the dominant form of causality is the formative process of development from an embryonic to a mature form. It follows that emergence has a particular meaning in Kant's thought. In Kant's systemic thinking, self-organisation means interaction between parts, and what emerges in this interaction is the developmental pattern of the whole. Since the system is unfolding what is already enfolded in it, this emergent developmental pattern is not unknown or unpredictable. The system does not move towards that which is unknown. What is unknown, however, is reality itself so the system hypothesis cannot be a claim that reality itself moves towards the known.

Note how this understanding of nature as system is quite consistent with the scientific method in that it is the human objective observer who identifies and isolates causality in natural systems and then tests hypotheses ('as if' or regulative ideas) about the purposive movement of those systems. It is not that organisms actually are systems or that they actually are unfolding a particular pattern in movement to a mature form. It is the scientist who finds it useful to think 'as if' they are. It is not that the laws are actually in nature but that the scientist is giving the laws to nature.

A very important point follows from this way of thinking about organisms, namely that it is *a way of thinking that cannot explain novelty* – that is, how any new form could come into existence. In thinking of an organism as unfolding an already enfolded form, Kant's systems thinking can explain the developmental cycle from birth to death but cannot explain how any new form emerges: that is, how evolution takes place. This is obviously a serious problem if what one wants to understand is creativity, innovation or novelty. The key point is that in Kant's systems thinking, causality is formative rather than transformative.

Also, Kant argued that the systemic explanation of how nature functioned could never be applied to humans, because humans are autonomous and have a soul. Humans have some freedom to choose and so the deterministic laws of nature cannot be applied to rational human action.

The autonomous individual

For Kant, the human body could be thought of as a system because it is an organism. As such, it is subject to the laws of nature and, when human action is driven by the passions of the body, then it too is subject to the laws of nature and so not free. However, when acting rationally, humans could not be thought of as parts of a system because then they would exist because of, and in order to maintain, the whole. A part of a system is only a part because it is interacting with other parts to realise themselves in the purposive movement of the emergent whole and the emergence of that whole is the unfolding of what is already enfolded, so excluding any fundamental spontaneity or novelty. If a part is not doing this then it is irrelevant to the system and so not a part acting to produce the whole. However, a part in this sense cannot be free: that is, it cannot follow its own autonomously chosen goals because then it would be acting for itself and not as a part. Furthermore, as parts of a whole that is unfolding an already enfolded final state, neither whole nor parts can display spontaneity or novelty. There can be nothing creative or transformative about such a system. This way of thinking, therefore, cannot explain how the new arises.

It follows that rational human action has to be understood in a different way. Kant held that human individuals are autonomous and so can choose the goals of their actions, and they can choose the actions required to realise them using reason. The predominant form of causality here is teleological: namely, that of autonomously chosen ends made possible because of the human capacity for reason. The principal concern then becomes how autonomously chosen goals and actions mesh together in a coherent way that makes it possible for humans to live together. This is a question of ethics, and Kant understood ethical choice in terms of universals: namely, those choices that could be followed by all people. We may call this *rationalist causality* (Stacey *et al.*, 2000).

So, Kant developed a systems theory with a theory of formative causality to explain how organisms in nature developed, arguing that this could not be applied to human action, and he also developed another kind of explanation for human action, involving rationalist causality. It is particularly important to note these points because, when later forms of systems thinking were developed in the middle of the twentieth century, they were directly applied to human action, and individuals came to be thought of as parts in a system called a *group*, *organisation* or *society*. It immediately follows that any such explanation cannot encompass individual human freedom. Nor can a systemic explanation encompass the origins of spontaneity or novelty. To explain these phenomena within systems thinking, we have to rely on the autonomous individual standing outside the system. In other words, change of a transformative kind cannot be explained in systemic terms – that is, in terms of

Box 3.1	Key concepts in Kantian thinking

- Organisms in nature can be thought about 'as if' they are systems.
- Systems are wholes consisting of parts interacting with each other in a self-generating, self-organising way and it is in this interaction that both parts and whole emerge without prior design.
- However, systems are 'purposive' in that they move according to a developmental pattern from an embryonic to a mature form of themselves.
- Causality may then be described as 'formative' in that it is the process of interaction between the parts that is forming the developmental path, unfolding that which was already enfolded from the beginning.
- Humans are autonomous rational individuals who are able to choose their own goals and the actions required to realise them.
- Causality may then be described as rationalist.
- Kantian thinking is fundamentally dualistic in that one kind of causality applies to an organism and another to a human individual.

interactions between parts of the system – with one important exception that I will come to in Chapter 10. Any transformative change can then only be explained in terms of the mental functioning of the individual.

There are two other points to be borne in mind about Kant's systems thinking. It is essentially dualistic: that is, it takes a 'both . . . and' form that eliminates paradox (Griffin, 2002) by locating contradictions in different spaces or time periods. So, with regard to knowing, there is *both* the known relating to phenomena *and* the unknown relating to noumena. With regard to the paradox of determinism and freedom, there is *both* the determinism of mechanism and organism in nature *and* the freedom of rational human action. Emergence is located in nature and intention in human individuals. Linked to this there is the essentially spatial metaphor underlying all systems thinking. *A system is a whole separated by a boundary from other systems, or wholes.* In other words, there is an 'inside' and an 'outside'. For example, one thinks of what is happening inside an organisation or outside in the environment. Or one thinks of the mind inside a person and reality outside it. The key concepts in Kantian thinking are summarised in Box 3.1.

3.4 Systems thinking in the twentieth century: the notion of human systems

Kant's thinking provoked many controversies and has continued to have a major impact on the evolution of Western thought up to the present time. This impact is evident in the major development of systems thinking in the twentieth century. Scholars in many different areas were working from the 1920s to the 1940s to develop systemic ways of thinking about physiology, biology, psychology, sociology, engineering and communication. This work culminated in the publication of a number of very important papers around 1950. These papers covered systems of control, the development of computer language, theories of communication (Shannon and Weaver, 1949) and the development of a new science of mind in reaction to behaviourism, namely, cognitivism (Gardner, 1985; McCulloch and Pitts, 1943). These ways of thinking amounted to a new paradigm: namely, a shift from mechanistic, reductionist science in which the whole phenomenon of interest was understood to be the sum of its parts, requiring attention to be focused on the nature of the part rather than the interactions between them. In the new paradigm of systems thinking, the whole phenomenon was thought of as a system and the parts as subsystems within it. A system in turn was thought to be part of a larger supra-system, its environment. The parts were now not simply additive in that they affected each other. The whole came to be understood as more than the sum of the parts. The focus of attention shifted from understanding the parts, or entities, of which the whole was composed, to the interaction of subsystems to form a system and of systems to form a supra-system. An essential aspect of this way of thinking is the *different levels of existence* it ascribes to phenomena. For example, individual minds are thought of as subsystems forming groups, which are thought of as systems forming an organisation, which is thought of as a supra-system. Here each level is a different kind of phenomenon to be understood in a different way.

The new systems theories developed along three pathways over much the same period of time:

- *General systems* theory (Boulding, 1956; von Bertalanffy, 1968) developed by biologists and economists. The central concept here is that of *homeostasis*, which means that systems have a strong, self-regulating tendency to move towards a state of order and stability, or adapted equilibrium. They can only do this if they have permeable boundaries that are open to interactions with other systems. This strand in systems thinking will be explored in Chapter 6.

- *Cybernetic systems* (Ashby, 1945, 1952, 1956; Beer, 1979, 1981; Wiener, 1948) developed by engineers. Cybernetic systems are self-regulating, goal-directed systems adapting to their environment – one simple example being the central heating system in a building. Here, the resident of a room sets a target temperature, and a regulator at the boundary of the heating system detects a gap between that target and the actual temperature. This gap triggers the heating system to switch on or off, so maintaining the chosen target through a process of negative feed-back operation. The impact of this strand of thinking on strategic management will be explored in Chapter 4.

- *Systems dynamics* (Forrester, 1958, 1961, 1969; Goodwin, 1951; Philips, 1950; Tustin, 1953) developed largely by engineers who turned their attention to economics and industrial management problems. In systems dynamics, mathem-atical models are constructed of how the system changes states over time. One important difference from the other two systems theories is the recognition that the system may not move to equilibrium. The system is then no longer self-regulating but it is self-influencing: it may be self-sustaining or self-destructive. The impact of this strand of systems thinking will be explored in Chapter 5.

These three strands of systems thinking began to attract a great deal of attention in many disciplines from around 1950, as did the new cognitivist psychology, and of course, computers. Engineers, bringing with them their notion of control, took the lead in developing the theories of cybernetic systems and systems dynamics, while biologists, concerned with biological control mechanisms, developed general systems theory. This systems movement, particularly in the form of cybernetics, has come to form the foundation of today's dominant management discourse, so importing the engineer's notion of control into understanding human activity. The development of systems thinking amounted to the rediscovery of formative causality. The move from mechanistic thinking about parts and wholes to systems thinking, therefore, amounted to a move from a theory of causality couched entirely in efficient terms (if–then) to one of both efficient causal links and formative causal process as found in Kant's philosophy.

It is important to note that in applying systems thinking to human action, all of the strands of systems thinking indicated above did exactly what Kant had argued against. They postulated that human action could be understood in terms of systems. Some of the systems thinkers at this time did explore the difficulties created by the fact that the observer of a system was also a participant in it in what is called 'second-order' systems thinking. This perspective will be considered in Chapter 9.

3.5 Thinking about organisations and their management: science and systems thinking

So far in this chapter, I have been describing the movement from revelation as a way of knowing to the Scientific Revolution with its rational way of knowing. I have talked about some of the reactions to the scientific method and to some key aspects of its development: namely, the move from mechanistic and reductionist ways of thinking to holistic and systemic ways of thinking. These developments have, of course, been reflected in thinking about organisations and their management during the course of the twentieth century.

Scientific management

The mechanistic and reductionist approach of the early Scientific Revolution is quite evident in what has come to be known as 'scientific management'. Frederick Taylor (1911) in the United States and Henri Fayol (1916) in Europe were the founding figures of scientific management and both were engineers. Taylor's central concern was with the efficient performance of the physical activities required to achieve an organisation's purpose. His method was that of meticulously observing the processes required to produce anything, splitting them into the smallest possible parts, identifying the skills required and measuring how long each part took to perform and what quantities were produced. His prescription was to provide standardised descriptions of every activity, specify the skills required, define the boundaries around each activity and fit the person to the job requirement. Individual performance was to be measured against the defined standards and rewarded through financial incentive schemes. He maintained that management was an objective science that could be defined by laws, rules and principles: if a task was clearly defined, and if those performing it were properly motivated, then that task would be efficiently performed. Fayol's approach to management was much the same. He split an organisation into a number of distinct activities (for example, technical, commercial, accounting and management) and he defined management as the activity of forecasting, planning, organising, co-ordinating and controlling through setting rules that others were to follow.

Management science equated the manager with the scientist and the organisation with the phenomenon that the scientist is concerned with. The particular approach that the manager is then supposed to take towards the organisation is that of the scientist, the objective observer, who regards the phenomenon as a mechanism. The whole mechanism is thought to be the sum of its parts and the behaviour of each part is thought to be governed by timeless laws. *An organisation is, thus, thought to be governed by efficient (if–then) causality and the manager's main concern is with these causal rules.* There is a quite explicit assumption that there is some set of rules that are *optimal*: that is, they produce the most efficient global outcome of the actions of the parts, or members, of the organisation.

There is, however, an important difference between the scientist concerned with nature and the analogous manager concerned with an organisation, which is not acknowledged in scientific management. The scientist discovers the laws of nature while the manager, in the theory of management science, chooses the rules driving the behaviour of the organisation's members. In this way, something like Kant's autonomous individual and the accompanying rationalist causality is imported into theories of scientific management, but with some important differences. First, it is only the manager to whom rationalist causality applies. It is he or she who exercises the freedom of autonomous choice in the act of choosing the goals and designing the rules that the members of the organisation are to follow in order to achieve the goals. Those members are not understood as human beings with autonomous choices of their own but as rule-following parts making up the whole organisation. Closely linked to this point about freedom is that of acting into the unknown. Kant argued that individuals make choices in the form of hypotheses about an unknowable reality and they discover the efficacy of these choices in acting. In its use in scientific management, rationalist causality is stripped of the quality of the unknown, and also of the ethical limits within which action should take place, to provide a reduced rationalist causality. In fact, scientific management does what Kant argued against. It applies the scientific method in its most mechanistic form to human action. Second, Kant's coupling of autonomous human action with universal ethical principles is absent in the rationalist causality of management science, which regards human action as a reflex-like response to stimuli in accordance with the behaviourist psychology of its time.

The ethical aspect appears to some extent in the reaction of the Human Relations School to scientific management. By the 1930s the view that Taylor and Fayol took of human behaviour was being actively contested by, for example, Elton Mayo (1945), a social psychologist. He conducted experiments to identify what it was that motivated workers and what effect motivational factors had on their work. He pointed to how they always formed themselves into groups that soon developed customs, duties, routines and rituals and argued that managers would only succeed if these groups accepted their authority and leadership. He concluded that it was a major role of the manager to organise teamwork and so sustain cooperation. Mayo did not abandon a scientific approach but, rather, sought to apply the scientific method to the study of motivation in groups.

From the 1940s to the 1960s behavioural scientists (for example, Likert, 1961) continued this work and concluded that effective groups were those in which the values and goals of the group coincided with those of the individual members and where those individuals were loyal to the group and its leader. Efficiency was seen to depend upon individuals abiding by group values and goals, having high levels of trust and confidence in each other in a supportive and harmonious atmosphere. In extending freedom to all members of an organisation and paying attention to motivational factors, the Human Relations school took up a fuller notion of rationalist causality.

Taking scientific management and Human Relations together, we have a theory in which stability is preserved by rules, including motivational rules, which govern the behaviour of members of an organisation. Change is brought about by managers when they choose to change the rules, which they should do in a way that respects and motivates others so that the designed set of rules will produce optimal outcomes. Organisations are thought to function like machines, achieving given purposes deliberately chosen by their managers. Within the terms of this framework, change of a fundamental, radical kind cannot be explained. Such change is simply the result of rational choices made by managers, and just how such choices emerge is not part of what this theory seeks to explain. The result is a powerful way of thinking and managing when the goals and the tasks are clear, there is not much uncertainty and people are reasonably docile, but inadequate in other conditions. Truly novel change and coping with conditions of great uncertainty were simply not part of what scientific management and Human Relations theories set out to explain or accomplish.

The principles discussed above were developed a long time ago, and they have been subjected to heavy criticism over the years, but they still quite clearly form the basis of much management thinking.

The shift to systems thinking

The wider paradigm shift from mechanistic to systemic thinking described in the previous section is also evident in theories of organisations and their management. For example, general systems theory was combined with psychoanalysis to develop a systemic understanding of organisation (*see* Chapter 6) which emphasises clarity of roles and task definition and equates management with a controlling role at the boundary (Miller and Rice, 1967). The influence of the cybernetic strand of systems thinking is even more in evidence (*see* Chapter 4). All planning and budgeting systems in organisations are cybernetic, in that quantified targets are set for performance at some point in the future, the time path towards the target is forecast and then actual outcomes are measured and compared with forecasts, with the variance fed back to determine what adjustments are required to bring performance back to target. All quality management systems take the same form as do all incentive schemes, performance appraisal and reward systems, management and culture change programmes, total quality management and business process re-engineering projects. The thinking and talking both of managers and organisational researchers, therefore, tends to be dominated by cybernetic notions. The third strand of systems thinking, namely systems dynamics, originally had little impact on management thinking but more recently it has attracted much interest as a central concept in the notion of the learning organisation (*see* Chapter 5). Here, instead of thinking of a system moving towards an equilibrium state, it is thought of as following a small number of typical patterns or archetypes. Effective management requires the recognition of these archetypes and the identification of leverage points at which action can be taken to change them and so enable management to stay in control of an organisation, in effect controlling its dynamics.

The shift from reductionist management science to holistic, systemic perspectives on organisations does not, however, entail any substantial challenge to the scientific method. The manager continues to be equated with the natural scientist, the objective observer, and just as the scientist is concerned with a natural phenomenon, so the manager is concerned with an organisation. Now, however, the organisation is understood not as parts adding to a whole, but as a system in which the interactions between its parts are of primary importance in producing a whole that is more than the sum of its parts. The manager understands the organisation to be a self-regulating or a self-influencing system and it is the formative process of self-regulation or self-influence (formative cause) that is organising the pattern of behaviour that can be observed. In the case of general systems and cybernetics, that pattern is movement towards a chosen goal, an optimally efficient state, and the pattern of behaviour is held close to this goal/state when the system is operating effectively. In the case of systems dynamics, the form towards which the system moves is a typical pattern or archetype enfolded in the system, which the manager can alter by operating at leverage points. In all of these systems theories, therefore, the final form of the system's behaviour, that towards which it tends, is a state already enfolded, as it were, in the rules governing the way the parts interact. The manager is the objective observer standing outside the system and through reason designs it, changes it, and sets objectives for it.

In the decades after 1950 the first wave of modern systems thinking about organisation, described above, paid as little attention as management science did to ethics, ordinary human freedom and the unknown nature of the final state towards which human action tends. As soon as one thinks of a human organisation as a system that can be identified or designed, one immediately encounters the problem that the identifier or the designer is also part of the system. This problem was recognised by the systems thinkers of the mid-twentieth century and later led to the development of second-order systems thinking (*see* Chapter 9). Also, some more recent developments of systems thinking (soft systems and critical systems) in the 1980s and 1990s actively took up the issues of participation and ethics, but they did so in a way that did nothing to alter the underlying theory of causality (*see* Chapter 9). The systems movement continues to build on a theory of rationalist causality applied to the understanding and design of organisations as systems that are governed by formative causality.

Back to the values task force

I started this chapter by referring to the task force appointed by the chief executive of a major international company. I suggest that the way he and the members of the task force were thinking about change in their organisation clearly reflects the history of systems thinking outlined in this chapter. They were taking it for granted that they, as autonomous individuals, could objectively observe their organisation, understood as a system, and change the values that drive its operation. In other words, they were assuming that they could enfold into the organisational system the purposes that it would then unfold. In doing this, they had lost sight of Kant's notion of a regulative idea. Instead of thinking that they could understand the system 'as if' it were unfolding a purpose they were hypothesising, they were thinking that their organisation was a system that really could/would unfold the purpose they determined for it. More than that, however, they were doing what Kant strongly advised against. They were applying the notion of system to the human actions that are the organisation, thereby thinking of the organisation's members, including themselves, as parts of the system. In this way of thinking ordinary human freedom to make a choice is lost sight of. However, all individuals in an organisation have some choice regarding the part they play in together forming the values that guide their behaviour. Attempts to determine these values for them are then bound to fail, if indeed individuals have at least some degree of choice. Furthermore, the systemic way of thinking cannot explain in its own terms the very matter that these managers were concerned with: namely the transformation of their organisation. This is simply because systems thinking cannot explain, in its own terms, novelty or creativity. What may seem, in this chapter, to be a rather abstract philosophical discussion is in fact a highly practical matter.

3.6 How systems thinking deals with the four questions

Systems thinking essentially seeks to understand phenomena as a whole formed by the interaction of parts. Whole systems are separated from others by boundaries and they interact with each other to form a supra-whole. There are thus different levels at which phenomena either exist or need to be thought about. These notions of wholes, boundaries and levels are central distinguishing features of systems thinking. How does this kind of thinking deal with the four questions posed near the end of Chapter 2 (page 37)?

The first question has to do with how interaction is understood. In systems thinking, interaction between parts produces the whole and the parts are relevant as parts only because they produce and sustain the whole. The form of causality is the formative process of interaction between parts. Process here means the process of producing a whole and participation means participating in the production of a whole.

The second question has to do with the nature of human beings. In systems thinking the answer to this question is a dualism. On the one hand, humans are thought of as rational, autonomous individuals who objectively observe systems and ascribe purposive behaviour to them. Causality here is rationalist and rational humans are free to choose. On the other, humans are also thought of as parts or members of the system being observed and so subject to formative causality. As such they cannot be free to choose but are subject to the purpose and formative process of the system. This problem has not gone unnoticed by systems thinkers but in Chapter 9 I will argue that the problem has not been resolved.

Taken together, the systems thinkers' answers to these two questions imply a particular way of thinking about human experience: that is, the patterning of interaction between people. The implication is that the cause of experience, the cause of the patterning of interaction between people, lies in some system, created by people, that lies above or below that experience. So, in the task force I referred to, the particular patterning of the interactions between people in the organisation was assumed to be caused by a system of values existing somehow outside the direct experience of the people interacting.

Turning to the third question to do with the method used to understand human action, it is clear that the method of the systems thinking so far discussed is that of objective observation. Generally, when applied to organisations, this is done in a realist way. People then think that systems actually exist in reality and organisations really are systems that have their own purposes. Organisations and systems are thereby reified – that is, understood to have an existence as things. Kant's idealist position on systems is thereby lost. However, in later critical systems thinking (*see* Chapter 9) Kant's 'as if' position has been recovered. Critical systems thinkers argue against the notion that systems actually exist and regard them as mental structures. Second-order systems thinking also moves away from simple objective observation and seeks to understand humans as participants in systems.

The fourth question has to do with paradox. Systems thinking originated as a dualistic way of thinking that eliminated paradox, for example by postulating one causality for nature and another for human action. Since Kant, systems thinkers have retained, often implicitly, a dual theory of causality, formative and rationalist, and applied them both to human action. They eliminate the paradox, not by different spatial locations, but in different temporal sequencing. First, managers are thought of as autonomous individuals subject to rationalist causality when they are determining the organisational system's purpose and then as subject to formative causality in their role as members of the system. In this way they preserve the 'both . . . and' structure of Kantian thinking.

3.7 Summary

This chapter has described some key aspects in the development of Western thought over the last four centuries. Its particular concern has been with the origins of systems thinking in Kantian philosophy and his articulation of the autonomous individual, as well as later developments in systems thinking and its application to human action around the middle of the twentieth century. The purpose has been to highlight the key aspects of systems thinking and the particular problems it poses when applied to human action. The main problem has to do with how, in system terms, we are to understand human participation, freedom and transformation.

Further reading

The origins and philosophical nature of systems thinking are reviewed in more depth in Stacey *et al.* (2000) and in Griffin (2002).

Questions to aid further reflection

1. What are the key elements of a system and what are the consequences of thinking about organisations in this way?

2. What are the distinctions between efficient, formative and rationalist causality?

3. How does the development of management thinking reflect changes in ways of thinking in the natural sciences?

4. In what way does systems thinking about organisations reflect a dualist, 'both . . . and' way of thinking and what are the consequences?

5. How would you explain learning, creativity, spontaneity and choice in the way systems thinking has been applied to understanding organisations?

6. Where in your own experience do you see organisational manifestations of the thinking described in this chapter?

Chapter 4

Thinking in terms of strategic choice
Cybernetic systems, cognitivist and humanistic psychology

This chapter invites you to draw on your own experience to reflect on and consider the implications of:

- The origins and nature of thinking that organisations are cybernetic systems.

- The origins and nature of thinking about the human individual in terms of cognitive and humanistic psychology.

- The origins and nature of thinking about human communication in terms of a sender–receiver model.

- The role of the objective autonomous individual observer who can control.

- The dual theory of causality implied by strategic choice theory.

- The requirement for predictability on which the theory of strategic choice depends.

- What it means to be practical in terms of strategic choice theory.

- The manner in which control, leadership and group behaviour are thought about in the theory of strategic choice.

- The technically rational process that is assumed in the theory of strategic choice.

- How the theory focuses attention and what this entails for what managers do.

It is important to understand the theories of cybernetic systems and cognitivist/humanistic psychology because they provide the key assumptions that tend to be taken for granted in the theory of strategic choice. Without this understanding it is not possible to reflect rigorously on the entailments of thinking in terms of strategic choice and so evaluate the prescriptions of the theory.

4.1 Introduction

The major part of most textbooks on strategic management is devoted to the prescriptions and analytical techniques of formulating and implementing strategic plans of one kind or another. In other words, they express the theory of strategic choice. What these textbooks devote very little attention to is the way of thinking that strategic choice theory reflects. The underlying assumptions of the theory are taken for granted rather than explored and so the entailments of making those assumptions are not examined. While this chapter gives a very brief description of the key elements of the theory of strategic choice, its main purpose is not to provide a comprehensive review but to explore the way of thinking reflected in that theory. This theory has strong critics and there has been a shift in thinking over the past two decades to notions of the learning organisation (*see* Chapter 5), but strategic choice is probably still the dominant theory of strategy and organisational change. You can hear it in the way that most management practitioners talk about strategy and change in their organisations, and you can read it in a great many of the books and articles written about strategy and organisational design and development.

According to the theory of strategic choice, the strategy of an organisation is the general direction in which it changes over time. The general direction encompasses the range of activities it will undertake, the broad markets it will serve, how its resource base and competences will change and how it will secure competitive advantage. The purpose of the strategy is to secure sustainable competitive advantage that will optimise the organisation's performance. This strategy is chosen by the most powerful individual in the organisation or by a small group of managers at the top of the management hierarchy – that is, the dominant coalition. The prescribed way of making the choice is first to formulate a strategy by following an analytical procedure to prepare a plan: that is, a set of goals, the intended actions required to achieve the goals, and forecasts of the consequences of those actions over a long period of time. Having chosen the general direction, or strategy, the managers at the top of the hierarchy are then required to design an organisational structure to implement it. The structure they design should be a largely self-regulating system in which people are assigned roles and objectives that will realise the chosen strategy. Implementation is the procedure of designing systems to ensure that the plans are carried out in the intended manner and periodically adjusted to keep the organisation on track to achieve its goals. A brief description of the formulation and implementation procedures is provided later in this chapter.

From this brief description it can be seen that strategic choice theory makes particular assumptions about how people interact with each other. They are thought to interact within a particular kind of system, which has been designed by the dominant coalition of managers in the organisation. This is a cybernetic system, the nature of which will be described in the next section of this chapter. The ability to predict is crucial to the ability to control an organisation understood as a cybernetic system.

Strategic choice theory assumes that it is possible for powerful individuals to stand outside their organisations and model them in the interest of controlling them. The theory assumes that organisations change successfully when top executives form the right intention for the overall future shape of the whole organisation and specify in enough detail how this is to be achieved. It prescribes the prior design of change and then the installation of that change. The theory of strategic choice therefore places the individual, and the rational choices made by the individual, at the very centre of its explanation of how organisations become what they become. The cause of an organisation's 'shape' and performance is the strategy rationally chosen by its most powerful members. It, therefore, immediately implies a particular theory of human psychology: that is, a theory of how humans know and act. The theory implied is that of *cognitivism*, which will be described later in the chapter. Furthermore, the need to motivate people to achieve objectives also implies a psychological theory of motivation and this is usually based on humanistic psychology. This will also be described later in this chapter.

The foundations of strategic choice theory therefore reflect a particular way of thinking about what organisations are and how they become what they become. This way of thinking derives essentially from Kant (*see* Chapter 3) and combines cybernetic systems theory with the cognitivist and humanistic psychological theories that the rest of this chapter will explore.

4.2 Cybernetic systems: importing the engineer's idea of self-regulation and control into understanding human activity

Cybernetics is an application of the engineer's idea of control to human activity. During the Second World War the superiority of the German air force led British scientists to consider how they might improve the accuracy of anti-aircraft defences. One of these scientists, Norbert Wiener, saw a way of treating the evasive action of enemy aircraft as a time series that could be manipulated mathematically using negative feedback to improve the gunner's predictions of the enemy plane's future position (Wiener, 1948).

Negative feedback and equilibrium

Negative feedback simply means that the outcome of a previous action is compared with some desired outcome and the difference between the two is fed back as information that guides the next action in such a way that the difference is reduced until it disappears. The effect is to sustain a system in a state of stable equilibrium. When anything disturbs a cybernetic system from its state of stable equilibrium, it will return to that equilibrium in a self-regulating manner if it is governed by negative feedback control. A commonly quoted example of a cybernetic system is the domestic central heating system.

A domestic heating system consists of an appliance and a regulator. The regulator contains a device that senses room temperature connected to a device that turns the heating appliance on and off. A desired temperature – that is, an external reference point – is set in the regulator by an observer outside the system. When the room temperature falls below this desired level, the control sensor detects the discrepancy between actual and desired states. The regulator responds to a negative discrepancy with a positive action – it turns the heat on. When the temperature rises above the desired level, the opposite happens. By responding to the deviation of actual from desired levels in an opposite or negative way, a cybernetic system dampens any movement away from desired levels. The system keeps the room temperature close to a stable level over time, utilising negative feedback.

Negative feedback and human action

Wiener and his colleagues held that negative feedback loops were important in most human actions – a loop in which the gap between desired and actual performance of an act just past is fed back as a determinant of the next action. If you are trying to hit an object by throwing a ball at it and you miss because you aimed too far to the right, you then use the information from this miss to alter the point at which you aim the next shot, so offsetting the previous error. In this sense the feedback is negative – it prompts you to move in the opposite direction. You keep doing this until you hit the object. Wiener and his colleagues thought that this negative feedback was essential to all forms of controlled behaviour and that breaking the feedback link led to pathological behaviour.

Another example is provided by the operation of markets. In classical economic theory, markets are assumed to tend to a state of equilibrium. If there is an increase in demand, then prices rise to encourage a reduction in demand and an increase in supply to match the demand. If demand then stays constant, so will price and supply. Any chance movement of the price away from its equilibrium level will set in train changes in demand and supply that will rapidly pull the price back to its equilibrium level. In other words, a cybernetic system does not have an internal capacity to change. Instead, any significant change is simply a self-regulating adaptation to some external, environmental change. *Dynamic equilibrium* is a movement over time in which a system continuously adapts to alterations in a continually changing environment.

However, the self-regulating operation of cybernetic systems is not as simple as it sounds. Cyberneticists realised that when negative feedback becomes too fast, or too sensitive, the result could be uncontrolled cycles of over- and under-achievement of the desired state. So, for example, you may be taking a shower and find the water too hot. This leads you to raise the flow of cold water. If you do not take sufficient account of the lag between your action and the subsequent drop in temperature you may increase the cold water flow again. This may make the water too cold, so you raise the flow of hot water, which then makes it too hot again. Unless you get the time lag between your action and its consequence right, the system will not stabilise. So, if a negative feedback control system is operating too rapidly, behaviour will fluctuate in an unstable manner instead of settling down to a desired level.

Those studying such systems therefore sought to establish the conditions for stability and instability in negative feedback control systems. As a result of this kind of work, governments came to accept that their attempts to remove cycles in the level of activity in the economy were usually counterproductive. Just as the economy was recovering from a slump, impatient governments tended to cut taxes and increase expenditure, so fuelling an excessive boom accompanied by rapid inflation. Just as that boom was collapsing on its own, fearful governments increased taxes and cut expenditure, so pushing the economy into a deeper slump than it would otherwise have experienced. To secure stability through negative feedback, you must be able to predict not only the outcome of an action but also the time lag between an action and its outcome. The design of a control system that works at the right speed and the right level of sensitivity relies upon such predictions. Given the ability to predict, it is then possible to specify in a precise mathematical way exactly what conditions will produce stable equilibrium for any negative feedback system.

The key point about all forms of equilibrating systems is that they are regular, orderly and predictable without any internal capacity to change. Such regular, orderly, predictable movement depends upon clear-cut links between cause and effect of the 'if–then' kind. Most theories of management and organisation have been developed within an equilibrium framework reflecting an underlying assumption that organisations should be designed as cybernetic systems.

Consider now how cybernetics has been applied to the control of organisations (Ashby 1945, 1952, 1956; Beer [1959] 1967, 1966).

Goal-seeking adaptation to the environment

According to cybernetic theory, two main forces drive an organisation over time. The first force is the drive to achieve some purpose: from this perspective organisations are goal-seeking systems and the goal drives their actions. The second force arises because organisations are connected through feedback links to their environments: they are subsystems of an even larger environmental supra-system. Reaching the goal requires being adapted to those environments. Thus, in the cybernetics tradition, organisations are driven by attraction to a predetermined desired state that is in equilibrium with the environment. The state a given organisation comes to occupy is determined by the nature of its environment.

For example, on this view, a company operating in, say, the electronics industry may be driven by the goal of achieving a 20 per cent return on its capital. In order to achieve this it must deliver what its customers want. If customers have stable requirements for standardised, low-cost silicon chips to be used as components in their own products, then the company has to adapt to this environment by employing mass-production methods to produce standardised products at lower costs than its rivals. It will have to support these production methods with particular forms of organisational structure, control systems and cultures: functional structures, bureaucratic control systems and conservative, strongly shared cultures. The company will look much the same as its rivals in the same market because the overall shape of each is determined by the same environment.

If, however, the electronics market is a turbulent one with rapidly changing technology and many niche markets where customers look for customised chips, then there will be very different kinds of organisation, according to cybernetics theory. A company will have to adapt by emphasising R&D and continually developing new products to differentiate itself from its rivals. It will support these production methods with particular forms of structure, control systems and culture: decentralised structures of separate profit centres, greater emphasis on informal controls, and change-loving cultures.

But how do organisations come to be adapted to their environments and achieve their goals?

Regulators

According to cybernetics, organisations deploy regulators that utilise negative feedback in order to reach their goals and the desired states of adaptation to their environments. The central problem is how to keep an organisation at, or near to, some desired state, and the answer to the problem lies in the design of the regulator: that is, the design of the control system. Cybernetics is the science of control, and management is the profession of control. There are two types of regulator: the error-controlled regulator and the anticipatory regulator.

If the regulator is placed so that it senses the disturbance before that disturbance hits the organisation, then it can take anticipatory action and offset the undesirable impact of the disturbance on the outcome before it occurs. An immediately recognisable example of this kind of regulator is of course a planning system. Such a regulator takes the form of sensing devices such as market research questionnaires or analyses of market statistics. On the basis of these, realistically achievable desired states are established. These desired states, or goals, are based on forecasts of sales volumes, prices and costs at some future point. Action plans to realise the selected goals in the predicted environment are also prepared: that is, patterns in future actions are identified. As the organisation moves through time it continually senses the environment, picks up disturbances before they occur and prepares planned actions to deal with them before they hit the organisation. This is ideal control without making mistakes: preventing deviations from plan occurring in the first place.

If it is not possible to establish such an anticipatory regulator, or if such a regulator cannot work perfectly, then a regulator must be placed so that it can sense the outcome once that outcome has occurred. This is the classic error-controlled regulator. An immediately recognisable example of this type of regulator is the monitoring, reviewing and corrective action system of an organisation. It is what an organisation's board of directors does each month when it meets to review what has happened to the organisation over the past month, monitors how the performance measures are moving and decides what to do to correct deviations from plan that have already occurred. Note, however, that even error-controlled regulators depend on some form of predictability. When you take a corrective action you have to be able to predict not only its outcome and the time delay between corrective action and its consequences but also the time lag between an event and its detection. To function effectively, cybernetic systems depend upon predictability at a rather detailed level.

An essential requirement for the most effective application of this whole approach to control, therefore, is the availability of quantitative forecasts of future changes in the organisation and its environment, as well as forecasts of the consequences of proposed actions to deal with these changes and the time lags involved. For self-regulating control to work adequately, the forecasts need to be at a rather detailed level of description and can only function, therefore, over a time span where this is possible. The tools available for such quantitative forecasts are those derived from statistical theory. Statistical forecasting methods are based on the assumption that the disturbances hitting the organisation from its environment take the form of groupings of large numbers of closely similar events that can be described by a probability distribution. It is implicitly assumed that uniquely uncertain events will be relatively unimportant.

Cybernetics sees the main cause of the difficulty in designing regulators not in terms of the uniqueness of events, but in terms of their variety, or complexity. Variety is the number of discernibly different states the environment can present to the organisation and the number of discernibly different responses the organisation can make to the environment. It is the function of the regulator to reduce variety, so retaining stability within a system, despite high variety outside it. In other words, the huge variety of disturbances presented by the environment must be neutralised by a huge number of responses such that the outcome can match the one desirable state selected in advance that will fit the environment. In order to be able to do this, the regulator must be designed to have as much variety as the environment; the number of potential responses must match the number of potential disturbances so that they can cancel each other out and produce a single desired outcome. This is Ashby's law of requisite variety: the complexity and speed of the firm's response must match the complexity and speed of change of the environment.

Cybernetics and causality

The law of requisite variety makes it unnecessary, according to the cybernetics tradition, to understand the internal feedback structures of the organisation and the environment. Cyberneticists recognised that feedback means circular causality – event A causes event B which then causes event A. They argued that one can determine the direction this circular causality takes for any pair of events simply by observing which precedes which in a large number of cases. However, when dealing with large numbers of interconnected pairs it all becomes too difficult. These internal structures are so complex that one cannot hope to understand them – they constitute a 'black box'. Note how an unquestioned assumption is being made here. Those arguing this position are assuming that there is always a specific cause for each specific outcome, the problem being that it is all too complex for us to understand.

The cyberneticists, however, argued that causal connections exist, but one does not need to understand them because one can observe a particular type of disturbance impacting on a system and also can observe the outcome of that disturbance: that is, how the system responds. If the regulator has requisite variety – that is, a large enough variety of responses to counteract the variety of disturbances – then it will normally respond to a particular type of disturbance in the same way. From large numbers of observations of such regularities statistical connections can be established between particular types of disturbance and particular organisational responses.

The importance of this notion of causal connection is that it allows the use of statistical techniques for control in a negative feedback way, despite system complexity so great that one cannot hope to understand it, at least according to the cyberneticists. What matters to them are pragmatic factors such as what is observed and what is done. It is not necessary to devote much energy to understanding and explaining, they claim, because observing and doing is what matters in a complex world. These writers were not concerned with the dynamic patterns of behaviour that organisations generated or with the complexities of the internal workings of the organisation.

Cybernetics, then, is an approach that seeks to control an organisation by using feedback but without understanding the feedback structure of the organisation itself. It sees effective regulators as those that cause the system to be largely self-regulating, automatically handling the disturbances with which the environment bombards it. It sees effective regulators as those that maintain continual equilibrium with the environment. The result is stable behaviour, predictable in terms of probabilities of specific events and times.

The key points on organisational dynamics made by the cybernetics tradition are summarised in Box 4.1. Whenever managers use planning, monitoring, reviewing and corrective action forms of control, they are making the same assumptions about the world as those made by cyberneticists. Whenever management consultants install such systems they too make the same assumptions. Whenever managers engage in trial-and-error actions in the belief that this will take them to an envisioned

Box 4.1	Cybernetics: main points on organisational dynamics

- Organisations are *goal-seeking*, *self-regulating* systems adapting to pre-given environments through negative feedback.

- Cybernetics thus takes a realist position on human knowing.

- The system is *recursive*. This means that it feeds back on itself to repeat its behaviour.

- It follows that causality is circular. However, although the causality is circular it is also *linear*. Cybernetics does not take account of the effects of nonlinearity. Causal structures cannot be understood because they are too complex. However, regularities in the relationships between external disturbances and the system's response can be statistically identified. Circular causality is thus recognised but then sidestepped by saying that it is too complicated to understand.

- Predictability of specific events and their timings is possible in a probabilistic sense. Disturbances coming from the environment are not primarily unique.

- Effective control requires forecasts and a control system that contains as much variety as the environment. Change must be probabilistic so that large numbers of random changes and random responses cancel out, otherwise unique small changes might amplify and swamp the system.

- No account is taken of positive, or amplifying, feedback. There is thus no possibility of small changes amplifying into major alterations.

- Behavioural patterns themselves, especially of the system as a whole, are not thought to be interesting enough to warrant special comment.

- The self-regulation process requires the system's actual behavioural outcomes to be compared with some representation of, or expectation about, its environment. There is an external point of reference according to which it is controlled. The system internally *represents* its environment and then responds to that representation.

- There is a clear boundary between system and environment, between inner and outer. Although the system is adapting to its environment, it is itself a closed system. It operates/changes with *reference to a fixed point at the boundary* with its environment.

- Its state is determined by flux in the environment expressed through the fixed point of reference. Instability comes from the environment.

- It is a homeostatic, or *equilibrium-seeking*, system.

- *History is not important* in that the current state of the system is not dependent upon the sequence of previous states, only on the 'error' registered at the regulator. The system does not evolve of its own accord. Any change must be designed outside the system and then installed.

- Effective organisations are self-regulating, an automatic mechanical feature flowing from the way the control system is structured.

- Success is a state of stability, consistency and harmony.

end-point in a turbulent environment – that is, whenever they implement the advice of writers such as Peters and Waterman (1982) – then they are assuming that the law of requisite variety is valid. The problem is that managers and consultants are normally not fully aware of what they are assuming. It is extremely important to be aware of these assumptions because, if life in organisations diverges significantly from them, cybernetic systems will not work. For example, if tiny unique changes can escalate through amplifying feedback, a cybernetic system will no longer be able to self-regulate.

Consider now how this systems theory is reflected in the prescriptions strategic choice theory provides for the formulation and implementation of strategic plans.

4.3 Formulating and implementing long-term strategic plans

Section 4.2 has described the assumptions about interaction that underlie strategic choice theory. This theory of strategic management is concerned with anticipatory and error-controlled regulators. Anticipatory regulation consists of the formulation of long-term strategic plans, and the implementation of these plans is based on the operation of error-controlled regulation consisting of various administrative and monitoring systems. The literature on strategic choice provides many prescriptions for formulating and implementing strategic plans (for example, Andrews, [1971] 1987; Ansoff, 1965, 1990; Barney, 1991; Porter, 1980, 1985). This literature is primarily concerned with formal, analytical procedures to do with planning and monitoring.

The words 'plan' and 'planning' are often used loosely by managers. For example, managers may say that they have a long-term plan simply because they have set out some long-term financial targets or because they have identified one or two specific actions that they intend to undertake – for example, make an acquisition. However, these words have more precise meanings in the theory of strategic choice. A strategic plan is a formally articulated choice of a particular future composition of activities and a particular market position for the whole organisation such that it will achieve an optimal level of performance in a future context. Strategic planning involves choosing aims and objectives for the whole organisation well in advance of acting. Strategic planning also involves managers sharing a common intention to pursue a sequence of actions to achieve that chosen future state. Before managers can intentionally choose an intended state and an intended sequence of future actions, however, they have to identify the future environment in which they are to achieve their aims – their intentions must be anchored to a specific future reality. In other words, managers cannot possibly plan unless they can also make reasonably reliable forecasts of the future time period they are planning for. The future must not only be knowable, it must be sufficiently well known in advance of required performance. The time span and the level of detail must be that which produces the required performance. A long-term plan requires long-term predictability, otherwise there is only a sequence of short-term plans.

Many managers will immediately realise that in a rapidly changing world they are rather unlikely to encounter the degree of predictability required to formulate long-term plans satisfying the definition just given. Some of them, and some writers on strategy too, then dismiss the whole approach as impracticable. Others argue that, while it may not be possible to plan the future in the way just described, it is still possible for them to choose a broad direction for their organisation. What is being suggested is that in practice a watered-down form of long-term planning is what is required. However, this still requires enough predictability to set a direction. The theory of strategic choice, however, goes further than simply setting some general direction and provides tools and techniques for doing more than this.

In addition to formulating plans, managers must set milestones along the path to the intended future state, couched in terms of results, if what they are doing is to qualify as controlling and developing an organisation's long-term future in the planning mode. This will enable the outcomes of actions to be checked and deviations from plan to be corrected. Action is both implementation of the planned sequence of actions and corrections to keep results on course. Only then is control being exercised in a planned manner. The ability to control by plan depends upon the possibility of establishing intention relating to the organisation as a *whole* and making predictions at the appropriate level of detail over the relevant time span.

Prediction is a process of analysing the past and the present and then using that analysis as the basis for forecasting the future. Once managers know something about the nature of their future environment, they can deduce what alternative action options might deliver their performance objectives. The rational criteria of acceptability, feasibility and suitability, to be discussed below, must then be applied to evaluate each option and select that option which best satisfies the criteria. This then becomes an organisation's strategy.

Since most organisations of any size consist of a collection of different activities organised into units, a distinction is drawn between corporate plans and business unit plans (Hofer and Schendel, 1978; Porter, 1987). The corporate plan is concerned with what activities or businesses the organisation should be involved in and how the corporate level should manage that set of businesses. In other words, corporate strategy is about a portfolio of businesses and what should be done with them. Business unit plans set out how a business unit is going to build a market position that is superior to that of its rivals, so enabling it to achieve the performance objectives set by the corporate level. In other words, business unit strategy is about the means of securing and sustaining competitive advantage. Since business units are generally organised on a functional basis – finance, sales, production, and research departments, for example – the business unit strategy will have to be translated into functional or operational strategies. The result is a hierarchy of long-term objectives and plans, the corporate creating the framework for the business unit, and the business unit creating the framework for the functional. Furthermore, this collection of long-term plans provides the framework for formulating shorter-term plans and budgets against which an organisation can be controlled in the short term.

The theory of strategic choice prescribes analytical criteria for evaluating strategic options. The evaluation criteria are intended to enable managers to conclude whether or not a particular sequence of actions will lead to a particular future state that will produce some target measure of performance. The criteria are there to enable managers to form judgements about the outcomes of their proposed actions before they take those actions. The purpose is to prevent surprises and ensure that an organisation behaves over long time periods in a manner intended by its leaders.

Evaluating long-term strategic plans

There are three very widely proposed criteria for evaluating long-term strategic plans and these are acceptability or desirability, feasibility, and suitability or fit. These are reviewed in the following sections.

Acceptability

There are at least three senses, it is argued, in which strategies have to be acceptable if they are to produce success. First, performance in financial terms must be acceptable to owners and creditors. Second, the consequences of the strategies for the most powerful groupings within an organisation must be acceptable in terms of their expectations and the impact on their power positions and cultural beliefs. Third, the consequences of the strategies for powerful groups external to an organisation must be acceptable to those groupings. Consider what each of these senses entails.

- *Acceptable financial performance.* Determining whether the long-term plans are likely to turn out to be financially acceptable requires forecasting the financial consequences of each strategic option: cash flows, capital expenditures and other costs, sales volumes, price levels, profit levels, assets and liabilities including borrowing and other funding requirements. The forecasts are used to calculate prospective rates of return on sales and capital in order to compare them with those required by owners and fund providers. This is not as simple as it sounds, because there are many different rates of return on sales and capital and the one used depends upon the purpose of use and also on accounting conventions. There are also many difficulties of measurement: for example, the problems of measuring depreciation, skill, knowledge and other costs and benefits that are not traded on markets. The analysis may therefore involve subjective judgements and disagreements that cannot be resolved by rational argument. Scenarios and simulations may be used to identify variables that performance is particularly sensitive to in order to manage risk.

- *Acceptable consequences for internal power groups.* If carried out, strategic plans may well change the way people work, whom they work with, what relative power they have, and how they are judged by others. Long-term plans could produce consequences that people believe to be morally repugnant or against their customs and beliefs in some other way. If this is the case, those plans are unlikely to succeed, because people will do their best to prevent the plans being implemented. The prescription is, therefore, to submit long-term plans to the test of acceptability in terms of the expectations, relative power positions and cultural beliefs of key individuals and groups within the organisation. In order to determine whether a plan is likely to be acceptable in cultural terms it is necessary to analyse people's shared beliefs. Analysis of the culture is thought to reveal whether options being considered fall within that culture or whether they require major cultural change. One would not necessarily reject options that require major cultural change, but then plans to bring this about would have to be formulated. It is also necessary to analyse the power structure of an organisation to determine whether plans are likely to be acceptable.

- *Acceptable consequences for external power groups.* Power groups outside an organisation also determine the acceptability of that organisation's strategies.

For example, a community pressure group may find the noise level of a proposed factory expansion unacceptable. Even if the factory itself turns out to be a financially acceptable investment, the total consequences for the image of the corporation could render the strategy unsuccessful. Another example is provided by the electricity and gas industries in the UK. To succeed, strategies of companies in these sectors have to be acceptable to the industry regulators and consumer pressure groups. A further example is where the strategies of one organisation could have damaging consequences for the distributors of that organisation's products or for the suppliers to that organisation. Such damage could provoke those distributors and suppliers to retaliate in highly detrimental ways. The reactions of competitors to strategies are also of major importance. Some strategies pursued by one company could provoke greater than normal competitive responses from competitors. Those competitors may regard the strategies of the first company as unfair competition and this could lead to price wars, hostile mergers or lobbying of the national political institutions, all of which could cause a strategy to fail.

Feasibility

Analysis may show that strategies are likely to be acceptable in terms of financial performance, and to major power groupings both within and outside an organisation, but yet fail because they are not feasible. To be feasible there must be no insurmountable obstacle to implementing a strategy. Such obstacles could be presented by:

- *Financial resources.* One of the immediately obvious resources that must be available if a strategy is to be carried out is the money to finance the strategy over its whole life. If a company gets halfway through a strategy, which is on target to yield acceptable performance, but nevertheless runs out of the funds to continue, then clearly the strategy will fail. The prescription is, therefore, to carry out a flow-of-funds analysis of the strategy options before embarking on any of them, to ascertain the probability of running into cash flow problems. A flow-of-funds analysis identifies the timing and size of the capital expenditures and other costs required for each project that makes up the strategy, and the timing and size of the revenues that those projects will generate. A flow-of-funds analysis makes it possible to calculate the break-even point, where a project, a set of projects constituting a strategy or a corporation as a whole makes neither a loss nor a profit.
- *Human resources.* In addition to financial resources, the availability of the right numbers of skilled people will also be a major determinant of the feasibility of strategic options. This makes it necessary for managers to audit the human resources inside their organisation, those available outside and the availability of training resources to improve the skills of people.

Suitability or fit

Having established that their strategies are acceptable and feasible, the next hurdle managers must cross to select an appropriate strategic plan is that of demonstrating that a strategy has a *strategic logic*. Strategic logic means that a proposed sequence of actions is consistently related to the objectives of the organisation on the one hand and matches the organisation's capability (including its structure, control systems and culture) in relation to its environment on the other. The idea is that all the pieces of the strategic puzzle should fit together in a predetermined manner – the pieces should be *congruent*. When this happens we can say that the strategies fit, that they are suitable. The prescription is to use analytical techniques to determine the strategic logic of a sequence of actions (Hofer and Schendel, 1978). The analytical techniques available to do this are:

- *SWOT analysis*. This is a list of an organisation's strengths and weaknesses indicated by an analysis of its resources and capabilities, plus a list of the opportunities and threats that an analysis of its environment identifies. Strategic logic obviously requires that the future pattern of actions to be taken should match strengths with opportunities, ward off threats and seek to overcome weaknesses.

- *Industry structure and value chain analysis*. Michael Porter (1980, 1985) has put the classical economic theories of market form into a framework for analysing the nature of competitive advantage in a market and the power of a company in that market, as well as the value chain of the company. These analytical techniques identify key aspects determining the relative market power of an organisation and its ability to sustain excess profits. Strategic logic entails taking actions that are consistent with and that match the nature of the organisation's market power. Industry structure is held to determine what the predominant form of competitive advantage, and thus the level of profit, is. Some market structures mean that sustainable competitive advantage can be secured only through cost-leadership strategies. Other structures mean that competitive advantage flows from differentiation. Strategic logic means matching actions to those required to secure competitive advantage. Value chain analysis identifies the points in the chain of activity from raw material to consumer that are crucial to competitive advantage.

- *Product life cycle*. To be suitable in market terms a strategy must take account of the stages in the product life cycle. Most products are thought to follow typical developmental stages: *embryonic* in which the product is developed; *growth* in which rapid market growth materialises, attracting other competitors; *shake-out* in which some of the competitors cannot compete and therefore leave; *mature* in which growth in the demand for the product slows and a small number of competitors come to dominate the market; *saturation* in which demand for the product stabilises and competitors have difficulty filling their capacity; and *decline* in which demand begins to switch to substitute products. These stages in the evolution of a product indicate different general types of strategies – different generic strategies. Which of these generic strategies is suitable is said to be dependent upon the stage of evolution of the product's market and the competitive strength of the company producing it. So, for example, a company with a strong capability should invest heavily in the embryonic stage and establish a position before others arrive.

- *Experience curves*. The idea of the experience curve is based on the observation that the higher the volume of a particular product that a company produces, the more efficient it becomes at producing it. The cost per unit therefore declines as volume increases, at first rapidly and then more slowly as the learning opportunities for that particular product are exhausted. As a company moves down the learning curve it is in a position to reduce the price it charges customers for the product because its costs are falling. These price and cost curves can be linked to the idea of a product life cycle and the different strategies that strong and weak competitors should pursue. In the early stages of product evolution, a strong competitor will achieve higher volumes than a weak one and so move further down the learning curve. This will enable the strong competitor to reduce prices faster, stimulating demand and so increasing volumes even more to move even faster down the learning curve. Soon, the weaker competitor, or the latecomer, will have no chance of catching up.

- *Product portfolio*. The earliest and simplest form of product portfolio analysis is the growth share matrix of the Boston Consulting Group (BCG) (Henderson, 1970). To analyse their organisation in this way, managers review their whole business, dividing it up into all its different products, or market segments, or business units. They then calculate the relative market share they hold for each product, or market segment or business unit. The relative market share provides a measure of the firm's competitive capability with regard to that product, segment or business unit, because a high market share indicates that the firm is well down the experience curve compared with rivals. Next, managers must calculate the rate of growth of the product demand or market segment. The rate of growth is held to be a good measure of the attractiveness of the market – the stage in its evolution that it has reached. Different combinations of market share and growth rates indicate which particular generic strategies should be followed. The suitable options will be those that have some balance between the different possibilities in terms of cash generation.

Implementing long-term strategic plans

Once long-term plans have been formulated and evaluated and the optimal ones selected, they need to be implemented. Implementation is primarily the design and installation of cybernetic systems as follows.

- *Designing organisational structures*. The structure of an organisation is the formal way of identifying who is to take responsibility for what; who is to exercise authority over whom; and who is to be answerable to whom. The structure is a hierarchy of managers and is the source of authority, as well as of the legitimacy of decisions and actions. The appropriate structure follows from the strategy that an organisation is pursuing and structure displays typical patterns of development or life cycles (Chandler, 1962). Embryonic organisations have very simple structures in which people report rather informally to someone that they accept as their leader. Growth strategy makes it necessary to change the structure to one based on more formal specialisation of functions and identification of authority and responsibility. This leads to the problem of integrating specialised functions so that the structure has to be made even more formal with clearer definition of lines of authority and communication. Strategies of diversification into new products and markets make it necessary to set up marketing and manufacturing organisations in different geographic areas. Further diversification leads to setting up largely independent subsidiaries in divisionalised or holding company structures.

- *Designing systems of information and control*. The information and control systems of an organisation are basically procedures, rules and regulations governing what information about the performance of an organisation should flow to whom and when. It also covers who is required to respond to that information and how they are authorised to respond, in particular what authority they have to deploy the resources of the organisation. To implement strategies, information and control systems are required to enable the flows of information that implementation requires and provide appropriate control mechanisms to enable managers to monitor the outcomes of the strategy implementation and do something if those outcomes are not in accordance with the strategy. Management control is defined as the process of ensuring that all resources – physical, human and technological – are allocated so as to realise the strategy. Control ensures proper behaviour in an organisation and the need for it arises because individuals within the organisation are thought not to be always willing to act in the best interests of the organisation. The process of control involves setting standards or targets for performance, or expected outcomes of a sequence of actions, then comparing actual performance or outcomes against standards, targets or expectations, and finally taking corrective action to remove any deviations from standard, target or expectation. The principal form taken by the control system in most organisations is that of the annual plan or budget. The budget converts strategy into a set of short-term action plans and sets out the financial consequences of those action plans for the year ahead. Control is then a process of regularly comparing what happens with what the budget said would happen. Budgets allocate the resources of an organisation with which different business units and functions are charged to carry out the strategy. Budgets establish the legitimate authority for using the resources of the organisation.

- *Installing and operating human resource systems.* Effective strategy implementation should occur when the people required to take action to this end are motivated to do so. One of the most powerful motivators is the organisation's reward system (Galbraith and Kazanian, 1986). Appropriate rewards stimulate people to make the effort to take actions directly relevant to an organisation's strategy. The way in which people's jobs are graded and the pay scales attached to these grades will affect how people feel about their jobs and the effort they will make. Differentials need to be perceived to be fair if they are not to affect performance adversely. Bonuses, profit-related pay, piecework and productivity schemes are all ways of tying monetary rewards to the actions that strategy implementation requires. Non-monetary rewards are also of great importance in motivating people. These rewards include promotion, career development, job enrichment, job rotation, training and development. They all help individuals to be more useful to an organisation while developing greater self-fulfilment. Simpler forms of reward are also of great importance: for example, praise, recognition and thanks. Training and development is an important implementation tool, not only because it motivates people, but also because it provides the skills required for strategy implementation (Hussey, 1991). The objectives of training and development programmes should be aligned with those of an organisation's strategy and those objectives should consist of measurable changes in corporate performance.

- *Culture change programmes.* Just as the reporting structure of an organisation should fit the particular strategy the organisation wishes to pursue, so too should its culture, the attitudes and beliefs that people within an organisation share. Just as structures need to fit a particular strategy and just as they tend to follow a life cycle from the simple to the functional to the divisional, so too do cultures according to strategic choice theory. Implementation may well therefore require that an organisation change its culture, and the conventional wisdom prescribes that such change should be planned. The reasons why people might resist a change in culture need to be identified and plans formulated to overcome the resistance. Participation, communication and training are all seen as ways of overcoming resistance. The process of overcoming resistance involves a stage called *unfreezing* when the existing culture is questioned, and is followed by a period of reformulation where people consider what new beliefs they need to develop and share with each other. Finally there is the re-freezing stage where the new culture is fixed in place.

- *Developing appropriate political behaviour.* It is inevitable that people in an organisation will sometimes come into conflict and, when they do, they engage in political behaviour (Pfeffer, 1981). Interdependence, heterogeneous goals and scarce resources taken together produce conflict. If the conflict is important and power is distributed widely enough, then people will use political behaviour, that is, persuasion and negotiation, to resolve their conflict. If power is highly centralised, then most will simply do as they are told – they will not have enough power to engage in political behaviour. The kinds of political strategies people employ to come out best from conflict are the selective use of objective criteria, the use of outside experts to support their case, forming alliances and coalitions, sponsoring those with similar ideas, empire building, intentionally doing nothing, suppressing information, making decisions first and using analysis afterwards to justify them, and many more. The above view of politics as a manipulative process of dubious ethical validity leads to the belief that steps should be taken to reduce the incidence of political behaviour. Such steps are those that reduce the level of conflict and the most powerful of these is to preach and convert people to a common ideology.

This section has very briefly summarised the general prescriptions, tools and techniques that have been put forward to formulate and implement the long-term plans embodying the strategic choices made by an organisation's dominant coalition. Condensing what is a huge body of literature in this way inevitably produces something of a caricature. There has been considerable research into the effectiveness of generic strategies and debates about many issues, some of which will be briefly reviewed in Section 4.6. There has also been some research into whether formal planning systems of the kind outlined above produce what they are intended to produce. The evidence is very far from conclusive. However, the summary presented in this section, although somewhat simplistic, does indicate the underlying way of thinking represented by strategic choice theory, which makes it very evident how heavily conditioned this way of thinking is by the notion of cybernetic systems.

The rational decision-making process put forward by the theory of strategic choice also implies a particular psychological theory, that of cognitivism, and a particular theory of human communication, namely, the sender–receiver model. In recognising that people need to be motivated in order to implement strategies, strategic choice theory also implies humanistic psychology. The next section explores the implicit assumptions about human psychology and communication.

4.4 Cognitivist and humanistic psychology: the rational and the emotional individual

The review of cybernetic theory in Section 4.2 has already brought out how cybernetics is a theory about human behaviour. It assumes that human beings are cybernetic entities and that they learn through an essentially negative feedback process. In fact, the development of cybernetic systems theory was closely associated with the development of cognitive science. Furthermore, both cybernetics and cognitivism were closely associated with the development of computers and technologies of communication.

Cognitive psychology and the sender–receiver model of communication

In 1943 McCulloch and Pitts (1943) published an important paper in which they claimed that brain functioning and mental activity could be understood as logical operations. They held that the brain was a system of neurons that functioned according to logical processing principles. The brain was thought to be a deductive machine, and this notion was applied to develop machines that could operate in the same way, namely computers. In essence, the claim was that human minds were cybernetic systems. So, a theory about the operation of the brain was fundamental to the development of computers and those computers then came to be taken as an analogy for brain functioning. Computers were developed to mimic what brains were thought to do and, this having been done, the brain was then thought to be like a computer: an essentially circular argument.

The next significant development in cognitive science occurred in 1956 at two meetings in Cambridge, Massachusetts, when Simon, Chomsky, Minsky and McCarthy set major guidelines for the development of cognitive science (Gardner, 1985). Their central idea was that human intelligence resembles computation so much that cognition – that is, human knowing – could be understood as a process of computing representations of reality, those representations being made in the form of symbols. Just as computers process digital symbols, so the human brain processes symbols taking the form of electrochemical activity in the brain. This is the central idea, just as it is with cybernetic systems. Humans are assumed to act on the basis of representations of their environment that are processed in their brains. Learning is a process of developing more and more accurate representations of external, pre-given reality utilising negative feedback processes. In a life experience of development and learning, human minds build up models, maps or schemas representing reality and then act on the basis of these models. Cognitivism focuses on the individual mind and claims that this mind is an information-processing device that is the basis of rational thinking. Human thinking is claimed to be an essentially calculating process that is highly rational when functioning properly. In focusing on rational choices made by powerful individuals, the theory of strategic choice is making just these assumptions about human psychology.

What should be noted here is the importance of internal representations of the external environment and the error-activated nature of the learning process that cybernetics specifies. These are central assumptions in a cognitivist approach to psychology and they have enormous implications for how human agency, groups and organisations are understood.

About the same time as the developments described above, Shannon and Weaver (1949) published an important paper on the science of human communication. What they proposed was a model of communication derived from telephony in which one individual formulates an idea in the mind, translates it into language and then sends it to another individual who receives the words and translates them back into the idea. If the translation processes are accurate and there is no 'noise' in the transmission, the communication will be effective. If there is any failure of communication, then the receiving individual sends a message or signal to the sender indicating a gap, which the sender must then try to remove. This sender–receiver model is clearly a cybernetic theory of communication and it has come to be the one underlying the dominant discourse on organisations. Strategic choice theory, then, is built upon the assumptions of cognitivist psychology and the accompanying sender–receiver model of communication.

Human beings are regarded, in strategic choice theory, as living cybernetic systems that can understand, design, control and change other cybernetic systems, including their own minds. The implication is that an individual human can stand alone as a system. Implicit in a cybernetic approach to human affairs, then, is the assumption that humans are monads, that is, autonomous individuals who can exist outside relationships with others. The individual is prior and primary to the group. Again, there is the assumption, dominant in Western thinking, of the primacy of the masterful, rational, autonomous individual. Box 4.2 summarises the main assumptions of cognitivism.

Humanistic psychology

Humanistic psychology was developed mainly in the United States as a reaction to what was felt to be the pessimism and conservatism of psychoanalysis. Humanistic psychology takes a basically optimistic view of human nature and its perfectibility. One of its roots was in inspirational religious revivalism, and it saw the main problem of human existence as the alienation of an individual from his or her true self. From this perspective people can be motivated by providing experiences for them in which they can experience more of their true selves. You see the influence of these ideas in the theories of motivation of Maslow and Herzberg, mentioned below. The prescriptions for establishing visions and missions that inspire people also arise from this kind of thinking about human nature.

So far, this chapter has reviewed the stages of formulation, evaluation and implementation of long-term strategic plans, which is the centrepiece of the theory of strategic choice. However, those writing in this tradition also recognise that the factors of human motivation and leadership affect how an organisation's strategy is implemented. For example, Peters and Waterman (1982) questioned the rational techniques of decision-making and control reviewed in this chapter, pointing to their limitations in conditions of turbulence. Instead, they emphasised human motivation, values, beliefs and the importance of leadership. They stressed the importance of working harmoniously together, and strongly sharing the same culture,

Box 4.2	Cognitivism: main points on human knowing and communicating

- The brain processes symbols (electrochemical pulses) in a sequential manner to form representations or internal templates that are more or less accurate pictures of the world. This means that the brain is assumed to act as a passive mirror of reality.

- The world so pictured by the brain can be specified prior to any cognitive activity. This means that the world being perceived would have particular properties, such as light waves, and it would be these already existing real properties that would be directly registered by the brain. The world into which humans act is found, not created.

- The templates formed are the basis upon which a human being knows and acts. Repeated exposure to the same light wave would strengthen connections along a specific neuronal pathway, so making a perception a more and more accurate representation of reality. This would form the template, stored in a particular part of the brain, against which other light wave perceptions could be compared and categorised, forming the basis of the body's response. Representing and storing are, thus, essentially cybernetic processes. There is a fixed point of reference, external reality, and negative feedback of the gap between the internal picture and this external reality forms a self-regulating process that closes this gap. Knowing, knowledge creation and learning are essentially adaptive feedback processes, as is communication between people.

- The biological individual is at the centre of the whole process of knowing and acting.

- Since all normal individuals have much the same biologically determined brain structures and all their brains are processing symbolic representations of the same pre-given reality, there is no fundamental problem in individuals sharing the same perceptions. They share perceptions by communicating in what is essentially an engineering process of transmission.

values, beliefs and vision of the future. Their prescriptions were to choose a vision of the whole organisation's future, convert people to believing in it, promote internal harmony by encouraging the strong sharing of a few cultural values, and empower people.

However, although critical of rational techniques, Peters and Waterman did not depart in any way from cognitivist assumptions about human nature, or in any essential way from the assumption that an organisation is a cybernetic system. This is evident when they talk about charismatic leaders who choose a vision of the future and certain core values that they then inspire others with, converting them into believing the vision and the values. If anything, the autonomous individual becomes even more heroic in their view of organisational change. The system is still cybernetic because it is controlled by referring to the vision and the values and damping down any deviations from them.

A number of similar theories of motivation have been put forward in the management literature on how to secure consensus, co-operation and commitment. For example, Herzberg (1966) pointed out that people are motivated to work in co-operation with others by both extrinsic motivators such as monetary rewards and intrinsic motivators such as recognition for achievement, achievement itself, responsibility, growth and advancement. Intrinsic motivation is the more powerful of the motivators and is increased when jobs are enriched – that is, when they are brought up to the skill levels of those performing them.

Maslow (1954) distinguished between: basic physiological needs, such as food and shelter; intermediate social needs, such as safety and esteem; and higher self-actualisation needs, such as self-fulfilment. Maslow held that, when the conditions are created in which people can satisfy their self-actualisation needs, those people are then powerfully motivated to strive for the good of their organisation.

Schein (1988) and Etzioni (1961) distinguished three categories of relationship between the individual and the organisation. The relationship may be coercive, in which case the individual will do only the bare minimum required to escape punishment. The relationship may be a utilitarian one where the individual does only enough to earn the required level of reward. Third, the relationship may take a normative form where individuals value what they are doing for its own sake, because they believe in it and identify with it. In other words, the individual's ideology coincides with an organisation's ideology. This provides the strongest motivator of all for the individual to work for the good of an organisation.

Pascale and Athos (1981) stressed organisational culture as a result of their study of Japanese management. They recognised that people yearn for meaning in their lives and transcendence over mundane things. Cultures that provide this meaning create powerfully motivated employees and managers.

What all these studies suggest is that an organisation succeeds when its people, as individuals, are emotionally engaged in some way, when they believe in what their group and their organisation are doing, and when the contribution they make to this organisational activity brings psychological satisfaction of some kind, something more than simple basic rewards. Others have argued that people believe and are emotionally engaged when their organisation has a mission or set of values and when their own personal values match those of the organisation. Organisational missions develop because people search for meaning and purpose and this search includes their work lives (Campbell and Tawady, 1990). To win commitment and loyalty and to secure consensus around performing tasks it becomes necessary to promote a sense of mission. The development of a sense of mission is seen as a central leadership task and a vitally important way of gaining commitment to, loyalty for and consensus around, the nature and purpose of the existing business. An organisation with a sense of mission captures the emotional support of its people, even if only temporarily. A sense of mission is more than a definition of the business: that is, the area in which an organisation is to operate. A sense of mission is also to be distinguished from the ideas behind the word 'vision' or 'strategic intent'. The word 'vision' is usually taken to mean a picture of a future state for an organisation, a mental image of a possible and desirable future that is realistic, credible and attractive. The term 'mission' differs in that it refers not to the future but to the present. A mission is a way of behaving.

The underlying assumption is that organisations succeed when individuals are motivated to perform, as individuals. The humanistic psychology on which the above writers draw accords the same primacy to the individual as cognitivism does. The difference is that the former places much more emphasis on emotional factors, predominantly of a positive inspirational kind. Note how leaders are supposed to choose appropriate motivators.

Box 4.3 summarises the key assumptions upon which are built humanistic views of knowing and communicating.

Box 4.3	Humanistic psychology: main points on human knowing and communicating

- The biological individual is at the centre of human experience and emotion and spirituality are fundamental to this experience.
- Each individual has a true self and is most motivated to act when such action realises the true self.
- Emotions, values and beliefs are fundamental and people work most effectively when they are in harmony with each other. Rational choice is a limited aspect of human experience.
- People yearn for meaning and transcendence of the mundane.
- Organisations will be successful when people are emotionally engaged and inspired by visions and a sense of mission and it is the role of leaders to choose these.

4.5 Leadership and the role of groups

From a strategic choice theory perspective, the primary focus is on the leader as one who translates the directives of those higher up in the hierarchy into the goals and tasks of the group. Leaders monitor the performance of the task in terms of goal achievement and ensure that a cohesive team is built and motivated to perform the task. Leaders supply any skills or efforts that are missing in the team and, most important of all, they articulate purpose and culture, so reducing the uncertainty that team members face.

When leadership is defined in these terms, the concern is with the qualities leaders must possess and the styles they must employ in order to fulfil these functions effectively and efficiently. Those who have put forward explanations of this kind on the nature of leadership have differed from each other over whether the effective leader is one who focuses on the task, or one who focuses on relationships with and between people. A related area of concern is whether the effective leader is one who is autocratic, or one who delegates, consults and invites full participation. The question is which style of leadership motivates people more and thus gets the task done better. Consider three prominent theories: those of Fiedler (1967), Hersey and Blanchard (1988) and Vroom and Yetton (1973). According to these theories, leadership styles are to be chosen by the individual manager and, to be successful, a style that matches certain pre-given situations must be chosen. The leader should arrive at the group with particular skills developed beforehand. The required personality, skills and styles (or, as they are sometimes called, competences) are supposed to be identified in advance to suit a foreseeable situation. Here, leadership is about motivating people and the concern is with the appropriate role of the leader in securing efficient performance of known tasks.

The relevance of the group

A group is understood to be any number of people who interact with each other, are psychologically aware of each other and perceive themselves to be a group. Formal groups in an organisation may be permanent – for example, the sales department; or they may be temporary, as is the case when special task forces or multidisciplinary teams are appointed to deal with a particular task. Whether they are temporary or permanent, formal groups have clear goals and tasks; it is the purpose of formal groups to find solutions to structured problems. They usually have appointed leaders – leaders and managers have power given to them. However, they may also be autonomous, self-managing or democratic work groups that elect their own leader and design their own approach to a given structured task.

Within, alongside and across the formal groups, there is a strong tendency for informal groups to develop. These may be horizontal cliques amongst colleagues on the same hierarchical level, vertical cliques that include people from different hierarchical levels, or random cliques. Informal groups develop primarily because of proximity (Festinger *et al.*, 1950): through the contacts people make with each other given their physical location in relation to each other, the nature of their work and the time pressures they are under. The immediate concern about these informal groups is whether they will support or counter the operation of formal groups. The concern is with motivating people to cohere into functional teams that will focus on clearly defined tasks, not dissipate energies in destructive informal groups. The concern is primarily with the authority, responsibility and performance of individual managers in carrying out their pre-assigned tasks. From this perspective, the interest in groups relates to the circumstances in which groups may be more effective than individuals.

The underlying assumption about the relationship between individuals and groups in the notions reviewed in this section is that of the objective observer standing outside the system of groups and teams. The explicit or implicit prescription is that leaders and managers should take this position too, identify the nature of the situation and select leadership styles and motivational factors that are appropriate in the sense that they fit the situation. In essence, this amounts to installing appropriate feedback loops in the organisation so that it operates like a cybernetic system.

As far as the relationship between individuals and groups is concerned, again it is clear how the primacy of the individual is assumed. Groups are made up of individuals and these groups then affect those individuals, meeting some of their needs but deskilling them in other ways. In order to prevent adverse effects of groups on individuals, leaders need to pay attention to factors to do with the environment of the group, its composition in terms of members and their sensitivity to group dynamics. Formal groups are to be preferred over informal ones. It is recognised that informal groups are inevitable but the mainstream view seems to be that they threaten control. This attitude towards groups reflects cognitivist and humanistic assumptions.

4.6 Key debates

Previous sections of this chapter have provided a very brief description of key aspects of strategic choice theory in order to bring out its underpinning way of thinking. This section explores some of the key debates that have arisen in the development of the theory. These debates, which have not questioned the underlying way of thinking with its taken-for-granted assumptions about organisations and human interaction, have had to do with:

- whether strategy determines organisational structure or whether it is structure that determines strategy;
- whether market position or the resource base of an organisation determines its competitive advantage;
- what the limitations of strategic choice are, particularly when it comes to uncertainty and the impact of cognitive frames in interpreting situations, leading to questioning the very possibility of strategic choice;
- process versus content leading to an emphasis on learning rather than simple choice.

A brief indication of some of these debates is provided in this section.

Market position and the resource-based view of strategy

Previous sections have described strategic choice as the choice of the overall direction and shape of a whole organisation and its parts for some long time period into the future. The central purpose of the choice is to secure sustainable competitive advantage for the whole organisation and this choice was thought to be the single most important cause of successful performance. Furthermore, it was held that the choice of market position was the single most important cause of competitive advantage. This view was based on neo-classical economic theory, particularly theories to do with industry structure. The idea was that managers needed to analyse and understand the structure of their industry or market and select strategies that were appropriate to that structure.

Others, however, also drawing on neo-classical economics, argued that market position alone was not the cause of competitive advantage and took a resource-based view of strategy. Here a firm is viewed as a blend of resources that enable certain capabilities, options and accomplishments (Wernerfelt, 1984), which determines competitive advantage far more than market position. One firm outperforms another if it has superior ability to develop, use and protect core competences and resources, which are the foundations for creating the future (Hamel and Prahalad, 1990, 1994). Internal capabilities are what enable a firm to exploit external opportunities, and competitiveness is a function of the exploitation and leveraging of these internal resources. Strategies are designed to capitalise on core competences and distinctive assets form the basis of creating a sustainable competitive advantage. Complementary interdependence makes a firm's capabilities difficult to imitate. Resource and competence are built up historically, evolving in a continuous way with cumulative effects. Capabilities are building blocks that can be combined in mutually reinforcing ways into unique capacities and the different unique combinations lead to different unique futures. To prevent imitation, attention is focused on intellectual capital, firm-specific practices, relationships with customers and other intangible ways of working together. Strategic intent relates to choices about competences to secure a desired future and success comes from focusing attention on a few primary success factors.

Hamel and Prahalad (1989) also stress the role of organisations in creating their own environments instead of simply adapting to them. They have studied a number of global companies in North America, Europe and Japan and they suggest that what distinguishes the noticeably successful (Honda, Komatsu and Canon, for example) from the noticeably less so (General Motors, Caterpillar and Xerox, for example) are the different mental models of strategy guiding their respective actions. This research questions one of the basic tenets of strategic choice: namely, the notion that successful organisations are those that fit, or adapt to, their environments.

Hamel and Prahalad found that the less successful companies follow strategic choice prescriptions and so seek to maintain strategic fit. This leads them to trim their ambitions to those that can be met with available resources. Such companies are concerned mainly with product market units rather than core competences. They preserve consistency through requiring conformity in behaviour, and they focus on achieving financial objectives. These companies attempt to achieve their financial objectives by using generic strategies, selected according to criteria of strategic fit, in order to secure sustainable competitive advantage. Hamel and Prahalad report that this approach leads to repetition and imitation.

By contrast, Hamel and Prahalad found that successful companies focus on leveraging resources – that is, using what they have in new and innovative ways to reach seemingly unattainable goals. The main concern of these companies is to use their resources in challenging and stretching ways to build up a number of core competences. Consistency is maintained by all sharing a central strategic intent, and the route to this successful state is accelerated organisational learning, recognising that no competitive advantages are inherently sustainable. Here, managers are not simply matching their resources to the requirements of the environment, leaving to others those requirements their resources are incapable of delivering. Instead, managers use the resources they have creatively, they create requirements of the environment that they can then meet, they push to achieve stretching goals and so they continually renew and transform their organisation. They question the idea of adapting to the environment, proposing instead creative interaction and stressing the importance of local learning, so suggesting a shift from classical strategic choice theory towards the perspective of strategy as a learning process, which will be taken up in Chapter 5.

While these authors question some assumptions of strategic choice theory, they preserve others. In particular, they continue to see organisational success as flowing from clear, prior, organisation-wide intention. They stress what they call *strategic intent*, a challenging, shared vision of a future leadership position for the company. This strategic intent is stable over time. It is clear as to outcome but flexible as to the means of achieving that outcome. It is an obsession with winning, and winning on a global scale cannot be secured either through long-term plans or through some undirected process of intrapreneurship or autonomous small task forces. Instead, success is secured by discovering how to achieve a broad, stretching, challenging intention to build core competences. However, in stressing intention, harmony and consistency, the resource-based view falls within strategic choice theory.

Uncertainty and the limitations to strategic choice

It has already been pointed out that cybernetic control depends on the possibility of making reasonably reliable forecasts of action outcomes and time lags involved at the required level of detail and over the required time span. When this is not possible, cybernetic control may still be effective if small and essentially random actions by the organisation can be relied upon to cancel out small and essentially random changes in the environment – the law of requisite variety. In other words, cybernetic systems require a fairly high degree of certainty about environmental change, either in the sense that a specific cause can be related to a specific effect or in the probabilistic sense of small changes cancelling out. This is the same as saying that cybernetic systems function effectively when they operate in rather repetitive environments.

Many writers on strategic management have, of course, been well aware of the uncertainty, ambiguity and conflicting goals that managers have to deal with and have developed different ways of understanding the nature of strategic choice. One influential example is the notion of logical incrementalism, which will be discussed in Chapter 7. Logical incrementalism represents a move from the more mechanistic view of classical strategic choice theory towards an understanding of strategy as a continual process of small incremental changes within an overall, chosen logic.

The view that competitive advantage could be sustained for long time periods was criticised by some who pointed to the rapid change in competitive conditions. They held that hyper-competition made it impossible to sustain competitive advantage for any length of time. Those taking this view argue that hyper-competition requires a new view of strategy (D'Aveni, 1995). From this perspective, one firm outperforms another if it is adept at rapidly and repeatedly disrupting the current situation to create a novel basis for competing. Hyper-competition requires a discontinuously redefined competitive advantage and radical changes in market relationships. Success is built not on existing strengths as in the resource-based view, but on repeated disruptions. This enables a firm to continuously establish new but temporary competitive advantages. Tactical actions keep competitors off-balance. Competitive advantage is temporary and firms destroy their own and others' competitive advantage. Organisation units and actions are loosely coupled and competition requires aggressive action unconstrained by loyalty and compassion. Successful strategies rely on surveillance, interpretation, initiative, opportunism and improvisation.

The writers in the organisational evolution tradition (Hannan and Freeman, 1989) went even further and questioned the ability of managers to choose the state of their organisation in any way. They took a neo-Darwinian view and held that organisations changed through random events that were then selected for survival by competitive selection.

Process versus content

Another debate arose between those who argued that strategy research focused too much on the content of generic strategies required to produce successful performance. Arising from the discussion of the limits to rationality, some argued for looking at how managers actually made strategy. They called for a focus on how strategies were constructed, the process, rather than what they consisted of, the content. The whole question of process will be taken up in Chapter 7. This emphasis on process was taken up by some as a move from simple choice to a view of strategy as a learning process. For example, Mintzberg (1994) made a direct call for a move from strategic choice and long-term planning to an understanding of strategic management as a process of learning. This perspective will be explored in Chapter 5.

4.7 How strategic choice theory deals with the four key questions

The purpose of this section is to reflect upon the underlying assumptions and reasoning processes of strategic choice theory, including the debates it has led to, in order to identify what it focuses attention on and the extent to which it helps to make sense of one's experience of life in organisations.

In Chapter 2 I suggested that the phenomena of interest when one talks about strategy are populations of organisations of various kinds that interact with each other. Each organisation is itself a population of groupings of individuals that interact with each other. These populations are continually changing in that new organisations and groups within them come into being, while already existing ones disappear altogether, merge with others, split apart, develop new activities, alter structurally, grow or decline. As they relate to each other in their groups, people experience enthusiasm and boredom, excitement and anxiety, anger and fear, jealousy and envy, fulfilment and disappointment, pleasure and frustration.

Making sense of the phenomena

Strategic choice theory makes sense of these phenomena from a realist position. In other words, the theory assumes a pre-given reality. Section 4.3 on the formulation and evaluation of a strategy shows how each step in the formulation process makes this assumption. For example, a suitable strategy is one that fits, or is adapted to a particular market. In order to determine whether or not this is so, the market must be analysed in terms of customer requirements, competitor positions, entry barriers and so on. These factors are treated as realities that already exist, not stories about a reality that is being socially constructed by those who are participating in that market.

In addition, to establish the suitability of a strategy, managers must forecast, envision or imagine the state of these market factors some years into the future. That future is talked about as a pre-given reality too. You can hear this when people talk about getting to the future first, or use the analogy of Columbus setting sail for America, or President Kennedy announcing the dream of putting a man on the moon. These are all metaphors of a future reality that already exists, waiting to be discovered rather than created. Another example of this realist position is the discussion of leadership. Different leadership styles are related to different situations and the recommendation is that individuals should choose a leadership style that fits the situation. Again, the situations and the styles already exist before any individual comes to take them up. They are not created in the act of leading but are discovered and adopted in advance. Emotion tends to be understood from a humanistic point of view as a source of motivating followers and workers, but the strategic choice itself focuses firmly on Kant's autonomous, rational individual.

Furthermore, strategic choice theory makes a particular assumption about the nature of causality. It assumes that linear causal links can be identified and that, therefore, predictions can be made. For example, it states that success is caused by choosing a strategy that is feasible, acceptable and suitable. Another example is provided by the understanding of groups. It is postulated that groups of people will function effectively as teams if certain environmental factors and certain kinds of members are chosen to form the group. Such linear causality is not the only possible view. Chapter 10 will review notions of nonlinear causal connections and look at theories indicating that it could be impossible to identify causal links at all in certain circumstances.

The point I am making, then, is that strategic choice theory takes a particular position in relation to the way that humans know anything, and the debates it has led to largely continue to do the same. As with any other position, this immediately moves the reasoning process down one avenue and excludes others. The result is to deal with the four questions posed in Chapter 2 in a particular way. Consider how strategic choice theory deals with these four questions.

The nature of interaction

In strategic choice theory, interaction is understood in systemic terms, where the entities comprising the system are organisations that interact with each other in industry groupings, or markets. An organisation is also thought of as a system that consists of people grouped into divisions, subsidiary companies, departments, project teams and so on, all of which interact with each other to form the organisational system. The immediate consequence is a tendency to *reify*: that is, to think of an organisation and a system as a thing.

The concept of a system in strategic choice theory is a very specific one. It is a cybernetic system: that is, a goal-driven, self-regulating system. The self-regulation takes the form of a negative feedback process through which an organisation adapts to its environment, that is, its markets. Negative feedback is a process of referring back to a fixed point of reference established outside the organisation. The market demand to which the organisation must adapt provides the fixed point of reference. The negative feedback works through the system, taking account of the difference between its offering and that market demand, so as to remove the difference. The organisation is itself also a cybernetic system consisting of groups of people. The fixed point of reference for these groups is the goals and targets set for them by their manager. Negative feedback operates by taking account of the difference between performance and targets, so as to remove the difference. Uncertainty, ambiguity and conflict are supposed to be dealt with largely by more elaborate negative feedback loops. Thinking about motivation, political activity and culture change is all in terms of negative feedback loops. Note how strategic choice theory takes no account of the effect of positive or amplifying feedback loops in human affairs.

The result is a theory that focuses primarily on the macro level with very little attention to micro interactions or micro diversity. In other words, differences amongst the system entities are averaged out. Interactions between the entities are assumed to be average, or at least normally distributed around the average. This allows the cyberneticist to disregard the dynamics of interaction between the entities of which the system is composed and concentrate on the system as a whole. What is then focused on is the regularities in the system's responses to changes in its environment. The system responds to differences between externally imposed goals and its actual behaviour. Or, it responds to differences between an expectation, or prediction, of some state it should achieve and what it actually does. In organisational terms, the focus of attention is on how the whole organisation responds to the actions of other whole organisations that constitute its environment. Little attention is paid to the differences in the people that belong to the organisation or the nature of their interactions with each other.

A single, whole organisation is the primary unit of analysis. Intention, or choice, is related to this whole. By focusing attention on a single organisation, 'the organisation', strategic choice theory tends to ignore the fact that other organisations are making choices too. What happens to one depends not only on what it chooses but on what all the others are choosing too. You can see the importance attached to a single organisation making choices for the whole in the emphasis placed on: strategic intent, choosing a vision, choosing financial targets, choosing a culture, choosing strategic management styles, and so on. The possibility of making such choices successfully depends heavily on the ability to predict at rather fine levels of detail and over rather long time spans. That in turn depends upon the possibility of identifying causal links between action and outcome at a rather fine level of detail over rather long time spans.

For example, to achieve financial targets, investments must be chosen to deliver those targets. The discounted cash flow method prescribed for choosing between alternative investments requires the forecasting of detailed cash flows over periods as long as 25 years. Whether an investment is a success or not depends on the fine detail of what it costs and what revenues it generates over many years, once it is in operation. Forecasts at a coarse level of detail, or for short time periods, will not capture the factors upon which success depends. The choice cannot then be made as prescribed, which is to make the choice in a rational way that takes account of the actual factors that lead to success. Success will not be the result of rational choice but will depend on the chance capturing of the most important factors in the coarse forecasts.

Strategic choice theory takes a particular view of organisational dynamics. Since it is a cybernetic theory, the dynamics are those of a move to stable equilibrium. Success is equated with stability, consistency and harmony. Instabilities arise largely in the organisation's environment.

Strategic choice theory is usually formulated in a way that focuses on the interaction between components and so ignores the richness of human relationships. In viewing people as parts of a system, it fails to take account of ordinary human spontaneity, which will always be affecting what happens. Cybernetic systems are incapable of any kind of novelty, innovation, creativity or transformation. They can only unfold what their designers, the observing humans outside them, put into them. The cause of the system's movement is the formative process of negative feedback. From this perspective, organisations are thought of as wholes formed by interacting parts. These parts exist in order to sustain the purpose of the whole and so cannot be free. The cybernetic system unfolds the purpose already enfolded in it, namely the target set from outside of it. Cybernetics cannot explain novelty or transformation.

Nature of human beings

This chapter has indicated how strategic choice theory is built on a particular view of human nature. It is assumed that individuals are essentially cybernetic entities. They make representations of a pre-given reality taking the form of regularities built up from previous experience and mentally stored in the form of sets of rules, or schemas, cognitive maps or mental models. Through experience they make more and more accurate representations, more and more reliable cognitive maps. This process is essentially one of negative feedback in which discrepancies between the cognitive map and external reality are fed back into the map to change it, closing the gap between it and reality. Strategic choice theory pays very little attention to emotion and the impact that this might have on how an organisation functions. To the extent that this theory does pay attention to emotion, it does so from a humanistic psychology perspective in which individuals are motivated by opportunities to actualise their true selves. Little attention is paid to the notion that unconscious processes might influence how people perceive and know anything.

So, when it comes to the micro level, strategic choice theory alternates between two views of human nature, the cognitivist and the humanistic. The former tends to be predominant when the theory focuses on control systems and the latter when it focuses on motivation, leadership and culture. The way both are used, however, has an element in common. It is implicitly assumed that the individual members of an organisation are all the same and that interactions between them are all the same. It is assumed that everyone responds in the same way to the same motivational factor, for example. Another example is the implicit assumption, when talking about leadership styles, that everyone will respond in the same way to a given leadership style. Differences between individuals, and deviant and eccentric behaviour, have no role to play in how an organisation evolves. Indeed, they are seen as dangerous disruptions to be removed by more controls or additional motivators. The emphasis is on everyone sharing the same values to produce uniformity and conformity. The very way members of an organisation are referred to as the staff, or the management, indicates how differences within the categories are obliterated while differences between them are highlighted.

There is an important consequence of this ignoring of individual differences and deviant behaviour that will be taken up in Part 3. Systems in which the entities and their interactions are all the same cannot spontaneously generate anything new. For strategic choice theory this means that the only possible explanation of creativity is located in the individual's intention to do something creative. How individuals do this is not explained in strategic choice theory. It is simply assumed.

Individuals feature in strategic choice theory primarily in terms of how they affect the organisation as a whole. Individuals make the choices and do the controlling. Individuals appoint people to roles and they put them into teams. They set targets for those teams and motivate, reward or punish people according to performance. An individual forms a vision and individuals articulate missions for others. Power is possessed by individuals who exert it over other individuals. In this way the individual is consistently held to be prior and primary to the group. While the organisation as a system is understood to be driven by formative causality, a different theory of causality applies to the humans who design it. This is the rationalist causality of the autonomous individual choosing goals and actions.

The point I am making here is that strategic choice theory implicitly makes a number of important assumptions about human beings that should not be mistaken for the 'truth'. They are all assumptions that can quite properly be contested and, when they are, the whole of strategic choice theory is questioned too (see Part 3).

Methodology and strategic choice

Both cybernetics and cognitivism take a realist position on human knowing. In other words, they assume that there is a reality to be dealt with that exists before people perceive it. They take the traditional scientific perspective of looking for laws, or regularities, to explain behaviour. They seek to apply the principles of logic. In doing this they take the position of the objective observer who stands outside the system of interest and makes hypotheses about it. They build models of the system to guide behaviour. The emphasis is on the ability to control. Little importance is attached to the notion that people may construct reality in their social interaction with each other. There is no notion of reflexivity and the position of understanding through participating. Individuals stand outside the system they are talking about and construct models of it as the basis for prescription and action. This has methodological implications for research and it has even more important consequences for how managers understand their role.

When a manager takes this position, that manager immediately assumes that it is his or her task to design and install some system, set of actions, motivators and so on. For example, the top executive is supposed to analyse the values of an organisation. This requires the executive to step outside the value system of which he or she is a part and look at it from the outside, as it were. The next step is to design and install a new value system. Another example is provided by the discussion of leadership styles. Again, the manager is required to step outside the situation and determine whether it is one in which a particular leadership style is required. If this differs from the one the manager currently practises, then the appropriate one must be installed.

Paradox

The theory of strategic choice pays no attention to the possibility of paradox, that is, the simultaneous presence of contradictory ideas. The primary example of this is the way in which people are implicitly regarded as parts of an organisational cybernetic system, and so not free, on the one hand, and yet also as autonomous individuals who can design it and so *are* free, on the other. This is not sensed as paradoxical at all. In fact any paradox has been eliminated in a temporal sequencing in which the human is first thought of as a part and then as autonomous.

Contradictions are to be solved, tensions and conflicts smoothed away and dilemmas resolved. In terms of what might be major paradoxes of organisational life, strategic choice consistently occupies one pole of the contradiction. Individuals and groups are not paradoxical, since groups simply consist of autonomous individuals. Predictability is emphasised and the possible implications of simultaneously present unpredictability are not seriously explored. Control is emphasised and freedom to act is made consistent with it through motivational factors. Order is required for success and disorder or any form of deviance or eccentricity is to be curbed and removed. Success is equated with rational choice and chance with the potential for failure.

Again, the point I am making is that strategic choice theory implicitly makes assumptions about opposing forces in organisational life that cannot simply be taken for granted. It is quite possible to take a different view and so construct a different theory.

Making sense of experience

The question now is how this theory assists one to make sense of one's experience of life in organisations. My experience is that, despite the rational analysis, the forecasts, the visions, strategic intents, team building and so on, organisational outcomes are very frequently surprising and unexpected. I find it very difficult to make sense of this experience by taking a strategic choice perspective, as indeed do many others as described in Section 4.6 above. The theory leads one to believe that it is possible to make choices that lead to organisational success if one follows the prescribed procedures. So, when managers follow the prescriptions and the surprising, the unexpected and the downright unpleasant occur, they are left with little option but to conclude that they, or more likely that other people, have been incompetent in some way. A variation on this is to blame the surprise on ignorance of enough facts. Alternatively, the blame might be placed on people who do not implement the strategic choice as required. When one makes sense of experience from the strategic choice perspective the most widespread response to the unexpected takes the form of some kind of blame.

The response is then to put more effort into gathering and analysing information to overcome ignorance. Or more intensive efforts are made to acquire the necessary competences to manage strategically and so avoid accusations and feelings of incompetence. Or new motivating and controlling systems are installed to prevent poor implementation and bad behaviour. When the surprise is a large one, these responses are usually accompanied by the removal from the organisation of individuals who are conspicuously associated with the surprise. However, none of these responses puts a stop to the whole sequence of events happening again. Instead, in my view, these responses raise levels of fear and place people under increasing stress. Is this inevitable or is there a problem with trying to make sense of experience from the strategic choice standpoint?

If you take the psychoanalytic perspective to be reviewed in Chapter 6, you might reach a different conclusion. It could be that many of the prescriptions of strategic choice theory are little more than defences against the anxiety of not being able to forecast and stay in control. If this is so, then they are not very good defences because, as I have just suggested, they may actually increase levels of anxiety. If you take the perspective that I will suggest in Part 3, you might conclude that it is the nature of organising itself that generates the unexpected and the surprising. Then it may be that no one is to blame but, rather, uncertainty needs to be accepted as an inescapable fact of life that need not provoke despair or paralyse action.

4.8 Summary

This chapter has reviewed the theory of cybernetic systems and the closely associated cognitivist theory of human behaviour upon which the theory of strategic choice is built. These theories are the foundations upon which the strategic choice theory of organisational change is built. Cybernetic systems depend upon the possibility of prediction over a long enough time period at a fine enough level of detail, if they are to achieve the control that is their central concern. Cognitivist psychology assumes that individuals are autonomous and that they learn in an essentially negative feedback manner. It emphasises heavily the logical capacities of the human being and it is these that enable choices to be made. These are central themes that run through strategic choice theory.

This chapter has also reviewed the rational, analytical sequence of steps prescribed by strategic choice theory for the formulation and evaluation of long-term strategic plans. The steps involve analysing and forecasting market development, as well as the financial, other resource or competence and power implications of alternative action options. The result should be a blueprint to guide the development of the organisation for some reasonably long period into the future. It is the template against which the actions of individual managers are to be measured. The assumption is that if the plan has been put together skilfully enough it will go a long way to ensuring the organisation's success. However, the formulated plan only provides the blueprint against which action is to be evaluated. Success requires effective implementation.

Implementation is in effect the construction of cybernetic systems. Detailed targets and objectives are derived from the strategic plan and hierarchical structures and detailed sets of procedures for measuring and comparing outcomes with expectations are designed to monitor movement towards the detailed objectives. Even 'softer' elements such as belief systems, power and management style are prescribed in much the same way.

The chapter then reviewed behavioural factors in organisations from a strategic choice perspective, primarily to do with the motivation of people working in the organisation and the nature of leadership. These were understood in terms of what amounts to negative feedback loops, displaying the way in which organisations are treated as if they are, or should be, cybernetic systems. In all of these areas the individual is treated as primary, displaying the underlying assumption of cognitivism and humanistic psychology. Another common assumption is that managers can and should take the position of independent observer and choose appropriate feedback loops in relation to motivation, leadership, politics and culture. Throughout, the assumption is that human beings behave like cybernetic systems themselves, the underlying tenet of cognitivism.

The conclusion I reach is that this theory provides a partial and limited explanation of how organisational life unfolds. It provides powerful explanations of, and prescriptions for, the predictable, repetitive aspects of organisational life over short time frames into the future. These are indeed very prominent and important aspects of organisational life. However, if you believe, as I do, that life in organisations is the interplay of the predictable and the unpredictable, the stable and the unstable, the orderly and the disorderly, then it provides a very partial explanation. On its own, it leaves one feeling puzzled by constant surprise and worried about the inability to stay in control that it prescribes. Creativity and innovation remain largely mysterious if strategic choice theory is the only way to understand organisations. The creativity and destructiveness of relationships between people is absent. It prescribes predominantly top-down processes, even when empowerment and self-managing teams are suggested. They are always the result of decisions made by those at the top of the hierarchy but, as those at the top know only too well, people rarely do exactly as they are told. These conclusions are not at all new – similar points have been made in the debate around strategic choice theory for a long time now. What is surprising, perhaps, is that despite the debate around it and the dubious evidence base for it, strategic choice theory continues to dominate most strategic management textbooks and features frequently in the ways in which practising managers talk about their organisation and its strategies.

Further reading

Richardson (1991) provides an excellent account of cybernetics and the use of feedback thinking about human systems. Baddeley (1990) provides a very good exposition of the cognitivist position and Varela *et al.* (1995) provide a cogent critique of cognitivism. To obtain further information on analytical techniques and models for evaluating strategies turn to Hofer and Schendel (1978) as well as Rowe *et al.* (1989) and Johnson *et al.* (2005). Also see Ansoff (1990) for a very different perspective from the one presented in this book. Hussey (1991) provides further material on management control and Goold and Campbell (1987) provide a thorough analysis of strategic management styles. Campbell and Tawady (1990) should be referred to for a greater understanding of the mission concept. For further detail on particular decision-making modes turn to Quinn (1978), Mintzberg *et al.* (1976) and Cohen *et al.* (1972). Good summaries of counter views are to be found in Hurst (1982). Hurst (1986), Argyris (1990), Schein (1988), Morgan (1997) and Mintzberg (1994) are well worth reading. For the resource-based view see Hamel and Prahalad (1989).

Questions to aid further reflection

1. What are the essential features of a cybernetic system and what assumptions does such a theory make about the world it is trying to explain?

2. If you think in the way suggested by the theory of strategic choice how would you explain what an organisation is?

3. What role does the notion of the objective observer play in cybernetic systems and cognitivist psychology?

4. What theory of communication is central to cognitivist psychology?

5. What taken-for-granted assumptions does the theory of strategic choice make about human individuals and the social world they live in?

6. What theories of causality are implied by the theory of strategic choice?

7. What does it mean to be practical if you subscribe to this theory?

Chapter 5

Thinking in terms of organisational learning and knowledge creation

Systems dynamics, cognitivist, humanistic and constructivist psychology

This chapter invites you to draw on your own experience to reflect on and consider the implications of:

- The importance and consequences of nonlinearity.

- The importance and consequences of positive feedback.

- What it means to think in terms of mental models.

- The consequences of the move from cognitivist to constructivist psychology.

- How control is presented as operation at leverage points.

- The dual causality to be found in organisational learning theories.

- The role of teams and of the social generally in learning processes.

- The role of leaders in learning and knowledge creation.

- The move to notions of organisations as living systems and the connection made to the mystical.

The ideas presented in this chapter are important because they constitute the assumptions on which theories of organisational learning are built. The recent popularity of notions of organisational learning and knowledge management reflects some realisation of the limitations of strategic choice theory. If one is to avoid naïve applications of learning and knowledge management prescriptions it is necessary to understand the way of thinking they reflect and understand the limitations of this way of thinking.

5.1 Introduction

Chapter 4 reviewed strategic choice theory, showing how its theoretical foundations are to be found in the theory of cybernetic systems and a primarily cognitivist view of human nature. According to this theory, organisations become what they become because of the strategic choices of their leaders. That chapter also described how a number of writers have taken issue with the strategic choice perspective and suggested instead that an organisation's strategic development could be better understood as arising in processes of learning (Mintzberg and Waters, 1985; Mintzberg, 1994). According to this theory, organisations become what they become because of the quality of their learning processes, and strategy and strategic direction are caused by such learning. It is the role of the leaders to design learning processes and inspire effective learning.

This chapter, therefore, explores the theoretical foundations of learning organisation theory and knowledge management which have attracted increasing attention since the early 1990s. This approach has much in common with strategic choice theory but there are significant differences. Most important, perhaps, is how it points to the limits of predictability to and more complex processes involved in strategising in organisations. The main theoretical difference is that learning organisation theorists employ a somewhat different theory of interaction. They still see interaction in systemic terms but the systems theory is systems dynamics rather than cybernetics. The same cognitivist view of human action is usually retained, however, although some writers move to a constructivist perspective and humanistic psychology becomes more important than it was in the theory of strategic choice. Strategic choice theory held that organisations change when their managers make choices about a wide range of issues. According to the theory of the learning organisation, change flows from a process of organisational learning. It is when people in an organisation learn effectively together and so create knowledge that it changes. However, the concern with control remains.

One of the most influential expositions of the concept of the learning organisation is that given by Senge (1990). Senge believes that an organisation excels when it is able to tap the commitment and capacity of its members to learn. He sees this capacity as intrinsic to human nature and he locates it in the individual, although he does see such learning as occurring when individuals experience profound teamwork. He identifies five disciplines required for an organisation that can truly learn:

- systems thinking;
- personal mastery;
- mental models;
- shared vision;
- team learning.

Each of these will be considered in the sections that follow.

5.2 Systems dynamics: nonlinearity and positive feedback

Senge understands organisations from the perspective of systems dynamics and holds that a learning organisation requires its people to think in systems terms. People should not think about their work purely in terms of their own roles. Instead, they should develop an understanding of the negative and positive feedback structure of the system of which they are a part. This should enable them to obtain some insight into the unexpected consequences of what they are doing. The purpose of thinking in systemic terms is to identify leverage points: that is, those points in the web of negative and positive feedback loops where change can have the largest beneficial effects. As in strategic choice theory, the purpose is to stay in control as much as is possible in a very complex system.

Systems dynamics has its intellectual roots in the same tradition as cybernetics. It is also built on the engineer's notion of control. However, from this common root and around the same time, it developed in a somewhat different way from cybernetics. While cyberneticists focused on the structure of negative feedback loops, those who developed systems dynamics sought to model the system as a whole in mathematical terms. The most important figures in this development were economists seeking to model economic cycles for whole economies or some aspect of them such as inventory cycles. Some of the most important figures here were Goodwin (1951), Philips (1950) and Tustin (1953). Systems dynamics thinking was also extended to industrial management problems (Forrester, 1958; Simon, 1952).

In their modelling work, systems dynamicists used *nonlinear* equations that incorporated *positive* feedback effects and generated rather complex dynamics. These models also display some cyclical behaviour that is due to the structure of the system itself, not just changes in the environment. However, just as with cybernetics, the system cannot spontaneously change, a matter I will return to in Chapter 10.

This section will give a brief review of some of the key concepts in systems dynamics, starting with the nature of nonlinearity.

Nonlinearity

Nonlinearity occurs when some condition or some action has a varying effect on an outcome, depending on the level of the condition or the intensity of the action. For example, the availability of inventories of goods in an inventory affects shipment rates of those goods, but the effect varies. When the inventory is close to a desired level, there will be virtually no impact of inventory levels on shipment rates. The firm ships according to its order inflow rate. However, when inventory is very low, inventory availability has a powerful constraining effect on shipments.

Instead of a system that operates only according to negative feedback, as in cybernetics, there is now a system that operates according to both positive and negative feedback. Systems dynamics therefore introduces the possibility that a system may display non-equilibrium behaviour as it flips between positive and negative feedback. The result is much more complex patterns of movement over time – that is, much more complex dynamics. Behaviour can now be cyclical and those cycles might be very irregular if the system is perturbed by environmental fluctuations. Systems dynamics was very important in understanding the nature of economic cycles, such as cycles in inventory and other forms of investment. Systems dynamics also points to the limits of predictability by introducing nonlinear circular causality, which makes it difficult to say what causes what, or what precedes what.

Perhaps the most important development of systems dynamics models for application to organisational and social policy issues has been by Jay Forrester (1958, 1961). His background was that of a servomechanisms engineer, digital computer pioneer and manager of a large R&D effort. He developed an approach to understanding human systems that is based on concepts of positive and negative feedback, nonlinearity and the use of computers to simulate the behaviour patterns of such complex systems. Feedback is the basic characteristic of his view of the world and he firmly links human decision-making to the feedback concept.

Production and distribution chains

Forrester has illustrated his approach by modelling the behaviour of production and distribution chains. A factory supplies a product, say beer, to a number of distributors who then ship it to an even larger number of retailers. Orders for the product flow back upstream from retailers to distributors and from them to the factory. The factory, the distributors and the retailers form a system, and the links between them are flows of orders in one direction and flows of product in the other. Each part of the system tries to do the best it can to maintain inventories at minimum levels without running out of product to sell. Each attempts to ship product as fast as possible. They all do these things because that is the way to maximise their individual profits. But because of its very structure – the feedback and lags in information flows – this system shows a marked tendency to amplify minor ordering disturbances at the retail level. An initial 10 per cent increase in orders at the retail level can eventually cause production at the factory to peak 40 per cent above the initial level before collapsing.

Peter Senge (1990) reports how he has used this example as a game with thousands of groups of managers in many countries. Even when people know about the likely consequences of this system, he has always found that the consequences of a small increase at the retail level are, first of all, growing demand that cannot be met. Inventories are depleted and backlogs grow. Then beer arrives in great quantities while incoming orders suddenly decline as backlogs are reduced. Eventually almost all players end up with large inventories they cannot unload.

Senge concludes that it is only by being aware of how the system as a whole functions, rather than simply concentrating on their own part of it, that managers can ensure that the extreme instabilities of the cycles are avoided. It seems, however, that these cycles can never be removed altogether.

Principles of systems dynamics

By running computer simulations of a great many different human systems, researchers in the systems dynamics tradition have identified a number of principles about complex human systems. These are set out below.

1. Complex systems often produce unexpected and counterintuitive results. In the beer game, retailers increase orders above their real need expecting this to lead to

bigger deliveries, but because all retailers are doing this, and because of lags in information flows, the unexpected result is lower deliveries.

2. In systems with nonlinear relationships, or with positive and negative feedback, the links between cause and effect are distant in time and space. In the beer game, the causes of increased demand appear at the retail end, distant in space from the factory and distant in time because of the lags in order flows. Such distance between cause and effect makes it very difficult to say what is causing what. Those playing the beer game always think that the fluctuations in deliveries are being caused by fluctuations in retail demand, when in fact they are due to the manner in which the system operates. The problem is made worse by many coincident symptoms that look like causes but are merely relational. This means that it is extremely difficult to make specific predictions of what will happen in a specific place over a specific time period. Instead, quantitative simulations on computers can be used to identify general qualitative patterns of behaviour that will be similar to those one is likely to experience, although never the same. Simulation here is being used not to capture the future specific outcome within a range of likely outcomes, but to establish broad qualitative features in patterns of behaviour.

3. Systems are highly sensitive to some changes but remarkably insensitive to many others. These systems contain some influential pressure, or leverage, points. Managers can exert influence at these points and so can have a major impact on the behaviour of the system. The problem is that they are difficult to identify. In the beer game, the leverage points lie in the ordering practices of retailers and distributors. Unfortunately these pressure points, from which favourable chain reactions can be initiated, are extremely difficult to find. More usually, it seems, systems are insensitive to changes and indeed counteract and compensate for externally applied correctives. So when retailers find that deliveries from the distributors are curtailed, they respond by ordering even more and so make the situation worse. Because of the natural tendency to counteract and compensate – that is, to move to stability – it is necessary to change the system itself rather than simply apply externally generated remedies.

The above points lead to the conclusion that attempts to plan the long-term future are likely to prompt counter-forces and lead to unexpected and unintended changes.

Archetypes of feedback processes

The strong possibility that systems will counteract correctives and produce unintended consequences makes it necessary for managers to analyse and understand the feedback connections in the system in order to understand the system as a whole. Through their simulations, systems dynamicists have built up a set of templates, or archetype feedback processes, that are very commonly found in organisations of all kinds. The purpose of these archetypes is not to make specific predictions of what will happen, but to recondition perceptions so that people are able to perceive the structures at play, to see the dynamic patterns of behaviour and to see the potential leverage in those structures. The templates are meant to be used in a flexible way to help understand patterns in events. For example, Senge describes an archetype called 'limits to growth', which occurs when a reinforcing positive feedback process is installed to produce a desired result (a positive growth loop) but it inadvertently creates secondary effects (a negative limiting loop) that put a stop to the growth. The 'limits to growth' structure is found wherever growth bumps up against limits. The most immediate response to this structure is that of pushing harder on the factors that cause growth. In fact this is counterproductive because it causes the system to bump even more firmly against the limits. The solution is to work on the negative loop, on relaxing the limits.

For example, a company may grow through introducing new products flowing from its R&D efforts. As it grows it increases the size of the R&D department, which becomes harder to manage. Senior engineers then become managers and the flow of new product ideas slows. Pressing for more new product ideas will simply lead to a bigger R&D department and that will exacerbate the management problems, so reducing the flow of new ideas. Instead, there is a need to rethink the whole process of developing new products and running R&D activities. The leverage point is the way in which the actual R&D effort is organised, and to see how this should be done one needs to understand the whole system of which R&D is a part.

Box 5.1 summarises the key points that the theory of systems dynamics makes on patterns of organisational change over time.

5.3 Personal mastery and mental models: cognitivist psychology

The second discipline required in a learning organisation is personal mastery. Senge does not mean by this some form of domination but, rather, a high level of proficiency such as that possessed by a master craft worker. Those who have personal mastery consistently obtain the results that they want and it requires commitment to lifelong learning. It is a process of continually deepening one's personal vision, focusing energy, developing patience and seeing reality objectively. He links it with spiritual foundations. The strongly humanistic flavour of his view of human nature is evident and takes the same line of inspirational motivation as that described in Chapter 4 in relation to strategic choice theory.

The third discipline required for the learning organisation is an understanding of the notion of mental models. These are deeply ingrained assumptions, or generalisations, often taking the form of pictures or images in individual minds. Individuals are mostly not aware of their mental models: they are hidden, or unconscious, mental constructions. Senge emphasises how mental models restrict perceptions, and points to Royal Dutch Shell, claiming that it developed the skill of surfacing and challenging the mental models of managers. Mental models are internal pictures of the external world, and he claims that individuals can learn to surface them and subject them to rigorous scrutiny. Institutional learning is a process in which management teams work together to change their shared mental models of their company and its markets. This is cognitivist psychology as in strategic choice theory.

According to cognitive science, humans are compelled by their limited brain capacity for processing new information to simplify everything they observe. They are unable to know reality itself; all they can do is construct simplifications: that is, mental models of reality. The influence of Kant (*see* Chapter 3) is very clear in this

Box 5.1	Systems dynamics: main points on organisational dynamics

- Organisations are goal-seeking feedback systems, but amplifying feedback loops and nonlinearity means that they are not self-regulating in the cybernetic sense. Instead, they are self-influencing and this may take a self-sustaining or a self-destructive form. They may be adapting to pre-given environments through negative feedback or diverging from them through positive feedback.

- Systems dynamics takes a realist position on human knowing.

- The system is recursive. This means that it feeds back on itself to repeat its behaviour.

- It follows that causality is circular. However, in systems dynamics causality is nonlinear. Causal links are distant and often difficult to identify.

- Predictability of specific events and their timings is very difficult, and this makes it important to recognise qualitative patterns.

- Control becomes difficult but if the structure of the system is understood, leverage points can be identified. These are points where efforts to change behaviour have the most effect. These points are difficult to find. Changes there might simply provoke compensating and offsetting behaviour.

- Instability is an essential part of what goes on and one cannot simply ignore it or write it off as something to be banished by negative feedback controls. There is too much evidence that this focus on negative feedback alone leads to unintended positive loops and unintended consequences.

- Behavioural patterns of the system as a whole are of great importance. Behavioural patterns can emerge without being intended; in fact they often emerge contrary to intention. The result is unexpected and counterintuitive outcomes. The systematic feedback structure of the organisation itself determines the pattern of behaviour over time.

- Because the analysis is conducted in feedback terms, there is still the notion of an external point of reference. The system still operates on the basis of representations of its environment.

- There is a clear boundary between system and environment, between inner and outer. Although the system is adapting to its environment, it is itself a closed system. It operates/changes with reference to a fixed point at the boundary with its environment, either amplifying or damping in relation to that fixed point.

- Its state is determined by its own structure as well as flux in the environment expressed through the fixed point of reference. Instability comes from within the system as well as the environment.

- The system is no longer homeostatic, or equilibrium seeking, but far more likely to be in nonequilibrium. However, left to its own devices, the system has a tendency to stabilise and so deteriorate in the face of change.

- History is important in that the current state of the system does depend upon the sequence of previous states. However, the system does not evolve of its own accord. Any change must be designed outside the system and then installed.

- The goal is still to achieve as much stability, consistency and harmony as is compatible with changing to adapt to the environment.

kind of thinking. When people look at a particular situation, they see it through the lens provided by the mental models built up through past experience and education. Humans approach each situation every day with a mindset, a recipe they have acquired from the past, that they use to understand the present in order to design actions to cope with it. When they take actions that fail to have the desired result, the reason often lies in the way the problem is perceived in the first place. The remedy is to amend the mental model, the perspective, the mindset, the paradigm with which the task is being approached.

Managers will not simply observe a given environment and a given organisational capability – that is, the facts. They, like all other humans, will sometimes inevitably invent, to some extent, what they observe. The whole process of simplifying and selecting means that the environment is in a real sense the invention and the creation of the managers observing it. It will then only be possible for managers to make sense of what they are doing after they have done it (Weick, [1969] 1979). In highly complex and uncertain situations, then, explanations of strategic management need to take account of the possibility that environments may be invented or created in managers' minds and that they can often only make sense of what they are doing with hindsight. This is a move from cognitivism to constructivism.

Constructivist psychology

Maturana and Varela (1987) argue for a constructivist view of human psychology. They hold that people do not simply respond to stimuli presented by the environment but select aspects of their environment according to their own identities. In other words, they enact, or bring forth, the environment that is relevant to them. This is a view of cognition – that is, of recognising and responding – that is active rather than simply passively registering what is already there. The world of an individual is an active construction by that individual of his or her own world, not a passive representation of a pre-given world. Each in a sense creates his or her own world.

This notion of selecting, or calling forth, a world is illustrated by the perception of colour (Varela et al., 1995). Primates have evolved a trichromate system for perceiving colour: that is, they possess one channel, or receptor, which responds to medium-wave light, another which responds to an excess of long-wave over short-wave light and a third to an excess of medium- over long-wave light. The colours perceived depend upon which receptors are dominant and which are dormant. Not all species, however, have trichromate systems. Squirrels and rabbits, for example, have dichromate systems – that is, two receptors – while pigeons and ducks have tetrachromate systems – that is, four receptors. These other creatures, therefore, cannot see the world of colour that humans see, and similarly humans are at a loss to know what the world of colour looks like to a duck or a rabbit. Which is reality? The question is meaningless, because specific evolutionary histories have produced one of a number of possible visual systems for each species. Evolutionary history has operated to select, to call forth or enact, one of a number of possible worlds for a particular species.

Maturana and Varela present evidence for their view that the human brain does not simply register stimuli but also creates patterns associated with them. The brain does not process information or act as a passive mirror of reality to form more or less accurate representations of the world. Instead, it is perturbed by external stimuli into actively constructing global patterns of electrochemical activity. Further-more, these patterns are not stored in specific parts of the brain, because each time a stimulus is presented to the body, the brain constructs a pattern anew that involves whole ensembles of neurons in many different parts of the brain. This leads Maturana and Varela to conclude that the nervous system does not simply represent a world; rather, it creates, calls forth or enacts a world. The world people act into is the world they have created by acting into it. In other words, Maturana and Varela adopt a constructivist perspective rather than the cognitivist one usually underlying the theory of strategic choice and many views of the learning organisation.

This change in the underlying theory of psychology is important because it presents a serious challenge to the cognitivist underpinnings of the theories of strategic choice and the learning organisation. It presents a view of mental process as one of perpetual construction, thereby moving away from the notion that brains faithfully represent an external reality and also any idea of the brain as storing and retrieving representations in any simple way. The Maturana and Varela perspective brings bodily action to the forefront and develops the notion of enactment: that is, of humans acting into what they have constructed.

However, the individual is still held to be primary and the theory is still a systems theory. They present a theory of autopoietic systems where the individual, understood as a system, is the fundamental unit of analysis and the conservation of individual identity is the fundamental principle. Here, individuals are bounded, self-determining entities. The constructivist position is not inconsistent with the notion of mental models, since it can be taken to be an alternative way of understanding how mental models are constructed. The individual mind is then functioning purely in terms of an identity, on one side of a boundary, constructing variations in itself, triggered by changes in other identities contained within their boundaries.

Enactment and sense making in organisations

One influential writer on organisations who adopts a constructivist approach is Weick (1995). He emphasises enactment and also the role of storytelling in communities of practice as processes of sense making, which have the following features:

1. Active agents place stimuli in some kind of framework so that they can comprehend, explain, attribute, extrapolate and predict. Weick often uses the metaphor of a map and talks about individual mental models.

2. Individuals form conscious and unconscious anticipations and assumptions as predictions of what they expect to encounter, and sense making is triggered when there is a discrepancy between such expectations and what they encounter. The need for explanation is triggered by surprise and takes the form of retrospective accounts to explain those surprises. Meaning is ascribed retrospectively as an output of a sense-making process and does not arise concurrently with the detection of difference.

3. Sense making is the process people employ to cope with interruptions of ongoing activity.

4. It is a process of reciprocal interaction of information seeking and meaning ascription: that is, it includes environmental scanning, interpretation and associated responses.

5. A distinction may be drawn between generic (collective) and intersubjective (individual-relating) forms of sense making.

Weick regards sense making as both an individual and a social activity, and argues that it attends to both how a 'text' is constructed and how it is interpreted, to both creation/invention and discovery. He argues that sense making is grounded in identity construction, where identities are constructed in the process of interaction between people. He emphasises its retrospective nature, where meaning is the kind of attention directed to experience. Sense making is a process of relating in which people co-create, or enact, their environment. This leads him to place particular emphasis on talk, discourse, conversation, storytelling and narrative. In this process, people notice, extract and embellish cues, which he regards as the simple, familiar structures from which people develop a larger sense of what may be occurring. For him, the metaphor of a 'seed' captures the open-ended quality of sense making because a seed is a form-producing process. He quotes Shotter (1983), who describes how an acorn limits the tree that grows from it to an oak tree but does not specify it exactly. Rather, it grows unpredictably. Notice here how this assumes a theory of formative causality (*see* Chapter 3).

Weick ascribes particular importance to novel moments in the process of sense making. He locates the origins of novelty in dissonance, surprise, gaps, differences, disruptions, unexpected failures and uncertainty. For him it is events of this kind that trigger sense making, which could produce novel explanations. He describes the process as one that involves emotion and is necessarily confusing. What he does not question is the split between individual and social and the dual causality that goes with it.

Box 5.2 lists the key points about knowing that are made by cognitivist psychology.

So far, I have been describing two theories of mental models: namely, the cognitivist theory in which mental models are internal representations of external reality, and constructivist theory in which mental models are active constructions that create the world that people act into. Whatever the perspective, however, learning has to do with changing mental models. A very influential theory of learning as change in mental models derives from the work of Bateson (1972) and later that of Argyris and Schön (1978). They distinguish between single- and double-loop learning.

Single- and double-loop learning

A person would function very slowly if for every action that person had consciously to retrieve and examine large numbers of previously acquired mental models and then choose an appropriate one. Experts therefore act on previously acquired models which have become unconscious. One process of learning, therefore, involves the repetition of an action in order to make the design of later similar actions an automatic process. The expert seems to use some form of recognisable pattern in a new situation automatically to trigger the use of past models developed in relation

---

Box 5.2	Constructivist psychology: main points on human knowing

- The biological individual is at the centre of human knowing.

- Individual brains do not represent a given world but rather actively select the world into which they act. They therefore create or enact their worlds.

- Sense making is triggered by discrepancies between what people expect and what they encounter.

to analogous previous situations. Experts do not examine the whole body of their expertise when they confront a new situation. Instead, they detect recognisable similarity in the qualitative patterns of what they observe and automatically produce models which they modify to meet the new circumstances. This is single-loop learning. Each time people act they learn from the consequences of the action to improve the next action, without having consciously to retrieve and examine the unconscious models being used to design the action.

Nonetheless, expert behaviour based on single-loop learning and unconscious mental models brings not only benefits; it also carries with it significant dangers. The fact that the mental models being used to design actions are unconscious means that they are not being questioned. The more expert one is, the more rapidly one acts on the basis of unconscious models. This means that one more easily takes for granted the assumptions and simplifications upon which the mental models are inevitably built. This is efficient in stable circumstances but, when those circumstances change rapidly, it becomes dangerous. The possibility of skilled incompetence (Argyris, 1990) then arises. The more expert people are – that is, the more skilled they are in designing certain actions – the greater the risk that they will not question what they are doing. It follows that they are more likely to become skilled incompetents. This gives rise to the need for double-loop learning. Here people learn not only in the sense of adjusting actions in the light of their consequences, but also in the sense also of questioning and adjusting the unconscious mental models being used to design those actions in the first place.

There may well be a difference between espoused models and models in use (Argyris and Schön, 1978). Experts are quite likely to say one thing and do another. The more expert people become in working together as a group, the more prone they are to do this. Ask managers what they do and most will say that they organise and plan. Observe what managers actually do and you may see that they dash from one task to another in a manner that is not very organised or planned.

When it is recognised that there are frequent differences between what expert managers say they are doing and what they are actually doing – differences of which they themselves are not usually aware – it can be seen how easy it is for managers to play games and build organisational defences against facing up to what is really happening (Argyris, 1990). For example, most managers espouse a rational model of action and believe that they should uncover the facts and consider a sensible range of options before they take action. Most espouse free and open discussions because that is a rational position to take. At the same time, however, there is a widespread norm in organisations requiring subordinates to withhold the truth from their superiors, especially if they believe that the superior will find the truth unwelcome and accuse them of being negative. Games of deception and cover-up are therefore played. Everyone knows they are being played but no one openly discusses what is happening, despite espousal of rational behaviour. Managers sometimes say one thing, but do the direct opposite, and rarely find this strange. Add to this the existence of skilled incompetence, and you can see how very difficult it will be to change these games and break down these defences. Attempts to explain how strategic management is actually carried out and to prescribe how to do it better will be misleading and perhaps dangerous unless they explicitly recognise the existence of skilled incompetence, the difference between espoused models and models in use, and the behavioural dynamics these lead to.

Double-loop learning begins when people question their own unique mental models and when together they start questioning the mental models they share with each other. As soon as they do this they arouse fears to do with failing to produce anything that functions in place of what they are destroying, as well as the fear of embarrassing themselves and others with questioning and discussion that may appear incompetent, or threatening or even crazy. As soon as such fears are aroused, people automatically defend themselves by activating defence routines of one kind or another. The raising of such defensive routines in an organisational setting is what is meant by 'covert politics'. It is a form of game playing that all are aware is going on but which all agree, tacitly, not to discuss (Argyris, 1990).

Defence routines become so entrenched in organisations that they come to be viewed as inevitable parts of human nature. Managers make self-fulfilling prophecies about what will happen at meetings, because they claim it is human nature; they indulge in the game playing, so confirming their belief in human nature. The defence routines, game playing and cover-ups can become so disruptive that managers actually avoid discussing contentious issues altogether. Even if this extreme is not reached, the dysfunctional learning behaviour blocks the detection of gradually accumulating small changes, the surfacing of different perspectives, the thorough testing of proposals through dialogue. When they use the control management model with the organisational defence routines it provokes, managers struggle to deal with strategic issues. They end up preparing long lists of strengths and weaknesses, opportunities and threats that simply get them nowhere. They produce mission statements that are so bland as to be meaningless, visions not connected to reality, and long-term plans that are simply filed. Or they may decide on an action and then not implement it.

Managers collude in this behaviour and refrain from discussing it. They then distance themselves from what is going on and blame others, the chief executive or the organisational structure when things go wrong. They look for solutions in general models, techniques, visions and plans. All the while the real causes of poor strategic management – the learning process itself, the political interaction and the group dynamic – remain stubbornly undiscussable.

People within an organisation collude in keeping matters undiscussable because they fear the consequences if they do not. Consultants too find themselves sucked into defence routines because they are nervous of the consequences of exposing them – they may be fired. The result of the defence routines is passive employees and managers, highly dependent upon authority, who are not well equipped to handle rapid change. In these conditions, managers produce vague, impractical prescriptions as a defence against having to do anything in difficult situations, such as 'we need more training' or 'we need a vision'. The organisation loses out on the creativity of people because of the management model it uses.

The way out of this impasse, proposed by Argyris, is for managers and managed to reflect jointly, as a group, on the processes they are engaged in. If this can be perceived as a challenge rather than a potential source of embarrassment and fear, then managers will be able to engage in double-loop learning.

Double-loop learning, then, involves changing a mental model, a recipe, a mindset, a frame of reference or a paradigm. It is a very difficult process to perform simply because one is trying to examine assumptions one is not normally even aware one is making. People will therefore keep slipping into single-loop learning because that is easier. But it is important to encourage double-loop learning since it is this that produces innovation. Managers who would innovate need constantly to be shifting, breaking and creating paradigms – they must engage in double-loop learning.

5.4 Building a shared vision and team learning: humanistic psychology

The fourth discipline of the learning organisation is that of building a shared vision. A shared vision inspires people to learn. It is a lofty goal and requires the skill of identifying inspiring pictures of the future. It is important that this vision should not be dictated but developed by people working together. The humanistic foundations of this idea are evident.

The final discipline of the learning organisation is that of team learning. Senge maintains that teams can learn, and when they do the intelligence of the team exceeds that of the individual members and produces extraordinary results. When this happens the individuals learn more rapidly too.

Teams and shared models

Managers do not act as isolated individuals but interact with each other in teams or groups. According to organisational learning theory, individuals learn to share the mental models they use simply by being part of a group. In this way they cut down on the communication and information flows that are required before they can act together. In particular, the more they share those implicit, expert models that have been rendered unconscious, the less they need to communicate in order to secure cohesive action. This sharing of implicit models is what is meant by the culture of the group or the organisation in learning organisation theory. Groups and organisations develop cultures, company and industry recipes or retained memories, as they perform together, in order to speed up their actions.

Individuals who are part of any group are put under strong pressure by group processes to conform, that is, to share the mental models of the other members. While this may have great benefits in terms of efficient action in stable conditions, it becomes a serious liability when conditions are changing rapidly. It then becomes necessary to question the implicit, unconscious group models that are being used to design actions. As conditions change, the unquestioned models may well become inappropriate. The powerful pressures that grow up within groups of experts to accept rather than question very fundamental values open up the strong possibility of skilled incompetence in group behaviour: of groupthink.

The kind of group that learning organisation theory focuses on is the team, and the key question is what kind of team performs double-loop learning effectively. The basic premise is that this will happen when people can engage in true dialogue rather than in the kind of defensive conversational cover-ups discussed in the previous section. This requires that members of a group trust each other enough to expose their shared assumptions to public scrutiny. It is held that this is possible only when the team is cohesive: that is, when there is good team spirit. Today, organisations spend considerable sums of money to provide social and training events where teams can be together in the belief that this fosters the required team spirit. In addition, attention is paid to the composition of the team in terms of different personality types. It is believed that a balance of different personality types will enable a team to function and learn effectively.

The basis of team learning is said to be dialogue and Senge's discussion of dialogue is based on the views of Bohm (1965, 1983; Bohm and Peat, 1989). According to Bohm, dialogue means the free flow of meaning through a group of people, allowing them to discover insights not attainable individually. This is a collective phenomenon that occurs when a group of people becomes open to the flow of a larger intelligence. Bohm talks about a new kind of mind that comes into existence. People are said to participate in this pool of common meaning, which is not accessible individually. He talks about the whole organising the parts. The whole here is this common pool of meaning, a kind of transcendent mind analogous to the idea in quantum physics that the universe is an indistinguishable whole. This is Bohm's idea of an implicate order that is unfolded by experience. The parts in this way of thinking are individual mental maps that guide and shape individual perceptions. Here, Bohm is clearly thinking in terms of formative causality, in which the future is the unfolding of what is already enfolded as implicate order, rendering any true novelty impossible. This idea of an already enfolded implicate order is expressed in the notion of a common pool of meaning, a kind of transcendent whole or group mind that people access when they interact with each other in dialogue. Bohm takes a perspective in which there is *both* a collective pool of meaning *and* an individual mind that is shaped by the common pool, quite outside individuals, in dialogue.

For Bohm and Senge, then, dialogue is a special kind of collaborative conversation, quite distinct from discussion, which is primarily competitive. Dialogue, as special conversation with a life of its own, is said to be rare nowadays and the call is for a return to ancient wisdom, to ways characteristic of so-called 'more primitive' people who used to practise it. North American Indians are often given as an example of the few people who still practise it today. Senge says that when we do (rarely) experience dialogue nowadays, it is a chance product of circumstance. So he calls for systematic effort and disciplined practice of the art of dialogue, which we need to rediscover to satisfy a deep longing. If we do it right we will all win. In order to do it right, people have to participate in a particular way: they must suspend, that is, be aware of, their assumptions; they must regard each other as colleagues and friends; and there should be a facilitator present who holds the context. Resistance and defensive routines are then diminished and dialogue can take place. Bohm claims that in these circumstances people can become observers of their own thinking and that, once they see the participative nature of their thought, they separate themselves from it. Conflict then becomes conflict between thoughts and not conflict between people. Dialogue, therefore, offers a safe environment in which it can be balanced with discussion. Dialogue becomes a new tool and a prescription for management behaviour (Isaacs, 1999), although Bohm himself thought dialogue was virtually impossible in hierarchical organisations.

Team learning also requires skill in identifying factors that block true dialogue. These blockages must be recognised and surfaced. Senge claims that it is teams rather than individuals that learn. It is important to notice how Senge handles this question of the individual and the team. It sounds as though he is making the group primary to the individual. However, this is not so. Although he says that it is the team that learns, when he develops what he means by team learning it is clear that he is saying that an effective team provides the context within which a number of individuals together learn more than they could on their own. It is still the individuals who learn. They arrive to form a team and the atmosphere of that team then affects their capacity for learning together. Part 3 will take a very different view of the relationship between the individual and the group, arguing that individual minds are formed by the group while they form it at the same time. This perspective also takes a very different view of the nature of conversation, avoiding the positing of a special form called 'dialogue' in the way that Bohm and Senge do.

The move to the mystical

For Senge, then, the notion of dialogue is an essential aspect of the learning organisation and it is understood as an activity enabling people to come into contact with a rather mysterious pool of 'common meaning'. This notion is greatly elaborated by one of Senge's collaborators, Scharmer, who outlines a theory of learning as the sensing and enacting of emerging futures (Senge *et al.*, 2005). Scharmer distinguishes between two different sources of learning and argues that both are required for organisations to succeed. He calls the first 'reflecting on the experiences of the past' and the second 'sensing and embodying emergent futures' *rather than* re-enacting the patterns of the past. One kind of learning is, therefore, relevant to the past and the other to the future.

The first kind of learning involves uncovering the past and bringing it into awareness as a process of 'presencing'. This occurs at the surface level of concrete experience. It is the cognitive process of downloading mental models and simply re-enacting old habits of thought. It also occurs below the surface level of action, involving the uncovering of common will and the changing of consciousness and then embodying the changes in the form of behavioural routines and procedures. In other words, this is close to single-loop learning. The second kind of learning, to do with the future, is called 'generative' learning, which is understood as cognitive processes involving the reframing of mental models: that is, double-loop learning. This requires the special conversational process called *dialogue*. It also requires imagination, which is described as becoming aware through the redirection of attention from an object to its source. Scharmer talks about generative learning as the deepest level and presents it as an essentially mystical experience, the manifestation, or coming into awareness, of a deeper, hidden reality. Here, individual intention is at one with the intention of the emerging whole. It is a process of bringing the emerging whole into reality 'as *it* desires', rather than as the ego desires, and this is what he means by the coming into presence of the emerging future.

Presencing is a process of becoming aware that involves taking off one's self-created cognitive filters, turning inward to the source of oneself, redirecting attention from current reality to an emergent reality, and letting go – that is, emptying or surrendering to a deeper, higher will. Scharmer then adds another stage, which he calls 'letting come'. For him surrender means switching from 'looking for' to 'letting come', a phase of quickening or crystallisation in which one allows the arrival of the highest possible future, the highest presence, the highest Self. What is received is an emerging heightened quality of will and a more tangible vision of what the individual and the group want to create. The language is strikingly mystical.

The key question for generative learning is how to access this level, for it is here that transformation occurs, where transformation is understood as the coming into presence of emerging futures. Scharmer emphasises that presencing is as much a collective phenomenon as it is an individual one, and by this he seems to mean that individuals fuse together into the collective when they reach this stage. Scharmer describes presencing as a mystery and says that it is a mode of relating in which the individual relates to the collective whole of the community, team and organisation. In this state people become more 'selfless' and become aligned with their true selves and with the intention of the emerging whole. Scharmer's understanding of generative learning, therefore, is one of accessing, even immersing in, a transcendent whole. It is essentially a mystical process in which there is participation in a mystical whole. This amounts to postulating a transcendent system and ascribing to it an actual intention rather than the 'as if' intention to be found in Kantian thinking. Emergence means bringing into being what this transcendent system desires.

For Scharmer, transformation is the enactment of a deep spiritual process in which individuals fuse into a common will. The origin of transformation, and thus novelty, lies in a transcendent whole that is brought into being, is presenced, by the basically meditative practices of a group of people. Individuals and groups are simultaneously transformed, but this is in no way paradoxical because the individuals and the group are fused. The process is the same and there is nothing contradictory in terms of individual and group. There is no mention of difference, conflict or power, which implicitly play no part whatsoever in the transformative process. The social is not thought of as a responsive relating of a co-operative/ competitive nature but as fusion in a transcendent whole. Participation means individuals participating in a transcendent whole.

The theory of causality is clear. Individuals fuse together and submerge in the 'whole', the transcendent system. This system is the formative cause of action in that action is clearly understood as unfolding the enfolded will of the whole. Scharmer suggests that this is transformative causality, but if it is then it is of a mystical kind.

Scharmer says that it is the role of leaders to choose the learning level at which to operate. The key challenge for leaders is how to enable teams to uncover layers of reality that will move them from one level of learning to another. Scharmer defines leadership as the activity of shifting the place from which a system operates and he defines this as shifting the conversation from talking 'nice' and talking 'tough' to reflective and generative dialogues. Generative dialogues lead to an intentional quietness or sacred silence. The only sustainable tool for leading change is the leader's self as the capacity of the 'I' to transcend the boundaries of its current organisation and operate from the emerging, larger whole, both individually and collectively. The leader's role is to create the conditions that allow others to shift the place from which their system operates. The leader, then, is understood as an autonomous individual standing outside the system and choosing the level at which to operate. Causality here is of the rationalist kind.

This immediately exposes the dual causality typical of systems thinking. There is a transcendent system of which individuals become a part in order to transform and there is an autonomous leader standing outside this and deciding whether to operate at that level. This is clearly 'both . . . and' thinking that eliminates paradox. The 'both . . . and' nature of the thinking is evident in the postulation of *both* a system with an actual intention/desire *and* autonomous individuals who create conditions for shifting the system.

So far, this chapter has been describing the key features and assumptions of organisational learning theories, focusing in particular on what has been the most influential variant of these theories, at least in terms of the impact on organisational practitioners. It started by identifying the theory of human interaction on which organisational learning perspectives are built. This is a view in which an organisation is understood as a system interacting with other systems in a supra-system, all understood in terms of systems dynamics. The chapter then identified the cognitivist and constructivist theories of individual psychology as the basis for understanding how individuals, as aspects of the system, learn. The important concept here is that of mental models and how learning takes the form of either single-loop learning where mental models remain the same or double-loop learning where individuals consciously engineer changes in their own mental models. Organisational learning theories identify what the obstacles to such double-loop learning are and present prescriptions for overcoming them. In essence, the prescription is to work in cohesive teams in a harmonious way using a special conversational form called *dialogue*. The chapter then went on to describe how easily this line of thought slips into mysticism, taking us back to what we started with, namely, the system, now understood as a mystical, transcendent whole into which 'good', selfless people submerge themselves. The reflection of humanistic psychology is clear.

Of course, not all organisational learning theorists make this move to the mystical. Others point to the importance of power, politics and vested interests in organisational learning. The next section looks at these perspectives.

5.5 The impact of vested interests on organisational learning

A previous section looked at how attempts to learn in a double-loop way can give rise to a number of fears, such as the fear of failing, of being embarrassed and of embarrassing others. These fears tend to trigger defensive routines, game playing and covert politics that block the learning. The whole point of double-loop learning is to bring about organisational change, and it is highly likely that change of an important kind will alter power relations between people. Change threatens vested interests and the prospect of losing power is likely to trigger action to prevent this from happening. That action is also likely to block the process of double-loop learning. In other words, the nature of an organisation's political system, the way in which power is used, is likely to have an important impact on its capacity to learn.

Authoritarian use of power

The authoritarian use of power may be relatively benign when it is based on legitimate positions in the hierarchy and exercised according to the accepted procedures of the organisation. This is likely to be accompanied by a group dynamic of compliance, especially when followers strongly share the same ideology. Compliance amounts to the suspension of intellectual and moral judgement about the appropriateness of superiors' choices and actions. People then willingly do what the powerful want (Bacharach and Lawler, 1980). Clearly this is incompatible with double-loop learning. Where power is exercised as force over unwilling followers the dynamic tends to be much more volatile. It is characterised by sullen acceptance, covert resistance and at times outright rebellion. Again, this is inimical to double-loop learning.

Collegial use of power

Highly authoritarian political systems based on mechanistic rules are, however, rather rare in practice. There is far more likely to be a complex, pluralistic, political system in which power is already spread around an organisation in groups with vested interests (Greiner and Schein, 1988). Thus, the typical modern corporation does not have a political system in which one or two powerful executives at the top control what goes on throughout the company. Instead, there are powerful subsidiary companies and powerful departments in many different parts of the organisation and those at the top have to sustain enough support to govern. Any change of notable significance is going to affect the balance of power, making one department, subsidiary company or management grouping weaker or stronger than it was before. Any sign of change will touch off fears that such power shifts might occur even before it is clear what they might be. People and groups will therefore start taking protective action as soon as they get wind of any possible change.

Any attempt to engage in double-loop learning, to change mental models, is likely to be just such a change, one that is directly concerned with changing power positions. It is therefore highly likely to touch off political activities that undermine and perhaps eventually destroy learning. The more people are persuaded to move to a consensus collegiate way of making choices, the more powerful groups with vested interests are threatened and the more likely they are to put a stop to the programme. The more managers try to head off this threat, the more they have to play by the rules of the political system they are trying to replace. If they do this they simply reinforce what they are trying to remove.

Power vacuums and organised anarchies

If managers do succeed in installing a collegial political system and the commitment management model, other behaviours may be activated by the shift in the distribution of power.

As authority and other forms of power are dispersed, as organisational structures are flattened, as job descriptions become looser and as the establishment of widespread consensus comes to be required before decisions are possible, so the likelihood of a power vacuum at the centre increases. It becomes more and more difficult for anyone to exercise much authority; more and more people have to be able to handle their own independence. In situations in which most people seek the comfort of dependence this could create serious difficulties. One way of understanding the consequences of changes in power distribution is provided by Greiner and Schein (1988).

Greiner and Schein relate changes in willingness to assert and to accept power to the consequent group dynamic. When both leaders and followers consent freely to the exercise of power, there is a high probability of active consensus. When the leader exerts power but the followers do not consent, then we get the behaviour of covert resistance. As the leader becomes less able or willing to exert power, while followers still look for a lead, then the behaviour is that of passive loyalty. If, in the same circumstances, the followers too become less willing to accept the exercise of power, the group's behaviour is characterised by peer rivalry. So the dispersal of power and the spread of participation could set off feedback loops in which declining central power leads to greater rivalry throughout the organisation, or to passive loyalty, both of which will block double-loop learning.

5.6 Knowledge management: cognitivist and constructivist psychology

The theory of the learning organisation discussed in previous sections is reflected in the more recent interest in knowledge management. Many argue that the global change towards the knowledge economy has major implications for the strategic management of organisations. First, professional knowledge workers need to be managed in different ways from manual workers in the industrial age. The argument is that to unleash the creativity of knowledge workers they must be empowered so that they can participate more fully in the development of the organisation and special measures need to be taken to ensure that individual knowledge becomes organisational knowledge. Many argue that this is to be done by codifying the knowledge held by key knowledge workers and by taking steps to retain their services. The new knowledge economy also has major implications for the nature of an organisation's assets. In the industrial age, accounting measures of asset values were close to the capital market valuation of the organisation because market pricing of the main assets, namely physical resources such as plant and equipment, enabled them to be measured. Managing the value of a corporation meant managing measurable physical assets and the 'human resources' who used them. In the new knowledge economy, however, knowledge is said to be the major asset and, since it is not directly traded in markets, it is not measured and recorded in corporate balance sheets. As a result, enormous gaps have opened up between the asset values recorded by a corporation and the value that capital markets place on the corporation itself. This creates problems for managing assets to produce shareholder value. The response to this has been a call to measure the intellectual capital of a corporation and manage its knowledge assets.

Nonaka's writings (Nonaka, 1991; Nonaka and Takeuchi, 1995) have exerted a major impact on the development of theories of knowledge creation in organisations (for example, Brown, 1991; Burton-Jones, 1999; Davenport and Prusak, 1998; Garven, 1993; Kleiner and Roth, 1997; Leonard and Strauss, 1997; Quinn *et al.*, 1996; Sveiby, 1997). Like Senge, Nonaka draws on the systems dynamics strand of systems thinking, including some concepts from chaos and complexity theories, which he treats as extensions of that thinking (*see* Chapter 10), and Argyris and Schön whose learning theories he traces back to Bateson (1972). In addition, he relies heavily on Polanyi's (1958, 1960) distinction between tacit and explicit knowledge.

Creating new knowledge

According to Nonaka (1991), new knowledge is created when tacit knowledge is made explicit and crystallised into an innovation, that is, a re-creation of some aspect of the world according to some new insight or ideal. New knowledge, according to Nonaka, comes from tapping the tacit, subjective insights, intuitions and hunches of individuals and making them available for testing and use by the organisation as a whole. For him, tacit knowledge is personal and hard to formalise. It is rooted in action and shows itself as skill, or know-how. In addition to being in technical skills, tacit knowledge lies in the mental models, beliefs and perspectives ingrained in the way people understand their world and act in it. Tacit knowledge is below the level of awareness and is therefore very difficult to communicate. The nature of explicit knowledge, however, is easy to understand: it is the formal and systematic knowledge that is easily communicated, for example in the form of product specifications or computer programs.

Nonaka gives an example of how tacit knowledge is to be tapped. In 1985 product developers at Matsushita could not perfect the kneading action of the home bread-baking machine they were developing. After much unhelpful analysis, including comparisons of X-rays of dough kneaded by the machine and dough kneaded by professionals, one member of the team proposed a creative approach. She proposed using a top professional baker as a model, so she trained with a top baker to acquire his kneading technique, and after a year of trial and error she was able to help her colleagues reproduce a mechanical kneading action that mimicked that of the professional. This example describes a movement between different kinds of knowledge, the tacit and the explicit:

- tacit to tacit as the product developer acquires the skill of the professional baker through mimicry;
- tacit to explicit as the product developer articulates the foundations of her newly acquired tacit knowledge to her colleagues;
- explicit to tacit as the colleagues internalise the knowledge and use it to alter their own tacit knowledge;
- explicit to explicit as the newly formulated product specifications are communicated to the production department and embodied in working models and final production processes.

Innovation then flows from a form of learning: that is, new knowledge creation, that in turn flows from moving knowledge between one type and another.

New knowledge starts with an individual, according to Nonaka. Tacit knowledge has to travel from one person to another, in a way that cannot be centrally intended because no one knows what is to travel, or to whom, until it has travelled. New knowledge can therefore be created only when individuals operate in empowered teams.

A key difficulty in the creation of new knowledge is that of bringing tacit knowledge to the surface of individual awareness, conveying tacit knowledge from one person to another, and finally making it explicit. This is so difficult because it requires expressing the inexpressible and this needs figurative rather than literal language. As new knowledge is dispersed through a group and an organisation, it must be tested, which means that there must be discussion, dialogue and disagreement.

The distinction Nonaka makes between tacit and explicit knowledge is derived from Polanyi (Polanyi and Prosch, 1975). Nonaka and Takeuchi maintain that 'knowledge is created and expanded through social interaction between tacit and explicit knowledge' (1995, p. 61) in the four modes of knowledge conversion described above. However, as Tsoukas points out, Polanyi was actually arguing that tacit and explicit knowledge are not two separate forms of knowledge, but rather that 'tacit knowledge is the necessary component of all knowledge' (Tsoukas, 1997, p. 10).

Another point to note is how Nonaka and Takeuchi (1995) talk about knowledge as embodied, rooted in experience and arising in interaction between individuals. They emphasise the importance of dialogue and discussion in this conversion process (p. 13), pointing to the importance of intuition, hunches, metaphors and symbols (p. 12). They see knowledge as essentially related to action and arising from a process in which interacting individuals are committed to justifying their beliefs. They talk about knowledge as justified belief closely related to people's values. They talk about the context of ambiguity and redundancy in which knowledge is created (p. 12). However, they then take their argument in a direction that leaves the importance of relationships and the social undeveloped and unexplored. Having emphasised the social, they locate the initiation of new knowledge in the individual when they argue that 'knowledge is created only by individuals' (p. 59).

In this way of seeing things, tacit knowledge is possessed by individuals and the knowledge creation at an organisational level is the extraction of this already existing tacit knowledge from individuals and its spread across the organisation by socialising processes. This leads to a rather linear sequential view of individuals passing tacit knowledge to others, primarily through imitation, then formalising and codifying it so that it can be used. The emphasis of Nonaka and Takeuchi on the individual as the origin of knowledge leads them to emphasise the organisation-wide intentional character of knowledge creation. Having emphasised the ambiguity of the situation in which knowledge arises, Nonaka and Takeuchi leave this behind and move to the strategic choice view of knowledge creation. Nonaka and Takeuchi do not pay much attention to the ever-present possibility of groups of people becoming stuck in some stable dynamic, or some fragmenting one that kills off the knowledge-creating process. What Nonaka and Takeuchi end up with, then, is a process for knowledge creation that can be managed and controlled.

Knowledge management writers focus attention on this process of translation but do not explain how completely new tacit knowledge comes to arise in individual heads.

5.7 Key debates

As with strategic choice theory, the notion of organisational learning has generated much debate. Two key debates are briefly reviewed in this section: representation versus enactment; and the learning organisation versus organisational learning.

Representation versus enactment

This is the debate between cognitivist and constructivist psychology, which has been mentioned above. Cognitivism takes the representational perspective in holding that the human mind constructs accurate representations of an already given reality. These representations are then built into mental models that form the basis upon which people act into the real world. Cognitivists accept that mental models can become inappropriate in a changing world and therefore become inappropriate for action requiring the double-loop process of learning in which mental models are changed. They accept that people are interpreting their world and in a sense constructing it through their interpretation. What they are constructing, their interpretation, can be appropriate in that it is an accurate interpretation of the real world or it may be inappropriate in the sense of an inaccurate representation. This is a view in which thought comes before action. Constructivism goes further than this and takes an enactment perspective in arguing that the human body actively selects what it is able to pay attention to and so constructs the reality into which it acts. This is a view in which thought comes after action in that the world is first constructed in action and then understood. These differences will be returned to in Chapter 9.

Learning organisation or organisational learning: the individual versus the group

Do organisations learn or is it individuals and groups in organisations who learn? If one thinks that it is individuals and groups *inside* an organisation that learn, then one focuses attention on individual and collective learning processes. If it is thought that it is organisations that learn, then attention is focused on what it is about an organisation that makes learning possible. A distinction along these lines is used by Easterby-Smith and Araujo (1999) to identify two strands in the literature to do with organisations and learning. They distinguish between the literature on *organisational learning* and that on the *learning organisation*. They say that the former 'has concentrated on the detached observation and analysis of the processes involved in individual and collective learning inside organizations' (p. 2). The literature on the learning organisation, on the other hand, is concerned with 'methodological tools which can help to identify, promote and evaluate the quality of learning processes inside organizations' (p. 2) and in so doing this literature identifies 'templates, or ideal forms, which real organizations could attempt to emulate' (p. 2). Easterby-Smith and Araujo argue that there is a growing divide between the two strands. Those writing in the organisational learning tradition are interested in 'understanding the nature and processes of learning' (p. 8). Those writing in the tradition of the learning organisation are more interested in 'the development of normative models and methodologies for creating change in the direction of improved learning processes' (p. 8).

Easterby-Smith and Araujo distinguish between a technical and a social strand in the organisational learning literature. The technical strand takes the view that organisational learning is a matter of processing, interpreting and responding to quantitative and qualitative information, which is generally explicit and in the public domain. Key writers in this tradition are Argyris and Schön (1978) with their notions of single- and double-loop learning. The social strand focuses attention on how people make sense of their work practices (Weick, 1995). This strand utilises Polanyi's distinction between tacit and explicit knowledge (Polanyi and Prosch, 1975). It focuses attention on the socially constructed nature of knowledge (Brown and Duguid, 1991), the political processes involved (Coopey, 1995) and the importance of cultural and socialisation processes (Lave and Wenger, 1991). The literature on the learning organisation also displays technical and social interests. The former tends to focus on interventions based on measurement and information systems, while the latter focuses on individual and group learning processes in a normative manner (Isaacs, 1999; Nonaka and Takeuchi, 1995; Senge, 1990).

However, the claim that *organisations* learn amounts to both reification and anthropomorphism. We slip into thinking that an organisation is a thing, even an organism or living thing, that can learn. To sustain the claim that an organisation is in any sense a living organism, we would need to point to where this living *body* is. Since an organisation is neither inanimate thing nor living body, in anything other than metaphorical terms, it follows that an organisation can neither think nor learn. But the alternative is not all that satisfactory either. To claim that it is only *individuals* who learn is to continue with the major Western preoccupation with the autonomous individual and to ignore the importance of social processes. One might try to deal with this objection by saying that it is *both individuals and groups* who learn. But that runs into the same objection as saying that organisations learn. The claim that *groups* learn is also both reification and anthropomorphism. Furthermore, to talk about individuals who learn *in* organisations or *in* groups is also problematic because, once again, this implies that the group and the organisation exist somewhere as a different 'place' or 'level' from people. If this were not so, how could people be *in* a group or organisation? Part 3 will suggest an alternative to thinking in these ways: namely, that learning is an activity of interdependent people, exploring in a different way the emphasis that writers such as Wenger place on the socially constructed nature of knowledge.

5.8 How learning organisation theory deals with the four key questions

At the end of Chapter 2, I posed four questions that I would ask of each of the theories of organisational change that this book is concerned with. They were:

1. How does the theory view the nature of interaction?
2. What view does it take of human nature?
3. What methodology does it employ?
4. How does it deal with paradox?

Then in Chapter 4, I examined the answers to these questions suggested by strategic choice theory. Consider now how they are answered from the organisational learning perspective.

The nature of interaction

Learning organisation theories see interaction in systemic terms just as cybernetics does. They are concerned with how components, entities or individuals interact to produce a system. They understand the system in the terms of systems dynamics, and this, like cybernetics, is a theory that focuses on the macro level. They identify the feedback structure of the system. It does not attempt to model the micro detail of the entities constituting a dynamic system. Two assumptions are implicitly made about these entities, events or individuals in systems dynamics (Allen, 1998a):

• First, it is assumed that micro events occur at their average rate and that it is sufficient to take account of averages only. Interactions between entities are then homogeneous.

• Second, it is implicitly assumed that individual entities of a given type are identical, or, at least, that they have a normal distribution around the average type. The entities, or events, are thus implicitly assumed to be homogeneous. Within a category, distinctive identities and differences are not taken into account.

These assumptions make it possible to ignore the dynamics governing the micro entities, events or individuals and model the system at the macro level. This is done by specifying the structure of negative and positive feedback loops that drive the system. For example, the beer distribution system, described earlier in this chapter, is specified in terms of damping and amplifying loops between orders, inventories and shipments between the different components of the system, namely customers, retailers, wholesalers and producers. Nothing is said about how customers, retailers, wholesalers and producers are organised or how they make decisions. This kind of model yields insight into the dynamics of the system as a whole and the possibility of unexpected outcomes. The way systems dynamics is used in learning organisation theory amounts to adding positive feedback loops to a cybernetic system.

However, there are also major differences compared with cybernetics. Because of the presence of positive feedback loops, the dynamic is no longer an automatic movement towards an equilibrium state. Instead, the system is a non-equilibrium one with the dynamics of fluctuating patterns that create considerable difficulties for prediction over longer time periods. However, it is claimed that, if the feedback structure of the system is understood, then leverage points can be located. Action at these leverage points makes it possible to control the system. In the end, however, the theory of causality underlying systems dynamics is formative cause just as it is with cybernetics. In systems dynamics the system unfolds archetypes already enfolded in it. People are still thought to be parts of a system and so not free. Because of its theory of causality, systems dynamics cannot explain novelty or creativity.

The nature of human beings

Learning organisation theory draws on cognitivist, constructivist and humanistic psychology to understand the nature of human beings. The cognitivist assumptions are particularly clear in that individuals are understood to act upon the basis of mental models built from previous experience and stored in the individual mind. They are representations of the individual's world. Part of each individual's model is shared with others and this forms the basis of their joint action together. The focus on the individual nature of these models, their representation function, the claim that they are stored and shared, the belief that they can be surfaced and subjected to rational scrutiny, are all hallmarks of a cognitivist psychology. However, the way in which mental models select some aspects of reality for attention and exclude others is a feature of a constructivist approach to psychology. The emphasis placed on individual vision and fulfilment, as part of the learning process, is evidence of the humanistic leaning in the theory of the learning organisation.

In all of these psychological theories the individual is held to be prior and primary to the group. Mental models are individual constructs that are shared with others. Effective teams are composed of a balance of different types of individual. Note, however, how differences between individuals do not feature in a fundamental way in the learning organisation theory. A small number of different categories may be identified but the difference is located between categories, while within those categories everyone is implicitly assumed to be the same. This is consistent with a systems dynamics approach in which micro entities are all assumed to be average and their interactions are assumed to be homogeneous. What I am trying to emphasise is this: cohesion and sharing are seen as the foundations of effective learning. There is no notion that deviant and eccentric behaviour might be essential to any creative and innovative thinking and behaving. In Part 3, I will be arguing that organisations change in novel ways through deviant behaviour.

The group is treated in a particular way. It consists of individuals and develops in phases, only some of which are conducive to members learning together as individuals.

So, learning organisation theory uses the same psychological theories as strategic choice theory but it does place more emphasis on emotion and relationships between people. It also identifies more clearly what may block people from changing and learning. Perhaps the importance of power receives more attention but power is still located in the individual. However, there is no fundamental change in the view of human action as one moves from the one theory to the other.

Methodology and organisational learning

The methodological stance in learning organisation theory is similar to that in strategic choice theory in some respects. A realist position is sometimes implied in which managers are assumed to be able to stand outside the system of which they are a part and think systemically about it. They are also supposed to be able to stand outside their own mental models, rigorously scrutinise them and then rationally change them. However, at other times an idealist position is suggested in that managers are assumed to respond not to the real world but to their idea of the real world as represented in their mental models.

Dealing with paradox

The notion of paradox does not play a fundamental part in learning organisation theory. Tensions, contradictions and dilemmas are certainly recognised but they are thought to be obstacles to learning and hopefully in the end resolvable. As with strategic choice theory, learning organisation theory takes a position at one of the poles of what seem to me to be fundamental paradoxes of organisational life. This is very clear in the case of the individual and the group. I argue above that this is not seen as a paradox at all. The individual is given primacy and understood to be in fundamental conflict with the group. This conflict must be resolved through building relationships of trust in teams if learning is to take place. Sameness and difference are not held in mind at the same time. For example, individuals within a personality category are treated as if they were all the same and all different from individuals in another category. Although unpredictability is pointed to, it is predictability and the possibility of control that are emphasised. As with strategic choice theory, order, stability, consistency and harmony are all seen as prerequisites for success and the role that the opposites of these might play in creativity is largely ignored.

Making sense of experience

The focus on learning, and what blocks it, provides a rich addition to strategic choice theory when it comes to making sense of my experience. I certainly recognise my own involvement in defence routines and political struggles. I also recognise the difficulty of learning in a fundamental way. However, I think the theory holds out a rather idealised picture of what it is possible for people in an organisation to do.

For example, Argyris (1990) reports that he has worked with large numbers of managers in many countries, coaching them to engage in double-loop learning. He reports that they find it difficult and rarely engage in it when they return to their workplace. Instead, they carry on with their win/lose dynamics and their defence routines. I think this immediately raises a question mark over his theory of learning as a change in mental models. Many organisations clearly do change, often in quite creative ways. How does this happen if double-loop learning is such a rarity? Furthermore, I wonder whether it really is possible for people to surface their mental models and change them. Where are they located? It is far from clear that brains store anything that could be correlated with a map or a model. If it is possible for people to identify assumptions of which they are unaware and change them, then why is mental illness so prevalent and difficult to deal with? I greatly doubt my own ability to identify whatever it is that makes me think the way I do, and then simply change it.

In the hurly-burly of organisational life, with its political intrigues and the possibility of losing one's job, is it at all wise to expose the defence routines that one is taking part in? If it is so important to do so, why is it so rare to find people doing it?

When I ask myself questions such as these, I have serious doubts about the practicality of the prescriptions this theory presents for successful organisational learning. For example, the kind of conversation that the theory of organisational learning presents is a special kind called *dialogue* which has the rather mystical tones of people participating in a common pool of meaning as if it were an already existing whole outside their experience. There seems to be no constructive place here for ordinary conversation. Also, participation has a special meaning – participation in some whole system outside our direct experience of interacting with each other (Griffin, 2002).

5.9 Summary

This chapter introduced systems dynamics theory and clarified how it differs from cybernetics. The most significant difference relates to the introduction of nonlinearity and positive feedback. The way in which positive feedback processes have been used to understand life in organisations was reviewed. From this it can be seen that a systems dynamics perspective presents a richer, more complex insight into the dynamics of life in organisations.

This chapter has also reviewed learning organisation theory. According to this theory, organisations are systems driven by both positive and negative feedback loops. The interactions between such loops tend to produce unexpected and often counterintuitive outcomes. Perfect control is not possible, but it is possible to identify leverage points where control may be exerted. Perhaps the most important loops relate to learning. Organisations learn when people in cohesive teams trust each other enough to expose the assumptions they are making to the scrutiny of others and then together change shared assumptions which block change. The theory identifies some important behaviours that block this learning process. Although learning organisation theory uses a different systems theory from strategic choice theory, its conceptualisation of that systems theory in terms of feedback loops keeps it close to cybernetics. Learning organisation theory is built on the same psychological theories as strategic choice theory. Control and the primacy of the individual are central to both.

Further reading

Richardson (1991) provides an account of the use of feedback thinking in human systems and Senge's (1990) book gives a summary of systems thinking. Rush *et al.* (1989) explain how personality types affect decision making, as do Belbin (1981) and Kiersey and Bates (1978). Argyris (1990) is important reading. Critiques of learning organisation theory from a system perspective are to be found in Flood (1999) and from a process perspective in Griffin (2002). Wenger's (1998) book on communities of practice is an important source for understanding the notion of communities of practice.

Questions to aid further reflection

1. What theory of causality is reflected in systems dynamics?
2. How is the conceptualisation of control different in systems dynamics from that in cybernetics?
3. What are the basic features of constructivist psychology?
4. What implications do theories of organisational learning and knowledge creation have for strategy?
5. Can organisations learn?
6. Do you think it is possible for people to change their mental models?
7. If double-loop learning is as difficult for people as some writers claim then how do organisations change?

Chapter 6

Thinking in terms of organisational psychodynamics

Open systems and psychoanalytic perspectives

This chapter invites you to draw on your own experience to reflect on and consider the implications of:

- The nature of unconscious group processes in organisational life and the part that they play in the activities of managing and strategising.

- How people in organisations deal with the experience of anxiety, particularly the social defences against anxiety that they employ and the effects these have on how an organisation evolves.

- The role of leaders and how this is co-created in groups, particularly in its neurotic form.

- The nature of groups and teams and the irrational processes that affect team formation and functioning.

This chapter is important because it draws attention to the unconscious, irrational and neurotic and the part that all of these play in the evolution of an organisation. It provides a fuller understanding of the leadership role and how it arises, particularly the negative aspects and the way leaders play a role in the fantasies of others, so providing a very different perspective from the charismatic hero view of leadership in learning organisation theory. This is a useful antidote to the generally idealistic view of teams taken in theories of the learning organisation.

6.1 Introduction

Chapter 4 explored the foundations upon which the theory of strategic choice rests: a theory of interaction to be found in cybernetic systems theory and a theory of human nature to be found primarily in cognitivism, but also in humanistic psychology. Then Chapter 5 examined the theoretical foundations of learning organisation and knowledge-creation theories. Here there is some shift from a theory of interaction based on cybernetics to one based on systems dynamics. However, the way systems theory is used retains a link with cybernetics through the conceptualisation of systems dynamics in feedback terms. There is much less of a shift in the basic theory of human nature. This remains heavily cognitivist, although with the addition of a constructivist slant by some writers in pointing to the way that mental models select features for attention, so constructing rather than purely representing experience. The reliance on humanistic psychology is even stronger than it is in strategic choice theory. Some writers also develop a link with Eastern spirituality so that participation comes to be understood as participation in a mystical whole that is greater than the individuals comprising it.

This chapter reviews a theory of organisational change that is built on both a different theory of interaction and a different theory of human nature. Interaction continues to be seen in systemic terms but this time from the perspective of general or open systems theory. The theory of human nature is provided by psychoanalytic perspectives. The chapter first reviews open systems theory and then turns to relevant psychoanalytic notions, before showing how they can be combined to shed light on life in organisations, primarily the obstacles to strategic choice and learning arising from unconscious group processes.

6.2 Open systems theory

Around the same time as the development of cybernetics and systems dynamics, there also appeared the closely related ideas of general systems theory. In a number of papers and books between 1945 and 1968, the German biologist von Bertalanffy put forward the idea that organisms, as well as human organisations and societies, are open systems. They are systems because they consist of a number of component subsystems that are interrelated and interdependent. They are open because they are connected to their environments, or supra-systems, of which they are a part.

Each subsystem within a system and each system within its environment has a boundary separating it from other subsystems and other systems. For example, the sales department in an organisation is a subsystem separated by a boundary from the production and accounting departments. One organisation such as IBM is a system separated by a boundary from the other organisations and individuals that form its environment. Within each system or subsystem, people occupy roles, they conduct sets of activities, and they engage in interrelationships with others. They do this both within their part of the system and in other parts or other systems. Each subsystem within a system and each system within an environment is open. It imports materials, labour, money, information and emotions from other subsystems or systems. It also exports outputs, money and information to other subsystems and systems.

Open systems explanations of managing and organising therefore focus attention on:

- organisations, industries and societies as systemic wholes;
- the behaviour of people within a subsystem or system;
- the nature of the boundary around a subsystem or system;
- the nature of the relationships across the boundaries between subsystems and systems;
- the requirements of managing the boundary.

The open systems concept provides a tool for understanding the relationship between:

- the technical and the social aspects of an organisation;
- the parts and the whole organisation (e.g. the individual and the group, the individual and the organisation);
- the whole organisation and the environment.

Negative feedback

Changing one component in an open system has knock-on effects in many other components because of the prevalence of interconnection. Changes in the environment have an impact on changes in the subsystems of an organisation. What happens in one system will affect what happens in another system and that in turn will affect the first.

One can see the importance of the insight provided by open systems theory if one considers how the technical subsystem of an organisation is interconnected with its social subsystem (Trist and Bamforth, 1951).

Scientific rational management tends to concentrate on the technical subsystem. This system consists of the techniques, technology and sets of tasks required to achieve the organisation's purpose. The prescription for success put forward by scientific management is to make the task subsystem as efficient as possible. So, if you introduce the latest technology for mining coal, for example, together with rules and regulations about quality and efficiency to govern the work of coal miners, then you should succeed according to scientific management. Success here depends primarily on the technical subsystem. The behavioural school of management, on the other hand, focuses primarily on the psychosocial subsystem. Its prescriptions for success stress the establishment of a social system in which people are motivated and participate in making decisions about the nature of the tasks and the technology. To succeed you must consult those who perform the organisation's primary tasks, involve them in decision-aking, and introduce reward structures that will motivate them to operate efficiently. Success here depends primarily on the social subsystem.

The insight that comes from open systems theory is that the technical and social systems are so interconnected that it makes no sense to regard one as dominant and the other as subordinate. Both subsystems have to be handled together in a manner that takes account of their interdependence. The importance of this interconnection was demonstrated many years ago in a study of the coal-mining industry in the UK by Trist and Bamforth (1951). In the late 1940s the British coal industry introduced the long-wall method of mining coal, which was more efficient than the previous method. The new technology, however, required changes in the set of tasks performed by coal miners. These changes broke up the cooperative teams in which miners were accustomed to working, teams that reflected their social arrangements in the coal-mining villages in which they lived. Because of the consequent resistance to working in the new way, the technology failed to yield its technical potential.

The message is that, if changes are to succeed, then they have to be based on a realistic understanding of the interconnection, or feedback, between the social and the technical subsystems. And that interconnection is not taken account of simply by introducing participation or reward schemes for individuals. Instead, general systems theory prescribes a match between the two subsystems, one that establishes stable equilibrium.

Like cybernetics and systems dynamics therefore, the general systems strand of thinking sees an organisation as a feedback system. It also sees that feedback system as one that maintains equilibrium with its environment, and between its parts, by utilising the mechanisms of negative feedback.

Conflicting subsystems

In general systems theory, open systems are thought of as having maintenance subsystems to sustain orderly relationships between the parts of the system (Lawrence and Lorsch, 1967). In an organisation this would be the management information and control systems and the cultures that keep people working harmoniously together. However, it is recognised that these maintenance systems are conservative by nature. They are intended to hold the system together; to prevent it from changing too rapidly; to keep it efficiently carrying out its main tasks. The inevitable consequence of this maintenance form of control is that the overall system and its subsystems become out of balance as time goes by and things change. They become out of balance with each other and with the environment.

However, organisations also have adaptive mechanisms that promote change so as to keep them in dynamic equilibrium with the environment. These two subsystems, the maintenance and the adaptive, inevitably conflict, but successful organisations sustain a stable balance between them, according to general systems theory. Note that general systems theory recognises a fundamental conflict inherent in the structure of the system, but assumes that successful systems deal with this by sustaining equilibrium.

General systems theory has made an important contribution to an understanding of the nature of managing and organising in a number of ways. It focuses attention on:

- interdependence, interaction and interconnection between parts of an organisation and between organisations;
- the importance of the boundaries between parts of an organisation and between one organisation and others;
- the roles of people within and across the boundaries and the nature of leadership as management of the boundary.

These ideas are summarised in Box 6.1.

Box 6.1	General systems theory: main points on organisational dynamics

- An organisation is an open system: a set of interconnected parts (individuals, informal groups, formal groups such as departments and business units) in turn interacting with other organisations and individuals outside it.

- Interconnection means that a system imports energy and information from outside itself, transforms that energy and information in some way and then exports the transformed result back to other systems outside itself.

- An organisation imports across a boundary separating it from other systems, transforms the imports within its boundary and exports back across the boundary. The boundary separates a system from its environment but also links it to its environment.

- Relationships across the boundary are always changing, the environment is always changing. The boundary therefore exercises a regulatory function: on the one hand it protects the system from fluctuations in the environment, and on the other it relays messages and prompts changes within the boundary so that the system adapts to its environment.

- It is the role of leadership to manage the boundary, to regulate so that the system is protected and changes adaptively.

- Successful management keeps an organisation adapted to its changing environment through a process of negative feedback producing stable equilibrium.

- Adaptation to the environment determines the stable equilibrium balance between differentiation and integration, between maintenance control systems and change, required for success. Organisational paradoxes are thus solved in a unique way determined by the environment.

- Success is therefore a state of stability, consistency and harmony.

I now want to move on from open systems theory to some relevant psychoanalytic concepts. I will return to open systems theory in Section 6.4.

6.3 Psychoanalysis and unconscious processes

In developing psychoanalysis, Freud focused attention on the unconscious. He believed that people repress dangerous desires and painful memories, but that this repression does not get rid of such desires and memories – they remain in the unconscious as determinants of behaviour. Repression is one of the major defences against anxiety: that is, a painful state of unease for which no clear reason can be found. It is also held that people's behaviour can be driven by unconscious group processes.

Unconscious processes in organisations

An unconscious group process is one in which a group of people engage without consciously agreeing to it or even realising that they are doing it. When groups of people are in this state, they find what is happening to them both puzzling and upsetting and it makes it impossible for them to engage in rational decision-making and learning. Covert politics is a defence against anxiety that people are more or less conscious of practising, but unconscious processes are defences they indulge in quite automatically without being aware of what they are doing. A group of people can make rational decisions and learn only when they are able to contain the anxiety of organisational life, as opposed to avoiding it through covert politics, on the one hand, or becoming overwhelmed by it in the form of unconscious processes, on the other.

When ways of thinking are challenged, people become anxious. That anxiety may rise to such high levels that people swing into automatic basic assumption behaviour – an unconscious process (Bion, 1961). When groups are dominated by basic assumption behaviour, they cannot learn and therefore their organisation cannot develop new strategic direction. On the other hand, if there is a good enough holding environment so that people can contain rather than submit to or avoid the anxiety, then insight and creativity may be generated by, and accompany, the anxiety of learning. Since all people behave in ways that are directed by unconscious as well as conscious processes, it is inevitable that, when they come together as a group, at least part of their behaviour in that group will be determined by those unconscious processes. In other words, unconscious group processes will inevitably be part of most decision-making processes in an organisation.

This proposition is not recognised in most explanations of managing, organising and decision-making. The role of unconscious processes is also firmly denied any explicit attention by many management practitioners. Such considerations tend to be dismissed as peripheral concerns for mature managers who are supposed to make decisions in largely rational ways. When unconscious processes are discussed, they are normally seen as peripheral influences on a decision, usually adverse influences, which must and can be removed.

More careful reflection, however, suggests that unconscious processes are so deeply embedded in human behaviour that it is only some completely inhuman, and therefore nonexistent, decision-making process that can occur in the absence of unconscious processes, or with those processes occupying a position of only peripheral importance. It is, therefore, a matter of importance for the effectiveness of strategic management to explore what impact these processes may have and how they come about. A psychoanalytical explanation is that, when humans are confronted by high levels of anxiety provoked by unfamiliar tasks and lack of leadership, they revert very easily to infantile mechanisms. They begin to behave according to patterns they learned as infants. So, first look briefly at an explanation of how infants cope with their world provided by the object relations school of psychoanalysis (Klein, 1975).

Infantile mechanisms

According to Melanie Klein's explanation (1975), infants are born with two powerful drives: the libido, or life force, which is the drive to love; and the morbido, or death wish, which is the fear of death and destruction, the feeling of persecution. The inner life of the infant is very simple – it is dominated by these two extremes of love on the one hand and persecutory fear on the other. The infant's perception of its external world is also very simple, consisting of two part-objects: a good part of the mother that feeds and comforts it and a bad part that denies it food and comfort.

The infant copes with this simple and also powerfully distressing world by splitting its inner life into a loving part that is projected on to the good part of the mother. The infant then identifies itself with that good part and introjects it back into itself. The same thing is done with the persecutory feelings and the aggression and hatred they arouse. These are all projected on to the bad part of the mother, and the infant identifies its own violent impulses with that bad part – it then introjects that bad part of the mother back into itself.

The infant projects its feelings and then perceives those feelings as coming from the outside object. It therefore reacts to the object in a manner provoked by the feelings that originally come from itself. So it projects its own fears of persecution and then reacts to the object projected upon as if that object is actually persecuting it. This leads to a reaction of hate and aggression, strengthening the feeling of persecution. If the projection affects the behaviour of the object, then the whole process becomes even stronger. It is through these processes that the character of the infant is formed. If it experiences loving responses to its loving projections then the loving side of its character is strengthened. If the persecutory projections are reinforced by lack of love and actual persecution then this side of the character is reinforced.

This first stage of infantile development is known as the paranoid–schizoid position. It is schizoid because the infant splits the external world and it splits its own internal world too. It is paranoid because of the persecutory fears of the infant. The infant deals with these fears by using the mechanisms of splitting and projective identification, putting what is inside its own mind out into some external object or person and then identifying with and reacting to what it has projected, and subtly influencing the one projected onto so that he or she behaves according to the projection. The infant copes with harsh reality by creating a fantasy world of separate objects, some of which are persecuting it. It is idealising the good parts and denying its own bad parts by projecting them, so building the external bad into a demon.

The infant who develops normally works through this position and comes to realise that the bad and good objects in its external world are really one and the same whole person. But for the infant, having learned how to defend against the earliest anxieties, these defences remain in the unconscious. In later life when people confront anxiety again, they are highly likely to regress to the infantile mechanisms of splitting the world and themselves into extreme and artificial categories of the good and the bad, projecting the parts of themselves they do not like on to others, so creating fantasies that have little to do with reality.

Once the infant realises that it loves and hates the same person, it is filled with anxiety because of the feelings of anger and hatred previously projected on to the mother. This causes the depressive position. The normal infant works its way through this position too, developing strong feelings of love and dependence on the mother, while seeking to make amends for previous bad feelings. It experiences hope from the more mature relationship with the mother. Once the infant can hold the depressive position – that is, hold in the mind the paradox of simultaneously loving and hating – then that child can go on to make reparative acts and have reparative feelings. If these are responded to with love, a lifelong cycle of experiencing guilt, making reparation and receiving forgiveness is put in place. Melanie Klein saw this as the basis of all later creative behaviour. So, it is when people are in the depressive position, when they can hold in their minds the paradoxes and ambiguities of organisational life, that they are able to engage in rational decision-making. When they regress from that depressive position to the paranoid–schizoid position, they become trapped in primitive ways of thinking and behaving. And this, it is held, happens to all of us when we cannot contain the anxiety of learning and when our environment provides us with no anxiety containment either.

Groups and infantile mechanisms

When mature, competent managers come together as a group, each is said to bring along the infantile mechanisms of dependence, idealisation, denial, splitting, projection and fantasising that have been learned as an infant and laid down in the unconscious. Anything that raises uncertainty levels and thus anxiety levels could provoke regression to those infantile mechanisms. Bion has provided an explanation of how these mechanisms are manifested in group behaviour (Bion, 1961).

Bion distinguishes between two important aspects of any group of people. The first aspect is the sophisticated work group. This group focuses on the primary task that it has come together to perform. So, a team of top executives has the primary tasks of controlling the day-to-day running of the business of the organisation and also the strategic development of that organisation. All groups are also at the same time what Bion called 'basic assumption groups'. A basic assumption group is one that behaves as if it is making a particular assumption about required behaviour. The assumption becomes most apparent when uncertainty and anxiety levels rise. What Bion is talking about here is the emotional atmosphere, the psychological culture, of the group. All groups of people have these two aspects: some task they are trying to perform together, accompanied by some emotional atmosphere within which they are trying to perform their task. That atmosphere can be described in terms of a basic assumption they are all making.

So, at any one time, a group of people may constitute a sophisticated work group characterised by a basic assumption on behaviour that occupies a kind of low-level background position, influencing the conduct of the primary task but not dominating or blocking it. Then, when uncertainty and anxiety levels rise markedly, the group can become suffused with and dominated by the basic assumption, a strong emotional atmosphere, or group culture, that blocks the group's ability to function as a sophisticated work group. The primary task will not be carried out, or it will be carried out in an ineffective manner.

Bion distinguished amongst three basic assumptions:

1. *Dependence*. Here the group behaves as if it has come together to depend on some leader. The members of the group seek a leader on whom they can depend. They abandon their individuality and critical faculties in favour of some kind of adoration of a charismatic leader. They actively seek a charismatic person who will tell them what to do. Charisma lies not in the person of the leader but in the interrelationship between the followers and the leader. In this state, members of a group will idealise the leader, expecting completely unrealistic performance from the leader. Groups working on this assumption are destined to be disappointed and will quickly denigrate and abandon the leader. This dependence is an infantile mechanism, because the members of the group are projecting their requirements for something to depend upon on to someone else. This projection

will in effect select the leader. Note how this raises a possibility not normally thought of in organisations. When a group is behaving in this mode, it is creating its own leader through projecting demands on to a person – it is not the leader who is creating the group. If the person selected for this projection does not cooperate or disappoints, then members of the group project their frustration and fear on to that person and begin to attack. This brings us to the second basic assumption.

2. *Fight/flight.* Here it is as if the group has come together for the purpose of fighting some enemy or for the purpose of fleeing from some enemy. Members project their desire for fight or flight on to someone to lead them in fight or flight. Once again they may rapidly become disappointed with and attack the leader. Groups in this state invent fantasy enemies in some other department or some other organisation. The energy goes into competition and win/lose dynamics or in scapegoating a member.

3. *Pairing.* Pairing is another mode in which a group might operate. Here it is as if the group has come together to witness the intercourse between two of their number that will produce the solution to their anxieties. The atmosphere here is one of unrealistic hope that some experts will produce all the answers.

Turquet (1974) added a fourth basic assumption:

4. *Oneness.* Here it is as if the group has come together to join in a powerful union with some omnipotent force that will enable members to surrender themselves in some kind of safe passivity. Members seem lost in an oceanic feeling of unity.

Once a group of people comes to be dominated by one of the basic assumptions, group members enter into volatile dynamics in which they switch, for apparently no reason, from one basic assumption to another. While people in a group are behaving like this, they are incapable of performing the primary task or acting as a work group. They cannot remember what they have just discussed; they go around and around in incompetent circles; they suck unsuitable people into leadership positions; they create scapegoats; they act on untested myths and rumours; they build fantasies and lose touch with reality. Individuals sink their individuality in group uniformity and become deskilled.

What provokes the switch from a work group with some background basic assumption, being used in a sophisticated way to support their task, to a group dominated by a basic assumption? The provocation seems to have a great deal to do with levels of ambiguity and uncertainty on the one hand, and with certain styles of exercising power on the other. If leaders abandon groups in times of great uncertainty and ambiguity, they will develop into basic assumption groups and become incapable of handling the uncertainty and ambiguity.

Note, however, that this is not clear-cut causality between a specific action – say, the withdrawal of power – and specific outcomes in behavioural terms. All one can say is that, when the nature of power in a group is changed so that people's requirement for dependence is frustrated, they will display general patterns of behaviour that can be labelled as fight/flight or some other label. It will not be possible to say what form such fighting or such flight may take, or when it will occur. The key points about the dynamics and unconscious processes are summarised in Box 6.2.

Box 6.2	Unconscious group processes: main points on organisational dynamics

- Any attempt to change an organisation in a fundamental way upsets the balance and nature of power and raises the levels of uncertainty and ambiguity so increasing anxiety.

- Increased anxiety unleashes unconscious processes of regression to infantile behaviour. Work groups become swamped with basic assumption behaviour in which they are incapable of undertaking strategic developments.

- A group of managers facing strategic issues is turning up the levels of uncertainty and ambiguity since these are characteristics of strategic issues. Such issues threaten power positions. It is therefore inevitable that strategic issues themselves will raise anxiety levels which could trigger basic assumption behaviour.

- In these circumstances it is quite likely that long-term plans, mission statements, visions and the like are simply being used as defence mechanisms. Perhaps people cling to a dominant paradigm despite all the evidence to the contrary because it is their main defence mechanism against anxiety.

- The dynamics of any real-life organisation are inevitably unstable, unless it is completely dominated by rules, fears or force, in which case it will atrophy and die. Strategic management proceeds as part of this unstable dynamic.

- Success has to do with the management of the context or boundary conditions around a group. The main factors that establish the context are the nature and use of power, the level of mutual trust and the time pressures on people in the group. The purpose of managing the context, or the boundaries, is to create an emotional atmosphere in which it is possible to overcome defences and to test reality rather than indulge in fantasy.

6.4 Open systems and unconscious processes

The combination of open systems theory and psychoanalysis originated at the Tavistock Institute of Human Relations. This was set up London in 1946 by a group of psychoanalysts from the Tavistock Clinic and social scientists from other institutions. During the 1950s and 1960s a distinctive approach to understanding life in organisations was developed by members of this Institute, for example Trist, to whom I have already referred, and Rice and Miller (Miller and Rice, 1967).

As I have already said, an open system exists by importing energy/materials from its environment across a boundary, transforming them and then exporting them back across the boundary (Miller and Rice, 1967). This boundary is seen as a region in which mediating, or regulating, activities occur not only to protect the system from disruption due to external fluctuations but also to allow it to adapt to external changes (Miller, 1977). The boundary region must therefore exhibit an appropriate degree of both insulation and permeability if the system is to survive. This makes regulatory functions at the permeable boundary region of central importance. In organisational terms, these regulatory functions are performed by leaders/managers at the organisation's boundary with other organisations. It is the activities of leaders and managers at the boundary that are key to the process of change. It then becomes quite logical to think about change in terms of rational design and to look for what might inhibit such rational designing activity. Disorder is seen as an inhibitor that must be removed. The disorder is due to the unconscious processes described in the last section.

Miller and Rice (1967) used Bion's (1961) insights to see a group of people as an open system in which individuals, also seen as open systems, interact with each other at two levels. At one level they contribute to the group's purpose, so constituting a sophisticated (work) group, and at the other level they develop feelings and attitudes about each other, the group and its environment, so constituting a more primitive (basic assumption) group. Both of these modes of relating are operative at the same time. When the basic assumption mode takes the form of a background emotional atmosphere, it may well support the work of the group but, when it predominates, it is destructive of the group's work. So, individuals are thought of as open systems relating to each other across their individual boundary regions. In this way they constitute a group, which is also thought of as an open system with a permeable boundary region. Furthermore, Miller and Rice argue that it is confusing to think of organisations, or enterprises, as open systems consisting of individuals and groupings of individuals. So, an inter-systemic perspective is adopted in which an enterprise is thought of as one open system interacting with individuals and groupings of them as other open systems.

Enterprises are seen as task systems – they have primary tasks that they must perform if they are to survive. There are various definitions of the primary task. It may be the task that ought to be performed. It may be the task people believe that they are carrying out. It may be a task that they are engaged in without even being aware of it and this probably means that it is a defensive mechanism. The primary task requires people to take up roles in order for it to be carried out, and the enterprise, or task system, imports these roles across its boundary with the system consisting of individuals and groupings of them. Roles, and relationships between roles, fall within the boundary of the task system. However, groups and individuals, with their personal relationships, personal power plays and human needs not derived from the task system's primary task, fall outside it: they constitute part of the task system's environment. So, there is one system, a task system, interacting with other systems, individuals and groups, and the groups are always operating in two modes at the same time: work mode and basic assumption mode.

When the individual/group system has the characteristics of a sophisticated group with basic assumption behaviour as a supportive background atmosphere, then it is exporting functional roles to the task system and the latter can perform its primary task. The enterprise, or task system, is thus displaying the dynamics of stability – that is, equilibrium or quasi-equilibrium. When, however, the individual/group system is flooded with basic assumption behaviour it exports that behaviour into the task system, so disrupting the performance of the primary task. Miller (1993) argues that this inter-systemic view encourages one to focus on interdependence: people supplying roles to enterprises and those enterprises requiring performance in role from people in order to survive.

Part of the task system, a subsystem of it, might be set up to contain imported basic assumption behaviour such as fight. Its primary task is then to operate as an organisational defence that allows the rest of the task system to carry out its primary task. Without such organisational defences, the task system as a whole would import fantasies and behaviours that are destructive of the primary task – the dynamics of instability. These undesirable imports are to be diminished by:

- clarity of task;
- clearly defined roles, and authority relationships between them, all related to task;
- appropriate leadership regulation at the boundary of the task system;
- procedures and structures that form social defences against anxiety (Jacques, 1955; Menzies Lyth, 1975);
- high levels of individual maturity and autonomy.

Most of these factors seem to emphasise design and some joint intention relating to the system as a whole. Furthermore, there is a strong implication that, while the dynamics of stability are a prerequisite for a functioning task system, the dynamics of instability are inimical to that functioning. There is little sense in this formulation of the creative potential of disorder. I am making this point here because the theory to be presented in Part 3 takes a different view on these matters.

Shapiro and Carr (1991) employ the above model in their interpretation of the role of the consultant. The consultant uses counter-transference feelings to formulate hypotheses about the transferential and projective processes at work in an organisation, and about the impact of basic assumption behaviour on the work of that organisation. Shapiro and Carr see the function of the consultant as one of feeding back those hypotheses into the life of the organisation and so fostering a collaborative, negotiated understanding and verbalisation of the unconscious, irrational processes at play. It is believed that this process enables the reclaiming of projections and distorted impressions of reality, so restoring to the group its work function. The consultants engage with and understand the complexity of organisational life by adopting an interpretive stance. This stance is seen as the most important element in creating a holding environment and they draw an analogy with a therapeutic setting: 'containment and holding ordinarily refer to symbolic interpretive ways in which the therapist manages the patient's (and his own) feelings' (Shapiro and Carr, 1991, p. 112).

Another feature of the holding environment, one that interpretation aims to secure, is the clarity of task, boundary and role. This is seen as containing, for example, sexual and aggressive feelings. Empathic interpretation affirms individuals in their roles and the resulting containment establishes a holding environment. This provides for safe regression, a shift from rationally organised words to the primitive distortions of fantasy images and simple metaphors which can then be articulated and so disarmed. The aim of interpretation is to move people from states of irrational anxiety and fantasy that distort work to the more reality-based taking of roles that support it.

According to Shapiro and Carr, the aim of the consultant's work is to identify whether an organisation is functioning according to its design. This will happen when members of the organisation understand their tasks so that roles within and across parts of the organisation can be legitimately authorised and fully integrated. This, in turn, requires clarification of authorisation from one level to another in the hierarchy and a structure of meetings to promote effective communication. Shapiro and Carr stress the need to develop a culture in which people bring their work-related feelings to legitimate forums where they can be made available for examination in relation to the work rather than discharged in informal subgroups. What they mean by an interpretive stance, then, is a collaborative verbalisation of unconscious processes leading to withdrawal of projections that might be adversely affecting task performance. The objection to informal subgroups seems to be based on the belief that, since they are based purely on personal relationships rather than on task, they are fertile ground for projections and basic assumption behaviour. Note how this model of organisational functioning leads to a focus on the legitimate relationships in an organisation.

6.5 Leaders and groups

In both strategic choice and mainstream learning organisation theory, leaders are assumed to be perfectly healthy, balanced people, who set the direction of the organisation for others to follow. However, as soon as it is recognised that basic assumption groups can very quickly emerge from work groups, the possibility arises that leaders can also be the creations of the group. It is quite possible that leaders are vainly trying to act out the fantasies that those in the management team are projecting. Leaders affect what groups do, but groups also affect what leaders do through processes of unconscious projection.

Leadership

Bales (1970) identified the emergence of two kinds of leaders in small task-oriented groups: the task leader, who gives suggestions, shows disagreement and presses the group to focus on task completion; and the social-emotional leader who asks for suggestions, shows solidarity and soothes tempers by encouraging tension release. These leadership roles are mutually supportive in that each helps the group solve different problems, provided that the role occupants can work together. Sometimes one person can combine both roles – the 'great man' leader (Borgatta et al., 1954). When specialist leaders of this kind do not emerge or cannot work together, then members begin to deal with their frustration in unconscious ways that lead to the emergence of scapegoat roles, enemy roles, messiah roles, and so on. Bion (1961) distinguishes between different types of leader in the basic assumption group: the fight leader, the flight leader, the dependence leader and the leader who symbolises some unrealistic utopian, messianic or oceanic hope. Bion points to the precarious position these leaders occupy. The important point here is that the leader is sucked into that position by the group and is controlled by the group, not the other way around as we usually believe.

An important distinction is that between the leader of a work group and a basic assumption leader. An effective leader is one who maintains a clear focus on and definition of the primary task. That task determines the requirements of the leader, who must continually struggle to synthesise, participate and observe. The effective leader operates on the boundary of the group, avoiding both emotional immersion and extreme detachment. Leaders are there to regulate transactions between their groups and other groups. Both immersion and distance make this impossible. When a group is dominated by basic assumption behaviour, it sucks into the leadership position one who is completely immersed in the emotional atmosphere, the basic assumption behaviour of the group. This leader is subjected to conflicting and fundamentally impossible roles – to provide unlimited nurturance, to fight and subdue imaginary enemies, to rescue the group from death and dissolution, to fulfil utopian or messianic hopes.

The kinds of roles that have been distinguished are those of the aggressor, the seducer who tries to seduce people into exposing their feelings and positions, the scapegoat, the hero, the resistors, the anxious participators, the distressed females, the respected enactors, the sexual idols, the outsiders, the prophets (Dunphy, 1968). These informal roles develop in order to contain and deal with internal conflict, the tension of fusion and individuation. Managers' choices and actions may have more to do with unconscious processes than any rational consideration.

Neurotic forms of leadership

Strategic choice and mainstream learning organisation theory focus on what leadership means when it is functioning well. However, leaders often do not function very well and quite often they are definitely dysfunctional. Such dysfunctional leadership has not attracted very much attention in most of the management literature, but it occurs frequently and it is therefore a matter of importance to understand something about it. Functional leaders assist in the containment of anxiety and thus help to create the possibility of learning, but dysfunctional, neurotic leaders may well become caught up, and drive others to become caught up, in neurotic defences that will block such learning.

Kets de Vries (1989) explains the nature of neurotic leadership in the following way. Everyone behaves in a manner that is affected by what one might think of as an inner theatre. That theatre consists of a number of representations of people and situations, often formed early in childhood, and those that have come to play the most important roles are core conflictual relationships. It is as if people spend much of their lives re-enacting conflicts that they could not understand in childhood, partly because they are familiar with them, and partly, perhaps, because they are always seeking to understand them. What they do, then, is project this inner play with conflictual situations out on to the real world they have to deal with. Leaders do this just as others do, the difference being that they project their inner conflicts on to a much larger real-world stage that includes their followers. A leader projects internal private dialogues into external public ones and these dialogues are about core conflictual themes from childhood. The particular neurotic style a leader practises will be determined by the nature of these core conflicts.

Followers also project their inner plays on to the leader and these leader/follower projections keep leaders and followers engaged with each other in a particular manner. Followers project their dependence needs on to leaders and displace their own ideals, wishes and desires on to them too.

The inner theatre in which leaders and followers join each other contains scenarios that are the basis of imagined, desired and feared relationships between them. There are typical scenarios that are found over and over again and they constitute typical dispositions, typical ways of defending against, repressing, denying and idealising particular leader/follower relationships. Everyone is said to use such devices and everyone has a number of prominent dispositions that constitute that person's neurotic style. This is quite normal and it becomes a problem only when people massively, compulsively and habitually use a rather small number of defences. This blocks their ability to relate to reality effectively and it is then that they might be labelled 'neurotic'.

Kets de Vries (1989) distinguishes amongst a number of such dispositions or neurotic styles as follows. Every leader will display a combination of some of these styles and it becomes a problem only when a rather small number of these come to dominate the behaviour of the leader and the followers.

- The *aggressive* disposition tends to characterise many who become leaders and rather fewer who are followers – aggression is often acceptable in leaders but creates problems for followers. Tough chief executives who are socially forceful and intimidating, energetic, competitive and power oriented fall into this category. People are not important to them and they want to dominate. They tend to be impulsive and to believe that the world is a jungle. They expect people to be hostile to them and they become aggressive in advance to counteract such expected hostility. Of course, their behaviour may well provoke the hostility they expect. Such leaders probably experienced parental rejection or hostility.

- The *paranoid* disposition is found frequently amongst leaders and less often amongst followers. Such people are always looking for hidden motives and are suspicious of others. They are hyper-vigilant, they keep scanning the environment and taking unnecessary precautions. They deny personal weakness and do not readily accept blame. They tend to be restricted and cold in relationships, with little humour. They are fond of mechanistic devices to measure performance and keep track of people. Such people may have had intrusive parents and may feel uncertain of themselves.

- The *histrionic* disposition is characterised by a need to attract the attention of others at all costs. Such people are alert to the desires of others, they are sociable and seductive with their sense of self-worth heavily dependent on the opinion of others. They love activity and excitement and tend to overreact to minor incidents, often throwing tantrums. Such people may have had difficulty attracting the attention of parents.

- The *detached* disposition is displayed when people find it difficult to form close relationships. They tend to be cold and aloof and this may be a response to parental devaluation.

- The *controlling* disposition is high in leaders and low in followers and it is displayed by people who want to control everything in their lives. They have an excessive desire for order and control. This is a way of managing hostile feelings that may have arisen from the behaviour of controlling parents. The resultant hostility may emerge as tyrannical ways of behaving or its opposite of submission.

- The *passive-aggressive* disposition tends to be found more in followers than in leaders. Such people are highly dependent but tend to attack those they depend upon. They resist demands for performance, they are defiant, provocative and negative, complaining all the time and demanding much from their leaders. They tend to blame others all the time; they are ambivalent and pessimistic. This difficulty might arise because such people find it difficult to assess what is expected of them. They are likely to have parents who presented them with conflicting messages.

- Other dispositions are the *narcissistic* one when people see themselves as exceptional and special; the *dependent* disposition in which people are excessively dependent upon others; and the *masochistic* disposition.

It is not just the style of the leader or the style of the followers on their own that determines how their joint behaviour unfolds. It is how the styles engage each other that will create the environment within which they have to work. So, an aggressive, controlling leader interacting with dependent, masochistic followers will produce a rather different context and pattern of behaviour compared with such a leader interacting with, say, passive-aggressive followers. These patterns of interaction will have a powerful impact on how effectively an organisation learns. Such neurotically based interactions, therefore, have to be understood as central to processes of management.

6.6 How open systems/psychoanalytic perspectives deal with the four key questions

This chapter now turns to how open systems/psychoanalytic perspectives answer the four questions posed at the end of Chapter 2. These were:

1. How does the theory view the nature of interaction?

2. What view does it take of human nature?

3. What methodology does it employ?

4. How does it deal with paradox?

You can compare how the theories surveyed in this chapter answer the questions with the kind of answers found in strategic choice theory (Section 4.7). You can also make comparisons with learning organisation theory (Section 5.8). Consider now how open systems/psychoanalytic perspectives deal with the questions.

The nature of interaction

Interaction within and between organisations is understood in systems terms as with strategic choice and learning organisation theory. While cybernetics analyses a system in terms of self-regulating negative feedback loops and systems dynamics takes account of amplifying positive feedback loops, open systems theory focuses attention on regulatory functions at the system's boundary. Essentially, these functions regulate the flows of imports into, and exports out of, the system so that the system adapts to its environment. The dynamics, the way the system moves, is therefore the same as for cybernetics: that is, a tendency to move towards stable equilibrium when the system is succeeding.

Open systems theory pays more attention to the micro level than cybernetics and systems dynamics do. In other words, it pays attention to the subsystems of which the whole is composed. This is especially so when it is combined with psychoanalytic perspectives, because these are very much concerned with the individuals and the groups that make up an organisation. The disorderly dynamics generated by individuals relating to each other in groups then become very important as an obstacle to the successful movement towards adaptive equilibrium. Those writing in the Tavistock tradition distinguish between the task/role system and the system of individuals/groups. The task/role system is a subsystem of the organisation, which is open to the other subsystem consisting of individuals and groups, and also open to the environment consisting of other organisations. When the imports from the individuals/groups subsystem are adequately regulated, the task/role subsystem can make rational choices about adapting to the environment of other organisations.

So, this is a theory that pays considerable attention to both macro and micro levels and it envisages both orderly and disorderly dynamics. The former is equated with successful adaptation to the environment and the latter as an obstacle to this process. The orderly operation of the task/role system is understood in much the same way as strategic choice or learning organisation theory. However, the attention to micro detail brings in very important processes that can disrupt the rational processes.

The theory of causality, however, is the same as that for cybernetics/strategic choice and systems dynamics/learning organisation – namely, formative cause. The emphasis is on already enfolded archetypes that are unfolded as the system develops. The same problems to do with ordinary human freedom and novelty follow. This open systems/psychoanalytic approach cannot explain how novel, transformative changes come about in systemic terms. These are matters that rely on some kind of explanation in terms of the individual.

The nature of human beings

The theory reviewed in this chapter takes a very different view of human nature from the mainly cognitivist and humanistic perspectives on which strategic choice and learning organisation theories are built. The main difference is the emphasis it places on unconscious processes, the effects of anxiety and the ever-present possibility of defensive and aggressive behaviour. Human ability to behave rationally and altruistically is seen as highly problematic and the capacity for learning as very fragile. Attention is focused on power and dysfunctional behaviour in a similar way to that found in organisational learning theories which emphasise defensive routines but which other writers in this tradition as well as in strategic choice theory largely ignore.

However, there are also significant similarities. First, the notion of representation is as central in psychoanalysis as in cognitivism. In other words, in both of these theories it is assumed that individuals' minds are internal worlds consisting of mental representations of outer reality upon which the individual then acts. However, the nature of the representations and the processes through which they are formed are very different. Consider what representation means in most psychoanalytic theories:

- In classic, Freudian drive theory, a representation is a conscious or unconscious idea that represents an instinct and as such it is the expression of some basic, inherited body function. So, here there is no notion of a more or less accurate picture of a pre-given external world. Instead, there is a unique expression of general bodily functions internal to the individual body, developed from the interaction of inherited instincts and actual experience. In early object relations theory (Klein, 1975) the notion of representation is developed in a different way. Representations are of part-objects and objects encountered in relationships. Object here is mainly a person or some part of a person and the nature of the representation is highly complex. It is not at all a more or less accurate picture of an external reality but rather an internal construct developed through experience on the basis of inherent, inherited fantasies common to all humans. The earliest object is that of the mother's breast and what is being represented is not so much the object itself as the experience and fantasised relationship with the object. Later object relations theorists (Bion, Winnicott, Fairbairn) placed much more emphasis on the relationships, as did attachment theorists (Bowlby, Balint), self psychologists (Kohut) and relational psychologists (Sullivan, Stern), for all of whom representations are primarily of relationships with other human beings.

- As with cognitivism, representations are made up of symbols that form 'internal' templates (drive derivatives, forbidden wishes, objects, relationships) which are the basis upon which a human being knows and acts. 'Internal' here refers not to the brain but to a mental apparatus or process. This is described in terms of mental components or agents – the ego, the id and the superego, various object and self-object representations, relational interactions that have been generalised. The question of where such an apparatus might be located, or where the fantasies and other psychological processes might actually be, is never addressed.

- As with cognitivism, representations are built up through a process of symbol processing but in psychoanalysis there is no suggestion that this is like a computer. Indeed, the process through which the representations are constructed becomes highly complex. Freudian drive theory emphasises processes of defence and suppression. Object relations theory presents highly complex mental processes of splitting, projecting, introjecting, identifying, idealising, denigrating, making reparation and so on. Attachment theorists, self and relational psychologists talk about processes of evocation, resonance, mirroring, attunement and empathy. All of these processes build up representations of objects and relationships.

- As with cognitivism, representing is a process of recovering or reconstructing templates from a memory bank but these now take different forms. They could be drive-driven wishes that are permissible in terms of external reality or suppressed wishes expressive of the pleasure principle. Or, they could be recoveries of past object relationships. Representing, as a process of comparing new stimuli with past representations of external, environmental features, receives little emphasis. Instead the representations are used to interpret reality and may well distort it in various transferential and projective processes.

The above usage of 'representation' clearly carries with it substantial implications. It postulates that the individual human mind is formed by the clash of inherited drives and social constraints, out of which there emerges a mental apparatus that mediates the clash. Later developments in psychoanalytic theory increasingly see humans occupying a world formed by relationships with other human beings, with representations of these relationships emerging from them and coming in turn to govern them. There is a separate entity that does this representing, namely a mind or psyche of the individual. These separate individual entities cannot easily share the same representations, because each individual uniquely constructs his or her own psyche. However, psychic processes are postulated that allow some degree of sharing of mental contents or states. These processes include projective identification, resonance, mirroring, empathy, attunement and, of course, talking.

There is a decentring of the individual in an inner sense in that the individual is not clearly in control of his or her mind, but, rather, is buffeted about by the id. However, in any external sense there is no significant decentring of the individual. It is true that the social prohibition is part of the process of structuring the psyche, particularly in the form of the superego, but groups arise when members identify with the same leader. There is no sense of individuals and groups co-creating each other. The social plays a part only in terms of the reality principle. This curbs the limitless drive for pleasure on the part of the individual, a drive that has to be mediated first by an ego and then by a superego. The process of mental structuring is essentially the feat of the individual infant as it copes with unconscious fantasy, proceeding from primitive dependence to autonomy. This is very much within the dominant Western paradigm of the autonomous individual.

To summarise: in cognitivism, constructivism, humanistic psychology and psychoanalysis, the individual is prior and primary to the group. With the exception of constructivism, all of the theories involve individuals building representations of reality. However, they do so in very different ways and build very different kinds of representations. Psychoanalysis, therefore, presents very different views on human nature and the ability of an individual to control his or her own mental processes. The impact of unconscious group processes on the individual's ability to think and act rationally receives a great deal of attention in this theory. The individual is primary in the sense that he or she is born with inherited drives and fantasies that are constrained by social forces.

Methodology

In strategic choice and learning organisation theory the researcher, consultant and manager are assumed to be able to stand outside the organisational system and to take the position of the objective observer. The perspectives in this chapter take a similar methodological stance, but with an important difference: the consultant, researcher and manager are assumed to stand at the boundary of the organisational system. In this position one is not so immersed in the organisational culture that one loses a rational, objective perspective. However, one is immersed enough to experience how being in that culture feels. These feelings are part of the information that can be used to understand the organisation.

Paradox

While strategic choice and learning organisation theory do not recognise paradox, it is central to a psychoanalytic perspective. The struggle amongst ego, id and superego is never resolved. The capacity to think and learn requires an individual to take the depressive position where it is possible to hold ambiguity and paradox in the mind. Creativity requires the individual mind to occupy the transitional space. This is essentially paradoxical since it is both fantasy and reality at the same time.

Making sense of experience

The perspectives in this chapter are particularly useful when it comes to making sense of experiences that feel stressful or bizarre. It might be possible to understand them by paying attention to the effects of anxiety on people's behaviour and how people defend against it. It also offers ways of understanding the nature and impact of dysfunctional leadership and inappropriate applications of power. The argument presented is that the processes described in this section affect how an organisation evolves. They are as important as rational choice in determining what happens to an organisation.

6.7 Summary

This chapter has reviewed open systems theory and psychoanalytic perspectives, pointing to how they focus attention on aspects of life that do not feature much in strategic choice and learning organisation theories.

The open systems/psychoanalytic approach opens up insights like these:

- Charismatic leaders and the strong cultures of dependence they provoke in followers may well be extremely unhealthy for organisations. Researchers (e.g. Peters and Waterman, 1982) may therefore note the presence of charismatic leaders and superficially conclude that this is the reason for success, when it might well be a neurotic phenomenon that is about to undermine the company.

- A cohesive team of managers may not be a healthy phenomenon at all. It may be an unhealthy and unproductive reflection of the fantasy of basic assumption groups acting out dependence or oneness assumptions. Again, researchers not considering an organisation from a psychoanalytic point of view may well conclude that such neurotic cohesion is a reason for success.

- The idea of the group or the management team may itself be a defence mechanism. So, faced by high levels of strategic uncertainty and ambiguity, managers may retreat into the 'mother figure' of the team for comfort and in so doing fail to deal with the strategic issues.

- Groups clearly do not have to have a purpose or even a task to function very tightly as a group, even if it is a misguided one. Again, signs of close teams should provoke suspicion, not praise.

- Groups or teams are a two-edged sword. People need them to establish their identity. They need them to operate effectively. But they can also deskill people.

- The desire for cohesion may well be a neurotic phenomenon.

- Plans and rigid structures and rules may all be defences against anxiety instead of the rational way of proceeding usually considered.

- One aspect of culture is the emotional atmosphere, the basic assumption, that a group of people create as they interact.

Further reading

Hirschhorn (1990) provides an important exposition of the role of the informal organisation as a defence against anxiety. I would also recommend Shapiro and Carr (1991) and Kets de Vries (1989), as well as Miller (1993), Oberholzer and Roberts (1995) and Gould *et al.* (2001). They all give deeper insight into the psychodynamics of organisations. Winnicott (1971) is also well worth reading.

Questions to aid further reflection

1. How do open systems differ from cybernetic systems and systems dynamics models?

2. What are the similarities and differences between psychoanalysis, cognitivism, constructivism and humanistic psychology?

3. From a psychoanalytic perspective, how would you understand the notion of the charismatic leader?

4. How would you understand the move to the mystical in organisational learning theory from a psychoanalytic perspective?

5. How would you think about teams from a psychoanalytic perspective?

6. How would you think about power from the open systems/psychoanalytic perspective?

7. What does it means to contain anxiety and how does this happen?

8. What is the nature of the relationship between the individual and the social in psychoanalysis?

Chapter 7

Thinking about strategy process from a systemic perspective
Using a process to control a process

This chapter invites you to draw on your own experience to reflect on and consider the implications of:

- The way of thinking reflected in systemic notions of process, practice and activity in organisational life.

- How the notion of rationality has been increasingly problematised over a number of decades.

- The possibility of choosing, shaping or influencing particular processes, practices and outcomes in organisational life and the possibility of remaining in control.

- The manner in which the concept of emergence is used in systemic views on process.

- The manner in which the activity-based view of strategy draws attention to the ordinary everyday activities of managers.

- The theory of time, which is reflected in systemic views on organisational processes and practices.

- The key debates in the process and activity-based literatures concerning the relative importance of macro and micro levels; formal and informal processes; as well as the tension between deliberately intended and emergent processes.

This chapter provides the basis for comparisons to be made with an alternative view of process to be explored in Chapter 12 below and begins to bring into focus matters that will be further developed in Part 3 of this book: namely, the importance of ordinary everyday activities of managers in processes of managing and strategising, which include conversation, political activities, emotion, improvisation and the connection with individual and collective identities. The concept of emergence, which is touched on in this chapter and developed further in Chapter 12, will become central to the chapters in Part 3.

7.1 Introduction

Chapter 4 reviewed the theory of strategic choice and its intellectual foundations in economics and systems thinking. The main focus of attention in this theory is on choosing the optimal market position and resource base required to gain competitive advantage and so produce successful performance for the organisation. The choice of the strategy and the effectiveness of its implementation are taken to be the cause of successful performance. This focus of attention, therefore, is on the *content* of strategy, that is, on *what* the strategy *should be*. The approach is highly prescriptive and it tends to take for granted the *processes* through which the strategy is said to be chosen and then implemented, that is, the *how* of strategy. The taken-for-granted processes are those of technical rationality, which tend to be regarded as unproblematic. The review of strategic choice theory ended with a brief look at some key debates provoked by this theory. The first was firmly within the theory itself and had to do with whether the market position was more or less important than the resource base in determining performance. The second debate amounted to a direct challenge to the theory, and those taking up the challenge argued that managers did not actually work in the technically rational manner assumed by the theory. For example, Mintzberg influentially argued for taking a more descriptive approach to strategy based on what managers actually did (Mintzberg, 1973, 1998) and his research into this led him to propose that, while some strategies were the result of *deliberate* choices made in a more or less rational manner, many others *emerged* (Mintzberg, 1987; Mintzberg and Waters, 1985) in processes of learning. What he and others were calling for was the focusing of attention on process, how strategies came about, rather than simply on content.

Chapter 5 then explored organisational learning processes, concentrating on the particularly influential theories of the learning organisation, while Chapter 6 considered how one might think about the psychological obstacles to learning in organisations from a psychoanalytic perspective. The intellectual foundations are to be found more in psychology and sociology than in economics, although the importance of systems thinking as foundational continues. This chapter looks more explicitly at how influential writers have dealt with issues of uncertainty, ambiguity, emotion and conflict in the move from strategy content to strategy process. Attention was drawn to the political nature and practical difficulties involved in strategising, learning, creating knowledge and dealing with problem issues to do with cognitive, psychological and emotional factors, as well as uncertain, even turbulent environments. To begin with, consider the critique that has been made of process as technical rationality.

7.2 Rational process and its critics: bounded rationality

The word 'rational' can be used in different ways and its use can cause confusion in discussions about management processes. It is important, therefore, to distinguish one meaning from another. The notion of 'rationality' can be thought about in two ways:

1. Rationality is a method of deciding that involves setting clear objectives, gathering the facts, generating options, and choosing one that maximises or satisfices (i.e. approximately satisfies) the objective. Irrationality here is any behaviour that is not preceded by fixing objectives and weighing up options based on observable facts. It involves rejecting that which cannot be tested by reason applied to objective facts. Rationality here is behaving and deciding only on the basis of propositions that can be consciously reasoned about, rather than on the basis of customs, norms, emotions and beliefs. Irrationality here consists not only of fantasy but also of behaviour driven by emotions and beliefs even if they are connected to an emotional and ideological 'reality'. We can refer to this meaning of rationality as 'technical rationality'.

2. Alternatively, rational could be a method of deciding and acting in what seem to be sensible ways which are reasonable in the circumstances and sane, rather than foolish, absurd or extreme. Rationality here is behaving and deciding in a manner connected to 'reality' in some sense and judged likely to bring about desired consequences. Irrationality consists of fantasy-driven behaviour, while rationality involves testing for reality where that reality may well be of an emotional, ideological or cultural kind.

It is quite possible, indeed highly likely, that thinking rationally in its broader sense will lead to the conclusion that technical rationality should be avoided: that is, it may be quite 'rational' in sense 2 to avoid being rational in sense 1. So, in a totally unpredictable environment, under strict time pressures, it would not be logical or sensible to try to make decisions in a painstaking manner that could never anyhow succeed in meeting all the criteria of rationality in its sense 1 meaning. You may achieve a better response from others if you base your behaviour on emotion and belief in certain circumstances. To do so would therefore be rational in sense 2 but not in sense 1.

When managers know what their objectives are, agree upon them and find themselves acting in highly stable, predictable situations, it could well be effective to make decisions and act on the basis of processes akin to technical rationality. I say 'akin' because, even in these circumstances, the limits to human cognition, as well as the inevitability of human emotion, make purely technical rationality impossible for the following reasons.

Given clear agreed objectives in relation to clear-cut problems, pure rationality requires the decision-maker to perceive the relevant objective facts in a direct manner. To perceive in a direct manner means to perceive without some kind of subjective interpretation that could open up the possibility of distortion. Having perceived the facts directly, the purely rational person would then have to store them in an exact form so that they could be processed later on without distortion. This would mean storing facts in categories that are precisely defined. Having memorised the facts in this fashion and having memorised the processing techniques required to manipulate them in much the same way, the rational person would then process the facts in a step-by-step fashion according to the rules of logic and select the action option that maximises the objective. The choice is predetermined by the facts and the problem is simply one of calculation.

However, as was recognised decades ago, humans do not perceive in this manner and they cannot therefore decide using a purely technically rational mode. Some kind of interpretation is always involved and it is highly questionable to think of the human brain/mind as some kind of information-processing device.

Bounded rationality, bureaucracy and dominant coalitions

Recognising the restrictive circumstance in which pure technical rationality could be applied, Herbert Simon developed the concept of bounded rationality (Simon, 1960). Bounded rationality is what might be called the weak form of technical rationality. Simon argued that managers could be rational only within boundaries imposed by resource availability, and by experience and knowledge of the range of options available for action. The collection, analysis and exchange of information all use resources, impose costs and are time consuming. It will therefore never be possible, or even sensible, to gather all the information and examine all the options. Instead of screening all the facts and generating all the action options before making a choice, managers, in common with all humans, take short-cuts. They employ trial-and-error search procedures to identify the most important bits of information in particular circumstances; they identify a limited range of the most important options revealed by the search; and then they act knowing only some of the potential outcomes of their actions. This means that they cannot take the action that maximises their objective. Instead they satisfice: they achieve the first satisfactory outcome they can in the circumstances. What they do then depends upon the sequence in which they discover changes, make choices and take actions.

Limited resources and the nature of the brain's processing capacity are also compensated for by the use of bureaucratic procedures (Cyert and March, 1963; March and Simon, 1958; Simon, 1960). As managers act together they develop rules of action and standard operating procedures in order to cut down on the need to make decisions afresh each time. Precedents are established and subsequent decisions are taken without having to repeat the search process anew. Decisions and actions come to be outputs of standard patterns of behaviour: that is, routines. For example, next year's budget is often determined largely by uprating this year's spend. New alternatives tend to be sought only when a problem is detected: that is, some discrepancy between what is expected and what happens. Once such a discrepancy is detected, a trial-and-error search for a new solution is undertaken. Since all possible outcomes are not known, the tendency will be to make incremental decisions: that is, decisions with consequences as small and containable as possible. By relying on bureaucratic roles and incremental decision-making, managers are able to reduce the levels of uncertainty they have to face. What they learn will be embodied in rules and procedures and these are used not to optimise outcomes, but to reduce uncertainty.

The lack of realism of the pure rationality model was recognised in other ways as well (Cyert and March, 1963). Although decisions and actions may flow from bureaucratic rules and precedent for most of the time, there are numerous occasions on which objectives and interests conflict. Which objectives are pursued will then depend on what the most powerful coalition of managers wants so that strategising becomes a political process.

The above paragraphs indicate how and why bounded-rationality/bureaucratic modes of deciding explain how managers actually strategise. However, like pure technical rationality, bounded rationality is still about solving problems, even though they may not be as clearly framed. The processes described are still step-by-step or algorithmic procedures, differing from those of technical rationality only in that they are routinised or heuristic – that is, involving rules of thumb to interpret and proceed by trial and error. An organisation is still seen as searching for satisfactory attainment of known objectives according to known criteria for success and failure.

What the bounded-rationality/bureaucratic explanations do is recognise economic constraints and take a more complicated view of human cognition; they recognise the limitations of human brain processing capacity. There is also some recognition of managing as problematic because of the need to interpret facts through some frame of reference. However, since this view of decision-making assumes that the outcomes of different possible action options are roughly known, it provides an explanation that is useful only in rather restrictive conditions.

7.3 Rational process and its critics: trial-and-error action

The previous section has described how one response to the problems identified with thinking about decision-making as technically rational is to say that decision-making in practice is a form of trial and error. For some this process amounts to a form of muddling through, while for others it does have a logic to it.

Muddling through, organised anarchy and garbage-can decision-making

Lindblom (1959) describes the process of strategic decision-making as incremental, taking the form of 'muddling through'. His observations are derived from decision-making in state sector organisations, but they are relevant to private sector organisations too. Since it is not possible, in complex situations, to identify all the objectives of different groups of people affected by an issue, policies are chosen directly. Instead of working from a statement of desired ends to the means required to achieve them, managers choose the ends and the means simultaneously. In other words, two different managers may choose the same policy or solution for different reasons.

This means that a policy cannot be judged according to how well it achieves a given end. Instead it is judged according to whether it is desirable in itself or not. A good policy is thus simply one that gets widespread support. It is then carried out in incremental stages, preserving flexibility to change it as conditions change. The policy is pursued in stages of successive limited comparisons. In this approach, dramatically new policies are not considered. New policies have to be close to existing ones and limited comparisons are made, making it unnecessary to undertake fundamental enquiries. The procedure also involves ignoring important possible consequences of policies – a necessary evil, perhaps, if anything is to be done. But serious lasting mistakes can be avoided because the changes are being made in small steps.

Cohen et al. (1972) have carried this kind of analysis of state sector organisations further. In their research, they found that universities and some state bodies were characterised by widely distributed power and complex, unclear hierarchical structures. The hierarchical structure was such that just about any issue could be taken to just about any forum, by just about anyone. According to Cohen *et al.*, these institutions were noted for widespread participation in decision-making, for ambiguous and intersecting job definitions, and a lack of shared cultural values across the whole organisation. Such organisations face high levels of uncertainty not only, or even primarily, because their environments are changing but because of the uncertainty of their technology. It is far from certain what good teaching is, for example, or what good medical care is. Such organisations, therefore, have to be collections of relatively free professionals, constituting what they called an 'organised anarchy' where decisions and their outcomes occurred largely by chance. The flow of choices over time was erratic and haphazard. There was a continuing flow of problems, opportunities, solutions and choices coming together in a largely haphazard manner. Choice was determined largely by chance, depending entirely upon the context in which it is attended to; the level of attention paid to it in the light of all the other issues; who was present and participated; how they participated and how others interpreted that participation. Looking back over this 'garbage can' mode of deciding, it will not be possible to say that the choice occurred because some individual or group intended it. In this sense, intention or purpose is lacking in the choice process. There is no overall rhythm to the process and the specific sequence of choices is random and without any pattern. The sequence of specific choices can shoot just anywhere because important constraints provided by unequal power, clear hierarchies and job descriptions have been removed. Action is then the result of habit, custom or the unpredictable influence of others. It is impossible to predict the choice without knowing all the small details of the context. Intention is lost in the flow of events and goals are the product of sense-making activities after the event.

What they are talking about here is *emergence*, but they ascribe it entirely to chance and assume that clear hierarchy, clear roles and clear tasks would prevent decisions 'just emerging'. When emergence is referred to in the organisational literature, it is frequently equated with the kind or organised anarchy presented by Lindblom and others: that is, as decision-making without intention where outcomes arise by chance. This view will be critically examined in Chapter 12, particularly the taken-for-granted view of emergence as chance and so the opposite of intention. Note how this description of collegial processes of decision-making reflects a particular ideology in which orderly rationality is implicitly valued while messier, more participative approaches are denigrated even though they may be regarded as necessary. However, in the public sector over recent decades this ideology has been completely countermanded by managerialism.

The search for error

Others took a less damning view of processes of trial and error. For example, Collingridge (1980) argued that effective decision-making in conditions of ambiguity and uncertainty amounted to a search for error and a willingness to respond to its discovery. Instead of searching for the right decision as you would when using a technically rational mode, you need to choose an option that can most easily be found to be in error, error that can most easily be corrected. In this way fewer options are closed off; you get more opportunities to adjust what you have done when the circumstances change.

For example, if you can forecast future electricity demand reliably, the right solution to increased demand may be to build one large power station now. If, however, the future demand for electricity is highly uncertain, it would be better to build a number of small power stations, spread over a few years. That way you will find it easier to check for error in your forecast of future demand and easier to correct for mistakes. You may only have to close a small power station instead of running a large one at low capacity.

This kind of approach requires a considerable psychological adjustment. Most of us are used to being judged on whether we made the right choice. If it turns out to be wrong we devote much energy to concealing this fact, or in justifying our original decision. Applying technical rationality in conditions of great uncertainty leads us intentionally to avoid the search for error and to delay its recognition. If we abandoned technical rationality in these circumstances and searched for error instead, we would have to admit mistakes as soon as possible and avoid trying to justify them. Here we are talking about a mature recognition that being wrong is a valuable learning exercise, and this is a very difficult proposition in modern organisations.

Trial and error – logical incrementalism

Quinn (1978, 1980) argued that there was a degree of logic to trial-and-error processes. His research into the decision-making process of a number of companies revealed that most strategic decisions are made outside formal planning systems, that is, outside the bounded-rationality mode of decision-making. He found that managers purposely blend behavioural, political and formal analytical processes together to improve the quality of decisions and implementation. Effective managers accept the high level of uncertainty and ambiguity they have to face and do not plan everything. They preserve the flexibility of an organisation to deal with the unforeseen as it happens. The key points that Quinn made about the strategic decision-making processes are as follows:

- Effective managers do not manage strategically in a piecemeal manner. They have a clear view on what they are trying to achieve, where they are trying to take the business. The destination is thus intended.

- But the route to that destination, the strategy itself, is not intended from the start in any comprehensive way. Effective managers know that the environment they have to operate in is uncertain and ambiguous. They therefore sustain flexibility by holding open the method of reaching the goal.

- The strategy itself then *emerges* from the interaction between different groupings of people in the organisation, and different groupings with different amounts of power, different requirements for and access to information, different time spans and parochial interests. These different pressures are orchestrated by senior managers. The top management level is always reassessing, integrating and organising.

- The strategy emerges or evolves in small incremental, opportunistic steps. But such evolution is not piecemeal or haphazard because of the agreed purpose and the role of top management in reassessing what is happening. It is this that provides the logic in the incremental action.

- The result is an organisation that is feeling its way to a known goal, opportunistically learning as it goes.

In Quinn's model of the strategy process, the organisation is driven by a central intention with respect to the goal, but there is no prior central intention as to how that goal is to be achieved; the route to the goal is discovered through a logical process of taking one small step at a time. In logical incrementalism, overall strategy emerges from step-by-step, trial-and-error actions occurring in a number of different places in an organisation; for example, some may be making an acquisition while others are restructuring the reporting structure. These separate initiatives are pushed by champions, each attacking a class of strategic issue. The top executives manage the process, orchestrating it and sustaining some logic in it. It is this that makes it a purposeful, proactive technique. Urgent, interim, piecemeal decisions shape the organisation's future, but they do so in an orderly logical way. No one fully understands all the implications of what they are all doing together, but they are consciously preparing to move opportunistically.

Quinn (1978) illustrates his concept of strategies being developed through a process of logical incrementalism as follows:

> When Exxon began its regional decentralization on a worldwide basis, the Executive Committee placed a senior officer and board member with a very responsive management style in a vaguely defined 'coordinative role' vis-à-vis its powerful and successful European units. Over a period of two years this man sensed problems and experimented with voluntary coordinative possibilities on a pan-European basis. Only later, with greater understanding by both corporate and divisional officers, did Exxon move to a more formal line relationship for what became Exxon Europe. Even then the move had to be coordinated in other areas of the world. All of these changes together led to an entirely new power balance toward regional and non-US concerns and to a more responsive worldwide posture for Exxon.   (Quinn, 1978, p. 10)

Processes of innovation

In more modern studies of the strategy process, this interest in trial-and-error decision-making continues. For example, Dougherty (1992) studied the *processes of innovation* arguing that they are processes of creating and exploiting knowledge, which involve exploration, research, strategic scouting, and the advice of a council of elders. It is these processes that link technological opportunities and markets. Garud and Van de Ven (1992) studied processes of trial and error in product innovation in one organisation over a period of twelve years and argued that, when ambiguity is high and resources are slack, managers avoid trial and error and simply carry on with their strategy even if it is producing negative outcomes. Here they are pointing to how organisations often lose the capacity to change and remain stuck in a strategy that once served them well but no longer does so. However, when ambiguity is low and there is little slack in resources, managers engage in processes of trial and error and so develop new strategies for their organisations.

7.4 A contingency view of process

In taking account of how uncertainty impacts on decision-making processes, a number of authors have related the appropriate decision-making processes to the context in which the decision has to be made. The process then becomes contingent on the situation. For example, Thompson and Tuden (1959) related the mode of decision-making to combinations of degree of clarity in causal relationships and the degree of agreement on objectives. Where causal connections are clear and objectives shared, the conditions are said to exist for managers to take decisions in a rational–logical way. As they move away from these conditions it is thought that it becomes impossible to apply rational logic and so they have to use some other approach. Thus, when causal connections are clear but managers conflict, then the decision has to be made in a political manner – those with the greatest power will prevail. The decision-making process here will be one in which managers build coalitions (Child, 1972, 1984; Cyert and March, 1963; Pfeffer, 1981). When managers are agreed on what they should be trying to achieve but the causal connections make it unclear how to do so, then they will have to use judgement and intuition. They will have to reason by analogy; they will have to think laterally and use trial-and-error, decision-making processes. The most difficult situation is where causality is unclear and objectives conflict. Here managers will have to decide in a way that combines intuitive individual judgements with political interactions in a group.

Perrow (1972) makes much the same point in suggesting a spectrum of problem-solving procedures with the analytic with its logical prearranged steps or rules at one end, while at the other end unique methods of solving a problem had to be created because the problem situations were unanalysable or unprogrammable. Problem-solving situations with few exceptions and thus little variability call for the analytic approach, but situations with many exceptions call for different, unique responses.

What emerges from these analyses of decision situation and appropriate decision-making mode is this: making a decision in a technical/bounded rational manner is only a possibility in the most restrictive of conditions. It will not be possible in conditions of disagreement, ambiguity and uncertainty where decision-making has to involve routines, judgements and politics and it is quite possible that organisations will show very little capacity for change. The implicit assumption throughout the work presented in this section is that managers are able to identify archetypal, typical situations and then rationally select appropriate processes, almost like tools, to use in making decisions. This is classic thought before action. It is common to present these theories of decision-making using Cartesian diagrams with the implication that process can be moved around. One process then is assumed to be required to move around or change another process – Chapter 12 will take up this issue of the doubling of process. It will also be argued in Chapter 12 that the thinking in this section takes a 'both . . . and' form, which eliminates paradox (*see* Chapters 2 and 3). The writers in this section present a manager as being in control of the decision-making mode to be employed.

Now consider in more detail the political and routinised forms that decision-making in organisations may take.

7.5 Institutions, routines and cognitive frames

The literature on what has come to be known as *strategy process research* (which includes the writers already described in this chapter) pays particular attention to the internal dynamics of organisations and their internal politics, thereby humanising the strategy process to some extent. More recently, the process view has been linked (Chakravarthy and Doz, 1992) to the resource-based view (*see* Chapter 4), which emphasises the importance of resources and competences, including practices and procedures, in determining competitive advantage. There is also a link to sociology (DiMaggio and Powell, 1991; Tolbert and Zucker, 1996), which is concerned with the behaviour of organisations as entities seeking legitimacy rather than competitive advantage. This link has come to be known as 'institutional theory' in which organisations are understood in terms of routines, norms, rules and processes of institutionalisation. This approach will be discussed in Chapter 9.

Other writers in the strategy process tradition emphasise the frame of reference of managers. In doing this, the understanding of the limitations of technical rationality as strategy process is expanded. The notion of bounded rationality sees decision-making as being mainly limited by the scarcity of time, resources and brain-processing capacity. However, it is not just the capacity of the human brain that is relevant here, because the way in which strategists think has the effect of filtering attention – managers only notice features and issues that their frame of reference, mental model or mental map predisposes them to notice. This point was made in Chapter 5 on the learning organisations. What might be called the *interpretive view*, therefore, takes cognitive limitations further to look at the limitations imposed by historically evolved ways of understanding and sense making. As mentioned in Chapter 5, Weick ([1969] 1979) argued that how managers scan and interpret their environment affects an organisation's strategic actions. Barr *et al.* (1992) explored the *process of managerial cognition* by comparing changes in the cognitive maps of top management over a 25-year period in a number of railway companies and related these to performance. They concluded that survivor companies were characterised by processes of continuous first- and second-order change (single and double-loop learning) in the cognitive maps of top managers. When top managers make timely adjustments to their mental models, they are able to make linkages between environmental change and corporate strategy and then organisational renewal is possible. Ginsberg and Venkatraman (1992) studied the *process of managerial interpretations* of technological innovations in 291 organisations and concluded that interpretations play a role in initiating strategic change while existing competitive posture influenced the implementation. Huff *et al.* (1992) explored the processes of inertia and stress in organisations using a simulation model and concluded that it is the initial level of inertia and stress rather than the external characteristics of stressors which influence strategic change.

Cognitive limitations, therefore, can lead to strategic drift. Here managers resist changes that conflict with their predominant way of understanding their organisation and its environment, until some crisis makes it impossible to continue doing so (Greiner, 1972; Johnson, 1987; Miller and Friesen, 1980; Mintzberg, 1989; Tushman and Romanelli, 1985). Before that, an organisation is driven down the same path by its own momentum, becoming more and more out of line with its environment. This gives rise to strategic drift. In other words, managers are caught in a fixed way of thinking. When that drift has taken an organisation too far from its environment, it then makes sudden revolutionary adjustments, rather than the incremental change Quinn talked about (see earlier in this chapter). These inevitably involve breaking the old frames its managers were working within and establishing new ones.

In his research into what managers actually do, Mintzberg (1973, 1998) challenged what he called the folklore of managerial activity:

- Instead of being reflective, systematic planners, managers work at an unrelenting pace, moving rapidly from one task to another.

- Instead of having no regular duties to perform because these are delegated, leaving room for planning, managers have to perform regular duties including rituals, ceremonies and negotiations.

- Instead of using aggregated information provided by formal management information systems, managers favour verbal communication and direct contact with people.

- Instead of being scientists, managers rely on judgement and intuition.

Mintzberg (1987) talks about strategy as an activity of crafting and argues that strategies arise from the grass roots wherever people have the capacity to learn and the resources to support this. He talks about umbrella strategy where senior managers deliberately provide broad guidelines and deliberately leave others to interpret and act upon them so that the strategy emerges in its specifics. He talks about the strategy being *deliberately emergent*. He also says that process strategy is deliberately emergent in that senior mangers deliberately control the process of strategy formation but leave the content to others. Sometimes, emergent strategies need to be uprooted while those that prove useful can be made deliberate and incorporated into formal strategy. Notice here how the process of emergence is thought to be one over which managers can exert some degree of control. A different view of emergence will be provided in Chapter 12.

An early expression of how politics, routines and cognitive limitations impact on strategy process is to be found in the work of Mintzberg. Mintzberg *et al.* (1976) analysed 25 decision-making processes situations characterised by novelty, complexity and open-endedness and concluded that a final choice was made in such situations only after lengthy periods that involved many difficult discontinuous and recursive steps. The need to make a decision is identified or prompted by signals from the environment or from the working of the organisation. The stimulus for a decision may be the voluntary recognition of a problem or an opportunity, or the result of some pressure or mild crisis, or the consequence of a major crisis that forces a decision. Many small stimuli may need to build up to some threshold before a decision need is identified and a decision triggered. However, if the stimuli for a decision fall outside the currently shared wisdom on what the business is about and how it should be conducted, then managers will ignore the stimuli. It will probably require a crisis to force a decision. Where managers identify a problem to which there is no clear solution there will be a tendency to ignore it. Problems for which there are matching solutions will tend to be dealt with. Note how the routine for recognising a problem depends upon the behaviour of individuals, is culturally conditioned, and involves political interaction. Once managers have recognised a problem, the diagnosis routine is activated. Old information channels are tapped and new ones opened. The diagnosis may be formal or it may be very informal. It may be skipped altogether. What managers are said to be doing here is trying to shape or structure the problems so that they may decide how to deal with them. The development stage involves search routines and design routines. The search routine is an attempt to discover a ready-made solution. These routines include simply waiting for an alternative to materialise, searching the memory of the organisation – that is, the solutions to problems that have worked before – scanning alternatives, hiring consultants and so on. Search is a step-by-step or incremental process beginning with the easiest search routine. The design routine consists of the steps taken to design a solution to the problem. Selection is often intertwined with the development stage and involves the routines of screening, evaluative choice and authorisation. The screen routine is used to screen out options that are clearly not viable. It is a superficial routine. The evaluation choice routine was not found to be one that involved the use of analytical techniques. The evaluation criteria were normally based on judgement and intuition. Managers dealt with information overload by using precedent, imitation or tradition. They made judgements on a proposal according to the reliability of the proposer rather than the project, on the track record of the manager. The final routine is that of authorisation and legitimation of the choices that individuals and groups have made.

The decision-making process identified here is a number of routines that have behavioural, political and learning aspects. The routines are affected by interruptions caused by environmental factors, by scheduling and timing delays as well as speed-ups generated by those involved in the process, by feedback delays as people wait for information and authorisation, and by cycling back to earlier stages in the process.

The writers in this section reflect a trend over the past few decades in which simplistic views of strategic choice and organisational learning are problematised, so challenging taken-for-granted views of managers being 'in control'. They point to how routinised strategising tends to become, so trapping managers into repetition leading to strategic drift. These views bring in the importance of interpretation and politics, judgement and evaluation. They continue, however, to present processes of decision-making in stages or phases and they also continue to sustain an ideology of being 'in control' despite implying how difficult this is.

7.6 Process and time

So far, this chapter has reviewed some key writings focusing on the strategy process where process refers mainly to the *cognitive activities of managers and the decision-making techniques* involved in formulating and implementing strategy. Process, however, always involves time in that it is concerned with sequences of changing events, that is, with history. I want to refer to two ways in which time is reflected in mainstream theory: namely, time as life cycle and time as linear from the past through the present to the future.

An example of the life-cycle theory of time is provided by the work of Greiner (1972) who presented a model of the life stages of an organisation in which the stages change in an incremental rather than a revolutionary way. He held that if companies are to sustain acceptable levels of performance then they must pass through five phases of growth, each of which is punctuated by a crisis. These phases and their related crises are as follows:

1. *Growth through creativity.* In the early stages of its life, when it has simple structures and is small, a company grows through the creative activity of small close-knit teams. At some point, however, the company faces the crisis of leadership. As the company increases in size it can no longer be managed in highly personal, informal ways.

2. *Growth through direction.* If the leadership crisis is successfully resolved through 'professionalising' the management, specialising its functions and setting up more formal systems, the company proceeds to grow in a centrally directed way. This leads to the crisis of autonomy. As the organisation gets bigger and bigger, employees feel restricted by the hierarchy and the top finds it more and more difficult to maintain detailed control.

3. *Growth through delegation.* If the autonomy crisis is successfully resolved through changing formal structures and decentralising, then growth proceeds through delegation. This brings with it a crisis of control. The top feels it is losing control and parochial attitudes develop in the divisions of the company.

4. *Growth through co-ordination.* If the control crisis is successfully resolved through installing systems to bring about greater co-ordination and co-operation, then the growth of the company proceeds. As it grows larger and more complex it is brought to the crisis of red tape. Increasingly bureaucratic controls create sharp divisions between head office staffs and operating divisions.

5. *Growth through collaboration.* Here the crisis of red tape is resolved through strong interpersonal collaboration and control through cultural sharing rather than formal controls. Greiner thinks that this growth stage may lead to a crisis of psychological saturation in which all become exhausted by teamwork. He thinks there may be a sixth growth phase involving a dual organisation: a 'habit' structure for daily work routines and a 'reflective' structure for stimulating new perspectives and personal enrichment.

Life-cycle theories point to the institutional rules or programmes that require development to proceed in the prescribed sequence. Note how the resolution of each crisis is itself a strategic choice made by individuals and how Greiner describes the resolution to each crisis in terms of more and more elaborate cybernetic systems. Life-cycle theory clearly assumes that the developing entity contains within it an underlying logic, programme or code that regulates the process of change and moves from a given origin to a mature stage. This theory, therefore, is an expression of Kantian systems thinking where the causality is formative (*see* Chapter 3). Time here is thought of in terms of a linear sequence with a clear beginning in an embryonic state proceeding step by step into the future to an already given end state. The present does not feature in any important way.

In models of planning and goal setting it is assumed that through a rational understanding of the past, autonomous individuals are able to choose a future and move to that future by taking step-by-step actions. There is a linear movement from the past to the future in which the present is simply a point separating the future from the past.

I will be referring back to the linear theories to time implicit in systemic views of organisations and their strategies when I come to an alternative understanding of process in Chapter 12.

7.7 Strategy process: a review

In reviewing the development of the process view of strategy so far described in this chapter, Chakravarthy and Doz (1992) argue that it is concerned with

> how managers can continuously influence the quality of the firm's strategic position through the use of appropriate decision processes and administrative systems. By the term administrative systems we mean the organizational structure, planning, control, incentives, human resource management, and value systems of a firm. The strategy process research subfield is concerned with how effective strategies are shaped within the firm and then validated and implemented efficiently. Moreover, the strategies of a firm must change in keeping with both new opportunities and threats in its environment and changes in its own competencies and strategic intent. The strategy process within a firm influences such adaptation and self-renewal. (p. 5)

The process subfield is thus distinct from the content subfield in that the latter focuses exclusively on *what* strategic positions lead to optimal performance. Both are interested in improving performance but the emphasis is different. While content research is concerned with the rationally chosen interaction of an organisation with its environment, the process subfield is concerned with interactions between people and groups of them within an organisation where that interaction could be rational, boundedly rational or even irrational. Process research is concerned with *how* an organisation achieves, maintains and modifies effective relationships between administrative systems and decision process, on the one hand, and competitive/resource positions, on the other hand. For example, Rajagopalan and Finkelstein (1992) explore the conditions under which an organisation's reward systems change and the linkages between such systems and strategic orientation. Floyd and Wooldridge (1992) researched the process of management involvement in the strategy process.

In commenting on the above quote from Chakravarthy and Doz, Schendel (1992) says that, since processes inevitably affect performance, there is an indirect causal connection so that both content and process researchers are interested in causal linkages to performance. He goes on to make the following points. The process researchers explore how effective strategies are shaped, validated and implemented where these are seen as separate activities. Shaping has to do with finding strategy and implementing has to do with using strategy – that is, with developing the administrative activities necessary to use strategy. Shaping need not engage the whole organisation but implementing does. However, some process researchers do not regard shaping and implementing as separate activities. Schendel argues that they then have to argue that strategy *merely emerges* from collective, random action in the everyday activities of an organisation. Schendel holds that this creates a problem of validation in that the only test of a particular strategy is its use – an essentially *ex post* view. He then says that without an *ex ante* prediction to be tested by *ex post* results there is no role for the management of strategy and no opportunity for the accumulation of knowledge. This is why process must include the validation step involving prediction in terms of what is expected to work. Validation of strategy found is thus essentially concerned with content. So, content and process can never be separated. The challenge is to select and use winning administrative processes to shape and use strategy to gain winning positions. He rejects any alternative as meaning that winning positions depend simply on luck.

Schendel's argument is based on the notion that thought comes before action. He also understands emergence purely in terms of chance. I mention these points here because they are commonly held views that will be critiqued from an alternative perspective on process to be developed in Chapter 12.

I want now to turn to more recent developments in researching the strategy process known as the activity-based view.

7.8 The activity-based view

In a special edition of the *Journal of Management Studies*, Johnson *et al.* (2003) argue that the process literature reviewed in previous sections of this chapter has defined process in terms of systems and processes of organisational wholes, which does not encourage probing into what goes on inside these wholes as practical activity and tools. In other words, the process literature takes a macro view of the organisation as a whole at the expense of the practical activity of the people involved. It follows that this literature does not pay much attention to managerial agency, tending to exaggerate its possibilities, on the one hand, and to place insufficient emphasis on how managers may become trapped in belief systems, on the other. Johnson *et al.* also say that the process literature has tended to be prescriptive, focusing on the overarching design of strategy and decision-making processes, but remote from what managers actually do. In addition, it sets up too sharp a dichotomy between content and process and lacks specific links between process and strategy outcome. Johnson *et al.* also question whether process research really helps managers in their strategising activities, such as how to run a strategy meeting. They call for a shift in the strategy debate towards a micro perspective, and by this they mean an emphasis on the detailed processes and practices of the day-to-day micro activities of organisational life that have to do with strategy. For them, practice is what goes on inside the process.

Whittington

In taking up such a challenge, Whittington (2002a) focuses on the formal activities of strategising rather than the informal processes that produce the emerging outcomes that Mintzberg has emphasised. The formal work of strategising encompasses data gathering and analysis, preparation of documents and presentations, project meetings, board meetings, conferences, workshops and away-days. It is performed by senior and middle managers, strategic planners, organisational development experts, management consultants, communication specialists, lawyers and investment bankers. Whittington distinguishes this work of formulation from that of implementation. He is concerned with where and how the work of strategising, both formulation and implementation, is done, who does it, what skills are required and how they are acquired, what the tools and techniques are, how the work itself is organised and how the products of this work are communicated and consumed. He argues that his interests are in tune with the interest in practice and communities of practice (*see* Chapter 5) in the literature (Brown and Duguid, 2001). For Whittington, practice has to do with the skills that people exercise in making do with the resources they have in their everyday lives and how this means focusing on people, their routines and their situated activities rather than abstract processes. The concern is with the local effectiveness of people and only indirectly with the performance of organisations as wholes. He is interested in the ability to enter strategic conversations and his practice perspective emphasises the creative improvisatory nature of the production and consumption of strategy.

Whittington (2002b) defines strategy content as the relationship between strategic choices and performance and strategy process as the activity in which strategies are formed and implemented (Rumelt *et al.*, 1994). He proposes an integrated model of strategic practice, consisting of three aspects, to complement the process and contents perspectives:

1. Strategy praxis (work), which is what strategisers actually do in a specific situation as distinct from general practices (*see* 3 below).

2. Strategy practitioners (workers), who participate in many activities, the praxis, and in doing so draw on a set of established general strategy practices (*see* 3 below).

3. General strategy practices (tools), which consist of what is done legitimately and what is done in a well-practised way through repeated doing. Practices refer to the social heritage of traditions, norms, rules and routines of a community, thought of as tools.

Whittington argues that there are those in the process perspective who emphasise strategy systems and decision processes in a fairly static sense (Chakravarthy and Doz, 1992) and those who emphasise change over time (Langley, 1999; Pettigrew, 1992; Van de Ven, 1992). For all of these writers, the analytical unit is the firm leading to a concern with the source of competitive advantage and performance in terms of superior financial outcomes. The practice perspective, however, is concerned with the relative diffusion of various technologies for doing strategy, focusing on practices: that is, tools. The question of performance has to do with a particular practice that performs well in terms of diffusion.

Salvato

Another writer in this field, Salvato (2003), starts with evolutionary models, developed by *economists*, in which organisations are understood to be collections of routines that are recombined in various ways over time (Nelson and Winter, 1982), so generating the variances upon which evolution depends. Some of these new combinations are selected, so providing new strategic configurations. This process of recombining routines provides the link between the micro and the macro. Salvato suggests that individual skills, rules of thumb, best practices and resources, as well as routines, are also drivers of strategic evolution. His main critique of evolutionary theory to date is that it lacks guidance on the interplay between managerial agency and organisational and environmental structure. To address this he proposes a *micro-sociological* account of strategic evolution in which strategic evolution is generated by *intentional* recombinations of what he calls 'core micro-strategies' with new resources and organisational routines. A core micro-strategy is an established *system* of interconnected routines, micro-activities and resources that characterise most of the organisation's strategic initiatives.

This model focuses attention on the importance of managerial leadership, micro-level processes and the resource base. He points to a tension between coherent organisational-level strategy (the *whole*) and the many fragmented activities (the *parts*) to be found in daily organisational life. When the whole is emphasised it becomes difficult to implement strategies in daily activities, but when the parts are emphasised people engage in the generation of variance in micro terms to the exclusion of higher-meaning processes, and so the organisation tends to drift. Salvato attaches central importance to the maintenance of balance between micro- and macro-activities. He also attaches great importance to managerial agency in guiding evolution. It is top management that continually recombines core micro-strategies in a process he calls the 'evolutionary engineering of knowledge'. Here he differs from the earlier evolutionary models, which attach little importance to managerial agency. For Salvato, managers can shape and engineer micro-strategies. While the building blocks of core strategies emerge from the routinisation of micro-activities across an organisation, the gradual recognition of an emerging meta-project by top managers allows them to formalise its emergence, for example through appointing project managers and organising workshops.

Regner

Regner (2003) argues that strategy process research has shown that the strategy literature provides broad descriptions of aggregates involved in strategy making such as culture, politics and individual cognitive processes. In doing so it makes clear that strategy making involves a variety of actors and contextual influences. However, it provides only an imperfect understanding of particular situations, because it does not pay attention to the micro level, particularly the practices of the actors involved. Although there is some writing on micro-politics, routines and interpretation modes, the practices of managers are usually described in vague terms such as artistic, creative, intuitive and crafting. Regner proposes the study of different categories of strategic activities in terms of their direction and the balance between exploration and exploitation. Regner is concerned with how managers inform themselves about strategies and how they make sense of them in terms of cognitive knowledge structures. This involves exploring the linkages between activity, understanding and strategic outcome.

Regner distinguishes strategy making at the centre of an organisation from that at the periphery. Strategy-making processes at the centre tend to be deductive, with a focus on industry levels and exploitation activities such as planning, analysis and standard routines. However, strategy making at the periphery tends to be inductive, with exploration activities such as trial-and-error, experiments, informal noticing and heuristic approaches. Regner's empirical work showed that strategies emerging in the periphery tended to be imprecise, vague and undefined in conditions of great uncertainty. Here strategies are impelled forward, often in secret, as the periphery tries to keep the centre away. They rely on knowledge rather than reports and forecasts and their activities are characterised by explorative enquiry. In the centre, however, activities are based on exploitation rather than exploration and tend to be confined to the existing organisation and industry. They rely on inference from history and emphasise the current knowledge structure.

Other writers

Jarzabkowski (2003) draws on activity theory according to which strategy *emerges* in the interaction of four components: the collective structures of an organisation; the primary actors, often equated with the top management team; the practical activities by means of which the actors interact; and strategic practices through which the interaction is conducted. She focuses on the formal practices of direction setting, resource allocation, monitoring and control. Such practices may distribute shared interpretations, so contributing to continuity, or they may mediate between contested interpretations leading to reinterpretation and change. She is therefore making a distinction between practice and practices, where the former is the *pattern of interaction* and interpretation *from which strategic activity emerges* over time (which is what Whittington calls 'praxis'), and the latter is habits, artefacts and socially defined modes of strategic activity through which strategic activity is constructed (which is what Whittington also calls 'practices'). Practices are the infrastructure generating the strategic activity which is practice (praxis). She seeks to explain continuity and change at the *activity system level* by focusing attention on practical activity. She draws on Vygotsky (1978) to argue that psychological development is a process of social interaction in particular historical and cultural contexts. Individuals attribute meaning to their own and others' actions through the interpretive interaction which enables them to engage in shared activity, which is practical because it is engaged in with an outcome in mind. She defines the context of such activity as an activity system, indeed the organisation is an activity system in which the components are actors, organisational structures (history, culture) and practical activities.

Maitlis and Lawrence (2003) argue that organisational strategising results from the interplay of organisational discourse and organisational politics and that there are certain forms of these that lead to strategic failure. They seek to understand the specific episodes of strategising, which they see as having four elements: an episode begins with the politics of taking a position in response to a specific strategic issue; then organisational members define a call of solutions; then the politics of assigning responsibility and accountability follow in which a specific instance of the general concept is developed; and the episode ends with the discursive construction of the strategic object, a specific strategy.

Brundin and Melin (2003) argue that the individual is central to the microactivities of strategising but that individuals are essentially interactive when it comes to strategy and that emotions are highly important in such interaction. Brundin (2002) holds that emotions are socially constructed in relationships and that they evolve in institutional and organisational contexts. As such, emotions are important in all organisational operations including the activities of strategising. Emotions are important in processes of change as is the organisational ability to acknowledge, recognise, monitor, discriminate and attend to emotions. The ways in which emotions are expressed and communicated by strategic leaders will affect the evolution of strategy.

Samra-Fredericks (2003) focuses attention on the practices of strategists and how they do social and political life through talking as an essentially relational–rhetorical process (Shotter, 1993). Samra-Fredericks observes and records the talk-based interaction of strategists, including the way they express emotions and speak of morals in lived experience. She draws on ethnomethodology and conversation analysis to highlight the linguistic skills of strategists. In such activity they build a shared definition of the future. It is in language that strategists establish a 'discourse of direction'. Her research points to how the effective strategist is one with the skills of persuading others in a community to take his or her own view of the past and the future as the basis of making decisions. This is accomplished in the skilful use of metaphor and the ability to articulate complex and tacit forms of knowledge. Language is taken as the dominant symbolic system for the accomplishment of social reality. She is concerned with showing how the micro, as human interaction, is linked to the macro, as social structure. She describes how this is done in conversation using rhetorical devices. The appropriate display of emotion is a key tacit resource in persuading others. In such processes, people's identities are invoked and contested.

Having summarised the criticisms of the strategy process perspective made by writers in the activity-based view, and having described the approach of the latter, I now want to go on to explore the underlying assumptions of both perspectives.

7.9 The systemic way of thinking about process and practice

This section explores the way of thinking underlying the process and activity-based views of strategy. While they differ in terms of the level of analysis, with the process view focusing on the macro level and the activity-based view focusing on the micro level, in my view they both reflect the same underlying way of thinking in that they both take a systemic perspective on process and practice. They are systemic in that they are concerned with what processes or activities produce a better whole or are diffused more effectively through the whole. In their interaction with each other, members of an organisation are assumed to be using processes, practices and activities, together thought of as an integrated system, to produce the position of an organisation, where the organisations is also thought of as a system. Consider, first, how the notion of process is presented in the process view.

Macro view of process

In the process view, process is taken to be specific categories of managerial action, namely, decision-making techniques/procedures and administrative systems. These may be formal, such as the approved planning and policy-making activities that produce deliberate strategies, or they may be informal, such as the political activities managers engage in, which are said to produce emergent strategies. Section 7.5 above gave further examples of the kind of processes writers in this tradition refer to: managerial cognition, interpretation and judgement; emotions of stress and inertia; innovation and the creating and exploiting of opportunities involved in this; reward systems; and management involvement. The process view seeks to explain *how managers use* processes such as these to adapt their organisation to its environment. There is a difference of view, however, as to how the decision-making techniques and administrative systems come about in the first place. Most writers in this field hold the view that the administrative systems and decision techniques are deliberately designed by managers, or at least that it is possible to do so if managers so choose, and this extends even to their own cognitive frameworks. Other writers argue that at least some of the systems and techniques emerge in the ongoing activity of managers and, by and large, they take this to mean that those systems and techniques evolve largely through chance, as in garbage-can decision-making and the evolutionary school. Alternatively, Mintzberg sees strategy and processes as deliberately emergent: that is, managers allow emergence to occur. However, emergent and deliberate are usually seen as polar opposites although they may be layered on to each other in the view of some, amounting to a doubling of process. From the deliberate perspective, design is a process being used to form processes of decision-making and administration, even of emergence. Of course, processes of designing processes of decision-making would themselves have to be designed, which is an even higher-level process, suggesting an infinite regress of processes. From the evolutionary perspective, evolution is a process producing chance variations in processes of decision-making which are subjected to another process: competitive selection.

Those taking the evolutionary or emergent perspectives naturally also hold the view that strategies emerge in what, for some, amounts to a form of muddling through, as in Lindblom's writing, or a form of garbage-can decision-making in the writing of Cohen *et al.* (1972). Many find this a 'no hope' situation because it excludes the possibility of managerial agency and influence. Those taking the deliberate design perspective say that managers *use* the administrative systems and decision-making techniques they have designed to shape, validate and implement strategies. The activity of shaping is the finding of strategies, validating is the activity of predicting what shaping and using will work, and implementing is the activity of using the strategy through developing administrative systems, for example. It is in using the strategy in this way that the organisation is adapted to its environment and renewed in what amounts to a life cycle, designed evolution or deliberately chosen emergence.

There are three important points to note about the deliberate strategy process being suggested here. First there is a further layering of process on process. The designed administrative systems and decision-making techniques, which are processes, are used to shape, find, validate, predict and implement, all of which are themselves processes. Then the latter layer of process is used to adapt the organisation to its environment, and this adaptation is itself also a process. The second point to notice is the theory of time underlying this view of process. Time takes a linear form moving from the past through the present towards the future, with the present as a point separating the past from the future. Managers inherit decision-making techniques and administrative systems from the past and then predict what processes will work in the future as the basis of designing the processes in the present. This is a view of phases through time in which managers first shape or find, then select the best design and then implement so that the organisation is then adapted to the environment. The third point to note is how process is equated with system. Managers are designing and using systems to adapt and change the organisation, which is also understood to be a system operating in a supra-system, the environment. The parts of the process/system are designed to be integrated, to fit together to produce an effective whole.

Micro view of process

Next consider the micro- or activity-based view. Writers in this tradition are concerned with the practices and activities that go on *inside the process* understood as a whole. They, or at least some of them, are therefore making a distinction between process, practice and activity and declare their interest in exploring practice and activity. So, Whittington (2002b) defines practices as the social heritage of traditions, norms, rules and routines that managers draw upon and use as tools in their strategising activities (praxis), which encompass data gathering and analysis, preparation of documents and presentations, project meetings, board meetings, conferences, workshops and away-days. Jarzabkowski (2003) makes a similar distinction although using slightly different terminology. So, for her, strategic practices are the means through which management interaction is conducted, such as habits, artefacts and socially defined modes of strategic activity, which include direction setting, resource allocation, monitoring and control. Strategic practices are the infrastructure that generates strategic activity as in Whittington. Strategic activity, which Jarzabkowski calls *practice* as opposed to practices, is the pattern of interaction and interpretation from which strategies emerge. The practices these authors talk about are often defined as skills, routines, norms, rules and tools.

What I find striking is that all of these activities fall within the definition of process used in the process literature subfield, the difference being that process is viewed from a macro perspective in that subfield while the activity-based writers talk about process from a micro perspective. Do they then also layer process on process as the macro-process writers do?

To answer this question, consider the distinction between practices and activities (praxis). It seems to me that this distinction reflects, to some extent, Giddens' (1976, 1979, 1984) sociological theory of structuration. According to this theory, as individuals interact with each other, Whittington's activity (praxis) and Jarzabkowski's practice, they build up a fund of knowledge that is largely tacit and embodied in institutions as rules of conduct, social structures, procedures, routines and so on, which constitute practices. Institutions, social structures, or practices, embody the previous experience of a community of people and form the framework within which individual agents will make subsequent choices. Giddens refers to this as a duality of structure and agency in which, in their ongoing dealings with each other as agents – that is, in their activities or practice – individuals draw on the resources provided them in the form of social practices that evolve in their use. Here we do not get layers of process but one recursive process in which activity as process is drawing upon process as practice while sustaining and changing that practice. In

Giddens' theory there are no levels with individual action at one level, the micro, and social structure at another, the macro. Instead they are on one level at which they recursively form each other. However, the writers in the activity-based tradition reviewed above do not go as far as Giddens because they retain the micro–macro split. In effect, their notion of practice can be understood as micro processes while their notion of practices is the same as that of the macro process of the process school. There are, therefore, two layers of process in which the lower level draws on the higher level for tools. What the activity-based writers do is provide a link between the micro and the macro in that they together form the organisation understood as a system.

It is clear that the activity-based view falls firmly within systems thinking just as the process view does. Jarzabkowski (2003) wants to explain continuity and change at the activity system level and understands an organisation to be an activity system whose parts are collective structures, primary actors, practical activities and strategic practices. Strategic activity emerges in the interaction of the parts of the organisations. Salvato (2003) argues that organisations evolve through the intentional recombination by managers of what he calls core micro-strategies, which he defines as a system of interconnected routines, micro-activities and resources. He regards organisation-level strategy as the whole that exists in tension with the many fragmented activities, the parts, in organisations. He uses the concept of emergence but argues that top managers can formalise emerging projects by appointing project managers and organising workshops. What is striking, for me, in this activity-based literature is how intention and emergence are no longer polarised as they are in the process literature. Instead, evolution and emergence themselves become subject to intention. This involves layering a process of intentional design on top of a process of emergence. Given the systemic and deliberate nature of processes in the activity-based view, the implicit theory of time remains the linear one to be found in the process literature.

I am arguing, then, that the activity-based writers have not departed in any essential way from the understanding of process to be found in the process literature. If process is the 'how' of strategy then, since both groups of writers are describing how strategy is done, they are both talking about process. Both are systems in which process basically means the interaction of parts to produce wholes. Both have the same view of time. Both make the psychological assumptions of cognitivism in which the individual is the primary unit with a mind inside and society outside.

However, in focusing attention on the local, daily, practical activities of managers, the activity-based writers bring a much richer perspective on process. Some of the writers focus attention on emotion (Brundin and Melin, 2003), and discourse and politics (Maitlis and Lawrence, 2003) as well as conversation (Whittington, 2002a). They draw attention to the detail of rhetorical skills of effective strategists (Samra-Fredericks, 2003) and the creative, improvisatory nature of daily managerial activity. The moral aspects of strategising and the connection with identity are also brought out (Samra-Fredericks, 2003). These are all aspects of managerial life that are central to the perspective to be presented in Part 3 of this book.

There are two other points to note about the systemic view of practice. The first has to do with causality. In the deliberate view of process, whether it is considered to be micro or macro, there is the same duality as in all the other systems theories so far considered in this book. There is the formative causality of the system itself and the rationalist causality of the individuals who design it. The theory of causality is different in the evolutionary process view where we might call the causality adaptionist in that what drives the evolution is adaptation of chance variations to the environment.

The second point I want to draw attention to is a consequence of the linear view of time. As soon as one takes a linear view of time, it seems natural to hold that sensible people first think and then act – thought comes before action. However, some authors, such as Weick, argue that thought comes after action. Yet others talk about thought, or reflection, in action. The argument is really about whether, in separating thought from action, one is to be placed in the past and the other in the future or whether to locate thought in action. In all of these cases the argument is based on the selection of an arbitrary beginning at which point either thought or action is located and both are attributed to autonomous individuals who may well be interacting with each other but are nevertheless autonomous. I make this point here because I will be returning to it in Part 3, which will introduce a different notion of time in which it is purely arbitrary to place thought before, after or at the same time as action.

7.10 Summary

The theory of strategic choice is primarily concerned with the content of strategy and implicitly assumes a technically rational process for formulating and implementing strategies. This chapter has reviewed the process view of strategy, which focuses on how strategies come about rather than what their content is. This literature critiques the technically rational mode of strategic decision making by pointing to the information-processing limits of the human brain and by taking an interpretive view in which the cognitive frameworks of managers, their mental models, restrict what they attend to, so making it possible for organisations to simply repeat old strategies and thus experience strategic drift. The process view focuses attention on the routines managers use in making decisions and the often trial-and-error nature of the strategy process.

The process view focuses attention at the macro level of an organisation as a whole and this has led to the critique presented by the activity-based view of how strategies arise. This view takes a micro perspective and attends to the daily practical activities of managers in their local situations. When this is done it becomes apparent that emotions play a part in strategising and other factors such as conversation and politics become important. The creative improvisational nature of strategising is emphasised.

The key debates in this literature can be summarised as follows:

• Should the process of strategising be understood at the macro or the micro level?

• Does strategy determine organisational structure or the other way around?

• Do individual agency or organisational structures and routines take primacy in the strategy process?

• Should attention be focused on formal decision-making processes or on informal ones?

• Are strategy and strategy processes primarily deliberate or emergent and can the latter be deliberately chosen, shaped or influenced?

Further reading

The 1992 special issue of the *Strategic Management Journal* edited by Chakravarthy and Doz provides a good overview of the process perspective on strategy. The 2003 special issue of *Journal of Management Studies* edited by Johnson, Melin and Whittington provides a good overview of the activity-based view.

Questions to aid further reflection

1. What do the concepts of process and practice mean in the process and activity-based views of strategy?
2. What traditions of thought and taken-for-granted assumptions are reflected in the notions of process, practice and activity in the process and activity-based views of strategy?
3. In your own experience, what do you find practical in the writings of the strategy process and activity-based views?
4. What are the similarities and differences between process and activity-based views of strategy?
5. Why is it problematic to think of strategising as a rational activity?
6. How do writers in this chapter use the concept of emergence?
7. What does it means to say that the writers reviewed in this chapter double process and why might this be problematic?
8. What does institutional theory add to our understanding of strategic management?
9. How do the views on the strategy process expressed in this chapter deal with the key questions posed in Chapter 2? These key questions are as follows: How does the theory understand the nature of human interacting and relating? What theory of human psychology, that is ways of knowing and behaving, does each theory of strategy and organisational change assume? What methodology underlies the theory? How does the theory deal with paradox?

Chapter 8

A review of systemic ways of thinking about strategy and organisational dynamics

Key challenges for alternative ways of thinking

This chapter invites you to draw on your own experience to reflect on and consider the implications of:

- Questioning the claim that there is a science of organisation and management.

- The manner in which the dominant discourse on strategic management deals with intention and emergence.

- The consequent polarisation of rational and more intuitive processes of strategising.

- Questioning the taken-for-granted assumptions that individuals are autonomous and organisations are systems.

- The approach taken to conflict and diversity in organisations.

The material in this chapter is important because it provides an argument countering the often quite explicit assumption that management is a science and that there is an evidence base justifying the prescriptions made for governing and changing organisations. In reviewing the literature on such evidence, the chapter concludes that there is no comprehensive evidence base justifying the claim that management is a science. If there is a science of organisation or management then it is clear that we have yet to find it. So what is the status of our knowledge on organisations and their management? What challenge does this question pose for developing alternatives to mainstream thinking. In terms of ideas, this chapter explores the manner in which mainstream theory polarises intention and emergence. It is important to understand this as the basis of a move in Part 3 to theories where there is no such polarisation. The chapter also identifies the ways in which understanding

organisation as systems will be challenged in Part 3. Another key mainstream assumption to be challenged in Part 3 is the way conflict and diversity are dealt with in mainstream thinking.

8.1 Introduction

Chapters 4 to 7 have reviewed what I am calling the dominant discourse on strategic management and the dynamics of organisational change. I now want to consider the status of the claim that it is a scientific discourse and reflect on where we have got to in what I regard as the key questions that have been debated within this discourse. The conclusion I reach from this reflection is that, after more than a century of research and development, the dominant discourse continues to provide a highly limited understanding of organisational life and that what is required is a different way of thinking about organisations and their strategic management. Chapter 9 will describe the most prominent alternatives to the dominant discourse. These alternatives focus attention, in different ways, on the essentially social nature of organisations, but none of them takes further our understanding of emergence, which I claimed, in the last chapter, would need to be a key foundation of a radical alternative to the dominant discourse. So, the chapters in Part 2 will consider a basis for an alternative way of thinking in the complexity sciences about emergence and Part 3 will explore a theory of complex responsive processes as an alternative way of thinking about organisations which takes analogies from the complexity sciences interpreted in terms of what might be called 'process sociology', placing great emphasis on processes of emergence.

However, before moving to alternative ways of thinking in later chapters, the next section of this chapter will consider the claim that there is a science of organisation and management. It will point to the absence of a scientific evidence base for the prescriptions of the dominant discourse, an absence which seriously undermines the claim to scientific status. This lack of evidence provides a powerful incentive to look for alternative ways of understanding organisational life. As a pointer to the kind of alternative required, section 8.3 in this chapter turns to what seems to me to be a key question of strategy process debated in the dominant discourse between those who claim that strategic management is a matter of intention and those who claim that strategies emerge. For the former, strategic management is the conscious, logical, rational process of analysing an organisation's environment and its internal capabilities and identifying how these may be aligned with each other to produce successful outcomes. This involves setting objectives and rationally deducing actions likely to achieve the objectives. For the latter – that is, those who emphasise emergence – strategic management is the process of organisational learning in which managers undertake trial-and-error activities. Such actions are provided with coherence by some kind of inspiring, overall vision guiding logically incremental steps in which strategies as patterns of action emerge. Managers may intentionally undertake trial-and-error steps within a logical framework, but the realised strategy is to a large extent a matter of chance.

Most leaders, managers and academics adopt a 'both . . . and' form of reasoning in holding that strategy is some combination of both intention and emergence. I am claiming that both of these processes, intentional planning and incremental learning, fall within the dominant discourse in that both explicitly and implicitly make much the same underlying assumptions. They take it for granted that the intending and the learning are performed by autonomous individuals. These autonomous individuals may formulate their intentions or conduct their learning in the teams and communities they form, from which they may even derive aspects of their identities, but they remain fundamentally autonomous as is reflected in psychological theories of cognitivism, constructivism, psychoanalysis and humanism. Furthermore, it is assumed on most sides of the debate that organisations are systems formed by autonomous individuals who must then be regarded as parts of a system. There is very little sense of a contradiction between these assumptions. Key to the successful functioning of planning and learning systems is the resolution of conflict and the establishment of fit, alignment and harmony which, more recently, involves respecting and valuing diversity. The above assumptions all reflect the implicit assumption of very particular theories of causality. The intentional view assumes mainly a theory of efficient, 'if . . . then' causality and the learning school assumes a systemic formative causality in which processes of incremental learning unfold the vision. These are both theories of causality which underlie the traditional scientific method of the natural sciences. While the intentional, rational planning side of the debate makes claims for the existence of a science of organisation and management, those on the learning side tend to be less sure of this, some of them claiming that management is more of a craft or an art. Others go even further and claim that that there is no science of organisation and management, with a few of those making this claim taking the view that strategising activities are largely mindless.

Running throughout the dominant discourse there is a taken-for-granted assumption made by most theorists that organisations are systems or that, at least, it is useful to think of them as if they were systems. Although this belief has not given rise to any significant debate within the dominant discourse, the chapters in Part 3 will develop a way of thinking which moves away from any systemic assumptions about individuals or organisations, and the third section of this chapter will therefore explore the different ways in which the notion of 'system' can be taken up. This will be followed by a short section which looks briefly at the way in which the dominant discourse identifies success with consistency, alignment and harmony and how this impacts on the recent interest in diversity in organisations. This will be contrasted with a different view of diversity and conflict in Part 3.

8.2 The claim that there is a science of organisation and management

In Chapter 1 I referred to the route which the new managerial class took to achieve professional status. This route was, and largely still is, one of identification with science, understood as a range of modified forms of the classical natural sciences. However, certainly from any traditional perspective, if any field of knowledge is to qualify as science then its propositions, predictions and prescriptions must be based on an extensive and comprehensive evidence base. So, what is the evidence base which entitles the theories of strategic choice and organisational learning to be called science? What is the evidence supporting the claims of those approaches to strategic management set out in the chapters of Part 2 that they do actually produce success?

The exploration of answers to these questions in this section starts with a consideration of what constitutes evidence. The evidence which commands the greatest support in the classical natural sciences is that which is generated by the exact repetition of large numbers of experiments in controlled conditions, such as a laboratory, which exclude any subjective bias. If the large numbers of exactly repeated experiments fail to disconfirm the proposition, prediction or prescription then it is taken as objectively valid for the time being. The evidence base in this case is comprehensive and rigorously generated objective findings. For some sciences, however, the application of the experimental method is not all that simple and, particularly when it is applied to human beings, special care needs to be taken to preserve objectivity. Medical science, for example, employs a double-blind procedure for testing drugs on live human bodies which involves one group taking placebos and the other taking the drug, with neither group knowing whether they are taking the drug or the placebo. Obviously, the disciplines of psychology, sociology, and organisation and management cannot conduct experiments in live situations – we cannot test a strategy using anything like the double-blind method, for example. Immediately, therefore, the meaning of evidence has to change as we move from the natural sciences to the discipline of human organisational management and the aim of objectivity becomes particularly problematic, leading to a long and voluminous debate on research methodology in this field (for example, Van de Ven and Johnson, 2006; Alvesson and Skoldberg, 2000; Alvesson and Karreman, 2000a; Alvesson and Karreman, 2000b; Guba, 2005; Guba and Lincoln, 1995; Heron and Reason, 1997; Lincoln and Guba, 1985).

Evidence in the disciplines of organisation and management is therefore garnered in a number of different ways:

- The analysis of statistical evidence is the closest to the methods employed in the natural sciences. Here, the quantitative financial, performance and other information which organisations are legally required to gather, as well as sales, market share, cost and other data organisations choose to gather, all provide the raw material of statistical analysis. Various methods developed in the disciplines of statistics and probability can then be applied to the data – for example, regression analysis – to produce statements of significance for proposed causal connections. For example, the proposition that formal methods of strategic management produce success can be tested in this way. There are, however, a number of difficulties. Not all the most significant variables in organisational life are quantitative, so efforts are made to represent qualitative variables with rough quantitative proxies. Then the statistics are often unreliable and always open to interpretation so that it becomes difficult to avoid subjective bias. There is also the matter of time period and sample size – it often proves difficult to get the necessary statistical information over long enough time periods or for large enough samples of organisations. Furthermore, there are no exact repetitions of organisational life. Any testing of relationships is thus probabilistic. To qualify as comprehensive and rigorous, statistical analyses should cover large samples of organisations over long time periods with similar events, and this is clearly extremely difficult to do and so rather rare in the massive literature on organisations and their management.

- Another approach to gathering evidence is to carry out surveys of actions and opinions and analyse the data produced to provide evidence relating to some proposition. There is a well-developed literature on the conduct and analysis of survey evidence and this method is often employed in organisational research. Obviously this form of evidence is characterised by a considerable degree of subjectivity.

- There is also the case study approach which produces more in-depth, more qualitative investigations into the decisions taken in an organisation, the main characteristics of the organisation and the ensuing development of that organisation. Once again, despite attempts at objectivity, the method is subjective in that it involves considerable degrees of interpretation on the part of the researcher. Case studies do not often cover large samples of organisations.

- There are enormous numbers of research papers published in the academic research journals which claim to find significant evidence for a few particular hypotheses selected for study using some or all of the above methods. However, much more rarely, are there studies which try to draw these disparate and often conflicting pieces of research into some kind of comprehensive review.

- Finally, there is the anecdotal evidence often provided in the memoirs of famous executives, which cannot really sustain a claim to being evidence in anything like a scientific way.

There are, therefore, considerable problems in producing the kind of rigorous and comprehensive evidence which is the hallmark of the classical sciences, and of course this difficulty has long been recognised in the dominant discourse. There is also another difficulty which does not attract attention in the dominant discourse and that is the implicit assumptions being made about the nature of causality in organisational life. The approaches to gathering and analysing evidence are almost always based on the assumption of efficient and formative causality. The problems caused by a different assumption on causality will be taken up in Chapter 18. However, the implicit claim is that despite the difficulties it is still possible to produce some degree of persuasive evidence and, indeed, that such evidence has already been produced. So, what then is the evidence base supporting the theory of strategic choice outlined in Chapter 4?

Evidence base for the theory of strategic choice

It has proved difficult to establish a link between *strategic planning* and superior performance. Somewhat surprisingly in view of the claim to science, there are relatively few studies of the effectiveness of strategic planning and those there are produce conflicting results. For example, a 1979 paper in the *Academy of Management Journal* (Wood and LaForge, 1979) concluded that formal planning procedures improved the performance of a sample of banks in the USA. This was followed by a paper in the same journal in 1980 (Kudla, 1980) which analysed the returns earned by shareholders of planning companies compared to non-planning companies and concluded that there was no statistical difference. Fairly sparse research from the early to late 1980s (for example, Armstrong, 1982; Greenley, 1986; Pearce et al., 1987) continued to provide conflicting evidence. A survey in 1990 showed that only 15 per cent of UK companies actually used long-terms plans as control instruments and even those 15 per cent monitored their plans against events such as building a factory rather than against performance (Goold and Quinn, 1990). In 1994 Mintzberg (1994) concluded that survey evidence for the success of planning processes was inconclusive, leaving largely anecdotal evidence which is hardly scientific. A few studies attempted to summarise previous research (for example, Miller and Cardinal, 1994; Brews and Hunt, 1999; Campbell-Hunt, 2000; O'Regan and Ghobadian, 2007) and their conclusions ranged from finding evidence for a positive link between planning and performance drawing on 26 previously published studies, to concluding that the theoretical positions of strategy needed to be supported, to finding in a sample of 656 firms that both planning and logical incrementalism improve performance especially in turbulent environments, to finding that although most SMEs now practised formal planning it was often little more than a paper exercise. It seems we have no idea whether formal strategic planning improves performance or not and yet most still do it.

One study (Short et al., 2006) sought to identify whether factors to do with a firm itself, or those to do with the strategic group of firms it belonged to, or to do with the industry it was part of, had most influence on both short- and long-term performance. The authors performed a statistical analysis of a sample of 1,165 firms in 12 industries over a seven-year period in the USA. The analysis showed that all three levels (firm, group, industry) were significantly associated with performance. The strongest effect was at the firm level, but the different levels had varying effects in relation to different performance measures, leading to the conclusion that the relationships were more complex than depicted in previous studies. What are we to make of this? The study seems to conclude that all the variables selected have an effect, but it is all more complex than was generally thought to be the case. Performance depends on the nature of the firm as well as the group and industry it is part of and it is difficult to say just how this is so. Then there are a number of studies of the effect of the board of directors and the CEO on performance (Dalton et al., 1998; Westphal and Frederickson, 2001; Mackey, 2008) which conclude that board composition and board leadership structure have not been consistently linked to performance (based on a review of 54 empirical studies), that it is not clear whether boards or CEOs have the greatest effects on strategy, that in certain settings the CEO impact is more important than industry or firm effects but only moderately more important than business-segment performance. We are, therefore, left wondering what to make of the impact of corporate governance and CEOs on organisational success.

There are also more specialist studies. For example, one looks at the effect of business planning on innovation (Delmar and Shane, 2003) by analysing 223 Swedish new ventures in 1998 and concludes that business planning is an important precursor to action. Another in-depth case study of the planning systems of eight oil majors (Grant, 2003) finds that the planning and emergent views can be reconciled, because these companies practise planned emergence in which strategic planning provided coordination through targets and corporate guidelines for decentralised strategy formulation. However, the author also concludes that these planning systems showed limited innovation and analytical sophistication. The element of subjective judgement in this kind of study stands out.

Two studies of the resource-based view of strategy reach rather different conclusions. One (Newbert, 2006) concludes that there is very little empirical work to support this view, while the other (Crook *et al.*, 2008) presents a statistical analysis of 125 studies covering 29,000 organisations which suggests that strategic resources have a significant impact on performance. A meta-analysis of studies into the effect of leadership development programmes (Collins and Holton, 2004) concludes that such programmes can improve knowledge and skill if front-end analysis provides assurance that the programmes offer the right development to the right leaders. This is an example of the many, many studies which claim to prove totally superficial hypotheses. Of course, if you provide the right development for the right people it will have some effect, but what on earth is the 'right' development and how are we to know who the 'right' people are in advance and what will be the knowledge which is 'improved'?

I can only conclude from all this that we simply cannot say what impact strategic planning has on performance and improvement. Nor can we say, in anything like scientific terms, whether boards of directors, CEOs, leadership development programmes, or anything else for that matter, have any identifiable effect on success, however we want to define it. We are left with assertions presented as evidence which actually reflect beliefs and ideologies of control and improvement. It seems fairly clear to me that the research reviewed above does not constitute the kind of evidence base required to qualify as a science in the traditional sense.

Next consider how organisational learning theory has fared in terms of an evidence base.

Evidence base for the theory of strategy as learning

Burgelman and Grove (2007) refer to a study by Collins (2001) which analysed the results of companies in the USA in order to identify which of them could be classified as 'great' companies. He defined a company as great if, after 15 years of continuous good results, it produced another 15 years of great results. This excluded most high-technology companies from the sample because they had not been in existence for 30 years. Of all companies that had been in existence for 30 years Collins could find only 11 who qualified as great companies. He claimed that such greatness depended upon: a paradoxical blend of personal humility and professional will; people willing to confront the facts; pursuing a simple core business and achieving the number 1 position; feeling passionate about profit; a culture of discipline and entrepreneurship; and the use of carefully selected technologies. Great companies push relentlessly in one direction. This is of course immediately recognisable as a simple restatement of the dominant discourse, particularly that concerned with learning processes. Burgelman and Grove point out that, since 2001, eight of the eleven members of the 'great' group have either been acquired or underperformed, leaving only three 'great' companies (Abott, Nucor and Walgreens).

There were earlier studies of the same type, most notably, that by Peters and Waterman (1982) which studied 43 excellent US companies, including names such as Disney, Boeing, and Kodak. The authors argued that these companies were successful because they all had eight attributes: focus on a core business; closeness to the customer; productivity through people; autonomy and entrepreneurship; hands-on, values-driven; bias for action; simple form and lean staff; simultaneous loose-tight properties. Just as Collins was to do nearly twenty years later, Peters and Waterman produced a recognisable re-statement of the dominant discourse, particularly factors to do with organisational learning. However, within five years two-thirds of the companies in the sample had slipped from the pinnacle, some to return later but others to disappear. Two years after the Peters and Waterman study, there was another (Goldsmith and Clutterbuck, 1984), this time of UK companies. The analysis produced a similar sample of excellent companies with much the same attributes and they suffered the same fate as their America counterparts. A Royal Dutch Shell study (De Geuss, 1988) found that the average life of the largest industrial corporations was 40 years. I am not aware of a more recent study, but corporations certainly do not seem to be living any longer than that and no one has been able to identify what leads to their survival or demise. Clearly the population of companies is a dynamically evolving one in which new ones are born and old ones die – in such a process looking for the excellent or great ones is bound to produce only short-lived examples.

So far, there seems to be very little evidence to back claims to have identified what constitutes successful strategic management. What other approaches to evidence are there?

Evidence-based management and implementation science

Over the last few years, some organisational researchers have been calling for an improvement in the management of organisations by adopting what they describe as *evidence-based management* (Pfeffer and Sutton, 2006; Rousseau, 2006; Rousseau *et al.*, 2008). Evidence-based management is defined as the translation of principles derived from research into management practices. Such principles are only credible if backed by clear research findings and the practices derived from them must suit the particular setting where they are to be applied to solve organisational problems. Evidence is defined as generalisable knowledge about cause–effect relationships derived from controlled testing and observation and the linking, measuring and analysing of the causal variables. These researchers claim that this approach to management promises more consistent attainment of organisational goals, because it is based on empirical knowledge. Managers are called upon to act on the facts rather than on beliefs, personal experience or politicking, and to continually test, probe and experiment with their approaches to the organisation. Although it is claimed that there is compulsive evidence that certain best practices based on research improve profitability, those writing about evidence-based management complain that there is unfortunately a poor uptake of practices shown by research to be effective, such as goal setting and performance feedback. Managers persist in practices which research shows to be largely ineffective, such as downsizing. However, Rousseau *et al.* (2008) note that, although there is an enormous amount of evidence concerning best management practice, there is very little synthesis of different studies of the same issues and practices. By synthesis they mean comprehensive accumulation, transparent analysis and reflective interpretation of all empirical studies pertinent to a particular question, which is what one would expect of an evidence base.

The evidence referred to by these writers relates to the nature of a particular problem situation and is concerned with whether a particular decision-making technique leads to the right answer or not. They are basically recommending that managers should gather information and base their decisions on an analysis of that information. This is hardly a novel notion. They do not ask why the uptake of this idea is so poor. They do not account for their conclusion that managers do not set goals nor do they produce much evidence to support this assertion – I cannot think of any managers in the modern world who are not setting and working to goals. If anything, the problem might be too much reliance on goals. The advocates of evidence-based management do not seem to be concerned with whether particular ways of thinking about the process of management are helpful or not. In particular, they produce no systematic synthesis of research evidence for their claim that evidence-based management leads to improvement. They simply restate the dominant discourse and make unsubstantiated claims that there is an evidence base without producing the actual evidence.

Another group of researchers are also much concerned with the question of an evidence base for management and describe their work as *implementation science*. These researchers are primarily concerned with the management of healthcare organisations, pointing to how medical practice is supposed to be evidence based but how management practices, which also affect patient care, seem to escape the need for an evidence base. A number of researchers concerned with the implementation of evidence-based medical guidelines have found that simply disseminating the evidence-based knowledge does not lead to automatic implementation. For example, recent evidence (Grol and Wensing, 2004) from the USA and the Netherlands indicates that 30–40 per cent of patients do not receive care according to current scientific guidelines and that for 20 per cent the care is not needed or is potentially dangerous. This has led a number of researchers to call for the development of an 'implementation science', which is a rigorous scientific study of what additional strategies need to be implemented to produce a greater uptake of best practice. They have established that organisational contexts and cultures play an important role in whether best practice is taken up or not. So, just as they seek to provide evidence-based medical guidelines they are undertaking research to provide evidence-based organisational initiatives to bring about the necessary changes in practitioner behaviour. However, they conclude that at present there is only limited evidence for claims of strategies that lead to improvement – they could not find any strategy where the effects could be predicted with much certainty and none of the improvement strategies produced consistent effects. The Centre for Quality of Care Research (WOK) in the Netherlands assessed 13 theories/models relating to implementing change including individual, group and organisational methods. The study concluded that there is still a lack of knowledge on the factors that are decisive in achieving particular types of changes, in particular target groups and settings, and so implementation interventions are left to chance. Grimshaw and Eccles (2004) recently conducted a systematic review of 235 studies of guideline dissemination and implementation strategies and found that while there was evidence of success in particular situations, there was little evidence that the particular implementation strategies associated with the success were generalisable to other behaviours and settings. They concluded that, while there are many change management methodologies in general organisational settings, their applicability to healthcare professional and organisational behaviour has yet to be established. It still requires the exercise of considerable judgment on the part of decision-makers to select interventions likely to succeed so that any important improvements seem to be a result of 'gut feel' rather than any scientific basis.

The evidence for particular management techniques/strategies

Research has been conducted on Total Quality Management (TQM) and Business Process Re-engineering (BPR). Some researchers (Hendricks and Singhal, 1997, 2000, 2001) have used the award of prizes for the implementation of total quality management programmes in industrial companies as a proxy for effective TQM. A sample of 400 such award winners between 1983 and 1993 in the USA was selected, and then publicly available accounting data and stock prices were analysed to test for changes in operating performance and income as a result of effective TQM and the consequent impact on long-run stock market performance. This analysis shows that the award winners produced operating income changes 48 per cent above a control sample of other companies over a ten-year period (six years prior to the award and three years after the award). The award winners showed higher growth in both employment and total assets. There is also some evidence that award winners did better on sales growth and some weak evidence that they were more successful in controlling costs. In a five-year post-implementation period, the award winners outperformed the control sample in stock market price terms. Some other studies in the 1990s have produced similar results. However, another piece of research (Taylor and Wright, 2002) analysed the perceived success of TQM in a cohort of 109 firms over a five-year period. Some 42, mainly small, firms had discontinued their programmes and the remaining 67 reported varying degrees of success. The conclusion from this data is that the size of the firm, the nature of its customer base, whether it holds ISO certification or not, all have no effect on TQM outcome. Boyne and Walker (2002) point to how governments across the world are promoting TQM in public organisations, but there are no empirical studies of the relationship between TQM and performance in public sector organisations. They conducted a critical review of 19 private sector studies of the relationship between TQM and performance and concluded that they do not provide comprehensive support for a positive impact of TQM on performance. Another study (Eskildson, 2006) of 150 successful organisational turnarounds in the USA concluded that typical TQM implementation strategies had limited impact. Analysis of a mail-based survey (Soltani and Pei-Chun, 2007) of 150 organisations in the UK affiliated to the European Foundation for Quality Management concluded that quality improvement programmes were perceived to be effective by managers. However, they also concluded that there was a major discrepancy between the rhetoric of these systems and the reliability of their practice. Surveyed organisations provide little evidence that they were developing a more strategic approach to managing the softer aspects of quality management.

It seems to me that there are repeated assertions in the literature that TQM has either succeeded or failed, but few are actually backed with evidence and the evidence there is provides a rather conflicting picture. There is now a claim that Six Sigma is replacing TQM and is much more successful, but again there is little evidence to support this claim. The story of Business Process Re-engineering is not any more promising and it is now widely regarded as having been a failure. What is striking is how sparse and inconsistent the evidence is. It hardly provides a scientific evidence base.

There has been some research on the link between human resource management (HRM) practices and organisational performance (Truss, 2001) which is critical of the use of quantitative techniques (Huselid *et al.*, 1997) to demonstrate a link between the 'High Performance Work Practices' of HRM and a range of individual and organisational outcomes variables. These cross-section studies rely on the answers of a single informant in each organisation to questions on practices and performance. The author of this research, Truss, took a longitudinal case study of Hewlett-Packard over a two-year time period, collecting data on many areas and conducting questionnaires and interviews with a number of people in the organisa-tion. She found that change takes place only slowly in HRM and those managing the change do not always get it right. The evidence on outcomes is conflicting, and informal processes of networking often override the formal HRM processes. Truss claims that, if she had simply used one cross-section method, she could easily have concluded that HRM practices produce successful outcomes at Hewlett-Packard, but the more varied methods and closer scrutiny over time reveals a much less clear picture in which it is difficult to find links between HRM practice and outcomes, not least because the HRM practices are often covers for what is actually happening informally. Another study (Ezzamel *et al.*, 2001) is instructive in this regard. It is an examination of the experience of managers at a plant in Northern England, who sought to re-engineer working practices in response to corporate-driven initiatives. They found this a very frustrating experience because employees practice all man-ner of individual and collective acts of resistance. They give a show of cooperating while behind the scenes they repeatedly undermine the initiatives. The employees were identifying with the earlier work practices and the new ones made little sense to them.

Next, consider the evidence base for the highly popular strategies of mergers and acquisitions. A study in 1997 (Akhavein *et al.*, 1997) found that large merged banks experienced a significant increase in profit and efficiency relative to other large banks, with most of the improvements coming from increasing revenues and shifts to higher-value products. A later study (Andrade *et al.*, 2001) noted that mergers over the 1973–98 period evoked positive stock market responses for both parties in mergers, suggesting that they create value for shareholders and also improve oper-ating performance. On the other hand, a study in 1998 (Amihud and Miller, 1998) pointed to how little evidence there was on the success or failure of bank mergers, particularly given the major increase in merger activity following deregulation. It seems that, while small banks might gain from mergers, large banks do not. The evi-dence for mergers and acquisitions of banks is sparse, contradictory and based on a few studies of small samples. The problem with 'evidence' relating to organisational actions is that it is highly context-and-time-period dependent. It is possible that a sample of banks engaging in mergers and acquisitions in a particular country may produce successful results for a short period only for it all to fall apart not long thereafter. I think we have to conclude that there is no reliable evidence to counter the clearly disastrous impact of large bank mergers and acquisition on the 2008 credit crunch. So what evidence is there of wider interest than just banks?

A paper in 1996 (Cartwright and Cooper, 1996) explored many studies of the impact on performance of mergers and acquisitions and concluded that these activities have a disappointing history. In 1997 researchers (Dickerson et al., 1997) analysed the impact of acquisitions on the performance over a long period of a large sample of quoted companies in the UK and concluded that acquisitions have a detrimental impact on company performance and company growth. Growth through acquisition yielded a lower return than growth through internal investment. A 2001 (Tichy, 2001) analysis of 80 empirical merger studies concluded that no more than a quarter of mergers increased consumer welfare, while another quarter increased profit at the cost of the consumer and reduced the value of the firm by half. The shareholders of the merger target win out, while those of the bidder break even upon announcement but lose out in the long term. In 2003 findings were published (King et al., 2003) showing that performance was not enhanced by acquisition activity in the USA and was negatively affected to a modest extent. A meta-analysis of empirical research into the variables leading to good post-acquisition performance (King et al., 2003) found that the acquiring firm's performance does not increase as a result of acquisition activity but tends to be reduced. A 2004 study (Andre et al., 2004) of 257 Canadian mergers and acquisitions between 1980 and 2000 showed that the acquirers significantly underperformed over the three-year post-event period. The study also found that cross-border deals performed poorly in the long run. Research published in 2007 (Ingham et al., 2007) pointed to the more than doubling of expenditure on acquisitions in the UK despite the consensus in the academic literature that this activity does not enhance performance. The authors drew on survey evidence from 146 of the UK's top 500 companies and concluded that large acquisitions do not enhance performance, although small acquisitions might not suffer from the same problems as large ones and so might be performance enhancing. The authors of this study also conducted a survey of executive opinions on mergers and acquisitions and found that, despite any evidence to the contrary, the executives felt that their organisation's performance was enhanced by acquisitions. The notion that managers are scientists looks extremely dubious. The continuing belief of executives that merger and acquisition activity enhances performance is surely an indication that actual management is far from scientific. The reality is that executives act on ideological bases, have their own agendas and pursue their own careers as part of trying to work toward success for the whole organisation.

The research over the last 30 years, therefore, has not been able to provide a reliable evidence base which would enable us to conclude that certain general approaches to organising produce consistent success. Given this lack of rigorous and comprehensive evidence for the propositions, predictions and prescriptions of organisational and management research, we must conclude that there is no objective basis for the claim that these disciplines are sciences in anything like the traditionally accepted definition. For me, the major problem with the equation of organisation and management with traditional sciences is that they are the sciences of certainty. They are about predictability, regularity and stability. Part 2 will examine what I regard as a more promising 'scientific' basis for management and organisation in what have come to be called the 'complexity sciences', which are clearly the sciences of uncertainty. A number of writers have turned to the complexity sciences as a basis for understanding organisations, and what attracts them, they say, is that these sciences move away from the reductionism of classical science to a much more holistic worldview. However, traditional science has long ago moved on from purely mechanistic approaches in developing systems theories along a wide front and these systems theories have come to play a much bigger role in the dominant discourse on organisations than reductionist views. The claim to be moving on from reductionism is often used rhetorically in complexity applications to justify these applications in a manner which overlooks how second-order systems thinking has already adopted hostility to reductionism and moved to interconnection and holism. The move to holism has already taken place and does not need to appeal to the complexity sciences. Instead, what I hope to stress is how the sciences of complexity can serve to give us greater insight into uncertainty and unpredictability. Similarly, some writers on the application of the complexity sciences to organisations contrast their own organic approach to the mechanical one they claim is typical of mainstream thinking. However, this distinction has long been explored in the management literature and there are now a number who claim that organisations are living systems. Again, the dominant discourse already encompasses organic approaches and so a turn to the complexity science is not necessary for this purpose. So in Part 2, I will be exploring just what it is about the sciences of uncertainty which might offer novel insights into human organisations.

The first conclusion of this chapter is that mainstream views on managing organisations do not contribute to a science but are, rather, a set of beliefs reflecting a particular ideology, and so sustain particular patterns of power relations. The second conclusion, I suggest, is that the claim to science was inappropriately based on the sciences of certainty and this suggests a move to the sciences of uncertainty which will be made in Part 2. In drawing on the sciences of certainty, mainstream theories polarise the relationship between intention and emergence in organisational life.

8.3 The polarisation of intention and emergence

Consider the point we have reached in the debate on whether to think of strategies as realisations of intentional, deliberate choices or as patterns of action emerging in processes of organisational learning, or as both. In his review of what he called the Design School of strategy, Mintzberg (1990) identified its key premises:

- Strategy formulation is a conscious rational process of thought followed in a controlled way by implementation.
- The strategy formulation process is the prime responsibility of the CEO.
- The purpose of the strategy is to align the internal capabilities of an organisation, its strengths and weaknesses, with its external position, its opportunities and threats, and this brings the Design School close to the Positioning School most notably developed by Porter who was also a writer in the Design School.
- Organisational values and ethics are recognised as important but given only secondary attention.

Mintzberg distinguished the Design School's processes of judgement from the Planning School's processes of analysis and the Entrepreneurial School's processes of intuition. He was critical of the thought-before-action structure of the Design,

Positioning and Planning Schools, pointing out how, in practice, thinking and acting proceed together so that formulating and implementing are not strictly sequential. In addition to the deliberate strategies which are sometimes formulated as suggested in the Design, Positioning and Planning Schools, Mintzberg points to the process of learning and discovery in which strategies as patterns of action emerge in processes of ongoing learning. For him, strategy is a combination of deliberate design and ongoing learning, particularly in unpredictable, turbulent environments. Trial, error and experience are major elements of the strategy process – he points to the evidence published in the mid-1980s that fewer than 10 per cent of American corporations implement intended strategies.

This critique provoked an extraordinary outburst from Ansoff (1991), regarded as the founder of the Planning School of strategy. Although Mintzberg nowhere completely dismissed the Design or any other prescriptive school, Ansoff said that Mintzberg consigned them all to the 'garbage heap of history'. Ansoff objected that this meant that his career of 40 years had not made a useful contribution to managers and he was replying to Mintzberg to salvage a lifetime's work. He then stated that he would provide a logical refutation of Mintzberg's position, based on empirical data of the success of the planning approach to strategy. In fact, he did not provide what could be accepted as a comprehensive scientific evidence base but gave an elaboration of what was in the end an ideology of planning in which he poured scorn on Mintzberg's emphasis on emergent strategy and learning processes. Mintzberg (1991) responded briefly. He drew attention to Ansoff's claims to be basing his work in science while that of Mintzberg was not scientific. He pointed out that despite the talk of 'facts' and 'factual evidence' there were 'in fact' no facts provide in the Ansoff piece, only opinions.

This exchange is illuminating because it typifies the rather few exchanges that have taken place when dominant approaches to strategy are critiqued. Those espousing the dominant approaches of intention and control always claim to be scientific, but they never produce what could stand up as a scientific evidence base because, as we have seen above, there is no such thing. The appeal to science is used as a rhetorical device on both sides of the debate. It has to do with claims to professional status and identity – note the point of having a lifetime of work being consigned to the garbage can of history. The debate is in the end ideological, reflecting issues of power relations and professional identity. For this reason, the periodic critiques of the dominant management discourse encounter ideological and power-based obfuscation and get nowhere.

While Mintzberg understood turbulent, unpredictable environments to mean that strategies could not be planned, Ansoff put forward measures of environmental turbulence and prescribed incremental strategic plans for low-level turbulence and strategic plans of discontinuity for turbulent environments, without addressing how managers were supposed to know which discontinuous plan to go for if they could not predict what would happen, as they cannot in turbulent environments. The writers in the organisational evolution tradition (Hannan and Freeman, 1989) went much further than Mintzberg and questioned the ability of managers to choose the state of their organisation in any way. They took a neo-Darwinian view and held that organisations changed through random events that were then selected for survival by competitive selection. What happens emerges in the competitive selection of chance variations in strategy as organisations evolve into an unpredictable future. Then we get the ongoing development of the more intuitive approaches which do not have to rely on prediction or control. For example, Chia and Holt (2006) contrast what they call a 'building' mode of strategy in which actors deliberately formulate purposeful strategies to realise desired outcomes, with a 'dwelling' mode in which strategies emerge non-deliberately in everyday practical coping which does not require intention and purposeful goal-orientation as people act in a manner consistent with past actions and experiences. They describe this practical coping as a primitive, mindless practical coping, of absorbed involvement in the world, which precedes any reflection, mental content or symbolic representation.

The strategy literature continues to polarise strategy as the deliberate realisation of intention, and strategy as patterns of action emerging in processes of muddling though, garbage-can decision-making, mindless coping or, less pejoratively, learning. Emergent strategy is almost always understood as random and arising by chance in rather messy processes which are often labelled as the opposite of rational. This is also true of probably the most influential articulator of emergent strategy, Mintzberg, who says:

> The interesting question, much like that concerning whether decision must lie behind action, is whether plan must lie behind pattern: because there is pattern, must there necessarily have been a plan? In other words, must strategies always be *deliberate*? Or can they *emerge*: that is, can pattern just form out of individual actions?
>
> (Mintzberg, 2007, 4)

Note the definition of emergence as *pattern just forming* out of individual action which is to be contrasted with its opposite of deliberate, intentional strategy. He has asked managers whether the strategy actually pursued by their company was what was intended five years previously or something else and, while some say 'yes' others say 'no' and most say 'something in between happened'. He goes on to argue that deliberate strategy is about control and that emergent strategy is about learning. In this learning process people learn their way into strategies action by action, decision by decision, and strategies may form without people even realising that this is happening. For Mintzberg, learning is trial and error, gradual, incremental change in which single projects set precedents that create patterns. Since managers always seek to exercise control over the strategy process we cannot get purely emergent strategies, which imply no control. Instead, sensible strategies combine the deliberate and the emergent. This implies some kind of choice between the process of emergence and the process of deliberate control. He regards strategy formulation as deliberate and strategy implementation as both deliberate and emergent. They are equal partners in the process. He says that it is difficult to imagine a total absence of intention as would be expected in purely emergent strategies (Mintzberg, 2007, p. 7). For him, emergent strategy is the same as strategic learning in much the same sense as Weick's 'sense-making' (Weick, 1979). Note how clearly emergence is identified with a lack of control, making it inconceivable that strategies might always emerge.

A third conclusion I reach in this chapter, then, is that the dominant discourse has not made much progress in dealing with intention and emergence. Part 3 will explore a way of making sense of organisational life in which intention/control and emergence are not seen as polar opposites. The claim will be that strategies always emerge, but they never *just form*, they do not just happen anyway and they are not random or chance occurrences. Instead, strategies emerge in the interplay of many intentions.

8.4 The belief that organisations are systems in the world or in the mind

There is another matter that has hardly been surfaced in the dominant discourse and that is the implications of thinking of an organisation as a system. Throughout the survey of the dominant discourse on strategic management and organisational dynamics in this Part 1 of the book, I have stressed the fact that all forms of this discourse make the assumption that organisations are some form of system. However, there are three reasons for claiming that it is not helpful to think of organisations as systems:

1. To think in terms of system is to think in terms of formative causality which cannot encompass novelty or creativity.

2. A system is a whole separated by a boundary from an environment and consisting of parts interacting to form the whole and themselves. A part is a part only in so far as it is necessary for constituting the whole. This means that, if you think of a human being as a part of a system, you are excluding from your theory of human agency, in all its good and terribly bad aspects, all that is truly human such as the capacity for some degree of choice and spontaneity.

3. The conceptual act of separating a system from an environment or a context is an act of creating an *inside* of the system and an *outside* of the system. This immediately implies an observer. The position of the observer as being outside the system was recognised by Bateson (1972) as problematic, and second-order system thinking attempted to widen the boundary to incorporate the observer. However, as Bateson recognised, this leads to an infinite regress in argument.

In Chapter 9 I will look at the way critical management studies (labour process theory) moves away from conceptualising organisations as systems or even believing that it is useful to think of organisations 'as if' they were systems. Then, in the chapters of Part 3 of the book, I will be reviewing the theory of complex responsive processes in which organisations are not thought of as systems. Instead, they are thought of as perpetual processes of interaction between persons over time. This move in thought is taken by some to mean that the notion of system in any form is being rejected: indeed, that the word 'system' has become a taboo. This is, of course, far too simplistic an interpretation, and so in this section I want to clarify what notion of system in the dominant discourse is being departed from in the theory of complex responsive processes. To make this clear, consider the different ways in which the word 'system' can be used:

1. A coherent, systematic whole of thought. For example, Hegel (1807) referred to his philosophy of the nature of thought and of the historical and social development of humans as his *system*.

2. A regulative idea or hypothesis about the nature of the development of phenomena in nature. For example, Kant (1790) held that it was useful to think of

living phenomena *as if* they were wholes formed by interacting parts to develop a mature form of that nature already present at their inception. He held that this way of thinking could not be applied to human action, because human actors are rational, autonomous individuals who cannot therefore be subject to, a part of, any system without losing their rational autonomy, their very selves.

3. A particular kind of conceptual model as in first-order, hard systems thinking with its general systems theory, cybernetic and systems dynamics models of human groupings as systems which came to be regarded as actually existing. Individuals came to be understood as parts of organisational and social systems.

4. A way of thinking about individual minds as information-processing devices. For example, cognitivist psychology is very much based on this systemic idea of the autonomous individual.

5. A way of thinking about human communication as a cybernetic system of transmission consisting of senders and receivers, both being autonomous individuals.

6. A living system. For example, Senge (1990) and Burke (2008/1982) both prescribe thinking about an organisation as a system that is actually living.

7. A particular kind of conceptual model as in second-order, soft, and critical systems thinking where the systems model is understood to be in the mind of the observer who thinks of organisations as if they were systems.

8. A complex system, the subject matter of Part 2 of this book, in which self-organisation at the level of the agents produces emergent order at the global level.

9. A tool or technique specifying rational sequential steps which observers and decision-makers should use to structure and shape the problem situations facing them, find rational solutions and make rational decisions. I have in mind here the aspects of soft and critical systems thinking that focus attention on tools and techniques for rational problem-solving by free agents, rather than thinking of organisations 'as if' they were systems. For example, these tools are prescribed for use by facilitators to facilitate rational discussion by groups of stakeholders to identity a plurality of ways in which problem situations can be understood as if they were systems.

10. A bureaucracy and hierarchy: that is, as a comprehensive, interlocking set of procedures and actions. For example, there are accounting systems, quality assurance systems, legal systems, property systems, health systems and transport systems.

In the chapters of Part 3, when I refer to 'systems thinking' I will be referring to meanings 3, 6, 7 and 8 which, although each is different to some extent, together present a way of thinking about the nature of an organisation as a system that is now completely taken for granted in the dominant discourse. I am identifying systems thinking in the dominant discourse with a particularly way of positing or thinking about an organisation as an organisation. I also include meanings 4 and 5 which provide compatible theories of the mental functioning of individual humans and the way they communicate. Meanings 3 to 8 have a number of important features in common. They provide coherent ways of modelling organisations as whole, global phenomena, which enable powerful members at an organisation's centre to 'read' the situation at the macro level across the whole organisation and make decisions in a rational manner, so ensuring some form of central control. However, all those models regard human beings as agents in, or parts of, a system which are simplifications taking the form of averages, probabilities and regularities. Such simplifications remove difference, and abstract from the detail of contingent situations and the complex detail of local interactions, which indeed are made rationally invisible by the focusing of attention on the abstraction. They all regard rational, cognising individuals as parts of the organisational whole. Process is understood as the interaction between parts to form the whole, which is then often thought of as exerting downward causal forces on the individuals. They all involve a split between observer and organisation, between problem and solution, between sender and receiver, and between decision and outcome. They all constitute abstractions which draw attention away from immersing in the local interaction of ordinary daily life in organisations. In Part 3 I will be exploring a way of thinking about organisations which does not appeal in any way to an understanding of organisation as a system with human parts, but rather thinks of organisation as ongoing local interactions of an ordinary kind in which population-wide patterns of organising emerge. The objection is to thinking about human beings in abstract ways as parts of a system split off from ordinary experience.

Meaning 1, a system of thought, and meaning 2, a hypothesis about systems in the natural sciences, are not meanings with which I am concerned when discussing organisations. When I refer to systems thinking, I am also not referring to meaning 10 about hierarchy and bureaucracy, since they are formal patterns of relationships and explicit generalised procedures which are unavoidable in organisations. While the concept of system contained in all of the meanings 3 to 8 has come to occupy a dominant place in the conceptualisation of the nature of organisation, this has not been accompanied, perhaps surprisingly, by the widespread use of the tools and techniques (meaning 9) developed by communities of systems thinkers in academia and the consulting world. At a recent conference of such practitioners in the UK, they were asked to vote on the importance of their offerings and their conclusion was that, while their work had not had zero impact, it also had not spread widely to become a method of making decisions and solving problems, despite its claims to rationality. People in organisations do not normally follow the steps proposed by systems practitioners nor do they follow 'rational' decision-making where rational is understood in a technical way. Instead, they engage in daily conversation, gossip, political negotiations, power plays, acts of resistance and pursuit of personal agendas: in short, local interaction. In addition, the powerful are hardly likely to enthusiastically back the use of techniques reflecting an ideology of freedom, democracy and emancipation of the people from oppression. Perhaps those presenting the techniques are not taking enough account of the patterns of power relations. However, systemic tools and techniques are often used on special occasions such as strategy 'away-days' or when large numbers are involved in highly visible problems. On these special occasions the tools and techniques (meaning 9) may be useful when they stimulate conversation. In moving away from systems thinking I am therefore not claiming that all the tools and techniques for promoting discussion should be dispensed with, although in my view they do run the risk of thought getting stuck at the abstract level of systems which avoids reflection on the messy reality of local interaction.

Although I am interested in developing a way of thinking which avoids thinking about organisations as if they were systems, I am not at all dismissive of using the notion of a system as a tool for approaching some specific problems. For example, systems thinking can be used very fruitfully to design flows of work. The system here is a tool that people use in their communicative interaction as a way of co-coordinating and accomplishing their work. In this view of system, the agent, the part of the system, is an activity not a person. For example, although Seddon (2008) very occasionally refers to the organisation as a system, he devotes most of his book to understanding the system as the way work is designed and managed and holds that this system governs performance. So he sees customers and the organisation's staff using the system to do their work. He distinguishes between value work – meeting the needs of the customer – and failure work, which is created when customers complain about the failure to meet their needs. He shows how one system design, one based on targets which are always arbitrary numbers, produces increasing levels of failure work. The design problem is to redesign the system to reduce failure work and focus on value work. Instead of targets, which he says should be scrapped, he measures the actual meeting of customer needs. Attending to this can lead to a failure to meet targets but it does satisfy the customers. Managing by targets leads to achieving the targets but failing the customers. We have here a system – the parts are tasks interacting with each other to produce the whole task of the organisation and performance; there is a boundary as customer demand flows in from outside the task system and customer service flows out. This is a very effective way of thinking about largely predictable but nevertheless highly variable work.

So I am not arguing against thinking of work flows as designed systems – to think like this brings a great improvement over ways of thinking that fail to see linkages. I am arguing against thinking of the organisation, as organisation, consisting of individual people as parts that produce the whole called the 'organisation' as a system. In Part 3 I will argue that an organisation is an evolving pattern of interaction, of activity between people who very frequently employ tools to accomplish this interaction – tools which they design and the design of which can provide a greatly improved understanding of the way tasks are connected as a system to produce purpose. But people are not a system – people employ a system in their action. This is important, because otherwise we tend to focus on the tool and ignore the people. Seddon shows clearly how the current system of organising work generates cheating. So he is taking account of the people, staff and customers, but does not write about them as being parts of a system, although this may well be what he thinks. For Seddon, taking a systems approach involves managers seeing workflows as a system. He says they need to think in flow terms of what is flowing from the outside into the system. This means starting with a study of demand to see what is working for customers now, for example, why customers call a local authority. Many workflow designs separate front and back offices (parts) and so involve transferring pieces of work from one to another. The call comes into the front office and dealt with by the back office. Seddon says this design blocks and slows down workflow. I think all of this is certainly very helpful. I am therefore not particularly engaged in a critique of system meanings 9 and 10.

It is the forms 3 to 8, which include theories of communication and the autonomous individuals, that I want to characterise as systems thinking in the dominant
discourse and challenge this by suggesting an alternative, complex responsive
processes way of thinking which I will cover in Part 3 of this book. So, the fourth
conclusion I reach in this chapter is that an alternative way of thinking about organisations needs to move on from thinking in terms of systems.

I now come to another issue recently taken up in the dominant discourse to do
with conflict and diversity. I will argue, in the next section, that these issues are not
adequately dealt with in the dominant discourse and that it will be important to
develop alternative ways of thinking about conflict and diversity in organisations.

8.5 Conflict and diversity

Running throughout the dominant discourse on organisation and management is
a clearly taken-for-granted assumption that successful performance depends upon
harmonious relationships between members of an organisation. This requires that
they 'buy into' the same inspiring vision, and follow the same behaviours reflecting
the same values. That assumption is part of the wider claim that organisational
success requires alignment of goals and strategies, as well as competences and competitive advantage, and consistency of implementation. Inevitable conflict, usually
understood to reflect undesirable 'politicking' and the pursuit of personal agendas
detrimental to the organisation, is regarded as an unfortunate distraction from successful functioning which requires action to resolve that conflict.

Most of the literature on organisations and their management, therefore, understands conflict as a characteristic of antagonistic relationships between people
characterised by hostility, fighting and sometimes the breakdown of cooperation.
Conflict is usually described as a struggle to neutralise, injure or eliminate the values,
status, power and resources of opponents (for example, Coser, 1956; Rapoport,
1976; Glasl, 1999). Writers in this tradition tend to say little about how conflict emerges and focus instead on how to prevent (Mastenbroek, 1987[1993];
Schermerhorn et al., 1991) or resolve it by handling misunderstanding and tension.
Some warn against suppressing conflictual feelings, because this could surface in
other forms, and advocate instead the bringing of differences into the open (Glasl,
1999). These writers categorise such antagonistic conflict into different types such
as instrumental, realistic or substantive conflict. Mastenbroek 1987[1993], for
example, identifies: instrumental conflicts about priorities, resulting from insufficient
communication and unclear division of responsibilities; social, emotional conflicts
relating to personal relationships, trust and self-image; negotiation conflicts arising
in the tension around sharing scarce goods; and power/dependency conflict reflected
in rivalry about position. Schermerhorn et al. (1991) distinguish between
substantitive conflicts, which are disagreements over ends and means, such as the
allocation of resources, distribution of rewards, and forms of policies and procedures, and emotional conflicts which involve feelings of anger, mistrust, dislike,
fear, resentment and personal clashes. They also distinguish between role conflict
which occurs when people are unable to respond to the standards of one or more
members of the group they normally work with; intrapersonal conflict; interpersonal

conflict; inter-group conflict; and inter-organisational conflict. Different prescriptions are then provided for dealing with these different types of conflict, the aim being to produce consensus and solve problems. Conflict resolution requires eliminating the underlying reasons for that conflict, and management techniques are provided to help the manager to solve the problem.

This approach to conflict in general is reflected in the more recent treatment of diversity in organisations. The globalisation of commerce and industry has had the effect of greatly increasing cultural diversity. Increasing emphasis on corporate social and environmental responsibility has added to the pressures. Furthermore, in North America and Europe there has been an enormous growth in legislation promoting equal opportunities and prohibiting discrimination on grounds of race, nationality, gender, sexual orientation and age. All of these developments create issues that leaders and managers cannot ignore and many have been trying to respond through the use of diversity programmes. These programmes became popular in the United States some time ago and apparently the majority of Fortune 500 companies have formal diversity programmes (Caudron, 1998). They are now also common in Europe. The aim of such programmes is to protect the rights of individuals and also to protect an organisation from expensive litigation, and this protection requires policing practices to ensure that organisational members are compliant. Clearly, these different protection needs can conflict. However, such conflict has to be resolved if the organisation is to be protected. Also, the approach to diversity is one that seeks to avoid surfacing the conflict inevitably aroused by diversity through preaching the need for tolerance and the respect for, even love of diversity. Some claim that diversity can be leveraged to drive business growth, attract the best talent and save costs, and they call for human resource directors to develop the business case for diversity-management programmes, drawing attention to the positive impact on profits and competitive advantage (Robinson and Dechant, 1997). Others claim that diversity enhances problem solving and increases creativity, and they point to the increasing number of organisations which try to increase the inclusiveness of under-represented groups through proactive efforts to manage their diversity as a successor to affirmative action (Gilbert et al., 1999). Analysis of the links between increased diversity and organisational performance (Richard et al., 2004) leads to the conclusion that management level heterogeneity can be a strategic asset in certain contexts. Such diversity can be exploited to gain competitive edge, and to this end managers should develop organisational capabilities that maximise the benefits of diverse human capital.

As with all other factors, the dominant discourse holds that the benefits of diversity are to be harnessed through planning with the aim of increasing voluntary inclusion. Diversity is to be managed and promoted because it is a 'good' thing that enhances performance. For example, a recent study (Marquis et al., 2009) provides a comprehensive review of the literature on diversity in organisations and conducts an analysis of the differences between corporations ranked highly for their diversity management programmes and those ranked highly for good HR practice without adopting diversity-management practices comprehensively. The authors conclude that senior managers are convinced that workforce diversity has a positive effect on business performance, although the empirical evidence for this is less than conclusive. However, realising this potential requires strong leadership commitment to diversity planning and implementation with formal mechanisms for evaluating and holding accountable managers and others for diversity outcomes. The authors claim that there are best practices, but that these on their own will not achieve a high level of diversity – other factors, such as firm size, have an impact too. Achieving more than surface diversity requires culture change, commitment and acceptance of difference. Diversity in management teams and the appointment of directors of diversity to run diversity offices focused on promoting diversity are also called for. Diversity, therefore, becomes an organisational objective, a variable to be improved by managerial action.

Diversity management is quoted as being a new paradigm for human resource management (Thomas and Ely, 1996). Thomas and Ely differentiate between the discrimination and fairness paradigm, the access and legitimacy paradigm and the learning and effectiveness paradigm. The latter is stated as the paradigm which gives rise to successful diversity initiatives, as defined by actual improvements in business performance. They talk of eight preconditions for making the shift:

1. leaders must truly value the variety of opinion and different perspectives of a diverse workforce;
2. leaders must recognise the difficulties that different perspectives present;
3. the culture must create an expectation of high standards and performance from everyone;
4. the culture must promote personal development through the design of jobs and the provision of training;
5. the culture must encourage openness to sustain debate and constructive conflict;
6. the culture must make people feel valued;
7. a well-articulated vision is essential to ensure work discussions stay focused on the accomplishment of goals;
8. it must be a egalitarian and non-bureaucratic organisation.

Typically, organisations take large-scale initiatives involving the establishment of working parties whose remit is to formulate strategies and design overall, global patterns of action to bring about respect for difference and diversity, as well as achieve equality and avoid discrimination. The approach to this work is to set global goals, prepare action plans covering communication and training and articulate the values leaders should propagate to realise the required outcomes. Here, people are thinking in macro terms about a global design which is to be rolled out across the organisation and applied in all local situations. This tends to obscure the political process involved, how people use such programmes to further their own ambitions, the conflict and power struggles generated by such initiative and how people can be trapped in their own procedures, leading to confusion about what they are actually doing.

In terms of likely benefits a recent article, taken from interviews with human resource managers of Fortune 100 companies, cited the five top reasons for engaging in diversity management as:

1. better utilisation of talent;
2. increased marketplace understanding;
3. enhanced breadth of understanding in leadership positions;
4. enhanced creativity;
5. increased quality of team problem solving (Gilbert and Ivancevich, 2000).

In another study the most frequently carried-out initiatives are: formal induction programmes for new recruits; criteria for selection and advancement that are open to all; and having a policy on equal opportunities. Most cited benefits included: retention of employees, enhanced organisational flexibility, improved public image, and better morale. Driving forces behind initiatives were: good personnel practice, legislation, business sense and organisational commitment to equal opportunities (Kandola and Fullerton, 1994). A comprehensive guide for all HR is available, which gives all the information needed to be successful.

In Chapter 10 of Part 2 I will be exploring how the sciences of complexity attach major importance to diversity as the source of evolution, creativity and novelty. Without diversity there can be no new developments. There is nothing inherently harmonious, however, about the meaning of diversity in the complexity sciences, and the role diversity plays can just as easily lead to that which is destructive as that which is creative. In the chapters of Part 3 I will be using this insight about diversity to appeal to process sociology in understanding how diversity is linked to conflict. This understanding is also one in which conflict is a condition for the emergence of the new, for the movement of thought. The theory of organisation and management developed in Part 3 – the theory of complex responsive processes, therefore, departs in a major way from the assumptions of the dominant discourse around conflict and diversity. The theory of complex responsive processes draws on the views of Elias and Mead for whom conflict is not understood simply in antagonist terms but is regarded as an inevitable aspect of all human relationships arising from the need to interpret generalised norms and idealised values – in particular, contingent situations – and from the fact that human interdependence means that all human relationships are power relationships. We come to see diversity as a social dynamic rather than a property of agents as we move from talking about general differences between people to talking about the interplay of diverse intentions, plans and unconscious behaviours. This necessarily means linking diversity to conflict and understanding both primarily in terms of power relations and identity formation in which ideology is central – matters that are conspicuous by their absence in the dominant discourse on conflict and diversity. We come to see that talking about living with, managing, promoting, respecting and embracing diversity is far too simplistic.

The fifth conclusion I reach in this chapter, therefore, is that the dominant discourse presents a sanitised view of diversity and prescriptions that amount to covering over the conflict that diversity inevitably generates. An alternative way of thinking, therefore, would need to address diversity and conflict more realistically.

In discussing the dominant discourse in Chapters 4 to 7, I have been drawing attention to various strands of work critiquing that dominant discourse, and I have argued that all of these remain based on much the same take-for-granted assumptions. There is, however, one strand of thinking I am aware of which departs from the foundational assumptions of the dominant discourse and this is known variously as *critical theory*, *critical structuralism*, *labour process theory* or sometimes just *critical management studies*. I think the main movement in thought here is away from a systemic notion of process to a more responsive temporal process of interaction between people. It is this notion of process that I will be taking up in the chapters in Part 3 of this book in developing a theory of organisations as complex responsive processes. This theory is concerned with very much the same issue as critical, labour process theory, often understood in much the same way. There are, however, some differences which the next chapter takes up.

8.6 Summary and key questions to be dealt with in Parts 2 and 3 of this book

This chapter has reviewed a number of important matters running through the dominant discourse surveyed in Part 1 of this book, because they are matters that represent major points of departure for the development of alternative, more useful, ways of thinking about organisations. This chapter has argued that useful alternative ways of thinking will need to be based in some way on the sciences of uncertainty rather than those of certainty. Second, they will need to avoid the polarisation of intention and emergence. Third, a useful alternative would avoid conceptualising an organisation as a system. Fourth, this alternative would avoid the dual rationalist and formative cause and, fifth, it would be based on a more realistic understanding of conflict and diversity. The review presented in this chapter suggests a number of important questions which will be dealt with throughout the chapters of Part 3:

- If management is not a science, what kind of knowledge can it claim to be?
- If organisations are not systems and cannot usefully be thought of as if they were, then how else could we think about them?
- If individuals are not autonomous then what are they?
- If organisations are not systems and individuals are not autonomous, how are we to think about strategy processes, particularly the linked oppositions of intention and emergence, and of macro and micro processes?
- If the assumptions of predictability, rationalist and formative causality limit our understanding of creative organisational evolution, then what theory of causality is more useful?
- Is strategic management primarily about problem solving or is it better understood as some kind of preoccupation in the organisational game?
- If it is too simplistic to think of human agents as rule followers, then how are we to think about rules.
- If it is too simplistic to treat conflict in terms of resolution and diversity as respect, all as instruments of improvement, then what role are we to understand them to play in participation in organisational life?
- What is the role of ideology and power in strategic management?

However, to end Part 1 of this book, Chapter 9 will look at discourses that do present alternatives to the dominant one by focusing on the essentially social nature of organisational life, although they do not move as far away from all the fundamental assumptions of the dominant discourse as I hope the chapters of Part 3 will.

Further reading

To explore further the matter of science and methodology in relation to management and organisation you could consult Tsoukas (1996), Alvesson and Skoldberg (2000) and Guba (2005). It is well worth studying the exchanges between Mintzberg (1990, 1991) and Ansoff (1991) on the debate between intention and emergence.

Questions to aid further reflection

1. What roles have emotion and the pursuit of individual agendas played in your experience of management?
2. In your own experience what role has conflict and diversity played in organisations?
3. If management is not a science what kind of knowledge can it claim to be?
4. If organisations are not systems and cannot usefully be thought of as if they were, then how else could we think about them?
5. If individuals are not autonomous then what are they?
6. If it is too simplistic to think of human agents as rule followers then how are we to think about rules?
7. How are we to think about diversity and conflict in organisations?
8. What part does power and ideology play in strategic management?

Chapter 9

Extending and challenging the dominant discourse on organisations

Thinking about participation and practice

This chapter invites you to draw on your own experience to reflect on and consider the implications of:

- A number of different discourses which depart in some respects from the dominant discourse outlined in previous chapters.

- How, in second-order systems thinking and social constructionist approaches, account is taken of the fact that humans cannot simply take the objective observer position in relation to human phenomena, because they are themselves participants in such phenomena.

- How social constructionist approaches, and notions of communities of practice, bring the social aspects of organisational life to the fore.

- How second-order systems thinking, social constructionist approaches, communities of practice theorising and labour process theory all focus attention on communication, culture, power, politics and ideology.

- The extent to which all of the approaches mentioned in this chapter depart from the dominant discourse's reflection of an ideology of efficiency and control.

- How the causal dualism of the dominant discourse continues to be assumed in some of the alternative discourse but disappears in others.

- The extent to which the alternative discourse continues to rely on or depart from individualistic psychologies.

- The emphasis placed on the validity of different viewpoints and multiple meanings in some of the alternative discourses.

- The view that alternative discourses take on time.

- The manner in which the alternative discourses deal with ethics.

The ideas in this chapter are important because they constitute discourses which depart in some important ways from the dominant discourse. These alternative discourses take the form of second-order systems thinking, social constructionist approaches, notions of communities of practice, ideas of the cultural formation of strategies and labour process theory. To varying extents, each of these alternative discourses focuses our attention on important matters that are ignored in the dominant discourse in important ways, primarily to do with the social nature of human activity, including power and ideology. It is this widening of focus that makes it important to read this chapter.

9.1 Introduction

Throughout the previous chapters in this part of the book, I have been grouping the ideas presented into what I have called 'mainstream organisational theory', but which I sometimes describe as the 'dominant discourse'. I claim that the ideas presented so far are dominant because people in most organisations nowadays talk together, explain and justify what they are doing in its terms. The discourse is dominant because if you do not talk in terms of visions, missions, targets, strategic plans, policy rules, performance, efficiency and improvement you will not be able to sustain your membership of the more powerful groupings in organisations today. This applies not just to commercial, private sector enterprise but now to all public sector organisations and even to charities and aid agencies. The ideas covered so far in this part have in an important sense colonised the most important public arenas in which questions of organising and governance are discussed and acted upon. This dominant discourse reflects a very powerful ideology of control, efficiency, progress and improvement which is simply taken for granted and difficult to discuss publicly. To question it is to take the risk of being marginalised. The dominant discourse also holds sway in most academic research establishments with the most prestigious journals tending to publish mainly papers reflecting mainstream theories, and research councils using criteria based on mainstream theories to award research funds. If you want a visibly successful academic career, you do not stray too far from the dominant discourse. The dominant discourse is based on a number of important assumptions that have emerged in the history of Western thought and now tend to be completely taken for granted.

1. The mainstream theories of the dominant discourse assume that agency is located primarily in autonomous individuals who act rationally and sometimes irrationally but nevertheless autonomously.

2. All mainstream theories assume that a group, organisation or society is a system, although some may admit that this is just a way of thinking about what organisations are. Groups, organisations and societies are thus thought of as entities outside human individuals who have minds as internal worlds. Individuals form groups and organisations which then act back on them.

3. Certain notions of causality follow from this spatial metaphor in which individual minds are *inside* persons and organisations are *outside* them. When individuals act as autonomous agents, their actions are caused by rational choice – rationalist

causality. When they act as parts of an organisational system they are subject to the formative causality of the system.

4. Mental and organisational systems can both be objectively observed and acted upon by observers.

5. Organisational change, strategy, flows from prior design, and the only alternative is chance happenings which are said to 'emerge'.

The dominant discourse takes its own ideology for granted, and through its mainstream theories largely sidelines matters to do with interdependence, unpredictability, power, ordinary day-to-day activities such as conversation and politics, and the richer fabric of social life.

There are, however, alternative discourses, and it is the purpose of this chapter to give a brief presentation of them. I have come to view all of the ideas described in the rest of this chapter as alternatives to the dominant discourse, for two reasons. First, none of the discourses presented in the next sections feature prominently in the public discussion of organisations and their management by influential organisational executives or by politicians and policy makers. These ideas are pursued in academic research, but usually as less central activities with their own specialist journals, only occasionally appearing in the most prestigious mainstream journals on, say, strategic management. These ideas are rarely presented in undergraduate programmes at business schools and usually only as special options in postgraduate degrees such as the MBA. I think this is a reflection of the challenge each of the ways of thinking described in this chapter presents to the dominant ideology of control and efficiency. Each of the ways of thinking presented below also questions at least one of the taken-for-granted assumptions upon which mainstream theories are built. The one taken-for-granted assumption which does not feature much in the critiques presented by the alternative discourses, however, has to do with the role of *emergence* in organisational life. This will become a central issue in the alternative way of thinking which will be developed in Part 3.

The first alternative discourse to be discussed will be second-order system thinking. This moves away from a realist belief in systems, regards systems as hypotheses – and so as ways of thinking rather than as existing things – and focuses attention on the observer of the system as also a participant in the system. Although individualist assumptions about human psychology are retained and although the duality of rationalist and formative causality continues, second-order system thinking presents a much richer picture of social interaction than the dominant discourse, including paying attention to culture and power in more reality-congruent ways. There is a significant ideological shift from an ideology of control and efficiency to one of participation and inclusion, and the postmodern idea of multiple discourses or realities.

The second alternative discourse is constituted by a number of social constructionist approaches, some of which leave behind the assumption of individual autonomy and give priority to the social. This is presented as a way of thinking about how social realities are constructed in human communication, and so focuses attention on conversation and ordinary daily life. The shift in ideology here is from control and efficiency to appreciative inquiry, inclusion, participation and the recognition of multiple discourses.

The third alternative presented is the work on communities of practice which also emphasises the social processes involved in learning and reflects the same kind of ideology as the previous two.

The fourth alternative is a few views which take unpredictability and habitual action seriously. So far, all of these alternative discourses think in terms of systems: strongly and obviously in the case of second-order systems thinking; to some extent in theories of communities of practice; less obviously in some social constructionist approach; and even less obviously in the work of Chia and Holt (2009).

When it comes to the fifth alternative discourse, labour process theory, there is an explicit move away from both individualism and systems notions. Labour process theorists argue against thinking in terms of systems, and seek to explain economic and political processes of control in terms of relationships between managers and workers. Here there is a major shift away from the ideology of the dominant discourse.

We turn now to second-order systems thinking.

9.2 Second-order systems thinking

The general systems, cybernetics and systems dynamics strands of systems thinking all departed from mechanistic and reductionist approaches in that they stressed dynamic interaction between parts of a system and between systems and between a system and its environment. However, they did not make a major move away from the radical separation of the observer (the subject and rationalist causality) from the observed (the object and formative causality). Like mechanistic and reductionist thinking, the first wave of twentieth-century systems thinking, often called 'hard systems thinking', assumes an objective reality that is objectively observed by an individual. The assumption is that the social world is made up of systems having a purpose, which can be objectively observed and modelled. The boundaries of a system are taken to be given by the structure of reality. In other words, reality is held to consist of systems in a realist perspective. Most hard systems thinkers forgot the 'as if' of Kant's regulative idea in relation to systems (see Chapter 3) and reified the organisation as a real system. This approach allows managers to imagine that their organisation is a system that they can control in an optimal manner. First-order systems thinking is concerned with intervening in the system to define clear goals, identify problems and propose rational solutions. This involves characterising a situation in terms of identifiable objects with well-defined properties; finding general rules that apply to situations in terms of those objects and properties; applying the rules logically to the situation and drawing conclusions as to what is to be done. The approach is consistent with the scientific method and it emphasises thought and its application as independent activities. It is concerned with transferable knowledge and it is based on the sender–receiver model of communication.

The last decades of the twentieth century saw a developing critique of first-order, hard systems thinking which led to the development of second-order systems thinking (cybernetics, systems dynamics and general systems theory). Second-order systems thinking is built on the understanding that human beings determine the world they experience (constructivist psychology) and this requires that we reflect upon how we operate as perceiving and knowing 'observers'. Second-order thinking is the continual attempt of managers and researchers to be aware of their own framework of understanding. One key name associated with the origins of second-order systems thinking is that of von Foerster (1984), who said that he was part of the universe and whenever he acted he was changing both himself and the universe. Another key name is that of Bateson (1972), who explored how the observer could be included in the system being observed. Bateson distinguished between learning Level 1, which is single-loop learning where mental models stay the same; learning Level 2, which is double-loop learning where mental models are changed; and learning Level 3, examples of which are religious conversion and deep personal change. A first-order cybernetic system is a deterministic mechanism that responds to gaps between target and actual and no learning is possible. To reach Level 1, the boundary of the cybernetic system has to be redrawn to include the human operator of the first-order system because it is the human who sets goals for the system. The human operator sets such goals according to some mental framework in his or her mind: that is, a mental model. The second-order system, therefore, now includes a person who can detect an error, a gap, between what he or she experiences and what he/she wants as determined by his/her habits, or mental model. The human operator can respond to this error and set a new goal for the system without in any way changing habits, mental models, or ways of understanding the world. In other words, the person's mental model, which remains the same, is now part of the higher-order system and this higher-order system can therefore learn to adjust behaviour. This learning is itself a cybernetic process in that experience of an error triggers a change in the goal set for the lower-order system. Mental models, then, are higher-order cybernetic devices that change the goals for the lower-order cybernetic system. Learning Level 1, or single-loop learning, is therefore made possible by including the objective observer's fixed mental model in a widened system. Although the process of changing mental models remains outside the definition of the Learning Level 1 system, the system boundary can be redrawn to include this observer's observing of him/herself performing the single-loop learning and if necessary he/she can choose to change his/her mental model in double-loop, Level 2 learning. However, the process for changing the mental model is now part of an even higher order system and the mental model requiring the boundary to redrawn yet again to include the process of changing mental models. Now, the observer is observing him/herself changing his/her preferences that trigger the choice to change his/her mental model – Level 3 learning. Bateson found he could not identify what this would be, fell back on mysticism – for example, religious conversion – and said that Level 3 was extremely rare. However, now there is the problem of defining the process by which the observer becomes aware of the need to change his/her preferences: that is, to choose to engage in Level 3 learning. The problem with second-order system thinking, then, is that it rapidly runs into an infinite regress and some kind of mysticism.

It seems to me that this problem of infinite regress is a sign that second-order systems thinking is not addressing the paradox of the observing participant, or the participating observer, but eliminating it through the device of redrawing boundaries and changing levels of description. Second-order systems thinkers tend to ignore the problem, claiming that in practice it would come to an end. The problem of infinite regress is fundamental to all forms of systems thinking simply because systems thinking is built upon a conceptual spatial metaphor. It always involves postulating a whole separated by a boundary from other wholes. There is always an 'inside' and an 'outside'. Drawing a boundary creates an 'inside', which has to be different to what is 'outside'. This cannot be other than a dualism in which one kind of causality applies to the inside and another kind to the outside. There always has to be something outside the system that is drawing the boundary around it and what that something is must eventually be a mystery. Systems thinking is fundamentally Kantian 'both . . . and' thinking. This matters in practical terms because it ends up with an appeal to mysticism. Part 3 of the book will move from systems thinking with its spatial metaphor to responsive processes thinking, which makes no use of concepts such as 'inside', 'outside' and 'boundaries'.

However, in drawing attention to the fact that the observer of a human system is also a human being, and so also a participants in the system, the critics of hard systems were taking a much more social, participative perspective. They also questioned early systems theories because they implied that organisations were physical entities like organisms with clear boundaries, structures and functions and this limited the domain of effective application. Allied to this was the criticism that hard systems theories presented individuals as deterministic, thinking machines and ignored the aspects of emotion, conflict, politics, culture and ethics. In other words, the critics of hard systems thinking were taking a much more social perspective. For example, Churchman (1968, 1970) focused on boundaries and ethics; Ackoff (1981, 1994) developed interactive planning; and Checkland (1981, 1983; Checkland and Scholes, 1990) developed soft systems thinking, arguing that very few real-world situations allowed one to think of them as systems with clearly defined goals and objectives. Later, critical systems thinking (Flood, 1990, 1999; Jackson, 2000; Midgley, 2000) grew out of the critiques of Churchman, Ackoff and Checkland and in emphasising power and participation, these theories have made a significant move away from the dominant discourse. This move will be taken further in Part 3 by moving away from thinking or organisations as systems.

As examples of the critical attitude towards the first wave of twentieth-century systems thinking, consider the work of Ackoff on interactive planning.

Interactive planning

Ackoff (1981, 1994) holds that obstructions to change lie in the minds of the members of an organisation: that is, in their mental models. He believes that it is not practically feasible to surface these mental models and change them as many learning organisation theorists believe. Instead, he argues that members of an organisation should participate in formulating an idealised design of the future they desire and create ways of achieving it. They should seek to close the gap between their present situation and this desired future. The central message is to plan or be planned for. Ackoff developed a method of interactive planning to do this, one that focuses on the participative development of scenarios for desired futures. The first step in the rather detailed process he proposes is systems analysis – that is, the formulation of a detailed picture of the organisation as it is today in terms of process, structure, culture and relationships with the environment. He is concerned with what can be done now to create the future.

Ackoff presents a version of strategic choice theory that emphasises not just the roles of leaders but also the participation of members of an organisation in making the strategic choice. It seems to me, therefore, that his perspective represents a shift in ideology from 'command and control' to teamwork and democratic participation. Ackoff is not explaining how managers and others actually do behave. Instead, he is prescribing what they should do to act more effectively. While Ackoff clearly continues within the theory of strategic choice, Churchman moves to a theory of organisational learning.

Churchman's critique

Churchman (1968, 1970) argued that human systems are best understood as systems of meaning (ideas, concepts, values) and learning. Churchman set out the conditions required for a system to be purposeful. Purposeful systems are characterised by a decision-maker who can produce change in performance measures, a designer whose design influences the decision-maker, a design aimed at maximising value and a built-in guarantee that the purpose can be achieved. He stressed the importance of critical reflection on system design and operation.

Notice here the distinction between decision-maker/designer and the system of ideas, concepts and values about which performance measurement decisions and design changes are made. The decision-maker/designer is clearly understood to be rationally seeking to maximise value and achieve a purpose through the system of ideas, concepts and values. The action of this decision-maker/designer is thus thought of in terms of Kantian autonomous individuals to be explained in terms of rationalist causality. However, the systems of ideas, concepts and values, which the autonomous individuals design and measure, must be subject to some other causality, for they are clearly not autonomous individuals. What causes the system's movement has to be the formative process of interaction between the ideas, concepts and values that produce the whole conceptual or value system. In other words, the conceptual and value system unfolds what the designers and performance measuring autonomous individuals have designed into them. Furthermore, the decision maker/designer is a participant in the ideas, concepts and values of the system. The decision maker/designer must think in terms of the ideas and concepts and act in accordance with the values in order to count as relevant to the system. If they deviate then they are no longer relevant to the construction of the social system of ideas, concepts and values.

Churchman's thinking, therefore, has the same structure as that of all the other systems thinkers so far reviewed in this part of the book: namely, that human interaction is first understood in terms of the rationalist causality of the decision-maker/designer and then in terms of the formative causality of the conceptual and value systems they have designed. In the former they are free to choose the design of the system and in the latter they are not, because they are subject to the formative causality of the system they have designed. This is not sensed as a paradox and no explanation is offered of how people manage to live with alternating between being free and being not free.

Churchman also placed great importance on moral practice. For him, the first step in systems thinking was to draw a boundary around the system, which is essentially a choice that opens up ethical questions because drawing a boundary always includes some and excludes others, dominating some and liberating others. For Churchman, the aim of systems thinking was to emancipate people from domination so that they could participate on a free and equal basis in the process of system design: that is, in the design of their own thinking. The way in which particular views are privileged over others was to be identified (Flood, 1990) and exposed so that people could be liberated from dominant worldviews (Phelan, 1999).

Churchman also stressed participation, debate and trans-discipline and trans-function teamworking. The response to the criticism that systems are designed by technocrats, who exclude people, is to focus on democracy and participation in the process of design. What this move does is substitute a democratic group for the individual designer of the system. The understanding of a system or the design of a system is now a task for a team in dialogue with each other. The method of their thinking and talking to each other is still supposed, however, to be systemic. So, the idea of human systems as systems of meaning is closely linked to an emphasis on participation as equality and an idealised, democratic freedom. The ideological basis of Churchman's thinking is thus quite transparent. It is based upon a belief in liberation and participation. It presents a prescription for better ways to manage human affairs. Churchman is not explaining what actually does happen, but is calling for a better way of making decisions.

Notice, however, that although Churchman is deeply concerned with participative social interaction and human freedom, he employs a framework that has problems with freedom. The autonomous individuals who are designing and making decisions about the systems of ideas and values are clearly free because they are choosing the system design. However, what they are designing is their own systems of ideas and value. If these systems are to mean anything to them then they and others must adhere to the formative purpose and process of the system. The ideas, concepts and values of the system must also be their ideas, concepts and values. As such, they cannot be free and this is why Kant warned against thinking of human action in terms of systems. The problem of freedom applies as much to the idealist position of Churchman as to the realist position of earlier hard systems thinkers. In the realist position people are actually taken to be parts of a real system, while in the idealist position the system is thought of as the mental construct of the people involved. However, even though the system is their own mental construction, the very act of this construction means that they must be thinking of themselves as parts of the system they are constructing, otherwise they are not really thinking in systems terms at all. Notice, also, a point already made about hard systems. Since the system, whether it be a real system or a system of ideas, is subject to formative cause, it cannot produce anything new. The source of novelty, therefore, lies in the individual and systems thinking does not explain how such novelty arises. This feature of dual causality and the problems it brings to do with freedom and novelty are also evident in Checkland's thinking.

Soft Systems Methodology

Checkland (1983) was critical of the positivist, engineering view of systems to be found in the three strands of systems thinking discussed in previous chapters of this part of the book. These views of systems took the realist perspective, regarding the world as actually consisting of systems having an objective existence. Instead, Checkland proposed that systems were the mental constructs of observers, in effect bringing back Kant's idealist view of the regulative, 'as if' nature of systems. For Checkland, the notion of systems related to the process of enquiry, meaning and intention, and he developed Soft Systems Methodology (SSM) as a reflection of this view. Notice how this approach implies the notion of the autonomous individual, the enquiring scientific observer who hypothesises about reality 'as if' it were a system.

SSM approaches a problem situation on the basis that people possess free will rather than being subjected to forces beyond their control and because of this they must be involved in any changes to the systems they create. Checkland is thus implicitly assuming some kind of rationalist causality, this time including emotion, as applying to human action. The implicit assumptions around human psychology are those of cognitivism. The aim of the methodology is to integrate multiple viewpoints of free participants in order to assist them *to predict and control the changes to their systems* in vague situations in which there are no agreed goals. The assumptions of rationalist causality and cognitivist psychology are again made clear.

The key phases of SSM are as follows:

1. An initial phase of analysis that should *not* be pursued in systems terms but should build up what Checkland calls a 'rich picture' of the problem situation. This is to avoid jumping too rapidly to conclusions about representing the situation in systemic terms.

2. In the next phase, a number of systems are drawn from the 'rich picture'. These are systems regarded as relevant to improving the problem situation and each system represents a particular viewpoint because it is not obvious which system design is appropriate to the particular problem situation. Notice here that Checkland is thinking in Kantian terms in that he posits a rich reality from which categories of the mind, called 'systems', are to be drawn to form understanding. Here, the autonomous individual is hypothesising systems as mental constructs just like Kant's regulative ideas, which impart 'as if' purpose to the system.

3. The third phase is the construction of a number of system models. These models are not blueprints for the design of an objective system but conceptual models contributing to a debate about change. This again is Kantian in that the conceptual models are subject to formative causality. The interaction of their parts, the concepts of which the system consists, produces the whole conceptual system, which unfolds the purpose ascribed to it by its designers. As soon as a designer defines a system in terms of the interaction of its parts, that designer enfolds in it that which is to be unfolded by it.

The second and third steps in Checkland's approach are essential if it is to qualify as systems thinking. One has to posit wholes formed by interacting parts within a boundary to qualify as thinking in systems terms. However, this very act of thought entails exactly the same causal dualism as that found in Churchman's version of systems thinking and brings with it the same problems to do with freedom and novelty. There are thus autonomous individuals, the designers of the system, who are subject to a causality of freedom of choice and there is the system they have designed, which is subject to formative causality. Soft systems thinking is thus clearly a form of thinking in terms of causal dualities. One implicitly thinks about oneself as designer in terms of a causality of autonomy and then one thinks of oneself as part of the designed system in some sense and so subject to formative causality.

In a later version of SSM Checkland identified two strands. The first was a cultural strand consisting of a view of the interventions and rules of clients, problems solvers and other stakeholders. This involves taking a cultural view of the social systems, roles, norms and values, as well as the politics and sources of power.

The second strand is the logical analysis. Both strands are modelled as systems and compared to the real situation to learn from differences.

Checkland, therefore, did not stop at the level of the cognising individual. In developing soft systems thinking, he advocated (Checkland, 1981; Checkland and Scholes, 1990) an interpretive approach to systems in which account is taken of the social rules and practices of participants in a problem situation. He defined a model, a learning cycle, with a number of steps that constitute the SSM, which is a methodology for systems designers to follow when facing soft, ill-structured problems *that include social practices, politics and culture.* Intertwined with this designed intervention is an investigation of the process of designing the intervention itself and the culture and politics this process involves. In other words, Checkland is taking account of the need for second-order systems thinking, or reflexivity, in which people seek to understand their own processes of interaction in systemic terms. In short, people are being advised to think of their interaction with each other as creating a system of values, culture, ideas, power interests, social relations and so on.

In SSM the subjective aspects of decision-making are brought into consideration and a number of different systems models are developed to make explicit the implications of different viewpoints so that the consequences of alternative courses of possible action can be compared. The purpose is to provide a systemic learning process in which participants can come to appreciate more fully their differing viewpoints and how they might come to some kind of consensus or accommodation as the basis of change. SSM does not seek to study objective facts or search for causal relations, because it views systems as the creative mental constructs of the human beings involved in the problem situation. Researchers and practitioners, therefore, need to understand subjectively the viewpoints and the intentions of all involved in a problem situation. SSM is a way of probing alternative worldviews and it uses specific models of systems to explicate those worldviews in specific situations rather than tries to identify the 'truth' about the nature of systems.

Note how Checkland is not explaining how people actually do go about dealing with life in organisations. Instead he presents prescriptions for dealing more effectively with problem situations. This heavily prescriptive rather than descriptive stance points to the underlying ideology to do with participation and the validation of alternative viewpoints.

In putting forward SSM, Checkland moved from a paradigm of goal seeking and optimisation, as in hard systems thinking, to a paradigm of learning, understood as the maintaining and development of relationships. Unlike Ackoff, Checkland does not seek to define an ideal future and identify ways of achieving it. Checkland moves from a positivist, functionalist philosophy to a phenomenological and interpretivist one, in which social reality is constructed and reconstructed in a social process in which meanings are negotiated. For him, an organisation is not an entity but part of the sense making of a group of people engaged in a dialogue. *Action is the managing of change in a set of relationships rather than taking rational action to achieve goals* (Checkland and Holwell, 1998). SSM helps to *manage relationships by orchestrating a process* through which organisational actors can learn about accommodations to each other that are feasible and desirable. Checkland provides lists of constitutive rules prescribing what constitutes a genuine soft systems study (Checkland, 1981; Checkland and Scholes, 1990), which ensures that the soft systems philosophy is carried out in practice. Managers are supposed to step out of

the hurly-burly of ongoing events to make sense of these events and apply structured, systemic thinking to them. The use of systems models is meant to facilitate
social processes of enquiry in which social realities are constructed. Notice here
how the underlying notion of autonomous individuals is subtly retained, although
Checkland distances himself from 'rational action to achieve goals'. There is still a
straightforward causality of individual freedom as evidenced in the managing and
orchestrating of relationships and the intentional use of systems models to facilitate
social processes.

Critical systems thinking

In their critiques of the approaches of Checkland, Ackoff and Churchman, Jackson,
Mingers, Flood and Midgley developed critical systems thinking. This section takes
the work of Midgley and Jackson as examples of this development.

Midgley (2000) is concerned with problem situations faced by people and his
question has to do with how they may be assisted by systems thinkers to deal with
those problem situations, understood in terms of wholes. As with all systems
thinkers, Midgley's approach is based upon the assumption that people are facing
a systemic problem or issue to which they must find a solution or answer in order
to act.

Midgley argues that systems thinkers seek to be as comprehensive as possible in
their analyses but, because everything is connected to everything else, it is impossible to be totally comprehensive. It therefore becomes essential to make boundary
judgements. For him, the making of boundary judgements is the core of systems
thinking; it is what he calls 'systems philosophy'. Boundaries are social and personal
constructs that define the limits of the knowledge to be taken as pertinent (first-
order system) and the people who may legitimately be considered as decision-
makers or stakeholders (second-order system). It is the inclusion of stakeholders that
yields the second-order system and this means that there are no experts and that far
from being comprehensive, systems thinking highlights the bounded nature of
understanding. However, systems thinkers need to widen boundaries so as to sweep
in more information because, even though understanding will never be comprehensive, it can be greater than what we currently have.

The perspective Midgley seems to be writing from is that of an agent (individual
or group) confronted with some situation in which that agent must make a decision
or choose an action. He advocates a particular approach to such a situation called
'systemic intervention'. This is an approach to analysing the situation by making
boundary judgements and the creative design of systemic methods of intervention to
enable agents to look 'outwards' at the situation understood as a first-order system
and to look 'back' to the knowledge-generating system (biological organisms, mind,
social group, society, etc.) in which the agents/stakeholders are embedded. He
understands the latter to be a second-order level or system. The first-order boundary judgement is one of including all those relationships judged to be pertinent to
the situation to be analysed and in relation to which action must be taken. The
second-order boundary judgement is one of including legitimate stakeholders –
that is, those who have the legitimate right to be involved in or be affected by the
situation or action. Boundary judgements are therefore matters of values and ethics
and particular attention has to be paid to who or what is being excluded or

marginalised. The excluded or marginalised can only be identified or understood in terms of a further boundary judgement. Although this involves infinite regress in theory, in practice people will not go on making boundary judgements but will act so that this is not a practical problem.

Since everything is connected to everything, there are multiple realities. It is, therefore, necessary to make many different boundary judgements in any situation and this requires using many different theories and methodologies. This underlies the prescription of the creative design of methods, which means tailoring a mix of methods (critical systems heuristics, viable systems model, etc.) to the situation and varying them during the work of systemic intervention. Systemic intervention is always purposive and the purpose is improvement, that is, the realisation of a desired consequence that can be sustained indefinitely.

This approach, it seems to me, has a number of key features:

- Thought in the form of reflection, analysis, determination of desired consequences, intervention design, all of which are either before or apart from action.

- How agents come up with creative boundary judgements and subsequent actions is not explained.

- Participation is systemic: that is, embedded in a knowledge-generating system. Despite moving to a second-order level – the knowledge-generating system – the whole implication is one of agents who step outside the first-order level when they look outwards at it and outside the second-order level when they look back at it. It is recognised that this involves infinite regress, but this is not regarded as a problem. In my view it is a serious problem because in practical situations people are trying to understand how to act creatively. When they start asking questions about who draws the boundaries, for example, the explanation tends to end up in mystical terms. This shuts down thinking with very important practical consequences. The infinite regress of systems thinking thus avoids explaining how novelty and creativity come about and also does not deal with the contradiction of freedom when individuals become parts of knowledge-generating systems.

- Midgley's argument reflects 'both . . . and' thinking. There is both the first-order and the second-order system. There are both systems and autonomous agents drawing boundaries.

- He implicitly assumes cognitivist/constructivist psychology.

Jackson (2000) says that systems thinking is a holistic way of thinking that respects profound interconnectedness and pays attention to emergent properties in reaction to the reductionism of positivist science. Jackson calls for systems thinking to put people, with their different beliefs, purposes, evaluations and conflicts, at the centre of its concerns. Systems thinking uses models to try to learn about behaviour and does not take for granted, or impose, boundaries on situations. Instead, it reflects upon and questions where the boundary has been drawn and how this impacts on the kind of improvement that can be made. It encourages different perspectives and values as contributing to holistic appreciation.

Jackson says that the core systems concepts are:

- Holism, which means either taking the whole into the models or continually reflecting on the inevitable lack of comprehensiveness in a system design.

- Knowledge as inevitably organised into cognitive systems, which are structured frameworks linking elements of knowledge into coherent wholes. System is the fundamental element in ordering human thinking. This indicates the basis of critical systems thinking in cognitivist psychological theories.
- Boundaries drawn in different ways according to different worldviews.
- Jackson seeks to re-establish the hegemony of systems thinking by developing a coherent multi-perspective, multi-methodological framework encompassing all strands of systems thinking.

Jackson wants to show that systems thinking is not confined to the functionalist thinking of the first wave of twentieth-century systems theories, but can contribute to radical and interpretive discourses. He believes that systems thinking must offer theoretical and methodological coherence in a world of multiple paradigms and clear, non-contradictory advice on how systems thinking can be put to use. Jackson defines the essence of critical systems thinking as critical and social awareness. Critical awareness is the differentiation of different strands and paradigms of systems thinking and social awareness is the understanding of the social contexts that lead to the popularity and use of the different systems methodologies.

Critical systems thinking seeks to address the problem created by the strengths and weaknesses of any particular systems approach depending upon the paradigm from which it is observed. Jackson develops what he calls the *System of System Methodologies (SOSM)* to encompass all methodologies and indicate how they create particular problem contexts, that is, how they depend upon different sets of assumptions.

Jackson distinguishes between method, methodology and meta-methodology in an ascending hierarchy. The method is the specific systemic tool applied in a particular problem situation. Methodology is the principles underlying methods, encompassing a number of methods. Meta-methodology is the relationship between methodologies. This meta-methodology includes all systems thinking in a pluralist framework that can be used to select a particular form of systems thinking, or some combination of them, or some combination of parts of them, as being appropriate to a particular problem context.

The SOSM, which is at the heart of Jackson's critical systems thinking, is thus a meta-methodological framework relating all systems methodologies to appropriate contexts: that is, according to the assumptions made about the nature of the problem. It brings pluralism to systems thinking by defining ideal problem contexts that differ from one another in a meaningful way. The existence of these ideal problem contexts implies, says Jackson, the need for a variety of problem-solving methodologies. Important differences in context should be reflected in differences of methodology.

The final element of Jackson's critical systems thinking is what he calls *Total Systems Intervention (TSI)*, which is described as a meta-methodology. This takes different views on the problem situation and combines different methodologies to address them in three phases: the creativity phase, where metaphors are used to stimulate thinking; choice of the appropriate systems-based methodology; and implementation, which is the use of a particular systems methodology to implement specific proposals. The tools of TSI, consisting of lists, metaphors and models, are available to assist this process and the outcome is co-ordinated change that brings about improvement.

The essentials of critical systems thinking are commitment, pluralism and emancipation or improvement. It aims to help individuals realise their potential. The point of pluralism is to enable the best use of methodologies, methods, models, tools and techniques in any intervention. Critical systems thinking is thus very clearly an ideology. It is not a description or explanation of what people in organisations are actually doing, but a set of prescriptions for how people should approach problem situations. The ideology is the commitment to pluralism, emancipation and improvement.

The causal duality characteristic of all of the systems thinking so far reviewed is apparent in Jackson's thinking. He writes about someone choosing an appropriate systems-based methodology. This immediately implies autonomous individuals subject to the causality of free choice. The person(s) choosing between different types of systems thinking are exercising some kind of choice based on their observation of context and systems methodology. Someone, the researcher, consultant or manager, has to form a judgement about the nature of the context of a problem situation and select the appropriate methodology. However, once the person has selected a methodology, that methodology is then applied to interacting humans, including the person(s) choosing the methodology. They are then subject to the formative causality of the system they have chosen. This is the dual causality and 'both . . . and' thinking that eliminates paradox. There is no sense in Jackson's discussion of the inherent paradox of observing that which includes oneself as participant.

Critical system thinking, therefore, has in common with all other forms of systems thinking the employment of central notions of wholes and boundaries. Difficulties with the concept of the whole are recognised and it is argued that they are inevitably incomplete. Difficulties with the notion of drawing boundaries and the infinite regress to which this leads are also recognised. However, these difficulties, and the inevitable causal dualism that goes with them, are not regarded as practically important. It is suggested that in practice they are overcome by pluralism.

Pluralism means taking many different perspectives on a problem situation and selecting those that are most helpful in a specific situation. The metaphor of lenses is often used. It is claimed that individuals have the capacity to change perspectives rather in the same way that one changes lenses in a pair of spectacles. The belief is that decision-making processes in groups, organisations and societies can be greatly improved if those involved avoid commitment to a particular perspective. Instead, they should engage in dialogues, hold their assumptions in abeyance and explore with each other different ways of understanding their situation. I would argue that this is a highly idealised notion and I do not think that it is possible for people to follow this advice. The perspective we take on the world is intimately tied up with our very identities and we cannot easily change who we are as if our identities were simply interchangeable lenses.

If the way we together make sense of our world is so much a part of who we are, is in fact a vital aspect of our identities, then putting on one lens after another would mean frequently changing identities, and pluralism implies that this is as easy as changing our spectacles. This is an idealised way out of conflict. People do not simply alter perspectives as if they did not matter – they kill each other for them because they are aspects of collective identity. Despite the concern with the social, with political action, power and freedom, the systemic way of looking at these does not accommodate their ordinary conflictual nature and it retains the primacy of the individual.

The development of second-order systems thinking about organisations has accomplished a radical questioning of the nature of the observer of a system and presented significant challenges to the dominant ideology of control and improvement by presenting an ideology of improvement linked to participation, emancipation, tolerance of multiple perspectives and rational decision-making which takes into account interconnections. It has developed techniques for formulating problems and making decisions in inclusive ways which may provoke conversation. It has presented models of organisational interconnections so as to promote greater understanding of organisational dynamics and useful analyses of workflows. While second-order systems thinking continues to take for granted the primacy of the individual agent, the next challenge to the dominant discourse to be discussed, social constructionist approaches, moves firmly from the primacy of the individual to the primacy of the social.

9.3 Social constructionist approaches

In this section three social constructionist positions will be briefly described. The first is institutional theory, already referred to in Chapter 7, the second is the more radical social constructionist position and the third is the theory of social identity. In institutional theory it is understood that meaning, as collective attributions of rationality and justice, is socially constructed through the sharing of practices between organisations. In their search for legitimacy organisations tend to become homogeneous. The more radical social constructionist approach to organisations focuses in interaction between members of an organisation on which people intentionally create new cultures and practices so that they come to develop different identities from each other (Pedersen and Dobbin, 2006). Consider first a brief outline of institutional theory.

Institutional theory

Institutional theory is concerned with the impact of wider social influences on organisational structures and practices compared to the more economics focused view of institutional economists such as Coase (1937) and Williamson (1975). Williamson developed a theory of transaction-cost economics to explain that organisations exist because they are more cost-effective ways of making transactions compared to market transactions. For these institutional economists, institutions come into being for reasons of economic efficiency. Institutional theory, on the other hand, understands institutions to be the historical and cultural contexts within which management practices are developed, and such contexts account for differences in practice from one sector or region to another. Organisations are not simply about efficiency nor do they simply adapt to their environments – they enact their environments (Weick, 1995) in the routinised practices and habits of a historically evolved culture, and institutional change is triggered by some crisis or failing of current institutional arrangements. Strategy is then understood as context dependent, as dependent on relationships between organisations, rather than as the choice of an autonomous organisation. Ideas and practices are adopted for symbolic reasons as managers seek support and legitimacy in a wider social setting, including relationships with government agencies and regulative authorities, which results in organisations becoming more and more alike.

In institutionalist theory (DiMaggio and Powell, 1991; Scott, 2001; Zucker, 1977), institutions are understood to be social arrangements, represented by systems of symbols, cultural scripts and mental models which are reflected in both cultural artefacts and individual cognitive constructions displaying awareness of the norms and rules that structure interaction between people. Institutions evolve regulative processes of incentives and constraints that shape social interaction and they provide stability, normative order and meaning to collective behaviour. Institutions are a set of legitimised roles of authority arising in constantly re-enacted practices and repeated social interaction which produces social patterns that reproduce themselves in a self-perpetuating manner. Institutions are formed in coercive, normative and mimetic processes of reproduction. Some institutionalist writers, for example DiMaggio and Powell, draw on Giddens' structuration theory according to which institutions emerge in a dynamic in which individuals' actions are shaped by the institutions they belong to and those individuals act on their institutional environment to transform the institutions. Institutionalisation is a political process depending upon the relative power of the actors. DiMaggio and Powell also draw on the work of Bourdieu to think in terms of an organisational field which is a community of competing, cooperating and regulating organisations with well-defined patterns of hierarchy. Such fields contain multiple influences, and can be fragmented through contention which emerges in the field. Organisational strategies are not autonomous decisions but are shaped by the field as organisations change to align themselves with other organisations in the field in a conscious claim for legitimacy and also in preconscious processes in which goals and behaviours are accepted as legitimate. Fields create managers' perceptions.

Critical theorists (Knights and Willmott, 2007) argue that institutional economics, institutional theory, evolutionary theory, network theory and virtual organisation theory broadly endorse the dominant discourse rather than challenging the status quo. They stress how institutional meanings are changed through power relations which reflect ideology. Institutionalisation is a process of persuading and building support, and so is political.

Relational co-construction and multiple narratives

Gergen (1999) presents what he calls the working assumptions of social constructionism:

- Language does not map or picture an independent world but, rather, a potentially unlimited number of descriptions and explanations with none being superior in terms of their capacity to map or picture reality. Everything humans have learned could be otherwise.

- Language and all other forms of representation gain their meaning from the ways in which they are used in relationships. The individual mind does not originate meaning, create language or discover the world. Relationships are prior to all that is intelligible.

- Relationships are based in wider patterns of practice, such as rituals and traditions. Relationships and reality are socially constructed and are limited by culture, history and human embeddedness in the physical world.

- Language constitutes social life, and without shared language descriptions social life is impossible. In the continuous generation of meaning together humans sustain life. Generative discourse transforms social life.

- The generation of the good is always from within a tradition and this requires reflexivity: that is, attempts to suspend the obvious and question assumptions.

Gergen points out that many participating in constructionist dialogues do not necessarily share these assumptions. He distinguishes social constructionism from constructivism, which focuses on the way in which the individual mind constructs what is taken to be reality (von Glasersveld, 1991) and from social constructivism in which individual minds construct reality in a way significantly formed by relationships (Vygotsky, 1978; Bruner, 1990). The social constructionist approach views the social as the process of articulating individual selves and the world. It is a challenge to the primacy and priority of the individual, in effect placing relationship, the social, as prior and primary. There is a strong ideological underpinning in that a shift to this way of thinking is held to promise better forms of social life (Gergen, 1999, p. 122). Shotter (1993) argues that human bodies participate in a ceaseless flow of relational activity which is spontaneous, effortless and performed without much self-consciousness. He describes this as joint activity, a third realm of human experience between subject and object, which is neither just action nor just behaviour but a 'dialogic space' at the boundary between one consciousness and another, the interweaving of unmerged consciousnesses. Joint action takes place when one's act is shaped by the act of the other so that none can be held accountable. It is in such relating that meaning and novelty arise. He describes the realm of joint action as one in which people jointly construct their actions, experienced as a 'third agency' with its own specific demands and requirements. This 'it', or responsive order, makes calls on participants.

When it comes specifically to organisations, many writing from this perspective understand social constructionism as a way of thinking rather than a set of techniques (Hosking and McNamee, 2006). Social constructionism focuses on relational practices of everyday professional life centring on dialogue. It is in these dialogical relational practices that people co-construct the ongoing realities of their organisational life together. In its radical forms, social constructionism adopts a postmodern stance in denying realist, modernist positions and grand narratives, pointing to how multiple realities, discourses and meanings are being constructed by groups of people as they coordinate their activites. This is said to call for an appreciative attitude of inquiry (Cooperrider and Srivastva, 1987), respect for diversity and avoiding the alienation of other forms of discourse. Instead of contesting facts, conflictual issues are approached as challenges in going on together. This is in reaction to the claim that truth is gained by opposition, argument and persuasion. Furthermore, the coordination of activities and the co-construction of meaning take place as local interaction, where local means particular contextual relations rather than universal ones. Meaningful actions are always emerging in local relationships. Local interactions lead to many different constructions, and this may be dealt with in some form of conflict in which one construction seeks to dominate others or, from a social constructionist point of view, the different construction can be viewed as resources for developing different kinds of relationship. Such process and choice bring power relations to the fore. Indeed, such processes construct self and other and self–other relations. Identity is understood as socially constructed.

Person and organisations are not viewed as separate entities but as relational realities that emerge in local interaction. Stability and change are ongoing reproductions of relational processes. Appropriate methods of inquiry are participative action research, collaborative inquiry, appreciative inquiry, narrative and storytelling approaches, open-space technologies and working with dialogue and drama. Social construction is understood as responsive and invitational action or performance taken place in both language and other forms of action involving human bodies. Power relations move from dominance to moral and communal relations where ethics is at the centre. There is a move from power over others to power to do something together. This leads to leadership theories that move away from the notion of the dominant proactive leader to a notion of leaders as responsive to social context (Grint, 2005). In this view leaders do not have the answers but seek to get followers to face their responsibilities.

The difficulties created by this elevation of the social become evident in discussions on responsibility. If actions are joint, how can an individual be held accountable? Both Gergen and Shotter hold that he or she cannot. McNamee and Gergen (1999) strongly argue that individuals should not be held responsible and accountable for their actions. They call for a move to a notion of relational responsibility, a 'we' that is to be held responsible for actions. In the same volume, Mary Gergen (1999) goes even further and suggests that the notion of 'responsibility' be dropped altogether in favour of 'relational appreciation'. Other social constructionists argue against this position, pointing to the difficulty of dealing with power, dominance, duplicity, deception and self seeking (Lannemann, 1999; Deetz and White, 1999).

Social constructionists argue that discourse transforms social life with change and novelty arising in the detail of bodily relating between individuals in discourse. In developing this kind of argument, social constructionists are moving away from the efficient and formative theories of causality underlying the dominant discourse. They are moving to a view of causality in which the future is under perpetual construction in the detail of interaction between persons. This move to a very different causal framework is, it seems to me, the prime strength of the social constructionist argument and it will be taken up in Part 3. However, social constructionists accord primacy to the social and so largely lose individual agency. A different way of understanding the relationship between the individual and the social will be presented in Part 3.

Social identity theory

Social identity theory (Tajfel, 1972; Tajfel and Turner, 1979; Ashforth and Mael, 1989; Fiske and Taylor, 1991; Hayes, 1994; Ellemers, 1993; van Knippenberg and Ellemers, 1993; Hogg and Abrams 1999; Hogg *et al.*, 1995; Korte, 2007) moves away from the individualistic psychological theories of mainstream thinking on organisations by emphasising the impact of social group membership on identity formation and hence the way people interact with each other. Since people belong to different groups, they have multiple selves or identities and which of these is expressed depends upon the group context within which people are interacting. Any society or organisation consists of diverse groups which differ from each other in terms of 'power, status, and influence' which is often expressed in inter-group conflict. Individual behaviour is thought to be directly linked to social processes. People classify information about their social contexts into orderly groups which they label, for example as Muslim or Christian, and this creation of stereotypes enables the simplification of vast quantities of complex information. Stereotypes are evaluated – for example, as good or bad – and group pressures operate to banish dissent, so establishing conformist, rigid ways of thinking as the price of belonging and thus securing identity. In establishing identities, these stereotypical categories create and define each individual's place in society – indeed, as mental representations, group attributes and evaluations of them form the basis of self-appraisal and judgements of others, in a sense constituting individual minds and determining how individuals relate to each other. Who a person 'is', his identity, therefore arises in the ongoing inter-group comparisons people are making and these are biased toward the groups to which a person belongs since it is from these that self-esteem is derived. Individuals use the stereotypes to accentuate the differences between groups of 'us' and 'them' so that 'they' are believed to look the same and act in the same way. Stereotypes are used to enhance the status of the 'in-group' and denigrate the 'out-group'. People are thought to be motivated by self-enhancement and this leads to power plays between groups.

The boundaries between social groups may be permeable, allowing people to move from one group to another in processes of social mobility. Individuals can then take up the dominant group's identity by changing the way they behave. However, if the boundaries are so rigid that individuals cannot discard an inferior social identity and acquire a more favourable one, they may call into question the legitimacy of group distinctions and so disturb social stability, leading to conflictual confrontation. Social identity theory, therefore, suggests organisational development will depend upon the strength of identification people have with groups in the organisation, the permeability of group boundaries, and therefore how easily organisational members can come to think of themselves in terms of different groupings.

Social identity theory, accordingly, posits reciprocal interaction between individuals and their social contexts in continuous processes that shape both the nature of the individual and the structure of their society, in an ongoing and transformative way. This focus on interlinked individual and social transformation distinguishes social identity theory from the individualistic psychological theories in the mainstream. However, in moving away from the modernist elevation of the individual above the social, social identity theory moves to the opposite pole and claims the primacy of society over the individual. The theory of complex responsive processes developed in Part 3 is based on the assumption that neither the individual nor the social are prior or primary, but that they are inseparable and interdependent processes of interaction.

Power is a central issue in social identity theory. Relationships between people are shaped by power plays between dominant and subordinate groupings characterised by in-group and out-group bias. This bias arises in cognitive processes of stereotyping and mental representations. This emphasis on relations of power and dynamics of inclusion and exclusion are also central to the theory of complex responsive processes to be developed in Part 3, but these processes are understood to emerge in wider processes of communicative interaction rather than in processes of cognitive representation.

From the perspective of social identity theory, an individual acquires an identity by cognitively assimilating the group stereotype in so aligning self-perception and behaviour with the relevant in-group stereotype. This emphasis on identify will also be a key feature of the theory of complex responsive processes to be developed in Part 3. However, the take on identity formation will be somewhat different. Rather than being some process of cognitive representation of in and out groupings, identity will be understood as ongoing habitual responses, emerging in social interaction, which constitute a felt unity of self as embodied histories of mutual responsiveness between the persons.

9.4 Communities of practice

Another approach to organisational learning and knowledge creation that has attracted considerable attention from organisational practitioners is the notion of communities of practice (Brown and Duguid, 1991; Lave and Wenger, 1991; Wenger, 1998). Wenger (1998) regards engagement in social practice as the fundamental process through which people learn and so become who they are, thereby making a close link between social practice and identity formation. Not only do people form communities of social practice, they are also formed by the process of learning in which they engage in their communities of practice. From this perspective, one can think of an organisation as a community of practice: that is, as a collective identity that shapes and is shaped by individual identities. An organisation then becomes what it becomes, it forms strategies, in the learning process of a community of practice.

Wenger builds a theory of *community*, social *practice*, *meaning* and *identity*, in which learning is a process of social *participation*. Learning is not simply an individual process but the lived experience of participation in local situations in the world as the production and reproduction of specific ways of *engaging* in the world. Through *local interactions*, learning *reproduces and transforms* the social structure in which it takes place and the *identities* of those who participate. For Wenger, practice is essentially an experience of everyday life, and meaning is located in the process of negotiating meaning. Practice is essentially the process of negotiating meaning in communities of practice, defined as those engaged together on a joint enterprise. It is this joint enterprise that distinguishes communities of practice from cultures and social structures. Practice is the source of coherence in communities of practice and it has three dimensions: *mutual engagement* in actions whose meaning is being negotiated; *joint enterprise*, which is a collective process of negotiation creating relations of mutual accountability; and *shared repertoire* consisting of routines, words, ways of doing, stories, gestures, symbols and genres. Wenger describes (1998, pp. 96–7) these three dimensions as 'interdependent and interlocked into a tight system' combining 'an open process (the negotiation of meaning) and a tight system of interrelations'. He talks about small perturbations rapidly having 'repercussions throughout the system' so that learning 'involves a close interaction of order and chaos'. Practice as a shared history of learning creates discontinuities between those participating and those not, and in so doing creates boundaries and also connections with other communities across boundaries. Wenger associates learning with *boundary* crossing. Furthermore, a practice is local but there are interactions between local and global *levels*. What I am stressing here is the way in which Wenger uses the terminology of systems thinking and its central concepts such as boundaries and hierarchical levels.

Running throughout Wenger's exposition there is the central role accorded to the negotiation of meaning which he understands to be a process, explicitly distancing his theory from functional, cybernetic or system-theoretical accounts. When he does this (Wenger, 1998, p. 286, n. 5), he means something quite specific. He wants to exclude things (like computers) from the status of participant in the negotiation of meaning. He does not want to think in terms of a total system in which both things and persons are actors. He wants to understand how meaning is negotiated, and only people can negotiate and recognise experience of meaning in each other. However, as I have already pointed to above, he does refer to the dimensions of learning as interlocked into a tight system, to interrelations between people as a tight system, and to the importance of boundaries. So it seems to me that while he mostly talks in terms of the process of negotiation, he does couple it with a notion of a system of interrelationship.

How does he think about the negotiation of meaning as a process? He argues that the negotiation of meaning is the interplay of two constituent processes that form a duality. He calls these processes *participation* and *reification*. Participation is an active process of human bodies, of human persons, engaging together in a practice. The actions are the personal and social acts of doing, teaching, talking, conversing, thinking, reflecting, feeling and belonging. Participation is a process characterised by mutual recognition, which is a source of identity. Reification is also a process of engagement with the world but this time it has to do with things. Reification is the production of the artefacts of a practice and they embody a long diverse process of reification. It is a process in which people project meanings on to the world and then perceive those meanings as existing in the world and having a life of their own. In reification we project ourselves onto the world, do not recognise ourselves in our projections and attribute to our meanings an independent existence. Reification *gives form to our experience*, so creating points of focus around which negotiation is organised. An understanding is given form and the form becomes the focus.

The processes of participation and reification are *both* distinct *and* complementary in that they come about through each other. The negotiation of meaning is the seamless interweaving of these two distinct and complementary processes and the experience of meaning is this duality. A duality is a single conceptual unit formed by two inseparable and mutually constitutive elements whose inherent tension and complementarity give the concept richness and diversity. Taken together, participation and reification are inseparable elements of the duality of the negotiation of meaning. This is not a paradox because, although they interweave at the same time in tension with each other, they are distinct processes in which there is no inherent contradiction and the tension between them is not transformed into a new dynamic. They are dual modes of existence through time because they exist in different realms (Wenger, 1998, p. 87). They continually converge and diverge, unfolding in different media. The duality operates as follows. Participation organises itself around reifications such as words. Conversation is said to be a powerful form of communication because it is the interweaving of participation, the action of talking to and mutually recognising each other, and of reification, the words or argument we are using. The words (reification) take advantage of shared participation to create short-cuts to communicational meaning, while participation produces and uses reification.

As I understand it, Wenger is saying that communities of practice are fundamentally social processes of negotiating meaning, which is the same as learning. Participation and reification are distinct processes, or modes of existence, operating in different realms, in different media with their own laws. However, they are also complementary and the process of negotiating meaning is the continuous interplay of the processes of participation and reification, which together constitute an inseparable, interwoven unity. The realm of participation is the actions and interactions of people. It is their doing, talking, thinking, feeling, reflecting and belonging. The realm of reification is another mode of existence, namely the process of projecting meaning on to objects: that is, artefacts, tools or abstractions treated as if they were things. In addition to material artefacts and tools, reifications are also all symbols, including language, and also any bodily expression of feeling, or communication such as glances and silences.

What Wenger is doing, I think, is moving from a micro-description of communities of practice to an abstract, macro-level explanation of the process. He provides a detailed description of the ordinary, daily experience of a woman engaged in a community of practice of claims processors. In constructing a theory to illuminate and explain their practice, he moves away from the daily lived experience and talks in terms of a model in which categories of macro processes 'participation' and 'reification' interact as the 'negotiation of meaning' to form meaning. In Chapter 16, I will make a distinction between first- and second-order abstractions. All thought requires abstraction – that is, a drawing-away from the detail of direct experience to form general categories or stereotypes. I will call this first order *abstraction*. Science performs a second act of abstraction when models consisting of first-order abstractions are built and used for explanatory purposes. It seems to me that Wenger builds such a model which I would describe as *second-order abstraction*. In doing this, he splits the experience of action and interaction into two distinct but complementary aspects constituting the unity of a duality. In other words he adopts a 'both . . . and' mode of thinking in that his view of experience as the negotiation of meaning consists of *both* participation *and* reification.

Wenger says that learning cannot be designed, but that it is a response to design. For him, designs then lead to a learning response and he implies some degree of control exercised by the designer over at least the occurrence of learning. Wenger's move to talking about designing participation and reification implicitly suggests that someone can step out of the processes and design the whole, while others in the community of practice are subjected to the designed aspects of participation and reification. This, it seems to me, creates a problem for personal freedom, because persons are subject to these macro processes of participation and reification which have a life of their own.

However, in its stress on the thoroughly social nature of learning processes and their role in identity formation, he makes a significant move away from the dominant paradigm. This move to the social will be very much the focus of attention in Part 3 of this book. However, the explanation it will put forward differs somewhat from that of Wenger. The first difference is that, while Wenger moves away to some extent from the notion of organisation as a system, he continues to refer to learning as a 'system' (although he does so mainly as a way of talking about participation); the notion of system is dropped altogether in the explanations of organisational life provided in Part 3. The second difference between Wenger's theory and the theory to be built in Part 3 is that, while Wenger explains learning processes in terms of a duality of reification and participation, the theory in Part 3 is built on a number of paradoxes rather than dualisms. For example, human communication is understood as the paradox of gesture and response, power as the paradox of enabling and constraining, and values as the paradox of compulsion and choice.

Now consider how some writers are considering the fundamentally unpredictable nature of organisational life and how strategies might emerge without design.

9.5 Unpredictability and strategy without design

Another move away from the dominant discourse involves accepting that the future is unpredictable. For example, Wiltbank *et al.* (2006) try to deal with the problem of unpredictability by separating prediction and control, advising managers to focus on factors they can control rather than those they can predict. They describe non-predictive techniques of control as generating favourable outcomes by creating a future market through cooperation and goal creation with others in a mutually persuasive process in which stakeholders commit to each other and continue shaping the vision and the opportunity. However, there is no explanation of what control means here or how managers are supposed to know if anything will succeed or not. Matters to do with conflict, politics, ideology, greed, power and unconscious processes are ignored in what amounts to a highly idealistic attempt to cover over the inability to control which follows from an inability to predict.

The debate has been joined by de Rond and Thietart (2007), who explore the extent to which strategic decisions reflect choice rather than circumstances. Choice is a judgement made by an individual as the basis of action: judgement causes the action, and the question becomes whether the action causes an intended outcome in a form of determinism with 'if . . . then' causality. The authors argue that a weaker form of determinism is provided by what they call 'causal background', which is the social and material context that constrains and informs choices: for example, ability, habit, know-how, experience, age, education, ideology, social structures, markets and technology. They suggest that causality is a necessary condition for choice in the sense of *if* a strategic choice is made *then* there is a change in the course of events. However, such choice does not fully determine the change in the course of events because outcomes also depend upon the context in which the choice is made: that is, on the causal background. Chance, also depending on the causal background, opens up new avenues for choices. Strategic choice, chance and context are thus inextricably intertwined in the production of strategic events. Sometimes, actors contribute to an unfolding situation, presumably the context or causal background, in which choices lead to success or failure, but the actors cannot accurately predict or control the unfolding situation. At other times chance plays an important role. Following Mintzberg, the authors regard strategy as a combination of deliberate and opportunistic moves affected by random events which can produce unexpected events that could not have been predicted. This leads to the view that 'strategy is likely to emerge from multiple, complex, interacting processes, only some of which are under managerial control' (de Rond and Thietart, 2007, p. 541). They talk about strategies emerging through chance rather than choice. Choices are made, but the strategy process develops a dynamic of its own which the choosers cannot fully control. In the strategy process, internal and external agents interact, tinker, hesitate, take advantage, and so on, in ways that combine rationality and intuition. Formality, structure and control provide processes of problem identification, search for solutions, selection and implementation, all in an orderly way. However, all of this confronts informality, lack of structure and autonomy in which solutions are the outcome of random, opportunistic processes between actors. They hold that strategy research needs to adopt a more reflective approach focusing on the micro level of ordinary decision-making.

Chia and Holt (2009) point to the usual way of understanding what happens in organisations, which is to see organisational consequences as the result of pre-existing, deliberate plans reflecting conscious choice and purposeful intervention. However, they argue that such direct deliberate actions aimed at realising goals eventually erode their own success, producing disastrous consequences. As an example, they cite the collapse of investment banks and ascribe it to the deliberate strategic intent of the banks. So, they argue for an alternative where organisational strategies should be understood as emerging in non-deliberate ways from the cumulative effect of coping actions performed by many, many individuals who are trying to respond constructively to the situations in which they find themselves. They claim that strategies emerge in indirect ways which are peripheral to specified ends.

In order to explain how the many, many coping actions amount to a coherent strategy, they refer to invisible coordinating forces that produce fruitful outcomes. Local coping actions give rise to strategic consistency in the absence of prior goals and this consistency comes about because of a latent, negative form of our knowing what we do not want, rather than what we want. They call for a 'bottom up' indirect or circuitous approach to strategy which stresses attending to small peripheral details. Sometimes what is deliberately designed does come to pass, but even when successful strategies emerge by chance, overall consistency is provided by unconsciously acquired, culturally shaped habits, which they understand in terms of Bourdieu's *habitus*: that is, durable transposable sets of dispositions. Strategic decisions are thus authored by invisible historical and cultural forces that are immanent in situations in which strategic ordering emerges spontaneously without any singular agency intending it. Spontaneous order emerges without intention, by chance, through the actions of multitudes mindlessly coordinating their actions with each other. Chia and Holt repeatedly contrast smooth unthinking spontaneous cooperation (Adam Smith's invisible hand) with deliberate attempts to impose order. They admit that it is difficult to explain what the invisible hand is, to make it visible, so that the invisible made visible remains an enigma. They trace this kind of thinking through the economist, Hayek, to Maturana and Varela's (1987) theory of autopoiesis where links between cause and effect become hard to identify, leading to the conclusion that there is some kind of immanent, self-generated intelligence which produces emergent order without design.

They claim that indirect, individual coping is more compatible with long-lasting success. This leads to prescriptions of approaching strategic situations indirectly and with more modesty in order to *allow* strategic priorities to emerge spontaneously through local ingenuity. Successful strategy emerges organically and infuses itself into the everyday actions of people, rather than being stated upfront. Instead of navigating, they suggest the metaphor of wayfinding – we know as we go. They call for strategic blandness (abandoning positions and grandiose preferences), a strategy-less strategy to keep open possibilities. They conclude that the best strategy for coping with chaos is to let individuals choose their next action based on their own sense of purpose. They reject the need for deliberate intention and pre-planning, and they call for an end to interfering with the world at a general or macro level and concentration on individual practical purposes. According to these authors, we are systems within systems, and the problem is that we are unaware of the wider self-organising systems we are part of. We should, therefore, redirect our attention from individual agency to the wider systems we are part of in order to develop systemic wisdom which is submission to open-ended interconnectedness.

Chia and Holt are clearly polarising the local and the global and taking up a position at the local emergent pole of the debate, rejecting the need for general overviews of the macro level, because such overviews cannot take into account unique circumstance. For them, the banks failed because their executives were focusing on macro overviews. They quote Scott (1998), who argues for the importance of macro generalisations and their paradoxical interplay with unique local actions, but interpret his work as justifying attention only to unique local situations. In Chapter 16 I will be arguing for the kind of paradoxical interplay of local interaction and global patterns that Scott is talking about. Chia and Holt ascribe the emergence of macro patterns to some invisible force which is difficult to understand or explain and, in doing so, I would say that they either implicitly assume formative causality – what the invisible force unfolds was already there from the beginning – or adaptionist causality in that what emerges is due to chance. In Part 3 of this book I argue for a theory of transformative causality in that what emerges does so in the interplay of intentions of people which amplifies small differences into potentially major changes. The cause of what happens is the interplay that none can control, and there is no polarity of intention and emergence since patterns emerge in the interplay of intentions. This means that the failure of the banks was a population-wide pattern that emerged in the interplay of many intentions, and it cannot be simply ascribed to banking executives focusing on direct macro interventions. Direct macro interventions were simply intentions that played into other people's intentions and it was this interplay that caused the pattern of failure. Chia and Holt equate strategic intent with the intellect and describe it as a conceit that is unable to appreciate any life outside the intellect. However, they then prescribe a choice, an intellectual choice, I would say, to abandon deliberate strategy in favour of adopting indirect strategy and allowing the emergence of strategies in local coping shaped by invisible forces. For me, the problem with the kind of argument presented by Chia and Holt is that, in polarising intention and emergence, they lose the paradox of the local and the global, and I will be looking at an alternative way of thinking involving the holding of that paradox.

Chia and Holt's work does move on from the dominant paradigm in focusing attention on how people are immersed in the social life of an organisation and just how much of their interaction is the expression of social habitus.

9.6 Critical management studies / labour process theory

Critical structuralism (labour process theory) regards organisations as political processes directly linked to the capitalist productive economy. In their recent textbook Knights and Willmott (2007) identify the intellectual basis of the critical approach in:

- Marx's analysis of the structure of capitalism. He maintained that capitalism involves a conflict of interests between owners (and their agents, managers) and labour. This is in direct opposition to the assumptions of the dominant discourse, which are that there is a unity of interests in modern organisations. This unity is represented by management who solve the problem of motivation through developing and applying knowledge. From the Marxist perspective, however, management engage in an ideology of motivation in order to control employees. People become alienated from what they produce, the processes in which they produce it, from each other and from themselves.

- Theories of the social construction of the self, drawing on the work of George Herbert Mead, and theories of the operation of disciplinary power derived from Foucault. Power shapes the ideals set for individual autonomy.

In the 1970s Braverman (1974) argued that scientific management was in reality a process of de-skilling driven by reduction in costs, worker resistance, and the intensifying of work. Braverman was emphasising the actual labour process in a move away from the idealisations of the dominant discourse. Burawoy (1979) drew attention to the use by managers of worker self-organisation. By 'self-organisation' he meant the use of bonus payments to create competitive games which relieved boredom and gave the impression of individual autonomy. Workers came to take the same instrumental approach as managers. Taking the idea of the social construction of the self, Townley (1994) draws on Foucault to argue that power relationships form the identities of individuals, rendering them controllable. Others (for example, Sewell and Wilkinson, 1992) argue that management initiatives, such as total quality management, increase the visibility of workers and so constitute forms of control.

This kind of theoretical approach leads to a view of organisational behaviour which emphasises essentially conflictual political processes in organisations, having to do with identity, insecurity, freedom, power, inequality and knowledge. In taking this processual approach, writers in the critical tradition move away from systems thinking, the foundation upon which the dominant discourse is built. They (for example, Knights and Willmott, 2007) argue that systems thinking produces abstractions that marginalise human beings and the political processes they engage in. Systems thinkers may differentiate between formal and informal organisations, but they tend to regard the latter as problems to be designed away. While systems thinking sees roles in organisations as being defined by consensus, critical theory regards them as patterned by negotiation and interpretation by all participants involved.

The development of complex responsive process theory in Part 3 of this book focuses attention on many of the same issues as the critical approach does, and it adopts the same attitude to systems thinking and an alternative concept of process. It also takes power as central, draws on Mead to understand human individuality and identity, and regards organisations as conflictual political processes of identity formation. However, the complex responsive process perspective is not based primarily on Marxist views of class conflict or Foucauldian notions of power, although both of these thinkers remain important. Instead the theory of complex responsive process combines the thought of Mead on communication and that of Elias on relations of power with insights on emergence and self-organisation (understood very differently from critical approaches).

9.7 Summary

This chapter has discussed the move to second-order thinking, pointing to how this presents a much fuller account of social processes, conversation and narrative. It shows considerable concern with matters of participation and inclusion based on a view of the co-construction of the realities into which organisational members act. However, it continues to rely on the concept of system as a way of thinking and seems to retain assumptions of individualist psychology. The chapter then reviewed various forms of social constructionist thinking about organisations which also develop a much more social perspective on organisational life without relying as explicitly on the notion of system. However, these perspectives seem to move from the priority accorded to the individual, granting it instead to the social. The chapter then went on to look at ideas of communities of practice. This too is a much more socially aware perspective on organisational learning. Others have moved from the dominant discourse by looking at consequences for thinking that flow from unpredictability and non-rational modes of interaction between people. Finally, the chapter briefly reviewed labour process theory which moves away from understanding organisations as systems and conceptualises them in terms of power relations and control. I think that all of these approaches challenge the dominant discourse because, although they may not move away from all the underlying assumptions upon which that discourse is built, they all develop important perspectives on the fundamentally social nature of organisational processes and the manner in which people learn together and deal with uncertainty. These are the concerns that the chapters in Part 3 will take up in an attempt to move on from all the fundamental assumptions of the dominant discourse identified at the end of Chapter 8.

Further reading

Flood (1999), Midgley (2000) and Jackson (2000) all provide thorough accounts of the more recent developments in systems thinking described in this chapter. Gergen (1999) is a thorough review of social constructionism.

Questions to aid further reflection

1. How does second-order systems thinking deal with the problem of infinite regress?
2. What ideologies do soft and critical systems thinking reflect?
3. What role does the notion of pluralism play in critical systems thinking?
4. How are social processes understood in soft and critical systems thinking?
5. What do social constructionist approaches contribute to our understanding of strategic management?
6. What are the implications of the notion of communities of practice for strategic management?
7. What do you think of strategies without design?
8. What conclusion does the theory of labour process lead you to regarding control in organisations?
9. How do the theories reviewed in this chapter deal with the four key questions posed in Chapter 2?
10. How does the concept of emergence feature in the alternative discourse described in this chapter?

Part 2

The challenge of complexity to ways of thinking

Part 1 of this book has described how the 1940s and 1950s saw the development of a number of closely related ideas. At much the same time, engineers, mathematicians, biologists and psychologists were developing the application of systems theories, taking the form of open systems, cybernetics and systems dynamics. These systems theories were closely related to the development of computer languages, cognitivist psychology and the sender–receiver model of communication. Over the decades that followed, all of these theories and applications were used, in one way or another, to construct ways of making sense of organisational life. The central themes running through all of these developments are those of the autonomous individual who is primary and prior to the group, and the concern with the control of systems. This first wave of twentieth-century systems thinking raised a number of problems that second-order systems thinking sought to address. One of these problems had to do with the fact that the observer of a human system is also simultaneously a participant in that system. This led to soft and critical systems thinking, which shifted the focus of attention from the dynamical properties of systems as such to the social practices of those using systemic tools in human activities. Ideology, power, conflict, participation, learning and narratives in social processes all feature strongly in these explanations of decision-making and change in organisations.

The 1970s and 1980s bear some similarities to the 1940s and 1950s in terms of the development of systemic theories in that mathematicians, physicists, meteorologists, chemists, biologists, economists, psychologists and computer scientists worked across their disciplines to develop new theories of systems. Their work goes under titles such as chaos theory, dissipative structures, complex adaptive systems, and has come to be known as nonlinear dynamics or the complexity sciences. What they have in common is the centrality they give to nonlinear relationships. Unlike the development of second-order, soft and critical systems thinking in the social sciences, this new wave of interest in complex systems has been very much concerned with the dynamical properties of systems as such. This has brought new insights into our understanding of systems functioning. Let me explain why this matters.

Part 1 explored the way of thinking reflected in the currently dominant discourse about organisations and their management. The dominant discourse is that way of talking and writing about organisations that is immediately recognisable to organisational practitioners, educators and researchers. It sets the most acceptable terms within which debates about, and funded research into, organisations and their management can be conducted. As such, it reflects particular, fundamental, taken-for-granted assumptions about organisational worlds that constitute 'commonsense' ways of thinking. If one is to be readily understood and persuasive in organisational and research communities, one must argue within the dominant way of thinking, or at least in ways that are recognisable within its terms. The aim of the chapters in Part 1 was to identify the different strands of the currently dominant discourse, including its critics, so as to clarify the differences and similarities in the ways of thinking that they reflect.

The strands of thinking about organisations identified in Part 1 were described as the theory of strategic choice, the theory of the learning organisation, open systems–psychoanalytic perspectives on organisations, and second-order systems thinking. Common to all of them is the assumption that organisations are systems, or at least that they are to be thought of 'as if' they are systems. The different strands of thinking assume different kinds of system with consequent important implications. In strategic choice theory the main assumption is that organisations are to be designed and managed as cybernetic: that is, self-regulating, systems. In theories to do with organisational learning it is mostly assumed that organisations are to be managed in recognition of their being systems of the systems dynamics type. In open systems–psychoanalytic perspectives, the system is assumed to be an open system. Second-order systems thinking, in contrast to the strands so far mentioned, draws on all these systems theories but usually does not regard any system as actually existing in the real world – they are all mental constructs.

Since organisations have to do with people, there always has to be some explicit, or quite often implicit, assumption about human psychology. Common to all of the strands of thinking in the dominant discourse is the psychological assumption that the individual is primary and exists at a different level from a group, organisation or society. Individuals, with minds inside them, form groups, organisations and societies outside them, at a higher level to them, which then act back on them as a causal force with regard to their actions. The different strands of the dominant discourse express this common assumption by drawing on different psychological theories which have important implications. Strategic choice and learning organisa-tion theories draw heavily on cognitivist and humanistic psychology and to a much lesser extent on constructivism. The open system–psychoanalytic perspective reflects the assumptions of psychoanalysis. Second-order systems thinking could draw on all of the mentioned psychological theories.

The chapters in Part 1 explored the differences between the ways of thinking of these different strands consequent upon their different assumptions about psycho-logy and the nature of systems. Just as important, however, are the entailments of what is common to all of them. They all make the following assumptions:

- There is some position external to the system from which powerful, rational indi-viduals can, in principle, objectively observe the system and formulate hypothe-ses about it, on the basis of which they can design the system to produce that which is desirable to them and, hopefully, the wider community. Usually this is quite taken for granted, although second-order systems thinking does grapple, unsuccessfully I argue, with the problem created by the fact that the external observer is also a participant in the system. Where the problematic nature of the assumption that individuals can design human systems is recognised, it is normally resolved by arguing that 'you', the powerful, rational individual, can at least set a direction or present a vision so that the system will produce reasonably desirable outcomes, or, failing even this, 'you' can design the conditions or shape the processes within which others will, more or less, operate the system to desired ends. If even this watered-down assumption is questioned, the immediate response is that the only alternative is pure chance, which leaves no role for leaders or managers.

- This first assumption amounts to one that rationalist causality is applicable to human action, although all of the strands of thinking in the dominant discourse recognise, in one way or another, the severe limitations to human rationality.

- The first assumption also immediately entails a further assumption about system predictability. A system can only be designed and operated to produce a desirable outcome set in advance if its operation is reasonably predictable. The purpose of the design and operation is to reduce uncertainty and increase the regularity and stability of system operation so as to make possible the realisation of the purposes ascribed to it by its designers. Success is equated with stability.

- Stability of system operation requires a reasonable degree of consensus between the individuals who are, or at least operate, the systems. What is required therefore is agreement on purpose and task and this is aided by strongly shared cultures and values. It is the role of leaders and managers to inspire, motivate and persuade others to act in the best interests of the 'whole'.

- The assumptions about predictability and stability immediately imply a particular theory of causality as far as the system is concerned and these are either efficient 'if–then' or formative causality.

- Causality is thus dual, with rationalist causality ascribed to designing individuals and formative causality ascribed to the system they design.

- The primary task of leading and managing is to be in control of the direction of the organisation, whether in a 'command and control' way or in some other more facilitative way in which others are empowered and invited to participate.

The way of thinking reflecting the above assumptions was developed primarily in relation to the private sector of Western economies. However, over the past few decades there has been a major shift in the form of public sector governance. Marketisation and managerialism have been imported into the public sector, and also into non-governmental organisations (NGOs) and charities, from the private sector. The private sector way of thinking about organisations now dominates these sectors too.

The assumptions common to the different strands of the discourse now dominant across all organisations reflects much more than the basis of intellectual argument. Even more importantly and more powerfully they reflect dominant ideologies. At the centre of this ideology is the belief in the possibility of, and the necessity for, *control*. This ideology has a long history in the West. It justifies the use of the natural sciences to control the resources of nature and the central concern with efficiency in organisations, even if people experience this as oppression. The domination of nature and the oppression of people in the interests of efficiency have, of course, been fiercely contested for some considerable time. This is evident in the ecological movement with its ideology of preserving the planet, in the human relations movement and humanistic psychology and its motivational ideology within organisations, in the call for empowerment, democracy, emancipation, pluralism and participative decision-making – for example in second-order systems thinking, and in the move to the mystical and the spiritual – for example in learning organisation theory.

However, all of these ideological responses to the domination and oppression that can flow from of an ideology of control are themselves dependent upon control. At issue is not control itself but the manner in which the control is to be exercised and the consequences it brings. Accordingly, the ecological movement expresses its ideology in a call for the control of industry and consumers in the interests of preserving the planet. The ideology of democracy, emancipation, pluralism and empowerment expresses the manner in which control should be exercised rather demanding that it should be abandoned. Indeed, the ideology of progress and improvement, more recently expressed in the public sector as modernisation, depends very heavily on the ideology of control. To question the ability of humans to be 'in control' is to question a belief that groups of well-meaning people can devise ways of improving whole sectors of human activity such as healthcare. Much the same is true of those who call for more attention to be paid to the spiritual and the mystical in organisational life in the interests of securing simpler, better ways for organisations to operate so that people can find fulfilling lives. Accompanying the ideologies both of control and participation is the ideology of large-scale improvement in human conditions and this includes the governance of organisations.

In challenging the dominant way of thinking about organisations, therefore, one is engaging in far more than an intellectual debate. To question a way of thinking is to question the dominant ideologies underpinning it and throw into confusion the sense people make of what they are doing and who they are, and at a very deep level. To question the ideology of control and improvement is not simply to question domination and oppression, but also to question the nature of our ability to preserve and improve the world we live in. It is to question some of the deepest beliefs people have about what it is possible for them to do for the good.

To claim, then, that the development of what have come to be called the 'natural complexity sciences' potentially presents a major challenge to ways of thinking, not just in the natural sciences but also in relation to human actions and organisations, is something of major importance which can be experienced as deeply threatening. Although they have their origins over a century ago, it is only since the 1960s that the complexity sciences have really begun to develop and only over the past two decades that they have attracted significant attention in both the natural and social sciences. They represent the most significant advance in the understanding of the nature of systems since the middle of the twentieth century. Since the currently dominant discourse on organisations is so heavily dependent on the first wave of system ideas, it is important to consider in what way the new systems theories support or contest those developed in the middle of the twentieth century.

For this reason the first chapter in this part, Chapter 10, briefly reviews some of the main ideas in the complexity sciences, while Chapter 11 considers how these ideas have been taken up by some writers on organisations. Chapter 10 also points to the different understanding different natural scientists have of complex systems. For some, complexity does not amount to science at all. Among those who do argue that their complexity work is scientific, there are some, perhaps the majority, who do not regard the insights of complexity theories as a major challenge to the natural science project of the past few hundred years to do with certainty and control. However, there are others who argue rigorously that complexity insights do present a major challenge to currently dominant ways of thinking and call for a radical re-thinking of the scientific project. So, what are the insights that might lead one to such a radical re-thinking?

First, complex systems display spatial patterns called 'fractals' and patterns of movement over time that have been described as 'chaos' or 'the edge of chaos'. These terms may be suggestive of fragmentation or utter confusion, but in fact they refer to the discovery of *coherent patterns* in what might have looked random and so without pattern. However, these patterns are not what we are used to. Fractals, for example, display a regular degree of irregularity so that within each space of stability there is always instability. Movement over time called 'chaotic' or at the 'edge of chaos' is movement that is regular and irregular, stable and unstable, at the same time. Such systems operate far from equilibrium where they have structure, but the structure is dissipating. In other words, complex systems are characterised by paradoxical dynamics. Most phenomena in nature, and all living phenomena, are held to be characterised by these paradoxical dynamics. This challenges the assumptions about stability and equilibrium in previous systems theories, the ones previously imported into the dominant way of thinking about organisations, which equate stability with success. If paradoxical dynamics have anything to do with organisations, then the dominant discourse's equation of success with stability would be open to question and we would have to explore the ways in which instability is vital in organisational life.

Second, systems operating far from equilibrium, in chaos or at the edge of chaos are radically unpredictable over the long term. They are characterised by predictability and unpredictability at the same time in the present, and over the long term their futures are unknowable when they are evolving in the presence of diversity. This challenges the assumption of previous systems theories that the movement of systems is predictable, or at least follows given archetypes. It is these latter assumptions that were imported to form the basis of the currently dominant way of thinking about organisations. If radical unpredictability is a characteristic of organisational life, we clearly need to re-think the most taken-for-granted prescriptions for managing organisations.

Third, the future of complex systems is under perpetual construction in the self-organising – that is, local interacting – of the entities comprising them. The long-term future of the whole system – that is, the pattern of relationships across whole populations of agents – emerges in such local interaction. *Emergence* means that there is no blueprint, plan or programme for the whole system, the population-wide pattern. In other words, the whole cannot be designed by any of the agents comprising it because they produce it collectively as participants in it. This challenges the assumptions made in previous systems theories about the possibility of taking the position of external observer and intervening in, even designing, the whole system. If the development of an organisation emerges in the local interaction of its members, then we will have to re-think all the approaches which suppose that powerful or well-meaning people can directly change the 'whole'.

Fourth, complex systems can evolve only when the agents comprising them are diverse. Evolution, the production of novelty, and creativity are possible only where there is diversity and, hence, conflicting constraints. Evolution as emergence occurs primarily through the self-organising – that is, local conflictual interacting – of the agents rather than by plan or central design which inspire harmony. This challenges the assumption of previous systems theories that functioning, developing systems are characterised by harmony where the pieces fit together. Again this challenges the previous systems theories imported into thinking about organisations.

If these four insights from the complexity sciences were to replace the assumptions of earlier systems theories in thinking about organisations, they would lead to a very different way of understanding organisational life. We would need to understand how people together are coping with fundamental unpredictability, how organisations as population-wide patterns are evolving in many, many local interactions, and what role diversity, conflict and non-average behaviour play in all of this. We would have to reconsider what we think we are doing when we formulate and implement strategic plans and design organisations, re-engineer processes, plan culture changes, install values, develop policies for the 'whole', and so on. In other words, we would have to re-think what we mean by 'control', because under the new assumptions no one would be 'in control'. It follows that no well-meaning group of people could directly improve the whole. One consequence of taking the radical insights of complexity theories seriously, then, would be the serious undermining of dominant ideologies.

However, others have a different take on what the complexity sciences mean for human action. Ecologists might take the challenge to the control paradigm as supporting their ideology on the basis of which they can resist the folly of treating nature as humans do. Others may see in the emphasis on local interaction support for their ideology of more caring relationships between people. Yet others may resonate with the unknowability of complex system futures and link this with something spiritual, while regarding emergence as linked to something mystical. Still others may find in the study and modelling of complex systems a different way to control systems and so sustain the control ideology.

In view of all of these possibilities it seems important to me to devote some effort to trying to understand just what different complexity scientists have to say and just how writers on organisations are using their work. That is the purpose of this part of the book.

Chapter 10

The complexity sciences

The sciences of uncertainty

This chapter invites you to draw on your own experience to reflect on and consider the implications of:

- Whether the traditional scientific project of certainty is undermined by the complexity sciences.

- The role of conflicting constraints in the functioning of complex phenomena.

- The relationship between local interaction and population-wide pattern.

- The different theories of causality implicit in models of complexity.

- The different ways in which theories of complexity are interpreted.

- Whether developments in the complexity sciences present key challenges to the fundamental assumptions previously imported from the natural sciences into thinking about organisations.

- The challenge that notions of self-organisation and emergence present to the possibility of whole system design to be found in mainstream thinking about organisations.

- The importance of diversity, difference and non-average behaviour in the generation of novelty and what challenge this presents to mainstream thinking about organisations.

It is important to understand the ideas presented in this chapter, because all of the theories of organisation reviewed in Part 1 rely on ideas that were originally imported from the natural sciences, and the complexity sciences could present significant challenges to these older imports. It is important, therefore, to consider the challenges presented by these more recent ideas for taken-for-granted ways of understanding organisations. The key ideas in this chapter will serve as analogies for the alternative way of thinking about organisations to be presented in Part 3. This chapter is thus an important transition from Part 1 to Part 3.

10.1 Introduction

For some 400 years now, since the times of Newton, Bacon and Descartes, scientists have tended to understand the natural world in terms of machine-like regularity in which given inputs are translated through absolutely fixed linear laws into given outputs. For example, if you apply a given force to a ball of a given weight, the laws of motion will determine exactly how far the ball will move on a horizontal plane in a vacuum. Cause and effect are related in a straightforward linear way. On this view, once one has discovered the fixed laws of nature and gathered data on the inputs to those laws, one will be able to predict the behaviour of nature. Once one knows how nature would have behaved without human intervention, one can intervene by altering the inputs to the laws and so get nature to do something different, something humans want it to do. According to this Newtonian view of the world, humans will ultimately be able to dominate nature.

This whole way of reasoning and understanding was imported into economics, where it is particularly conspicuous, and also into the other social sciences and some schools of psychology. This importation is the source of the equilibrium paradigm that still today exercises a powerful effect on thinking about managing and organising. That thinking is based on the belief that managers can in principle control the long-term future of organisations and societies. Such a belief is realistic if cause-and-effect links are of the Newtonian type described above, for then the future can be predicted over the long term and so can be controlled by someone – they can get organisations and societies to do what they want them to do.

The basis of this approach to both nature and human action is that of *determinism*, in that there are fixed laws causally connecting an action and a consequence, and also *reductionism*, in that the laws governing the movement of phenomena can be discovered by identifying their smallest components and the laws governing the movement of these small components. One comes to understand the whole phenomenon through understanding the smallest components in the belief that the whole is the sum of its parts. It follows that in this approach the micro aspects of phenomena are of crucial importance.

The notion of systems, first put forward by Kant, represents a very important addition to this way of thinking in that it focuses attention not simply on the parts but on the *interaction* between them. The whole, then, becomes more that the sum of its parts, and functioning wholes are stable. This represents a major move away from simple reductionism, and the chapters in Part 1 of the book have traced how the notion of systems has been taken up in thinking about organisations and their management. The move from reductionism is thus a move from the micro to the macro. The systems theories represented in Part 1 model phenomena at the macro level of the whole.

However, this movement from reductionism to systems, from micro parts to macro wholes, did not amount to a move away from determinism. Cybernetic, general systems and systems dynamics models are all deterministic, so that nature and human action are both still understood to move according to fixed laws but now the laws take account of interaction. The same idea about the possibility of human control persists both in relation to nature and human action. Stability continues to be the key characteristic.

The move to systems thinking is also not necessarily a move away from linear causality. Cybernetic and general systems models continue to be based on linear relationships, although they do envisage the possibility of a linear connection between cause and effect being followed by a linear connection between the effect acting back on the cause, so leading to circular connections. In the review of the systems dynamics model, however, Chapter 5 pointed to how it differed from both cybernetics and open systems theory in the emphasis it placed on nonlinearity and non-equilibrium states. In other words, systems dynamics took account of relationships where the effects of a cause could be more or less than proportional to that cause and where there could be more than one effect for a single cause, or more than one cause for an effect. When systems dynamics came to be used in learning organisation theory, the nonlinearity was incorporated by adding positive feedback loops to the negative feedback that formed the basis of cybernetic systems. As a consequence of this nonlinearity, links between cause and effect can become distant and hard to identify, prediction becomes more difficult and so systems dynamics models can produce unexpected outcomes. Control, therefore, becomes more problematic, but it is held in learning organisation theory that control over the whole system is still possible if one recognises archetypal behavioural patterns and acts at leverage points.

The next two sections of this chapter are concerned with much the same kind of nonlinear relationships that systems dynamics was originally concerned with. These sections introduce two branches of what have come to be called the complexity sciences, namely, the theories of mathematical chaos and dissipative structures. Both of these theories have been developed since the 1950s and provide models that are essentially an extension of systems dynamics. Just as in systems dynamics, the models of chaos and dissipative structure theory focus on the macro level and both are nonlinear and deterministic. Because they are deterministic, the relationships in the models do not themselves change, develop or evolve, although the system they produce does develop as that which is enfolded in the relationships is unfolded by the interaction of its components. It follows that it is problematic to apply these theories in any direct way to human relationships, since humans do learn and evolve. However, the theories of chaos and dissipative structures may have some value as metaphors and they do extend the insights into systems dynamics significantly.

These insights can be claimed to be so fundamental as to challenge the scientific project of control, based on predictability and certainty, which has prevailed in the West now for hundreds of years. Both of these theories demonstrate the fundamental unpredictability of nonlinear interaction in conditions required for change, rendering long-term forecasting impossible. Both of these theories identify a paradoxical dynamic, a paradoxical movement through time, in which stability and instability cannot be separated. Instead, they constitute a new dynamic that one would have to call *stable instability* or *unstable stability*. Uncertainty becomes a basic feature of nature and the possibility of control is seriously compromised. Furthermore, dissipative structure theory shows that a system can only move from one pattern of behaviour to another of its own accord if it operated far from equilibrium. Here the system can amplify irregularities in its interactions with the environment called 'fluctuations', break symmetries and spontaneously produce a shift from one pattern of behaviour to another which cannot be predicted from the previous pattern. Instability is shown to be fundamentally necessary for a system to change of its own accord. The preoccupation with equilibrium and stability in both the natural and social sciences is thus severely challenged by theories of chaos and dissipative structures. The manner in which systems models have been applied to organisations and the prescriptions deduced from them are thus severely challenged by the development of chaos and dissipative structure theory.

Section 10.4 takes up another branch of the complexity sciences – namely, the theory of complex adaptive systems developed by scientists working at the Santa Fé Institute in New Mexico, who formulate systemic behaviour in agent-based terms. Here there are no equations at the macro level. Instead, the system is modelled as a population of agents interacting with each other according to their own local 'if–then' rules. This theory of systems differs from all of those so far surveyed in that it focuses attention at a lower level of description – namely, the micro level of the individual agents that form the system. The models demonstrate how local – that is, self-organising – interaction yields emergent order for the whole system and also, in certain conditions, evolution in the form of emergent novelty. These models focus on a system's internal capacity to evolve spontaneously because of micro diversity. Here self-organisation refers to local interactions between agents in the absence of a system-wide blueprint, rather than the collective response of the whole system as in dissipative structure theory.

Consider first what is meant by mathematical chaos theory.

10.2 Mathematical chaos theory

Chaos theory (Gleick, 1988; Stewart, 1989) is concerned with the dynamical properties of the same kind of models as systems dynamics. It can, therefore, be regarded as an extension of systems dynamics. A systems dynamics model consists of a set of interrelated nonlinear equations which model the movement over time of some phenomenon at the macro level. The concern is with how the whole phenomenon is changing over time. The model is such that the calculated output of one period is taken as the input for the calculation of the output of the next period. The model is thus *iterated* over time and the pattern of movement of these iterations is studied to identify dynamical properties. This description applies to the models used in chaos theory too. Those studying systems dynamics models showed how, for particular parameter values, the model produces perfectly stable, predictable movement over time. The model produces one pattern of equilibrium behaviour. In the language of chaos theory this is referred to as a 'point attractor' in that the model settles down at one equilibrium point. At other parameter values, the model produces perfectly stable, predictable cycles of movement from a peak to a trough and back again. In the language of chaos theory this is a 'cyclical', or 'period two, attractor'. At yet other parameter values, a systems dynamics model can produce explosively unstable behaviour. In the language of chaos theory this might be referred to as 'high-dimensional chaos', a pattern of fragmentation.

It is important to note that these attractors of stability and instability are a consequence of the internal structure of the model itself, and are not simply due to changes occurring in the environment. Those using systems dynamics models in organisations have explained the changing dynamics of the model in terms of feedback where negative feedback produces the stable equilibrium of a point attractor and positive feedback produces instability. However, strictly speaking, this is not feedback in the cybernetic sense, because there is no comparison with an external reference point which is then used as an input to the next calculation so that system change is due to environmental change. However, in the systems dynamics models, the whole output of one calculation is 'fed back' into the calculation for the next period without any comparison with an external reference point so that systems change is due to the internal structure of the model.

What has so far been said about systems dynamics models applies to chaos theory models too. What chaos models reveal is an important property of these models that had not been noticed before. Between parameter values at which the system is stable (point or cyclical attracts) and values at which it is unstable (high-dimensional chaos), there are values at which the system moves in a manner that might appear to be random, but on closer examination a pattern is revealed. This pattern is regular irregularity, or stable instability, and this means that it is predictably unpredictable. In other words, the dynamics, the pattern of movement, is paradoxical and it has been given the name of *strange attractor* or *fractal* or *low-dimensional chaos*. It is tempting to understand this pattern as a balance between stability and instability, or as a flipping back and forth between negative and positive feedback, or as a tension between stability and instability. However, descriptions such as these lose the paradoxical nature of the dynamic. The strange attractor called *mathematical chaos* is not a little bit of stability and a little bit of instability, but a completely different dynamic in which instability and stability are inextricably intertwined so that in every stability there is also instability and they cannot be separated out. Taken together in this way, stability and instability no longer mean what they did in their separate states. Note that 'chaos' here does not mean utter confusion but pattern that we are not used to noticing or thinking about.

When a system moves according to the chaotic pattern of the strange attractor, it is highly sensitive to initial conditions. Precisely where the calculation starts matters a great deal. This means that a tiny difference, an error or fluctuation, in the input of one period can escalate over subsequent periods to qualitatively change the pattern that would otherwise have occurred. This creates enormous practical difficulties for long-term prediction; in fact it is impossible to make long-term predictions when a system's movement is mathematically chaotic.

Models of mathematical chaos have been used to explain many natural phenomena: for example, the earth's weather system. Models of weather systems consist of nonlinear relationships between interdependent forces such as pressure, temperature, humidity and wind speed that are related to each other by nonlinear equations. To model the weather system, these forces have to be measured at a particular point in time, at regular vertical intervals through the atmosphere from each of a grid of points on the earth's surface. Rules are then necessary to explain how each of the sets of interrelated measurements, at each measurement point in the atmosphere, moves over time. This requires massive numbers of computations. When these computations are carried out, they reveal that the weather follows a *strange attractor*, which is the technical term for a mathematically chaotic pattern.

This means that the weather follows recognisably similar patterns, but those patterns are never exactly the same as those at any previous point in time. The system is highly sensitive to small changes and blows them up into major alterations in weather patterns. This is popularly known as the 'butterfly effect' in that it is possible for a butterfly to flap its wings in São Paolo, so making a tiny change to air pressure there, and for this tiny change to escalate up into a hurricane over Miami. You would have to measure the flapping of every butterfly's wings around the earth with infinite precision in order to be able to make long-term forecasts. The tiniest error made in these measurements could produce spurious forecasts. However, short-term forecasts are possible because it takes time for tiny differences to escalate. Chaotic dynamics means that humans will never be able to forecast the weather at a detailed level for more than a few days ahead, because they will never be able to measure with infinite precision. The theoretical maximum for accurate forecasts is two weeks, something meteorologists are nowhere near reaching yet.

Although the specific path of behaviour in chaos is unpredictable, that behaviour does have a pattern, a qualitative shape. So the specific path of the weather is unpredictable in the long term, but it always follows the same global shape. There are boundaries outside which the weather system hardly ever moves and, if it does so, it is soon attracted back to the pattern prescribed by the attractor. Some weather conditions do not occur – snow storms in the Sahara desert or heat waves in the Arctic. There is a pattern to weather behaviour because it is constrained by the structure of the nonlinear relationships generating it.

Because of this, the system displays typical patterns, or recognisable categories of behaviour. Even before people knew anything about the shape of the weather's strange attractor, they always recognised patterns of storms and sunshine, hurricanes and calm and seasonal patterns. These recognisable patterns are repeated in an approximate way over and over again. They are never exactly the same, but there is always some similarity. This means that it is not possible to identify specific causes that yield specific outcomes, but the boundaries within which the system moves and the qualitative nature of the patterns it displays are known. The very irregularity of the weather will itself be regular because it is constrained in some way – it cannot do just anything. The resulting self-similar patterns of the weather can be used to prepare appropriate behaviour. One can buy an umbrella or move the sheep off the high ground. People can cope with the uncertainty and the lack of detectable causal connection, because they are aware of self-similar patterns and use them in a qualitative way to guide specific choices.

Throughout the 1970s and 1980s the principles of chaos were explored in one field after another and found to explain, for example, turbulence in gases and liquids, the spread of some diseases and the impact of some inoculation programmes against some diseases. The body's system of arteries and veins follows fractal patterns similar to the branching pattern generated by the mathematical models. The growth of insect populations has chaotic characteristics. The leaves of trees are fractal and self-similar. The reason for no two snowflakes ever being the same can be explained using chaotic dynamics. Water dripping from a tap has been shown to follow a chaotic time pattern, as does smoke spiralling from a cigarette. One of the most intriguing discoveries is that healthy hearts and healthy brains display patterns akin to mathematical chaos. The heart moves into a regular rhythm just before a heart attack and brain patterns during epileptic fits are also regular. It seems that chaos is the signature of health.

The properties of low-dimensional deterministic chaos have been found to apply to nonlinear systems in meteorology, physics, chemistry and biology (Gleick, 1988).

Economists and other social scientists have been exploring whether these discoveries are relevant to their disciplines (Anderson *et al.*, 1988; Baumol and Benhabib, 1989; Kelsey, 1988). There are some indications that chaos explanations may give insight into the operation of foreign exchange markets, stock markets and oil markets (Peters, 1991).

It is important to note that chaos theory models of systems, just as with systems dynamics models, do not have the internal capacity to move spontaneously from one attractor to another. It requires some external force to manipulate the parameters for the system to move from a point attractor to a cyclical one and then to the strange attractor. Finally, it is important to note a related point about causality. Causality continues to be formative, just as it is in systems dynamics. The chaos model is unfolding the pattern already enfolded in its mathematical specification. Such systems are incapable of spontaneously generating novelty.

The conclusion, then, is that very simple nonlinear relationships, perfectly deterministic ones, can produce highly complex patterns of behaviour over time. Between stability and instability there is a complex 'border' that combines both stability and instability. Note that, although the word 'chaos' is being used, it does not mean the utter confusion, the complete randomness it usually means in ordinary conversation. On the contrary, mathematical chaos reveals patterns in phenomena previously thought to be random. It is just that the patterns are paradoxically regular and irregular, stable and unstable.

The central insight from chaos theory is that, in certain circumstances, iterative, recursive, nonlinear systems operate in a paradoxical dynamic which makes it impossible to make long-term forecasts, for practical reasons. The next section continues the exploration of deterministic dynamical systems by briefly describing the theory of dissipative structures.

10.3 The theory of dissipative structures

Prigogine (Nicolis and Prigogine, 1989; Prigogine and Stengers, 1984) has demonstrated in laboratory experiments how nonlinear physical and chemical systems display intrinsically unpredictable forms of behaviour when they operate far from equilibrium. He identified a fundamental relationship between fluctuations, or disorder, on the one hand, and the development of orderly forms, on the other. A nonlinear system far from equilibrium escalates small changes, or fluctuations, in the environment, causing the instability necessary to shatter an existing behaviour pattern and make way for a different one. Systems may pass through states of instability and reach critical points where they spontaneously self-organise to produce a different structure or behaviour that cannot be predicted from knowledge of the previous state. This more complex structure is called a *dissipative* structure because it takes energy to sustain the system in that new mode. Consider what happens when a system moves from equilibrium to a far from equilibrium state.

A liquid is at thermodynamic equilibrium when it is closed to its environment and the temperature is uniform throughout it. The liquid is then in a state of rest at a global level – that is, there are no bulk movements in it – although the molecules move everywhere and face in different directions. In equilibrium, then, the positions and movements of the molecules are random and hence independent of each other. There are no correlations, patterns or connections. At equilibrium, nothing happens and the behaviour of the system is symmetrical, uniform and regular. This means that every point within the liquid is essentially the same as every other and at every point in time the liquid is in exactly the same state as it is at every other: namely, at a state of rest at the macro level and randomness at the micro level. However, when the liquid is pushed far from equilibrium by increasing the heat applied to it, small fluctuations are amplified throughout the liquid. So, if one starts with a layer of liquid close to thermodynamic equilibrium and then begins to apply heat to the base, that sets up a fluctuation or change in the environmental condition in which the liquid exists. That temperature change is then amplified or spread through the liquid. The effect of this amplification is to break the symmetry and to cause differentiation within the liquid.

At first the molecules at the base stop moving randomly and begin to move upward, those most affected by the increase in temperature rising to the top of the liquid. That movement eventually sets up convection so that those molecules least affected are displaced and pushed down to the base of the liquid. There they are heated and move up, in turn pushing others down. The molecules are now moving in a circle. This means that the symmetry of the liquid is broken by the bulk movement that has been set up, because each point in the liquid is no longer the same as all others: at some points movement is up and at other points it is down. After a time, a critical temperature point is reached and a new structure emerges in the liquid. Molecules move in a regular direction, setting up hexagonal cells, some turning clockwise and others turning anti-clockwise: they self-organise. What this represents is long-range coherence where molecular movements are correlated with each other as though they were communicating. The direction of each cell's movement is, however, unpredictable and cannot be determined by the experimenter. The direction taken by any one cell depends upon small chance differences in the conditions that existed as the cell was formed.

As further heat is applied to the liquid, the symmetry of the cellular pattern is broken and other patterns emerge. Eventually the liquid reaches a turbulent state of evaporation. Movement from a perfectly orderly, symmetrical situation to one of some more complex order occurs through a destabilising process. The system is pushed away from stable equilibrium in the form of a point attractor, through bifurcations such as the limit cycle, and so on towards deterministic chaos. The process is one of destruction making way for the creation of another pattern.

What I have been describing is a laboratory experiment used to explore the phenomenon of convection. When it comes to that phenomenon in nature, rather than in the laboratory, there is an important difference. In the case of convection in nature there is no experimenter standing outside the system objectively observing it and turning up the heat parameter as there is in the laboratory experiment. Instead, the patterns of convection in the earth's atmosphere and oceans are caused by variations in the earth's temperature, which are in turn partially caused by the convection patterns. Outside the laboratory, the system itself is changing the parameters and it is this that the experiment is trying to model.

Self-organisation is, therefore, a process that occurs spontaneously at certain critical values of a system's control parameters and it involves the system organising itself to produce a different pattern without any blueprint for that pattern.

Emergence here means that the pattern produced by self-organisation cannot be explained by the nature of the entities that the system consists of or the interaction between them. What is important is that there should be fluctuations – that is, non-average impacts from the environment – otherwise the system cannot spontaneously move to a different attractor. The different pattern that emerges is a dissipative structure in that it easily dissolves if the system moves away from critical points in its control parameters. An equilibrium structure requires no effort to retain its structure and great effort to change it, while a dissipative structure requires great effort to retain its structure and relatively little to change it.

Prigogine (Nicolis and Prigogine, 1989; Prigogine and Stengers, 1984) has established that nonlinear chemical systems are changeable only when they are pushed far from equilibrium where they can become dissipative systems. Dissipative systems import energy and information from the environment that then dissipates through the system, in a sense causing it to fall apart. However, it also has structure and it is capable of renewal through self-organisation as it continues to import energy and information. A dissipative system is essentially a contradiction or paradox: symmetry and uniformity of pattern are being lost but there is still a structure; dissipative activity occurs as part of the process of creating a different structure. A dissipative structure is not just a result, but a process that uses disorder to change, an interactive process that temporarily manifests in globally stable structures. Stability dampens and localises change to keep the system where it is, but operation far from equilibrium destabilises a system and so opens it up to change.

It is important to note here that the kind of system described in the section on chaos theory cannot spontaneously move of its own accord from one attractor to another. Something outside the system has to alter the parameter for this to happen. However, with the kind of system described in this section such a spontaneous move is possible because the system is sensitive to non-average interaction with its environment (Allen, 1998a, 1998b).

Note, however, that these are deterministic systems modelled at the macro level just as is the case in chaos theory and that neither of these systems evolve. Formative causality still applies, but now the dissipative system can move spontaneously from one enfolded attractor to another. The suggestion is that a spontaneously changeful system is one that is constrained from settling down into equilibrium, a completely different finding from that usually assumed.

When Prigogine (1997) considers the wider implications of his work, he poses an important question: 'Is the future given, or is it under perpetual construction?' One could express the question thus: 'Is causality to be understood as formative or is it to be understood as transformative?' Prigogine sees the future for every level of the universe as under perpetual construction and he suggests that the process of perpetual construction, at all levels, can be understood in nonlinear, non-equilibrium terms, where instabilities, or fluctuations, break symmetries, particularly the symmetry of time. He says that nature is about the creation of unpredictable novelty, where the possible is richer than the real. When he moves from models and laboratory experiments to think about the wider questions of evolution, he sees life as an unstable system with an unknowable future in which the irreversibility of time plays a constitutive role. He sees evolution as encountering bifurcation points and taking paths at these points that depend on the micro details of interaction at those points. Prigogine sees evolution at all levels in terms of instabilities with humans and their creativity as a part of it. He pronounces the end of certainty for the scientific project and the intrinsic uncertainty of life, calling for a new dialogue with nature.

So a key discovery about the operation of deterministic iterative nonlinear systems is that stable equilibrium and explosive instability are not the only attractors. Nonlinear systems have a third possibility: a state of stable instability far from equilibrium in which behaviour has a pattern, but it is regularly irregular and intrinsically uncertain. That pattern emerges without any overall blueprint through self-organisation. It is important to note how the nature of self-organisation and emergence is conceived in these theoretical developments. Self-organisation and emergence are thought of as the collective response of whole populations. These are properties of the system itself, not the consequences of some external agent first applying positive feedback and then applying negative feedback.

When it operates in the paradoxical dynamic of stability and instability, the behaviour of a system unfolds in so complex a manner, so dependent upon the detail of what happens, that the links between cause and effect are lost. One can no longer count on a certain given input leading to a certain given output. The laws themselves operate to escalate small chance disturbances along the way, breaking any direct link between an input and a subsequent output. The long-term future of a system operating in the dynamic of stability and instability at the same time is not simply difficult to see: it is, for all practical purposes, unknowable. It is so because of the structure of the system itself, not simply because of changes going on outside it and impacting upon it. Nothing can remove that unknowability.

If this were to apply to an organisation, then decision-making processes that involved forecasting, envisioning future states, or even making any assumptions about future states, would be problematic in terms of realising a chosen future. Those applying such processes in conditions of stable instability would be engaging in fantasy activities. It follows that no one can be 'in control' of a system that is far from equilibrium in the way that control is normally thought about, because no one can forecast the specific future of a system operating in stable instability. No one can envision it either, unless one believes in clairvoyance, prophecy or mystical visions. No one can establish how the system would move before a policy change and then how it would move after the policy change. There would be no option but to make the change and see what happens.

Prigogine's theory of dissipative structures takes a radical step from systems dynamics and chaos theory. Like systems dynamics, Prigogine's models are cast in nonlinear equations that specify changes in the macro states of a system and, like systems dynamics and chaos, the system is assumed to be a non-equilibrium one. In addition, however, the assumption that micro events occur at their average rate is dropped. In other words, the 'noise', or 'fluctuations', in the form of variations around any average are incorporated into the model (Allen, 1998a, 1998b). Prigogine's work demonstrates the importance of these 'fluctuations', showing how fluctuations impart to a nonlinear system that is held far from equilibrium the capacity to move spontaneously from one attractor to another. He calls this 'order through fluctuations' and shows how it occurs through a process of spontaneous self-organisation.

10.4 Complex adaptive systems

A complex adaptive system (Gell-Mann, 1994; Holland, 1998; Kauffman, 1995; Langton, 1996) consists of a large number, a population, of entities called *agents*, each of which behaves according to some set of rules. These rules require each individual agent to adjust its action to that of other agents. In other words, individual agents interact with, and adapt to, each other and in doing so form a system which could also be thought of as a population-wide pattern. For example, a flock of birds might be thought of as a complex adaptive system. It consists of many individual agents, perhaps thousands, who might be following simple rules to do with adapting to the movement of neighbours so as to fly in a formation without crashing into each other, a population-wide pattern called 'flocking'. The human body might be thought of as a complex adaptive system consisting of 30,000 individual genes interacting with each other to produce human physiology. An ecology could be thought of as a complex adaptive system consisting of a number of species relating to each other to produce patterns of evolving life forms. A brain could be considered as a system of 10 billion neurons interacting with each other to produce patterns of brain activity across the whole population of neurons. Complexity science seeks to identify common features of the dynamics of such systems in general.

Key questions are these: how do such complex nonlinear systems with their vast numbers of interacting agents function to produce orderly patterns of behaviour across a whole population? How do such systems evolve to produce new orderly patterns of behaviour?

The traditional scientific approach to answering these questions would be to look for general laws directly determining the population-wide order and governing the observed evolution of that population-wide order. The expectation would be to find an overall blueprint at the level of the whole system, the whole population, according to which it would behave or to identify some global process governing the evolution of the system. This is the kind of macro approach common to all the branches of systems thinking reviewed so far in this book, including chaos and dissipative structure theory. Scientists working with complex adaptive systems take a fundamentally different approach. They do not look for an overall blueprint for the whole system at all: instead, they model individual agent interaction, with each agent behaving according to its own local principles of interaction. The interaction is local in the sense that each individual agent interacts with only a tiny proportion of the total population, and it is local in the sense that none of them are following centrally determined rules of interaction. In such interaction, no individual agent, or group of agents, directly determines the rules of interaction of others or the patterns of behaviour that the system displays or how those patterns evolve and neither does anything outside the system. This is the principle of self-organisation: agents interact locally according to their own principles, in the absence of an overall blueprint for the system they form.

A central concept in agent-based models of complex systems is that this self-organising interaction produces emergent population-wide pattern, where emergence means that there is no blueprint, plan or programme determining the population-wide pattern. What happens is the emergence and maintenance of order, or complexity, out of a state that is less ordered, or complex – namely, the local interaction of the agents. Self-organisation and emergence can lead to fundamental structural development (novelty), not just superficial change. This is 'spontaneous' or 'autonomous', arising from the intrinsic iterative nonlinear nature of the system. Some external designer does not impose it – rather, widespread orderly behaviour emerges from simple, reflex-like rules.

Since it is not possible to experiment with living systems in real-life situations, complexity scientists use computers to simulate the behaviour of complex adaptive systems. Some scientists argue that computer simulations are a legitimate new form of experiment, but others hold that they show nothing about nature, only about computer programs.

How complex adaptive systems are studied

In the computer simulations each individual agent is an individual computer program. Each of these programs is a set of operating rules and instructions concerning how that program should interact with other individual computer programs. It is possible to add a set of rules for evaluating those operations according to some performance criteria. It is also possible to add a set of rules for changing the rules of operation and evaluation in the light of their performance. Another set of rules can be added according to which each individual computer program can be copied to produce another one. That set of replicating rules could take the form of a rule about locating another computer program to mate with. Another rule could instruct the first to copy the top half of its program and the second to copy the bottom half of its program and then add the two copies together. The result would be a new, or offspring, program. This is known as the *genetic algorithm*, developed by John Holland of the Santa Fé Institute.

You can see how such a procedure could model important features of evolution, in that a population of individual computer programs interact with each other, breed and so evolve. The result is a complex adaptive system in the computer consisting of a population of agents, each of which is a computer program. Each of the agents in the simulation – that is, each individual computer program, is made up of a bit string, a series of ones and zeros representing an electric current that is either on or off.

The inherent patterning capacity of interaction

Those who have developed the study of complex adaptive systems have been most interested in the analogy between the digital code of computer program agents and the chemical code in the genes of living creatures. One of their principal questions has been this: if in its earliest days the earth consisted of a random soup of chemicals, how could life have come about? You can simulate this problem if you take a system consisting of computer programs with random bit strings and ask if they can evolve order out of such random chaos. The answer to this question is that such systems can indeed evolve order out of chaos and this chaos is essential to the process.

Contrary to some of our most deep-seated beliefs, disorder is the material from which life and creativity are built, and it seems that they are built, not according to some overall prior design, but through a process of spontaneous self-organisation that produces emergent outcomes. If there is a design, it is the basic design principles of the system itself: namely, a network of agents driven by iterative nonlinear inter-action. What is not included in the design is the emergent outcomes, the emergent pattern, which this interaction produces. There is inherent order in complex adap-tive systems which evolves as the experience of the system, but no one can know what that evolutionary experience will be until it occurs. In certain conditions agents interacting in a system can produce not anarchy, but creative new outcomes that none of them was ever programmed to produce. If this has anything to do with human action, then even if no one can know the outcome of their actions and even if no one can be 'in control', we are not doomed to anarchy. On the contrary, these may be the very conditions required for creativity, for the evolutionary journey with no fixed, predetermined destination.

According to this view, evolution is, then, not an incrementally progressive affair occurring by chance as in neo-Darwinism, but a rather stumbling sort of journey in which a system moves both forwards and backwards through self-organisation.

Fitness landscapes

You can see why this is so if you think in terms of fitness landscapes, a concept Kauffman (1995) has used to give insights into the evolutionary process. Picture the evolution of a particular species, say leopards, as a journey across a landscape characterised by hills and mountains of various heights and shapes, and valleys of various depths and shapes. Suppose that movement up a hill or mountain is equiva-lent to increasing fitness and moving down into a valley is equivalent to decreasing fitness. Deep valleys would represent almost certain extinction and the high peaks of mountains would represent great fitness for the leopards. The purpose of life is then to avoid valleys and climb peaks.

The shape of the landscape

What determines the shape of this landscape, that is, the number, size, shape and position of the peaks and valleys? The answer is the survival strategies that other species interacting with leopards are following. So, leopards could potentially inter-act with a large number of species in order to get a meal. They could hunt elephant, for example. However, the elephant has a survival strategy based on size, and if leopards take the elephant-hunting route they will have a tough time surviving. Such a strategy, therefore, is a move down into a rather deep and dead-end sort of valley. Another possibility is to hunt rather small deer. In order to achieve this the leopard might evolve the strategy of speed, competing by running faster than the deer. To the extent that this works it is represented by a move up a fitness hill. Or, the leopards may specialise in short-distance speed plus a strategy of camouflage. Hence their famous spots. This strategy seems to have taken them up a mountain to a reasonably high fitness peak.

The evolutionary task of the leopard species, then, is to journey across the fitness landscape in such a manner as to reach the highest fitness peak possible, because then the leopard stands the greatest chance of surviving. To get caught in a valley is to become extinct, and to be trapped in the foothills is to forgo the opportunity of finding one of the mountains.

Moving across the landscape

So, how should the leopard species travel across the landscape to avoid these pitfalls, given that leopards cannot see where the high peaks are? They can only know that they have reached a peak when they get there. Suppose the leopards adopt what strategy theorists call a *logically incremental strategy* (*see* Chapter 7) – that is, they adopt a procedure in which they 'stick to the knitting' and take a large number of small incremental steps, only ever taking a step that improves fitness and avoiding any steps that diminish fitness – they are driven by efficiency. This rational, orderly procedure produces relatively stable, efficient, progressive movement uphill, consistently in the direction of success. Management consultants and academics in the strategy field would applaud leopards following this procedure for their eminent common sense. However, a rule that in essence says 'go up hills only and never downwards' is sure to keep the leopards out of the valleys, but it is also almost certain to get them trapped in the foothills, unless they start off with a really lucky break at the base of the highest, smoothest mountain, with no crevices or other deformities. This is highly unlikely, for a reason I will come to.

The point to note here is that the rational, efficient way to move over the short term is guaranteed, over the longer term, to be the most ineffective possible. What is the alternative? The alternative is to abandon this nice, neat strategy of logically incremental moves and travel in a somewhat erratic manner that involves sometimes slipping and tumbling downhill into valleys out of which a desperate climb is necessary before it is too late. This counterintuitive and somewhat inebriate method of travelling across their fitness landscape makes it likely that the leopards will stumble across the foothills of an even higher mountain than the one they were climbing before. So, cross-over replication, sex to us, makes it more likely that we will find higher mountains to climb than will, say, bacteria, which replicate by cloning, precisely because of the disorder of mixing the genetic code rather than incrementally improving it.

The whole picture becomes a great deal more interesting when you remember that the fixed landscape I have been describing for the leopard is in fact a fiction, because the survival strategies of the other species determine its shape and they are not standing still. They too are looking for peaks to climb and every time they change their strategy, then what was a peak for the leopard is deformed and could become a valley. So, if the leopard increases its short-distance speed and improves its camouflage, it moves up towards a fitness peak on its landscape. However, if the deer respond by heightening their sense of smell, then that peak certainly subsides and may even turn into a valley.

The evolutionary journey for all species, therefore, is across a constantly heaving landscape and it is heaving about because of competition. Competition ensures that life itself never gets trapped. Species come and go but life itself carries on, perhaps becoming ever more complex. It is this mess of competitive selection that is one of the sources of order, the other being the co-operative, internal process of spontaneous self-organisation. This possibility occurs in a dynamic known as 'the edge of chaos', which is the pattern of movement which is both stable and unstable at the same time. One property of the edge of chaos is known as the power law, which means that many small perturbations will cascade through the system but only a few large ones will. In other words, there will be large numbers of small extinction events but only small numbers of large ones. It is this property that imparts control, or stability, to the process of change at the edge of chaos.

Systems characterised by dynamics that combine order and disorder, which operate at the edge of chaos, are capable of evolving while those that are purely orderly, those that operate well away from the edge of chaos, cannot evolve. At the edge of chaos, systems are capable of endless variety, novelty, surprise – in short, creativity. Systems that get trapped on local fitness peaks look stable and comfortable, but they are simply waiting for destruction by other species following messier paths. Kauffman gives precise conditions which generate the dynamics of the edge of chaos. The dynamic occurs only when the agents are numerous enough and richly connected to each other. Agents impose *conflicting constraints* on each other and it is these that provide control to the movement of the system.

Kauffman is arguing, then, that the manner in which competitive selection operates on chance variations depends upon the internal dynamic of the evolving network – that is, upon the pattern of connections, the self-organising interaction, between the entities of which it is composed. The fitness landscape is not a given space containing all possible evolutionary strategies for a system, which it searches for fit strategies in a manner driven by chance. Rather, the fitness landscape itself is being constructed by the interaction between agents. The notion of fitness landscape, its ruggedness, becomes a metaphor for the internal dynamic of a system, not an externally given terrain over which it travels in search of a fit position. These internal properties of the network are the connections between its entities and these connections create conflicting constraints. The internal dynamic is thus one of enabling cooperation and of conflicting constraints at the same time, a paradoxical dynamic of cooperation and competition at the same time. Notice how connection, constraint and conflict are all essential requirements for the evolution of a system.

While no agent is 'in control' of the evolution of the system, it is nevertheless evolving in a controlled manner and the source of this control lies in the pattern of conflicting constraints. This is a very important point, because it is the conflicting constraints that sustain sufficient stability in a network at the edge of chaos.

However, the interests of complex adaptive systems modellers are not confined to such major questions as the evolution of life. The complex adaptive system model has been applied to many other phenomena too.

Simulating populations of homogeneous agents

Take a simple example of a complex adaptive system: namely a flock of birds. Reynolds (1987) simulated the flocking behaviour of birds with a computer program consisting of a network of moving agents called Boids. Each Boid follows the *same* three *simple rules*:

1. Maintain a minimum distance from other objects in the environment including other Boids.
2. Match velocities with other Boids in the neighbourhood.
3. Move towards the perceived centre of mass of the Boids in the neighbourhood.

These three rules are sufficient to produce flocking behaviour. So, Boids, each interacting with a relatively small number of others according to its own local rules of interaction, produce an emergent, coherent pattern for the whole system of Boids.

There is no plan, or blueprint, at the level of the flock. There is no overall intention in relation to the flock, for the population as a whole, on the part of any Boid. Each does what it is required to do in order to interact with a few others and orderly behaviour emerges for the whole population. Flocking is an attractor for a system in which entities follow the three rules given above.

Note how all agents follow the *same rules*. Each agent is the same as every other agent and there is no variation in the way they interact with each other. Emergence here is, therefore, not the consequence of non-average behaviour, as was the case with dissipative structures in the last section. Instead, emergence is the consequence of local interaction between agents. Unlike dissipative structures, and because of the postulated uniformity of behaviour, these simulations cannot spontaneously move, of their own accord, from one attractor to another. Instead, they stay always with one attractor and show no evolution.

However, more complicated simulations of complex adaptive systems do take account of differences in agents or classes of agents and different ways of interacting. These simulations do then show the capacity to move spontaneously from one attractor to another and to evolve new ones. This is demonstrated by the simulation called Tierra (Ray, 1992).

Simulating populations of interacting heterogeneous agents

Organic life utilises energy to organise matter and it evolves, developing more and more diverse forms, as organisms compete and co-operate with each other for light and food in geographic space. An analogy to this would be digital life in which central processing unit (CPU) time organises strings of digits (programs) in the space of computer memory. Computer programs are then used as the analogue of living organisms. Would digital life evolve as bit strings and interact and compete for CPU time?

This is the question explored by Ray (1992) in his simulation. In this simulation, Ray, the programmer, designs the first digital organism, which he calls a *creature*, consisting of 80 instructions on how to copy itself. The first creature is thus a string of digits of a particular length. The programmer also introduces a mechanism to generate variety into the replicating process, taking the form of random bit flipping to simulate random mutations in evolution. It follows that, as the creature copies itself, the new copies will differ from the original one and, as they copy themselves, each subsequent copy will differ from them. The programmer also introduces a constraint in the form of scarce computer time, which works as follows. Agents are required to post their locations in the computer memory on a public notice board. Each agent is then called upon in turn, according to a circular queue, to receive a slice of computer time for carrying out its replication tasks. The programmer introduces a further constraint on agent life span. Agents are lined up in a linear queue according to their age and a 'reaper' lops off some of these, generally the oldest. However, by successfully executing their programs, agents can slow down their move up the linear queue, whereas flawed agents rise quickly to the top.

The only task agents have is that of replicating in a regime of scarce CPU time and what happens is that new modes of doing this evolve. In other words, different categories of replication method appear. These changes can be observed in numerical terms by watching changing patterns of dots on a computer screen. An analogy is then drawn between this digital interaction and the biological evolution of species and the simulation is described in these biological terms. For example, categories of agents are said to develop their own survival strategies. It is important to remember that this is an analogy drawing attention to changes in categories of agent in the digital medium and changes in categories of species in the biological medium.

What happens in the simulation?

The simulation was set off by introducing a single agent consisting of 80 instructions. Within a short time, the computer memory space was 80 per cent occupied by these agents but then the reaper took over and prevented further population growth. After a while, agents consisting of 45 instructions appeared, but they were too short to replicate. They overcame this problem by borrowing some of the code of longer agents in order to replicate. This strategy enabled them to replicate faster within their allocated computer time. In other words, a kind of parasite emerged. The use of the term 'parasite' is obviously an analogy.

Although the parasites did not destroy their hosts, they were dependent on them for replication. If the parasites became too numerous in relation to hosts, they destroyed their own ability to replicate and so declined. In the simulation, the parasites suffered periodic catastrophes. One of these catastrophes occurred because the hosts stopped posting their positions on the public notice board and in effect hid so that the parasites could no longer find them. Some hosts had, thus, developed an immunity to parasites by using camouflage as a survival strategy. On the other hand, in hiding, the hosts had not retained any note of their position in the computer memory. So, they had to examine themselves to see if their position corresponded to the position being offered computer time, before they could respond to that offer. This increased the time they needed for replication. However, although not perfect, the strategy worked well enough that the parasites were nearly wiped out.

Then, however, the parasites developed their own memories and did not need to consult the public posting board. Once again, it was the parasites' turn to succeed. Later, hyperparasites appeared to feed off the parasites. These were 80 instructions long, just like the hosts, but they had developed instructions to examine themselves for parasites and feed off the parasites by diverting computer time from them. These hyperparasites worked symbiotically by sharing reproduction code: they could no longer reproduce on their own but required cooperation. This cooperation was then exploited by opportunistic mutants in the form of tiny intruders who placed themselves between replicating hyperparasites and intercepted and used hyperparasite code for their own replication. These cheaters could then thrive and replicate although they were only 27 instructions long. Later, the hyperparasites found a way to defeat the cheaters, but not for long.

How the simulation is interpreted

I would like to emphasise, once more, what is happening in this simulation. After the simulation has run for some time there are a number of bit strings, each arranged into operating instructions requiring them to replicate in a particular way, often in interaction with other bit strings. These bit strings fall into categories and all within a category replicate in the same way, while bit strings in another category replicate in a different way. In complexity language, each of these categories is an attractor and there are a number of different attractors in the system. To put it another way, there is micro diversity in the total population of bit strings. During one round of replication – that is, during a given short time period – the bit strings carry out their instructions, one after the other, and as they do so bits in some of the strings are randomly flipped. Over a series of runs the bit flipping and the interaction between the bit strings result in rearrangements in the bit strings themselves. In other words, new arrangements of bit strings appear: that is, new categories of replicating instructions. At the same time older categories disappear because of the procedure of competitive removal of some of them. Once begun, this evolution continues even when the random bit flipping, that is, chance, is turned off. Self-organisation is then the driving force of evolution.

In summary, the population of bit strings is a population of algorithms, or logical procedures. What running the simulation demonstrates is the logical properties of iteration (replication) and local interaction of algorithms (self-organisation in the absence of a blueprint for the whole) in the presence of random mutation and competitive selection. The simulation shows that it is logically possible for self-organisation, mutation and selection operating iteratively to display evolution – that is, emergent novelty that is radically unpredictable. This evolution is characterised by both destruction of some categories and emergence of new ones.

Anything more that is said about the simulation is an interpretation by way of analogy. So, Ray uses the simulation as an analogy for biology and calls the bit strings *creatures*. One category of bit strings is called *hosts* and another is called *parasites*. If the interpretation is done carefully, it may provide insight. For example, it may indicate that new biological forms can emerge from a process of self-organisation, not just by chance. If done carelessly, it could produce unwarranted claims. It is, therefore, important to take great care in using insights about self-organisation and emergence in relation to organisations. The question becomes one of how to interpret, in organisational terms, the logic of iterative, nonlinear interaction between replicating algorithms and their self-organising and emergent properties. Even more fundamental is the question of whether it even makes sense to try to do this.

Some major insights

It seems to me that this simulation provides some major insights into the nature of complex adaptive systems.

First, this system produces evolving population-wide order that comes about in a spontaneous, emergent way through the local interaction of diverse agents. The evolving population-wide order has not been programmed and there is no blueprint, grand design or plan for it. Furthermore, this spontaneous self-organising activity, with its emergent order, is vital for the continuing evolution of the system and its ability to produce novelty. However, what form that order takes – that is, the population-wide pattern of behaviour, the system-wide strategies – cannot be predicted from the rules driving individual agent behaviour. The strategies are emerging unpredictably in co-evolutionary processes. First the strategy is small size, but then parasites change the rules and the most successful strategy becomes feeding off others. Then, the hosts change the rules and the better strategy is camouflage. But the parasites change the rules of the game again and the best strategy becomes the development of a local memory. Competition and conflict emerge and the evolution of the system is driven by agents trying to exploit each other, but the game can go on only if neither side succeeds completely, or for long, in that exploitation.

From this perspective, the evolution of life in the universe occurs primarily not through random mutations selected for survival by the forces of competition as in Darwinism, but through an internal, spontaneously self-organising, co-operative process that presents orderly forms for selection by the forces of competition. Selection is not made by freely operating competition that chooses amongst random little pieces, but by a competitive process constrained to choose amongst new forms emerging from a co-operative process. Life in the universe, and perhaps life in organisations, arises from a dialectic between competition and cooperation, not from unconstrained competition.

Causality

In Kant's philosophy, the scientist understands organism in nature as wholes consisting of parts. It is in the self-organising interaction of the parts that those parts and the whole emerge. The scientist understands the development of such a system by hypothesising that it is developing according to some 'as if' purpose, usually that of the whole realising a mature form of itself – formative causality. Although the first wave of twentieth-century systems thinkers did not develop Kant's idea of systems as *self-organising* wholes, emphasising self-regulation and self-influence instead, they did implicitly adopt the formative theory of causality. In the more recent wave of complex systems theories, chaos and dissipative structure theorists also produce models of systems which unfold attractors already enfolded in the equations specifying them, although dissipative structure models do bring back the notion of self-organising wholes that can spontaneously move from one enfolded attractor to another. Homogeneous complex adaptive systems model self-organising processes at the micro level but, because the agents are all the same, the theory of formative causality continues to apply.

However, heterogeneous complex adaptive systems, where the agents differ from one another, do what none of the other systems can. They display the capacity for spontaneous evolution to new forms, the unknown. Causality, therefore, is transformative. In other words, such systems take on a life of their own. This creates a problem for the notion of the 'whole' because here the 'whole' is never finished but always evolving. One then has to talk about incomplete or absent wholes, notions that make rather dubious sense. It amounts to saying that there is something that is a whole but is not yet a whole and never will be. Heterogeneous complex adaptive systems then begin to point to a problem with one of the central concepts of systems thinking: namely, 'wholes'. The notion of a system with a life of its own brings other problems. If the system model has a life of its own how can we be confident that it actually models what it is supposed to? Surely the model and what it is trying to model would diverge as each takes on a life of its own? Also, what would it mean for individual members of an organisation to think of themselves as parts of an organisational system that had a life of its own?

Models of complex adaptive systems differ significantly from all of the system models so far reviewed in this book. All the other approaches model phenomena at a macro level, paying little or no attention to the nature of the entities comprising the system, while complex adaptive systems model agent interaction at a micro level. In all of the other macro-system models, with the exception of dissipative structures, interactions with the environment are assumed to be average or distributed around an average. It follows that only the dissipative structure models and complex adaptive systems with homogeneous agents have the internal capacity to move spontaneously from one given pattern of behaviour to another given pattern of behaviour. In all of the other system models, including dissipative structures and some complex adaptive system models, agents are implicitly or explicitly assumed to be homogeneous, or average. Such systems have no internal capacity to spontaneously evolve and so are incapable of novelty. All of these models can move only within one attractor and novel change has to come from outside the system. It is only when agent diversity is introduced – for example, in heterogeneous complex adaptive system models or in Allen's complex evolutionary models to be referred to in the next chapter – that the system can produce novel forms: that is, evolve.

The new emerges in these models when the system displays the dynamics of the edge of chaos, where the differences between entities, micro diversity, are amplified. Here the system produces not only the new but avalanches of destruction as well, with many small and few large extinction events. In the review of all of these systems theories there has been a move from models that are linear, equilibrium seeking and lacking in any micro diversity to those that are nonlinear, far from equilibrium and full of micro diversity. The most striking change in the properties they display is the capacity for spontaneously developing new forms.

So far in this chapter, I have described my interpretation of what some branches of the complexity sciences mean and why I think it is important to take account of them with regard to organisations. However, the complexity sciences are in their infancy and there is by no means one monolithic view of what they mean. In this chapter I have drawn heavily on what I see as one important strand of thinking in these sciences exemplified by the work of Prigogine, Kauffman and Goodwin. However, there are natural complexity scientists who take a different view. The next section will therefore consider the nature of these differences. In the next chapter I will explore how those differences appear in the way researchers and writers are using the concepts in relation to organisations.

10.5 Different interpretations of complexity

A key concept in the sciences of complexity is that of *emergence*. The complexity sciences have revived interest in the concept of emergence which had aroused interest in the early part of the twentieth century, but then came to occupy a position very much at the margins of Western thinking. Hodgson (2000) and Goldstein (1999, 2000) provide short histories of the use of the concept of emergence in philosophy and science.

The philosopher George Lewes (1875) seems to have been the first to use the word 'emergence' in a scientific sense when he distinguished between *resultants* of components which could always be traced to steps in the process of interaction of components, and *emergents* when the outcome could not be traced to steps in component interaction. This was taken up by the philosopher Conway Lloyd Morgan (1927, 1933) who developed an idea of emergent evolutionism and defined emergent properties as non-additive, unpredictable results of complex processes. In other words, emergence was taken to denote processes of evolution in which a whole could not be deduced from or reduced to its component parts. Morgan emphasised how emergence produces novelty in the sense of something that had not been in being before as opposed to developmental processes which unfold something already there. This way of thinking about evolution involved a shift from mechanical to organic ways of thinking and from any form of reductionist thinking in which wholes were to be understood in terms of aggregation of their parts to some form of organisational or holistic thinking. Morgan argued that evolution occurred at both the level of biology (the genes) and at the social/cultural (institutional) level where the latter could not be reduced to the former. Others picked up on Morgan's formulations: for example, Alexander (1920) and Broad (1925) in the UK and Wheeler (1926) and Whitehead (1926) in the USA. However, this strand of thinking did not command attention for long because it provided no clear explanation of how emergent phenomena actually came about, and so the concept of 'emergence' came to be regarded as a metaphysical one in an age in which metaphysics came into disrepute – it was submerged by the positivist and reductionist phase of Anglo-American Science. However, the concept survived on the fringes of biology and social science. The institutional economist Thorsten Veblen was influenced by Morgan's ideas and held that institutions were dependent upon individuals but could not be reduced to them, although he did not use the term 'emergence' explicitly. In their reviews both Hodgson and Goldstein seem unaware of the use that the sociologist Norbert Elias (1939) made of the concepts of self-organisation and emergence in his explanation of social evolution.

Then in the post-war period, social and natural scientist, Michael Polanyi (1960), and biologist, Ernst Mayr (1988), along with others, revived the idea of emergent properties. The former argued that the laws governing higher levels could not be governed by the laws of isolated particulars, and Mayr argued that a new, unpredictable whole emerges when complex components are assembled. Then, with increasing momentum in the 1970s and onwards, the concept of emergence became central to the thinking of complexity scientists, intent on explaining and exploring processes of emergence. For some the notion of emergence is not so much an explanation as a description which points to patterns exhibited at a macro level and amounts to the need to move to the macro level and its unique dynamics for explanation.

It is these different interpretations of emergence that lead to different views on what the complexity sciences are about. There are at least four important and closely related matters on which those working in the field of complex systems take different positions. These four matters are:

- The significance of self-organisation.
- The nature of emergence.
- The importance of unpredictability.
- The implications for the scientific method.

To illustrate how views on these matters differ (Griffin *et al.*, 1998; Stacey *et al.*, 2000), consider the views of some leading figures in the field of complexity, namely,

Langton (1996), Gell-Mann (1994), Holland (1998), Kauffman (1995), Goodwin (1994) and Prigogine.

Langton

Langton (1996) specifies the simple rules of interaction that each agent in his system will follow and then observes the behaviour that emerges, stressing the radical unpredictability of the pattern that emerges. The inability to provide a global rule, or algorithm, for changes in the system's global state makes it necessary to concentrate on the interactions occurring at the local level. It is the logical structure of the interactions, rather than the properties of the agents themselves, which is important.

He retains the notion of processes of information manipulation, of computation, found in the field of artificial intelligence (AI) but locates them at the level of the agents rather than at the global level as AI does. This establishes a strong link with cybernetics and cognitivism. In both of the latter, the manipulation and processing of information is a central concept. For Langton, the system as a whole is no longer a cybernetic one but is composed of cybernetic entities which function in a cognitivist manner in that they process information. Algorithms drive the behaviour of the agents, although no algorithm can be identified for behaviour at the global level. This retention of an essential cognitivist view of the world has important implications for the ease with which the insights generated by Langton's work can be assimilated into management discourses based on systems thinking.

Langton holds that his approach is both mechanistic and reductionist, but in a new sense (Langton, 1996). What Langton appears to mean by this is that the old mechanism is one in which the components could be added to arrive at the whole in a linear manner. Parts have functions that fit together uniquely to determine the whole. The new mechanism he is talking about is one in which the parts interact according to recursive rules to produce a whole that is radically unpredictable. However, the system remains mechanistic in the sense that the recursive rules are computed, and it is this running of the programme that yields the resultant whole. The mechanism is the rules and the reduction is to the rules, so that there is nothing left unexplained. Intervention at local levels gives rise to global-level dynamics and this affects the lower levels by setting the local context within which each entity's rules are involved. The behaviour of the whole system does not depend upon the internal details of the entities, only on the details of the way they behave in each other's presence.

So, Langton's position on methodology is one that stays close to scientific orthodoxy. The methodology remains deterministic, reductionistic and mechanistic. However, he stresses the radically unpredictable nature of emergent order. For him, self-organisation is an algorithmic interaction of a cybernetic kind and emergence is a fundamentally important phenomenon.

Gell-Mann

Gell-Mann (1994) says that all complex adaptive systems acquire information about their environment and their interactions with it. These systems identify regularities in their environments and their interactions, which they condense into models on the basis of which they then predict and act (p. 318). The cognitivist frame of reference and its cybernetic underpinnings are, in his view, therefore clear.

Gell-Mann does not talk a great deal about self-organisation and emergence – at least not in the book that most now use when importing his ideas into organisation theory. When he does, he relates these concepts very much to structures emerging from systems characterised by very simple rules (p. 100). He uses the word 'apparently' to limit the notion of the complex and describes self-organisation as a process of following *simple rules*. This makes it very easy to assimilate what Gell-Mann says into systemic perspectives on the nature of organisations. What Gell-Mann is doing is downplaying the importance of self-organising process and emergence and focusing on competitive selection as the driver of evolution in complex adaptive systems. This is made clear by the importance he attaches to 'frozen accidents'. Evolution occurs by chance, but once a new form has emerged as an accident, it is frozen and so characterised by regularities which make it predictable (p. 229).

So, like Langton, Gell-Mann stays with orthodox scientific methodology. He emphasises the importance of chance in the evolution of complex adaptive systems. Although this implies long-term unpredictability, Gell-Mann seems to me to downplay the implications of this and focuses instead on regularities and predictability. His emphasis on 'frozen accidents' and competitive selection is close to the orthodox ideas of neo-Darwinism, as is his lack of emphasis on self-organisation and emergence, which he clearly does not see as radical concepts. Despite talking about the importance of interaction, he retains the primacy of the autonomous individual in the sense of agents and systems that individually represent a world and then act autonomously on those representations. For me, the potentially radical implications of complexity theory are readily assimilated by Gell-Mann into scientific orthodoxy. Complexity theory, in his version, is an interesting extension of orthodoxy. This, and the explicitly cognitivist frame of reference he works within, makes it almost inevitable that the importation of his work for theorising about organisation will not pose any radical challenge. Also, the kind of emphasis he places on simple rules has proved to be very popular amongst many of those who have applied the theory of complex adaptive systems to organisations. The validity of doing this will be explored in Chapter 11.

Holland

Holland (1998) is particularly concerned with nonlinear, agent-based models and he sets out the procedure for designing such models. The first step is to shear away irrelevant detail, because the model must be simpler than that which it models – he is looking for simple laws (p. 46). He then talks about specifying the mechanisms through which entities, or agents, relate to each other and how these mechanisms form the building blocks of the model. The configuration of the building blocks determines the state of the model at any particular moment and transition functions determine how it changes state. These building blocks make predictability and planning possible (p. 11).

Holland's cognitivist frame of reference is quite explicit, as is his deterministic and reductionist approach to science. He clearly takes the position of the independent observer of a system and talks about models needing to follow the designer's intent. Repeatedly he talks about focusing on the time spans and the levels of detail that allow the uncovering of regularities and unchanging laws. He stresses how *simple rules* of interaction yield emergent pattern, how rules generate perpetual novelty. However, he rapidly follows such statements with others in which he says a phenomenon is emergent only when it is recognisable and recurring, although it may not be easy to recognise or explain. So, he points to chance, unpredictability and novelty and then rapidly backs away from these notions to advocate concentrating on time spans and levels of detail where predictability is possible and 'novelty' is regular.

The emphasis he places on the autonomous individual also comes out very clearly when he describes the individual agents in his models. He says that these agents must have strategies – that is, prescriptions telling them what to do as the game unfolds, approximating a complete strategy that tells them what to do in all possible situations. For Holland, emergent patterns are predictable and regular. He points to how chaos theory is used to explain why it is that the long-term future of nonlinear systems is unpredictable. He accepts this but then takes the example of the weather system and says that because meteorologists do not know all the relevant variables, they simply do not work at the level at which chaos would be relevant. They simply start their forecast afresh each day and chaos does not matter (p. 44).

What Holland does, then, is to dismiss the importance of long-term unpredictability and holds that it is possible to get by through focusing on the short term. What I see here is someone pointing to radical unpredictability, emergent novelty through a radical notion of self-organisation and then immediately assimilating it into orthodox science and so neutering its implications. Again, I would argue that the principal route through which this is achieved is the retention of a cognitivist perspective on human knowing. As with Gell-Mann, I would argue that, in the hands of Holland, complexity theory represents an interesting development of orthodoxy in the natural sciences. I am not trying to say that this is unimportant. I am simply pointing to the reasoning process being employed. Holland's views, even more so than Gell-Mann's, are immediately and easily assimilated into systems-based management thinking.

Kauffman

Kauffman's (1995) work has much in common with that of Gell-Mann and Holland but in some important respects it is radically different. The similarity is in his method. He simulates abstract living systems consisting of large numbers of autonomous adaptive agents in terms of information-processing systems. What he does is quite close to Langton's work. Once again, the agents and their *rules of interaction are simple* and, from this simplicity of interaction, complex novelty emerges. As with the others, his agents are cybernetic entities, cognitivist in nature. His methodology and the underlying cognitivist assumptions make it just as easy to import his modelling approach into systems-based theorising about organisations. However, the conclusions he draws from his work are radical. He emphasises the importance of self-organisation in evolution, calling it a *second-ordering principle*, and attaches greater importance to it than to random mutation or natural selection. He places emergent novelty at the centre of life and as a consequence accepts that one has to give up the dream of predicting the details. Instead, one has to pursue the hope of explaining, understanding and, perhaps, predicting the emergent generic properties of a system.

The radical position Kauffman takes up here is contrary to management orthodoxy in many ways and it is this kind of perspective I will be interested in exploring in relation to organisations in Part 3.

Goodwin

Goodwin (1994) also holds the radical implications of complexity theory, particularly emphasising relationship and participation. Like Kauffman, Goodwin rejects the neo-Darwinian view of evolution. Goodwin takes the organism, rather than the gene, as the fundamental unit in biology. He thinks in terms of a network of interacting genes located within an environment, or context, which he calls the *morphological field*. This context is a constraint on the possible patterns of expression by the genetic network. By ensuring that parameter values fall within certain domains, genes contribute to the stability and repeatability of a life cycle, the biological memory, or heredity. However, organisms are entities organised dynamically by developmental and morphogenetic fields. Fields are wholes actively organising themselves. Goodwin relocates agency away from interacting individual components and places it at the level of the whole.

Prigogine

Prigogine sees the radical potential more than anyone, perhaps, as he speaks of a new dialogue with nature in which the purpose of science would not be that of dominating and controlling nature.

A review

On the one hand, there is what seems to me to be an orthodox perspective, typified by the views of Holland and Gell-Mann and to some extent by those of Langton. From this perspective, a complex system is understood in somewhat mechanistic, reductionist terms and is modelled by an objective observer in the interests of predicting its behaviour. Self-organisation is not seen to be a new ordering principle in the evolution of the system. Evolution occurs through random mutation and competitive selection. The radical unpredictability of emergent new forms is not emphasised. The system is modelled as a network of cybernetic and cognitivist agents: they represent regularities in the form of schemas, the equivalent of mental models; they store those representations in the form of rules and then act on the basis of those rules. Complexity is reduced to simplicity and much emphasis is placed on complex patterns emerging from simple rules.

On the other hand, there is what seems to me to be a radical perspective on the nature of complex systems. This is typified by the views of Kauffman and Goodwin, and, even more so, Prigogine. From this perspective, self-organisation, rather than random mutation, plays the central role in the emergence of new forms. Those new forms emerge and they are radically unpredictable.

The more orthodox viewpoint can be brought to bear on organisational issues within a cognitivist view of human psychology and a systemic perspective on interaction. The result, I hope to show in the next chapter, is a theory of organisation that uses the terminology of complex systems but stays firmly within dominant systems-based thinking about organisations. Potentially radical insights from complexity theory are easily assimilated into the orthodox discourse. This is done by selectively concentrating on time periods and levels of detail that are predictable and talking about self-organisation and emergence as if they could be controlled by managers. When this is done, what is lost is the invitation to explore what managers do when time spans and levels of detail are radically unpredictable. In the next chapter, I will be exploring how some writers have been doing just this, in my view. In Part 3 I will be exploring the consequences for organisational theory of the radical perspective on complexity within a framework of human psychology that is different from cognitivism, constructivism, humanistic psychology and psychoanalysis. I will be reviewing a responsive processes rather than a systemic way of making sense of life in organisations, a way that draws on analogies from the more radical expositions of complex adaptive systems with heterogeneous agents.

10.6 Summary

This chapter has reviewed a number of developments in theories of systemic behaviour, namely chaos, dissipative structures and complex adaptive systems.

Chaos theory is a theory of systems that focuses on the same level of description as systems dynamics; that is, both focus on the level of the system as a whole. They both make assumptions about the entities comprising a system and their interactions, particularly with the environment. The assumption is that both the entities and their interactions are average, or normally distributed around an average. Dissipative structure theory develops the notions of self-organisation and emergence. It models the system of interest in terms of nonlinear mathematical equations governing state changes at the macro level of the system, just as systems dynamics and chaos theory do. However, unlike these last, dissipative structure models incorporate fluctuations, or variety, in exogenous variables, or micro events. In other words, fluctuations in the sense of non-average behaviour in the system's environment are incorporated in the former and not in the latter. The result is the phenomenon of self-organising order through fluctuations and, given the presence of non-average behaviour, the system has the internal capacity to move spontaneously from one attractor to another. Note also that self-organisation in dissipative structure theory is a collective response of the whole system. It takes the form of correlations and resonances between the entities comprising the system that emerge as new patterns or order.

Complex adaptive systems theory models interaction between many agents comprising a system. It sets out the logical structure of algorithmic – that is, digital-code-based, interaction – and derives the properties of such interaction through the method of computer simulation. The digital code interaction is then used as an analogy for some other kind of interaction. For example, digital code is used as an analogy for the genetic code of biological organisms. The properties of digital code interaction are then taken to apply to biological code. In other words, an act of interpretation is required in order to utilise the insights derived from the logic of digital code interaction in relation to some other kind of interaction.

Further reading

On chaos there is the classic account of how chaos was discovered and what it means by Gleick (1988), and also Briggs and Peat (1989) and Kellert (1993). A more mathematical but accessible treatment is Stewart (1989). On self-organisation it is useful to read Prigogine and Stengers (1984), Davies (1987) and Nicolis and Prigogine (1989). Useful reviews of complexity theory are provided by Waldrop (1992), Casti (1994), Cohen and Stewart (1994), Goodwin (1994), Kauffman (1995) and Levy (1992). Boden (1996) provides a useful review of the philosophy and methodology of complex adaptive systems.

Questions to aid further reflection

1. What do the terms self-organisation and emergence mean?
2. What is meant by conflicting constraints and what part do they play in the functioning of complex adaptive systems?
3. In what way might the theory of complex adaptive systems present an alternative to the neo-Darwinian theory of evolution?
4. What theories of causality are reflected in different theories in the complexity sciences?
5. What do you see as the major differences between alternative interpretations of complexity theories?
6. How might notions of self-organisation and emergence challenge mainstream theories of organisation?
7. In what way do the dynamics of stable instability and the possibility of radical unpredictability challenge mainstream theories of organisational change?
8. What role does diversity play in theories of complexity and what implications does this have for thinking about life in organisations?

Chapter 11

Systemic applications of complexity sciences to organisations
Restating the dominant discourse

This chapter invites you to draw on your own experience to reflect on and consider the implications of:

- The different quantitative and qualitative ways of applying the complexity sciences to organisations.

- What new and challenging insights some of the approaches to complexity and organisations have to offer.

- How some of the applications of the complexity sciences to organisations may simply continue to reflect the position of the external objective observer of a system and so lose the potentially radical insights coming from the natural complexity sciences.

- How many applications retain the central concern of organisational theorists with control.

This chapter is important because it invites reflection on how insights coming from the complexity sciences are being taken up by some writers on organisations and how these insights may be easily subjugated and absorbed into the dominant discourse on organisations. Understanding the material in this chapter aids in understanding the distinction to be made in the approach to management in Part 3 of the book which draws on relevant insights from the complexity sciences in a different way.

11.1 Introduction

Chapter 10 argued that during the 1970s and 1980s the complexity sciences developed further the thinking about the fundamental dynamics of systems. These new systems theories, like the first wave of twentieth-century systems theories in the 1950s, have been developed largely by natural scientists. I have argued that they are potentially radical in that they point to the self-referential, self-organising capacities of such systems. What this means is that agents in a complex system interact locally with each other on the basis of their historically evolved capacities, and this local self-referring, self-organising interaction itself generates emergent new forms of the whole system in the absence of any blueprint or programme for that whole. These insights are a radical departure from earlier systems theories in that new forms are now seen to emerge from local interaction rather than global laws or blueprints, but only in the presence of diversity. The emphasis is placed on the local, differentiated, evolving relationships between entities rather than on some view of the whole and its properties. This potentially displaces the externally observing cognising individual from the central position occupied in the application of the earlier systems theories to human organisations. Furthermore, the creative novelty that emerges in this fashion is fundamentally unpredictable. This raises question marks over the nature of control, another central feature of the application of earlier systems theories to organisations.

However, in the last chapter I also tried to show how some interpretations of the theory of complex systems in the natural sciences do not depart from cybernetics in many ways. This is because, in some formulations, the agents making up a complex adaptive system are defined in cybernetic and cognitivist terms. Furthermore, complexity theories continue, of course, to be systems theories. Despite the radical potential of some complexity theories, stressed by a few, most of the natural scientists working in this area seem to me to remain, more or less, within a basically orthodox perspective on science and, of course, all of them continue to think within the systems paradigm. Organisational theorists using chaos and complexity theory also continue to think in terms of systems and, I suggest, most of them focus on those expositions of the natural complexity sciences in which agents are cybernetic entities. They therefore continue with an individual-based psychology drawn from cognitivism, constructivism or humanistic perspectives. With the notable exceptions of the work of Allen and Marion discussed below, most organisational complexity writers avoid exploring the implications of radical unpredictability and so retain conventional notions of control. They therefore continue to argue within the dominant ideologies of control, harmony and conformity. I will explain what I mean by looking at some books and papers that use notions from complexity theory.

11.2 Modelling industries as complex systems

One approach to applying theories of complexity to organisations is to use the mathematical and modelling techniques of the natural scientists to model the dynamics of whole industries. This section looks at three examples of this. The first uses chaos theory, the second makes considerable use of fitness landscapes and the third draws on Prigogine's work.

The application of chaos theory to industries

Levy (1994) simulates an industrial supply chain using nonlinear equations of the type that can produce mathematical chaos and concludes that the model can be used to guide decisions concerning production location, sourcing and optimum inventory levels. Levy focuses his analysis on the macro level, arguing that industries can be modelled as dynamic systems that exhibit both unpredictability and underlying order. He notes the point that human systems are not deterministic and that human agency can alter social system, but believes that 'chaotic models can be used to suggest ways that people might intervene to achieve certain goals' (p. 169).

He concludes that, although short-term forecasting is possible, long-term planning is impossible and says that this has 'profound implications for organisations trying to set strategy based on their anticipation of the future' (p. 170). He concludes that strategic plans should take account of a number of scenarios and that firms should not focus too narrowly on core competences. For him, strategy becomes a set of *simple* guidelines that influence decisions and behaviour. This is the notion of '*simple rules*' so popular amongst those applying complexity theories to organisations. Furthermore, firms need to change these guidelines as industries and competitors change. Levy also says that the system as a whole must be understood if one is to understand indirect and counterintuitive means to an end.

Notice how this argument proceeds. It recognises the impossibility of long-term prediction but then, instead of asking how managers are actually now proceeding in the absence of reliable forecasts or foresight, the issue becomes how managers should foresee a number of scenarios and set simple guidelines. The notion seems to be that complex systems can be managed if one can identify the right set of simple rules. He also recommends, just as the systems-dynamics-based theory of the learning organisation does, that organisations must be understood as a *whole* and that this can be done by computer simulation. For him, goals are to be achieved through indirect means. So, here chaos theory is being used to model an operational system at the macro level in order to aid decision-making. Levy clearly equates the manager's role with that of the model builder or programmer who stands outside the system and controls it.

I think that the radical potential of theories of complexity for organisational theory tend to be obscured by approaches of this kind because of the direct application of concepts from the natural sciences with no interpretation of what they mean in the human domain. This is a problem if you are interested in the nature of organising and managing in terms of human relationships. Attempts to model people as an impersonal collective driven by rules immediately loses the rich texture of emotional and embodied relating. The idea that an organisation can be modelled and then influenced and controlled is implicitly cognitivist and cybernetic. What is lost here is the question of what it is like for a manager to be a member of a complex system, interacting at a local level, when it is not possible to see the organisation as a whole or know where it is going.

How industries explore fitness landscapes

Marion (1999) describes the development of the microcomputer industry and uses it to illustrate his perspective on organisational complexity. He describes how mainframe computers became commercially available in 1952 and how, in the mid-1960s, microprocessors were developed and incorporated in hand-held calculators. Small packets of technology were, therefore, emerging in a moderately coupled network of industries over the 1950s and 1960s. Then, in 1975, MICS produced the first microcomputer, the Altair, which was cheaper and more accessible to a wider market than mainframes. Microcomputers had a different architecture from mainframes and calculators, and during the initial stage of market development competition in the microcomputer sector had more to do with architectures than with anything else. There were, and still are, only two architectures. One is based on the Intel chip and the other on the Motorola processor. A number of operating systems were built around these chips: CP/M; the Apple system; IBM DOS; and systems for the Commodore, Tandy, Texas Instruments, NCR, NEC, Olivetti, Wang and Xerox microcomputers. The early market niche for microcomputers was thus crowded with architectures and operating systems when, in 1981, IBM entered the microcomputer market. The entry of IBM immediately put the fastest-growing operating system, CP/M, out of business. By the mid-1980s IBM's architecture was dominant and others adopted it in order to survive. At the same time, Apple introduced the Mac, which was not as cumbersome or as difficult to learn as DOS. Later, Microsoft brought some simplicity to DOS but it is still not able to match the elegance and simplicity of the Mac. During this period microprocessor technology was also developing: the earliest processors were 4-bit and were soon replaced by 8- and then 16-bit processors. By the mid-1990s, 32-bit technology was dominant.

Marion describes a development, then, in which there were a few people dreaming of microcomputers in 1974, a great many people wanting one by 1976 and explosive growth in the ensuing two decades. It looked as if microcomputers had suddenly appeared out of nowhere. However, the pieces were coming together long before microcomputers were ever envisioned: microcircuits, microprocessors, ROM and RAM memory chips were being used in calculators, while computer language logic was being documented in mainframes. The microcomputer was built from these pieces.

Marion uses the Kauffman framework described in Chapter 10 to make sense of these developments. He argues that bits of already existing technology come together as emergent microcomputers just as Kauffman argued that emerging connections between molecules became the chemical basis of life. He continues with Kauffman's framework to argue that the early microcomputer niche was occupied by a large number of architectural species. These early producers were small organisations driven by a few engineering personalities. They were relatively simple organisations, lacking much internal complexity and having few internal connections. They also displayed relatively few connections with other players in the niche, since producers specialised in sub-niches – for example, Apple in the education market and Commodore at the low end of the home market. Competitive interaction was thus limited. Kauffman's models show that such patterns of connection produce highly unstable, chaotic dynamics and this was evident in the rapid and unpredictable development of the microcomputer market in the early days. The industry was characterised by frequent and strong shocks, or large avalanches of extinction.

Then, in the 1980s, the number of players in the architecture field diminished until IBM DOS and Mac dominated that field. In addition, the entry of an internally complex organisation, IBM, and the rapid growth and development of Apple, meant that internal complexity rose: that is, there was a greater number of connections between agents within the competing organisations. At the same time, the number of connections between organisations in the niche increased because both of the main players competed with each other in all of the market niches. In Kauffman's models this pattern of connections produces the dynamic at the edge of chaos. Marion argues that the intertwining of stability and instability at the edge of chaos was also characteristic of the microcomputer industry at the end of the 1980s and on into the 1990s, when changes became much smaller and more incremental, with large extinction events a rarity. IBM DOS came to dominate the architecture niche, despite the technical superiority of the Apple Mac. This is technological 'lock-in', which occurs as more and more users come to rely on a particular technology so that the costs of change become too high and users stay with the technology they have, even if it is inferior. However, there was still change as the number of microcomputer producers increased, IBM lost its market dominance and Microsoft increased its power. The changes, of course, continue to this day.

Marion is showing how an industrial network evolves through its own internal dynamic to the edge of chaos. He emphasises the radical unpredictability of such evolution and the continuing unpredictability when a network operates at the edge of chaos. He draws on three characteristics to reach this conclusion. The first is sensitive dependence on initial conditions (*see* Chapter 10), which he argues can be seen in the sensitivity of human interaction to small events. Unpredictability here is due to human inability to monitor and observe infinite detail. Second, he refers to Prigogine's work on potential energy and Poincaré resonances to argue that intrinsic unpredictability is also a feature of complex systems. Third, he brings in the power law (*see* Chapter 10) to argue that, despite its great stability and robustness, a network at the edge of chaos will be subject to many small, and a few large, extinction events and that these are impossible to predict.

He argues that all of these factors are sources of radical unpredictability in the evolution of human networks that makes it impossible for an individual to be in control of such a network. In other words, no single organisation in the industrial network chooses the future direction of the industry, and this means that it cannot choose its own evolution either. This suggests that managers who claim to be planning the future of their organisation will not actually be doing so. Furthermore, no single organisation can choose the dynamics of the industry as a whole and therefore no organisation can choose its own dynamic either. In the early stages of the development of the microcomputer industry, the dynamics were chaotic because of the large number of simply structured competitors, loosely connected to each other. None of them chose this. It flowed from the nature of the interaction between them. The entry of IBM was a deliberate choice but the reduction in the number of competitors and the increase in the range of competitive interaction between the survivors was not simply IBM's choice. It depended upon what the others did too. The evolution to the dynamic at the edge of chaos was co-created through the interaction of the organisations, not chosen by one in isolation. Outcomes and dynamics continued to change in unpredictable ways, outside the power of individual organisations to choose, as the number of microcomputer producers increased and Microsoft gained greater power over the market. More recently, the power of Microsoft was challenged by lawsuits and freely available operating systems on the Internet.

Marion is making an important point here, because many who take up complexity theory in relation to organisations may accept that organisations cannot choose future outcomes but then claim that they can deliberately choose the dynamic in which they operate.

However, Marion also repeatedly stresses that unpredictability does not lead to the conclusion that it all happens by chance or that there is no control. Attractors at the edge of chaos are bounded and demonstrate a family-like similarity. Therefore, it is not possible for just anything to happen. He also argues that the power law is itself a form of control because, at the edge of chaos, the numbers of extinction events both large and small are smaller than they are in the dynamics of stability, on the one hand, and instability, on the other. Because of the relatively small number of large extinction events, change spreads through a network in a controlled manner. In the other dynamics, change spreads through the network in a highly destructive, continuous manner.

Marion, therefore, focuses at the macro level of a whole industry and talks about a population of impersonal organisations (IBM and Apple for example) interacting with each other in a self-organising manner, driven by an urge to survive. He is talking about this population and the organisations of which it consists as if they were no different from a population of organisms. However, what are these organisations? They are not organisms, or anything like organisms, but, rather, patterns of joint human action. Marion reifies organisations and treats them as if they are things, or organisms, apart from, or outside of humans, interacting according to principles that apply to them at a macro level, split off from the humans that constitute them. The principles governing these systems are taken to be the same as those governing non-human systems.

To this Marion adds the deliberate purposefulness (teleology) of human beings, by which he means what has been called *rationalist causality* in Part 1. The result is that humans, acting according to rationalist causality, find themselves having to act within a system that is somehow independent of them, operating according to the causal principles of self-organisation. The latter considerably restricts the scope humans have for realising their intentions. Patterns in human action, then, emerge as the 'both . . . and' paradigm of both human choice and a system with a life of its own.

Marion's assumptions about human psychology are clearly individual centred and cognitivist. He argues that social behaviour arises from the selfish needs of the individual. Selfishness is local and personal, an individual trait that does not depend upon any external force. Humans are said to cooperate because that is the best way of achieving individual goals. In addition, he says that humans assign meaning to symbols and mental constructs that catalyse human action to create complex social structures. This clearly places the individual as fundamental, and thought before action. Before there can be the social there have to be individual humans with their selfish interests, and before they act, they think and make selfish choices.

However, another part of Marion's argument does pick up on a radical insight coming from complexity theory. He argues that the very nature of the irrational and the random is essential to the emergence of novel structures. He ties creativity and the emergence of novelty firmly to the unpredictable aspect of the dynamic at the edge of chaos. He argues that without irrationality there would be stagnation. He sees irrationality as the social equivalent of the Poincaré resonances that Prigogine regards as essential to the emergence of new structures in nature. Diverse and surprising order in the world arises because life takes unexpected directions. Marion thinks about human learning as a process of tinkering, often without much thinking. People tinker, and as they do so they sense patterns. These patterns organise their perception and understanding, and as they tinker further those perceptions and understandings restructure, which in turn affects what people observe. He claims that learning occurs because humans are irrational. Perfectly rational decision-makers have nothing to discover and hence nothing to learn. Heroic leaders do less than we think they do, but they do act as symbols of a cause and they do rally unified behaviour. However, having taken a radical position on causality, predictability, equilibrium, limits on human ability to change social processes through deliberate action alone, and so in many ways decentring the individual, Marion ends up with a view of human psychology and social relating that is not particularly radical, apart from the way he stresses the irrational and the need for deviant behaviour.

Complex evolutionary models of industries

Allen and his colleagues (for example, Allen, 1998a, 1998b; Allen *et al.*, 2006) work in the tradition of Prigogine (*see* Chapter 10) to argue that change in organisations occurs through an ongoing process of co-evolution in which behavioural types interact with each other. Allen argues that the underlying mechanisms of such evolution involve micro diversity within a system and it is this that drives ongoing, emergent, qualitative changes in systems and structures. He draws on Darwinian theory in saying that there are selective effects of interaction and also mechanisms that discover new strategies or niches. He also says that human intention, calculation and belief may channel diversity into a narrower range than that which the random micro diversity of nature would produce.

Diversity is defined in terms of the number of qualitatively different types of individuals, each type having different attributes. As an organisation evolves, changes occur in both the attributes internal to each type and the configuration of interactions between types. Individuals are thought of as bundles of attributes reflecting a type and organisations are thought of as bundles of these individual types, with societies being bundles of organisations. These levels of individual, organisation and society co-evolve and the diversity of each level emerges in the co-evolutionary process, driven by diversity at the level below. Evolution requires the invasion of a population by new behaviours which grow to a significant level in the system.

This conceptualisation allows the construction of a mathematical model consisting of differential equations where each equation generates growth rates for a different type in a population and where the growth rate of each type depends to some extent on the growth rates of competing types. The model shows that a new type can only invade the system, the system can only evolve, if it is unstable – stability makes invasion by a new type, and thus evolution, impossible. The model is used to demonstrate that evolution generates coherent diversity and that micro diversity at one system level drives the evolution of the system level above it.

So, a model of macroscopic equations of population dynamics is used to describe how evolution works. This model starts with the assumption that each agent in a type is the average across that type. Errors are then introduced into the replication of the behaviours, or strategies, of agents within a type, amounting to a relaxation of the assumption of averages across a type. This takes account of micro diversity within a type, that is, of non-average agents. Then the model shows how error making, or ignorance, is a robust way of exploring for new strategies.

The conclusion is that, when agents are in a new domain, then learning/exploration leads to better overall performance, despite the opportunity cost of error making; but in a domain which is not new, exploitation rather than exploration produces better overall performance. Allen suggests that industries display similar dynamics to the model as they gradually switch from exploration to exploitation. The models show that there is no such thing as an optimal strategy, because as soon as one strategy becomes dominant then it will be vulnerable to the invasion of some other strategy.

The model is developed to explore the dynamics of economic markets. Potential customers are modelled in terms of their revenue, recognising that this means ignoring different desires and needs of individuals. The model shows how an ecology of strategies emerges indicating that agents are not susceptible to adopting the same strategy, contrary to the prescriptions for best practice or benchmarking to be found in the organisational literature. Diverse behaviours and learning rules lead to more rapid evolution of market structure at a lower cost than benchmarking. However, the explorations/innovations tried out at a particular time cannot be logically deduced because their overall effect cannot be known ahead of time.

The conclusion is that a system of co-evolving agents with underlying micro diversity, or idiosyncrasy, automatically leads to the emergence of new structures, and the general implications are that:

- error-making diffusion leads to successful performance and innovation;
- the whole process leads to the evolution of a complex community of types of agent;
- successful and sustainable evolutionary systems are those in which there is freedom and encouragement of exploration – they are more cooperative than competitive;
- uncertainty about the future allows actions that are exploratory.

The same authors (Allen *et al.*, 2005) use a macroscopic model to show how non-linear responses can generate new (false) information which can break symmetries and lead to evolutionary change. They take the problem of policemen trying to catch criminals. In the first model they assume that the policemen carry out the random 'stop and search' of people when they seem to be acting suspiciously. Micro diversity is introduced by assuming that there are two types of people – pink and blue. These two types commit exactly the same average rate of crime. However, in actuality there are fluctuations, small deviations around the average, so that in one period pinks commit a higher rate of crime and in others the blues do. On average the rate is the same, but for particular sampling periods there is some purely chance variation around the average. Over a long period, the deviations around the average will cancel out if the police stop and search pinks and blues randomly. The statistics they collect on their arrests will reflect the underlying real rates of crime over a reasonably long sampling period.

However, to improve performance the police authorities introduce targets for arresting criminals and reward policemen according to target achievement. The police gather statistics on crime rates over a particular sampling period during which it just happens that more pinks than blues are arrested. So, policemen form a theory that crime rates are higher in the pink population and so focus more attention on stopping and searching pinks. This turns into a self-fulfilling prophesy because the greater police effort in relation to pinks does lead to the arrest of more pinks than blues. Also, the blues may come to feel that they can more easily escape detection and so actually commit more crimes than the pinks, but this fact escapes detection by the police because they are focusing their attention on the pinks. The statistics the police collect will then show that pinks commit much more crime than blues when in fact the opposite is the case. This false information will lead to even more effort being directed at the pinks so leading to the vicious circle of a self-fulfilling prophesy. Complex systems evolve into an unknowable future sometimes with unwanted consequences. The authors argue that uncertainty and surprise are essential features of life itself.

This kind of macro modelling yields important insights which are often counter-intuitive. For example, the models show that following best practice benchmarks actually harms strategic exploration and that apparently rational strategies developed to meet targets can have highly distorting effects on activity. The models can there-fore be used to generate provocative generalisations. The interesting question then becomes just how people in organisations use such articulations of *generalisations* in their context-specific situations. However, I argue that macro models cannot capture the detail of unique, context-specific detail of human interaction and so cannot explain how people actually make particular such generalisations in their specific situations. This will be a matter of concern in Part 3 of the book. Also, while the models considered above make an important move to explore the consequences of diversity, mathematical models cannot deal with the full diversity of human behaviour. For example, in modelling markets, the models mentioned above cannot capture differences in the preferences and tastes of individual consumers. Part 3 will also be concerned with the actual diversity of human action in our experience.

Although Allen's models are extremely useful in generating provocative insights, they can quite easily be subtly reproduced as theories of strategic choice and the learning organisation, cast in a new vocabulary. I suggest that this happens because of the continued employment of the language of systems and the adoption of an essentially cognitivist view of human psychology, emphasising the primacy of the individual who knows through making representations of reality and behaves on the basis of these representations. This is an essentially cybernetic view of human know-ing and behaving, one that is entirely compatible with systemic management and organisational theory. The result is that the potentially radical implications of the models may not be realised in relation to the management of organisations.

To illustrate what I mean, take Allen's (1998a) analysis of the fishing industry. He contrasts the conclusions produced by equilibrium (cybernetic system), systems dynamics, self-organising, and evolutionary models of that industry. The equilib-rium model produces a policy recommendation to constrain fishing effort at, or just below, the maximum that yields a sustainable fish population. However, the dynam-ics of the fish population and fish markets rapidly render any selected sustainable level of fishing highly inaccurate. A systems dynamics model allows for variations in fish populations and in economic conditions. However, the model uses average data for all of these factors and so cannot capture spontaneous change.

Allen then introduces 'noise' into the equations to represent random fluctuations in fish populations to construct a model of the systems dynamics kind. This model produces boom-and-bust oscillations in fishing fleet catches. On the basis of this model, management should concern itself with overcoming this cyclical behaviour rather than discussing fishing quotas. Allen then introduces a variable to represent the rate of response of the fleet to fish availability, another for the level of technology and yet another for price responsiveness, to construct a model of the self-organising kind. Now there is still a boom-and-bust attractor, but in addition, another attractor emerges, one of a small high-priced niche where fish becomes a luxury food.

Allen also incorporates different levels of information acquired by each fishing fleet and different attitudes to risk into the self-organising model. He assumes that fishing fleets are boundedly rational decision-makers and so imports cognitivism as his theory of human psychology. The model demonstrates that optimal use of information increases profit in the short term but not necessarily in the long term. Cautious optimisers get locked into the existing situation while more adventurous risk takers open themselves to the possibility of finding new strategies. The model identifies a tendency to follow short-term profit-maximising strategies at the expense of the long term.

Finally, Allen specifies what he calls an evolutionary complex model, which introduces different types of boats and fleet behaviours. The result is a model that can be used to explore the relative effectiveness of different strategies (1998a, p. 33). From this analysis, he reaches the conclusion that sustainability lies not in efficiency, or in allowing free markets, but in creativity. Creativity is rooted in diversity, cultural richness and the will and ability to experiment and take risks. Another conclusion is that uncertainty is inevitable.

Allen very clearly demonstrates the importance of diversity in generating new forms as he moves from one way of modelling the fishing industry to another. He clearly identifies the radical nature of models that incorporate high levels of diversity. However, what he suggests as application in terms of management falls quite easily into the systemic management discourses reviewed in Part 1. For example, his whole methodology implies a cognitivist view of human beings who use rational constructs to explore scenarios with the intention of gaining insight. This easily allows one to sidestep the possibility that management itself is an evolving process. The implication is that managers can step outside their system and model it as the basis of making decisions to manipulate it. The insights he produces are radical but the prescriptions are not. However, in saying this I do not in any way diminish the importance of the generalised insights that complex evolutionary models generate. I am simply arguing that they need to be taken further in terms of the detail of actual human experience in organisations.

11.3 Understanding organisations as complex systems

In this section, I will look briefly at a number of publications that import theories of chaos and complex adaptive systems into theorising about organisations in a qualitative way, as opposed to the quantitative modelling of whole industries explored in the last section.

Thietart and Forgues

Thietart and Forgues (1995) review chaos theory and conclude that mathematical chaos can be found 'when there is the simultaneous influence of counteracting forces' (p. 23). The authors then review relevant literature on organisations to show that organisations are characterised by counteracting forces. Some of these forces push an organisation to stability: namely, the forces of planning, structuring and controlling. Other forces, however, push an organisation towards instability and disorder. These forces include innovation, initiative and experimentation. They argue that when these forces are coupled they produce the chaotic organisation. On this basis, Thietart and Forgues present a number of propositions based on the theory of chaos, such as:

- Organisations are potentially chaotic.
- Organisations move from one dynamic state to another: namely, stable equilibrium, periodic equilibrium or chaos.
- Forecasting is impossible, especially at a global scale over the long term. Change, therefore, has an unpredictable long-term effect.
- When in the chaotic state, organisations are attracted to an identifiable configuration.
- Similar actions taken by the same organisation will never lead to the same state.

They conclude that the interaction of forces of stability and change can create chaotic dynamics, which they define literally as 'deterministically induced random behavior' (p. 28), which they say has an underlying order and so leads to new stabilities. The prescription then becomes to 'let chaos develop because it is the only way to find new forms of order' and 'look for order but not too much, because it may be a source of chaos' (p. 28).

There are a number of points to note about this kind of analysis. First is the level at which the analysis is conducted, namely the macro level of the organisation as a whole. Second, it adopts the position of the objective observer. Third, there is a hint of an underlying cognitivist perspective in that organisations, presumably those who manage them, are assumed to be able to choose how much chaos or order to have. There is the notion that the role of managers is to move their organisation between different dynamic possibilities. I would like to sound a note of caution in pursuing this kind of analysis. Chaos theory is a theory of deterministic systems, but human action is not deterministic. The behaviour of people is not driven by unchanging rules. The 'rules', if that is what they are, change as people learn.

Morgan

Morgan (1997) uses chaos and complexity theories as the basis of one of his metaphors for organisations: namely, the organisation as flux and transformation. He points to the order that can emerge from interaction governed by a few *simple rules* and equates these simple rules with his notion of 'minimum specs': that is, avoiding a grand design and specifying a small number of critical variables to attend to. He says the minimum specs define an attractor and create the context within which the system will move to it.

There are problems with this idea of 'simple rules'. If the requirement is some new form, the rules, or the context, that will produce that form do not yet exist. If emergence depends critically on small changes, then there is no way to specify what they are in advance. You could not ensure that you have detected all of them or measured them accurately enough. Morgan passes over this and recommends that managers should manage the context and allow self-organisation to do the rest. Here again there is the notion of manager not as participant in a difficult-to-understand complex system but as one who stands outside it, identifies the minimum specs and then creates the context for it to produce self-organisation. Note the talk about a manager 'allowing it to happen'. This seems to assume that self-organisation is some new form of behaviour an individual can choose rather than a different way of understanding how people have always behaved.

Morgan also recommends identifying the small changes, or leverage points, that will transform the system. I have already explained why I think that this does not fit with the notion of a complex system. He also recommends identifying the existing attractor: that is, locking an organisation into a stable position and identifying whether it should be changed. If it is to be changed, then managers are supposed to work out how the transition is to be achieved and how small changes can be used to do so. In advance, they are supposed to identify what the new ground rules are supposed to be. They must consider how they are going to manage through the 'edge of chaos'.

For me, the essentials of cybernetics and cognitivism are all firmly in place in this argument. The focus is on the autonomous individual who stands outside the system and in effect controls it, even if in a much looser way than is often supposed. The reasoning remains, I think, firmly within the systemic tradition and the invitation to explore a radical perspective is passed by.

Nonaka

Nonaka (Nonaka, 1988a, 1988b, 1991; Nonaka and Takeuchi, 1995) also uses chaos theory in his perspective on creation of knowledge in organisations (*see* Chapter 5). Nonaka and Takeuchi use the words 'self-organising' but in a very different way from my understanding. They see self-organisation not as the local interaction of agents that produces emergent patterns, but rather as the unconstrained activity of autonomous or free individuals. They describe a self-organising team as a structure in which individuals can be free to diffuse their ideas (p. 76). They link this with Morgan's (1997) 'minimum critical specifications'. In complexity theory, self-organisation is a process in which agents interact locally on the basis of their historically evolved identities. They are constrained by the need to interact and this does not imply the kind of freedom that Nonaka talks about.

A key insight from complexity theory is that of the paradoxical dynamics of stability and instability at the 'edge of chaos'. Again Nonaka and Takeuchi use similar words, but they equate chaos with crisis and assign to top management the role of injecting it into the organisation in order to break down routines, habits and cognitive frameworks. I cannot see any justification for equating mathematical chaos with human crisis.

Sanders

Sanders (1998) claims that chaos and complexity are everywhere in organisations and talks about the need to master them, claiming that the complexity sciences provide a way to 'anticipate, respond to, and influence change as it is emerging and before a crisis arises' (p. 7). She talks about observing the system, so implicitly taking the position of manager as objective observer rather than participant, and moves immediately to prescriptions for success.

She says that it is possible to identify any system's initial conditions, because systems are deterministic, but that it is difficult to predict their future states, because they are nonlinear. This statement is clearly wrong. It is in practice impossible to forecast the long-term state of the kind of system she is talking about precisely because it is not possible to identify the initial conditions to the infinite exactness required. Infinite precision is required because the nonlinear structure of the system may amplify even the tiniest failure to identify and measure precisely the initial conditions. Without this, long-term prediction would be possible *because* the system is deterministic. Determinism is a theory of causality and it implies nothing whatsoever about the ability to measure initial conditions.

She then says that despite an inability to make predictions of long-term states it is possible to provide qualitative descriptions of whole system behaviour over time. This is true, but only for the attractor the system is currently drawn to. It would not be possible to describe any new attractor that some system was capable of spontaneously jumping to, until the jump occurred. Furthermore, human systems are not deterministic because, even if there are 'rules' governing them, these rules change over time. If one is to think of the human in terms of systems then one at least needs to think of them as learning, evolving and producing new forms. In other words, they have to be thought of as moving to entirely new attractors, the 'shape' of which cannot be 'seen' before the move is made. So, you can only 'see' the shape of the attractor you already know about. To the extent that strategy is about producing creative, innovative new forms of business, it would not be possible, in terms of complexity theory, to 'see' that form before it emerges.

As far as I understand it, what I have summarised above is the conceptual core of the whole book and underlies all the prescriptions it makes. Sanders clearly takes the stance of external objective observer who sees an organisation as a chaotic system. Implicitly, she is prescribing this as the stance that a manager should take too. Managers are supposed to look at the system as a whole and then identify the pre-existing order, the strange attractor, hidden in apparent disorder. Then they are supposed to detect new initial conditions and take hold of them – master them, she says, before they do something that is unexpected. Not only is the manager to be the objective external observer but also the heroic individual who can master chaos and find hidden order. Unpredictability is mentioned and then, in effect, ignored. The words are from complexity science but the concepts are from cybernetics and cognitivism. In the process, any new insight is lost and orthodox prescriptions are simply presented in different language.

Consider now how Shona L. Brown and Kathleen M. Eisenhardt (1998) apply complexity theory to management in their book, called *Competing on the Edge: Strategy as Structured Chaos*.

Brown and Eisenhardt

Brown and Eisenhardt appeal to a central concept from complexity theory: namely, the 'edge of chaos', which they define as being only partially structured. This immediately loses the paradoxical notion of contradictory forces that can never be resolved, replacing it with a simple balance: too much structure gives stability and too little produces chaos. Being at the edge also means *letting* a semi-coherent strategy emerge from the organisation: that is, one that is not too fixed, nor one that is too fluid. They turn to that favourite of organisational complexity writers, the notion that a few simple structures 'generate enormously complex adaptive behaviour – whether flock behaviour among birds, resilient government (as in democracy), or simply successful performance by corporations' and argue that the 'critical management issue at the edge of chaos is to figure out what to structure, and as essential, what not to structure' (p. 12).

These authors take the notion of the edge of chaos across into organisations and immediately collapse it into one of organisational structure, which then becomes a choice for managers to make. The choice is to install just enough structure to move their organisation to the edge of chaos where it can experience relentless change. Self-organisation is equated with adaptiveness and the notion of local interaction amongst agents producing emergent outcomes is lost. The analogy of the birds is used and then quite effortlessly coupled with successful organisations.

However, flocking is one attractor for bird behaviour, one that already exists. The few simple rules that produce it will not produce spontaneous jumps to new attractors. Surely, success for corporations over the long term requires just such a move to new attractors. Furthermore, a key feature of the edge of chaos is the *power law*. This means that small numbers of large extinction events occur periodically while large numbers of small extinctions events occur. There is no guarantee of survival at the edge of chaos, only the possibility of new forms emerging that might survive. Nowhere do the authors mention this power law. Instead, they make a simplistic equation between being at the edge of chaos and success.

They reduce human behaviour to a few key rules and assume that these can ensure success. The authors provide a questionnaire that managers can use to identify whether they are at the edge of chaos or trapped in one of the other dynamics (pp. 30–1). They give examples from their research of a company in each of these states and, of course, the only successful one is reported to be at the edge of chaos. They then give prescriptions for moving to the edge, if they are not already there. Managers should foster frequent change in the context of a few strict rules. They should keep activity loosely structured but at the same time rely on targets and deadlines. They should create channels for real-time, fact-based communication within and across groups.

So, the strategic choice now relates less to outcomes and more to a few simple rules, frequent changes to keep people on edge and fact-based communication channels. Why is it necessary to appeal to complexity theory for these prescriptions?

I think I have said enough to show that, once again, researchers have made some very loose interpretations of what complexity theory means and quite easily subsumed it into orthodox organisational theory. The prescriptions and the descriptions rely implicitly on cybernetics and cognitivism, even though the language is drawn from complexity theory. The result is a watered-down strategic choice theory.

Wheatley

Griffin (2002) provides a critique of Wheatley's (1999) reliance on chaos and complexity theory. He points out how she sees chaos and complexity theories as providing an insight into the simplicity of all living systems in nature. If leaders come to understand their organisations as living systems, they will be able to use the insights from chaos and complexity theories to find a much simpler way of organising human affairs. For her, it is by recognising and working with the living system, by participating in a higher-level whole, that leaders can achieve a more human and a more creative organisation. She also attaches much the same importance to the notion of vision as learning organisation theorists do, but she understands vision as a field of real but unseen forces influencing human behaviour. Having conceived of an organisation as a living whole in which people participate, Wheatley argues that those people exhibit a self-organising capacity just as in nature's living systems. Wheatley suggests that organisations are quite literally alive and must be understood, using the complexity sciences, just as other living systems in nature are thought of.

For Wheatley, the essence of living systems is the *simple rules* according to which they function. If leaders of organisations are to lead in a simpler way then they must identify the simple rules and they can do this by turning to the complexity sciences, which she sees as the rediscovery of ancient wisdom. In her thinking about leadership, Wheatley clearly displays the 'both . . . and' thinking of causal duality. There is a living system having it own purpose and an autonomous individual, the leader, also having purpose, and what she is arguing for is for leaders to align their individual purpose with that of the greater living whole. For her, it is an overriding system that assures the emergence of order and she often refers to this in mythological terms: for example, as the order of Gaia emerging from Chaos. Wheatley affirms the mysterious nature of this level of system, and being a part of such a system is what participation is about. She speaks of finding the self in participation in higher wholes. Not to participate, she says, leaves one isolated as an individual. Those who participate in the whole are 'healthy'. Ethical action is equated with conforming and submission to harmonious wholes (*see* Griffin, 2002, for extended critique). Note how her view of organisational life is essentially the same as learning organisation theory and emphasises the rather mystical aspects of that theory (*see* Chapter 5).

Lewin and Regine

Griffin (2002) discusses the work of Lewin and Regine (2000), who also state that organisations are living systems, which they understand as complex adaptive systems, drawing on the work of Stuart Kauffman. They are concerned with the individual's soul being allowed to be present in the workplace and with the emergence of the collective soul of the organisation, thereby displaying the same kind of dualistic, 'both . . . and' thinking as Wheatley. Individuals are *both* agents in complex adaptive systems, where the simple rules governing their interactions have to do with ensuring *caring* relationships, *and* have souls, that is, they are autonomous individuals responsible for their actions in a way that is independent of the self-organisation of the complex adaptive system. There is a distinction between individuals as agents in the system making choices that are caring and participative, so contributing to the health of the system (organisation), and individual agents making other choices which are selfish and make the system (organisation) an unhealthy place to work in.

For Lewin and Regine, the implication of the complexity sciences is that leaders must come to a new understanding of themselves, putting aside their egos to serve others. The new form of leadership requires nothing less than a personal conversion, which is a painful process of learning to let go of the illusion of control. However, they also talk about the leader as the one who changes the culture. The leader, on the one hand, is capable of changing the culture and, on the other hand, must give up the illusion of control.

Just as Wheatley did, so Lewin and Regine emphasise the 'few simple rules' idea, arguing that rich, creative, complex behaviour emerges from a few simple guidelines. They, along with so many others, cite the Boids simulation (*see* Chapter 10), which reproduces flocking patterns on the basis of only three simple rules of interaction among individual agents. They argue that when leaders formulate a few simple rules and leave the rest to self-organisation they will unleash human creativity. However, as Chapter 10 made clear, simulations based on a few given rules produce no creativity whatsoever. What the simple rules thinking represents is simply a different form of control (Stacey *et al.*, 2000).

Lewin and Regine express the source of commitment and ethical action in terms of idealised wholes. Individuals must give up themselves in order for this whole to emerge, which then becomes the basis for the action already taken. This means that the participants are not focused on the everyday potential emerging from conflict and difference, but rather on an idealised and harmonious whole. Again, what Lewin and Regine present is little different from the more mystical aspects of learning organisation theory.

Pascale

Pascale (Pascale *et al.*, 2000) also claims that organisations are living organisms, and that, as such, they are complex adaptive systems. It is not just a metaphor for organisations. Nevertheless, he uses the terminology in both metaphorical and literal senses. For example, he views the mathematical term 'attractor' as a key concept in understanding complex adaptive systems but also uses it in the metaphorical sense of a 'vision' drawing the organisation forward. In a manner that is very similar to that of Lewin and Regine, Pascale describes the leader as being in a 'both . . . and' position. Operational leadership is to be applied in conditions of relative equilibrium. Adaptive leadership, on the other hand, makes happen what would not otherwise have happened. The individual leader must choose the appropriate form of leadership. It is taken for granted that the leader can observe the system from outside and choose amongst possible alternatives to apply to the system.

However, Pascale differs significantly from Wheatley and Lewin and Regine in his focus on conflict as the most important quality of relationship in looking at the organisation as a complex adaptive system. The leader, again from a position external to the system, judges when adaptive leadership is necessary and then considers how much the system needs to be disturbed. Pascale says that this is achieved by communicating the urgency of the adaptive challenge, establishing a broad understanding of the circumstances creating the problem, clarifying why traditional solutions will not work and keeping up the stress until guerrilla leaders come forward with solutions. Leaders intentionally generate anxiety and tension when an adaptive style is called for. They push their organisation to the edge of chaos. Social interaction is driven by conflict but the leaders introduce the source of the conflict into the team.

Griffin (2002) argues that Pascale and his co-authors present a view of leadership that is unethical in Kant's sense. To induce crisis into human teams in order to take advantage of 'productive' self-organisation for the survival of the whole is using humans as a means to an end and so contravenes Kant's ethical imperative.

Beinhocker

Beinhocker (2006) argues that organisations are complex adaptive systems because they are made up of individual agents who interact dynamically with each other: their rules of behaviour and networks of utterances adapt to changes in the environment and their interactions produce macro-level patterns of behaviour. Organisations are complex adaptive systems nested in the larger complex adaptive systems of the industry and the economy. More specifically, organisations are goal-directed, boundary-maintaining, socially constructed systems of human inter-action. This means that organisations are designed and built for a purpose – namely, to achieve a goal and this is done by actions that close the gap between current and desired states. Organisations are open thermodynamic systems in which goals drive activities that lower entropy inside relative to outside: they carry out thermo-dynamically irreversible transformation on matter, energy and information. So, from this perspective, organisations are actually existing systems which process informa-tion to produce wealth which is the fit order of knowledge.

Furthermore, like all complex adaptive systems, organisations evolve. For Beinhocker, evolution is an information-processing algorithm, essentially a search process across some fitness landscape which ideally takes a rugged rather than smooth or fragmented form. Evolution is an algorithm of differentiation, selection and amplification which creates fit design without a designer. Evolution combines an adaptive walk (exploitation) with random jumps (exploration) to explore the landscape which is a design space of all possible designs coded as schema to be read by some schema readers as the basis of interactions which produce both schema and readers. The interactors are code for building blocks in the schemata. In the case of organisations the landscape is the space containing all possible business plans and evolution is the algorithm for searching this space which is done by managers as readers of business plans and so as interactors. They explore the space of plans using a combination of deduction and tinkering amounting to trial and error learning. Business plans have components, key building blocks taking the form of physical technologies and social technologies. Business plans describe strategies of combing the building blocks of physical technologies and social technologies. Strategies are characterised by the Red Queen effect, which means that in order to stand still in a dynamic environment you have to keep running faster and faster.

In practical terms, managers need to create adaptive strategies and for this they require adaptive mindsets. They need to pursue a portfolio of strategies as experiments, set aspirations understood as levers, avoid distortions stemming from internal politics and bureaucracy by improving the quantity, quality and speed of information flow and by creating the right environment for selecting actions. Managers need to create mechanisms which tell people what kinds of behaviours will be rewarded. Managers are supposed to know which initiatives are promising and which are not, through explicit market feedback. Individuals have mental models, are over-optimistic and block change, and can be grouped into into 'rigids' and 'flexibles'. Culture is rules of behaviour, norms which emerge, but inherent tensions in cultures make it virtually impossible for norms which balance individual performance with cooperation to arise organically without strong leadership that manages the tensions. It is the role of leaders to create the kind of conditions – that is the social technology and the social architecture – which unleash the power of self-organisation and emergence.

It is striking how Beinhocker's use of the models of complex adaptive systems starts by abstracting organisations from ordinary human interactions, reifying them into the equivalent of physical systems which lower entropy by managing information. When human persons are introduced, they are taken to be information-processing cognitive systems that resist change and are over-optimistic. The culture governing their behaviour emerges, but managers and leaders must create the conditions which will manage any tensions that emerge. Managers need to create experimental strategies which will be adaptive. The result is simply a re-presentation of the dominant discourse in somewhat different language.

Recent research papers applying complexity science to organisations

Research papers published in professional journals on management and organisation make much use of the concepts of self-organisation and emergence. Most of them (for example, Haynes, 2003; Carlisle and McMillan, 2006; Coleman, 1999; Meek *et al.*, 2007) understand *self-organisation* to be a special process or force in organisations, which takes the form of self-determination by individual members of the organisation. Most writers say that self-organisation is a form of organisation in which there is no central controller within the organisation and no external controller either. Self-organising agents behave in exploratory and experimental ways and do not have complete knowledge of the circumstances surrounding their actions. This is contrasted with deliberate control exercised through formal and informal power, through the authority and feedback processes of bureaucracy, and through the work routines which discipline human interaction. Too much deliberate control is held to be counterproductive, and the emphasis should be shifted to self-organisation. Instead of regarding self-organisation as a threat to order, it should be seen as a creative force which must not be suppressed but harnessed and used for the good of the organisation. Self-organisation, defined as the opposite of central control, is equated with self-governance, empowerment, and teamwork in which individuals manage themselves within clear boundaries and bottom-up decision-making, all of which must be balanced with top-down control to avoid chaos. Network organisations are the preferred form and organisations have to find the right dynamic mix of collaboration and competition. The understanding of the concept of *emergence* continues in the same vein (for example, Robertson and Caldart, 2008; Anderson, 1999) where it is the unpredictable arising of global, higher-level, properties from lower level self-organisation which is understood in terms of simple rules of agent behaviour. This view is taken to justify a new model of an organisation which focuses on utilising emergent dynamics as opposed to hierarchical direction and control (for example, Twomey, 2006; Downs *et al.*, 2003; Campbell-Hunt, 2007; Gershenson and Heylighen, 2003; Goldstein *et al.*, 2008; Hodge and Coronado, 2007; Mitleton-Kelly, 2006; Anderson and McMillan, 2003). This new model takes the form of a shared decision-making process governed by organisation-wide principles and intentions with managers acting as catalysts for emergence at all levels. Emergent strategy, practised by entrepreneurial organisations, is understood to be distinct from formal planning processes. Such emergent strategy requires the management of context and the creation of conditions which foster emergence, such as steadfast relationships, rewards for communication at all levels, allowing multiple representations, encouraging the telling of stories and risk-taking. These are the conditions that encourage spontaneous self-organisation within which strategies may emerge. However, although the outcomes that emerge from the dynamic interplay of networks and groups can only be partially planned, it is held that clear and consistent underlying principles, shared and aligned at all levels, make it possible to achieve intended patterns and avoid chaos. Such organisations are said to operate at the edge of chaos, a state which can be intentionally achieved. Others (for example, Pascale *et al.*, 2000; MacIntosh and MacLean, 1999; Sanders, 1998; Wheatley, 1999; Lewin and Regine, 2000) present yet another variation on this theme, appealing to the notion of dissipative structures which are said to rely on deep structure for the order they display. This deep structure is a quasi-permanent, invisible sub-structure that remains largely intact while manifest, observable structures break down at bifurcation points. Deep structure is equated with a few simple rules in organisations that define business logic and operate as organising principles. Change occurs in an organisation when these hidden simple rules are surfaced, reframed and then enacted during the chaotic transformation characteristic of a bifurcation point. The role of managers is to manage this deep structure and, in doing so, they condition the emergence of new deep structures. By operating on deep structures, managers can have a limited influence on the outcomes of self-organisation rather than simply relying on the spontaneous, random and unpredictable self-organisation of systems in nature.

So, on the one hand, these writers are identifying self-organisation as an impersonal force which must be harnessed and used, and then, on the other hand, they equate this with empowerment and looser forms of organisation. Furthermore, the force of self-organisation, according to these writers, only produces creative good outcomes. But in the science, self-organisation is not a force at all – it simply refers to local interaction and calling it a 'force' immediately obscures this local interaction behind a kind of mysterious global force. This then means that we have passed by the invitation to explore the organisational reality of local interaction. Since the prescriptions of empowerment and loose organisational forms can be found in the dominant discourse, there is no need to look anywhere else for explanation or justification. In fact the conceptualisation of self-organisation as a force or an alternative form of organisation simply re-presents the dominant discourse in new jargon. The 'both . . . and' structure of the dominant discourse is retained as both top-down control and bottom-up decision-making, the problem being one of balance with no hint of paradox. This all makes no addition or challenge to the dominant discourse. In the same way as self-organisation, emergence is regarded as some kind of force to be deliberately brought about by managers by creating the right conditions. It is striking how in these developments of the notion of emergence people and their ordinary activities simply disappear. In my understanding emergence does not refer to a force that someone can operate on or a process that someone can use another process to shape or condition. As I understand it, emergence refers to pattern arising across a population that is not the realisation of a prior design or plan for that population-wide pattern but flows from many, many local interactions. This notion of emergence is completely nullified in the writing of most who apply the concept of emergence to organisations. As a result, they simply re-present the dominant discourse in different language.

There are widespread prescriptions for fostering the conditions for emergence, moving the organisation to the edge of chaos and allowing / unleashing the power of self-organisation. These views of self-organisation and emergence are taken to justify the rejection of hierarchical, command and control organisational structures and their replacement with more fluid network structures based on simple rules (Ashmos *et al.*, 2002). However, those presenting such views are usually quick to explain that this does not mean abandoning control. For example, Meek *et al.* (2007), researching complex metropolitan administrative systems, subscribe to another widely expressed prescription calling for simple design principles, said to underlie self-organising systems, which involve keeping routines and rules few and simple so that managers need not totally abandon control for self-organisation and top-down for bottom-up decision-making. Policy-makers should choreograph the interrelation between the varieties of elements of concern to them (Edelenbos *et al.*, 2008).

A number of writers applying the complexity sciences to organisations adopt a contingency approach (for example, Allen *et al.*, 2006; Boisot, 2000; Burgelman and Grove, 2007; Sommer *et al.*, 2009). The claim is that, since it is possible to make predictions in stable environments and repetitive businesses, it follows that standard planning and rule-abiding strategic actions and processes are applicable. However, in situations where technology and the environment are changing rapidly, it is not possible to predict, and rule-changing strategies of experimenting, developing agility, adaptability and co-evolution are called for in organisational forms of decen-tralisation, networks, project teams, empowerment and innovation. It is pointed out that it will normally be impossible to predict shifts from rule-abiding to rule-changing strategies, which means that managers must maintain a mental state of constant alertness. However, even in turbulent environments intention, as commonly owned visions for the future, is said to be central because, even if not realised, intention provides fast feedback. Sword (2007) argues that uncoordinated self-organisation destabilises systems, since even tiny conflicts can set off a cascade that destabilises the system. She argues that avoiding or resolving conflict too early may prevent system adaptation while, by tipping the system into chaos and then back to the edge of chaos, conflict can stimulate innovation and information exchange, which allow change to flourish. Throughout these prescriptions there is the clear notion of the manager making rational decisions and acting on forces of emergence and self-organisation, designing loose structures and encouraging interaction. The language is a little different in that managers are now said to 'choreograph' and 'create' condi-tions, but in the end the leaders are still making choices which they can still realise, as in the dominant discourse, if they follow what are called 'complexity principles'.

Notions of self-organisation and emergence raise questions about the nature of leadership. Some (for example, Lichtenstein *et al.*, 2006) argue that leadership is not in or done by leaders but is rather an emergent outcome of relational inter-actions between agents. Leadership is the expediting of processes which combine interdependent actions of agents into a collective venture. Leadership is a systems phenomenon transcending individuals, and relationships are not defined in terms of hierarchies but of interaction between heterogeneous agents across a network. Individuals and groups are said to 'resonate' with each other in the sense of sharing common interests, knowledge, goals, worldviews and histories. Agents respond to pressures from leaders and others and struggle with conflicting needs. These tensions generate system-wide emergent learning, the conditions for which can be enabled by leaders. A distinction is drawn between leadership as the product of interactive dynamics in which knowledge, preferences and behaviours change, and leaders who influence the process of dynamic interaction. Interactions are thought to be governed by rules and mechanisms for changing the rules, one of which is leadership events which produce a new identity. They recommend the use of computational modelling to better understand the dynamic of leadership, arguing that complexity leadership theory expands the potential for creativity and positive change. Complexity leadership is more than simplistic notions of empowerment. Instead, complexity leadership encourages all members to be leaders and 'own' their leadership to evoke greater responses from everyone. Complexity leadership theory provides an unambiguous pathway for driving responsibility downward, setting off self-organisation and innovation. This removes a significant pressure from formal leaders, allowing them to attend more directly to identifying strategic opportunities. Complexity leadership creates new managerial strategies, such as the introduction of low levels of tension to create adaptive change. Complexity theory calls for much greater attention to be paid to relationships.

This view of leadership still presents the highly idealised notions to be found in the dominant discourse, even though it is cast in relational terms. Leaders enable the learning of others, they influence the process of dynamic interaction, they encourage all to be leaders and they drive responsibility down the hierarchy. These quite conventional prescriptions, it seems to me, have no clear link with complexity sciences or with what self-organisation and emergence mean. The leaders are still supposed to use one process, such as influencing and driving, to operate on another process, the learning of others and their dynamic interaction as self-organisation and emergence.

Other complexity writers (Surie and Hazy, 2006) continue within the dominant discourse when they identify generative leaders as visionary and charismatic people who promote clear and effective communication, and limit signal noise so as to reduce and absorb complexity. They help to evolve a language all can understand and they ensure goals are specified and interactions aligned to system goals. Generative leaders are open to collaboration; they adopt modular organisational systems and foster problem-solving and innovation. They evolve and enforce rules that govern the system's dynamic by fostering and sustaining generative relationships through structuring situations and managing interactions. Effective leadership creates a system which brings together appropriate individuals and knowledge and allows them to interact with minimal friction. The focus must be on the process, because outcomes are uncertain and leadership affects the simple, local rules governing agent interaction. Innovation flows from how interactions are managed and regulated. The steps managers can take are the partitioning of tasks to allow effort to be structured within a confined context rather than allowing attention to be distracted. Generative leaders promote information flow and feedback and they distribute problem solving efforts more widely. Innovation can be institutionalised in the form of simple rules which operate locally to solve problems. Interactions must be regulated to prevent a complexity catastrophe. This is simply a re-statement of the empowerment strand of the dominant discourse in the jargon taken from the complexity sciences.

Yet others (Schreiber and Carley, 2006) model an organisation as a complex adaptive system using a multi-agent network model. They recognise a paradox of organisations needing to stimulate emergent collective action but also needing to use bureaucracies to control outcomes for exploitation. Emergence is here set up as the opposite of control. Postmodern leadership accommodates the paradox by combining managerial, adaptive and enabling leadership roles. Complexity leadership theory focuses on the latter two. Adaptive leaders shape the overall communication structure and help advance the co-evolution of human and social capital. Human capital appreciation takes the form of knowledge flows in informal networks of social interactions in the conditions created by enabling leadership. It all sounds very familiar and very distant from organisational reality.

The problem with 'living systems' and 'simple rules' as a theory of organisation

Griffin (2002) makes a number of criticisms of those who present a theory of organisations as living systems. First, those proposing this view frequently make emotive appeals for a return to ancient wisdom, supposedly now made scientific by the complexity sciences. However, it is far from clear that the ancients were any wiser than we are, or that the complexity sciences are rediscovering this ancient wisdom, including Far Eastern spirituality. These are simply assertions. Second, the suggestion that an organisation is a living system sets up a whole outside the experience of inter-action between people, a whole to which they are required to submit if their behaviour is to be judged ethical. This distances us from our actual experience and makes it feel natural to blame something outside our actual interaction for what happens to us. It encourages the belief that we are victims of a system, on the one hand, and allows us to escape feeling responsible for our own actions, on the other. Or it alienates people. They come to feel that they are insignificant parts of some greater whole and that there is nothing much they can do about it. The third difficulty is that organisations are not things at all, let alone living things. They are processes of communication and joint action. Communication and joint action as such are not alive. It is the bodies communicating and interacting that are alive.

Those prescribing 'simple rules', as the new way to manage complex organisations, hope to accomplish two rather attractive states. On the one hand, they hope that simple rules will replace complicated procedures, plans and other forms of bureaucracy, so freeing people to act creatively. On the other hand, they implicitly hope that this replacement of a bureaucracy by autonomous people freely following a few simple rules will not erode the control of the leaders. What these writers tend not to notice is the ideological basis of their prescription. This is an ideology of harmony in which people voluntarily submit themselves, often somewhat mystically, to a greater living whole in which they display caring behaviour and get in touch with their true selves, their souls. Griffin (2002) points to how this distracts our attention from the essentially conflictual nature of human interaction and so covers over inevitable power relations. Griffin draws on Mead's (1923) distinction between cult and functional values (*see* Chapter 15). Cult values are idealisations in which real-life obstacles to what we want to achieve are ignored. Cult values provide a feeling of enlarged personality. Functionalised values are interpretations of cult values in ordinary, real-life situations. On the rare occasions in which humans do directly follow the simple rules (cult values) without functionalising them, they form a cult. However, organisations are rarely cults. Mostly, they are collectives of people who are interpreting or functionalising the cult values in their interactions with each other.

Those prescribing 'simple rules' in this way usually draw on the Boids simulation (*see* Chapter 10) to justify their view that simple rules can generate complex behaviour. This demonstrates a complete misunderstanding of the Boids simulation. In that simulation, all the Boids are the same – they are homogeneous. They each precisely follow the same three simple rules and only those three rules. They do not interpret or functionalise them. They are the equivalent of cult values directly applied to conduct and they can only produce one pattern of complex behaviour: namely, flocking. The Boids are in no sense free, just as the members of a cult are not free. If they were free, then each Boid would be interpreting or functionalising the three rules in their own unique way and they would then not flock. They would produce some other pattern and we cannot know what that pattern is until we see it.

If the leaders of an organisation do prescribe a few simple rules (cult values) for the members to follow, then it is highly likely that the members will interpret or functionalise the values in many different ways. The overall pattern of behaviour they would produce would be unpredictable. The simple rules prescription can, therefore, not be a means for retaining control and as the leader tries to influence the interpretations, more and more rules must be added. If, on the other hand, people did slavishly follow the simple rules then they would constitute a cult, which is incapable of creativity.

I am here emphasising the need for a careful study of what the complexity simulations are actually doing before jumping to simplistic prescriptive conclusions.

11.4 How systemic applications of complexity sciences deal with the four key questions

The above sections have briefly reviewed some of the literature taking a complex systems view of organisations. Some employ the simulation methods of complexity scientists to model organisational processes at the macro level of the industry or the organisation as a whole. Others use the theory of complex systems as a metaphor that gives insight into the management of organisations. The analysis here is usually at the macro level, but sometimes at a more micro level. In the latter case, the emphasis tends to be on prescription rather than analysis.

I would like now to do what I did in relation to the main theories of organisation reviewed in Part 1 of this book and examine how the theories surveyed in this chapter deal with the four questions posed at the end of Chapter 2.

The nature of interaction

As with strategic choice, organisational learning, knowledge management and psychoanalytic perspectives, the writers in this section understand interaction in organisations in systemic terms, this time in terms of chaotic or complex systems. Analysis of these systems may be at a macro level in which diversity in agents and their interactions is not postulated. In that case, the system may follow equilibrium attractors or some strange attractor, but it does not have the internal capacity to move from one attractor to another. In this regard, there is relatively little difference from systems dynamics. What is different is the identification of strange attractors and the use of the concept of self-organisation to explain how movement around the strange attractor emerges. Alternatively, the system may be modelled on a macro level but also take account of some micro diversity. In this case, the system does display the internal capacity to move spontaneously from one attractor to another or to evolve new ones. Self-organisation is then understood as the process that produces emergent novelty. This is a major difference from all of the other systems models reviewed in this book because here the system takes on a life of its own.

It seems to me that the literature reviewed in this chapter mainly uses the first of the above complexity models: namely, the one that does not place microdiversity at the centre. This is evidenced by the focus on identifying a few simple rules and on someone operating on the conditions, or model parameters, to move the system to the edge of chaos. Apart from Allen and Marion, it is rare for those utilising complexity theory to talk about the importance of diversity, which in human terms amounts to deviance and eccentricity, as central to that kind of self-organisation that might produce emergent novelty. As a result, the causality of the system is always formative. Those who do focus attention on diversity point to transformative causality, but do not develop the implications of this move.

Complex systems at the edge of chaos display the dynamics of order and disorder, stability and instability, regularity and irregularity, all at the same time. When this is interpreted in organisational terms, by the authors reviewed in this chapter, it is often translated as 'crisis'. I suppose that from an orthodox perspective it might be crisis. However, the dynamics of the edge of chaos are not at all the dynamics of crisis, but rather, of paradox and ambiguity. For me, this connotes a mature ability to hold a difficult position, not a state of crisis. Those who equate the edge of chaos with crisis then prescribe the injection of crisis into an organisation. Surely, this is a misinterpretation of what complexity might mean in human terms.

The nature of human beings

The applications of complexity theory to organisations reviewed in this chapter all make implicit assumptions about human psychology. These are drawn from cognitivist and humanistic psychology. This is evident in the emphasis placed on the individual. This means that the notion of a complex system is being interpreted in organisational terms from the same psychological perspective as those theories based on cybernetics and systems dynamics. Given the tendency also to interpret complex systems from the orthodox perspective, it would be surprising to find enormous differences between the theories surveyed in this chapter and those of strategic choice, organisational learning and knowledge management. Again, the exception is provided by the work of Marion and Allen who, although implicitly retaining individual-centred psychological theories, emphasise unpredictability and diversity as generalised insights.

Methodology and paradox

The methodological position of the theorists reviewed above is no different from that of those proposing strategic choice, learning organisation and knowledge management theories. They all take the position of the objective observer, understood in terms of rationalist causality, who stands outside the system and models it in the interest of controlling or, at least, influencing it. The prescriptions derived from these theories all implicitly place the manager in the same position. It is the manager who must produce and impose the few simple rules that will produce the desired attractor. It is the manager who must alter the parameters, or create the conditions, that create the edge of chaos dynamics. This is then simplistically equated with success.

Although paradox seems to me to be at the heart of what the dynamics at the edge of chaos means, it does not feature at the centre of the theories described in this chapter. The paradox of observing participant is eliminated in the 'both . . . and' thinking of dual causality (Griffin, 2002).

Focusing attention

The approaches using chaos and complexity theory reviewed in this chapter focus attention on much the same factors as the systemic theories reviewed in Part 1 of this book, apart from Allen and Marion. There is the same emphasis on the agency of the autonomous individual. There is the same concern with control. There is the same downplaying of the importance of unpredictability and diversity. There is the same belief in the possibility of an organisation moving according to some organisation-wide intention.

It seems to me that what is happening is this. Complexity theories, particularly those modelling systems with a life of their own, have potentially radical implications for thinking about organisations. The most radical potential implication, it seems to me, is to question systems thinking itself. Continuing to think of human interaction as 'system' makes it impossible to move away from all the other systemic theories and the problems with them that Kant identified so long ago. Added to this, the theories of complex systems are combined with a cognitivist theory of human behaviour. Cognitivism has close links with cybernetics and systems dynamics and, as soon as the cognitivist perspective is brought to bear, cybernetics and systems dynamics assumptions come with it. The result, I think, is theoretical developments that start off with radical promise but then rapidly slip back into the same systemic theories as those reviewed in Part 1. It seems to be very hard to hold on to the radical perspectives of complexity theory while retaining the perspective of systems, the assumptions of cognitivism and the methodology of the objective, external observer.

11.5 Summary

This chapter has reviewed the way in which a number of writers are interpreting chaos and complexity in organisational terms. Most claim that complexity science leads us away for the determinism and reductionism of the old science and focuses our attention on interaction and holism. In fact, this kind of move has long since been made by both first- and second-order systems thinking. It is this kind of thinking that is far more evident in the dominant discourse. So, if there were to be any serious challenge coming from the complexity sciences, it would need to be a challenge to first- and second-order systems thinking. However, the common approach of those taking up complexity in relation to organisations is to retain a systems view of interaction and a cognitivist approach to human psychology and to interpret chaos and complexity from that perspective. This amounts to retaining the assumption of the autonomous, even heroic, individual and the prescription of the manager as the objective observer of the organisation as a system. I have argued that the result is the re-presentation of strategic choice, learning organisation and knowledge management theory in a different vocabulary. The emphasis on control and organisation-wide intention remains intact. For me, this means that the opportunity to explore what it means to operate as a participant in a setting in which the future is unknowable is lost. No further understanding of the process of how strategy might emerge from local interaction is obtained. The interpretation of chaos and complexity thus remains within management and organisational theory orthodoxy. The essentially dual causality, formative and rationalist, remains.

Part 3 of this book reviews a very different way of interpreting the insights of the complexity sciences for organisations. This moves from systems thinking to thinking in terms of responsive processes.

Further reading

For further reading I suggest Axelrod and Cohen (1999), Goldstein (1994), Wheatley (1999) and Zimmerman (1992). In addition to those reviewed in this chapter, other recent publications you might want to refer to are: Wood (2000); Ralls and Webb (1999); Lissack and Roos (1999); Rycroft and Kash (1999); Baets (1999); Petzinger (1999); Stickland (1998) and Kelly and Allison (1999). An in-depth critique of the use of complexity theories can be found in Griffin (2002). There is also a journal called *Emergence: Complexity and Organization*.

Questions to aid further reflection

1. How are organisational complexity writers using the notions of self-organisation and emergence?

2. How does the property of unpredictability feature in the work of organisational complexity writers?

3. How is the notion of the 'edge of chaos' taken up by organisational complexity writers?

4. What are the consequences of emphasising the 'simple rules' idea?

5. What is the implicit ideology in the work of many of the organisational complexity writers?

6. How does the notion of diversity feature in the work of organisational complexity writers?

7. What does a complexity view of leadership add to our understanding.

Part 3

Complex responsive processes as a way of thinking about strategy and organisational dynamics

When organisational practitioners and researchers talk and write about an 'organisation', no matter what perspective they take, they are all basically talking about groupings of people engaged in some kind of joint activity that has some purpose – which could be to search for some purpose. Fundamental questions immediately arise which have to do with *what* an organisation is and *how* it is becoming *what* it is *becoming*. As soon as we try to enquire into these questions of what and how, the controversy begins. To introduce Part 3 of this book, I first give a brief summary of the position taken in the dominant discourse in relation to this controversy in order to clarify how the chapters in Part 3 will provide a different perspective.

Part 1 of this book explored how those engaged in the dominant discourse, including most of those critical of it, explicitly or implicitly assume that the people comprising an organisation are independent, autonomous individuals, or at least come close to this position when they are acting rationally. In other words, human action is understood in terms of the individual-centred psychologies of cognitivism, constructivism, humanistic psychology and psychoanalysis in which individuals are understood to have minds inside them which either represent or select the world outside them. It is, therefore, assumed that an organisation exists, or at least is thought of 'as if' it exists, outside of the individuals comprising it. In their joint activity individuals create, choose, design, shape or give direction to an organisation which is understood to be a system of one kind of another. An organisation is thought of as a system, at a higher level than the individuals, having properties of its own and acting back on the individuals as a cause of their actions. Once taken, this view leads to particular ways of answering the fundamental organisational questions posed above of what and how.

All strands of the dominant discourse on organisational strategy are concerned, if only implicitly, with *how* an organisation is *becoming* – this is the concern with *strategy as process*. *Process* refers to the administrative systems and decision-making procedures managers use to formulate and implement strategy *content*. It refers to the routines, habits, frames of reference, interpretive schemas, cultures, political activities, learning activities, norms and values of the organisation. It can also refer to informal conversation, storytelling and engagement in communities of practice. There is debate around which of these aspects of how an organisation is becoming are more important than others. However, whatever the debate, it seems to be taken for granted that individuals, in their joint activity, create, choose, design, shape or give direction to the processes of organising and/or the conditions which will produce the desired processes and outcomes – for example, when they are said to design administrative systems and decision-making techniques, which are processes, to shape, find, validate, predict and implement, all of which are themselves processes, or when they condition emergence and create the conditions which will unleash self-organisation. When they cannot control the outcomes of organisational strategies, it is assumed in the dominant discourse that managers and leaders can at least control the dynamics of organisations. All the perspectives in Part 1 were also concerned with *what* is becoming, usually referred to as *strategy content*. Strategy content is taken to mean a description of an organisation's position in a market and of the resources, competences, skills, information and knowledge that the organisation uses to take that position. There is debate about which aspects of content are more or less important than others and whether the content should be expressed in formal plans or in vaguer visions, missions and directions. All of this, both content and process, is what strategy means in the dominant discourse.

Underlying this understanding of strategy is the ideology of control. From the strategic-choice perspective, leaders and dominant coalitions choose the process and the content of strategy for an organisation in order to ensure acceptable performance. From the learning perspectives, this ability to simply choose in rational ways is questioned and, instead, leaders and managers are understood to shape and influence the learning process that produces strategy content. The argument between the two approaches is not about *whether* leaders and managers can be 'in control' of an organisation but *how* they are able to exert such control. This possibility depends crucially on the nature of organisational dynamics. It is possible for someone to be 'in control' only if the dynamics, the patterns of movement over time, are reasonably stable and thus predictable. This possibility has been vigorously contested, as described in some of the chapters in Part 1. The critics argue that strategy content and process are not simply deliberately chosen, shaped or influenced by leaders and managers, because they emerge to a significant extent. This argument holds that, in a sense, strategy is being chosen for leaders and managers by chance changes in the environment and their role is to fit into these changes. For me, this critique remains firmly in the dominant discourse, because it takes the same view on the importance of predictability. If it is possible to predict then we can choose and if we cannot predict then we have no choice but to adapt to chance. Here deliberate choice and emergence are seen as polar opposites. We either choose in orderly ways because we can predict the consequences of our actions or when we cannot predict the consequences of our actions we are reduced to inertia or some form of organisational anarchy, muddling through and garbage-can decision-making. Neither side in this debate questions whether predictability is indeed a prerequisite for order.

The dominant discourse is conducted primarily at the macro level of the whole organisation or the whole industry. Strategy process is concerned with how process and content are to be chosen, shaped or influenced for the organisation as a whole. The link to the micro level of the ordinary everyday activities of organisational members is understood to be provided by the inspirational, motivational, target-setting and performance-monitoring activities designed or influenced by leaders so that their strategies will be implemented by the organisational membership. There are those who are critical of top-down, command-and-control approaches to strategic management and they call for those at the top to arrange for, or at least allow, involvement, democracy, empowerment and bottom-up forms of strategic management, latterly erroneously described as 'self-organisation'. Empowerment is understood as the top giving away some of their power. However, in order to prevent the immediately feared anarchy this could lead to, bottom-up proposals are quickly accompanied by the requirement that those at the top should set some direction, guidelines or logic within which the empowered must act. So, here the link between the macro and the micro is partially reversed, with the micro activities now shaping and influencing the macro level but only within guidelines set at the macro level. However, in my view, this critique does not depart from the dominant discourse, because the relationship between micro and macro is still understood in terms of different levels, and it is only a very few who advocate bottom-up management without any top-down management – most call for some balance between the two. Chapter 8 in Part 1 did draw attention to the recent call made by activity-based strategy theorists for attention to be focused on the micro level of ordinary, everyday management activity. These writers identify the need to explain the link between this micro activity and the macro level but, as far as I can see, have not yet provided a satisfactory explanation of this link. Just as the dominant discourse takes for granted polarised distinctions between intention and emergence, between unpredictability and order, so it takes for granted the opposition between micro and micro levels. All of these distinctions are ultimately reflections of the separation of the individual and the organisation as system.

The dominant discourse reflects a way of thinking that has its origins in the natural sciences, particularly in the importation of systems thinking after the 1950s. Part 2 of this book explored more recent developments in understanding dynamics of systems in the form of the complexity sciences. A radical interpretation of these sciences leads to the following conclusions. Complex systems display the capacity to change and produce new forms only when they operate in a paradoxical dynamic of stability and instability at the same time. The properties of this dynamic are such that small differences can escalate into major, completely unpredictable changes, so creating new forms and destroying others at the same time. This creative destruction emerges in processes of self-organisation. Self-organisation means local interaction between the agents comprising the complex system, and what emerges is the form of the system where emergence means that the form arises in the complete absence of any plan, blueprint or programme for it. The emergent form is due entirely to the self-organising activity of the agents. New forms can emerge only if the agents differ from each other enough – diversity is essential for the evolution of the new. In Chapter 10 I suggested that it is possible to understand these properties in terms of local interaction between agents producing emergent patterns across a whole population.

These findings are of major importance, in my view, because they challenge the dominant discourse's most fundamental assumptions. From a complexity perspective, stability, harmony and consensus cannot be equated with success and unpredictability is fundamentally unavoidable, making it impossible to talk about being 'in control'. The 'whole' is not designed or chosen in advance because it emerges in local interaction. Such emergence is in no way a matter of chance, because what emerges does so precisely because of what all the agents are doing or not doing. There is nothing mysterious about emergence. Orderly global forms, which I will usually call population-wide patterns, do not come about by chance or mystery but as basic properties of local interaction. The cause of the global order is the connections between the agents, where connections mean that agents impose conflicting constraints on each other. It is constraint and conflict in local interaction that impart order to the 'whole' so constituting a mode of control. The cause of new global form, new population-wide patterns, is the diversity of the locally interacting agents. This explanation of emergence challenges the equating of emergence with chance and some form of anarchy or muddling through to be found in the dominant discourse. It supports the call for an activity-based perspective on strategic management which focuses attention on the micro, local interactions of people in an organisation. Furthermore, it offers a different understanding of the link between micro and macro – the macro emerges in the micro. In fact, the distinction between the macro and the micro as different ontological levels dissolves and with it further taken-for-granted distinctions between intention and emergence, unpredictability and order, individual and organisation also dissolve.

Part 2 then reviewed how a number of writers are interpreting the finding of the complexity sciences in terms of human organisations. Some writers apply some aspects of the complexity sciences to the macro level of the whole organisation or industry. I argued that mostly they do so in a way that does not take seriously enough the radical challenge presented by insights from the complexity sciences and so slip back into the dominant discourse. Chapter 11 referred to two exceptions to this conclusion in the work of Allen and of Marion. Both of these writers emphasise fundamental unpredictability and how essential micro diversity is for the emergence of new forms. In doing this, they present major challenges to the dominant discourse on organisations and strategic management and, particularly in the case of Allen's work, point to the limitations of systems models themselves. However, in focusing on the macro level, their work does not reach the ordinary, everyday human diversity of organisational life. Many writers do focus on the micro level but, as I argued in Chapter 11, they tend to apply the less radical interpretations of the complexity sciences and so mainly re-present the dominant discourse in a different language.

The purpose of Part 3 of this book is to explore how we might interpret the radical insights of the complexity sciences in terms of human action. Human agents differ from those studied in the natural complexity sciences in fundamentally important ways. Human agents are unique and, therefore, diverse persons who are conscious, self-conscious, emotional, rational, irrational, often spontaneous beings capable of some choice. Furthermore, in their local interaction, human agents are capable of perceiving and articulating something about the population-wide patterns they are implicated in and even of desiring different population-wide patterns. This is something that the agents of complexity models cannot do. Any interpretation of complexity insights must be firmly based on these attributes of human agents and that is what the chapters in this part will seek to do. This requires returning to the most basic assumptions we make when we talk about organisations.

I started this introduction to Part 3 by stating that an organisation is groupings of people engaged in joint activity having some purpose. The dominant discourse assumes that those people are independent, autonomous individuals. The argument of this part departs immediately from this position by claiming that such independence and autonomy is a fiction because human persons are always fundamentally and inescapably interdependent. This shift in assumption from autonomy to interdependence leads to a move away from the individual-centred theories of cognitivism, constructivism, humanistic psychology and psychoanalysis to a view of the individual self as thoroughly social through and through. Individual selves are formed by social interaction as they form such social interaction at the same time. There is no possibility of human society without human minds and there is no possibility of human minds without human societies. The distinction between psychology and sociology dissolves. Mind is no longer thought of as existing inside a person and nor is society thought of as existing outside a person as a system. Instead, both mind and society are thought of as the actions of human bodies and this way of thinking has no need for concepts such as 'system'. Instead, the focus of attention is directly upon the responsive manner in which human persons interact with each other, hence the label 'complex responsive processes of relating' which will be applied to the perspective taken in this part. A caution is necessary at this point. In talking about human relationships I am not just talking about something 'good' simply because human relationships are frequently very 'bad'. The term 'complex responsive processes of relating' refers to both the good and the bad and is concerned with how we might understand them.

Once taken, this view leads to very different ways of dealing with the fundamental question posed at the start of this introduction which has to do with *how* an organisation is becoming *what* it is *becoming*. In the dominant discourse, process (the how becoming) refers to the administrative systems and decision-making procedures managers use to formulate and implement strategy content. From the complex responsive processes perspective, process refers to the fundamental processes of human interaction – namely, communicative interaction between interdependent persons taking the form of the conversation of gestures. The very fact of interdependence means that this ongoing conversation is at the same time processes of power relating which are sustained by ideologies. Furthermore, in their ongoing conversational power relating, persons are always forming intentions and making choices evoked and provoked by each other, and these intentions and choices always have an ideological basis. Processes then refer to conversation, power, choice and ideology, which may be patterned as routines, procedures and so on. However, what it is important to focus attention on is not simply the routine or the procedure, but the complex responsive interactions between persons which may have a routine pattern. Strategic processes are then understood as basically conversational forms of power relating based on ideology and reflected in intentions and choices.

Since the persons comprising an organisation are interdependent, it follows that none of them can simply choose what is to happen to all of them. What happens to all of them will emerge in the interplay of their intentions, and no one can be in control of this interplay. The shift from the assumption of autonomous to interdependent persons immediately challenges the whole basis of strategic choice theory. Strategy as a population-wide pattern of action cannot be chosen by anyone, but rather emerges in the interplay of individual intentions and choices in local interactions. Here there is no polarisation of deliberate intention and emergence, and emergence has nothing to do with chance. Instead, emerging patterns are becoming what they are becoming because of the interplay of many, many intentions in many, many local situations. This presents radical challenges to the dominant discourse in all its forms, because it questions the ability of leaders and others to change the 'whole' in any direct manner. They may be articulating desires for the population-wide pattern, the 'whole', but this will be a gesture into the ongoing conversation and what happens will depend upon the responses evoked in many, many local inter-actions. All *anyone* can ever do, no matter how powerful, is engage intentionally, and as skilfully as possible, in local interaction, dealing with the consequence in an ongoing manner as they emerge. Many practical activities such as organisational change programmes, strategic planning, the nature of leadership, the meaning of control, and so on, need to be re-thought if one takes this perspective.

In fact, the shift in the focus of attention to the basic forms of human interaction leads one to reformulate the fundamental question of how an organisation is becom-ing *what* it is becoming. The question changes to one to do with *how* a group of interdependent people are becoming *who* they are *becoming*. The strategy process (how becoming) has already been referred to above as basic human interaction, but now for strategy content we ask about *who* instead of *what* simply because we are talking about people and not abstract systems.

When we talk about organisational strategies, we are taking about what kind of joint action people are undertaking, about what purpose it is meant to achieve and what the actors desire it to be. When we talk about organisational dynamics, we are talking about patterns of movement in this activity and its purposes over time and how the actors involved are engaged in, and thinking about, this movement. In other words, we are talking fundamentally about who people think they are and what they think they are doing together; who they want to be, what they want to do together and what they desire to achieve. When it is put this way, we can immediately see that organisations and their strategies are fundamentally about the identities of people. Identity is the answer we give to the question, 'who are you and what are you doing?' and when asked this question we usually reply with some description of the groups or organisations we belong to and what kind of work we do in them. At strategy 'away-days', groups of managers talk about what kind of business they are in and how they might want to change it; what kind of image their organisation has, how they might wish it to change and sometimes how they are thinking about all of this. In doing this, they are talking about identity: their own identities. From a complex responsive processes perspective, then, strategy content is dynamic patterns of emerging continuity and potential transformation of col-lective identities which are inseparable from individual identities. Put like this, the distinction between content and process dissolves.

Chapter 12 will explore what I mean by responsive processes and how this notion differs from systemic process reviewed in Chapter 8. Systemic process is interaction between parts that produces a system or whole outside of the parts. For example, the human individual may be thought of as a cognitive system consisting of inter-acting mental models and the group is then a supra-system of interacting indi-viduals. In the notion of responsive processes, there is no 'inside' or 'outside', no 'whole' or 'boundary'.

Chapters 13 to 17 will explore the communicative, power-relating, ideological and choice aspects of complex responsive processes of relating between persons. Chapter 18 will explore how thinking in responsive process terms focuses attention in relation to strategy and organisational dynamics. Moving from systems thinking to responsive processes thinking about strategy and organisational dynamics has a number of important consequences. Strategy ceases to be understood as the realisa-tion of someone's intended or desired future state for the whole organisation. It ceases to be understood as the intentional design and leveraging of whole organisational learning and knowledge-creating systems. Instead, strategy is understood as evolving patterns of simultaneously collective and individual identities. Evolving identities are understood to emerge in the local communicative interacting, power-relating and ideology-based choices of the people who constitute an organisation.

The focus of attention is then not on some abstract systemic whole, but on what people are actually doing in their relationships with each other in the living present. It is in these relationships that strategy as evolving identity continually emerges. It is in interaction, particularly ordinary, everyday conversation, that members of organisations perpetually construct their future as continuity and potential transformation at the same time.

Chapter 12

Responsive processes thinking
The interplay of intentions

This chapter invites you to draw on your own experience to reflect on and consider the implications of:

- An alternative to systemic ways of thinking about process in human action. I call this alternative view 'responsive processes' in order to distinguish it from the notion of systemic process discussed in Chapter 8.

- The fundamental assumptions upon which this alternative notion of process is

based and its location in the historical tradition of Western thought.

- The concepts of self-organisation and emergence in human action.

- The key differences between the notions of systemic process and responsive processes of human action.

This chapter provides foundational concepts required to understand the theory of complex responsive processes of human relating and the explanation it provides of strategising and organising, which will be developed in later chapters. I believe it is very important to understand the nature of responsive processes and how this notion differs from systemic process, because it leads to a very different way of thinking about what an organisation is. As soon as one takes one view rather than the other, one inevitably goes down a particular path of thought and action. From a systemic process perspective it is easy to think of an organisation as a thing separate from people, a thing that managers can give direction to, and move about in time and conceptual space. As soon as one takes a responsive processes view one goes into a way of thinking about organisations as nothing more or less than patterns of inter-action between human persons. These two different starting points lead to very different ways of thinking about what it means to manage, strategise and lead, which will be explored in some detail in Chapters 13 to 17. In broad terms, the difference is as follows. If you think from a systemic process perspective about what you are doing as leader or manager then you will believe that you can and should take an objective viewpoint from outside your organisation as a whole or the part of it that you are responsible for. From this viewpoint you will be concerned with designing, or at the very least, shaping, influencing or conditioning organisational process. You will understand process in terms of administrative systems and decision-making procedures. You will be concerned with changing the whole system and the whole process. However, if you take the alternative perspective on process, you will understand what you are doing as leader or manager as participating in relationships with other people. You will understand that there is no objective, external position in relationships, only the subjective–objective, involved–detached, participation in relating to others. You will understand your work as influencing, perhaps even manipulating, other people, not some abstract system or process, in order to get things done. You will understand what you are doing as processes of communication with others, as patterns of power relations between you, as choices based on ideological criteria: in short, as the politics of ordinary daily life. From the systemic perspective one's thinking is abstracted from the direct experience of relating to others, while in the responsive processes perspective that relating, both good and bad, is at the centre of one's attention. Moving from the systemic to the responsive perspective challenges the belief that 'you' can be 'in control' and directly change the whole. Instead, it invites you to reflect on what you are actually doing in the ordinary, everyday political activities of leading, managing and organising.

12.1 Introduction

Social, responsive processes thinking developed in reaction to Kantian philosophy, so by way of introduction I will first briefly summarise some points made in Chapter 3 about Kant's thought. Kant thought in terms of dualisms:

- On the one hand, there is reality, the noumenal, which is unknowable, and on the other hand, there is the appearance of reality, the phenomenal, which is knowable.

- On the one hand, there are subjects – that is, autonomous individual humans, who can freely choose goals and actions through their reasoning capacity and are therefore subject to rationalist causality. On the other hand, there are objects, the natural phenomena, which human subjects can know because they have innate mental categories by means of which they can classify and causally connect phenomena.

Kant argued that humans come to know phenomena by means of the scientific method, which means that they take the position of the objective observer external to the phenomena to be known, formulate hypotheses about them and then test the hypotheses in experimental action. These hypotheses can take the form of mechanistic 'if–then' rules – that is, efficient cause, in the case of inanimate matter – or they can take the form of regulative ideas in relation to organisms, which means that the objective observer ascribes an 'as if' purpose to organisms, understood as systems. Kant defined a system as a self-organising whole consisting of parts which interact with each other to form both themselves and the whole. Furthermore, the whole develops over time in a purposive manner as it moves from its embryonic to its mature form in developmental stages – the causality is formative. The system is understood as unfolding the purpose or mature form ascribed to, or enfolded in, the idea of the system.

What Kant was doing here was *presenting a particular notion of process, systemic process, involving a particular notion of time*. Process here is the interaction of parts to form a whole and time takes a linear, life cycle form. Chapter 8 explored just how this systemic notion of process pervades the literature on the process- and activity-based views of strategy. According to Kant, then, organisms in nature are understood to move according to the formative, systemic process of the system – that is, formative cause – and the human subject can take a rational, external position. The result is another dualism:

- Human action is understood to be subject to *rationalist* causality and nature is understood to be subject to either *efficient* or *formative* causality.

The essence of Kantian thinking, therefore, is the dualism. This way of thinking has a 'both . . . and' structure in which one side of the dualism applies at one time or place and the other side of the dualism applies at another time or place. First, one side is the figure and the other the background and then this is reversed. The effect of this dualistic, figure–ground way of thinking is to eliminate paradox. Locating the opposites of the dualism in a sequence avoids the need to hold the two together *at the same time*, which is the essence of paradoxical thinking (Griffin, 2002).

Although Kant had cautioned against thinking about human action as a system, because this was incompatible with the autonomy of the individual, all of the systems thinkers of the twentieth century have ignored this caution and applied systems thinking not only to nature but to human action and interaction as well. The *how* of strategy, the process, is then thought to be designing, shaping and influencing the system as a whole and its process. The content of strategy is thought of as the pattern of intended movement of the system and intended changes in the process over time by a regulator or controller standing outside them. Strategy, here, is all about moving systems and designing process.

This chapter explores an alternative to systems thinking about organisations. The philosopher Hegel argued against Kant's dualisms and their elimination of paradox. Instead, for him, thought was essentially paradoxical. Unlike Kant, who located human knowing in the innate capacities of the individual mind, Hegel presented a view of human knowing that is essentially social and, as later chapters will explain, this immediately signals a move away from individual-based views of human psychology. In doing this, Hegel was in effect developing a notion of processes that differed fundamentally from Kant's notion of systemic process. Hegel's notion of processes is a social one, essentially involving the interaction of human persons in what I would call *responsive* processes of struggling for mutual recognition as participants. Here there is no external viewpoint and everything any of us does is as a participant in some interaction with others. This alternative view of processes indicates a different notion of time from the linear one of Kant's systemic process, a matter I will take up later in this chapter. From a responsive processes perspective, the *how* of strategy is thought of as social processes of interaction between conscious and self-conscious persons in which their very identities emerge. The content of strategy is thought of as patterns of interaction: that is, as iterated identity. Strategy, here, is all about sustaining and changing identity: that is, who we are and what we are doing together.

The next section of this chapter briefly reviews Hegel's thinking and how the sociologists Mead and Elias thought in essentially the same terms. The section after that suggests that the insights of the natural complexity sciences can be interpreted in human terms using the kind of social, responsive processes thinking that derives from Hegel and Elias, rather than the dominant systemic process theory implicit in the writings of most others who appeal to the complexity sciences (*see* Chapter 11).

This chapter seeks to clarify the sense in which systemic and responsive processes thinking provide two incompatibly different ways of understanding human organisations. Later chapters in this part will point to some of the consequences of thinking in responsive processes terms about strategy and organisational dynamics.

12.2 Responsive processes thinking

In the late eighteenth and early nineteenth centuries, the philosophers known as Romantic idealists (Fichte, Schelling and Hegel) moved from Kant's split between the knowing subject and the object to be known and argued that the object of knowledge was constituted by the *process of knowing* performed by the subject or self. Subjects, then, were together mentally creating their knowledge of the world of objects and of themselves at the same time. The Romantic idealists were particularly concerned with self-consciousness where the subject is an object to itself. It is the self that is real and all experience is carried back to this immediate experience of the self so that the reflexive position becomes central. This immediately challenges the external objective position and claims instead that knowledge is socially constructed in the interaction of interdependent, conscious and self-conscious persons. Kant held that the mind encountered contradictions when it attempted to go beyond the phenomenal world to the noumenal and these contradictions were warnings of a mind going beyond its limits. For the Romantic idealists, however, contradictions were inherent in the movement of thought. The Romantic idealists moved away from a Kantian innate logic, with already given forms of thought outside of experience (transcendental), to a dialectical logic in which human consciousness and self-consciousness as experience are central to knowing. Furthermore, individual selves and social relations were understood to be intimately interconnected and *experience was understood as historical, social processes of consciousness and self-consciousness*. This represented a powerful break with the notion of the autonomous individual and innate, transcendental, pre-given knowing. From the Kantian perspective it is possible to take a position external to social interaction and to observe it objectively. From the perspective of the Romantic idealists this is not possible, because all self-conscious persons are always participating in social activity even when they think they are observing it from an external position.

Hegel

In Hegel's philosophy, the development of thought takes place through *conflict* between persons and the world of *our experience is the world we are creating in our thought*. Hegel held that one cannot begin, as Kant had done, with an isolated individual subject experiencing the world and then ask how a world of objective experience gets built up out of the inner world of purely subjective, individual representations as in systems and mental models. Rather, one must begin with an already shared world of subjects making judgements in the light of possible judgements by other subjects: in other words, interacting responsively. Hegel also emphasised the notion of *mutual recognition* to argue that there was an intersubjective unity of mutually recognising agents: in other words, agents acting responsively. He argued against any separate realm outside experience. In this, he moved decisively away from the Kantian notion of a system, which others had directly applied to human interaction, lying outside direct experience of such interaction and causing it.

For Hegel, the notions of person and subject are historically specific and are given content only by the social institutions in which each individual achieves social identity through interdependence and mutual recognition. Mind or consciousness is manifested in social institutions – that is, ways of life, which give identities, self-concepts, to individuals. Each person is self-consciously, purposively directing herself or himself, but each is also dependent on others at the same time. How we come to understand our own desires, interpret their intensity and priority, how we categorise objects to satisfy our desires, is not fixed or determined by our natures or the real world but depends on the concepts we employ and these are socially evolved. Self-determination by a free subject can only occur through other persons who are also self-determining subjects and are doing the same. Another self-conscious subject offers resistance to the realisation of my desires by testing or challenging me and my self-world conception. It is inevitable that two self-determining, self-conscious subjects will conflict and struggle.

Hegel argued that individuals are fundamentally social practitioners and what they do, think or say takes form in the context of *social practices*, while these practices provide the required resources, objects of desire, skills and procedures. In contrast to Kantian thinking, where there is a duality of the individual and the social, Hegel presents a perspective in which they cannot be separated. Indeed, individual consciousness and self-consciousness arise in the social relations, which they are simultaneously constructing. This is clearly a paradoxical perspective in which individual minds are simultaneously forming and being formed by social relations. This presents a different notion of causality, which we may call *transformative* causality (Stacey *et al.*, 2000).

The move from systemic to responsive processes thinking is, therefore, fundamentally a move from a dualistic theory of rationalist–formative causality to one of transformative causality. These different notions of causality are summarised in Table 12.1.

The Kantian and Hegelian ways of thinking have continued to influence sociologists, psychologists and organisational theorists up to the present time. The sociologist Mead continued in the Hegelian tradition and worked out in detail how one might think of mind, self and the social in a responsive processes way, and this will be explored in Chapter 13. First, however, consider how another sociologist, Elias, who was also influenced by Hegel's thought, reflects the notion of social, responsive processes in his sociology.

Elias

Following the tradition of Hegel, Elias did not think about the relationship between the individual and society in terms of any spatial distinction between inside and outside, as in systems thinking. He argued that, while the notion of a receptacle

Table 12.1 Comparison of different ways of thinking about causality

	Nature of movement	Cause of movement
Efficient cause	Corrective repetition of past in order to realise an optimal future state	Universal, timeless laws of an 'if–then' kind
Rationalist cause	Towards rationally chosen goals for the future in order to realise a designed, desired state	Human reason
Formative cause	Unfolding of enfolded mature form in order to realise that form in the future	Self-organising systemic process of unfolding in developmental stages
Transformative cause	Iterated interaction perpetually constructing the future in the present in order to express continuity and potential transformation in identity at the same time	Responsive processes of local interaction between entities in the present

containing something inside it might be applicable to the physical aspects of a human being, it could not be applied to the personality or the mind (Elias, 1991, p. 480). In rejecting the notion of the individual mind as an 'internal world', he also argued against thinking of the social as an organic unity or supra-individual with a 'group mind' developing through stages of youth, maturity and old age to death (pp. 5–6). Instead, he pointed to the essential interdependence of people. Elias also usually avoided any kind of systemic formulation, arguing that such formulations abstract from experience. Instead, he understood both individual and social purely in what I am calling 'responsive processes terms'. He did not think of the individual and society as first existing and then subsequently affecting each other (p. 456). He suggested that we can see the connection between individual and social more precisely if we refuse to abstract from the processes of their development, of their becoming. Elias also argued against concepts of society as some kind of 'whole', arguing that the social life of human beings was full of contradictions, tensions and explosions rather than being more or less harmonious as the concept of a 'whole' implies. Furthermore, while the concept of a 'whole' implies something complete in itself, societies are always more or less incomplete, remaining open in time as a continuous flow (p. 12). What Elias is doing here is moving completely away from any notion of human interaction as a system and any notion of some 'whole' existing outside of that interaction and causing it. Instead, he is focusing entirely on the processes of interaction between human bodies. Elias argued that the concept of the whole applied to human action simply created a mystery in order to solve a mystery.

In order to understand the nature of human interaction, Elias made a detailed study of changes in the way Western people have experienced themselves over hundreds of years and pointed to how social order *emerges* in interactions between people.

The emergence of social order

Elias argued that what we now call 'Western civilisation' is not the result of any kind of calculated long-term planning. Individual people did not form an intention to change civilisation and then gradually realise this intention through rational, purposive measures. It is not conceivable that the evolution of society could have been planned, because that would suppose that modern rational, calculating individuals with a degree of self-mastery already existed centuries ago, whereas Elias's research shows that such individuals did not exist then but were, rather, themselves the products of social evolution. Societal changes produced rational, planning kinds of individuals, not the other way around. In medieval times people experienced their self-consciousness in a completely different way, in a completely different kind of society, compared with the way we experience our self-consciousness in modern society. Elias concluded that the development of a society was not caused by 'mysterious' social forces but was the consequence of the interweaving, the *interplay* of the intentions and actions of many, many people. He talked about the moves of many interdependent players intertwining in ways that none of them could control no matter how powerful they were. However, despite the development of a society being unplanned and outside the immediate control of its members, the interplay of individual plans and intentions nevertheless produced an orderly pattern of development, tending in a particular direction (Elias, 1991, pp. 146–7).

So, Elias argued that change in society occurred in an unplanned manner but nevertheless displayed a specific type of order. His research demonstrated how the constraints imposed by others were converted into self-restraints and how many human bodily activities were progressively pushed behind the scenes of communal social life and invested with feelings of shame. Elias explained how the growing interdependence of people caused by the increasing division of labour and specialisation of tasks could only be sustained by the increasing self-control of those interdependent people. In other words, increasing interdependence, taken together with the increasing state monopolisation of violence, came to be reflected in the very personality structures of people. The 'civilising' process is one of increasing self-control, bringing with it the benefits of social order but also the disadvantages of neurotic behaviour associated with such self-control and increasing anxiety of contravening social norms. Furthermore, this civilising trend is easily reversed by any threat to, or breakdown in, social order. Although this transformation of societies and personality structures could not have been planned and intended, it was not simply a sequence of unstructured changes (Elias, 2000, p. 365). Elias looked for an explanation of how it was possible that orderly population-wide formations, which no human being had intended, arose in the human world:

> It is simple enough: plans and actions, the emotional and rational impulses of individual people, constantly interweave in a friendly or hostile way. This basic tissue resulting from many single plans and actions of men can give rise to changes and patterns that no individual person has planned or created. From this interdependence of people arises an order sui generis, an order more compelling and stronger than the will and reason of the individual people composing it. *It is the order of interweaving human impulses and strivings, the social order, which determines the course of historical change; it underlies the civilizing process.*
> (Elias, 2000, p. 366)

Although it is highly unlikely that Elias was ever aware of the complexity sciences, what he is describing here is what complexity scientists call *self-organisation* and *emergence*. Elias is arguing that individuals and groups are interacting with each other, in their local situations, in intentional, planned ways. However, the widespread, population-wide consequences of the interplay of these intentions and plans cannot be foreseen by any of them – long-term, population-wide patterns emerge without an overall plan or blueprint. Elias explains that long-term consequences cannot be foreseen because the interplay of the actions, plans and purposes of many individuals constantly gives rise to something that has not been planned, intended or created by any of those individuals. Elias pointed to the important fact that individuals pursuing their plans are always in relationship with each other in a group or power figuration. While individuals can plan their own actions, they cannot plan the actions of others and so cannot plan the interplay of plans and actions. The fact that each person depends on others means that none can simply realise their plans. However, this does not mean that anarchy, or disorder, results. Elias talks about a trend or direction in the evolution of the consequences of the interweaving of individual plans and intentions. In other words, he is talking about self-organisation and emergence. We can understand what he is talking about by reflecting on almost any story of developing organisational life over time. One of my favourite examples is provided by events how we might understand recent developments at British Airways back in 2005 as the interplay of intentions.

The interplay of intentions in the airline industry in 2005

Gate Gourmet is a catering company in the UK owned by a corporation in the United States. Some years ago, a group of executives at British Airways (BA) chose to outsource the provision of all of its in-flight meals and chose Gate Gourmet as its sole provider because this was the least-cost solution. Here, in their local interaction, executives form BA's plan to outsource, while another group of executives at Gate Gourmet interact locally to plan their bid for the contract, and in the interplay of these plans a different population-wide pattern of supplying in-flight meals emerges. So far, it looks as if the interplay of plans produces the population-wide pattern that all had intended. However, by mid-2005 executives at Gate Gourmet were coming under pressure from another group of locally interacting executives at their parent company to stem the large losses they were making from supplying BA meals. Notice the local interaction on both sides of the Atlantic. In August 2005, in response, the directors of Gate Gourmet decided to reduce costs by making 670 employees redundant, intending to replace them with cheaper labour from Eastern Europe. Here we have another Gate Gourmet plan emerging in the interplay with the intentions of executives on the other side of the Atlantic. The 670 staff who packed meal containers for the in-flight services were predominantly Sikh women who lived in a close-knit community, organised around a Sikh temple near to Heathrow airport. When these women were abruptly dismissed, they angrily informed members of their families and the wider community. That night there was a meeting in the temple. Notice the population-wide pattern emerging in the interplay of the intentions of executives and workers. Many of the husbands of the dismissed women happened to work for BA as luggage handlers at Heathrow. At the meeting in the temple they agreed to form picket lines outside Gate Gourmet to interrupt the delivery of meals to BA flights and also to call a wildcat strike of BA luggage handlers. So here we have the workers' plans arising in their local interaction. On the next day, within hours, managers at BA found that the only way to deal with the escalating situation was to ground all of their flights around the world. Here another BA plan emerges in response to the interplay of the plans of Gate Gourmet's executives and workers. For days after this, thousands of passengers were stranded at airports around the world and even months later meal services on BA fights were still not back to normal and a large dent had been made in BA profits. Another population-wide pattern has emerged.

Here we have an example of the interplay of intentions that Elias talked about. Executives at BA intended to outsource the provision of meals. Executives at Gate Gourmet intended to reduce its labour force. The affected members and others in their community intended to take action against this. In response, executives at BA intended to ground all its flight. However, the overall, widespread pattern of the interaction between all the players was not intended by anyone but, rather, emerged in the many local interactions between all of those involved. If we think of strategy as a widespread pattern of actions over time, we can see the emergent nature of the individual strategies: that is, intentions of all involved. Instead of thinking about strategy in terms of an isolated organisation making choices, we can see from this example how the choices, intentions, decisions, strategies of all are all responses to what the others involved are doing. Together they are creating the ongoing processes of local interaction, aspects of which could be described as 'strategising', and it is in the interplay of these local actions that population-wide patterns emerge and we could call these 'strategies'.

When I use this example at workshops with managers I get a rather typical response. These managers immediately start treating the story as a case study in which they identify the mistakes made by the BA executives. They should not have relied on one supplier, for example. Participants at my workshop would, of course, not have done this and so the unfortunate outcome would not have occurred. Or people shake their heads and point to the events as a clear example of what happens when thinking breaks down. What these responses reflect, of course, is the dominant discourse with its taken-for-granted assumption that competent executives can and do devise strategies which produce the outcomes they want. It seems difficult to hold on to the notion that the interplay of intentions can lead to the emergence of what no one wants. The selection of this story of BA might have the unfortunate implication that emergence applies only to bad outcomes, breakdowns, and losses. However, consider another story, this time one of classic entrepreneurial success.

The development of Facebook

Mezrich (2009) tells the story of Mark Zuckerberg, founder of Facebook in which his shareholding is currently worth billions of dollars. I will summarise the story in a fair amount of detail as an invitation for you to notice how intentions are playing into each other to produce emergent outcomes.

Mark was an 18-year-old undergraduate student at Harvard University in 2003, majoring in computer science, when he met and formed a friendship with another undergraduate student, Eduardo Saverin, at a Jewish Fraternity group called Alpha Epsilon Pi. Mark had a reputation as a computer hacker listed by the FBI and as a person who had turned down a $1 million job at Microsoft in order to come to Harvard. It was this reputation that had attracted Eduardo to Mark. Around this time Mark broke into Harvard University's computer system and copied over the photographs of every girl on campus from the databases. He then created a website which he called *Facemash.com* and which enabled subscribers to compare the pictures of the girls and vote for the one they thought was the hottest, the votes being used to calculate who the hottest 'chick' on campus was. He emailed the website address to a few of his friends, asking what they thought of it and then went to one of his classes. On his return he found that his computer screen was frozen because it was acting as a server for *Facemash.com*, a development which both surprised and alarmed him. The friends to whom he had emailed the website address had in turn passed it to their friends and it had rapidly spread through the student body. However, the address also found its way to members of the Institute of Politics and to members of a women's-issues organisation called Fuerza Latina. From there it seems that someone had forwarded it to the Association of Black Women at Harvard and to *Crimson*, the college newspaper. In less than two hours the site had logged 22,000 votes and 400 students had gone on the site in the last 30 minutes. Mark had not meant this to go out before he found out about the legality of copying the pictures and he feared that he was in big trouble. We can see here how Mark forms a rather frivolous intention to create a particular kind of website and a perhaps humorous intention to send it to his friends. They intentionally send it to others, some of whom intentionally send it to women's organisations whose members intentionally respond in an outraged manner. What emerges is a pattern of interaction, which we can call a 'scandal', which Mark and his immediate friends certainly did not intend, particularly given the punishment that might be inflicted on Mark.

Elsewhere on campus at this time, twin brothers Tyler and Cameron Winklevoss, members of the secretive Porcellian, Harvard's oldest all-male club and sons of a very wealthy father, as well as champion rowers who would go on to compete in the 2008 Olympics, were developing a secret project with Divya Narendra – another intention. The project was to establish a website called the Harvard Connection to put Harvard's social life online, making it possible for busy men like Tyler and Cameron to meet girls without wasting time going to parties and wandering around the campus looking for girls. However, to set up such a website they needed a computer expert to write the code. Finding such a person was Divya's job. As they sat discussing the problem in the canteen, Divya drew attention to an article in the *Crimson* which reported on *Facemash.com* and the voting on girls. The *Facemash.com* website had aroused much opposition from feminists' groups on the campus and the traffic on *Facemash.com* had clogged the university's bandwidth so that professors could not get their emails. Mark had closed the site down but was having to face the consequences of stealing the pictures. Mark looked like the right person to develop the Harvard Connection website. So an unexpected intention emerges in response to the outcomes of Mark's and others' intentions.

After Mark's disciplinary hearing, the Winklevoss twins sought him out and told him what they were trying to do on Harvard Connection. Mark liked the idea of a website to meet girls and felt the programming would not present a problem. The Winklevoss twins told Mark that they thought the site would make money and they wanted Mark to be at the centre of it. For the next two months the partnership seemed to be going well but after that no real progress was forthcoming. The Winklevoss twins and Divya put pressure on Mark but still nothing happened. By January 2004 Mark met up with his friend Eduardo again and outlined how the *Facemash.com* idea could be extended to enable male and female students to find out about each other in an informal, friendly online community. He saw this as a sort of exclusive social network – you could only get on the site through recommendation of someone already a member. Real online social circles could be created by the people themselves putting up their own pictures and profiles and inviting their friends to join. He proposed to call it Facebook. Eduardo knew that there was a similar but not very good website called Friendster which was not exclusive and few at Harvard used it. He also knew about the MySpace site which was growing rapidly but it was not really about communicating. Mark mentioned the project proposed by the Winklevoss twins but he regarded it as simply a dating website to enable men to find sexual partners. Mark had decided that this was not worth his time. Eduardo had money and agreed to fund the development of the social networks site, providing $1,000 in the first instance. Mark set up a company owned 70 per cent by him and 30 per cent by Eduardo, who Mark thought should be chief financial officer. By the end of the month Facebook was ready to go, and Eduardo thought it should be introduced to members of his fraternity club, Phoenix. Two weeks later, 5,000 members had signed up, representing 85 per cent of Harvard's undergraduates. So here we see the interplay of the intentions of the Winklevoss twins, Mark, Eduardo producing the emergent outcome called *Facebook.com*, part of a wider emerging pattern of electronic social networks. No one is following step-by-step procedures to deal with a problem situation and no one is formulating any kind of strategic plan for a new organisation or a whole new industry.

To return to the story – the Winklevoss twins complained to Larry Summers, President of Harvard and former US treasury secretary that Mark had stolen their idea in contravention of Harvard rules. Summers said that it was a personal issue between them and Mark and had nothing to do with the university. Meanwhile, Facebook was not only changing Harvard's social scene – it was spreading to other colleges. Eduardo wanted to push it with advertisers but Mark wanted to keep it a fun site. He slept through advertising and marketing meetings arranged with sponsors by Eduardo. Then Mark and Eduardo agreed to meet Sean Parker, a 24-year-old Silicon Valley entrepreneur, only four years older than Mark. Sean, who had never been to college, was one of the creators of the website, Napster, while he was still at High School which enabled college students to get the music they wanted. Eventually this failed, but Sean started another site called Plaxo. Sean told them that 85 per cent of Stanford students had joined Facebook within 24 hours of an article appearing in the *Stanford Daily*.

By the summer of 2004, only months after the setting up of Facebook, Sean had persuaded Mark to move to Palo Alto near Silicon Valley in California where he lived in a quiet suburban house with a team of young programmers. Eduardo, still funding Facebook, had gone to New York to take an internship at an investment bank and so was not involved in the day-to-day activities of Facebook. Sean sought to ally himself with Mark in order to build the billion-dollar business that had so far eluded him. Eduardo quit his investment bank job on his first day and then managed to get advertisers for Facebook. He was concerned about Sean's growing importance and the way he was approaching the business through taking Mark to one party after another to meet fundraisers and celebrities. Facebook had more than 500,000 members by August 2004. There was now a need for more servers, full-time staff and permanent offices and lawyers and this required more funds than the $18,000 that Eduardo had so far invested. Eduardo therefore returned to New York while Mark carried on partying with Sean in San Francisco. Mark tried to persuade

Eduardo to move to California but he refused. Sean introduced investors without Eduardo, who then wrote an angry letter to Mark and then froze the company account. So, following Sean's advice, Mark re-incorporated Facebook as a Delaware company to protect it from Eduardo and Mark put his own money into this company. Next, the Winklevoss twins took out a lawsuit against Mark which would use up $200,000 in legal defence costs. Mark and Sean then went to see Peter Thiel founder of PayPal and head of venture fund Clarium Capital. Thiel provide $500,000 seed money in exchange for 7 per cent of the reincorporated company and a seat on the board. Sean also became a shareholder. Eduardo would still get his 30 per cent but this would be diluted if he did not contribute and accept that he could not be the head of business. Eduardo went back to Harvard to complete his degree. By April 2005 Facebook was everywhere in America. Facebook then issued new shares to Mark, Sean and others but diluted Eduardo's holding to almost nothing. Sean was to be the new president of the company and Eduardo was edged out. By July 2009 there were 250 million users and the company was worth billions of dollars.

The book by Mezrich, from which this story has been taken, is based only on Mezrich's interviews with Eduardo and has therefore been criticised for being biased and not factual. This highlights the problem of trying to tell or find out what actually happened – all players have their story and each differs from to some extent from others, especially relating to feelings, ethics and power. So, usually, the so-called factual accounts focus on agreed upon events and rationally reconstructed stories of the past which brush aside emotions, unethical conduct and anything which might be called irrational. However, what the stories make clear, no matter whose particular version is taken, is how population-wide patterns of internet interaction have emerged in many local interactions between a number of people such as Mark, Eduardo, Sean, the Winklevoss twins and many others. There is no polarity of intention and emergence, because patterns are emerging in the interplay of many intentions, reflecting all kinds of emotions and ethical or unethical actions. This is a very different picture of creativity and innovation in organisations to that presented by the dominant discourse.

Facebook and national politics

Those who developed Facebook could have had no idea that it and other internet social networks would actually play a significant role in the US Presidential election of 2008. That role was not included in any strategic plan on the part of the Facebook organisation. I have drawn on an article in the *Sunday Times* on 25 May 2008 for the following account. Senator John McCain's 2002 campaign finance law set a maximum of $2,000, later raised to $2,300, for individual donations to party politics. This ended the era of a few big donors funding elections, including presidential elections, and meant that it was crucial to get as many people as possible to contribute to campaign funds. In the 2004 election the George W. Bush campaign had organised 'rangers' and 'pioneers' to get people together in living-room fundraisers and barbeques. In the same year Howard Dean had used the internet to raise money for his presidential nomination campaign and raised $50m, a tactic copied by John Kerry in his contest with Bush. By the 2008 campaign all candidates were on Facebook and had MySpace profiles. Obama's staff focused on raising funds on internet social networks, targeting not the maximum $2,300 but

$200 contributions. They transformed their websites into social networking zones and raised millions of dollars for campaign funds. The websites also served as focal points for organising campaigners and supporters. Obama generated more than 1.5 million individual donors. At his big events his staff collected email addresses and then sent emails asking for contributions and support. This approach made contact with the young and encouraged support and voting turnouts form the young in a way never before experienced. Also individuals loaded videos for and against Obama on YouTube and other sites, and this became very important in the election. Neither Hilary Clinton nor John McCain showed the same awareness or skill in operating on internet social networks which had become a new force in politics. The claims of politicians can now be immediately scrutinised and commented upon by ordinary people on social networking sites constituting a kind of political vetting procedure.

What we see here is the ongoing, never-ending interactions between the intentions of many, many people, in many, many local interactions in which population-wide patterns of political campaigns and Presidential elections emerge. Now consider two rather more mundane stories of the interplay of intentions.

Broken guitar

In an article in *The Times* on 22 July 2009, called 'Revenge is best served cold', the story was told of a Canadian musician, Dave Carroll, who in early 2009 took a United Airlines flight. As he waited for its departure, he saw baggage handlers throwing his guitar around on the tarmac. When he reached his destination, he found that the neck of his highly prized, expensive guitar had been snapped. He asked for compensation but was fobbed off by one department after another until he reached the customer complaints manager, Mrs Irlweg, who flatly dismissed his claim. Carroll then promised to write three songs, shoot a video for each and post them online. His first song called 'United Breaks Guitars' has now been played 3.5 million times on YouTube, causing Carroll to be invited to go on every major news network in the USA. The song created enormous bad PR, and United Airlines' share prices fell by 10 per cent, costing shareholders $180 million (equivalent to 51,000 replacement guitars). The second song came out in late July 2009 and was about Mrs Irlweg, who had become a national hate figure. Again we have a story of the interplay of rather minor intentions escalating into population-wide emergent patterns of some consequence. It is only with the benefit of hindsight that we can say that it could have been avoided.

Last day of drinking on the Tube

In June 2008 the new Mayor of London, Boris Johnson, banned the drinking of alcohol on London's underground railway transport system in response to growing vandalism and violence perpetrated on passengers. The ban was due to come into force at midnight on Saturday, 31 May 2008 (*Evening Standard*, 2 June 2008, 'Protestors pledge more anti-Boris booze-ups'). However, not everyone was happy with this development. For them, the Conservative Party Mayor, Boris, symbolised all that they hated and they felt he was ruining their London. So, a 26 year-old, Alexander Graham, set up a page on Facebook headed 'Circle Line Party – Last Day of Drinking on the Tube'. This attracted more than 1,000 Facebook members. Another group was set up by 19-year-old Dan Collins called 'Final Tube Booze Party' and this attracted 4,000 members. The groups proliferated: Anti-Boris Tube Crawl; One Final Tube Booze Party; the Circle Line Cocktail Party; London Underground's Last Ever Party; and Last Round on the Underground. Huge numbers of people turned up for the Tube Ban Drink Parties and they soon spiralled out of control. Although rowdy fun for the most part, some began to vandalise carriages as drunken people fought and vomited. The police had to intervene and arrest 17 people as well as having to clear up the huge mess at some tube stations. A messy party at Liverpool Street Station seems to have brought the evening to an end with chants of 'Boris is a wanker', while others sang songs made famous by the Village People and did the conga across the platforms. Others plastered the place with 'Free Tibet' stickers leading to chants of 'Dalai Lama'. Then someone started smashing bottles and the police swooped to restore order. The Mayor claimed that the Circle Line parties had vindicated the alcohol ban, but his opponents felt he ought to apologise to those who had been assaulted, abused and arrested when all they were doing was trying to have fun. So the unplanned and unintended consequences of Facebook continue to emerge in many local interactions.

Intention and emergence are not polarised

It is important to note how Elias does not polarise intention and emergence and how intention and emergence are not polarised in the above stories. I pointed out in Chapter 8 how writers in the process and activity-based strategy traditions polarise intention and emergence. They argue either that emergence means that everything happens by chance or that emergence is such that it can be designed, conditioned or at least influenced by powerful, effective individuals with intention. Elias takes a completely different view. People interact with intentions but their intentions will differ – indeed, each of these intentions is a response to the intentions of others – and so what happens emerges in the interplay of all of their intentions. Intention and emergence are thus in play at the same time without either being opposed by or subordinated to the other. No one can get outside of the interplay and so there is no doubling of process in the sense of someone using a process called influencing to shape a process called interplay or emergence. All that *everyone*, no matter how powerful, can do is to continue participating with intention and continually negotiate and respond to others who are also intentionally doing the same. It is in this ongoing, intentional, local interaction of strategising that the population-wide patterns of strategy emerge.

Elias talked about essentially paradoxical processes in which individuals form groups while being formed by them at the same time. This is a fundamentally different way of thinking compared with the dualism of individual and social to be found in systems thinking. In Elias's process theory, change occurs in paradoxical transformative processes – change is self-organising, emergent processes of perpetually constructing the future as continuity and potential transformation at the same time. Elias argued that we cannot identify self-organising social order with the order of nature, or with some kind of supra-individual. Instead the order arises in specific dynamics of social interplay in particular places at particular times.

If it makes sense to think of societies and their 'strategies' in this way, then there is no reason why we could not think about organisations in this way too and this is what the rest of the chapters in this part of the book will be doing. We can come to understand how organisational strategies emerge unpredictably in the interplay of many different intentions and, as such, emergence is not a matter of chance. What emerges does so precisely because of what all involved do and do not do. This notion of emergence presents a serious challenge to the dominant discourse on strategy and organisation, which assumes that leaders or others can directly change some whole system, process or population-wide pattern in an intentional manner. The whole notion of planned global change programmes 'rolled' down organisations begins to look rather like a fantasy.

Elias developed his process sociology during the 1930s and 1940s well before the emergence of the complexity sciences. He continued to develop his theories until his death in 1990, but it is unlikely that he knew anything about the developments in the natural complexity sciences. However, these sciences provide considerable support for what Elias was arguing. What these sciences are pointing to is the ubiquitous presence in nature of the unpredictable emergence of order in disorder through processes of spontaneous self-organisation or, to put it another way, the emergence of population-wide patterns in local interactions. The sociology of Elias, and some others in the Hegelian tradition, therefore provides an alternative to systems thinking for interpreting the insights of complexity theories into human terms.

12.3 Chaos, complexity and analogy

The complexity sciences present an ongoing, rigorous exploration of what self-organisation and emergence mean and in doing so represent a departure from some of the scientific foundations long ago imported into organisational thinking. They offer an important source of understanding the concepts of self-organisation and emergence (for a history *see* Chapter 10) and, since these concepts are central to the responsive processes perspective, it becomes important to draw on what the natural complexity scientists have to say. The purpose of this section, therefore, is to explore how the abstract relationships studied in the complexity sciences might provide analogies for human interaction understood from the perspective of Elias's process sociology and also the work of Mead. This will involve taking abstract relationships from the domain of natural science complexity theories and interpreting them in the human domain by taking account of the distinctive features of human agents. Unlike agents in the natural sciences or in the computer simulations described in Chapter 10, human agents are conscious and self-conscious, they form intentions and have some freedom of choice, they display emotion and spontaneity, and they have the capacity to articulate the population-wide patterns emerging in their local interactions, even desire different ones, and these desires and articulations affect their local interactions at the same time as they are being articulated and desired. These are all matters to be taken up in subsequent chapters.

First, however, consider whether it is reasonable to regard chaos and complexity theories as source domains for analogy with human interaction.

Chaos theory

Chaos theory (*see* Chapter 10) is concerned with the properties of iterative, deterministic, nonlinear mathematical relationships (i.e. algorithms) in which the output of one iteration becomes the input of the next. In other words, the current state is determined by referring, through a deterministic nonlinear algorithm, to its own previous state. At some values of a control parameter, such models display a strange attractor called *chaos*, a paradox of stability and instability, predictability and unpredictability, at the same time. However, the pattern of movement takes one, and only one, form – namely, that of the particular strange attractor generated by the particular algorithmic relationship specified. Furthermore, mathematical models are not reality but simply logical structures created by mathematicians. The physicist, meteorologist, chemist, biologist, or any other scientist in any other field, then has to interpret how these abstract logical structures might apply to the field they are interested in. They do this by calling upon what is already known, through scientific experiments, about the phenomena in their field of study. They also perform new experiments suggested by chaos theory in order to provide empirical support for the claim that the abstract mathematical models they have developed do apply to the phenomena in their field of interest.

In Chapter 11, I referred briefly to the work of some economists and organisational theorists who adopt exactly the same approach. They use data on macro events, such as foreign exchange rates, to explore whether the mathematical equations of chaos theory fit the data. As soon as they do this, they make implicit assumptions about the nature of human interaction. They assume that human beings are such that patterns in their interaction can be described at the macro level in terms of deterministic equations. Alternatively, some organisational theorists use the properties revealed by the mathematical models of chaos as metaphors to describe organisations. For example, Chapter 11 reviewed the work of a number of researchers who describe an organisation as 'chaotic'. As soon as they do this, they too are making the implicit assumptions about the nature of human interaction just described.

It is very important not to jump straight from a mathematical model to an application in a particular field without examining how the model is being interpreted in that particular field. In other words, the implicit assumptions being made about human action when chaos theory is applied to organisations need to be made explicit if one is to think rigorously. If one applies chaos theory directly to any form of human action, including organisations, then one is assuming that human interaction is deterministic or, at least, can be thought of 'as if' it is. This immediately means that one is assuming away any form of human freedom: that is, any possibility of individuals making any kind of choice or learning from experience. Since this is so directly contrary to our experience, it follows that chaos theory cannot be directly applied to human action. Furthermore, chaos theory cannot offer analogies for human action. In *reasoning by analogy*, we take relationships, without any attributes, from one domain and argue that these relationships apply in some other domain. The relationships in chaos theory are abstract relationships between mathematical symbols of a deterministic kind yielding abstract patterns in those symbols: for example, patterns called *strange attractors*, *fractal* or *mathematical chaos*. I have already argued that we cannot take abstract deterministic relationships as analogous to real human relationships, because that would amount to assuming that humans do not exercise choice. However, we might still want to reason using metaphor. When we *reason by metaphor* we take the attributes of phenomena in one domain to another domain without taking the nature of the relationships. So, one could use chaos theory to provide metaphors for human interactions. For example, one might want to say that human interactions are patterned like the paradoxical patterns of mathematical chaos, strange attractors or fractals. Chaos theory, then, can only ever provide what might be experienced as provocative metaphors, which might give us some kind of poetic insight into patterns of human action. The same conclusion applies to dissipative structure theory because it too is based on deterministic models.

Complex adaptive systems theory

The theory of complex adaptive systems differs from chaos and dissipative structure theory in that it reveals the properties of iterating the interaction between separate algorithms representing entities comprising a system, rather than those of iterating algorithms modelling the system as a whole. The former focuses at the micro level while the latter focuses at the macro level. Chapter 10 distinguished between two substantially different kinds of complex adaptive system simulation. The first is where the algorithms, or agents comprising the system, are all the same as each other, as for example in the Boids simulation (Reynolds, 1987), and the second is where the agents differ from each other, as for example in the Tierra simulation (Ray, 1992).

Complex adaptive systems with homogeneous agents

In some simulations of complex adaptive systems, the agents are algorithms, or computer programs, that are all the same as each other. For example, Reynolds' simulation of Boids consists of a number of computer programs, each comprising the same three instructions that organise the interaction of each computer program with other programs. Furthermore, the algorithms or computer programs are cybernetic entities. This is so because one of the algorithms, for example, requires each agent to keep a target distance from its nearest neighbours. The actual distance from a neighbour is compared with the target and the difference is fed back so as either to increase or to decrease the distance. The agents in complex adaptive systems of this homogeneous kind are deterministic, cybernetic algorithms.

The simulation then reveals that this interaction between each individual algorithm with some others – that is, local interaction between them – yields a population-wide pattern in the relationship between all of them. They clump together. When each algorithm is represented as a dot on the computer screen, the clumping pattern can be seen and the programmer can observe how it persists in various forms over time. Reynolds then makes an interpretation. He calls each individual algorithm a 'Boid' and he calls the population-wide pattern they produce 'flocking'. He makes a further interpretation when he suggests that the Boids are logically equivalent to real birds and that the model points to how real birds produce flocking behaviour. He then points to how a few simple rules of local interaction can yield emergent population-wide patterns of a very complex kind, without the need for any overall blueprint to determine the population-wide patterns. Each algorithm interacting with a few others at their own local level of interaction is sufficient to produce a population-wide pattern of relationships between all of them. What the iteration of their interaction reveals is the *emergence* of a coherent collective pattern: that is, an attractor for the whole system.

There is a very important point to note about simulations, such as the Boids one, where each interacting symbol pattern, or agent, is the same as all the others. This is interaction where there is no diversity amongst the symbol patterns, no non-average interaction between them, no noise, no fluctuations in Prigogine's terms. Because of this lack of diversity, the simulation cannot display spontaneous moves from one attractor to another, nor can it spontaneously generate a new attractor (Allen, 1998a, 1998b). The symbol patterns, or rules, always yield the same attractor, and change can occur only when the programmer changes the individual algorithms. Furthermore, each of the agents is a deterministic cybernetic system, a set of rules, a blueprint. In other words, such a model cannot explain novelty because it has no freedom of choice and does not evolve of its own accord, and because it is deterministic it cannot be applied to human action other than metaphorically.

Each individual Boid is itself a blueprint, doing only what its programme enables it to, and it is constrained by that programme from doing anything else. These agents cannot be said to be organising themselves in some kind of individual manner with connotations of doing whatever they please. They are constrained by the need to interact locally with each other. In fact, self-organisation does not mean that something is organising itself. It means local interaction. Furthermore, emergence does not mean that some pattern arises by chance. Emergence means that population-wide patterns arise in local interaction in the complete absence of a blueprint, program or plan for that population-wide pattern. The global pattern is what it is because of the manner in which the agents interact locally and this is not a matter of chance. The overall pattern of interaction is said to be emerging because there is no blueprint for it.

Organisational interpretations

Some organisational theorists interpret simulations like the Boids to suggest that if a manager wants his or her organisation to produce an overall pattern, or strategy, of a highly complex kind, then it is not necessary to formulate and implement an overall strategy. Instead, the manager should establish a few simple ground rules, and this is held to unleash the power of self-organisation and allow emergence to happen. In this interpretation, the manager is, without any explicit justification, equated with the programmer. Reynolds, the programmer, took the position of the objective observer, standing outside the pre-given reality of birds flocking, and induced rules that might produce flocking. He then simulated them in the computer and showed that they do produce the equivalent of flocking. This is what the manager is now supposed to do. Implicit in the prescription to formulate a few simple rules that all in the organisation are to follow is the notion that the manager must first choose which attractor he or she wants the organisation to be drawn to. The manager then has to induce the few simple rules that will produce it.

However, note the consequence of this. Assuming for the moment that an organisation is a system and that people do follow rules, then if the manager succeeds in identifying the *right* set of rules and people do follow them, the required attractor will emerge. However, this is all that will emerge. The organisation will follow this attractor until the manager changes the rules, because a system in which the separate entities are all following the same rules does not possess the capacity for spontaneously moving to another attractor, nor does it possess the capacity to generate new attractors spontaneously. The prescription ensures that the organisation will not be creative. The only change from strategic choice theory is that the manager is now relieved from having to formulate detailed overall plans. This is not a radically different insight, since it was long ago concluded that detailed long-term plans were not very helpful in turbulent times and that what managers needed to do was set the direction in the form of a few guidelines or a vision.

Now, consider whether complex adaptive systems, such as the Boids one where all the agents are the same, can provide a source domain for analogies with human behaviour. The abstract relationships in such systems are relationships between cybernetic entities defined as deterministic, simple rules. It follows that such complex adaptive systems cannot provide analogies with human interaction for exactly the same reasons as chaos and dissipative structure theories cannot: humans are not cybernetic entities. In addition, if people really are to follow rules then they will need rules to interpret the rules in a particular contingent situation. Then they will need rules to select the appropriate rules of interpretation, and so on in infinite regress. Furthermore, if people following rules keep altering their interpretations even according to rules, rather than following them rigidly, then they are no longer following a given set of simple rules and so they will not produce the attractor enfolded in the first rule set. It follows that simulations with homogeneous agents can only ever provide metaphors that may or may not provoke thinking about human interaction. The most immediately obvious metaphor is the human cult or fascist power structure – here people do follow simple rules, for a time at least.

Complex adaptive systems with heterogeneous agents

Now consider another simulation in which the interacting algorithms (agents) do not all follow the same rules and can change from one iteration to another. This means that the algorithms in the population fall into different categories, so that difference is located between categories and sameness within a category. An example of this kind of system is provided by the Tierra simulation in Chapter 10. In the Tierra simulation, each agent is an algorithm consisting of 80 instructions specifying in detail how the algorithm is to copy itself. The programmer then introduces a mechanism to generate diversity – namely, random mutation in the copying of an algorithm, and selection criteria – namely, limited computer time available for replicating and a limited total time period over which an individual algorithm has the opportunity to replicate. The programmer then runs the program and observes what happens.

A population-wide pattern rapidly emerges in the form of an increase in the number of algorithms. The attractor is one of exponentially increasing numbers, which eventually impose a constraint on further replication. The population-wide pattern is continually moving from sparse occupation of the computer memory to overcrowding. The algorithms are also gradually changing through random mutation and so they are gradually differing from each other – increasing diversity is appearing. Before long a new attractor appears in the form of shorter algorithms with only

40 instructions. Now there are distinctively different kinds of algorithms: namely, long ones and short ones. The constraints on computer time favour smaller ones and the emerging population-wide pattern is now decline in the number of long algorithms and increase in the number of short ones. The system has spontaneously produced a new attractor. Later, another kind of algorithm emerges, taking the form of instructions to read the replication code of neighbouring algorithms. Another new attractor has emerged, which is usually understood to be a system where agents are at one level and the global system is at a higher level.

However, we could think about what is happening in this simulation in another way. We could say that new forms of individual algorithm and new overall patterns of the population have emerged at the same time. There can be no population-wide pattern of increase and decline without simultaneous change in the length of some individual algorithms. There can be no sustained change in individual algorithms without the population-wide pattern of increase and decline. Individual algorithms and the population-wide pattern can be said to be forming and being formed by each other, at the same time. Here we do not need to say that the agents are forming a system at a higher level. Instead, we could argue that agents and population-wide patterns are emerging at the same time and that neither constitutes a system. This is very much the argument presented by Elias in relation to individual human agents and populations in the previous section.

The important point is that the programmer has not programmed the new attractors in advance. They emerge because overall, global, population-wide pattern is emerging through the local interaction of the agents (self-organisation) within the constraints that the programmer has set, but the programmer is not able to predict what the global patterns will be before they emerge. The new emerges through self-organisation (local interaction), not prior design of the whole. Here, again, I am avoiding an interpretation involving systems and levels because I want to explore a responsive processes perspective, rather than a systemic one, for the reasons provided by Elias and outlined earlier in this chapter.

This simulation is very different from the Boids one. The latter displayed only one population-wide pattern and could not spontaneously move to another or generate a novel one. The programmer would have to change the individual agents for this to happen. In the Tierra simulation, however, there are spontaneous moves to emergent new individual algorithms and population-wide patterns. The programmer did introduce a mechanism for generating diversity in the replication process in the first place, but once diversity has appeared, the random-generating device can be turned off and the evolution continues without it.

Note how the agents are not feedback mechanisms in that they do not compare their actual state with some target; instead, each refers back to itself as it interacts locally with others, as when some use the code of others. The key point here is that the agents are different from each other and the nonlinearity of the iterating interaction can amplify tiny differences into major qualitative changes in population-wide pattern. This micro diversity is what enables both the population-wide pattern and the individual algorithms to simultaneously evolve in the sense of producing emergent, unpredictable, novel forms (Allen, 1998a, 1998b). Note that the agents and the interactions between them are not deterministic, but evolving, and that the capacity for evolution arises because of the presence of microdiversity in the interaction between diverse entities.

Important points to note

With models of the heterogeneous kind just discussed there is the possibility of reasoning by analogy about human action. This is because the agents in these models are not deterministic or cybernetic, but evolving. One can, therefore, explore the transfer of abstract relationships from the model domain to the human domain and this will require some kind of interpretation that adds human attributes. While agents in the models interact in the medium of digital symbols, humans interact in the medium of other kinds of symbols, particularly those of language.

The computer simulations demonstrate the possibility of digital symbols arranged as algorithmic rules interacting locally (self-organising) in the dynamics at the edge of chaos to produce emergent attractors of a novel kind, provided that those symbol patterns are richly connected and diverse enough. Natural scientists at the Santa Fé Institute and elsewhere then use this demonstration of possibility in the medium of digital symbols as a source of analogy to provide explanations of phenomena in particular areas of interest such as biology. My argument is that the abstract, nonlinear, iterative relationships of heterogeneous complexity models are analogous to the interactive processes of social evolution proposed by Elias.

Analogies

I suggest the following analogies:

- *There is **no** analogy between the programmer of the complex adaptive system model and anything in human interaction.* There is no possibility of standing outside human interaction to design a program for it, since we are all participants in that interaction and cannot control the interplay of our intentions. When Ray and others use a model of complex adaptive systems to simulate life, they are quite clearly trying to simulate the evolution of a process where there is no outside programmer or designer. They are trying to model self-organising and emergent phenomena in nature: that is, phenomena that evolve without design. Since they are using a model for this purpose, they naturally have to design the model, at least initially. However, they do not propose any analogy in nature for the modeller of the system – on the contrary, they argue that there is no designer outside nature. If one is trying to understand human organisations as self-organising and emergent phenomena then one cannot find an analogy for the programmer.

- Furthermore, following the arguments of Elias, I suggest that *there is no analogy between systems and humans.* Throughout Part 1 I pointed to the ways in which it is inappropriate to think of human interaction in systems terms, since that perspective reifies what are ongoing processes and ascribes a causality to human action that does not take account of individual capacities to choose actions, and that does not explain the possibility of novel forms. Furthermore, the simulations of heterogeneous complexity models begin to pose problems for systems thinking, even though they are models of systems. For example, as I have explained above, these simulations can be understood in a way that does not involve hierarchical levels, which is a central concept in systems thinking. Then there are problems created for that other central concept in systems thinking, namely the 'whole'. Heterogeneous complexity models take on a life of their own: that is, they evolve in unpredictable and novel ways. It follows that the 'whole' is not there until it has emerged, and since it is always evolving it is never complete. One then has to talk about incomplete or absent wholes and this begins to undermine the usefulness of the very concept of the whole itself. The explanation for the unpredictability and the novelty has nothing to do with the 'whole'. It lies in the *intrinsic properties of the process of interaction between diverse entities*. The notion of a model that takes on a life of its own also creates problems for the use of the models. If one is modelling a phenomenon with a life of its own, the phenomenon and the model will soon diverge from each other. The usefulness of the model is then restricted to the insight it gives into the general nature of the dynamics. The points I have been making above apply to all systems, whether one thinks of a system as mechanistic or as a living organism.

- With regard to human action, the *analogy begins with the individual agent*. The abstract agents in the form of computer instructions on how to relate to other agents are taken by analogy to the human domain by interpreting the concept of the human agent in terms of the human characteristics of consciousness, self-consciousness, emotion, desire, anxiety, capacity for imagination, excitement and spontaneity and ability to choose within limits.

- Central to understanding the agent is the *interaction* of agents in the complexity models, which is analogous to the interdependence of individuals and the interplay of individual human intentions and plans described by Elias earlier in this chapter.

- Furthermore, the *digital symbols of the complexity models are taken as analogies* for the symbols humans use to interact with each other. In other words, it is the aspects of responsive processes in the complex adaptive system models that I suggest provide analogies for human interaction, not the systemic aspects of those models. In the models, digital agents interact with each other by exactly *following rules*. This is analogous to the rule following that human agents perform, but careful interpretation will need to be made of what it means in the human sphere to follow a rule.

- From a responsive processes point of view *there are no levels of operation*, only degrees of detail in which the phenomenon of interest is examined. Elias's description of societies forming individual minds while being formed by them at the same time is analogous to populations of algorithms forming individual algorithms while being formed by them.

- *The patterns that emerge across a population* of digital agents are analogous to the population-wide patterns (social) which emerge in local interaction in organisations. Chapter 13 will explore processes of societies forming individual minds while being formed by them at the same time, which is analogous to populations of algorithms forming individual algorithms while being formed by them.

- Finally, the *transformative causality* displayed by interaction between heterogeneous entities in the complexity model is analogous to the transformative causality that Elias posits in relation to interaction between people. This represents a move away from the dual causality of the theories described in Part 1 to the paradoxical transformative causality of 'forming and being formed by at the same time' that will be the basis of the theory developed in the subsequent chapters of this part.

What I hope to do in the subsequent chapters of Part 3 is to explore the implications of taking a responsive processes view of human action rather than a systemic one. I want to explore what happens when organisational analogies are sought for in simulations in which there is agent diversity and hence the spontaneous capacity to change. Instead of thinking about the manager as the analogue of the programmer, I would like to consider the consequences if the manager is a participant in responsive processes of relating, and human interaction is thought of not as a system or a network but as responsive processes. Since humans do not always adapt to, or fit in, with each other, it might then be useful to think of human relating not as adaptive but as responsive. I will suggest that the human analogues for complex adaptive systems in the simulations are *complex responsive processes* of relating in organisations.

Table 12.2 summarises the different ways in which complexity theory is used as a source domain for systems and responsive processes thinking.

What is to be gained by drawing analogies between complex adaptive systems and human interaction is a clearer understanding of self-organisation and emergence and a strong argument that coherent, population-wide patterns can emerge from many, many local interactions. Other insights of importance have to do with unpredictability, the importance of diversity and conflicting constraints and the paradoxical dynamics in which novelty can emerge.

Having explored how analogies might be drawn and what insights they might give about human processes of interaction, I want to turn to another key aspect of process: namely, time.

12.4 Time and responsive processes

From a responsive processes perspective, people interact with each other locally and in doing so produce population-wide patterns for which there are no global blueprints or programs. Furthermore, local interactions are iterative – that is, they are perpetually reproduced – and they are nonlinear, which means that differences, even very small ones, from one iteration to the next are potentially amplified to produce novelty. One consequence of thinking in these terms is that *time* is immediately of the essence, because one is thinking of iteration or reproduction from one period to the next in which the patterns of interactions in the present depend upon the history of interactions in the past and expectations of the future.

Mead (1932, 1938) distinguished between two ways of thinking about the past. First, the past may be thought of as real events that are independent of any present. On this view, the investigation of the past is a reconstruction, belonging to the past, of real events that unquestionably occurred in the past. Our investigation of the past is a process of slowly and imperfectly deciphering what actually happened. This past is then the background for, the constraint on, dealing with the issues we face in the present. We refer to a given past out of which the issues we are now dealing with have arisen. However, we know that a particular reconstruction of the past is questioned and reinterpreted at some later date – each generation rewrites history: indeed, each of us tends to reinterpret our own past from time to time. Any present interpretation of the past is therefore open to doubt. This leads to the second view

Table 12.2 Human analogues of simulations of heterogeneous complex systems

Computer simulations	Systemic analogue in organisations	Responsive processes analogue in organisations
The programmer	CEO	None
The whole is a complex adaptive system	The whole is a complex adaptive system	None
Consisting of locally interacting (self-organising) algorithms	Consisting of interacting individuals said to be organising themselves, with minds	Complex responsive processes of relating between persons interacting locally (self-organising) in the medium of symbols (see Chapter 13) where the symbols are
Arranged as rules and called agents	Arranged as schemas and mental models as basis of individual as agent	Arranged as narrative and propositional themes that organise experience (see Chapter 15)
Reproduced through replication with random mutation	Reproduced through individual choice to change mental models	Reproduced through interaction with conflict, negation, misunderstanding and deviance as source of transformation (see Chapters 13 and 14)
What emerges is forms of algorithm and population-wide patterns at the same time	What emerges is the organisational system and the detail of action which can be shaped from an external position	What emerges is population-wide patterns as themes in conversations that are individual mind and group at the same time as well as figurations of power relations (see Chapters 13 to 15)
Novelty emerges at the edge of chaos, i.e. paradox of stability and instability in processes of self-organisation	Edge of chaos defined as crisis and stress in which self-organisation and emergence can be intentionally unleashed to produce novelty	Novelty emerges as re-patterning of conversational themes in paradoxical processes of human interaction simultaneously predictable and unpredictable, continuity and transformation (see Chapters 13 and 15). Self-organisation is local interaction between persons
Radical unpredictability	Unpredictability played down	Radical unpredictability
Attractor	A vision, etc., as something that draws the system towards it	A population-wide pattern such as a routine, habit, some generalisation or idealisation such as a social object or cult value (see Chapter 13) which has to be made operational in local interaction
Boundaries set by programmer	Boundaries set by CEO, i.e. simple rules	Emerging constraints of power relations and dynamics of inclusion and exclusion (see Chapter 14)

of the past, not as a given to be discovered but as a meaning to be formulated anew. Here, the significance or meaning of past events is to be found in, that is, belongs to, the present rather than to the past. In other words, we know the past through the present. Furthermore, the future is implicated in that the knowledge we gain of the past, the hypotheses we form about the past, depend upon the viewpoint of the present, which will change in the future. In other words, the future will change the meaning of the past. In this way we *construct different pasts* and one past displaces and abrogates another. There are coincidences and events that are relatively permanent, and this makes possible a translation from one historical account to another, but these coincidences are not the object of our knowledge.

Mead, then, is arguing that each present has a different past in that in each present we interpret the past differently because we have a different viewpoint and so construct different meanings of past events. The reality of the past that gets into our experience is thus different, depending upon our present standpoint. Mead says that the only alternative is to think of our experience in terms of being a reflection of a transcendental reality. The perspective he suggests is one in which the past can only reach us through our own current frame of reference within which we are interpreting our own present and determining our future.

What Mead is doing here is pointing to *iteration*: that is, the reproduction and potential transformation of the past in the present. He is pointing to the time structure of the present in which the movement of present experience is that of forming and being formed by our reconstruction of the past while forming and being formed by our expectation of the future, all at the same time in the present. In complexity terms we might say that it is the nonlinear nature of this iteration that makes possible both continuity and potential transformation at the same time. Mead explicitly links this time structure of the present to the notion of emergence as the appearance of unique events.

Clearly, human experience is also experience of what Prigogine (1997) called the 'arrow of time', in the sense that we all know that what has been said cannot be unsaid, and what has been done cannot be undone. We cannot go back in time and unsay or undo. We can only go forward in time and elaborate on what we have said or done. It is also our experience that interacting with each other in one way immediately precludes all alternative ways of interacting, and that what happens next will be different from what might have been if we had interacted in one of these alternative ways. It is because the past is not a given but a perpetual construction in the present that we cannot go back to the past. It is because of the potential for small differences to escalate that we cannot retrace our steps. In other words, it is because time has the structure of the living present that we also experience the arrow of time.

Human interaction in the present is thus simultaneously forming and being formed by the past and the future. In other words, the arrow of time means that time moves only from the past through the present to the future because of the iterative nonlinearity of interactions and the bifurcations they encounter. In relation to human action, the arrow of time has an important temporal implication. It means that the present has a circular time structure in that the present both forms and is formed by the past and the future at the same time. The arrow of time then means that the movement of human experience in the present has the circular self-referential time structure of reconstructed pasts and imagined futures. We may call this the living present, which is very different from the notion of the 'here-and-now', which explicitly excludes the past and the future in focusing entirely on present feelings.

12.5 The differences between systemic process and responsive processes thinking

In dictionaries, the word 'process' is defined as 'going on, being constructed over time, a series of changes, a series of operations, or a course of action'. For the philosopher Whitehead (1978), process refers to *how entities become* what they become. Process, then, refers to some kind of movement over *time* in which entities are *becoming*. I think that there is a further implication, given a universe of inter-dependent entities, and this is that the movement of process always involves some kind of interaction between entities. So at its most basic, I take process to be the ongoing, interactive movement (the *how*) of entities over time through which these entities become, individually and collectively, the coherent patterns of activity (the *what*) that they are. Process is interactive movement, the *interaction* of entities, and what these interactions are continually producing or creating is the coherent *pattern* of the entities themselves both individual and collective.

Consider how systemic and responsive processes perspectives interpret the key terms of this general definition of process in substantially different ways.

The *entities* in systemic process are defined as parts of a system. These *parts interact* over time, *the process*, to produce a bounded whole, the coherent *pattern*, which actually exists, or is thought of 'as if' it exists, at a higher hierarchical level than the parts. In other words, the whole is more than the sum of the parts, has additional properties and can act back on the parts as a causal force in their interaction, giving meaning to the parts. In the organisational literature on systemic process, reviewed in Chapter 8, the parts were defined as routines, core micro-strategies, micro-practices, procedures and many similar concepts. In their inter-action, sometimes called *recombination*, these parts are said to produce an activity system, or an organisation as a system, which is a coherent pattern. The parts themselves may also be thought of as subsystems produced by the interaction of sub-parts. For example, the sub-parts could be individuals or the mental models through which individuals interpret the nature of the organisational whole and its environment. In this systemic process view it is some kind of system which is *becoming* what it becomes.

From the perspective of responsive processes, however, the *entities* are embodied human persons and the movement, the *how*, is the *interacting*, the relating, *between persons* in their ongoing responding to each other. *Process* is understood as respon-sive acts of mutual recognition, where recognition is not simply good since persons may recognise each other and themselves as superior or inferior, as attractive or repugnant. The coherent *patterns* that are being produced in such interaction are not 'wholes' outside the interaction but the coherent patterns of the interaction itself, of the process itself. Nothing is being produced above, below, behind or in front of the patterns of interaction, of the process. Patterns of interaction simply produce further patterns of interaction, individually and population-wide. What are *becoming* are the individual and collective identities of the persons interacting. Furthermore, in the responsive processes view, categories of pattern such as routines are instances of more fundamental patterns: namely the thematic patterning of com-munication (*see* Chapter 13), the patterning of power relations between people (*see* Chapter 14), and the patterning of the ideologically based choices people make (*see* Chapter 14). So, in firmly grounding the notion of processes in interaction between human persons, the responsive process perspective makes central the iterative pro-cesses of communication, power and ideologically driven choice. This perspective, then, focuses attention not on abstract wholes or administrative procedures but on the actual micro, local interaction between people in the living present in which people may imaginatively construct 'wholes' felt as the unity of experience, especially the experience of value (*see* Chapter 14).

Second, notice how the systemic perspective on process is based on a spatial metaphor of 'inside' and 'outside'. The parts of an organisational system are inside the whole system, which is outside the parts, and outside the system there is its environment. Of course, the activities of the parts take place in a physical, spatial setting, but in a systems view they also take place in conceptual space: that is, the system itself is thought of as a space. Furthermore, process itself is often thought about conceptually as spatial. This can be seen in Chapter 8 when writers refer to what is going on 'inside' the process. This conceptual spatial distinction immediately leads to the notion of an observer who can perceive the system or the process from the outside, as it were, and so can shape or influence the process and what goes on inside it. This leads to talking about a process called shaping which shapes another process called routines (*see* Chapter 8). In systemic process thinking there is a doubling of process – some process shapes, influences or conditions another process.

In the responsive processes view, although the activities of interdependent people obviously take place in a physical setting, space, there is no notion of the activities themselves being inside or outside of anything – mental activity, for example, is not thought of as being inside a person as it is in systemic process thinking. Responsive processes thinking is not based on a notion of conceptual space. Furthermore, there is no external objective observer, only participants. Participation also means something completely different in the two approaches. In systems thinking, people are thought to participate in a system, a whole. In responsive processes thinking, participation means direct interaction between persons in local situations in the living present. So, the methodological position is a participative one rather than one based on the objective observer. In responsive processes thinking there is no doubling of process – there is only one process: namely, interaction between persons which is creating the patterns in their interaction. Since persons can only participate in their interaction with each other, there is no outside position from which anyone could use another process to shape or influence the processes of interaction – any influence is exerted through relations between people in the interaction itself.

Third, the spatial metaphor and the taken-for-granted linear theory of time renders time itself a relatively unimportant aspect of systemic process. Instead, the systemic perspective focuses attention on routines, procedures and analytical tools. Systemic process thinking is built upon a linear notion of time in which the past is factually given, the future is yet to be unfolded and the present is simply a point dividing the two. It is based on linear phases or stages of development.

Responsive processes thinking, however, takes a circular, paradoxical view of time. This means that the past is not actually given, but is being reiterated, retold in the present in the light of the expectations people are forming in the present for the future. Expectations for the future are affecting how the stories of the past are being retold and those stories are affecting expectations for the future, all in the present. In a sense the future is changing the past just as the retelling of the past is changing the future, all in the present. The present is thus living in the sense that it has a time structure incorporating both the past and the future. The *living present*, the present we actually live in, implies the arrow of time because you cannot tell the same story twice – you cannot return to the past. Systemic perspectives look for how the system moves over linear time, while the responsive processes approach asks about the narrative patterns being created in each living present, how narrative patterns are moving over time.

Fourth, in systemic process thinking, causality takes a dual form. The individuals designing the system, with its routines and values, are subject to rationalist causality, which means that the cause of their actions lies in their rationally chosen objectives. The system itself is subjected to formative cause, which means that the operation of the system unfolds the form already designed into it in a move from an embryonic to a mature state.

Responsive processes thinking is based on a different theory of causality. In responsive processes thinking, the theory of causality is unitary and transformative in that patterns of interaction emerge as continuity and potential transformation at the same time in the iteration of interaction itself. The future is thus under perpetual construction in the interaction between people, and it is the processes of interaction between differences that amplifies these differences into novelty. The explanation of novelty lies in the properties of the processes of interaction.

Fifth, it can be seen immediately that systemic and responsive processes thinking make completely different assumptions about human psychology. The former is based on the individualistic psychologies of cognitivism, constructivism, humanistic psychology or psychoanalysis, while the latter takes a relational, social perspective on individual psychology, a point that will be explained in Chapter 13.

Sixth, in systemic process thinking, practice means the system of routines, cultural traditions and so on that individuals use as tools in their practices or praxis. From the systemic view, experience is the formulation and testing of hypotheses about an objective world understood in terms of systems, where the system is outside experience, a hidden reality or given categories such as mental models.

In responsive processes thinking, individuals are social practitioners through and through in that their very selves emerge in social practice. Practice is the local activity of bodily interaction as communication, power relating and evaluative choice. Generalisations such as routines and cultural traditions are to be found only in their particularisation in local interaction (*see* Chapter 13). As for Hegel, experience is the historical, social processes of consciousness and self-consciousness, the world we are creating in our thought.

Seventh, the systemic view places thought before action, while from the responsive processes point of view there is no necessary sequence because interaction is continuous over time.

Eighth, from the perspective of responsive processes, population-wide pattern emerges in local interaction rather than being intentionally created by a plan. The systemic process perspective takes the view that population-wide pattern, understood as a system, can be intentionally planned, or at least the process producing it can be shaped from some external position.

The differences between systemic process and responsive processes are summarised in Table 12.3.

12.6 Summary

This chapter has presented arguments for interpreting the relevance of complexity theories for organisations from a responsive processes perspective rather than the systemic process point of view discussed in Chapter 8.

Table 12.3 The differences between systemic process and responsive processes

	Systemic process	Responsive processes
Entity	Parts of a system, which could be individuals, routines, etc., and which can be thought of as subsystems, such as mental models. Psychological assumptions are those of individual-centred cognitivism, etc.	Embodied interdependent human persons. A social, relational view of human psychology is taken
Process	Interaction of parts	Responsive acts of mutual recognition by persons
What is becoming	The system, a bounded whole which exists at a higher level than the parts, has properties of its own, and acts causally on the parts	Coherent patterns of interaction, of the process itself. Patterns of interaction produce further patterns of interaction and nothing else. These constitute individual and collective identities
Causality	Dual causality of the rationalist, objectively observing autonomous individual and the formative cause of the system unfolding a mature form of itself imputed by the observer	Transformative causality in which continuity and potential transformation emerge at the same time. The potential for transformation arises in the capacity of nonlinear interaction to amplify difference and in the inherent possibility of spontaneity in human agents
Theory of time	Linear view of time where past is factually given and future is yet to be unfolded in developmental stages	Time as the living present in which both accounts of the past and expectations for the future are formed in the perpetual construction of the future in the present
Conceptual space	Spatial metaphor of parts inside the system and the system outside the parts	No spatial metaphor in that human action itself is not inside or outside of anything. So there is no society or organisation at a level higher than human interaction
Emergence	Not central to the process and, where used, equated with chance happenings as the opposite of intention	Central to the process of human interaction where emergence is understood in terms of the interplay of human intentions. Emergence is not seen as the polar opposite of intention and what emerges does so because of the interplay of what people intend to do, not by chance
Doubling of process	Autonomous individuals can stand outside a process, such as strategising, and shape it, that is, use another process to shape a process	No doubling of process since there are only the processes of human interaction and no one can take an external vantage point in relation to this
Practice	Practice is a system of routines, etc.	Practice is the local, social activity of communication, power relating and evaluative choice
Experience	The use of tools and techniques to make decisions and act	Historical, social processes of consciousness and self-consciousness in interaction with others. The world we together create in our thought
Organisation	A thing to be moved around	Patterns of relating in which one can only participate

Systems thinkers use the word 'process' to mean the interaction of parts of a system to produce that system, whether that system be real or a mental construct. In human terms this amounts to the assumption that, in their interaction, people either actually are a system or that they understand their interaction as if it were a system. Here a macro perspective is taken, which I have signalled by using 'process' in the singular when referring to systems views. It is easy then to reify 'process' and talk about shaping and choosing it. In responsive processes thinking, the interaction between persons is understood to produce further interaction between them. In responsive processes thinking, people are thought of not as parts producing a system but as interdependent persons producing patterns of relationships, which produce them as selves at the same time. In the kind of responsive processes thinking I am talking about there is no notion of system at all. In talking about this perspective I have used 'processes' in the plural to indicate the micro perspective being taken, in which the macro emerges not in one monolithic process but in many local processes of local human interaction which cannot be reified and talked about as if they could be influenced from the outside.

From a responsive processes perspective, there is also no notion of hierarchical levels in human action. Instead of thinking that individuals produce organisations as another level, which shapes their identities, individual identities and the organisational are thought of as the same responsive processes. In responsive processes thinking, people interacting are intrinsically social and what they produce is further interaction with widespread, population-wide patterns, not some higher-level system or whole. In systems thinking, emergence relates to levels in that interaction at one level produces an emergent system at another level. In responsive processes thinking, relationships are emerging in relationships and the question of levels does not even arise.

Responsive processes thinking involves moving away from any form of systems thinking when it comes to human action and focuses on:

- The detail of local interaction between diverse people in the living present as patterning of experience, emergent identity and transformation.

- Interaction in the form of conversation and how it patterns experience in narrative-like forms. This emphasises the importance of the informal and the narrative rather than the prescriptive and instrumental.

- Ideology as the basis of evaluative choices made by persons.

- The importance of conflicting constraints emerging as power and the dynamics of inclusion and exclusion and the links to how people deal with anxiety.

- The emergence of population-wide patterns in the local interaction of interdependent persons.

- The simultaneous emergence of continuity and novelty, creation and destruction, in the iteration of nonlinear interaction and its amplification of small changes.

By patterns of interaction, then, I mean the activities of interdependent people and these activities can be categorised in many different ways. For example, such patterns may take the form of routines as in the process and activity-based literature, but now they are thought of not as systems but as the patterns of activities of human persons iterated over time.

I will be arguing that a perspective along these lines forms a coherent way of thinking that directs attention to the narrative forms of human experience. The focus is on lived experience in local situations in the present, paying particular attention to the diversity of relationships within which individual and organisational identities emerge. The practical implication of such a move is that we focus attention directly on patterns of human relating and ask what kind of power relations, ideology and communication they reflect. We ask how themes such as planning or routines are becoming in ordinary daily life. We look beyond the already given, beyond the tools, to the ordinary, everyday nature of human interaction in organisations.

Further reading

The arguments presented in this chapter are explored in Stacey et al. (2000) and Stacey (2003, 2005). Also see Stacey (2009). Further information on the differences between Kantian and Hegelian thinking can be found in Ameriks (2002).

Questions to aid further reflection

1. What do the terms 'systemic process' and 'responsive processes' mean and what are the key distinctions between these notions?

2. How would you articulate different notions of process, practice and experience in human action generally and in organisational life in particular?

3. In what traditions of thought are the notions of systemic process and responsive processes located?

4. What does it mean to reason by analogy?

5. On what analogies with the complexity sciences does the notion of responsive processes draw?

6. What do the concepts of emergence and self-organisation mean to you and how would you take them up in thinking about human action?

7. Elias argued that change in societies is unplanned and emerges in the interplay of intentions. Would it make sense to think of organisations in the same way?

8. What difference would it make to thinking about the nature of organisations and the strategising of managers if you think in terms of responsive processes? For example, would it be possible for a leader to change the culture or values of an organisation?

9. In your own experience, can you trace out how what actually happens in organisations emerges in the interplay of many intentions?

Chapter 13

The emergence of organisational strategy in local communicative interaction
Complex responsive processes of conversation

This chapter invites you to draw on your own experience to reflect on and consider the implications of:

- Thinking of organisations not as things or systems but as dynamic patterns of relationships, good and bad, between people.

- Understanding patterns of relationships in terms of ordinary, everyday conversation between people in their local interaction with each other in which they form their intentions to act and make their choices.

- How the attributes of being human persons – consciousness, self-consciousness, spontaneity, emotion, aggression, choice – arise in the social conversation of gestures and what difference this makes to thinking about the activities of strategising in organisations.

- The difference between the sender–receiver model of communication found in the dominant discourse and the understanding of communication as conversation in the complex responsive processes perspective.

For more than 50 years now a vast literature on strategy and organisation has been explaining organising and strategising in a particular way and presenting prescriptions for success based on these explanations. This dominant discourse, described in Part 1 of this book, is based on the assumption that an organisation can be thought of as a system for which leaders and managers can more or less choose the strategic direction and/or design, influence or condition the process which will determine that direction. Over this period there has been an enormous expansion in management education delivered both by business schools and expensive training and development programmes for leaders and managers. The great majority of these educational programmes operate firmly within the dominant discourse. To present anything else is dismissed as theoretical as opposed to practical. Over much the same period there has been a significant, research-backed critique of the explanations and prescriptions of the dominant discourse, but this has not, by and large, questioned the fundamental assumptions of that discourse, nor has it dented the still common belief amongst organisational practitioners that they should be able to do what the dominant discourse prescribes even if they may not really be doing it properly yet. Although at first mainly confined to the private enterprise sector, over the past two decades this dominant discourse has now taken over public sector governance in the form of managerial systems to improve performance. This too has attracted criticism which has had very little effect in deflecting or modifying managerialist forms of governance. What is striking, however, is that after more than about 100 years of research (see Chapter 9), the approaches found in the dominant discourse have not delivered what they promise. Commercial organisations still fail as much as they did in the 1960s, or the 1860s for that matter, and the debates about public sector performance and the more and more frenetic calls for improvement are all replays of what one could hear in the 1960s. Limited research indicates that mergers and acquisitions do not fulfil their promise of improvement. It is widely known that culture change programmes, business process re-engineering, quality improvement programmes, and many others, come and go without producing what they promised. And yet commercial organisations have grown and proliferated, expanded across the globe and delivered ever more varied and advanced products and services as their activities have contributed to growing pollution and cultural clashes across the globe. In many countries, public sector services have expanded rapidly and increased in sophistication as healthcare and education become more widely available. It seems that improvement and deterioration come about at the same time, despite the huge question marks over the impact of the prescriptions of the dominant discourse. The question this raises for me has to do with the adequacy of dominant ways of thinking about what is happening. On the one hand, we have the surprising, unpredictable but recognisable, creative and destructive evolution of organisational life, and, on the other, we have a dominant way of thinking according to which it all ought to be happening in a stable, orderly and purely progressive way according to some leadership choices, otherwise it is all a matter of chance. I think the ideas presented in this chapter are important because they offer a way of escaping this dichotomy between order and disorder, predictability and unpredictability, choice and chance, and so provide a way of thinking about what people in organisations already do in all its creative and destructive aspects. This perspective does not present prescriptions for some new, more successful form of organisation. It is concerned with how we might *think* more usefully and more satisfyingly *about what we already do* in the knowledge that when we think differently we inevitably act differently, which may or may not improve matters.

13.1 Introduction

Chapter 12 suggested a move from systemic ways of thinking about organisations to one in which organisations are understood in terms of responsive processes of interaction between human persons. It drew on complexity sciences to suggest that we might think of organisations and their strategies as population-wide patterns that emerge in the interplay of local, responsive interaction. It was suggested that complex adaptive systems with heterogeneous agents could provide a source domain for analogies with human interaction, but that this would involve an interpretation grounded firmly in the attributes of human agents, such as consciousness, self-consciousness, spontaneity and choice. The purpose of this chapter is to carry out that task of interpretation using the work of Mead.

Mead (1934) argues cogently that human consciousness and self-consciousness emerge in the conversation of gestures. He holds that mind, self and society all arise simultaneously in the same social, conversational processes. His work, therefore, explains in detail how the attributes of being human arise in social interaction, so providing a way of interpreting the analogies from the complexity sciences as far as human action is concerned. It is in communicative interaction, in conversation with each other, that humans accomplish whatever it is that they accomplish. Organisation is conversation and organisation and strategy emerge as the patterning of conversation. Furthermore, in exploring the work of Mead, this chapter will be arguing that it is far more than organisational strategies which emerge in local conversational interactions – what also emerges is the ongoing iteration of the selves of the interdependent people who are members of the organisation.

If one adopts this approach, one comes to think about organisational communication and strategy in very different ways from the theories described in Part 1. Communication is understood as ongoing, responsive conversation, and strategy comes to be understood as the evolving patterns of individual and collective identities. Strategy is about what people in organisations do and who they are and this is exactly what identity means. Strategy is about the evolution of what people in an organisation do and how they become who they become. One then takes a very different position in the debates about: intention versus emergence and the meaning and consequences of organisational planning activities; macro (population-wide) versus micro (local) with its implications for top-down and bottom-up strategy processes; formulation (thought or theory) versus implementation (action or practice). Dominant ways of thinking about what it means to lead and control, to manage change and knowledge, to manage improvement in quality and performance, to design organisations and change values, are all brought into question. This chapter and the next three will outline the basis of this challenge; its implications will be dealt with more fully in Chapters 17 and 18.

An important general point about the responsive processes perspective to be explored in this and subsequent chapters is that *it is a way of thinking about what we already do*. It is not about prescribing what people ought to be doing or about labelling what they are doing as futile or foolish. The point is to try to understand and explain what we are already doing in an uncertain world of experience that we are creating in our interaction, some of which might look foolish and futile but may nevertheless be serving a purpose. The importance of a different way of thinking, a different explanation of what we are already doing, is not that it immediately leads to another prescription, but that it focuses attention on aspects of what we are doing together that have been invisible to us, especially that made invisible by determined efforts to be 'rational'. In focusing attention differently we may find ourselves doing things differently. So what does this chapter focus attention on that is not often taken seriously? It focuses on the ordinary, everyday local interactions, particularly conversational interactions, which are mostly ignored when talking about organisation and strategy and dismissed as 'just talk'. The purpose of this chapter is to focus on conversation as the basic activity of local interaction, leading in the next chapter to an exploration of the interplay of intentions, in which emerge population-wide patterns of relating called strategy. The claim is that conversation is *the* activity of organising. Organisational change is change in conversation.

This chapter now turns to complex responsive processes of human communication.

13.2 Human communication and the conversation of gestures: the social act

Mead (1934) proposed a way of thinking about communication which differed markedly from the cybernetic sender–receiver model discussed in Chapter 4. According to the latter model, a thought arises in one autonomous individual's mind which is encoded in language and transmitted to another autonomous individual who then decodes the language so that, when communication is good, the thought in one mind is transferred to the mind of another. If there is a gap between what was transmitted and what was received, then further transmissions are required to close the gap. Here meaning lies in the word – that is, in the vocal gesture of the one making the gesture; the part played by the receiver is simply one of translation until the same meaning is received as was transmitted. It becomes very important, then, to get the communication 'right'. This model is reflected in the dominant discourse when people in organisations talk about insufficient, good and bad communication. When people in organisations complain about poor communication they are usually thinking in these terms. In this model, communication begins with the sender and ends with the receiver, implying a linear view of time.

Mead, however, did not think in terms of a sender and a receiver. Instead he thought of one body making a gesture to another body where the gesture calls out, or evokes, a response from that other body. That response is itself a gesture back to the first body which, in turn, evokes a further response. What we have, then, is ongoing responsive processes, which Mead called *the conversation of gestures*, where beginnings and endings are purely arbitrary. The conversation of gestures is temporal, social processes in which the fundamental unit is the social act consisting of gesture and response, where these are phases of the social act and cannot be separated from each other, because together they constitute meaning in the following way.

Mead gave an example of a very simple act of communication between two dogs to explain this point about the social constitution of meaning. One dog makes the gesture of a snarl and this may call forth a counter-snarl, which means 'fight'; or the gesture could call forth flight, which means victory and defeat; or the response to the gesture could be crouching, which means submission and domination. Meaning, therefore, does not lie in the gesture alone but in the social act as a whole. In other words, meaning arises in the responsive interaction between actors; gesture and response can never be separated but must be understood as moments in one act. Meaning does not arise first in each individual, to be subsequently expressed in action, nor is it transmitted from one individual to another but, rather, it arises in the interaction between them. Meaning is not attached to an object, formed as a representation, or stored, as in cognitivism, but is created in the interaction. Immediately, knowing becomes an aspect of interaction, or relationship. Here meaning is emerging in the action of the living present (*see* Chapter 12) in which the immediate future (response) acts back on the past (gesture) to change its meaning. Meaning is not simply located in the past (gesture) or the future (response) but in the circular interaction between the two as the living present. In this way the present is not simply a point but has a time structure. Communication is then a social, relational process, so that poor communication means inadequate interaction.

The process of gesture and response between biological entities in a physical context constitutes simple cooperative, social activity of a mindless, reflex kind. At this stage, meaning is implicit in the social act itself and those acting are not conscious of that meaning.

Consciousness

For consciousness to arise, Mead argued that our mammal ancestors must have evolved central nervous systems that enabled them to gesture to others in a manner that was capable of calling forth in themselves the same range of responses as in those to whom they were gesturing. His hypothesis has been borne out by much research into the functioning of the brain (Damasio, 1994, 1999) and by the identification of 'mirror neurons' (Gallese, 2001), as well as by research into the behaviour of primates, particularly apes (de Waal, 2006). Mead held that a gesture would evoke a response in the gesture to that evoked in the responder if, for example, the snarl of one called forth in itself the fleeting feelings associated with counter-snarl, flight or submissive posture, just as they did in the one to whom the gesture was being made. The gesture now has a substantially different role. Mead described such a gesture as a *significant symbol*, one that calls forth the same response in the gesturer as in the one to whom it is directed. Significant symbols, therefore, make it possible for the gesturer to 'know' what he or she is doing. If, when one makes a gesture to another, one is able to experience in one's own body a similar response to that which the gesture provokes in another body, then one can 'know' what one is doing.

Possessing this capacity, the maker of a gesture can intuit, anticipate and to some extent predict the consequences of that gesture. In other words, he or she can know what he or she is doing, just before the other responds. The whole social act – that is, meaning – can be experienced in advance of carrying out the whole act, opening up the possibility of reflection and choice in making a gesture. Furthermore, the one responding has the same opportunity for reflecting upon, and so choosing, from the range of responses. The first part of a gesture can be taken by the other as an indication of how further parts of the gesture will unfold from the response. In this way, the two can indicate to each other how they might respond to each other in the continuous circle in which a gesture by one calls forth a response from another, which is itself a gesture back to the first.

As individuals interact with each other in this way, the possibility arises of a pause before making a gesture. In a kind of private role-play, emerging in the repeated experience of public interaction, one individual learns to take the attitude of the other, enabling a kind of trial run in advance of actually completing or even starting the gesture. Will it call forth aggression, fright, flight or submission? What will be the consequences in each case? In this way, *rudimentary forms of thinking develop, taking the form of private role-playing*: that is, gestures made by a body to itself, calling forth responses in itself. Mead said that humans are fundamentally role-playing animals.

Consciousness, therefore, arises in interaction, and the body, with its nervous system, becomes central to understanding how we 'know' anything. I want to stress how Mead is arguing that individual human consciousness, mind, arises in the social act, in communicative interaction, so that there cannot be the one without the other.

Language

Mead then argued that the gesture that is particularly useful in calling forth the same attitude in oneself as in the other is the vocal gesture. This is because we can hear the sounds we make in much the same way as others hear them, while we cannot see the facial gestures we make as others see them, for example. The development of more sophisticated patterns of vocal gesturing – that is, of the language form of significant symbols – is thus of major importance in the development of consciousness and of sophisticated forms of society. Mind and society emerge together in the medium of language. However, since speaking and listening are actions of bodies, and since bodies are never without feelings, the medium of language is also always a medium of feelings.

As soon as one can take the attitude, the tendency to act, of the other – that is, as soon as one communicates in significant symbols – there is at least a rudimentary form of consciousness. The nature of the social has thus shifted from mindless co-operation through functional specialisation to mindful, role-playing interaction made more and more sophisticated by the use of language as silent conversation with oneself. Meaning is now particularly constituted in gesturing and responding in the medium of vocal symbols, but these vocal symbols are always aspects of a process that always includes the 'symbols' of feeling. Mind, or consciousness, is the gesturing and responding action of a body directed towards itself as private role-play and silent conversation, and society is the gesturing and responding actions of bodies directed towards each other. They are thus the same kind of process.

It is important to note here that the conversational processes of communication described by Mead are not some kind of social determinism and they do not function in some perfect manner. Although I have the physiological potential for calling forth in myself similar responses to my gestures as those evoked in others, there is no guarantee that I will 'get it right', certainly not at the first attempt. This is because there is no fixed causal connection between my gesture and the response evoked in you, which is why Mead's theory is not a form of social determinism. There is no fixed causal connection, because at the same time as your response is evoked by my gesture it is also selected by you in a manner that reflects your experience of a lifetime of interacting with others. Although I may be able to anticipate something of the kind of response you may make, I can never be sure because I can never know your life history in full and, even if I could, there is always the possibility of some surprising, spontaneous response from you. Furthermore, the response that my gesture to you evokes in me is also, at the same time, selected by my own lifetime of experience so that what is evoked in me may have to do more with me than with you. The possibility for miscommunication is thus substantial and can only be dealt with in ongoing conversation as we try together to clarify what we mean. This is not a cybernetic feedback process, as in the sender–receiver model, but an ongoing, conversational negotiation of meaning.

Comparison with the sender–receiver model of communication

Mead's mode of communication is thus profoundly different from the sender–receiver one. The sender–receiver model encourages us to believe that good communication will enable us to 'get it right'. So if I translate my thought clearly into language, if there is no 'noise' in transmission caused, for example, by distorting emotions, and if you translate my clear words clearly into thought, then our communication will be good. Or if the communication does not succeed at first then 'feedback' from the receiver will enable the sender to provide a more precise communication. On this view, a leader or manager who is a good communicator will be able to send a message to all the members of an organisation and they will immediately understand it. However, people in organisations frequently complain that communication is not good enough and the response is to blame the sender or the receiver. This leads to a call for improvement in communication skills, involving the development of language and presentational skills and of detached attitudes to objective communication. This, it is believed, will lead to improved communication in an organisation. In terms of strategy it then becomes important to formulate clear plans and communicate them clearly so that people will implement them. Implementation problems are frequently blamed on poor communication.

However, in Mead's model of communication, when I make a gesture to a number of people, I can rely on its calling forth many different responses from others, all of whom have different life histories. Since the meaning does not lie in my words alone but emerges in the words and the responses they evoke in others taken together, it follows that I can only know the meaning of what I say in your responses to them. There is no point in blaming you, or your blaming me, because we are having to carry on exploring just what it is we mean – this is the very nature of communication. Sending me for training in communication skills can, therefore, have only a very limited effect in terms of improving the communication between us, because you are implicated too. From this alternative perspective on communication it is no use for a leader, or manager, to imagine that they have sent a clear message and leave it at that. Communication ceases to be a one-off event that someone can get right and becomes instead an ongoing conversational process in which meaning is being clarified and, in the course of such clarification, is actually evolving in potentially novel ways. From this perspective, one can no longer think of the strategic plan as a one of communication which must be got right. Instead, one comes to see the activities of strategising as ongoing conversational processes, essentially involving emotion and fantasy, as well as reason and all the other aspects of conversation.

I think leaders, managers and others will act differently with regard to communication and communication skills training if they take this different perspective on communication.

The generalised other

Mead takes his argument further when he suggests how the private role-play/silent conversation of mind evolves in increasingly complex ways. As more and more interactions are experienced with others, so more roles and wider ranges of possible responses enter into the role-playing/silent conversational activities that precede the gesture, or to be more accurate, are continuously intertwined with public/vocal gesturing and responding. In this way the capacity to take the attitude of many others evolves and this becomes generalised. Each engaged in the conversation of gestures can now take the attitude of what Mead calls the *generalised other*. Eventually, individuals develop the capacity to take the attitude of the whole group, or what Mead calls the game or the social attitude. The whole of society, in a generalised form, then enters the mental processes of each interdependent person. In a fundamentally important way, this constitutes a powerful form of social control through self-control. The result is much more sophisticated processes of cooperative interaction. There is now mindful social behaviour with increasingly sophisticated forms of cooperation. The next chapter will continue with the exploration of the nature of the generalised other, while the rest of this chapter looks at how Mead explains self-consciousness and then considers further points on the nature of conversational activity in organisations.

Processes of self

In understanding self-consciousness Mead talked about processes in which a person takes the attitude, the tendency to act, of the generalised other, or the group, to himself as an 'I', where that attitude is the 'me'. It is important to bear in mind that Mead was saying something more than that the self arises in the attitude, the tendency to act, of specific others towards oneself. Mead was talking about social, generalising processes where the 'me' is generalised tendencies across a whole community or society to act to me as a person. For example, what it means to be an individual, a person, a man or a woman, a professional, and so on, does not arise in relation to a few specific people but in relation to a particular society in a particular era. We in the West think of ourselves now as individuals in a completely different way from how people in the West thought of themselves four hundred years ago and in a different way from people in other cultures. In what Mead called the 'I–me' dialectic, then, we have *processes* in which the generalising of the 'me' is made particular in the responses of the 'I' for a particular person, at a particular time, in a particular place. For example, I may take up what it means to be a man in my society in a particular way that differs in some respects from how others see themselves as men in my own society, in other societies and at other times.

What is happening here is the linking of the attitude of generalised other, of the whole group, organisation or society, with a 'me' in becoming an object to oneself. The 'me' is one's perception of, one's feelings towards, the configuration of the gestures–responses of the others/society to one as a subject, or an 'I'. A self, as the ongoing relationship between 'me' and 'I', as well as an awareness of that self – that is, self-consciousness – emerges in a life history of social interaction, which includes organisational interaction, and continues to evolve throughout life. Mead argues, very importantly, that the responses of the 'I' to one's perception of the attitude of the group to oneself (the 'me') are not givens but are always potentially unpredictable in that there is no predetermined way in which the 'I' might respond to the 'me'. In other words, each of us may respond in many different ways to our perception of the views that others have of us. Mead's argument, therefore, is not a form of social determinism, because the possibility of individual spontaneity means that the response of the 'I' is not given. The response is simultaneously called forth by the gesture of the generalised other and selected or enacted by the responder on the basis of past history reconstructed as the present, always with the possibility of spontaneous variation. In other words, the response of the 'I' is both being called forth by the other and being enacted, or selected by the history, biological, individual and social of the responder. Society's gesture, as 'me', calls forth an 'I' response, but only a response I am capable of making and that depends upon my history. There is a tension of movement in the response, a tension of selection/enactment and evocation/provocation at the same time. The process is one of emergence in which the future of my self is being perpetually constructed and it does not ultimately locate the source of personal change in the individual alone.

Mead's concept of the 'I' is sometimes interpreted as the spontaneous impulse of the body (Joas, 2000). However, in complex responsive processes terms, the 'I' is no less social than the 'me' simply because they cannot be separated from each other. The dialectical 'I–me' process evolves – it has a history. This means that in any present, the 'I' response reflects a history of social engagement. It is the capacity for imagination and reflection that brings small differences in the 'I' response to the 'me' gesture from one present to another and it is the amplifying propensity of nonlinear interaction that escalates these small differences into transformations of the self.

It is essential, if we are to understand the important point Mead makes, not to split the 'I' and the 'me'. They are inseparable phases of one act. The self then is understood as an ongoing activity, an ongoing temporal process of 'I' responding to 'me'. It is not that there is a true self called 'I' which is seen in the mirror of the social 'me' or that the 'I' engages in some kind of conversation with the 'me' as the voices of other people. In Mead's formulation there is no given, true self. Instead a self is continually iterated, continually emerges in interaction with others and oneself. This self is truly social through and through (Foulkes, 1948). Mead is not denying unique individuality but explaining how such uniqueness emerges in social processes of interaction. What he is clearly denying is any notion of an autonomous self. Elias said much the same when he claimed that the individual was the singular of interdependent people while the social was the plural.

The social, in human terms, is highly sophisticated processes of cooperative and competitive interaction between people in the medium of symbols in order to undertake joint action. Such sophisticated interaction could not take place without self-conscious minds but neither could those self-conscious minds exist without that sophisticated form of cooperation. In other words, there could be no private role-play, including silent conversation, by a body with itself, if there was no public interaction of the same form. Mind/self and society are all logically equivalent processes of a conversational kind. The result is self-referential, reflexive processes of sophisticated cooperation and competition in the medium of symbols that constitute meaning. These processes, always involving the body and its feelings, both enable and constrain human actions. All of these interactions, private and public, are processes in which humans act within a physical, non-human environment using tools and technology in a cooperative manner. In so acting within the context, humans affect that context, which simultaneously affects them, enabling them to do what they do, and constraining them from doing other things. Individual selves/minds emerge between people, in the relationship between them, and cannot be simply 'located' within an individual. In this way of thinking, individual minds/ selves certainly exist, and very importantly so, but they emerge in relationships between people as iterated processes rather than arising within an individual. The notion of conceptual space with a mind inside a person and society outside is completely avoided in this way of thinking.

What relevance does this view of mind and self have for organisations and the activities of strategising? Organisations and the work activities of their members are social activities which play a very important part in the lives of all of their members. Organisations are ongoing patterns of relating between people in which their very minds and selves are sustained and continue to evolve in important ways. If one thinks in this way then it becomes very difficult to regard people in organisations as *its* 'human resources', on the one hand, or as autonomous individuals for whom the organisation should provide special opportunities for their self-actualisation, on the other. People's selves are sustained and evolve in the ordinary, everyday work activities they undertake in their local interactions with each other. Changes in hierarchical reporting structures, divisional or subsidiary company groupings, procedures for accountability, control systems, objectives and targets, performance appraisal systems, to name but a few, will all have implications for how people experience their selves. Changes in how one experiences one's self are bound to be highly emotional and anxiety provoking and this is highly likely to lead to responses which are difficult to understand and may even seem to be bizarre. There are many practical questions which this view raises for managing change and managing people which I will return to later in this chapter and in Chapter 14. First, however, consider a further development of Mead's argument.

Having set out Mead's basic theory of human consciousness and self-consciousness as social processes of conversation, we now turn to a more detailed exploration of ordinary conversation in organisations.

13.3 Ordinary conversation in organisations

Ethnomethodologists (Garfinkel, 1967; Goffman, 1981) study the finely ordered detail of local interaction, including an analysis of the detailed flow of ordinary conversation (Jefferson, 1978; Sacks, 1992; Shegloff, 1991).

The turn-taking/turn-making nature of conversation

Conversation analysts have used recordings of ordinary conversations to build up a picture of how conversation is patterned and how it produces orderly interactions between people. What they point to, as the fundamental organising principle of conversation, is the process of turn taking. Turn taking is at the heart of all social activity in that it establishes a temporal and spatial location for social interaction. From it flows the back-and-forth rhythm of social relationships. Turn taking

> creates the rhythms of daily life, from the formal, public rituals and ceremonies of ancient religions and national states to the most intimate of human intercourse.   (Boden, 1994, p. 66)

Sacks' (1992) research pointed to the way in which turns to speak are valued, distributed across speakers, competed for, abandoned and held on to. Turn taking is, thus, one of the important ways in which power differentials are established and sustained in conversations, very much a reflection of the processes to which Elias points (*see* Chapters 12 and 15). Turn-taking processes are self-referential as participants respond to each other in a back-and-forth way with reference to their own histories and the history of the communities they are embedded in. The response of one calls forth a further response from another, in turn calling forth a response from the first, always simultaneously selected on the basis of the life histories of all involved. The processes of turn taking are also reflexive processes since who takes turns reflects each person's individual history and the history of the community they are members of.

There is no objective position external to the conversation from which someone can control, shape, influence or condition the conversational processes of turn taking and turn making. All are participants and none of them can get outside the conversation, observe it and control it, at least without destroying its very nature as ordinary, everyday conversation. Each participant can, of course, reflect on the emerging pattern of the conversation and its turn-taking, turn-making processes, but each reflection is always itself an activity within the ongoing conversation. Elias (1987) drew a distinction between *involved* and *detached* participation. By involved he meant highly emotional, rather unaware participation and by detached he meant a less emotional, more aware, more reflective participation. He also made clear that neither form of participation is ever encountered in pure form. Conversational participation is always a paradox of involved detachment or detached involvement where the emphasis may shift from more to less detachment or involvement, but never completely. The point is that there is no process external to the conversation. Anyone's influence can only be exerted through participating in the conversation in some involved–detached way. There is no possibility of the doubling of process from this perspective (*see* Chapters 8 and 12).

Furthermore, conversational processes are ones of local interaction in the sense that each participant is acting on his or her own local organising themes. This local interaction produces emergent patterns of meaning for participants in the sense that there is no blueprint for that meaning. I am suggesting, then, that conversations are complex responsive processes. Speakers take turns which are organised by certain principles that have themselves emerged out of the history of interaction in the community to which the speakers belong.

The principles of turn taking have to do with how one person speaks at a time; how it may, or may not, be permissible to interrupt or talk over others; how the number and order of speakers varies; how turn sizes vary; how turn transition is accomplished; what kind of gaps and overlaps occur in turn taking; how the turns themselves are allocated. These organising principles evolve, and so come to differ from one historical period to another and from one locality to another. For example, in many organisations the most senior executive is automatically granted more and longer turns than anyone else, and in others one may notice that men take more turns than women.

Sacks and others have also pointed to the manner in which turns tend to be organised into what they call 'adjacent pairs'. So conversational exchanges may be organised into greeting–greeting, question–answer, invitation–acceptance (rejection), summons–answer, request–response and so on. Speakers create turns with recipients in mind and listeners are motivated to hear their turn, all in local interaction. Speakers tend to pursue a response until they are acknowledged, and those being addressed are under pressure to respond to the meaning emerging between them. This requirement to respond does not mean that grammatical sentences are always used. In fact, ordinary conversation is characterised by grunts, other noises such as 'mm', pauses and fragments of sentences. The listener is thus co-creating the meaning by a constructive process of filling in. The result is the highly associative nature of ordinary, everyday conversation.

Boden talks about different kinds of conversation:

> From the basic elements of conversational turn taking, what Sacks and his collaborators proposed was that other speech exchange systems such as meetings, classrooms, interviews, debates, and even the most ritual of ceremonies would span a kind of continuum. The central differences between casual, freely occurring conversation and the kinds of exchanges listed depend primarily upon such issues as: allocation and duration of turns, selection and order of potential speakers, and designation and order of topic, as well as a specific method for ensuring that each speaker is heard and that discussion does not break down into mini conversations. In meetings and on conference calls, the structuring methods of turn-taking are indeed modified . . . but the core of organizational communication remains this simple, reciprocal and self organizing system.
>
> (Boden, 1994, pp. 72–3)

In their sophisticated, associative turn taking, participants in conversation co-create meaningful patterns over time which can be described as themes.

The thematic patterning of ordinary conversation

Each member of a group has his or her own personal organising themes that have been taken up in the silent conversation, or mind, of that individual. They reflect his or her own personal history of relations with, and between, others in the community he or she lives in. As soon as members of a group meet each other, they all actively, albeit largely unconsciously, select, and so organise, their own subjective experience of being in that place, with those people, at that time. However, what those particular themes are at that particular moment will depend just as much on the cues being presented by others as upon the personal history of a particular individual. Each is simultaneously evoking and provoking responses from others so that the particular personal organising themes emerging will depend as much on the others as on the individual concerned. Furthermore, since everyone is also, largely unconsciously, taking the attitude of the generalised other in all their interactions, particular organising themes of individuals also depend on the wider communities of which they are members. Put like this, it becomes clear that no one individual can be organising his or her experience in isolation, because all are simultaneously evoking and provoking responses in each other and simultaneously taking up the attitude of the generalised other. Together they immediately constitute intersubjective, recursive processes. These are continuous back-and-forth circular processes in which themes emerge that organise the experience of being together out of which further themes continuously emerge.

Relationships between people in a group can then be defined as continuously iterated patterns of *intersubjective themes that organise the experience of being together*. These themes emerge, in variant and invariant forms, out of the interaction between group members as they organise that very interaction. I want to stress, however, that I am not suggesting that these themes are disembodied interactions. Although the themes emerge between people, and therefore cannot be located 'inside' any individual, the experience is nevertheless always a bodily one. I am suggesting, then, that both personal and group themes always arise between people in a community, but are always at the same time experienced in individual bodies as changes, marked or subtle, in the feeling tones of those bodies.

From this perspective, themes interact in many, many local situations in which patterns of relating continuously emerge both locally and across populations. These patterns are changes in the themes organising local interaction as group members seek to negotiate with, and respond to, each other in some way as members of a community. The patterns of organising themes are continually iterated in self-referential, reflexive ways.

Another important point to be made here about organising themes is that they arise in a particular place at a particular time. The bodies interacting with each other in a group are located in a wider context of a community and a society that has a history. This means that the group/individual themes are resonating with wider themes that organise the experience of being in a community and a society at a particular point in its history. The themes arising in a particular group, at a particular time, will thus be influenced by the figuration of power relations in the wider grouping (*see* Chapter 15). They will also reflect the pattern of control over economic resources and, therefore, the material, technological and physical nature of the place at a particular historical moment.

So, organising themes are continuously arising in the interaction between people, while simultaneously being experienced in their bodies, located in a particular community, in a particular place, at a particular point in the history of the community and the group. Note that this is very different from saying that members of a group share the values of the community and the society in which they are located. It is saying that at a particular time there will be salient themes organising the experience of being together in a community. They will evoke themes organising the experience of being together in a particular group. The theme evoked in the group might be quite different from group to group. For example, a theme organising the experience of being together in a community might have to do with condemning asylum seekers. Groups of established residents and groups of asylum seekers in the community will not be sharing a common theme. However, each group will be responding to the same theme in a different way.

The thematic patterning nature of ordinary, everyday conversation can be very easily seen by asking a group of people to play a word game. One member of the group is asked to start with any word he or she chooses and the others are asked to respond. What always happens is this. One word almost always triggers a response, usually by association, from another person and that response triggers yet another and so on. Within a very short time, a theme emerges. For example, the theme may have to do with the weather, with body parts, with places, with moods, or whatever. Some people may try to break the associative links, and if they succeed another theme begins to emerge. Even when people try very hard not to associate but to keep breaking the links, it turns out to be rather difficult to keep it going. This is exactly what happens in ordinary conversation: a theme emerges and the talk swirls around this theme, until some remark triggers the emergence of some other theme. The dynamic, the pattern of movement over time, has the paradoxical characteristics of regularity and irregularity at the same time. What themes will emerge and how they will change are not predictable. However, there are coherent themes, order, even though there is no plan or blueprint for them. And the themes do not come about by chance. They emerge in what people are doing and not doing both intentionally and unconsciously.

Intention

Intention is a communication between people, and like any other communication it is expressed in conversation. It is a particular kind of theme and it organises experience just as any other theme does. Intentional themes may also be expressed explicitly or implicitly in a narrative themes (*see* Chapter 16). All of these intentional themes are gestures that provoke or evoke responses in others. Those articulating the intention then find that these responses, in turn, evoke or provoke responses from them and they will not be able to know in advance just how these responses, and response to responses, will evolve. The theories of strategic choice and organisational learning, as well as psychoanalytic perspectives on organisations, take intention for granted. They assume that the formation of an intention is the starting point of action, as thought before action. Intention is not problematic. People simply decide as autonomous individuals because of an innate capacity to do so. However, when one comes to regard intention as a theme that organises the experience of being together, it becomes clear that intentions emerge in relationships just as any other organising themes do. Intention, then, emerges in the conversational life of a group of people. A single individual does not simply 'have' an intention. Rather the intention an individual expresses has emerged in the conversational interaction with others. Intention and choice are not lonely acts but themes organised by, and organising, relationships at the same time. Everything that everyone does, or does not do, matters in what is always local conversational interaction. So what are we doing and not doing in organisational conversation?

Rhetoric

Shotter (1993) talks about experience being organised in what he calls the rhetorical-responsive conversations of ordinary, everyday life. What he means by this is that people continually account for themselves to each other. They continually respond to what others are doing and try to persuade others to take the position they want. This conversational activity organises experience. Shotter explores how groups of people come to a more articulate grasp of their practices from within their ongoing conduct of them. Shotter and Katz (1997) talk about a relational-responsive form of understanding between people in their ordinary everyday conversation. In their ordinary forms of language they:

> deconstruct the routine links and relations between things once constructed and then taken for granted. In this way, new possibilities are revealed. People do this in the directive use of words: by saying 'Look at that', 'Look at this', people can lead others and themselves to notice important features of their circumstances. In ordinary conversation, people arrest or interrupt each other in order to deconstruct and destabilise so that they can make new distinctions and so create new knowledge. They also use analogies, metaphors, and other ways of making comparisons to develop new ways of talking. It is in talk like this that people are moved.
>   (Shotter and Katz, 1997, p. 5)

Here Shotter is pointing to the *rhetorical* nature of ordinary conversation. This is a very important point: new knowledge can emerge in ordinary, everyday conversation as people go on together and seek to persuade and negotiate with each other. As mentioned in Chapter 7, Samra-Fredericks (2003), arguing in the emerging tradition of activity-based strategy, has drawn on Shotter's work and on an analysis of the conversational activity of strategising to indicate how the rhetorical skills of the strategiser are key to the influence exerted.

Rhetoric is the art of persuasion and Springett (1998) categorises rhetorical ploys as follows:

- Those that influence the direction of conversation. Under this heading, he includes statements that invoke a sense of purpose, as when someone says, 'these are *the* objectives'. Then there are silencing moves such as not responding to a point made but rapidly raising another. There are also moves that block a direction, such as 'this is really Stone Age stuff'. Some moves contract the line of conversation, such as 'let's concentrate on the key points'. Other moves expand the line of conversation, such as 'there must be other ways to think about this'. Yet other moves give emphasis, such as 'this is the way we must go'.

- Those that provide frames of reference. This takes place when someone uses other companies as examples of the successful application of their ideas.

- Those that make claims to be the truth, such as 'the latest research shows', or 'customers feel'.

- Those that destabilise, such as 'Does that really add anything?'

- Those that influence beliefs about what is real and possible. Examples are making the intangible seem tangible, such as talking about a merger as a 'marriage', referring to a company as if it were a person and using statements like 'let me walk you through this'. Another example is a move that implies pre-existence, such as talking about unlocking a company's potential.

- Those that construct urgency, such as 'there is a short time window'.

The point is this: without even being aware of it, people in ordinary conversation may be using conversational devices to dismiss the opinions of others and close down the development of a conversation in an exploratory direction. If this way of talking to each other is widespread in an organisation, it will inevitably keep reproducing the same patterns of talk. The use of some rhetorical device is, therefore, one of the most important blockages to fluid conversation and thus to the emergence of new knowledge. Other rhetorical devices, however, could have the effect of freeing these blockages. The use of rhetorical devices is thus of major importance in influencing what people talk about and do. This is how strategy happens and what change is about.

Conversation, strategy and change

Shaw (2002) draws attention to the importance of ordinary conversations in organisations as the processes in which change emerges. In such ordinary conversations, what is being talked about is often unclear in many respects and the lack of clarity is the very reason for having the conversation. We come to know what we are talking about from within the development of the conversation itself, even when a topic has been agreed in advance. Shaw argues that ordinary conversations do not take the form of one person saying something, others listening in order to understand what is said, and then formulating a response. Instead, people speak into one another's responses, so responsively shaping what they say in the very process of conversing. When people understand what they are doing in conversation as clarifying information, reaching shared understandings, developing orderly agreements and plans and capturing outputs, they lose awareness of the ongoing mutually constructive nature of what they are doing together. Shaw argues that the widespread demand that management meetings should be carefully planned and prepared actually kills the spontaneity of ordinary conversation in which new meaning can emerge. She points out how consultants and managers try to agree, in advance of starting a conversation, on the ground rules for good communication, such as listening carefully, respecting the views of others, suspending judgements and surfacing assumptions. The result is a set of idealised rules that change the nature of the conversation and limit its ordinary spontaneity.

As a consultant, Shaw seeks to foster fluid, more spontaneous conversation through the way in which she participates in ordinary conversations in organisations. She does not decide in advance what role she is going to take at a meeting. Instead, she joins the meeting and leaves unspecified what the rules of interaction should be. After the meeting she does not try to abstract what had been learned, nor does she make summaries and action plans to provide feedback to anyone anywhere. She argues that as people continue to meet and talk with others in other settings they will remember what was relevant in previous conversations. She does all this to avoid the rigidity that people impose on meetings in organisations and to restore something of the ordinary spontaneity of conversation.

What Shaw is drawing attention to is those aspects of processes of change that are excluded in orderly accounts of organisation change initiatives. She is drawing attention to the importance of ordinary conversation in processes of change, and such ordinary conversation is characterised by random as well as intended encounters. As people go about conversing in an ordinary manner, they purposefully make connections with others but often without a set of clearly defined objectives. They participate in situations where they have only an incomplete grasp of what is happening. In doing this ordinary process of relating, they are forming and trans-forming, they are perpetually constructing their future in the living present.

The point, then, is that whatever people do is accomplished in local con-versational interaction which always has some thematic pattern that organises the experience of being together. Themes trigger other themes that trigger yet others in repetitive ways that often have some potential for transformation given that any small difference from one iteration to another could be escalated into a different theme. In talking about ordinary conversation in this way, I am saying something about the dynamics of conversation, that is, the patterns of movement over time.

13.4 The dynamics of conversation

As argued above, the thematic patterning of conversation is iterated over time as both repetition and *potential* transformation at the same time. However, this potential need not always be realised. When it is not, the themes emerging in and organising the conversation become highly repetitive and, when this happens, conversation loses its lively, energising characteristics as a group of people may get stuck in repetitive, emotionally dulling exchanges (Foulkes, 1948). Change can only emerge in fluid forms of conversation. However, it is important to understand that fluid conversation is not some pure form of polar opposition to repetition. Rather, 'fluid' conversation refers to thematic pattering, which is paradoxically repetitive and spontaneously transforming at the same time. The repetitive aspects of conver-sational patterning promote continuity, imparting the stability to social relations required to enable people to go on together. This kind of stability is what is meant by the term 'social structure'.

Social structure is usually defined as the repetitive and enduring patterns of recur-ring relations between people in their ongoing dealings with each other. Examples of social structures are economic phenomena such as patterns of relationships between the owners of capital and the providers of labour. Markets are patterns of relationships between suppliers and demanders of goods and services and as such constitute social structures. Other examples of social structures are state and government functions; legal relationships; technological development; the family; religious practices; language; demography. Institutions and social structures are characterised by repetition and endurance reflected in widely accepted discourses. Organisations may be thought of as institutions with a significant element of formal description of roles, relationships between members and the tasks they perform. Closely linked to the ideas of social structure, institutions and organisations are the notions of habits, customs, traditions, routines, mores, norms, values, cultures, paradigms, beliefs, missions and visions. These are all ideas about the repetitive, enduring practices of people in their ongoing dealings with each other in institu-tional life.

From a complex responsive processes perspective, these are all social acts of a particular kind. They are couplings of gesture and response of a predictable, repeti-tive kind. They do not exist in any meaningful way as a thing in a store or artefact anywhere. Social habits and routines, values and beliefs are emerging aspects of the thematic patterning of interaction between people. Habits here are understood not as shared mental contents but as history-based, repetitive communicative inter-actions, both private and public, reproduced in the living present with relatively little variation. They are aspects of the continually iterated interactions between people. In other words, they are habitual themes organising the experience of being together. However, even habits are rarely exactly the same. They may often vary as the contexts and participants in interactions change. In other words, there will usu-ally be some spontaneous variation in the repetitive reproduction of patterns called 'habits' and it is this that creates the *potential* for transformation. An important factor sustaining habitual, repetitive conversation, one which blocks more fluid, spontaneous conversation, is anxiety.

Anxiety

Anxiety is a generalised form of fear. While fear has a known cause, anxiety is a very unpleasant feeling of general unease, the cause of which cannot be located. Chapter 6 on psychoanalytic perspectives reviewed the important contribution that these perspectives make to an understanding of the organisational effects of anxiety. First, there are the defences people use to avoid feeling anxious. These may take the form of structures and procedures having the ostensible purpose of enabling some rational task, but actually operating as defences. For example, people may prepare forecasts of future states that are impossible to predict and develop strategic plans on the basis of these forecasts. Such plans may then have little impact on what is actually done but, by creating a sense of certainty, they defend people against the anxiety of feeling uncertain. The result is stable, repetitive conversational dynamics around strategies that are simply a continuation of what is already being done. An alternative form of defence is what Bion (1961) called *basic assumption behaviour*. Here people in groups are overwhelmed by volatile fight, flight, dependence and other dynamics that disable their thinking capacity. Conversations are organised by fantasy themes that produce highly unrealistic conversational stability or con-versational disintegration. The former are present when the basic assumption is dependence and the latter when it takes the form of fight–flight.

Chapter 6 also introduced the important psychoanalytic concept of 'good enough holding'. Here conditions are such that people are able to live with the simultan-eous excitement and anxiety of conversations that test the boundary of what they know. The 'good enough holding' of anxiety is an essential condition for the fluid, spontaneous conversational dynamics that are the analogue of the edge of chaos. I suggest that 'good enough holding' is a quality of the themes organising the experi-ence of relating. When these take the form of trusting interaction, they are them-selves then forms of 'good enough holding' that enable people to live with anxiety. In other words, when the quality of relating is characterised by trust, conversation can take more fluid forms. This interpretation of 'good enough holding' differs from the psychoanalytic interpretation in that it does not locate the 'good enough' in a leader or a consultant (Stapley, 1996), but in the quality of conversational inter-action itself.

Closely related to the 'good enough holding' of anxiety is the matter of the qual-ity of power relations (*see* Chapter 15). Themes organising relating between people may be highly constraining so that power relations have the qualities of force, authoritarianism, dictatorship, and so forth. The responses that these qualities evoke are either submission or rebellion. The former produce highly repetitive, stable conversational patterns, while the latter produce disintegration in communication. Sometimes, the themes organising the relating between people impose very little constraint. This is equivalent to saying that relational ties are very weak and, therefore, patterns of conversation are likely to be disrupted. The conversational dynamics are disintegrative. It is a critical range that is associated with fluid conversation, this time a critical range in the constraining qualities of relating.

The crucial distinction I am making here is that between more fluid conversation and patterns of conversation that take on a repetitive, stuck form. This is crucial, because it is only in the former that potential creativity – that is, emergent new patterns of conversation, lies. A healthy, functioning organisation is one in which its members continually respond to each other and to members of other organisations – they provoke and evoke responses from others and react to the provocations and evocations of others so as to survive in an uncertain world of experience. For this to happen, communication must flow freely and not get caught in repetitive themes. This means that the themes organising experience must interact so as to flow continually along new pathways. An ailing organisation is one in which communication is blocked.

The capacity for emergent new ways of talking is fundamental to organisational creativity. This being so, it is a matter of considerable strategic importance to pay attention to the dynamics of ordinary conversation. The purpose of this attention is not to control the conversation or somehow produce efficient forms of it, but to understand it so as to participate more effectively. The dynamics of more fluid, spontaneous conversation rely on enough trust and ability to live with anxiety, as well as power relations that are both co-operative and competitive at the same time and rhetorical conversational practices that do not block exploration. Key questions become: what conversational practices block fluid, exploratory conversations? What practices trap groups of people in highly repetitive conversations?

13.5 Leaders and the activities of strategising

So far, this chapter has argued that organisations are patterns of interaction between interdependent persons. Processes of human interaction are fundamentally conversational in nature. Not only do people accomplish and change their joint activities in these processes, their very identities are sustained and potentially transformed in them too. Conversational dynamics in organisations are thus of primary importance. Whether such conversational dynamics take the form of stuck, repetitive patterns or of more fluid, spontaneous ones depends upon the nature of power relations between people, the way they find it possible to deal with the inevitable anxieties of organisational life and the conversational practices, particular rhetorical practices, they have evolved together. Repetitive conversations block the emergence of innovative strategies, while more fluid forms of conversation create the possibility but by no means the guarantee that creative strategies will emerge. The activity of strategising is also, on this view, fundamentally conversational.

A particular view of the role of leader follows from the claim that creative organisational strategies are more likely to emerge in more fluid, spontaneous forms of conversation. Instead of understanding the role of leadership purely in terms of directing and exhorting followers, one comes to see leadership in perhaps humbler but no less skilful or important terms. Given the power relation of the leader to others, he or she is in a particularly well-placed position to create opportunities for conversation that may foster greater spontaneity. Such spontaneity is likely to be fostered through the manner in which the leader handles a situation, encouraging others to create and shape the situation rather than simply giving instructions. The founder of group analysis, Foulkes (1964) took the view that it was the primary role of the therapy group conductor to deepen and widen communication in the group through the manner of his or her participation in the group. What Foulkes has to say could just as easily be applied to leaders in other situations where it is important to help create fluid forms of conversation. Foulkes called upon the leader to apply the

> minimum of instructions, of program or of rules, and maximum of freedom in self expression, a maximum of active participation in what is going on. The keynote . . . is informality and spontaneity of contributions which leads to what I have described as 'free-floating discussion'. The conductor gives a minimum of instructions and there are no set topics, no planning. While he is in the position of a leader, he is sparing with leading the group actively. He weans the group from wanting to be led – a desire which is all too strong – from looking upon him as an authority for guidance. (Foulkes, 1964, p. 40)

This situation promotes active participation that awakens interest and communication in an atmosphere enabling people to search for meaning for themselves. The group provides support by sharing anxiety, and the leader lets his or her own contributions come in response to the members of the group. The leader is a participant, whose aim is to encourage others towards taking responsibility. He or she resists the inevitable idealisation of the leader and seeks to replace submission with co-operation and explorative conflict. For Foulkes, the leader has self-confidence that comes from modesty, courage, social responsibility. The leader *participates* in the simultaneously social and individual processes of exploring together our way of life as members of our organisation. However, although he or she participates as others do, there is also a very important difference: namely, that he/she is more powerful. This power difference is a very important part of the relationships between everyone in the group. The leader almost always comes to occupy an important part in the fantasy lives of others, no matter how much he or she tries to resist this. The skilled leader pays particular attention to the unconscious aspects of the communicative interaction between group members and seeks to avoid taking for granted or exacerbating power differentials, all in the interests of encouraging more fluid forms of conversation. This does not involve abdicating power in any way nor does it mean that the leader never moves into highly directing roles where appropriate.

13.6 Summary

This chapter started by looking at Mead's explanation of how the important human attributes of consciousness and self-consciousness emerge in local social interactions. He argued that such interactions take the form of the conversation of gestures in which the very selves of interdependent people are constituted. Local interaction between people in organisations can, then, be understood to be fundamentally conversational in nature. Drawing on ethnomethodological studies, the chapter pointed to the turn-taking and turn-making structure of conversations. It went on to describe how meaningful themes emerge in ordinary conversation which organise the experience of people being together. Organisational strategies can be understood as such emerging themes. On this view the dynamics of ordinary everyday conversation become of crucial importance for the qualities of the activities of strategising. The emergence of novel strategies depends upon the practice of more fluid, spontaneous forms of conversation. The possibility of such conversational dynamics occurring depends up the conversational practices that have evolved in an organisation, on the manner in which anxiety is dealt with and on the nature of the power relations between people.

Further reading

Useful further reading is provided by Burkitt (1991), Shotter (1993), Steier (1991), Stacey (2001, 2003), Shaw (2002) and Shaw and Stacey (2005). Also Boden (1994) and Samra-Fredericks (2003) develop insights into the importance of conversation. Alvesson and Karreman (2001) explore the meaning of linking knowledge and management. Sarra (2005) writes about organisational development in the National Health Service from the point of view of communicative interaction.

Questions to aid further reflection

1. In what ways does Mead's theory of communication differ from that to be found in the dominant discourse on organisations?
2. What does self-consciousness mean in Mead's theory?
3. Why would fluid forms of conversation be important in strategising?
4. What role does anxiety play in strategising?
5. If fluid conversation is important for the emergence of novel strategies then what is the role of the leader?
6. How would you understand your own involvement in the strategising activities of your organisation?

Chapter 14

The link between the local communicative interaction of strategising and the population-wide patterns of strategy

This chapter invites you to draw on your own experience to reflect on and consider the implications of:

- Thinking of organisations as social rather than physical objects.

- Thinking of organisational strategies as generalised population-wide patterns of activity that emerge in many, many local interactions.

- Thinking about the interplay of intentions as the connection between local interac-

tions in organisations and population-wide patterns of activity called 'organisational strategy'.

- The meaning of emergence in human activity.

- Control as social processes rather than anyone being 'in control'.

The last chapter looked in some detail at the nature of local interaction in organisations, arguing that it is fundamentally communicative. The argument was that all the activities of organising, including those of strategising, are conversational processes. It is in local conversational processes that the population-wide patterns that we call 'strategy' actually emerge. However, people in organisations also have the ability to notice and interpret emerging population-wide patterns, and what they notice and how they articulate their interpretations have an impact on how they interact locally with each other. Strategising, as patterns of local interaction, forms population-wide patterns of strategy while being formed by them at the same time. The ideas in this chapter are important because they constitute a way of thinking about the paradoxical processes of strategising and strategy which in the dominant discourse would be described as the link between micro and macro. The way of thinking presented in this chapter reverses the usual connection made between strategy and change. In the dominant discourse, a desired population-wide pattern is formulated first and then implemented as the cause of population-wide change. If one argues that emergence applies to human action then this direct causal link from a global plan to local change is impossible. In the approach adopted in this chapter it is in local change that new population-wide patterns of strategy emerge. If a plan for a population-wide pattern cannot be the cause of it, if local interaction is the cause of it, then what effect does the population-wide pattern have on local interaction? This is the question explored in this chapter.

14.1 Introduction

Chapter 12 explored a responsive processes way of thinking about *how* organisational strategies, understood as population-wide patterns of activity, arise. It drew on traditions of Western thought exemplified by the philosophy of Hegel and the sociology of Elias, who both emphasised the essential interdependence of human persons and how their patterns of activity could only be understood in terms of the history of responsive interactions between them. The key point made in this chapter is that individual persons and groupings of individual persons make choices and act with intention in expectation of realising some future population-wide pattern of activity which they desire, and they call this a *strategy*. However, the fact that they are always interdependent means that there can be no simple realisation of such desire or strategy. The population-wide patterns of activity will always *emerge* in the *interplay* of the desires and intentions of all of them. Since it is extremely unlikely that all will have the same desires and intentions, the interplay of intentions is an essentially conflictual process, in the sense of ongoing exploration and negotiation, taking the form of cooperation or manipulation, and sometimes hostility, aggression, competition, revolution or war. While each person or group may, *perhaps*, be more or less able to control their own desires and intentions, none of them will be able to control the desires and intentions of everyone else all of the time. It follows that no one can be 'in control' of the interplay of desires and intentions or even fully understand that interplay. Clearly, then, no individual person or grouping of persons, no matter how powerful, can choose the population-wide patterns of activity that will continually materialise. Instead, the actual, realised, ongoing, population-wide pattern of activity will continually emerge, where this means that the ongoing realised pattern of activity is not caused by any plan or blueprint for it – the pattern that emerges is not the pattern that anyone planned, although what they were all planning is clearly crucial to what actually emerges. That emergent pattern is caused by the ongoing responsive adjustment of the individual plans and actions of persons to each other. It is caused by the interplay of desires and intentions.

Chapter 12 also argued that this view is supported by the properties of complex adaptive systems consisting of heterogeneous agents. Using this idea, serious natural scientists have shown that evolving, coherent, population-wide patterns do emerge in local interaction between agents (self-organisation or interplay) when those agents are richly connected to each other, so imposing *conflicting constraints* on each other, and when they differ sufficiently from each other, so displaying *diversity*. When these conditions are met, the dynamics, the patterns of movement over time, of both local interactions and population-wide patterns, take the form of regular irregularity (edge of chaos), which has the property of *amplifying small differences* into novel patterns. So, there is nothing mysterious or inexplicable about the emergence of population-wide pattern in local interaction, nor is it due to chance. Emergence is caused by what agents do as they impose conflicting constraints on each other in which their diversity, the small differences between them, is amplified. Elias's painstaking research provides us with a means of understanding how these abstract ideas from the complexity sciences can be understood in terms of the evolution of human communities and this is, of course, what organisations are.

In the dominant discourse, strategy is mostly defined in terms of the desire and intention of some individual person, or group of persons, and the definition stops there. It is then the obvious next step to ask what process persons do or should employ to formulate and implement their chosen desire or intention, or at least to learn together how to do so, in order to realise their desire or intention. What materialises is, here, by and large, thought to be caused by the intention when carried out competently. Where such realisation of strategic intention fails and something else happens, it is ascribed to chance and called *emergent*. The responsive processes perspective does not stop the definition of strategy at the point of individual, or collective, desire or intention because it is concerned with the interplay of different desires and intentions. The realised strategy is caused, not by any individual or collectively shared desires and intentions, but by their interplay. This is in no way to diminish or downplay the importance of individual or collective desires and intentions, because without them there could, obviously, be no individual or joint actions and so no interplay with the individual or joint actions of others. The interplay is not some abstraction but the embodied interaction of human persons acting with intention and also often quite unconsciously without intention.

If one is *not* to stop the definition of strategy at the point of individual intention then how are we to use the word 'strategy'? I will be using the word 'strategy' to mean *generalised articulations* of the ongoing *pattern of activity* that people in an organisation are engaged in. For example, they may be engaged in a pattern of activity to which the label 'outsourcing' could be attached. Or, they could be engaged in a pattern of activity called 'wildcat strikes'. Furthermore, the ongoing pattern of activity of people in an organisation clearly also includes what intentions they are forming, how they are forming them and what *thinking* they are *doing* as they desire and intend. In other words, the distinctions between thought and action, planning and implementation, doing and thinking, all dissolve.

In the following chapters, then, strategy refers to generalisations about the ongoing, population-wide patterns of activity of interdependent people and those population-wide patterns continually emerge in the ongoing local strategising activities as the interplay of the desires and intentions of all involved, both as members of a particular organisation and as members of other organisations they interact with. What now becomes important is to explore just what is meant by the interplay of intentions – that is, by the local interaction of persons – just what is meant by the emergence of population-wide patterns, and just how such patterns are related to local interactions. That is the purpose of this chapter and the next one.

Chapter 13 focused on local interaction as communicative interaction. People accomplish whatever they accomplish in communicating with each other. That chapter explored how such communication might be understood from the perspective of Mead who understood communication as the conversation of gestures, by which he meant ongoing everyday, local activities of bodies gesturing to each other in the process of which they are evoking and provoking responses from each other. Meaning, or knowledge, emerges in these iterated social processes of gesture and response: that is, conversation. What I mean by local interaction, therefore, is fundamentally these complex responsive processes of conversation between human bodies, whether in each other's presence or using technologies such as writing and email.

This chapter is concerned with the extension of Mead's argument to understand how the local interaction of conversation is linked to population-wide social patterns. Mead also argued that such conversation was social process and as such always reflected the history of the communicators' communities. In other words, human local communicative interaction always involves the population-wide patterns that have evolved over time in the many, many local interactions of the past. These population-wide patterns are present in all current actions as generalisations and idealisations, also referred to by Mead as social objects and cult values, which are continually taken up by people in their local interactions. In other words, in local communicative interaction, local patterns of interaction are being formed by population-wide patterns – generalisations and idealisations – while at the same time forming them. Pattern is emerging locally and globally at the same time, all in local communication in which the interplay of intentions means making particular to a particular situation that which is general and idealised. This chapter will be exploring just what the meaning might be of this possibly unfamiliar way of thinking about the meaning of the relationship between the local and the global, the micro and the macro.

To say that both local and population-wide patterns *emerge* at the same time is to say that both are arising and evolving into the unknown without any plan or blueprint. In other words, the emerging patterns are paradoxically predictable and unpredictable at the same time and over the long term fundamentally unknowable in their important detail. If this is so, then people can certainly articulate these patterns in generalised and idealised terms once they have occurred and we know that they do – these hindsight articulations are the stories about the past that we take up in the living present (*see* Chapter 12) as a basis for forming our next intentions.

But what of foresight? If the world of experience we create in our interactions with each other is stable and regular enough, then foresight can mean predicting future local and population-wide patterns in general. However, if the world of experience we create in our interactions is paradoxical and fundamentally unknowable in the long run, as the perspective being discussed here claims, then foresight cannot be equated with prediction. However, this does not mean dismissing foresight or any form of discussion about possible futures as futile. What it does mean is reflecting more deeply on what foresight means in a fundamentally uncertain world of experience. It could mean desiring, imagining, fantasising about, dreaming of, having premonitions of, speculating about, having expectations for, even omnipotently claiming certain knowledge of, future population-wide patterns. These are all fundamentally important human motivations to act, and no theory trying to explain what we actually do could possibly dismiss them. Such 'foresight', taking the form of stories about dreams or expectations for the future, will have no less impact on action taken in local interaction as the living present than the stories told with hindsight. Chapter 12 referred to the circular structure of the living present in which stories about the future affect the stories told about the past which affect stories about the future, all as the basis of the intentions we form and the actions we take in the present. This notion of the present does not dismiss either the past or the future but indicates how both are aspects of the living present, the present in which we always live.

Consider now how, according to Mead, local communicative interaction and population-wide patterns are interconnected.

14.2 Human communication and the conversation of gestures: processes of generalising and particularising

As we saw in the last chapter, Mead sought to understand the complex social acts in which many people are engaged in conversation through which they accomplish the tasks of fitting in and conflicting with each other in order to realise their individual and collective objectives and purposes. People do not come to an interaction with each other afresh each time, because they are born into an already existing, socially evolved pattern of activity and they continue to play their part in its further evolution. This leads Mead to his concept of the *generalised other*. In order to accomplish complex social acts, it is not enough for those involved to be able to take the attitude of the small numbers of people they may be directly engaged with at a particular time. They need to be able to take the attitude of all of those directly or indirectly engaged in the complex social act. It would be impossible to do this in relation to each individual so engaged, but humans have developed the capacity to generalise the attitudes of many. In acting in the present, each individual is then taking up the attitude of a few specific others and, at the same time, the attitude of this generalised other, the attitude of the group, the organisation or the society. These wider, generalised attitudes are evolving historically and are always implicated in every human action. In play, the child takes the role of another, but in the game the child must take on not only the role of the other but also that of the game: that is, of all the participants in the game and its rules and procedures. The generalised other is the taking of the attitude of all other participants in general.

We learn early on in life to take the attitude of the generalised other as, for example, when one's mother says, 'What will *people* think of you if you do this or say that?' Here one's mother is not warning one to take account of how particular people will respond to us, but how people in general in our society will respond to us. We care about what others think of us and about the consequences of their not thinking well of us – ongoing existence requires the recognition of others simply because we are all interdependent persons. We continue throughout life to care and this provides a powerful constraint on what we do and so a powerful form of social control. We begin to see here how, despite the inability of anyone to be in control, there are powerful forms of social control expressed most effectively as socially acquired self-control so that the only alternative to someone being in control is not anarchy, muddling through or garbage-can decision-making. It is only when social habits break down, as for example in the recent flooding of New Orleans or the aftermath of the Iraq war, that anarchy ensues.

Taking the attitude of the generalised other

It is important here to note what Mead means by '*attitude*'. He does not mean simply an opinion; he means a 'tendency to act'. In taking the attitude of the generalised other we are therefore taking into account the established tendencies to act towards us and each other of people in general in our group, organisation and society. However, we are always having to interpret what these generalised tendencies to act might mean in the specific, contingent situations we find ourselves in. We cannot simply, directly apply the generalisation, because in each present time period, in each contingent situation, we will find it necessary to make the general particular to that time and situation. This will inevitably lead to conflict in that we will differ from each other on just how to make the generalisation particular in each present time period and situation. Such conflict requires us to carry on exploring with each other just what our differences are and negotiating the meaning of the generalisation; and it is this conflictual, explorative process of particularisation that makes possible the further evolution of the generalisation as tiny variations in the particular way the generalisation is taken up are amplified across a population over time. We can immediately see the superficiality of the notion, taken by some from the complexity sciences (*see* Chapter 11), that people should follow simple rules. Simple rules are generalisations, and there is nothing simple at all about the processes of making particular such generalisations.

To see what the above argument means in terms of human action, consider the activity of smoking cigarettes. A person who undertakes this activity inevitably affects others in the immediate vicinity and so, in order to carry on in an ordinary way with those others, has to take the attitude of those specific others – that is, the tendency of those specific others to act towards the smoker – and they too find they have to take the attitude of the smoker. We are talking about what the parties directly involved have to take account of in each other's actions in order to go on being together. If we are dining together at a restaurant and I want to smoke at the table, I have to take account of how you might react and you will have to take account of how I might react if you protest. To go on together we each have to take the attitude of the other. However, there is more to it than this, because people in general in the wider society have a generalised tendency to act towards each other with regard to the activity of smoking. What can we say about the attitude of the generalised other here? Well, if we go back some 70 years to the period of the Second World War, the attitude of the generalised other could be described as permissive, even encouraging of the activity of smoking. For example, the military authorities gave cigarettes to members of the armed forces in the belief that smoking calmed people down in very difficult circumstances. In lighting a cigarette in a specific situation, say a restaurant or cinema, a person would take account of the attitude of the specific others in the vicinity and, at the same time, quite unconsciously take account of the permissive attitude of the generalised other at that time, and others in the vicinity who were not smoking would do the same. So in a specific restaurant or cinema a smoker would probably feel perfectly entitled to light up and most others would feel that it was quite acceptable for this to happen.

However, as the years went by, the attitude of the generalised other with regard to smoking evolved and became more complex. Groups of people in the medical research community produced evidence of harmful effects of smoking, not just on smokers but on those around them. Other groups of people entered into the discussion, particularly over the past twenty years, accelerating over the past five years. Gradually over these years, and increasingly so over the past few years, the tendency of people in general to act in relation to smokers has shifted to one of prohibition, even hostility, and this shift in the attitude of the generalised other has been codified in the law. Now a person lighting a cigarette has to take the attitude of those in the immediate vicinity and the attitude of the generalised other and in doing so knows that he or she is acting in a way condemned by people in general. Non-smokers now feel perfectly justified in condemning the practice of smoking and refusing permission for others to smoke near them. How is the smoker going to deal with the attitude of the generalised other in specific situations: for example while waiting for a bus near a bus shelter? I might feel quite justified in lighting a cigarette in the open air but those nearby might feel that it is quite unjustified. We are both accepting the general attitude of prohibition but conflicting around what this means in the specific situation of the area around a bus shelter.

This is an example of how people take up the attitude of the generalised other across a whole society, indeed across many societies, and of how the generalised other evolves. However, the processes in this case are just as much in operation in all of the ordinary, everyday activities of people in any organisation. So, for example, a manager arrives at the office on Friday to find that a member of his staff has not reported for work and, furthermore, has not telephoned to explain the absence, as required by company policy. Some hours go by and the manager telephones her to find that her mobile phone is switched off and he cannot contact her. In deciding what to do next, he will find himself taking account of the attitude of the absent staff member and the attitude of other staff members. Will they be supportive of her or, given that she frequently fails to attend work on a Friday, or will they be annoyed by any failure to take action against her? He will also, largely unconsciously, be taking the attitude of the generalised other – in general, people in this society do not approve of people who stay away from work for no good reason and do not explain why they are doing so. This attitude is codified in company policies and, since she has done it before, the generalisation would be to take disciplinary action.

However, in this specific, contingent situation, on this particular Friday morning, in this particular office, how is this generalisation to be made specific? For example, the absent staff member is a single mother abandoned by her partner who has great difficulty caring for her young daughter and, furthermore, she has produced letters from her doctor saying that she is suffering from depression. These contingent aspects of the situation call out other generalised attitudes to do with protecting single mothers, not discriminating against those with mental problems, and so on. In deciding what to do, then, this manager is making particular to this situation the generalisations so far mentioned. Furthermore, over the past few years all of these generalisations have been evolving as new specific situations are encountered and many have been codified in law.

Mead's theory of the evolution of groups and societies in processes of communicative interaction between persons provides us with a way of understanding organisations that focuses upon the ordinary, everyday activities of people, rather than abstracting from them and regarding people as the resources of an organisation, which is what most other explanations of organisations do. I want to stress that this focus on people is in no way an idealisation of people and their relationships with each other nor is it a fundamentally ideological position, although of course it has ideological implications. This is because no claim is being made that relationships between people are essentially good. Mead's theory of the conversation of gestures, in which generalisations are made particular, is as much an explanation of war, corruption, abuse and all the other terrible ways people relate to each other, as it is of caring, loving relationships.

From Mead's perspective we come to understand organisations as patterns of interaction between people which evolve over time in those processes in which people are making particular the generalisations, and in the course of which those generalisations evolve. The strategies of an organisation are those generalisations and the strategies, therefore, evolve in the ordinary, everyday processes in which people interpret and negotiate with each other what the strategies as generalisations mean in specific contingent situations and what implications these meanings have for what to do next. For example, consider a commercial organisation where the strategy is described as one of delivering, to customers, mobile telephones of a quality consistently higher than the competition, on time, and at competitive prices, while generating acceptable profit without compromising the safety of staff or customers. It may also be part of the strategy to do all of this in an ethical, socially responsible and environmentally aware manner. All of this may well have been codified in the form of strategy documents, procedural manuals and administrative systems such as financial budgeting and quality monitoring. However, what we are talking about here are generalisations that have emerged from numerous past conversations, including formal meetings, as well as actual production experiences. Now, at a particular time, on a particular day, particular people in the assembly operation encounter a quality problem with a particular component. To sustain quality they should stop the assembly operation but then they will not meet time deadlines and profits will suffer. This is, of course, a common problem encountered when strategy requirements conflict as they inevitably do. It will be necessary for those involved to make particular decisions about these generalisations. Would it be better to take a small risk on quality and meet the time deadline, or not? If similar problems are more frequently encountered, the manner in which they are dealt with in particular situations may well come to be expressed in a reformulation of the generalisation. It is in this way that the generalisations evolve in further conversations on how to deal with the conflict.

Conflict

This perspective, then, brings conflict to the fore. It is not just that the generalisations may conflict with each other but that the particular people involved in the particular, contingent situation may well conflict with each other on how to interpret the generalisations and how to take them up at this particular moment. The movement of strategy occurs in the negotiation of such conflict. Groot (2005) draws a conceptual distinction between explorative conflict and polarised conflict. Conflict is usually understood as the polarised form. Here people take up opposed positions and hold on to them in an overt power struggle in which one side holds out to win at the expense of the other. When Mead is emphasising conflict he does so in its explorative sense. Explorative conflict is conversational, negotiating processes in which people explore how to interpret generalisations and negotiate different interpretations with each other to make them particular. Such explorative conflict always has the potential, but not the necessity, of polarisation.

In the evolution of organisations, then, many generalisations emerge which are taken up, or particularised, in people's local interactions with each other and in the course of which the generalisation evolves. This is a point of major importance. Mead draws attention to paradoxical processes of generalisation and particularisation at the same time. Mental and social activities are processes of generalising and particularising at the same time. Individuals act in relation to that which is common to all of them (generalising) but responded to somewhat differently by each of them as each living present (particularising).

Social objects

Mead's (1938) discussion of what he called a 'social object' is yet another formulation of the generalising and particularising processes discussed in previous sections. Mead distinguished between a physical object and a social object. A physical object exists as a thing in nature and is the proper object of study in the natural sciences, while a social object is the proper object of study in the social sciences and this object exists only in human experience. While the physical object can be understood in terms of itself as a thing, the social object has to be understood in terms of social acts. Mead referred to markets as an example of a social object. When one person offers to buy food, this act obviously involves a complex range of responses from other people to provide the food. However, it involves more than this because the one making the offer can only know how to make the offer if he is able to take the attitude, the tendency to act, of the other parties to the bargain. All essential phases of the complex social act of market exchange must appear in the actions of all involved and appear as essential features of each individual's actions. The activities of buying and selling are involved in each other.

As another example, take a National Health Service trust in the UK. From a complex responsive processes perspective this organisation is the iterated patterning of communicative interaction between large numbers of interdependent persons and groupings of them – when asked what they do, their answer is that they work in a hospital. Some are employees and belonging to the trust is an aspect of their identities, the 'we' aspect of each of them. Furthermore, they are not simply members of the trust, because each of them also belongs to groupings of doctors, nurses, porters, managers, and so on – when asked who they are, their answer is that they are doctors, hospital porters, and so on. Even in these grouping there are subgroupings – for example surgeons – and even within that there are groupings – say, heart surgeons – when asked who they are they reply that they are heart surgeons. All of these groupings give rise to the 'we' identities of their members, providing them with a powerful sense of identity or self. Others are receiving attention as patients and so belong to the group of the 'sick'. Yet others are relatives of the 'sick' and so belong to yet another group, perhaps, 'carers'. And of course each of these groups consists of subgroups, such as the diabetics, the mentally ill, the Aids patients and so on. They too take aspects of their identities, albeit often more temporarily, from belonging to these groups. For all of those mentioned, such identities constitute how they are recognised by others in the wider society. All of these people continually interact with each other in a coherent manner, moment by moment, every day, because each has the largely unconscious capacity to take the attitude, the tendency to act, of all the others in the hospital game. We have some expectation of what will happen when we enter a hospital as a patient. We have some expectation of how doctors, nurses, administrators and porters will act. And so do all of them of us and each other. What we are all doing is taking up the attitude of the 'game'. We are all taking up, in our interactions, the social object that is the hospital organisation. As an organisation, the hospital does not exist as a thing. Rather, it is only to be found as patterns of interaction in our experience. This must be so if we are to interact coherently. Try to imagine what it might be like to be rushed to a modern hospital in London from a remote jungle village somewhere in South America.

However, taking up the social object in our interactions is not a perfect process, because it is not the actualisation of something given and the expectations of all involved will not therefore fit in easily with each other. As generalisation, the social object will have to be made particular in each particular, contingent situation and this will inevitably lead to some kind of conflict. Nurses and physicians, for example, might well take up the social object in their actions in different ways so that they will conflict and there will be complaints.

Social objects, as generalisations, can also be idealised, becoming what Mead called a 'cult value', a matter to be discussed in Chapter 15. I mention this concept here in relation to the hospital example, because nowhere will the conflict caused by making some generalisation particular be greater than when this generalisation is also a cult value. For example, how will the cult value 'treat all patients equally' be taken up in Ward A at the Royal Free hospital at 15.25 on 14 May 2010 in relation to patients X and Y by doctor L and nurse M? Also, it is more complicated than this because there will be more than one cult value and they may well conflict with each other. Nowadays, hospitals take up cult values to do with performance, quality assurance, risk management and evidence-based treatment. These frequently clash with other cult values such as vocation, collegiality, causing no harm, professional freedom and personal responsibility. People then have to negotiate their way through inevitable conflicts in ways that inevitably transform their identities. This becomes especially pressing when the scope for particularising the generalised cult values is more and more severely restricted by shifts in power relations, as in the concentration of policy making, monitoring and control in the hands of central government. People must comply, or at least be seen to comply, to avoid public humiliation, shame and even annihilation of identity. Identities, which can only be sustained in the recognition of important others, may come to be characterised more by appearance and spin than substance. Compliance may mean submerging values that may feel more important, leading to feelings of alienation and a lack of authenticity because to survive we may have to deceive. All of this will have enormous implications for the strategy of hospital improvement. As is now very evident, it is by no means guaranteed that formulating a strategy of health improvement and implementing it through administrative systems of monitoring will have sustainable effects. This is hardly surprising when one takes account of the local particularising of generalised strategies such as 'healthcare improvement'.

It is important to notice how Mead used the term 'object' in a social sense as a 'tendency to act' rather than as a concept or a thing, which are meanings appropriate to physical objects. In a social setting, then, Mead used the term 'object' in tension with the usual understanding of object as a thing in nature. The pattern, or tendency, which Mead calls an 'object' is in a sense an object in that it is what we perceive in taking it up in our acting, but this is a perception of our own acting not a thing. We seem to have a strong tendency to reify patterns of acting and this makes it important to emphasise that Mead's social object is not a thing.

Mead, therefore, defined a social act as one involving the cooperation of many people in which the different parts of the social act undertaken by different individuals appear in the act of each individual as a social object. The tendencies to act as others act are present in the conduct of each individual involved and it is this presence that is responsible for the appearance of the social object in the experience of each individual. A social object is only to be found in the conduct of the different individuals engaged in the complex social act. The social object appears in the experience of each individual as a stimulus to a response not only by that individual but also by the others involved – this is how each can know how the others are likely to act in general situations and it is the basis of coordination. A social object is thus a generalised gesture taken together with many tendencies to respond in particular ways. Social objects are common plans or patterns of action related to the future of the act. Social objects have evolved in the history of the society of selves and each individual is born into such a world of social objects. Individuals are forming social objects while being formed by them in an evolutionary process.

What Mead is talking about here is the manner in which population-wide patterns of action are generalisations that can only be found in the particular local interactions between people. Generalising is the same as both articulated and unconscious population-wide patterning and particularising is the same as local interacting.

Social control

Mead linked social objects to social control. Social control is the bringing of the act of the individual person into relation with the social object. The social act is distributed amongst many, but the social object appears in the experience, the selves, of all of them. Social control depends upon the degree to which the individual takes the attitude of the generalised other: that is, takes the attitude which is the social object. All institutions are social objects and serve to control individuals who find them in their experience. So the social tendencies to act feature as key aspects of the individual selves comprising a group, organisation or society as the basis of self-control.

Mead's notion of social object has something in common with the notions of social structure, habit and routine. What was distinctive about Mead's approach to these matters, however, was how he avoided positing social structure as a phenomenon that exists outside individuals. Social objects are generalisations that only have any existence in their particularisation in the ordinary, everyday interactions between people as the living present. Box 14.1 summarises the key points about social objects.

Box 14.1	Key points about social objects

- Social objects are *generalised tendencies*, common to large numbers of people, to act in *similar ways in similar situations*.

- These generalised tendencies to act are iterated as each living present as rather repetitive, *habitual patterns of action*.

- In their continual iteration, these general tendencies to act are normally *particularised* in the specific situation and the specific present the actors find themselves in.

- Such particularising inevitably involves *conflictual processes* of interpretation as the meaning of the generalisation is established in a specific situation.

- The possibility of *transformation* of social objects arises in this particularising because of the potential for *spontaneity* to generate variety in human action and the capacity of nonlinear interaction to *amplify* consequent small differences in their particularisation.

- While physical objects are to be found as things in nature, social objects can only be experienced in their particularisation in complex social acts as the living present. Social objects do not have any existence outside of such particularising social acts.

- The self is a social object and since social objects appear in the actions of individual people, the processes of particularising the general constitute social control.

Mead's view of control stands in contrast to how control is thought about in the systemic perspectives underlying the theories reviewed in Part 1 of this book. From the systemic perspective, control is usually equated with someone being 'in control', and this control is effected by cybernetic system forms of monitoring where actual outcomes are compared with targets and action is taken to close the gap. From this perspective the only alternative to someone being 'in control' through the use of monitoring procedures is anarchy or some form of muddling through. What Mead is making clear is that there are far more widespread and powerful forms of social control which do not involve any individual or powerful group of individuals being in control. The only alterative to someone being in control through operating monitoring process is not anarchy or muddling through simply because humans are social animals – that is, they are dependent upon each other, which requires each to unconsciously take up the generalised other, the social object, in their particular interactions with each other as aspects of their very selves. It is only when normal social relations break down that social control is disrupted – for example in the aftermath of a war, during riots or in the aftermath of major natural catastrophes such as hurricanes and flooding.

14.3 The relationship between local interaction and population-wide patterns

In all his formulations of human communicative interaction, Mead presented the same paradox: gesture and response are inseparable phases of one social act; generalising and particularising are inseparable phases of social objects; the 'I' and the 'me' are inseparable phases of the social self. It is in the ongoing activity of gesturing and responding, of generalising and particularising that meaningful patterns of interaction between people arise, including their very selves. I suggest that these meaningful patterns take the form of iterated, emerging, narrative and propositional themes that organise the experience of being together (*see* Chapters 12 and 13). Such themes are iterated as each present taking the paradoxical form of habit, or continuity, and potential transformation at the same time. The essentially reflexive nature of human consciousness and self-consciousness means that we have the capacity to reflect imaginatively on these patterns, both local and population-wide, articulating both the habitual and the just emerging transformations and, in doing so, either sustain the habitual or reinforce the transformation of habit.

Imaginative constructs

In our reflection we generalise the tendencies we experience across many present situations, creating imaginative 'wholes' that have never existed and never will (Dewey, 1934). What we are doing in creating these imaginative 'wholes' is constructing in our interaction perceptions of unity in the patterning of our interactions. That imaginatively perceived unity is then a generalised tendency to act in similar situations in similar ways. What is emerging is the imaginative generalisation that is one phase of what Mead calls *social object*. The other phase, which is inseparable from the generalisation, is the particularising of the general in the specific contingent situations we find ourselves in. The general population-wide pattern can only be found in its particularisation in our local interaction, and that particularising inevitably involves conflict. In reflecting upon our patterns of interaction, in generalising those patterns and in imaginatively constructing some kind of unity of experience, we employ the tools of writing to codify habits or routines – for example, as law – and even design changes in them. However, any intentionally designed change can only ever be a generalisation, and what that means can only be found in the particularisation: that is, in the interplay between the intentions of the designers of the generalisation and the intentions of those who are particularising it.

Given the points made above, we can now understand what we mean by 'local interaction' and 'population-wide pattern' and how they are related to each other. Population-wide pattern is the imaginatively created unity across a whole population that we perceive in our patterns of interaction – it is the activity of generalising as one phase of social object. Local interaction is the particularising of the general, of the imaginatively constructed unity of our experience across the whole population we are part of. However, these are phases of one social act and can never be separated. The general is only to be found in the experience of the particular – it has no existence outside it. The processes of particularising are essentially reflective, reflexive, emotional, imaginative and potentially spontaneous. It is possible for individuals and groups of individuals, particularly powerful ones, to intentionally articulate and even design a desired generalised pattern, but the particularising involves an interplay of many intentions and values, and this interplay cannot be intended or designed, except temporarily in fascist power structures and cults (*see* Chapter 15). Furthermore, the generalisations will further evolve in their particularisation. In short, the population-wide and the local are paradoxical processes of generalising and particularising at the same time.

This point about the particularisation of generalisations is of great importance and reinforces, for me, the inappropriateness of simply applying the notion of complex adaptive systems, or any notion of systems for that matter, to human interaction. In complex adaptive systems, the agents follow rules – in effect, they directly enact generalisations. If humans simply applied generalisations in their interactions with each other, there would be no possibility of individual imagination and spontaneity and hence no possibility of creativity. We would simply be determined by the generalisations. It is in the essentially conflictual particularising of the generalisations, which have emerged over long periods of human interaction, that socially constructed, interdependent persons display spontaneity, reflection, reflexivity, imagination and creativity as well as conflict.

Spontaneity

Spontaneity, it seems to me, should be distinguished from impulse. In humans, impulse is an unreflective compulsion to do something, on the 'spur of the moment', as it were. Impulsive actions, however, are still socially formed and reflexive. Humans are reflexive in that their actions are formed by their own histories. Whatever we do, whether impulsive or not, depends upon who we are, upon identity/self, which is socially formed. Humans are also socially reflexive in that what they think and what they do is formed by the group, community, society they are part of, which have histories. This social reflexivity is also shaping whatever we do, impulsive or not. Spontaneity is often spoken of as if it were the same as impulse and the opposite of reflection in that spontaneous action also has that 'spur of the moment' quality. However, this is to chop out one event from an ongoing flow of interaction. I would argue that if we pay attention to the interactions preceding the arbitrarily selected moment of spontaneous interaction, we find people exploring the situation they face in ways that are reflective, and it is because of this 'preparation', as it were, that someone takes spontaneous action, having the appearance of 'on the spur of the moment'. What distinguishes this kind of spontaneous interaction from mere impulse is that it is a skilful performance, not just a historically, socially conditioned reaction. Spontaneity is what makes it possible for people to deal with the unique contingencies of the situations they always face. Spontaneity generates variety in responses, often as small differences that have the potential for being amplified in interaction. In other words, human spontaneity is closely associated with the possibility of transformation and novelty in human interaction (Friis, 2004; Larsen, 2005). Spontaneity in humans, I would argue, is reflexive, just as impulse is but, unlike impulse, the spontaneous act emerges in a history of skilful, reflective performance. Furthermore, spontaneity is never simply located in the individual, or the 'I', because the 'I' can never be separated from 'me', the social.

This perspective leads to ways of understanding what organisations are and what form the strategising activities of managers takes. Our understanding of organisational life might be enhanced by the notion of social object as generalised tendencies on the part of large numbers of people to act and the notion that such generalisations must be particularised in essentially conflictual processes in specific situations at specific times.

Organisations as social objects

What Mead presents is a complex, nonlinear, iterative process of communicative interaction between people in which mind, self and society all emerge simultaneously as the living present. Mead is concerned with local interaction as the present in which population-wide patterns emerge as social and personality structures. If one takes the complex responsive processes view, then one thinks of the emergence of long-term, widespread, coherent patterns of relating across a population emerging in the local processes of relating. It follows that there is no need to look for the causes of coherent human action in concepts such as deep structures, archetypes, the collective unconscious, transcendental wholes, common pools of meaning, group minds, the group-as-a-whole, transpersonal processes, foundation matrix, the personal dynamic unconscious, internal worlds, mental models, and so on. Instead, one understands human relating to be inherently pattern forming – it is its own cause.

Consider what organisations are usually thought to be. From a legal point of view, an organisation is a legal person. It is legitimised, under the laws of the land, by a legally recognised and binding constitution specifying purpose, procedures to be followed, hierarchical offices to be taken up, authority to be granted, and membership criteria and categories. This legal person has legal rights and obligations and it can be sued and punished. However, it is by no means necessary, and certainly not sufficient, to posit an organisation as a *legal* person. Some organisations are not legal persons at all. Indeed they are illegal, as is the case, for example, of a terrorist organisation or a drug-smuggling ring. Furthermore, the *person* part of the definition is highly problematic, although very useful, because without it we would have extremely ambiguous, cumbersome and muddled laws of contract and this would obstruct our joint activities. It is, therefore, a convenient *fiction* to think of an organisation as a person for legal purposes but it does not really get us to what an organisation is in our experience.

If we listen to how people talk about an organisation and read how the word 'organisation' is used in the now vast literature on the subject, it is striking how frequently the word 'it' is used in referring to an organisation. There is a powerful tendency to reify an organisation as an 'it' that somehow has a separate existence from the individuals who comprise it. We tend to talk about an organisation as actually existing as a thing, as a system. However, when we come to look for this 'thing', I think we are hard put to find it. People go even further than this and talk about an organisation as an organism, as a living system. They anthropomorphise it, treat it as actually being a person in ascribing purposes and direction to it. They claim, for example, that organisations learn. However, when we come to look for this organisational organism or person, we are hard put to find a body that qualifies as living. Organisations are not things, because no one can point to where an organisation is – all one can point to is the artefacts used by members of organisations in their work together. In our experience of ordinary, everyday life, we do not encounter an organisation as a thing, let alone a living thing with purposes of its own.

What we are doing in thought when we talk in the way just outlined is treating an organisation 'as if' it were what Mead called a 'physical object' and often we forget the 'as if' nature of our construct. An alternative way of thinking would be to regard an organisation as a social object. In other words, we then think of an organisation as the ongoing patterning of the relationships between those who are members of the organisation and, indeed, between them and members of other organisations. The organisation is nothing more or less that the iterated ongoing processes in which people are together particularising the generalisations in terms of which they perceive their organisation. An organisation then exists as an emergent phenomenon taking the form not only of practical activities, but also, very importantly, the form of an imaginative construct emerging in the relationships between the people who form and are formed by organisation at the same time. Patterns of relationships and imaginative constructs are as 'real' as anything to be found in our lives: indeed, they are essential to the meaning of our lives. It is for this reason that I am using the term *imaginative construct* to distinguish what I am talking about from a mere 'fiction', however useful that may be, and from the notion of 'fantasy' with its connotations of some individual experience that stands in contradiction to 'reality'. We together construct the imaginative, not in some individual process of introspection or fantasising, but in our continually iterated local relationships with each other. This immediately brings us to the fundamentally social nature of imagination and so of organisation. We understand organisations as emerging patterns of communicative interaction between people, as ongoing 'conversations' in which emerge themes that organise our experience of being together. As people interact locally with each other, moment by moment, they form patterns of activity. They iterate, in a sense repeat, these patterns of communicative interaction as the living present, and it is this activity of communication across the population of members that constitutes the experience of organisation.

Organisations are the ongoing patterning of conversations, so that changes in conversations are changes in organisations. Usually, when talking about organisations, people refer to procedures, roles, tasks, and the activities of monitoring, planning and budgeting. They talk about organisations in terms of technologies, bundles of resource and positions in markets, and dismiss ordinary conversation as 'just talk'. I think that in doing this they are focusing attention on what are only the tools we use in our ongoing local interactions with each other. If we think of organisations as social objects, we avoid mistaking the tools for the organisation and see them for what they are: namely, the tools we use in the activities of organising.

Mead's notion of social object as generalised tendencies to act is the same as the population-wide patterns I have been referring to, and his notion of particularising such generalisations is the same as the processes of local interaction I have been referring to. Drawing on analogies from the theory of heterogeneous complex adaptive systems, I have suggested that population-wide patterns, or social objects, emerge in many, many local interactions. Mead explains the processes by which social objects, as generalisations, are made particular in many, many local interactions. This is what the activity of management is all about – it is the activity of making generalisations particular. The processes of management as particularising are interpretive and conflictual, and it is in such local interaction that social objects continue both to be reproduced and to evolve – that is, population-wide patterns are iterated in local interactions as continuity and potential transformation at the same time. So, it is not simply that population-wide patterns emerge in local interaction, but also that population-wide patterns are themselves taken up as particulars in local interactions – they are mutually constitutive. Furthermore, humans can articulate and even codify the population-wide patterns emerging in their local interactions and these articulations are themselves important aspects of local interaction.

This leads to a different way of thinking about formulation, or thought, and implementation, or action. This is a distinction widely made in the ways of thinking about organisations and strategy reviewed in Part 1 of this book. From the above discussion one concludes that such a distinction is purely arbitrary. The activity of particularising the general cannot be described simply as either formulation (thought) or implementation (action). This is because the activity of making the general particular involves interpretation, conflict and negotiation, all of which are actions that involve thinking. Generalising also cannot be simply categorised as formulation or implementation, because the generalisation is emerging in the local interactions of particularising and the activities of articulating and codifying the general are themselves actions requiring thought. Instead of an arbitrary beginning described as 'formulation' and an arbitrary end described as 'implementing' we have ongoing processes of formulation and implementation, thinking and acting, at the same time.

Analogies from the complexity sciences

In the last chapter I took local interaction between human persons to be analogous to the concept of self-organisation in the theory of complex adaptive systems. To recapitulate, self-organisation in heterogeneous complex adaptive systems means that:

1. each agent interacts with only a small fraction of the total population of agents and in that sense agents only ever interact locally;

2. each agent interacts with others on the basis of its own historically evolved, local organising rules or principles rather than according to population-wide general rules set for each agent by some designer external to their interaction;

3. agents in their diversity are thereby locally constraining each other in conflicting ways and such constraining is an important source of order.

So I am arguing that local interaction between human agents as conversation, as in Mead's thought, and the interplay of intentions, as in the thinking of Elias, is fundamentally self-organising in the sense of points 1 to 3 set out above, with an important addition in the case of human agents: namely, their ability to particularise generalisations of population-wide patterns in their local interaction. Then, by further analogy I am arguing that just as global, population-wide patterns of interaction emerge and evolve in self-organising interaction in abstract models of complex systems, so population-wide patterns of interaction between people emerge and evolve in local human interaction. In both cases, emergence means that the global or population-wide patterns are not the consequence of any plan, programme or blueprint for that population-wide pattern. Simulations of complex adaptive systems demonstrate that this is possible in principle, and the work of both Mead and Elias indicates just how this happens in the case of human agents. Also, by yet another analogy, I am arguing that, just as global and local patterns in complex adaptive systems both evolve together when the agents are diverse, so in human interaction both local and population-wide patterns evolve together because of human differences, which inevitably bring with them conflict, just as both Mead and Elias argue.

It may be argued that the way I have draw the analogies in the previous paragraph ignores the following aspects of human interaction:

1. Some human agents – namely, leaders – might be said to interact with a whole population of agents in an organisation or society.

2. While most other agents may be interacting with only a small fraction of the total population, they do not do so simply on the basis of their own historically evolved local organising principles, but also, to a significant extent at least, on the basis of generalised, population-wide rules such as the laws of society, and the visions, objectives and norms of an organisation, as well as its plans, routines, procedures and administrative systems.

3. Agents are constrained not simply by the conflicting constraints they place on each other but by the need to conform harmoniously to the population-wide rules specified in 2 above.

However, if we take account of the arguments about the social act of gesture and response, and of the relationship between the general and the particular as social object, it becomes clear that points 1 to 3 in the above paragraph present too simplistic a picture of human interaction for the following reasons:

1. When we look at how leaders or dominant coalitions interact with whole populations of people in an organisation or society, we find that they can only do so in essentially the same way as anyone else. All any of us can do, including leaders and members of powerful coalitions, is gesture and respond to others. When the powerful and the charismatic are said to be interacting with a whole population, what they are doing amounts to only one phase of the social act: namely, the gesture – the responses of all the individual members of the population are required to complete the social act. As Mead cogently argued, the meaning does not lie in the gesture taken on its own. The meaning emerges only in the gesture of the powerful taken together with the second phase of the social act: namely, the responses of the many to whom the gesture is made. Such responses can only be made in many, many local interactions in which those gestured to discuss what the gesture of the powerful means and, since there are many, many local interactions, there will be many, many conflicting responses and accompanying meanings. The responses all occur in local interaction on the basis of local organising principles to do with, for example, emotion and individual histories as well as the generalised other/social object, which is always involved in local interaction. The powerful will then find that they must in turn respond to these many, many responses and meanings. What they thought their gesture meant might turn out to provoke surprising, unpredictable responses, which they will then have to deal with. Furthermore, both their original gesture and their responses to the responses to that original gesture will all arise in their own local interaction. No matter how powerful a person is, that person always interacts directly with a small number of close colleagues, and their intentions emerge in such local interactions. So, the powerful do not interact directly with large numbers of people after all, because all they can do is undertake one phase of the social interaction – namely, the gesture – while the response arises indirectly in many other local situations. Human interaction remains fundamentally local despite the enormous differences in the visibility and power of different human agents.

2. The gesture made by the powerful can only ever be some articulation of a generalisation, perhaps one which is just emerging or one which is desired, wished for, or dreamt of. So the powerful are articulating the nature of social objects or their desires for it. Such generalisations or social objects must be made particular in many, many local, contingent situations. So, people in an organisation are not simply following generalised rules but are continually interpreting and negotiating them with each other in local situations. This involves the spontaneity of the 'I' and the interplay of intentions.

3. People rarely conform harmoniously to general principles. Instead they make them particular in conflictual processes of the interplay of intentions.

Then when we take account of other organisations, or populations, with which people in any organisations have to interact, there is a further interplay of intentions. In a fundamental sense we are talking about local interaction (self-organisation) and emergence when it comes to human interaction.

I find that there is a typical response whenever I suggest to a group of managers that they might think of themselves, and also their chief executive officer (CEO), as participants in essentially self-organising processes – that is, local interaction from which population-wide patterns and imaginatively constructed unities of experience emerge. They claim that if they cannot be the designer of the whole and if they cannot know the outcomes of what they are doing in terms of directly causing the whole, then they have no role. They claim that they would simply give up if they thought that population-wide patterns emerged and the 'whole' was an imaginative construct. Alternatively, they point to examples of CEOs who do form overall intentions for their organisation, who set out compelling visions and missions and do thereby transform their whole organisation. They conclude that the notion of self-organisation as local interaction does not apply to them. Why do they think this?

It seems to me that they are immediately understanding self-organisation in terms of the individual: the unquestioned assumption of the primacy of the individual. Self-organisation is taken to mean that it is the individual members of the organisation who organise themselves without the direction of their leaders. This then leads to the view that self-organisation is all or some of the following:

1. Something that happens no matter what anyone does. This means that there is no point in doing anything. One should simply sit back and just wait for fate or destiny.

2. Full-blown democracy in which all agents are equal and nothing is done without complete consensus.

3. Anarchy in which everyone does whatever they please.

4. The empowerment of the lower echelons in the organisation and then leaving them to get on with it.

5. The disempowerment and incapacitation of the higher echelons who no longer have a role.

It is important to stress that the notion of self-organisation as it is employed in complexity theory does not mean any of these things. People think it does because they hear these words from the perspective of the autonomous individual and think that it means that individuals are organising themselves without any constraint. However, if you look carefully at the simulations intended to demonstrate the nature of self-organisation you will notice two points.

First, there are conditions that simultaneously enable and constrain the interactions between agents. Take the Tierra simulation (Ray, 1992) discussed in Chapter 10. Agents are enabled to replicate because computer time is allocated to them, but this is also a constraint because they only have limited time. In organisations, all members are both enabled and constrained by the availability of resources. In the simulation, agents are constrained by the mode of replication and by the competitive selection applied to them. In the simulations, the programmer imposes all of these constraints, but in the reality the programmer is trying to model, they all emerge in evolving interaction. So self-organisation is certainly not a constraint-free form of behaviour. In organisations, people constrain each other (*see* Chapter 15 on power) and they are constrained by each other and the generalised other/social object, which constitutes key aspects of their very selves.

Second, that which is organising itself is not the separate individuals on their own. In fact, self-organisation does not involve anything organising itself – it means local interaction. Population-wide patterns of relationships are emerging at the same time as the nature of the agents is changing, all in local interaction. The agents are forming and being formed by population-wide patterns of relationships. Once this perspective is taken there is no justification for making any of the interpretations of self-organisation in points 1 to 5 above. Instead:

1. Far from there being no point in doing anything, everything one does in one's local interactions, including nothing, has potential widespread consequences. Far from population-wide patterns being a matter of fate or destiny, they are the co-creation of all locally interacting agents.

2. There is no reason at all why agents should be interacting in a democratic way. They might, but they might not. Indeed, what it means to interact democratically, as a generalisation or idealisation, will need to be continually negotiated in local, contingent situations. Furthermore, they are not all equal in a simulation such as Tierra. Some are pursuing more powerful strategies than others, in terms of survival. There is certainly no requirement for consensus but, rather, the tension between competition and cooperation is expressed as conflict.

3. There is no anarchy, because no agent can do whatever it pleases. There are a number of constraints, not least those provided by the actions taken by other agents.

4. There is no connection whatever between empowerment of the lower echelons in an organisation and self-organisation, a matter I will explore next.

5. There is also no connection whatever between disempowering the higher echelons and self-organisation, also to be explained in the next section.

14.4 The roles of the most powerful

Understanding organisations and their strategies as social objects that emerge in local communicative interaction immediately raises questions about the role of leaders. Since many equate emergence with chance, they immediately conclude that it implies no role for leaders. This section will argue that this is not so.

To repeat: self-organisation means that agents interact locally with each other according to their own local principles of interaction, where those local principles have evolved in a life history and include the historically evolved generalisations of their community that have become aspects of their personality structures. This means that as agents they respond to each other according to their own historically evolved capacity to respond. They are enabled to respond in certain ways and constrained from responding in others by that capacity, which has emerged from their histories of interacting with others in which social objects have become aspects of their very selves. Some agents will have developed wider-ranging capacities for taking the attitude of others and of the social object than others. Some will have evolved capacities that enable them to respond more effectively and more successfully than others do. In organisational terms, some members will have more knowledge and more understanding than others and so the power ratio will be tilted toward them. Some agents interact with more agents than others. Some are able to stand back and understand something of the larger processes in which they are participating, which does not mean that they are stepping outside those processes and understanding them from the perspective of the objective observer. Instead they are reflecting, as participants, on the nature of what is happening in the situations in which they are participating.

In organisational terms, then, the top executives have more power than others: that is, a greater capacity to instruct, persuade or even force others to do what they want. Furthermore, those top executives interact with a great many more people than the less powerful. A CEO may communicate with, and issue instructions to, hundreds of thousands of others in his or her organisation through email, for example. A CEO might form certain views about the nature of his or her organisation, the nature of leadership, the direction the CEO would like it to go in, a vision or a mission for it and so on. These are all actions the CEO is taking that are likely to call forth some kind of response from many others in the organisation. A small group of powerful people at the top of an organisation might, after many local interactions, take a decision to enter a new market or to negotiate with a small group of powerful people in another organisation to merge with it. All of these actions would evoke and provoke multiple responses from others, both within and outside the affected organisations. If the pattern of these responses were simply the expression of some overall blueprint then we could not talk about self-organisation or emergence. However, if others were responding according to their own local capacities to respond, we would be talking about self-organisation and emergence.

The point I am making is this. Small groups of very powerful people at the top of an organisation allocate resources and in so doing both enable and constrain other members of the organisation. They design sets of procedures and hierarchical reporting structures but always in local interactions in which they are responding to what has just been happening. They legitimise some actions and not others. They gesture to very large numbers of others. They make statements about visions and missions. They make decisions and take actions that greatly affect a great many others. What they cannot do, however, is programme the responses those others will make. They cannot control the interplay of intentions. The powerful may identify what kind of responses they would like by making statements about values and required cultures and behaviours. They may try to motivate others to adopt all of this. They may have desires and dreams. However, people will still only be able to respond according to their own local capacities to respond, and the most powerful will find that they have to respond to the responses that they have evoked and provoked. This is what I think self-organisation means in human terms. It is a process of interaction that is ever present in all human situations and would only cease if people really did respond like automatons to statements about the values and behaviours they were supposed to display.

For example, suppose the chief executive of a major multinational corporation announces his new vision of the 'corporation as global leader in network solutions'. Perhaps one hundred thousand people around the globe hear the gesture and a great many feel called upon to respond in some way. However, the meaning of the vision, like the meaning of all gestures, does not lie in the gesture taken on its own. What it means will be created in the responses. Will most just pay lip service to it and carry on doing what they were doing before? If they do not, just what will they do? The gesture may call forth the response of many meetings around the globe as people discuss what it means and what they are supposed to do about it. The meaning of the chief executive's gesture, and its impact on the organisation, will emerge in many local situations, including his or her own, in the living present of conversations around the globe.

From a complex responsive processes perspective, no one can determine the dynamic of interaction within an organisation, because that dynamic depends upon what others both within that organisation and in other organisations are doing. In other words, an individual, or a group of individuals, powerful or otherwise, can make gestures of great importance, but the responses called forth will occur in local situations in the living present and from these there will emerge the population-wide patterns of strategic activity that perpetually constructs an organisation's future.

The focus of attention, in trying to make sense of what happens, shifts from the chief executive's statement, or new tool, to the processes in which the statement or tool arises and to the many, many local situations in which they have their effects. Instead of taking it for granted that powerful chief executives actually individually change organisations directly through their intended actions, the complex responsive processes perspective focuses attention on the communicative processes in which the mere presence of, the images of and the fantasies about leaders all affect local processes of communicative interaction in the living present from which emerge the population-wide patterns that are organisations. Emergence, then, has very little, if anything at all, to do with chance. No one can shape, influence or condition emergence.

14.5 Summary

The key question addressed in this chapter had to do with understanding the basic structure of the local (self-organising) interaction between human agents as persons and the connection between such local interaction and the emergence of population-wide patterns, an organisation being an example of such a pattern.

Mead's work provides an explanation of human interaction in which such interaction is understood to be communication between human bodies, taking the form of the conversation of gestures where the fundamental unit is the gesture–response as inseparable phases of the social act. What is profound about Mead's thought is that it explains how the basic attributes of being human emerge in such social communication. His theory is also able to provide a convincing explanation of how population-wide patterns emerge in local, human communicative interaction. Local interaction always occurs in a social situation which has evolved to its present through a history. The social is generalised tendencies on the part of large numbers of people to act in similar situations in similar ways through taking the attitude of the generalised other/social object. These generalisations must be made particular in contingent situations and it is this particularising activity that constitutes the local, communicative interaction of negotiating meaning which always involves explorative and sometimes polarised conflict. It is in this conflictual negotiation, involving spontaneity, that small differences can occur and be amplified across a population.

The consequence of thinking in this way is that we come to understand organisations as social objects, as iterated patterns of interaction. The key argument is that strategies and organisational changes emerge in local interaction understood as conversation. This requires us to re-think what we mean by most organisational activities such as strategising, leading and many more. The next chapter will turn to the power and ideology aspects of local interaction and the consequences for emergent population-wide patterns.

Further reading

Useful further reading is provided by Stacey (2005) and Shaw and Stacey (2006). Williams (2005) writes about the experience of national education policies in local interaction

Questions to aid further reflection

1. What do you understand 'population-wide pattern' and 'local interaction' to mean and how are they related to each other?
2. In what ways does Mead's idea of control differ from that to be found in the dominant discourse on organisations?
3. What is a social object in your experience?
4. Can you think of population-wide patterns that have emerged in local interaction?
5. What happens in your organisation when leaders issue statements on visions, missions and values?

Chapter 15

The emergence of organisational strategy in local communicative interaction

Complex responsive processes of ideology and power relating

This chapter invites you to draw on your own experience to reflect on and consider the implications of:

- The processes of idealisation in forming the cult values of an organisation and interpreting them in specific, contingent situations.

- The ideological basis of choice and intention in organisations.

- The nature of power relations in organisations and the ideologies that sustain them.

- The impact of the inclusion–exclusion dynamics of power in organisations.

- The role of inclusion–exclusion processes in identity formation.

- The part that gossip plays in sustaining ideologies and power relations in organisations.

- The implications of power relations and ideology for the local activities of strategising and the population-wide patterns of strategy that they produce.

This chapter carries further the exploration of processes of local interaction understood as conversation, drawing attention to how figurations of power relations emerge in ongoing communicative interaction and how these patterns of power relations are sustained by ideologies. It points to an understanding of choice, decision-making and intention in organisational life as all fundamentally ideological in nature and reflective of power relations. This chapter is important because it introduces two further key aspects of complex responsive processes of relating in addition to conversation. In doing so it makes power and ideology central to an understanding of organisational life, aspects of experience that do not receive this prominence in the dominant discourse on organisation and strategy. We come to understand strategy as the evolving collective identities of people in organisations reflecting the pattern of power relations between them and the ideologies that sustain these patterns. We come to understand local interaction as not just the particularising of generalised population-wide patterns but also the functionalising of idealisations of these patterns understood as values and ideology. We come to understand population-wide patterns: that is, strategies, as generalisations and idealisations.

15.1 Introduction

Chapters 13 and 14 described how Mead drew attention to the human capacity to generalise the attitude, the tendency to act, of people in groups and societies and how each person takes up such generalisations, or population-wide patterns of action, in each specific local situation in which they interact with other people. General tendencies to act are thereby made particular in each specific situation, through interactive processes of essentially conflictual negotiation and compromise. They do all of this in conversation with each other, and it works primarily because, through the life histories of the individuals involved and through the history of their communities, these generalised tendencies to act have become central aspects of their very selves. Socialising processes have instilled self-control in persons, and this is the basis of modern social order. Socially instilled self-control is a far more important source of the controlled behaviour of people in groups, organisations and societies than the instructions of the more powerful, the procedures of an organisation or even the law. However, individual persons do not act in ways that are simply socially determined because of the human capacity for choice and spontaneity.

This chapter is primarily concerned with the processes of human choosing reflected in the formation of intentions and the processes of decision-making. Central to understanding processes of choosing, intending and making decisions is the nature of ideology. This chapter will, therefore, be concerned with how we might understand the formation of values and norms, the implications they have for power relations, and the impact they have on choices, intentions and decision making in organisations. The argument will be that ideologies and the power relations they sustain are central to the local communicative interactions of strategising in which the population-wide patterns of strategy emerge.

This chapter draws on the work of Mead and Dewey to understand ideology and on that of Elias to explore the nature of power relations. Chapter 14 drew attention to Mead's explanation of how the generalisations of social objects are made particular in ordinary everyday, specific, contingent situations in which people in organisations find they have to act. Mead also drew attention to another important human capacity: humans have a powerful tendency to idealise social objects – that is, to idealise generalisations of population-wide patterns. He argued that in idealising social objects people form cult values, an idea to be explored in the next section.

15.2 Cult values

Mead (1923) held that people not only generalise habitual patterns of interaction to imaginatively construct some kind of unity of experience, usually understood as some kind of 'whole', they also inevitably idealise these imaginatively constructed 'wholes'. Mead pointed to how people have a tendency to individualise and idealise a collective and treat it 'as if' *it* had overriding motives or values, amounting to processes in which the collective constitutes a 'cult'. Mead described such idealisations as 'cult values' that emerge in the evolution of a society and said that they were the most precious part of our heritage. Cults are maintained when leaders present to people's imaginations an idealised future for the 'whole' – that is, free of conflicts and constraints, evoking in individuals who belong to it a sense of enlarged personality in which they can accomplish anything simply through their belonging to an idealised group in which they participate and from which they derive their value as persons. For example, a collective consisting of supporters of a football club displays the tendencies Mead was talking about. Simply belonging to the club and watching the team playing generates feelings of euphoria in fans, of belonging to the 'best', even though they are sitting in front of a television screen miles away from the very small number who are actually playing the game. The same kind of feeling of enlarged personality is experienced when one's country is selected to host the Olympic games or wins a war. Belonging to a major corporation elicits the same feeling of enlarged personality in many people. The visions articulated by leaders of countries and corporations are examples of idealisations of the 'whole' which promise a utopian future shorn of all obstacles to its realisation – 'we will be number one'.

It is important to stress immediately that cult values can be good or bad or both. Cult values would include 'ethnic purity' and 'loving your neighbour'. Mead points out that the processes of idealisation are far from unproblematic and could easily lead to actions that others outside the cult will come to regard as bad, even evil, as in 'ethnic purity'. On the other hand, cult values to 'end poverty' could lead to actions that others will come to regard as good, even saintly.

If cult values are applied directly to action, without allowing for variations contingent on a specific situation, those undertaking such action form a cult in which they exclude all who do not comply. Members of 'cults' forget the 'as if' nature of their constructed unity of experience, the 'whole', and act in a manner driven by the cult's values. Mead was pointing to the dangers of focusing on the cult values themselves, on the values of the personalised institution or system, and directly applying them as overriding universal norms, conformity to which constitutes the requirement for continuing membership of the institution.

Normally, however, idealisation is accompanied by functionalisation. Idealisations, or cult values, can become functional values in the everyday interactions between members of an institution rather than being simply applied in a way that enforces the conformity of a cult. For example, the cult value of a hospital might be to 'provide each patient with the best possible care'. However, such a cult value has to be repeatedly functionalised in many unique specific situations throughout the day. In other words, specific healthcare professionals, in specific places, at specific times will have to decide how to interpret the meaning of 'best possible care' in the face of competing demands for time and other resources. As soon as cult values become functional values in real daily interaction, conflict arises and it is this conflict that must be negotiated by people in their practical interaction with each other as they act on present interpretations of cult values. For example, a cult value to do with the sacredness of life may be directly and rigidly applied by people in an anti-abortion group who deny that there are any circumstances whatsoever in which abortion is to be allowed. Such cult members have been known to murder doctors who defy this cult value. However, for many people the cult value of the sacredness of life is not directly applied, leading to conflict regarding the circumstances in which abortion may be permissible – the conflict may be around whether abortion should be allowed up to 20 weeks after conception or up to 24 weeks. Functionalising of values is the enactment of values in the ordinary, local interactions between people in the living present.

In many healthcare organisations today, the notions of 'modernisation', 'improvement' and 'performance' have taken on the status of cult values. Government ministers present to people's imagination a future for healthcare in which such care is of a continuously improving quality, and equally available on demand to everyone with very little waiting time. This 'vision' is presented in such a way that the difficulties in achieving it go unmentioned. However, when practitioners try to functionalise such cult values, they are confronted with shortages of resources and many other relational problems which mean that they find it impossible to deliver the idealised future. They find they have to functionalise the undoubtedly worthy cult values and this gives rise to conflicting priorities.

Mead presented a paradoxical formulation in his distinction between cult and functional values. The idealisation must be functionalised in specific contingent situations – the meaning of the idealisation is only to be found in the experience of its functionalisation. In its functionalisation the ideal inevitably become less than ideal.

We may employ the tool of writing to articulate and codify our idealisations in the form of ethical propositions, myths and inspiring narratives. They may be presented as intended, crafted vision statements for a corporation, for example. However, although someone can design and intentionally present statements about values, they can only ever be cult values that have no meaning on their own. In other words, the cult value is the first phase of a social act that can never be separated from the other phase: namely, functionalising the cult values.

As well as being generalisations, then, social objects may also take the form of *idealisations* or cult values. Such values have the effect of *including* those who adhere to them and *excluding* those who do not, so establishing collective or *'we' identities* for all of the individuals in both groupings. Social objects/cult values are thus closely linked to *power*, a matter to be discussed later in this chapter. Social objects as generalised/idealised tendencies to act in similar ways both enable and constrain the actors at the same time. Social objects/cult values are thus forms of *social control* reflected in figurations of *power relations* between people.

Furthermore, cult values provide the evaluative criteria people use to make choices. We normally do not choose our actions in a technically rational manner but on the basis of what we believe, often unconsciously, to be 'right'; and we derive these beliefs from the social milieu in which we have grown up and live. The ideological basis of out choices of action have become so ingrained in who we are that we are mainly unaware of just what this ideological basis is. This point about the ideological basis of choice is of great importance, because ideology deeply conditions the way we think about what we do, or should do, in organisations. For example, the ideology of control underpinning the dominant discourse about organisations goes largely unremarked. The demand for control ceases to be examinable as a belief and becomes taken for granted as 'reality', so closing down explorative processes of new thinking. The manner in which personal experiences of value arise is not explored and, instead, leaders of organisations are called upon to provide appropriate values for people and to inspire them with 'compelling visions of the future'. When they do this, leaders are actually articulating cult values, which may or may not be 'good'. What is overlooked, however, is the need to functionalise the cult values. On the contrary, the prescriptions usually call for the conversion of people so that they all share and act upon the same values. It is not realised that this is in fact a prescription for the formation of a cult through processes that can easily amount to propaganda, even brainwashing. Fortunately, visions, missions and value statements are usually simply acknowledged in public while privately people express their cynicism. What is also not questioned is how experiences of value arise and whether it is indeed possible for leaders to provide genuine value experiences for other people in an instrumental manner.

Recognising that many of today's prescriptions for leaders could amount to the potential formation of cults, that actually it is impossible to prescribe genuine values for other people except through intense propaganda and brainwashing, thus has considerable practical implications for currently dominant ways of organising, leading and strategising.

The question then is how cult values arise and how they evolve.

15.3 Desires, values and norms

The work of Joas (2000) is helpful in understanding how cult values arise and evolve. He draws on the thinking of the American pragmatists (Dewey, 1934; James, 1902; Mead, 1934) to make a distinction between desires/preferences, values/ideals and norms.

Turning first to desires, a distinction can be made between first- and second-order desires (Frankfurt, 1971). First-order desires or preferences are:

- fluid and particular bodily impulses expressed as unreflective action;
- experienced as compulsive motivations for actions;
- lacking in evaluative criteria and so not intrinsically linked to ethics or morals.

However, humans also have desires that are directed to their desires and could be called *second-order desires*. In other words, humans can desire to have desires, or not, and they can desire that their desire should be strong enough to influence their will. We can desire to be different from who we are. Desires directed to our desires arise in reflective self-evaluation so that human desiring is essentially reflective and self-evaluative and so essentially social because the self is social. For human action it is not possible to take desire (bodily impulse, or first-order desire) on its own because of the human capacity, essentially social, to formulate the desirable and the judgement or evaluation that this always involves. Only in the rarest of circumstances, I would argue, do humans simply act on bodily impulse – there is almost always some kind of discrimination arising in a history of social interaction, although that discrimination could quite easily have become unconscious. This discrimination inevitably implicates norms and values. So what are they and how do they arise?

Norms are:

- evaluative in that they provide criteria for judging desires and actions;
- obligatory and constraining. They therefore restrict opportunities for action. We experience them as compelling in a restrictive sense;
- intimately connected with morals in that they provide criteria for what *ought* to be done, what is *right*.

Norms, then, provide a basis for evaluating and choosing between desires and actions. Elias ([1939] 2000) was particularly concerned with how norms emerge and evolve as people in a society become more and more interdependent and as the use of violence is monopolised by the state. He explained how desires are taken more and more behind the scenes of daily life as more detailed norms emerge about what can and cannot be done in public. These norms become part of individual personality structures and adherence to such norms is sustained by the social process of shame. Norms, therefore, are constraints arising in social evolution that act to restrain the actions and even desires of interdependent individuals, so much so that the constraints become thematic patterns of individual identities. In complex responsive process terms, norms are themes organising experience in a constraining way. However, norms are inseparable although different from values. First, consider how values differ from norms and then how inseparable they are, despite the differences.

Joas uses the words 'values' and 'ideals' interchangeably and identifies their characteristics as:

- evaluative in that they provide general and durable criteria for judging desires, norms and actions;
- attractive and compelling in a voluntary, committed sense. They motivate action and open up opportunities for action. Values attract us, giving life meaning and purpose, and so are not experienced as restrictive. They are the highest expression of our free will, presenting a paradox of compulsion and voluntary commitment at the same time;
- intimately connected with ethics in that they provide criteria for judging what *is* the *good* in action, differentiating between good and bad desires, good and bad norms.

Values are essentially concerned with what it is good to desire. When we reject a perfectly realisable desire because we believe it is unacceptable then we are distinguishing between higher and lower virtues or vices, profound and superficial feelings, noble and base desires. Such evaluations indicate a life we hold to be of higher value, a view of the kind of person we want to be.

Joas drew on Dewey (1934), a friend and colleague of Mead, to argue that values, as inspiring, attractively compelling motivations to act towards the good, are continually arising in social interaction as inescapable aspects of self-formation. Values are continually arising in our ongoing negotiation with each other, and ourselves, in our going on together. It follows that values are contingent upon the particular action situations in which we find ourselves. Although values have general and durable qualities, their motivational impact on action must be negotiated afresh, must be particularised, in each action situation. Dewey combines such an intersubjective understanding of self- and value-formation with experiences of self-transcendence. The communicative interaction in which self is formed is more than a means to coordinating action; it opens human beings up to each other, making possible the experience in which values and commitments to them arise. Shared experiences overcome self-centredness producing altruism, which is a radical readiness to be shaken by the other in order to realise oneself in and through others. This opening, or transcending, of the self is the process in which genuine values arise.

Dewey also brings the role of imagination and creativity into the genesis of values and value commitments. Imagination idealises contingent possibilities and creates an imaginary relation to a holistic self. While imaginary, this relation is not an illusion or a fantasy. Idealisation allows us to imagine a wholeness that does not exist and never will but seems real because we have experienced it so intensely. This is not a solitary but a social process. The will does not bring about the imagined wholeness; rather, the will is possessed by it. The voluntary compulsion of the experience of value and value commitment feels to come from outside of ourselves, to be not of our own positing but of something higher than us.

So, here, values are understood as the 'imaginative constructs' of 'wholes'. Indeed, organisations as idealised patterns of relating between human beings can be thought of as 'wholes': that is, as the imaginative constructs that people take up together in their coming together in joint activity. Here, I am referring to a conceptual whole in a very different way to that found in systems thinking. In systems thinking the conceptual whole is a system arising in the interaction of conceptual parts within a conceptual boundary. This is a way of conceptualising an object. From the responsive processes view, 'whole' does not refer to a system of any kind but to a felt experience of unity in interaction with others in a society. The whole is thus not a creation or co-creation of some *thing*, some third, but a *feeling* arising in a human body in relating to other human bodies in joint activity. The unity of experience only exists in the iteration of interaction, not as any thing outside it. The argument is that we construct a unity of experience in processes of idealisation in which we experience some group of people to whom we belong as an 'it' to which we together ascribe idealised properties. For example, we may idealise 'the academy' and ascribe to it idealisations (cult values) such as free speech. The whole that I am referring to is a feeling involving the experience of value and the co-creation of cult values. This is very different to thinking of a whole as a system with parts. The feeling of unity as the experience of ideology does not have parts interacting to form a whole. The whole of the unity of experience does not exist other than in the mind and even then it exists only in its expression in the interaction of human bodies with each other and there is no need to think of any of this as a system.

The description of values and value commitments in the last section may easily be taken as meaning that values are unequivocally good. However, as indicated in the discussion above, this is not so. The notions of cult values, the power dynamics of inclusion and exclusion they involve, and the way in which groups of people may get caught up in destructive unconscious processes of self-loss, focus our attention on the darker aspects of values/ideals and value commitments. These processes point to the particular problems that arise from the tendencies to idealise imagined wholes and submerge oneself in imagined participation in them.

Notice the paradoxical nature of the theory of values so far outlined. Values arise in processes of self-formation and self-transcendence at the same time. Values arise in critical reflection and in experience beyond conscious deliberation at the same time. Values arise in intense actual experience of interaction and in idealising acts of imagination at the same time. Values may be good or bad or both, depending upon who is doing the judging.

Values do not arise either from conscious intentions or through justification and discussion, although such intention, justification and discussion may be applied later. Genuinely experienced value commitments cannot be produced rationally, and authentic values cannot be disseminated through indoctrination. A purpose in life cannot be prescribed. Instead, the subjective experience of values arises in specific action contexts and types of intense experience. Values and value commitments arise in the process of self-formation through processes of idealising key intense experiences and through the imaginative construction of a whole self to yield general and durable motivations for action directed toward what is judged as the good. These generalised idealisations must always be particularised in specific action situations as people negotiate their going on together if they are to avoid a cult.

Values cannot be prescribed or deliberately chosen by anyone, because they emerge, and continue to be iterated, in intense interactive experiences involving self-formation and self-transcendence. To claim that someone could choose values for others would be to claim that this someone could form the identity, or self, of others and form the self-transcendence of others.

If one takes the above view of what values are and how they arise, then the pre-scriptions of the dominant discourse that require leaders to form an organisation's values become highly questionable. Such approaches could not create authentic experiences of value and value commitment involving a mature capacity to func-tionalise them in contingent situations. All they could do, when effective as pro-paganda, would be to create the dangerous conformity of a fundamentalist cult. Alternatively, leadership activities claiming to be formulating values may only amount to the prescription of norms as obligatory restrictions rather than the voluntary compulsions of values. Even these norms would have to be functionalised in con-tingent situations unless people felt so threatened and afraid that they could do not other than rigidly comply in what would then be a fascist power structure. The less harmful consequence of attempts to instil values is the cynicism usually provoked by such attempts. The way one thinks about values and norms thus has profound consequences for what one does in organisations.

Now consider how norms and values together constitute ideology.

Norms, values and ideology

In complex responsive processes terms, values are themes organising the experience of being together in a voluntary compelling, ethical manner, while norms are themes of being together in an obligatory, restrictive way. Furthermore, in complex respon-sive process terms, norms and values constitute a paradox. When humans interact, they enable and constrain each other at the same time. It is the actions of human bodies that enable and constrain. However, in their ongoing negotiation of these enabling–constraining actions, all are taking the attitude of others, specifically and in a generalised/idealised way. In other words, they are continually negotiating the evaluations of their actions. The criteria for evaluation are at the same time both obligatory restrictions, taking the form of what they ought and ought not to do (norms), and voluntary compulsions, taking the form of what they are judging it good to do (values). The evaluative themes forming and being formed by human interaction are norms and values at the same time, together constituting ideology.

Ideology can be thought of as an imaginative 'whole' – that is, simultaneously the obligatory restriction of the norm and the voluntary compulsion of value, constituting the evaluative criteria for the choice of actions. As such it is largely habitual and so unconscious processes of self and social at the same time. If people in a group rigidly apply the ideological 'whole' to their interactions in all specific, contingent situations, they co-create fascist power relations and cults which can easily be taken over by collective ecstasies. The result is to alienate people from their ordinary everyday experience and so create a false consciousness. Alternatively, if the ideological 'whole' is so fragmented that there is little generalised/idealised tendency to act, then people will be interacting in ways that are almost entirely contingent on the situation, resulting in anarchy. Usually, however, people particularise/functionalise some ideological wholes in contingent situations and this is essentially a conflictual process of negating the 'whole', which always involves critical reflection.

From a complex responsive processes perspective, there are no universals outside of human interaction, but this does not mean that norms and values are purely relative in an 'anything goes' kind of way, because generalisations and idealisations can only be found in their particularisation in specific interactive situations. This always involves negotiation of conflict; power relating, in which 'anything goes' is impossible.

From a complex responsive processes perspective, desires, values and norms are all understood to be particular narrative and propositional themes emerging in interaction and at the same time patterning that interaction. Norms are constraining aspects of themes, providing criteria for judging desires and actions. Emotions, such as shame and fear of punishment or exclusion, provide the main constraining force. Values, on the other hand, are highly motivating aspects of themes that arise in particularly intense collective and individual experience, involving imagination and idealisation, and serving as the basis for evaluating and justifying desires and actions, as well as the norms constraining them. Emotions such as altruism, gratitude, humility self-worth, guilt and outrage provide the attractive, compelling force of value experiences. For each person, these intense value experiences are particularly linked to interactions over a life history with important others, such as parents, who are perceived to enact values ascribed to them. These important others cannot unilaterally prescribe such values, because they emerge in the relationship. However, while the separation of values and norms is an aid to understanding, it is an abstraction from lived, practical experience in which norms and values are inseparable aspects of the evaluative themes, the ideologies, which are the basis of our choices of actions.

Ideology and healthcare

Consider the points made above in relation to government policy on the National Health Service in the UK. The NHS can be thought of as a collective identity, a 'we' identity that is inseparable from the 'I' identities of all who work for it and all concerned with its governance. Such an identity is a social object – that is, generalised tendencies to act in similar ways by large numbers of people in similar situations. On closer inspection, however, there is not one monolithic identity, one social object, but many linked ones. Each hospital, for example, has a distinctive identity, as do the groups of different kinds of medical practitioners and managers who are its members. There are, therefore, many social objects, many generalised tendencies by large numbers of people to act in similar ways in similar situations. Furthermore, the medical profession, the NHS and the many different institutions and groupings the NHS composed of are all idealised. Cult values, such as 'providing free health-care', 'doing no harm', 'providing all with the highest standard of care' and 'providing the same standard of care in all geographical locations to all classes of person', are essential features of what the NHS means. 'Performance' and 'quality' are recent additions to these cult values. The generalisations and idealisations can all be recorded in written artefacts, sound recordings and films as propositions and/or narratives. These artefacts may take the form of policy documents, legal contracts, procedures, instructions from the Department of Health, and so on. Such artefacts are then used as tools in the communicative interaction and power relating between members within the NHS and between them and those concerned with its governance. However, the artefacts recording the generalisations and idealisations are just artefacts, not the generalisations and idealisations themselves. Whether recorded or not, the generalisations and idealisation only have any meaning in the local interactions of all involved in each specific situation – they are only to be found in the experience of local interaction.

So, for example, when groups of policy makers in the Department of Health and each of the main political parties get together to decide what to do about the NHS, they are clearly interacting locally. What they will be reflecting upon and discussing are the generalisations and idealisations of the NHS or parts of it. They may issue a consultation document to large numbers of people for comment. This is then taken up for discussion in the professional bodies representing different groups in the NHS. Again, the discussion is local interaction, as is the subsequent negotiation of changes in any of the policies. What they are discussing and negotiating in this local interaction is changes to population-wide patterns, to the generalisations and idealisations. Eventually a policy statement is produced and instructions sent to, say, all of the hospitals in the country, setting out what new targets they must meet in order to demonstrate quality and performance and in what way they will be punished if they do not. What I have been describing is processes of local interaction, local negotiation, in which emerge articulations of the general and the ideal as far as the NHS is concerned. The processes are ones in which people have been trying to design the general and the ideal, and in the way they currently do this in the UK they reflect a particular way of thinking about the NHS. In setting targets and establishing monitoring process they display a way of thinking derived from cybernetics systems. They are trying to design and install a self-regulating system.

However, the NHS is not a self-regulating system, but many local patterns of interaction in which the general and the idealised are continually emerging as continuity and change from one iteration of the present to the next. What then becomes important is how people are taking up, in their local interactions, the generalisations and idealisations articulated in the artefacts of written instructions and procedures. The meaning cannot be located simply in the gesture that these artefacts represent but only, at the same time, in the myriad responses this gesture calls forth. In a specific situation on a specific day, there may simply not be the physical capacity to achieve the targets set. In each specific situation there will always be conflicts on what the targets mean and how they are to be adhered to. The target might then become something that has to be avoided, manipulated and even falsified. For example, a specific decision might be to meet, say, a target of reducing waiting lists, by sending people home too early after an operation, leading to a rise in re-admissions. The global generalisation that the policy makers designed is thus being transformed in the local interaction so that it comes to mean something different – instead of uniform high performance it might come to mean 'cover up' and 'deceit'.

As the unexpected emerges in many, many local interactions, the population-wide pattern is transformed and, of course, in their local interactions, the policy makers are reflecting upon this. They may then conclude that the now burgeoning number of targets is proving too much of an embarrassment and should be scrapped. However, still thinking in system terms, they feel that they must design some other form of generalisation to stay in control and secure adequate performance. The proposal is then that 700 targets should be abandoned, only to be replaced with 22 qualitative standards. Once again, however, the meaning does not lie on the generalisation alone but in its particularisation in many local situations.

The argument I am presenting here has an immediate implication for processes of policy making and strategising. This is that the almost exclusive focus on the design of a generalisation/idealisation in policy making will lead to continual cycles of surprise. Greater attention needs to be paid to processes of particularising if policy makers are to avoid some of the endless policy reversals that characterise policy making, at least in the NHS.

What is the part a leader plays in all of this? Leadership arises in social processes of recognition (Griffin, 2002) in which, in imagination, the leader can be recognised as embodying the idealised whole. The leader is not actually designing the values and persuading others to commit to them, although this is how it might appear. Instead, the leader is actually participating in the intense experience in which the values are arising and in which he or she comes to be imagined as embodying them. He/she and others may be so caught up in the process that they all lose sight of the imaginative nature of their construct. The leader is then idealised as a person and denigration is never far away. Leadership as a social object and cult value will be explored in the next section.

15.4 Ethics and leadership

Griffin (2002) argues that, from a systemic perspective, leaders are understood as autonomous individuals who formulate visions and values to be directly applied to an organisational or cultural system. In other words, the whole system is reified in thought and ascribed intentions or qualities such as 'harmonious', 'caring' or 'soul'. They are then understood as idealised wholes, which provide leadership to those individuals participating in them. The result is a dual notion of leadership being provided *both* by individual leaders, who define the values and purpose of the whole system, *and* by a system, which incorporates those values and purposes as the leading principles its members are to follow. Individuals following the principles of the whole are regarded as 'good' or 'compassionate', while those who do not are characterised as 'bad' or 'selfish'. In other words, leadership and ethics become matters of explicating the rules or qualities of the harmonious whole and of individuals conforming to it. Griffin is drawing attention here to how notions of leadership are inextricably interwoven with questions of ethics.

Griffin argues against this view of leadership and ethics because he says that it eliminates paradox and mystifies leadership, abstracting ethics from direct experience and locating it in some kind of external, idealised whole. As a result, people experience themselves as the victims of the systems they think they have created.

Griffin traces systemic thinking on ethics and leadership back to Kant's categorical imperative. By this, Kant meant that the principles behind an ethical action would reflect a universal law. Autonomous individuals could objectively observe their own conduct, just as they could objectively observe nature, and judge their actions, which could be understood 'as if' they were actions that could be performed by everyone. As people proceed in this way, different formulations of the categorical imperative emerge: for example, 'treat others as you want them to treat you' and 'do not treat other people as means to an end since all people are ends in themselves'. These imperatives have the character of universals but they do not dictate what to do in any specific situation. In specific situations people have to choose what to do by formulating hypothetical imperatives and then, in their acting, testing them against the categorical imperatives, also using such a procedure to justify what they have done. In this way it is thought that, just as we can progressively build up a body of knowledge about the timeless universal laws governing nature, so we can progressively build up a body of knowledge on timeless, ethical imperatives for human conduct. Ethics here is firmly based on the reasoning capacity of the autonomous individual, who can discover the universal principles of good conduct through what amounts to the scientific method.

Kant, then, presented a notion of ethics as a body of universal imperatives that already exist, just as natural laws do, to be discovered by autonomous individuals, just as natural laws are, and expressed in a body of timeless ethical imperatives, just as natural laws are timeless and universal. From this perspective, the principles of actions do not depend upon social or natural contingencies, nor do they reflect the bias of the particulars of individuals' plans for their lives, the particular desires, aims or aspirations that motivate them. It is this notion of ethics that forms the basis of traditional business ethics today – a notion of universal codes of conduct discovered or formulated by autonomous rational individuals as the basis upon which they are to judge their own and each other's conduct. In this way of thinking, the leader is an autonomous individual, as is everyone else, charged with developing ethical behaviour.

Contrary to Kant (*see* Chapter 3), however, systems thinkers today apply the notion of systemic wholes to human interaction. This leads to an ethics that is quite contrary to Kant in that now autonomous individuals are required to participate in, submit themselves to, some larger whole or greater good. No longer are the autonomous individuals trying to discover in their actions what the ethical imperatives reflecting the not-to-be-defined whole are. Instead they are required to submit themselves to the visions and values revealed to them by their leaders. In doing so, they lose their autonomy. In the Kantian sense of autonomy, the endorsement of the vision statements of top management by others is in effect the surrender of autonomy. In organisational theory of this kind, it is only senior managers who are leaders in the Kantian sense of being fully autonomous individuals and they allow others to share in this autonomy. Participation becomes participating in the leadership of the leaders, where that leadership is the values ascribed to the organisational system.

Griffin suggests that the theory of complex responsive processes of relating provides an alternative way of thinking about leadership and ethics. Here participation is the direct interaction of persons with each other, not participation in some whole. This is an approach that stays with our experience of interaction and regards the ethics of action as processes of perpetual negotiation that do indeed depend upon personal desires, aims and aspirations as well as natural contingencies. These processes of communicative interaction are ones in which we together create what happens to us and they are such that small differences can be amplified to transform population-wide patterns. What each of us does matters even though we cannot know what the outcome of our actions will be. Griffin regards this as an empowering perspective that also makes it impossible for one to escape the responsibility for one's own actions by ascribing the causes of what happens to some whole system outside of our direct experience of interacting with each other. He argues that instead of leading us to feel hopeless, victimised or rebellious, this perception encourages us to pay attention to what we are doing and to believe that this is effective in some way, even though we cannot know how.

Griffin draws on Mead (1934) to develop this argument. For Mead, those who emerge as leaders are those who display a greater spontaneity and have a greater ability to deal with the ongoing purpose or task for which others are interacting. The leader is an individual who is able to enter into the attitudes of others, so enhancing connection and interaction between group members. Notice how this notion of a leader does not simply locate leadership in the individual by ascribing leadership purely to the personal attributes of the leader. This is because the leader is actually constructed in the recognition of others. It does not matter what leadership attributes one has if no one recognises them; and, of course, one cannot be a leader if one does not recognise the recognition of others and so recognise them. Leaders, therefore, emerge in complex responsive processes of mutual recognition.

Mead refers to the way in which groups tend to recognise the leader role in those who have acquired a greater spontaneity, a greater ability to deal with the unknown as it emerges from the known context. Mead argued that the ethical interpretation of action is to be found in the action itself, in the ongoing *recognition* of the meanings of actions that could not have been known in advance. In other words, ethical meaning does not reside in external universals to be applied to interaction but continually emerges in the interaction itself. Ethics are being negotiated in the interaction. Moral advance, for Mead, then consists not in adapting individuals to the fixed realities of a moral universe, but in constantly reconstructing and recreating the world as individuals evolve.

The distinction between cult and functional is relevant to understanding leadership (Taylor, 2005). One aspect of a leader is his or her idealisation as cult leader. This idealisation is functionalised in the role of the leader in the everyday conflicts of interaction. The functionalised role of leader emerges in the interaction and those participating are continuously creating and recreating the meaning of leadership themes in the local interaction in which they are involved. However, there always remains a strong tendency for a group to idealise the leader, who thereby becomes a cult leader – that is, leader of a group of people directly enacting idealised values, cult values, to which they are subtly pressured to conform to. This blocks the functionalising of the ideals, which is what an organisation needs in order to come alive in the present.

Chapter 11 referred to the way in which many people are using complexity theories to justify the formulation of simple rules and their application to an organisational system as an alternative to detailed plans. The hope seems to be that through specifying simple rules, we can still get the whole to do what we want it to. From the complex responsive perspective, these simple rules are cult values and what really matters is how they are functionalised in daily life. It is this functionalising that brings in the conflict and uncertainty, which will defeat our hope of controlling the whole unless it is indeed a cult.

The next section turns to the matter of how ideologies sustain relations of power.

15.5 Power, ideology and the dynamics of inclusion–exclusion

In order to go on together, people have to account to each other for what they do. In other words, the maintenance of relationship imposes constraint. However, at the same time, relationship enables. Elias (1991) argues that power is not a thing that someone possesses and is not simply force or violence but, rather, power is a structural characteristic of all human relationships in that it reflects the fact that we depend on each other and so enable and constrain each other. Power is this activity of enabling and constraining each other. The basis of power is *need*, so that when we need others more than they need us for love, money, status, or whatever, then they have more power over us than we have over them. However, this is never absolute because the power of the more powerful depends upon the recognition of the less powerful that this is indeed so. Furthermore, if those others come to need us more than we need them, then the power ratio shifts in our favour – power relations are dynamic. Elias expresses his relational view of power as ongoing processes of configuring power relations between people. Communicative cooperation arises in the process of people holding each other accountable for their actions in some way. They act towards each other in a manner that recognises their interdependence and so negotiate their actions with each other. Without this, relating breaks down.

The immediate consequence of such interdependence is that the behaviour of every individual is both enabled and constrained by the expectations and demands of both others and themselves. To carry on participating in the communicative interaction upon which an individual's very life depends, that individual has to rely on the enabling cooperation of others. At the same time that individual has to respect the wishes of others and those wishes will frequently conflict with his or her own. Communicative interaction is, thus, power relating as the patterning of enabling and conflicting constraints.

Elias explores how people, because of their interdependence and the way their actions intermesh, form figurations while those figurations form them. To illustrate this he uses a number of game models to demonstrate the relational character of power in a simplified form (also see Dopson, 2001). These are game contests in which the relative power of the contestants is explored to bring out the features of various power figurations. He starts with a game in which two groups of antagonists face each other in an all-out struggle in which there are no rules. For example, two groups might struggle with each other for limited food resources. When one group does something – say, raids the territory of the other group to steal their cattle – then that other group will have to respond to this, perhaps by mounting a counter-raid or building better fortifications, or entering into an alliance with a third group. It is because of this continuing need on the part of all groups to respond to what the others are doing that they obviously depend on each other – there can be no cattle raiders if there are no farmers who possess cattle, and farmers who possess cattle would not have to build fortifications if there were no cattle raiders. Groups perform a function for each other, even if such a functional relationship is not desired, and the way each group is internally organised reflects their expectation of what they will need to do next. One group, the raiders, will probably organise themselves into a pattern of a fierce leader commanding warriors, while the other, intent on improving fortifications, will probably show greater functional differentiation with soldiers distinguished from builders and both distinguished from ruling groups. Each group then is serving a function for the other even in patterns of hostility – they need each other as enemies if they are to conduct skirmishes. 'It is not possible to explain the actions, plans and aims of either of the two groups if they are conceptualized as the freely chosen decisions, plans and aims of each group considered on its own, independently of the other group' (Elias, 1970, p. 77).

The central question relates to how people have come to be able to regulate their interdependence so that they need not resort to all-out struggle as a regular pattern of interaction. This can be explored by comparing a number of games in which the strength differential between two playing groups diminishes. As the power ratio declines, the possibility of either of the groups controlling both the other group and the course of the game diminishes. This game becomes more like social processes and as this happens it resembles less and less the implementation of individual plans: 'to the extent that the inequality in the strengths of the two players diminishes, there will result from the interweaving of moves of two individual people a game process *which neither of them has planned*' (Elias, 1970, p. 82). The social cannot be reduced to the individual, and it is because of this that no one in the game can control its evolution. The explanation has to do with the constraints they place on each other and the unpredictability of their responses to each other.

As the number of players in each playing group increases, some groups of players might disintegrate, splintering into a number of smaller groups, which move further and further apart from each other, playing the game without trying to cooperate or compete with each other. For example the weaker groups might migrate to new territories where they can live independently of other groups, at least for a time. On the other hand, the splinter groups could carry on playing with each other, but in doing so they will develop a new power figuration of interdependent groups, in which each may have some autonomy but will also have to develop forms of cooperation as they compete with each other for certain resources. If this happens, it becomes even less helpful to try to understand the evolution of the game in terms of individual plans – it will be even less possible for any grouping to control the course of the game. It is also possible, of course, that as the number of players in a group increases, they could choose to remain together but this will require a much more complex figuration in which a two-tier group might develop with one subgroup being rulers, say, while the other becomes the common people, so that a specialisation develops. Special functionaries now coordinate the game: representatives, delegates, leaders and governments which together form a smaller group, playing directly with and against each other. However, they are also bound together in some way with the mass of players, the second tier. Both levels depend on each other, but the distribution of power between them can vary. Elias then explores what happens when the power differentials decline.

> Even in a game with no more than two tiers, the figuration of game and players already possesses a degree of complexity which prevents any one individual from using his superiority to guide the game in the direction of his own goals and wishes. He makes his moves both *out* of the network and *into* the network of interdependent players, where there are alliances and enmities, cooperation and rivalry at different levels.   (Elias, 1970, p. 86)

This game analogy demonstrates the evolving effects of interdependence on power figurations and the ability to control the game and, in so doing, points to explanations of the kinds of processes in which the functions of upper and lower classes in, say, Western Europe changed as the power differential diminished. The game analogy also points to explanations of the processes in which the financial sectors of most countries have become increasingly differentiated and interdependent over the last few decades, making it impossible for any group of players – financial institutions, borrowers and lenders, regulators and governments – to control the evolution of the global financial game. Despite this, however, we continue to blame one or other of the groups of players for what happened so that they can be punished, and we also continue to ascribe the problem to the system, calling for it to be re-designed so that it all 'never happens again'. In their explanations of what is happening people use metaphors

> which oscillate constantly between the idea that the course of the game can be reduced to the actions of the individual players and the other idea that it is of a supra-personal nature. Because the game cannot be controlled by the players, it is easily perceived as a kind of superhuman entity. For a long time it is especially difficult for the players to comprehend that their inability to control the game derives from their mutual dependence and positioning as players, and from the tension and conflicts inherent in this interweaving network. (Elias, 1970, p. 92)

The game analogy shows clearly how social evolution is an emergent change in patterns of relationships across a population arising in many local interactions, but this insight is clouded by the persistent tendency of the dominant discourse to either locate the cause of change in an individual or in some 'whole' outside the direct experience of interaction. Increasingly elaborate chains of connections between people produce shifting power figurations leading to processes and outcomes which are more and more difficult to understand and intend.

Newton (1999, 2001) also points out how organisations can usefully be thought about in terms of Elias' game of power and the effects it has on agency. It follows from the nature of the game that no one agent or group thereof can determine history over the long term, because their intentions and actions are always moderated by those of others on whom they depend. There is, thus, no simple relationship between strategy and outcome, because the outcome results from the interweaving of intentions and outcomes. Something comes into being that was not intended or planned by anyone but nevertheless emerges from the interweaving of their actions. Organisational change is change in interdependency networks, and human subjectivity, self, identity and agency are intimately tied up with historical changes in interdependency networks. So, the way we express emotions, emotional self-control are all the result of the historical evolution of patterns of power relations that flowed from increased interdependence and the monopolisation of violence. Power relations are built into subjectivity as we learn how to behave as children, where such subjectivity is tacit and unthinking. This is different from the taken-for-granted, ahistorical view of subjectivity in organisational theory which reflects the notion of atomistic individuals. Newton argues that writers on corporate culture (for example, Deal and Kennedy, 1988) promote individualism and a romantic view of collectivism as teams in an attempt to artificially engineer a sense of shared mission and values. This may be a response to the demise of a sense of the collective – if it existed why manufacture it? Individualism becomes a sham, since members must adhere to corporate values as a cover for hierarchy. Newton claims that Eliasian analysis also suggests that there is no separation between micro-analytical concern with emotion and subjectivity and macro-analytical concerns with power figurations. Emotional expressions are interwoven with patterns of power relations. Increasing interdependence causes emotional control. Elias stresses the unplanned nature of ordering and change where strategic outcomes flow from interweaving of actions of numerous players.

Other writers (van Iterson et al., 2001) suggest that Eliasian analysis shows the intricate connection between macro-societal developments such as state formation and micro-level changes in morals, manners and mentalities. They suggest that we can only understand strategy and change in the light of this interconnection, and they call for greater exploration of Eliasian analysis in understanding organisations in the light of changing figurations of power. So consider some further important implications of the figurational view.

The dynamics of inclusion and exclusion

Power differences establish groupings in which some people are 'included' and others are 'excluded'. Power is thus felt as the dynamics of inclusion and exclusion. These dynamics feature prominently in Elias's process sociology.

Elias and Scotson ([1965] 1994) studied events following the influx of a working-class group into a new housing estate in the UK, adjacent to an older estate that was also occupied by working-class people. Although there was no recognisable difference between the two groups, hostility soon appeared, and persisted for a very long time, in which the older, established inhabitants denigrated the newer ones. The simple fact of having been there longer meant that the established group had a degree of group cohesion and collective identification that the newcomers lacked. The established community had developed norms and values that gave them the gratifying consciousness of belonging to a group of higher value with the accompanying contempt for the other groups. The established group had come to think of themselves as a 'we', a group with common attachments, likes, dislikes and attributes and this had emerged simply because of their being together over a period of time. They had developed an identity. The new arrivals lacked this cohesive identity, because they had no history of being together and this made them more vulnerable. The more cohesive group therefore found it easy to 'name' the newcomers, to categorise them, and ascribe to them hateful attributes such as being dirty or liable to commit crimes. The two groups were unconsciously bound to each other in such a way that the members of one of them felt impelled, and had sufficient power resources, to treat those of another group collectively with a measure of contempt, and the other group accepted it because they lacked cohesion.

So, although there was no obvious difference between the two groups, one group unconsciously used the fact that the other was newly arrived to generate hatred and so maintain a power difference. Furthermore, this was, in a sense, 'accepted' by the newcomers who took up the role of the disadvantaged. The established group ascribed the 'bad' characteristics of the newcomer group's 'worst' section to the group as a whole while ascribing to themselves the characteristics of their 'best' section. Population-wide ideological patterns had emerged in the conversation within and between both the established and the newcomer groups, and this ideology established, and continued to reinforce, membership categories and differences between those categories.

One of the principal ways that power differentials are preserved, then, is the use of even trivial differences to establish different membership categories. It is not the difference itself but rather the ideological form that stirs up hatred in the interests of sustaining power positions in a dynamic of inclusion and exclusion. Dalal (1998) points out how this as an unconscious process in that the hatred between the groups emerges essentially in local interaction as patterns that no one is really aware of or actually intends. It should also be noted that what I have been describing is an everyday occurrence in less dramatic ways in all organisations. For example, when we debate differences in our theories, or when we talk in particular ways in ordinary, everyday life we are often using differences to sustain power relations.

There are other aspects of ideological themes that also serve to preserve power differentials in essentially unconscious ways in local interactions. A key aspect of ideology is the binary oppositions that characterise it and the most basic of these is the distinction between 'them' and 'us'. Ideology is thus a form of communication that preserves the current order by making that current order seem natural. In this way, ideological themes organise the communicative interactions, the conversation, of individuals and groups. As a form of communication, as an aspect of the power relations in the group, ideology is taken up in that private role play, that silent conversation, which is mind in individuals. So, while diversity is essential for the evolution of novelty, such diversity can easily become polarised and stuck, so blocking the emergence of novel patterns of relating.

Note that ideology here is thought of as being mutually reproduced in ongoing communicative action rather than anything shared or stored. Here, ideology is not some fundamental hidden cause located somewhere. It is not stored anywhere, transmitted and then shared. Rather, it is patterning processes – that is, narrative themes of inclusion and exclusion organising people's experience of being together in perpetual reproduction and potential transformation. Ideology, as population-wide pattern, exists only in the speaking and acting of it in local situations.

The processes so far described in this section are ubiquitous in organisations and are key aspects of local interactions of managing and strategising. People working in, say, the finance department of an organisations experience themselves as a 'we', and may regard those who work in, say, the public relations department as 'them', ascribing lesser value to what they do. People working in an operating subsidiary of a large corporation regard themselves as 'we' who earn profits, while 'them' at the head office are pen-pushing parasites. When people are reorganised into new departments or subsidiaries, they normally experience feelings of loss of identity, which can lead to resistance, even sabotage. When a large corporation makes an acquisition, the 'them' and 'us' dynamics become very powerful and often constitute the main reason for the failure of attempts at integration. The power dynamics of inclusion–exclusion and the ideological processes underlying them thus have a profound impact on emerging population-wide patterns of realised strategy.

It becomes important, then, to understand how ideological themes and the power relations they justify are created and sustained in organisations. How this happens is a crucial aspect of the local interactions of strategising. Gossip is a potent means of sustaining ideological patterns and power relations in organisations.

Gossip

Elias and Scotson pointed to how ideology emerges in local interactive processes of gossip. Streams of gossip stigmatise and blame the outsider group while similar streams of gossip praise the insider group. The gossip builds layers upon layer of value-laden binary pairs such as clean–dirty, good–bad, honest–dishonest, energetic–lazy, and so on. Gossip plays a significant role in maintaining identity. The same point applies to the 'inclusion–exclusion' dynamic created by particular ways of talking – for example, talking in terms of complexity, in terms of psycho-analysis, in terms of making profit, and so on. Such gossip and other ways of talking attribute 'charisma' to the powerful and 'stigma' to the weak, so reinforcing power differences. In established, cohesive groups, streams of gossip flow along well-established channels that are lacking for newly arrived groups. The stigmatisation, however, only sticks where there is already a sufficiently large power difference. Again, these are social relations that are reflected in the private role-play of individual minds, conferring feelings of superiority on the powerful and feelings of inferiority on the weak. Eventually, however, the weak or marginalised groups will probably retaliate with what may be thought by others to be unreasonable vigour.

Elias stresses the importance of streams of gossip in sustaining the group fantasy, showing how closely praise-gossip and blame-gossip are interlinked. A close-knit group, with its high power ratio, has more opportunities for effective gossip, and the more people feel threatened or insecure, the more gossip becomes fantasy of a rigid kind. Thus, gossip of praise for the charismatic and blame for the disgraced becomes part of the individual personality structures of both groups.

I am drawing attention to Elias's explanation of gossip as the means by which people sustain ideologies, which in turn sustain relations of power and patterns of inclusion–exclusion, because gossip is an essential feature of local interactions in all organisations. Many managers tend to dismiss gossip as 'idle chatter' that has no connection with the activities of strategising. They think gossip is only harmful and steps ought to be taken to minimise it. Gossip is undoubtedly often harmful but it can never be removed from human relating and it is not just harmful, because it serves a purpose in organisations. It is in activities of gossiping that ideologies and figurations of power relation are sustained but also potentially transformed, in making sense of strategising activities and how these play a part in the emergence of population-wide patterns of realised strategy, it is important to understand the effect that gossiping is having on what is happening in an organisation in terms of patterns of inclusion–exclusion which powerfully affect local activities of strategising. The dynamics of inclusion and exclusion are accompanied by powerful emotions that also impact on local strategising activities.

Emotional aspects of inclusion and exclusion

Any change in the processes of communicative interaction must at the same time constitute a shift in power relations and, therefore, a change in the pattern of who is 'included' and who is 'excluded' and so shifts in ideology. Such shifts generate intense anxiety and communicative interaction is recruited in some way to deal with this anxiety. These ways may be highly destructive of effective joint action and may even completely disrupt the reproduction and creative transformation of coherent communication. All of this is understood, from a complex responsive processes perspective, to be essential to the strategising activities of managers.

Elias and Scotson argued that inclusion–exclusion processes are expressed as differentials of cohesion and integration, which are sources of power differentials. There is a complementarity between one group's charisma and another's disgrace and this sets up emotional barriers on the part of the former to any contact with the latter, as well as processes within each group, as follows. All belonging to an established group participate in its charisma in return for which they have to conform or else suffer the humiliation of exclusion. The charismatic group uses language that deeply hurts the members of the disgraced group and this has a paralysing effect on the latter's members. Stigmatisation involves a person's image of his/her group's standing amongst others and therefore of his/her own standing. The silent voices of members of the disgraced operate as the ally of the dominant group, because the disgraced have come to believe what is said about them.

The power differential with which the disgraced comply, even agree, is essential to enable the stigma to be driven in. The disgraced often act out the aspersion cast upon them, such as being dirty and noisy, because they know they can annoy the established in this way. Power confers on a group much more than economic advantage, because the struggle is about the satisfaction of needs to do with esteem and identity. The outsiders suffer deprivation of identity and of meaning. Elias talks about the peculiar helplessness of groups unconsciously bound together in these dynamics of inclusion and exclusion. The processes that keep the disgraced in place are those of humiliation and shame.

Shame, panic and anxiety

According to Elias (Smith, 2001) the roots of civilisation are firmly planted in the soil of shame, which includes self-disgust, inhibition, isolation and fear. Shame is produced by any kind of transgression against the rules of society that others can 'see'. As people become more self-disciplined and self-aware, their thresholds of repugnance rise. Shame is in turn rooted in the body and, because human metabolism cannot be easily controlled (blushing, sweating), people feel vulnerable in a civilised society, which pushes such bodily expressions behind the scenes of social life so that when the body plays its tricks the person gets blamed for infringing norms. Ironically, feelings of shame trigger many of the bodily responses that cause shame in the first place. Threats of exposure and exclusion involved in organisational surveillance techniques and in organisational change trigger feelings of insecurity and shame that can have a big impact on what people do in organisations.

Aram (2001) links shame with panic, which is a response to the fear of potential embarrassment. She argues that panic is simultaneously relationally constructed and individually experienced, and may be thought of as a response to anxiety that serves the purpose of not dealing with the situations provoking that anxiety. The fear of the fear is translated into panic. She also links panic to waiting for something to happen, dreading it and avoiding it until it 'arrives'. Panic is, then, an investment of energy into not feeling and not knowing that leads to exactly that which is being avoided. Panic is associated with strong desires to be with others, with avoiding being alone and ascribing great importance to what others think, so that withdrawing from interaction with others is experienced as particularly difficult. The fear of being on one's own, out of control and in constant need of support makes it extremely difficult to relax. It is not necessarily any change itself that leads to panic, because when that which is being unconsciously avoided does happen, the panic symptoms diminish and the capacity to manage is found. It is the phase before a change – namely, the waiting period – which is experienced as panic. This waiting is felt to be an unconscious immobilising fear that past experiences are about to recur. People who suffer panic usually end up feeling exactly that which they are actively trying to avoid. They are highly invested in trying to maintain a strong, 'in control' sense of self and they feel humiliated when they realise how affected they are by others and how important others are in helping them maintain a sense of self. They fear dependence, yet are highly dependent. They long for relationships yet are often intimidated by them and tend to have fractious and unsuccessful ones.

Aram regards this interlinked process of panic and shame as a response to deep-rooted fears to do with inclusion and exclusion and the consequent potential for being humiliated and shamed. Panic arouses feelings of shame and humiliation because it is taken as a sign of weakness and immaturity. Anxiety generated by endlessly waiting and preparing to be abandoned and rejected, reflecting past experience, is replaced with panic, anger, rivalry and fear of closeness.

The points about the emotional aspects of power relations and inclusion–exclusion dynamics and the role that gossip plays in them are highly relevant to the local interaction of strategising. These processes are ubiquitous and are rarely paid much attention. They become particularly relevant during reorganisations, mergers and acquisition but they feature in all processes of decision-making.

15.6 Complex responsive processes perspectives on decision-making

This section will consider how the dynamics of power and ideology affect decision-making processes in organisations. First consider the key arguments presented so far in this chapter.

Earlier in this chapter, I referred to Elias's understanding of power as a central characteristic of every human relationship which flows from the fact that people are interdependent and so need each other, some more than others. Power, there-fore, arises in the relative difference of need, in an irremovable inequality between people. More specifically, power is those aspects of human activities through which people are continually enabling and constraining each other's actions. Drawing together the discussion in this chapter on power and its ideological basis, we could identify the nature of this enabling–constraining activity in the following terms:

- Forming and continuing to belong to groups are essentially activities of including some people and excluding others and much of this activity is unconsciously motivated. Such activity is experienced by people as feelings of inclusion and exclusion. Accompanying and inseparable from these activities are the activities, primarily gossiping, of labelling groups of people in terms of polarised attributes so as to differentiate 'us' and 'them'. These differentiating activities express ideo-logical themes that organise the experience of being together, so defining the 'we' identities of all. All of these activities are enabling in that they create feelings of belonging that make it possible for people to cooperate more easily with each other within a particular group. At the same time these activities are constraining in that, to continue to belong to a particular group, it is necessary for members to conform to the group ideology. Activities of inclusion and exclusion also enable competition between groups while at the same time constraining cooper-ation between them. These activities are emotionally highly charged. The experi-ence of inclusion and belonging generates feelings of affection and loyalty towards other members of the 'in' group and any criticism or threat to one's group quickly arouses aggression. The mere threat of exclusion, and so loss of identity, arouses feelings of shame and humiliation, anxiety and even panic. People unconsciously defend themselves, individually and collectively, in the mostly unconscious manoeuvres of what psychoanalysts have referred to as *basic assumption behaviour*, scapegoating and other forms of fantasy-driven behaviour (*see* Chapter 6).

- The activities of enabling and constraining can also be described in terms of coop-eration and competition and this immediately directs attention to human motiv-ations of altruism, empathy, compassion and acceptance, on the one hand, and self-centredness, envy, jealousy and rivalry, on the other hand. Some emotions and motivations are enabling of cooperation and others constrain interaction into competitive forms. There can be no pure form of enabling cooperation with its attendant emotions or of competition with its attendant emotions. Both are always present at the same time and which is more evident fluctuates over time. Of particular importance in organisational terms is the cooperation and com-petition around which discourse, and the ideology it reflects, is to dominate, because this is the largely unconscious basis of power figurations.

- Other aspects of enabling activities are fantasising and imagination, while acting and thinking in defensive ways may well be constraining.

- Activities of enabling and constraining are inevitably conflictual activities. Explorative conflict may well be enabling, while polarised conflict may be constraining.

In making these distinctions it is necessary to stress that each describes a paradox. Human relationships are enabling and constraining, including and excluding, cooperative and competitive, imaginative and defensive, at the same time. This chapter has also argued that enabling and constraining activities always reflect some ideology, some interplay of norms and values. Enabling and constraining activities also always reflect the choices people are continually making as they select one action rather than another in response to the actions of others. They make these choices, often unconsciously, on the basis of evaluative criteria provided by ideology. Such evaluative choice is simply another term for decision-making.

From the perspective of complex responsive processes, then, decision-making is understood primarily in terms of the ideological, power, emotional and social processes briefly summarised in the points above. This way of thinking about decision-making stands in contrast to that of the dominant discourse as described in the chapters of Part 1. In the dominant discourse, a decision is normally thought of as preceding an action and the making of a decision is usually thought of in terms of the step-by-step thinking activities of rational, autonomous individuals. Despite the continuing critique of rationality in the dominant discourse, decision-making continues to be described as a *programmatic* activity. There are stages leading to the making of a decision that can be identified with a specific point in time. Action then follows. From the complex responsive processes perspective, choices, decisions and intentions are inseparable from other forms of action. Indeed they continually emerge in response to all forms of action in ongoing ways that make it arbitrary to select a particular point in time when the decision was actually made. A particular point in time when the decision is legitimised by some authority in the hierarchy can, of course, be identified, but this is not the same as deciding, which is an ongoing emotional, conversational activity of enabling and constraining reflective of ideology.

15.7 Summary

Ideology can be thought of in paradoxical terms as the simultaneous voluntary compulsion of value and the obligatory restriction of norm. Ideology provides criteria for choosing one action rather than another – decision-making – and it serves as the unconscious basis of power relations, making it feel natural to include some and exclude others from particular groups, thereby sustaining the power difference between those groups. Ideology is the ideal made functional in specific situations always involving conflict.

We start from the position that humans are fundamentally social beings where this means that they survive and get done whatever they need or wish to get done in relation to each other. To relate to others is to communicate with others. By social, then, we essentially mean ongoing activities of communication between bodies in which they together accomplish whatever they accomplish. The social is the patterning of communicative interaction. To understand communication we turn to Mead and his notion of the conversation of gestures. Human communication takes the form of gestures calling forth responses from others and at the same time calling forth similar responses from oneself. In other words, communication takes place in significant symbols. Furthermore, in communicating, people take not only the attitude of the other but also always the attitude of the generalised other (group or game) and of the 'me', all encapsulated in the concept of social object as generalisation which is only to be found in the activity of particularising. This amounts to saying that consciousness and self-consciousness are social phenomena. Here communication, consciousness and self-consciousness are all social activities rather than individual representations. This is so in another sense too: namely, the tendency to idealise collectives, ideas, concepts, theories, physical objects, other people, etc. This leads to the notion of cult values which must be functionalised. The generalisation (social object)/idealisation (cult value) are major aspects of the consciousness and self-consciousness of everyone so that mind and self are patterned as social processes while they pattern social processes at the same time. Another way of talking about the enabling/constraining nature of social object and cult value is to talk about power. Elias points out that power is a characteristic of all human relating and is felt as the dynamics of inclusion and exclusion in which identity is formed. Ideology sustains patterns of power relations. Ideology, power relations, inclusion–exclusion forming identities and processes of gossip are all essential features of the local interaction of strategising and decision-making.

Further reading

Joas (2000), Griffin (2002), Stacey (2003) and Griffin and Stacey (2005) provide more detailed treatment of the points made in this chapter. Elias and Scotson ([1965] 1994) is important reading. Also look at Dopson (2001) and Newton (1999, 2001). Willmott (1993, 2003) argues that linking leadership and culture amounts to an extension of control which is masked by high-sounding language. Williams (2005) writes about leadership, power and problems of relating. Lacey (2006) explores the experience of power, blame and responsibility in the Health sector. Mowles (2008a, 2008b) discusses values in international development organisations. Drabæk (2008) draws attention to compromising as processes of moving forward in organisations. Billing (2008) reflects on the role of propaganda in organisational change.

Questions to aid further reflection

1. How would you describe the cult values of the organisation you work for and what do you notice about the ways in which they are functionalised?

2. Do you experience values as voluntary compulsions and norms as obligatory restrictions? Give examples from your own experience.

3. Where in your work do you notice the power dynamics of inclusion–exclusion and what effects do you think they have?

4. Do you think that factors to do with identity affect your work in organisations?

5. How do you think about the connections between organisational strategy and power, ideology and identity?

6. What part do you think gossip plays in organisations?

Chapter 16

Different modes of articulating patterns of interaction emerging across organisations

Strategy narratives and strategy models

This chapter invites you to draw on your own experience to reflect on and consider the implications of:

- How people construct their experience together as narrative-like patterns.

- How human agents are pre-occupied in social and organisational games.

- How human agents, reflect on, think about and make sense of their experience through abstracting from that experience in narrative forms and also in the form of maps and models.

- What it means to talk about a 'whole' organisation.

- What it means to talk about the 'long term future'.

- The role played in the iteration and potential transformation of strategy narratives and models by the tension between legitimised and shadow ideologies expressed in local conversational interactions.

- How people construct narrative strategy and strategy maps in both formal and informal conversations.

- The part played by conscious and unconscious processes in strategy narratives and strategic maps and models.

This chapter seeks to develop an understanding of what people in organisations are actually doing in their strategising activities. Strategising activities are not confined to formal meetings with agendas specifically identified as 'strategic' and devoted to discussing propositions about markets and resources. Wider ranges of communicative interactions are involved as people talk together in informal, shadow ways about who they are and who they are not, who they want to be and who they do not want to be, what they are doing and not doing, and what they desire to do and not do. As they talk together in a whole variety of ways, they co-create their experience which takes the form of narrative-like patterns in their own local interactions from which emerge population-wide patterns across societies and organisations. Human agents have the capacity to reflect upon, think about and make sense of these population-wide patterns. They are able to conceptualise these patterns as 'wholes': that is, as unities of experience, and articulate what they think these 'wholes' are. They can form desires and 'visions' for particular kinds of 'wholes' and make choices about those desires, forming intentions to act in ways that they believe will actualise their desires over the 'long term future'. These activities are essentially what most people mean when they talk about 'strategy', and this chapter seeks to understand the ordinary, everyday local activities of strategising in organisations in which human agents act upon desires and intentions for global, long-term futures. It is important to read this chapter, I think, because it attempts to bring together the ideas about human agency explored in previous chapters in Part 3 to present a way of understanding, from a complex responsive processes perspective, which is specifically focused on what we are doing when we strategise.

16.1 Introduction

What I have been doing in the last few chapters is developing a way of understanding how human agents actually carry out their agency. What is it that we are doing day after day in organisations? I have been inquiring into how we communicate with each other as the basis of everything we do. I have been exploring how in communicating with each other we are inevitably constructing and expressing figurations of power which are expressed in what we do and how these patterns are sustained by ideologies, by what we believe in. I have been describing how we are endlessly choosing and intending much of what we do and also unconsciously selecting what we do. I have been explaining how, in doing all this, we take up in our local interaction with each other global tendencies to act developed over long time periods in the history of our community and the history of our own lives. I now want to move on to how we can understand the nature of the global patterns that emerge in all this local interaction, which will then serve as a basis on which to consider more specifically, in Chapter 17, what it means to strategise and how we might understand what strategy is.

Chapter 2 identified the primary concern of strategy as that of understanding how an organisation becomes whatever it becomes. Part 1 of this book explored how this primary concern is expressed in the dominant discourse. Most of those engaged in this dominant discourse understand the matter of an organisation becoming whatever it becomes as essentially a concern with the 'whole' organisation, understood as some entity separate from the individuals forming it, over the 'long term' future. From this perspective, the fundamental roles of leaders and managers have to do with specifying what this 'whole' should become and they are advised to do this by following rational analytical procedures and/or engaging in learning, inspirational, visioning and motivating processes, followed by the design and operation of implementation systems. For some, what the 'whole' is to become is defined in terms of its resource base and its position in a market and whether or not it is successful in terms of some performance criteria. This leads to a debate about how an organisation becomes a successful performer. Some argue that this 'how' is a process of rational, strategic choice, while others point to how problematic such rational choice is for human beings and answer the 'how' question in terms of processes of organisational learning, which encompass politics, culture, cognition, emotion and many other factors. While these views may question straightforward strategic control of the 'whole' organisation by top managers, their proponents largely retain some claim for managerial ability to shape, influence or condition the 'whole' processes of learning. Organisational change, therefore, flows from activities of designing, and the dominant discourse is primarily concerned with prescriptions for what people in organisations ought to do to achieve success. The alternative most frequently put forward within the dominant discourse seems to be some form of local muddling through in which an organisation becomes what it becomes largely through chance, and reliance on this is regarded as highly questionable. Chapter 9 at the end of Part 1 described alternatives, such as social constructionism and critical management studies, which presented ways of understanding the kind of supposed muddling through as social activities, and so not simply to be dismissed.

In Part 3 of this book, Chapters 12 to 15 have presented an alternative view of the primary concern of strategy identified in Chapter 2. According to this view, what organisations become emerges in the local activities of people acting strategically in organisations, which is essentially the local activity of ordinary, everyday politics in which people continually negotiate with each other what they are trying to achieve and how they wish to proceed. The 'whole' emerges as patterns in activities across the populations of organisational members and it emerges in the interplay of the intentions, plans and strategies of all of those members. To put the same idea in slightly different words: people in an organisation are continually negotiating with each other what they want to be and what they want to do together – that is, their identities. These identities emerge in the interplay of different desires and intentions for what people want to be and what they want to do together. The consequence of the interplay of local activities is thus the emergence of both local and population-wide patterns in that activity which we call strategising. Here strategy is a pattern in a stream of interactions which can be understood as continually emerging group/organisational identity. Chapter 14 was specifically concerned with how the local activities of strategising are always forming and at the same time being formed by the 'whole' – that is, population-wide patterns of strategy understood as social objects and the identities of groups, organisations and societies. That chapter pointed to how people, particularly powerful people, might articulate desires and intentions for population-wide patterns, but the impact such articulations have will always emerge in local interpretations which no one can control. No one, therefore, can design the 'whole'. The alternative view presented in Part 3 is, consequently, not overtly prescriptive but is concerned with inquiring into and understanding what people in organisations are already doing to function, often very creatively, in conditions of great uncertainty in which they have very limited abilities to control what emerges in the interplay of all of their intentions.

However, strategy, leadership and management are all notions that have to do with intentional activities aimed at governing, sustaining, changing and improving 'whole' organisations, industries, economies and societies. The activities of strategising, leading and managing are generally supposed to be concerned with intentional operation on the global, or what I have called 'population-wide' patterns. How are we to think about these activities if we come to think that no one can realise an intention for the global and, indeed, that the very concepts of 'global' and 'whole' are problematic? Since many people are clearly involved in activities of intending, visioning, and planning, any useful way of understanding organisational life must include a way of making sense of what such activities are all about and what impact they have. Such an understanding is the central purpose of this chapter.

To start with, we need to be clear on the different meanings evoked by the notion of the 'whole'. In the dominant discourse the 'whole' is generally taken to be a 'system'. For many, the 'whole' as system actually exists and in their strategising leaders and managers are thought to provide this actually existing, even living system with some form of direction. For others, the 'whole' system cannot be said to actually exist, and instead it is a way of thinking. The claim is that it is useful to think about the whole 'as if' it existed but to retain awareness of the hypothetical nature of this construct. The 'whole' is then some hypothesis about the nature of an object called an 'organisation'. Since this object, in the real world or in the mind or both, cannot be known 'in itself', it is thought of 'as if' it were a system. The complex responsive process perspective moves away from any notion of system in the world or in the mind, but this does not mean that there is no notion of the 'whole'. Complex responsive processes theory seeks to explain what people in organisations are actually doing, and since people in organisations talk and think about the 'whole' organisation, it is necessary to make sense of what they are talking about. From the complex responsive processes perspective, the 'whole' is understood to be the social activity of together imaginatively constructing a felt sense of the unity of experience. The 'whole' here is temporal responsive processes of creatively imagining, not a spatial metaphor. 'Whole' here is not cognitive construct or scientific hypothesis but an emotional social activity of imagining. Organisations are patterns continually emerging in iterated forms across a population of people identified with an organisation, and people try to make sense of these patterns by articulating them. In doing this they are seeking to express some feeling of the unity of their experience. We do not simply experience one thing after another in a random disconnected way but, rather, we experience some kind of continuity, some kind of ongoing unity, in what we and others are doing in an organisation and the wider society it is involved in. This experience of unity requires acts of human imagination in which we generalise population-wide patterns, imaginatively ascribe a unity to them and then idealise this 'whole'. This imaginative activity is of the greatest importance because, in articulating social objects and cult value, it is repeatedly taken up by many, many people in the particularity of their local interactions. This chapter will be exploring how people construct the 'whole' as the unity of experience in the activity of strategising activity. We come to a notion of an organisation as both emerging population-wide patterns in ongoing local interacting and imaginative constructing.

Strategy is usually taken to refer to the 'whole' over the 'long term future' and the second important notion in this view is, therefore, that of time. The view of time taken in the dominant discourse was presented in Chapter 7. This is a linear view of time which can be conceptualised as a straight line moving from a factually given past into an intended future with the present simply being a point separating the past from the future. Then Chapter 12 presented a view of time consistent with a responsive processes way of thinking. Here time is nonlinear in that all action takes place in the present; it is in the present that we live and act. But we act in the present on the basis of what we tell ourselves happened in the past and on the basis of what we expect or intend for the future, all in the present. We find that our expectations are influenced by our stories of the past and that our stories of the past are at the same time influenced by our expectation for the future. So in imaginatively co-constructing a felt unity of experience, a 'whole', we are in essence co-constructing mutually influencing narratives of our past actions and future expectations.

In developing an understanding of what we are doing when we express our imaginative constructions of the 'whole' organisation, economy or society, I first want to look in some further detail at what we are producing together in our lived experience of interacting locally with each other. I want to suggest that human persons are continually co-creating their experience in essentially narrative forms. Ask anyone who they are and they respond with a narrative. Each of us is an autobiography. Ask people in an organisation what it is all about and how they come to do what they do and they tell you a story. Ask them what the strategy has been and they tell you a story of expansion, acquisition, downsizing, or whatever. In an ordinary, everyday way, therefore, strategy is a narrative of identity co-created by people in an organisation. The next section of this chapter explores the manner in which ordinary, everyday conversation forms and at the same time is formed by emergent themes which construct narrative patterns of experience. The section after that considers how we might think of our activities as ones of immersing ourselves in the narrative patterns of our experience, of being pre-occupied in the game.

However, in their preoccupation with the narrative or game of their experience, people have the capacity to reflect upon the narrative or game as a 'whole', as a unity of experience, and one way they can do this is to selectively simplify, generalise and stereotype their experience in the form of stories and narratives, which inevitably represent an abstraction from the full, direct experience. This form of reflection will be the concern of section 16.4 below. More recently, particularly in Western modernity, people have developed ways of thinking and reflecting, epitomised by the natural sciences, in terms of propositions, maps and models that amount to a further abstraction from their direct experience. This mode of reflection will be considered in section 16.5 below.

In all such reflection, people form desires and intentions for some population-wide patterns or identities rather than others and such desires motivate their local actions. I have been suggesting that, in reflecting upon population-wide patterns, people imaginatively construct 'wholes' called 'organisations' which essentially involves abstracting from experience. I think of this as first-order abstraction. I will suggest that, when people present, aims, goals, visions and plans for 'whole' organisations, economies and societies, they are engaging in second-order abstracting. We can understand activities of strategising as activities of both first- and second-order abstracting and at the same time as activities of immersing in the ordinary political games of organisational life in which we construct identity narratives. These ideas will be explored in Chapter 17.

Consider then how the narrative themes of experience emerge in ordinary everyday conversation in organisations. It is this experience and the felt 'whole' it produces which becomes the object of thinking and reflecting.

16.2 The emergence of themes in the narrative patterning of ordinary, everyday conversation

From a complex responsive processes perspective, *ordinary, everyday conversation*, in both its public/vocal (social) and private/silent (individual mind) forms, is the key human activity as far as acting jointly is concerned, and it is in this conversational activity that experience emerges as themes organising the experience of people being together while at the same time those themes are organising the ordinary, everyday conversation. These themes can take a number of forms – for example, fantasies, myths, rituals, ideologies, cultures, traditions, routines, habits, gossip, rumours, discourses, speech genres, dialogues, discussions, debates, presentations, and scientific propositions, maps and models.

If one takes the perspective that an organisation is patterns of conversation (relational constraints), then an organisation changes only insofar as its conversational life (power relations/ideology) evolves. Organisational change is the same thing as change in the patterns of conversation and therefore of the patterns of power relations and ideology. Creativity, novelty and innovation are all the emergence of new patterns of conversations and patterns of power relations and ideological themes. In other words, the strategic direction an organisation follows emerges as a pattern in the way people talk and in their talking configure power relations. Note that public, vocal conversations (group relationships) and private, silent conversations (individual minds) are both aspects of the same phenomenon. Change in one means some kind of change in the other at the same time. Organisations and their individual members change together. It is not a matter of changing the people first and then changing the organisation. Change is possible when conversational life is fluid and spontaneous and impossible when conversational life remains stuck in repetitive themes.

The key questions then become: how do themes organise the narrative experience of organisational life? What facilitates and what blocks the emergence of new patterns, new narratives, of conversation? What facilitates the stability and continuity of organisational life? In response to these questions consider first how particular kinds of themes, which emerge in ongoing conversation, organise the experience of life in organisations according to what can and what cannot be talked about. Here I want to draw a distinction between what I have called *legitimate and shadow themes* emerging in ongoing conversation.

Legitimate and shadow themes

There is no organisation in which it is possible to talk freely and openly to just anyone, in any situation, about anything one likes, in any way one chooses and still survive as a member. Organisations are patterns of relationships between people, and these relationships impose powerful constraints on what it is permissible to say, to whom and how, if one is to be included rather than excluded. Sometimes it is quite acceptable to behave in particular ways but quite unacceptable to freely and openly discuss that behaviour or the reasons for it. Alternative presentations of such behaviour and different reasons for it cover up the 'real' events even though most engaged in them may well know that this is what is happening. This is the basis of the distinction I make between *legitimate* and *shadow* themes that organise the narratives of experience.

Legitimate themes organise what people feel able to talk about openly and freely. They organise conversations in which people give acceptable accounts of themselves and their actions, as well as imputations about the actions of others. They are the kinds of conversation you readily engage in with others, even if you do not know them well. Shadow themes organise conversations in which people feel able to give less acceptable accounts of themselves and their actions, as well as of others and their actions. They are the kinds of conversations you would engage in only informally, in very small groups, with others you know and trust. Shadow themes, taking the form of gossip, organise what people do not feel able to discuss freely and openly.

The distinction between legitimate and shadow themes is intimately related to ideology, which can be either official or unofficial. It is ideology that legitimises a conversation. In particular, it is the ideology sustaining current power relations that makes conversation feel natural, acceptable and safe – that is, legitimate. One would normally expect that ideology to be official: that is, the values that are publicly pronounced as those people are to live by. This official ideology may well exert a powerful influence on what may or may not be freely spoken about. However, it need not necessarily determine what may or may not be done. Despite the official ideology, people may behave in ways consistent with unofficial ideologies, even though they cannot talk about how their actions are justified by their unofficial ideologies. Instead, they will have to find some other, plausible reason consistent with the official ideology. When people engage in shadow conversations, they also do so on the basis of some unofficial ideology that makes it feel natural and justifiable to talk as they do, but this time secretly. Shadow narratives then emerge as strategies organising experience.

Legitimate conversational themes are legitimate, then, because they conform to official ideologies. The opposite of legitimate is, of course, that which is illegitimate or illegal. This is not what I mean by shadow themes in organisations. Shadow themes form conversational narratives – that is, power relations – which are not legitimate but also not illegitimate or illegal. Shadow themes/power relations are shadow because of the manner in which they are expressed in conversation. Such conversation always takes place informally between small numbers of people and their distinguishing feature is that they do not conform to the official ideology. Official ideologies provide the main support for existing patterns of power relations. Some unofficial ideologies may collusively support current power relations, whereas others seek to undermine them and both can be taking place at the same time. This does not mean that shadow conversation only takes place between the less powerful. The most powerful participate in them too, and indeed skilful participation in shadow conversation plays a major role in sustaining the relations that render them more powerful.

Let me give an example to clarify the distinction. Although the organisation I am about to describe is fictional, it is nevertheless constructed from experiences in a number of real organisations.

Equal opportunities

A company's board of directors consists of eight men and the group of 30 senior executives who report to them also consists entirely of men. However, there are

12 women in the group of 150 senior managers reporting to the senior executives, mostly in the human resources, public relations and marketing functions. For the past ten years the directors have emphasised the company's formal equal opportunities policy for recruitment and promotion and its policy on the harassment of women and minorities. Virtually everyone in the organisation is aware of this official ideology of equality – for example between men and women – and it exercises a powerful constraint on what may be talked about freely and openly. It is widely felt to be unacceptable to talk freely and openly about whether women, for example, are in general suitable for the most senior positions. It is also unacceptable to ask openly why there are no women in the upper echelons despite the equal opportunities policy or why they are concentrated in particular functions. Even the twelve senior women managers in the company do not feel that it would be wise to talk openly about such matters lest the most senior men should feel accused of hypocrisy, which might prompt them to seek some form of retribution. A powerful theme organising experience here has to do with the danger of pointing openly to, let alone questioning, the policies of equal opportunities and harassment in any way. What all are doing here is co-creating an official narrative of transparency and equal opportunities.

This is what I mean by themes organising the legitimate experience of being together. Some of these themes are formal, propositional and quite conscious in nature, such as the policy statements on equal opportunities and harassment. Others are narrative, informal and possibly unconscious in nature. The unconscious aspect may lie in the reasons why the women managers do not challenge top executives. For example, it might be a fantasy that the latter would interpret any comment as an accusation of hypocrisy. It is legitimate in this organisation to talk openly and freely only in terms of the equality that is part of the official ideology, but it is also quite legitimate to appoint only men to the upper echelons. In other words, it feels right and natural to appoint men only, but it does not feel right to talk openly about this. Note here how the ideology and underlying current power relations are a mixture of official ideology of equality and unofficial ideology of inequality.

However, people do talk about inequality in private, but only to those whom they trust and expect to agree with them, or in the form of a joke. For example, some of the directors and senior managers can be heard to tell disparaging jokes about women, occasionally in the presence of one of the twelve female managers. Female managers also sometimes make disparaging remarks about men, often in their presence. Because the exchanges take place in the form of jokes, any serious intention underlying them can be denied if need be. Privately, a few men express their unwillingness to report to a woman. Although women are sometimes interviewed for director and senior executive posts, a good reason has so far always been found for not appointing them. In each separate case, the reasons produced are indeed plausible but the pattern over a long period of time is curious. The senior women managers also talk in private, often amongst themselves but also with male colleagues who are known to be sympathetic. They talk about glass ceilings and hypocrisy.

These are all examples of what I mean by shadow themes that organise the experience of being together. These conversations express the organisation's unofficial ideologies. Unofficially, some have an ideology that does encompass discrimination and yet others believe that the top executives are hypocrites. Note how the themes organising shadow conversations are mainly narrative in nature. Also, note the unconscious aspect. Those making decisions not to appoint women are usually not

cynically ignoring the equal opportunities policy and most of them would strenu-
ously, and probably quite genuinely, deny that they are discriminating. After all,
they provide very careful and convincing reasons why they have not appointed a
woman in each separate case. The female managers may not be aware of how they
are colluding in maintaining the situation by their public silence.

Clearly, unofficial ideologies are undermining official ideology. It is also easy to
see that one powerful unofficial ideology, in part unconscious, is sustaining current
power relations in which men get the top jobs. It can also be argued that the unofficial ideology of the women and some of the men who support them contributes
to sustaining current power relations. It looks as if official ideology is about changing current power relations and unofficial ideologies are resisting this. However, a
different argument can be made. In today's social climate, it would be unacceptable
not to have public policies about equal opportunities and harassment. It is also
probably helpful to have them from a legal point of view as a protection in the event
of litigation. The policies may well be providing an official ideology that meets the
requirements of public opinion and in the process covers up the unofficial ones that
really make behaviour feel right. This interpretation is strengthened when one of the
human resources directors recounts how he raised the topic of equal opportunities
over two years before it was incorporated in personnel policies. He did so privately
with a few of his colleagues to get the necessary support to take it to the board. His
most persuasive argument was the weight of public opinion.

I am using this example to argue that it is neither the official nor the unofficial
ideologies on their own that are sustaining current power relations. Rather, it is the
complex interplay between them, between legitimate and shadow organising themes,
that sustains current power relations. I am also using it to point to how what is the
officially stated ideology today in fact emerged from shadow conversations some
time ago.

I want to take this example one step further. A few of the female managers become
increasingly frustrated and begin to talk privately about how they can influence the
situation. Some of them talk, as people do, at dinner parties about their experience
of discrimination in the workplace. A guest at one of these dinner parties is an
influential journalist, well known for her championing of women's rights. She interviews the chairman and writes a sarcastic piece in a major newspaper about the all-
male top management at this particular company. Most people in the company talk
about the article and they now feel able to talk more openly and freely about why
there are so few women in top management. What was a shadow conversation
has now emerged into the legitimate arena. A few months later two women are
appointed to the senior executive ranks and a prominent businesswoman is
appointed to the board as non-executive director. Clearly, the meaning of the equal
opportunities policy has changed and with it the pattern of power relations. What I
am illustrating here is the complex interplay between shadow and legitimate themes
organising experience in an organisation and how new themes, new meanings, can
emerge in this interplay. This interplay has generated greater diversity and variety
in the management of the company.

The importance of deviance

The distinction between legitimate and shadow is important, because the tension
between the two is the potential source of the diversity that is critical to the

capacity to change spontaneously in novel ways. Conversational shadow themes, then, are those organising themes/power relations that are in some sense deviant and this deviance encompasses the despicable and the destructive, on the one hand, and the heroic and the creative, on the other. Shadow communications take the form of ordinary, everyday conversations, gossip, rumour, inspirational accounts, stories that express humour and the grotesque, tales that take the form of elaborate social fantasies or touching personal experiences. Shadow communications shape and are shaped by power relations, some of which collusively support, and others of which covertly undermine, the legitimate. I am suggesting that the potential for the emergence of new organisational direction arises when legitimate and shadow themes are in tension. In other words, creative potential arises from the subversion of legitimate organising themes by shadow themes. What emerges then is new forms of conversation: that is, shifts in power relations, new strategy narratives.

Unofficial innovation

Consider another example of the interplay between legitimate and shadow themes. Fonseca (2001) reports a development in a water utility in Lisbon. The manager and his colleagues in the Operations and Maintenance Department talked about the waste involved in having to consult many different maps showing the location of utilities in the streets before they could carry out any repairs on the water supply system. They decided that it would be a good idea to digitise all the existing maps so that repair crews would only have to consult one up-to-date map. However, the manager of the department knew that investment priorities lay elsewhere and that any request for funds for the digitisation project would be turned down. Without approval, the manager nevertheless started the project, freeing up some time for the four engineers who were enthusiastic and finding small amounts of funding from other budgets.

The project could not be talked about openly and freely to anyone because it was not in the legitimate arena. This did not mean that no one else knew about it. Senior managers did know about it and tolerated it. However, it still could not be talked about openly. Conversations about it were organised by shadow themes. The reason is obvious. The official ideology on control was one in which the use of resources had to be approved by senior executives. It is immediately evident how such a control ideology sustains current power relations and how going around the approval procedures subverts them. After some time, the project reached a stage at which there was enough evidence of its potential usefulness to seek and obtain official approval. As it further developed, it led to significant shifts in power relations between different departments in the organisation. The complex interplay of shadow and legitimate themes led to the emergence of a new technology. This sequence of events clearly takes the form of narrative.

Challenges from the margin: public and hidden transcripts

In using the term 'shadow', I am connecting to Elias (1989) when he talked about people challenging the official ideology from the margin (see Chapter 15). Conversations in the shadow are conversations at the margin. I am also trying to capture the point Bhaktin (1986) makes about 'carnival'. Frequently, conversations in the shadow take humorous forms. Conversations in the shadow are a form of play. It is in the complex interplay of legitimate and shadow themes that ordinary, everyday conversations create the narratives of experience.

Scott (1990) presents a different formulation of the distinction I am making between legitimate and shadow conversational themes. He explores how subordinate groups of people often have to adopt a *strategic pose or public transcript* when dealing with the more powerful, but how they also find other ways amongst themselves of expressing what they think and feel. He refers to the latter as *hidden transcripts* and argues that contradictions and tensions expressed in the hidden transcripts and between them and the strategic pose/public transcript have a major impact on what happens. In other words, it is vital to understand the nature of local political interactions if one is to understand wider social evolution. The problem with studying the hidden transcripts is that they are usually clandestine and so closed to outsiders. However, they are frequently expressed more publicly in disguised form as rumours, gossip, folktales and jokes. Scott argues that these apparently innocuous and anonymous forms of discourse are disguised ideological insubordination which provides a reasonably safe critique of power. Civility requires us to smile and exchange routine pleasantries, especially when others have the power to harm or reward us, even if we privately despise those others. Especially in the face of domination, people will express themselves in their public transcripts in ways which are ritualised and stereotypical. The public transcript will be a performance masking the hidden transcripts which will often irrupt in ways that catch the more powerful off guard. Eventually the hidden transcripts may be expressed publicly, and Scott argues that when this happens it is often experienced as a breach of etiquette, even a symbolic declaration of war. The frontier between public and hidden transcripts is a constant struggle between the dominant and the subordinate.

We can see this distinction between public and hidden transcripts quite clearly at play in the modern National Health Service in the UK. The public transcript is cast in terms of targets, visions, values, strategies and the implementation of plans to achieve the targets, keeping the organisation on message going forward. Managers and others in the service strike a strategic pose in which they subscribe to the public transcript. In private, however, the hidden transcript comes out as people try to work out how to achieve targets given resource constraints. Waiting times are met by occasional 'massaging' of the figures, by discharging people early, and by cancelling follow-up appointments. The forms of resistance identified by Scott are much in evidence for those who look – the gossip, the jokes about leaders and so on. These hidden transcripts and the forms of resistance they embody are having just as much effect on the delivery of healthcare to the public as the public transcript is having. What happens does so in the interplay of public and hidden transcripts or what I have called the 'legitimate' and the 'shadow' themes organising our experience of being together in organisations. The purpose of the public transcript is to provide an appearance of unanimity and of keeping discord out of sight, while the hidden transcripts are forms of resistance. The strategies of resistance all involve some form of concealment, disguise and anonymity and they take the form of gossip, rumour, deferential performances covering over hidden acts of aggression, euphemisms concealing what is actually being done, grumbling and expressing disguised bits of the hidden transcript publicly.

The dominant discourse on strategic management reviewed in Part 1 makes a similar distinction to that between legitimate and shadow themes, but covert politics were understood as unfortunate distractions which ought to be removed. From a complex responsive processes point of view covert politics are inevitable in human interaction and, whether they produce behaviour that is good or bad, creative or destructive depends upon the ideology one subscribes to. A distinction was also made in the dominant discourse between other aspects of organising: the formal and the informal, with the former being privileged, and the conscious and unconscious, again with the former being privileged. From a complex responsive processes perspective there is no immediate privileging of one aspect over the other. Consider how these aspects are defined and then how they differ from the legitimate–shadow distinction.

Formal and informal

All of the theories reviewed in this book draw much the same distinction between the formal and the informal aspects of an organisation. The formal is identified in terms of an organisation's purpose, its mode of fulfilling its purpose – that is, its task – and the individuals who are assigned roles in carrying out the task. The formal organisation is defined in terms of the role it promises to fulfil in its larger community and it is defined in terms of those formally authorised to be its members. The organisation's identity here is defined in terms of formal propositions as to membership, roles and relationships between roles, tasks and purposes.

The informal organisation consists of all relationships not formally defined by people's roles or clearly related to their tasks. All personal and social relationships fall within this category. These personal relationships extend into other organisations, making it difficult to define the membership. As everyone knows, no organisation can function without these informal relationships, and an organisation, therefore, has to be understood in terms of both formal and informal relationships.

In the terms I am using in this chapter, some of the themes that organise the experience of being together, and therefore some aspects of power relations, may be described as 'formal'. These are often propositional themes, frequently expressed in written form setting out reporting structures, procedures and policies of various kinds. The propositions model the hierarchy and the bureaucracy and set out the official ideology. However, the formal organising themes also encompass some of a more narrative kind. For example, there are unwritten understandings of how people should conduct themselves at formal meetings and the kind of deference they should display in conversations with those more senior to them in the hierarchy. The themes that organise informal experience almost always take a narrative form as the informal strategy narratives of an organisation.

Note that this distinction between formal and informal is very different from the distinction between legitimate and shadow. The former distinction relates to the degree of formality and the latter to the degree of legitimacy.

Conscious and unconscious

Learning organisation theory distinguishes between assumptions people are aware of and those that they are not aware of. The concept of mental models used in this theory postulates that most of the content of the models is below the level of awareness. A distinction is also drawn between tacit (unconscious) and explicit (conscious) knowledge. Psychoanalytic perspectives distinguish between what members of an organisation do consciously and what they do unconsciously and it attaches particular importance to the notion of unconscious group processes. This theory pays attention to the impact of unconscious fantasy on how people experience being together, particularly the unconscious deployment of defences against anxiety. A complex responsive processes perspective also draws attention to the unconscious processes in which people are unaware of how they use ideology to justify power relations and patterns of inclusion and exclusion (*see* Chapter 15).

People are usually conscious of the formal propositional statements that organise their experience of being together. Reflective members of a group are also usually aware of a number of the narrative themes that are organising their experience of being together. However, most of the themes organising experience are likely to be unconscious. It is unusual for people to struggle publicly to identify what these themes are. Certain categories of themes are particularly likely to be unconscious and will be linked with other themes that protect them from exposure to consciousness. In Chapter 15 one such category was identified around the unconscious preservation of power relations through talking and acting on differences that are used to stir up hatred. This is the dynamic of those who are 'in' and those who are 'out'. While people will be aware of who is 'in' and who is 'out', what they tend to be unaware of is the purpose this categorisation is serving. People in groups also unconsciously categorise experience into binary opposites that become entrenched as ideologies, which make their behaviour seem right and natural. Here the ideology may be conscious but its dubious basis will be unconsciously excluded from consideration. Then the very categorising and logical procedures of language work to highlight certain differences and obliterate others in what is ultimately an arbitrary way. The difference is conscious but what it obliterates becomes unconscious.

The dynamics of conversational themes

The institutional themes organising the experience of being together tend to take the formal, conscious, legitimate form and they have the effect of limiting the connections between people, so preserving stability. Hierarchical reporting structures in an organisation are an example of this. In hierarchical structures, people mainly interact with their immediate superior, who in turn interacts with a person higher up in the hierarchy. This clearly cuts down on the number of connections. The accomplishment of hierarchy, habits, routines, customs and traditions is to replace many potentially conflicting constraints with a few in the interests of ongoing joint action. When current power relations are sustained by this means, stability emerges. Social structures, cultures, bureaucratic procedures and hierarchical arrangements emerge, often as intentions and designs, in local communicative interaction. This is a way of thinking about, say, hierarchy that is more encompassing than the usual way of simply identifying it as a designed structure. What is more encompassing is the inclusion of hierarchy and decisions about hierarchy in the wider process of communicative interaction.

The social process may be one that patterns communicative interaction as clusters of strong connections linked to other clusters by much weaker connections. Such clusters of strong connections would constitute institutions and organisations, in turn patterned as clusters of strong connections with weaker links to others, for example, as departments and project teams within an organisation. This could be understood as an intrinsically stabilising process in that it reduces numbers of connections and hence the numbers of conflicting constraints. In this process, closely linked clusters establish power differences both within and between clusters, so constraining both those within the cluster and those in other clusters. The strong connections take the form of habits. In this way powerful institutions and organisations emerge that constrain the choices open to people.

However, institutionalisation as formal, conscious, legitimate themes organising the experience of being together is only one aspect of the process. At the same time experience is also being patterned by, for example, informal, unconscious, shadow themes. These too form clusters as people organise themselves into shadow pressure groups in organisations, sometimes displaying the kind of fluid communication between people that tends to be stifled by institutionalised themes. These pressure groups and their shadow themes will frequently be antagonistic to institutionalised themes, and it is in the tension and the conflict between them that change in institutionalised themes emerges.

16.3 Narrative patterning of experience and preoccupation in the game

What I want to draw attention to in the discussion of the previous section is the fundamentally narrative-like patterning of ordinary, everyday conversation. The associative, turn-taking processes of ordinary, everyday conversation produce emergent, co-created narrative as one person tells an anecdote, expresses an opinion or takes some other action that evokes some evaluative comment from another, an associated anecdote or opinion from a third and some other kind of gesture from a fourth, as together they co-construct narrative themes. Such conversation is ongoing without the beginning or the end which we associate with stories and narratives – hence my use of the term 'narrative-like' to describe them. Narrative themes structure the historical and current experience of being together, so creating personal and group realities (Gergen, 1982; Shotter, 1993). Our social interactions are patterned as narratives and each self in such interaction is an autobiographical narrative. Narratives, sometimes including propositional statements within them, are always constructed in local conversational interaction, and population-wide narratives emerge in many, many local interactions. Furthermore, as they iterate particular narratives in their local interaction, people are taking up the population-wide narratives that have already emerged and in so doing further evolving these narratives. The generating of the population-wide narratives, including the cult values they reflect, are being particularised in the local creation of particular narratives. In such ordinary conversation, we are together constructing our experience as narrative.

In other words, social objects and cult values (*see* Chapter 15) take a narrative-like form. There are other concepts that get at much the same phenomena as social objects and cult values, and it is worth briefly reviewing them here because they help to bring out the nature of our experience of the narrative-like thematic patterns we are together constructing, patterns which are at the same time constructing us. Two similar notions are those of *habitus* and of *the game*.

Preoccupation in the game

Bourdieu (1998) makes a distinction between two modes of experience and thought. In the first mode, human agents are thought of as acting on the basis of reasons so that, once the reason is found, the coherent set of principles governing a series of actions becomes apparent and it is possible to see pattern in what might have looked like random actions. Bourdieu contrasts this notion of the reasonable agent with one in which agents act on the basis of interests. He relates this to the notion that in their ordinary activities, agents are engaged in a game which they take seriously and regard as worth the effort because they have an interest in it; they are invested in it and they participate in the game, recognising the game and the stakes. In this mode, they are preoccupied by the game rather than acting rationally to achieve goals. Bourdieu relates the game to the habitus (see also Elias, 1978) in which people live: that is, the habitual social customs and ways of thinking into which they are born. We acquire our interest in particular social games through our living in the society we are born into. Our minds are structured by this social experience which is imprinted in our bodies as a feel for the game. Bourdieu talks about agents

> being invested . . . in the stakes existing in a certain game, through the effect of competition, and which only exists for people who being caught up in that game and possessing the dispositions to recognize the stakes at play, are ready to die for the stakes which, conversely, are devoid of interest for those who are not tied to that game and which leave them indifferent.   (Bourdieu, 1998, pp. 77–8)

Of course, much of this is unconscious as agents embody schemes of perception on the basis of which they act rather than setting objectives for what they do. Agents

> are not like *subjects* faced with an object (or, even less, a problem) that will be constituted as such by an intellectual act of cognition; they are, as it is said, absorbed in their affairs (one could also say their doing): they are present at the coming moment, the doing, the deed . . . which is not posed as an object of thought, as a possible aimed for in a project, but which is inscribed in the present of the game.   (ibid., p. 80)

He explains how having a feel for the game, embodying it, based on a sense of history and skill in anticipating the moves of others allows us some mastery over the unfolding game.

> It is true that most human behaviors take place within playing fields; thus they do not have as a principle a strategic intention such as that postulated in game theory. In other words, social agents have 'strategies' which only rarely have a true strategic intention as a principle.   (ibid., p. 81)

Bourdieu poses an opposition between a preoccupation as anticipation immediately present although not yet perceived and a plan as a design for the future requiring the mobilisation of actions to bring this future about. This is directly relevant to the dominant discourse on change in organisations which focuses attention almost entirely on the design and the plan, so encouraging us to ignore how we are actually preoccupied by the organisational game. We are absorbed in the affairs of the organisation in our local interactions, conducting skilful performances which give us some mastery of organisational continuity and change. However, we could be covering over the limitations to such mastery by focusing attention only on the design. Bourdieu's analysis suggests that, while the individual with the capacity for powerful individual agency exercised in a rational, detached way is what is publicly presented, the reality of ordinary interaction is that of participating, largely unconsciously, in games, in the habitus in which we live.

Bourdieu, therefore, polarises intention as a design for the future, on the one hand, and preoccupation in the local interactions of the game, on the other, expressing a strong preference for the latter. This is the same kind of polarisation as that found in the work of Mintzberg (*see* Chapter 8) who polarises deliberate and emergent strategy, although he does see realised strategy as the outcome of both. I want to describe now a view of strategy in which this paradox is central.

The paradoxical nature of strategising processes

We can only interact with each other locally and that local interaction always reflects population-wide generalisations (social objects)/idealisations (cult values) most of which we are not conscious of. In other words, in our local interaction we are normally preoccupied in Bourdieu's sense and we are always reflecting the habitus in which we live. I want to use the term *immersing* to describe what we are doing as we act locally, preoccupied in the game, in ways which unconsciously reflect the generalisations and idealisations, the habitus of our society. The word *immersed* means to be absorbed in some interest or situation where one devotes oneself fully to some interest or situation, throwing oneself into that situation and to engage others to be so immersed. Immersing is an activity of bringing together, filling in, expanding, elaborating, complexifying and taking into account greater detail and diversity. In other words, it is what Bourdieu calls our 'preoccupation' with the game, our experience of the habitus in which we live, our direct involvement in our ordinary, everyday local interactions. Such activity, essentially ideology-based acts of choice, inevitably generates conflict.

Immersing, therefore, refers to activities taking the form of:

- the ordinary, everyday politics of life. This is our ongoing negotiation with others, including our attempts to persuade and manipulate those others using techniques ranging from the use of rhetorical ploys to emotional blackmail and the techniques of domination.

- the patterning of the power relations between people. Patterns of power relations between people reflect the dynamics of ideologically based group inclusion and exclusion which establish individual and collective identities.

- acts of politeness and face-saving. Analysis of the micro interactions of individuals in a workplace reveals how politeness is a fundamental aspect of power relations (Holmes and Stube, 2003). Politeness is essential to maintaining good social relations and takes the form of political acts required to gain the cooperation of others, especially powerful others. Civility requires us to smile and exchange routine pleasantries, especially when the other has the power to harm or reward us, even if we privately despise that other. In local interaction people are testing, challenging, supporting and undermining so as to shift or sustain patterns of power relations. Mostly we do this by avoiding direct confrontational challenges, but use instead socially acceptable, polite ways involving humour, irony, sarcasm and social banter. How to do this will depend upon the evolved habitus, the generalisations and abstractions across a population.

- practising the arts of resistance (Scott, 1990). Subordinate groups of people in organisations often have to adopt a strategic pose when dealing with the more powerful in which they express compliance in the 'public transcripts' (legitimate themes in the dominant discourse) couched in terms of abstractions. But they also find other ways of expressing what they think and feel amongst themselves in 'hidden transcripts' (shadow themes) in which they block, subvert and countermand the abstract categories imposed upon them. The contradictions and tensions expressed in the hidden transcripts, and between them and the strategic pose, have a major impact on what happens.
- denial, scapegoating and blaming as defensive ways of living with the anxieties of ordinary, everyday life. Talking in terms of second order abstractions may serve the purpose of providing social defences against anxiety in organisations.
- the spontaneity and improvisation required of us if we are to respond appropriately in the unique contingent situations we so often face.
- the attachment to others, as well as the empathy with, and trust in, those others, which enables us to find fulfilment in what we do and also aggression, competition, rivalry, mistrust and hatred.
- the creative imagination of alternative ways of living and doing and the inevitable destruction of others' ways of living.
- altruism and generosity as well as selfishness and meanness.

So in the local interaction of making the general specific and the ideal functional in conversation with each other, in their preoccupation with the game, people are negotiating their next actions in ways that have emerged and continue to emerge and evolve as narrative and propositional themes of power, identity and ideology.

However, we also have the capacity to become aware of our preoccupation with the game, to reflect upon our practical action, which expresses the habitus in which we live, in an effort to make conscious sense of what we are doing. To live simply immersed in this way would be to live a life devoid of all thought, reflection or meaning making. Thought, reflection and meaning-making are all activities of *abstracting*, the opposite of the activities of immersing. The most common understanding of abstract is that it denotes theory as the opposite of something practical, but in its original sense it means 'to abstract', 'to draw away from, to separate from'. All forms of thinking about and reflecting upon experience necessarily involve abstracting or drawing away from that experience which becomes an object of perception, not simply the subject of experience. Abstractions are articulations of both local and global patterns of interaction. They are attempts to describe social objects, cult values, habitus and the game rather than just participating in them. However, such activities of articulation always occur in local interaction and it is in such local interaction that the meaning of these abstractions emerges. Experience is thus an inseparable interplay between the activities of immersing and abstracting, of participating and reflecting in which each is simultaneously forming and being formed by the other.

Since humans have always sought to make meaning, they must also always have been paradoxically immersing and abstracting from experience in explorative forms of reflecting on the generalisation and idealisation of experience and articulating them in narrative and philosophy. People made, and continue to make, sense of the population-wide patterns of interaction they lived in through the stories they told and the myths they recited from generation to generation. We still articulate the general/ideal in stories, rumours, and fantasies about distant powerful figures despite social and individual evolution of the past centuries. The point about the narrative forms of our articulations is that they stay close to our experience of local interaction in that they provide descriptions and accounts of that local interaction itself, even in mythical form. Articulations of these generalisation and idealisations in narrative form involves selecting and simplifying and in that sense, *abstracting* from experience. However, the selection is not only simplification but also elaboration. Narrative articulations of experience require interpretation in particular contingent situations. Their aim is not simplicity, standardisation and uniformity – as we shall see below in later forms of abstracting – but rather their aim is the opening-up of accounts of experience for greater exploration in order to develop deeper understanding.

However, the conscious simplifying generalisation of narrative does amount to abstracting from – that is, simplifying and generalising – the detail of each uniquely experienced situation. Insofar as the characters and situations in stories are stereotypes, narratives abstract from and categorise the detail of experience. Furthermore, thought is essentially an act of categorising and generalising. So, people do not think entirely in terms of specific objects such as this table or that table, but instead they think in terms of a general and, therefore, abstract category of tables. There were always philosophers and theologians who articulated formal simplifications, generalisations and categories of experience concerned with perceiving, knowing and acting ethically. Metaphysics involved abstracting from unique experience to signify hidden causes. Philosophy sought to explain the experience of perception, of knowing and relating in abstract modes that opened up exploration and interpretation so elaborating further reflection on experience.

Human thought, therefore, has always been paradoxical acts of immersing and abstracting at the same time, and for most of human history it is the narrative form of abstraction that has been most prominent. The next section reviews the nature of narrative and the section after that takes up later forms of abstraction which merged in the scientific revolution and the formation of nation states.

16.4 Reflecting on experience: the role of narrative and storytelling

In the previous two sections I have been describing ways of thinking about how we are together constructing our experience in narrative-like forms. I have pointed out how we also reflect upon our experience. The narrative-like emergence of our experience can be an object for our thought and reflection not only on what each of us is doing but on what we perceive to be the 'wholes' we are together producing. That reflection can be articulated in narrative and propositional terms (Tsoukas, 1997).

When we articulate our experience in propositional forms, we make causal and prescriptive statements about experience, such as: *if* you shout *then* people will get angry; *if* you improve the quality of your product *then* the volume of sales will increase; *if* you ban smoking *then* most people will obey; *if* the money supply is increased *then* inflation will occur. However, people cannot rely entirely on propositions in the form of procedures, manuals, and so on to do their jobs adequately. They also need to draw on narrative knowledge embodied in the informal stories they tell each other about their work (Brown and Duguid, 1991). A number of organisational researchers have therefore taken an interest in the role of stories and narratives in organisations (Boje, 1991, 1994, 1995; Grant *et al.*, 1998). Narratives and stories constitute sense-making processes in organisations, and stories, often considered to be a subset of the category of narratives, can be understood in different ways (Gabriel, 1998):

- Storytelling is a traditional activity in which storytellers tell their stories to members of a community so preserving folklore. These stories are fluid and evolving and their primary purpose is entertainment. Linked to folklore there are fairy tales, myths and legends which may be didactic, carry sacred meaning or some moral injunction and explain, justify and console.

- From a modernist perspective, stories, myths fairy tales and legends, are all seen either as fiction opposed to factual, objective information, or as highly subjective accounts of personal experience. Stories here are marginalised as sense-making processes, being rejected completely on the grounds of having no connection to fact, or they are taken to represent hidden subjective experience which can be revealed through interpretation. The purpose of the story here may be to provide people with a vehicle to evade the controls of society, even laugh at them.

- For postmodernists, stories, not facts, make experience meaningful and are the privileged mode of sense making. Here all human experience is a story of some kind and stories influence the way people talk. Boje (1991, 1994, 1995) sees storytelling as an institutions' memory, which is continually recreating the past. For him stories are in continuous flux, taking the form of fragments of conversation.

Narrative, however, is more complex, taking the form of stories and evaluations of these stories which convey understandings of our experience. The point is that both narrative and propositional themes emerge in conversation and that conversation and experience are organised by both. Although much underplayed in the dominant discourse, narrative articulations of experience are of enormous importance and constitute major forms of knowledge. Both narrative and propositional articulations of patterns emerging in our conversation organise the experience of relating in a number of ways – for example, by: selecting what is to be attended to; shaping how what is attended to is to be described; selecting who might describe it; accounting by one to another for their actions; articulating purpose in the form of themes expressing intentions; and justifying actions in the form of themes that express ideology.

This section considers storytelling as a mode of articulating reflections on emergent experience. A story is an account of a sequence of specific actions, feeling states and events, while a narrative is a story line linked by reflections, comments upon, and categorisations of, elements of the story line. So, a narrative contains within it a story but it is a more complex form of communication than a story because it involves some kind of evaluation.

Bruner (1986, 1990) has identified some of the key features of narrative. Narratives create a sense of temporality in experience, linking present experiences to past ones and pointing towards the future evolution of the experience. They focus upon departures from what is expected, from what is taken for granted as ordinary and acceptable, and thereby they reinforce cultural norms. Stories that simply recount expected routines are not particularly interesting, but those that describe the unexpected are, and such stories usually have a 'moral' that reinforces the culture or ideology of the group. Stories also impart something about the subjectivity of the narrator or about the subjectivity of the characters in the story. In other words, they disclose some aspects of individuals' silent conversations and provide the means for people to experience each other's subjectivity.

People also use stories to describe and deal with ambiguity. Bruner (1990) points to the essential ambiguity of stories themselves in that it is quite difficult to tell just what is fact and what is fiction in a story, thereby opening up the possibility of the fantasy potential to which Elias attached so much importance with regard to human interaction. An essential aspect of narrative, therefore, is the scope it offers for the exercise of imagination and the spinning of fantasy. Bruner also emphasises the constructive role of the listener in storytelling, because people do not just listen to stories. They select and fill in meanings and, indeed, storytelling techniques employ devices to encourage this active participation in the co-construction of meaning in narratives. Bruner talks about stories as 'trafficking in human possibilities rather than settled certainties' (1986, p. 28).

Sarbin (1986) points out the link between narrative and feelings: emotional states are located in narratives and passions are 'storied'. McCleod (1996) emphasises the problem-solving function of stories in that they are used to put chaotic experiences into causal sequences and explain dilemmas and deviations:

> In co-constructed narratives, the listener or audience may feed their own alternative accounts into the story that emerges, or may seek clarification by asking questions. So, the act of telling a story makes available a communication structure that not only conveys a sense of a world of uncertainty and ambiguity, but also provides a means of reducing dissonance and re-establishing a sense of control and order, by assembling an account that becomes more complete or ordered through the process of being told. (p. 37)

So, in constructing a story and a narrative of our experience of local interaction and our perceptions of the emergent population-wide patterns, as a form of thought and reflection on what we are doing, we are in a sense simplifying that experience, categorising characters and situations into stereotypes. This enables us and others to go more deeply into our own experience, elaborating and developing it in unexpected ways. Although, of course, stories can also be used in dogmatic ways – for example, in some religions where they must be taken as literally true, sometimes on pain of death. Clearly these narrative simplifications close down on reflection of experience and prohibit any kind of imaginative elaboration.

However, social evolution over the last 500 years in Western Europe has produced the modern, rational, calculating, planning, individual agent (Taylor, 2007; Elias, [1939] 2000; Scott, 1998). A central feature of such modern individuals is their capacity to reflect and to think in objective propositional, simplifying, rational ways indicated in section 16.3 above as the first mode of thinking and acting identified by Bourdieu.

16.5 Reflecting on experience: the role of second-order abstracting

Social evolution produced modern agents who engage in a kind of generalising about their experience, articulated primarily in propositional forms, which was not available to pre-modern individuals. What emerged we could say was a particularly rigorous form of simplification, a stronger form of *abstracting* from the experience of local interaction than before. In addition to generalising through the identification of categories of experience, articulated in narratives and philosophical arguments, which we might call *first-order abstracting* from the experience of local interaction, there was an added generalisation expressed in the mapping and modelling of relationships between the categories, which we might call *second-order abstracting*. This is a form of simplification by abstraction which manipulates the categories of first-order abstractions and therefore operates at yet another remove from direct experience. This abstraction from the abstraction of categories of experience makes it easier to split the second-order abstraction off from the experience through reification and so lose the sense of the paradox of immersing and abstracting at the same time. Second-order abstracting activity seeks to simplify, standardise and measure, so reducing elaboration, multiple interpretations and mystery. The consequent clarity and uniformity makes it much easier to exert some control on the activities of others from a distance.

In our ordinary, everyday local interaction with each other, in which we accomplish all our joint activities, we always have been and still are *immersing* ourselves in the experience of such interaction and at the same time we are *abstracting* from that experience by simplifying, generalising and categorising in the forms of narrative and philosophy as *first-order abstracting*, and also in the modern world we are frequently articulating generalisations/idealisations of the categories of experience as maps and models which can be described as *second-order abstracting*. Local interaction in the modern world, therefore, necessarily includes the formulation and interpretation of second-order abstractions as one aspect of what we are doing together in organisations. Certainly, to be included in groups of managers one must be a skilled participant in the dominant discourse conducted in terms of second-order abstractions. In our immersion, our preoccupation in the game of ordinary, everyday organisational life, we are together meaningfully patterning our interactions by drawing upon both the first- (narrative) and second-order (models and maps) abstractions which have evolved in our community, and in so doing we are together changing the abstractions in our local interaction. We are largely unconscious of how we are relying upon abstractions and find it difficult to notice just how readily we reify them and so cover over our preoccupation in the game.

This activity of second order abstracting involves:

- *Objectifying* and categorising. Here phenomena from celestial bodies down to social patterns, modes of thinking and individual human feelings are placed in well-defined bounded 'spaces' where differences within categories are obliterated and all difference is located at the boundary.

- *Measuring* the quantitative aspects of these categories (and nowadays the qualitative too by means of quantitative proxies) using *standardised* measures.

- *Averaging* out differences within categories and interactions between categories.

- *Analysing* the data so produced using mathematical, statistical and other analytical techniques.
- Selecting regularities and stabilities and forming hypotheses about relationships between entities, particularly *causal connections* often involving, by deduction, some hidden mechanism or whole.
- *Modelling*, forecasting, specifying probabilities with given distributions of variances, mapping, articulating rules and schemas.
- *Prescribing rules*, laws and moral norms.
- *Setting targets*, planning, monitoring and envisioning.

The scientific method is the paradigmatic example of the activity of second-order abstracting. It is also an essential activity for governing the modern state and modern organisations, because its aim to standardise and so remove diversity to make activities legible to people at some central point, so enabling some degree of central control.

How the modern state came to rely on second-order abstractions

Scott (1998) provides a number of examples of how the modern state has come to rely on what he calls 'state simplifications', which are what I mean by *abstractions*. The modern state with its increased centralisation relies heavily on tax revenues to function and it has therefore had to develop an efficient method of taxation. Until fairly recently in Western Europe, tax collecting was rather arbitrary and open to cheating. It often involved force and relied heavily on the local knowledge of tax collectors. The principal problem of reforming the most important of the taxes in earlier times, the tax on land wealth, was that the practices of land tenure were extremely intricate and varied considerably from one local context to another – very different tenure arrangements could be encountered geographically very close to each other. Detailed local knowledge was required in order to know what it was possible to collect, hence the need for local tax collectors, and any attempt to rationalise and centralise tax collection was blocked by the impossibility of those at the centre gaining knowledge about all the varieties of tenure arrangements. The locals would always be able to conceal the real situation from uninformed central tax collectors. In Scott's terms, the property-owning system was illegible to the state, and so a centralising state could only succeed if it could impose a legible property system. This meant that economic activities and all landed wealth had to be identified, measured and attached to some individual or group of individuals. Measuring wealth and changing tenure arrangements was a major political act. It would be necessary to impose the reforms, because a simplified, unified and transparent property system would profoundly shift existing patterns of power relations and so, naturally, any reforms would be resisted.

An important move in the reform of the property systems of Europe occurred first in Holland, Denmark and France around the Napoleonic era: cadastral maps of rural areas were prepared. A cadastral survey is one on a scale sufficiently large to show accurately the extent and measurement of every field or other block of land, thus precisely identifying land boundaries. However, accurate measurement of the immense variations across small areas was not possible. The maps had to be simplifications of some kind, and the more orderly the actual land tenure practices the more useful the maps would be. Surveyors then pressed locals to consolidate their disparate holding of strips of land into neater farms which could be measured. So the act of measuring was producing patterns of tenure that could be measured. Measuring was more than a detached scientific act; it was a social, political act as are all acts of measuring human activity. Simplified and consolidated tenure was the ideal, but what actually happened in each local situation still varied as locals carried out unauthorised consolidations or appeared to be operating according to authorised consolidations while they continued to farm their strips as before. However, although not accurate, the abstraction and universality of the maps applied the same objective standard across the populations. The cadastral map, therefore, makes local conditions legible to the state but only in a highly simplified way, because the actual wealth and its taxable capacity depends on its detailed production capacity, still only known to the locals. No matter how much detail the map makers include, the maps inevitably remain simplifications based on averages, while farmers rarely experiences average crops or average rainfalls. Uniform administration requires standardised measurements and calculations, but they cannot reflect the actual complexity of the farmer's experience.

Scott emphasises how what seems to be an objective, scientific, value-free activity of measuring and classifying, in fact, established new institutions administering title deeds, fees, applications and other matters. The maps were changing the world in many respects to accord with what could be measured and in doing so they were shifting patterns of power relations in which administrators became more powerful and cultivators less so. This early application of measuring, standardising, establishing a property system provides us with important insights into what we are still doing today in the dominant discourse. The dominant discourse lays great emphasis on simplifying and abstracting in an attempt to bring about the uniformity which enables some control from a distance. Attempts at centralised control do require some imposition of uniformity and in so doing shift patterns of power relations, which has an effect on shaping behaviour. As an example, take the government targets for the National Health Service in the UK. In the 1990s the government imposed waiting-time targets on all hospitals in England and Wales, and some ten years later most hospitals were indeed meeting those targets. Apparently the setting of uniform targets does shape behaviour.

However, standardising, mapping and modelling inevitably leaves behind real people, replacing them with simplified averages. So, the activity of second-order abstracting produces articulations of generalisations and idealisations in relation to hypothetical wholes which have the effect of focusing on what is believed to be important across a whole population and this could and often does render invisible the experience of local interaction. This is by no means a criticism, because without the activity of second-order abstracting there could be no modern state or policies of improvement, nor would it be possible to govern large organisations. In reflecting an ideology of order, rationality, harmony, design, control and improvement, the activity of second abstracting does change the world and is essential for the kind of lives we live in modernity. However, second-order abstracting does render rationally invisible the disorder, diversity, deviance, conflict, compromise, manipulation, cheating, trickery, power plays, concealing and revealing of ordinary, everyday experience which also changes the world and so also needs to be understood.

The activity of second-order abstracting necessarily involves the postulating of an entity outside our local experience and we easily come to believe that it actually exists, that we can be outside it, observe it and then 'move' it around, or that it is the only possible way to think. This kind of belief in second-order abstractions is the foundation of today's dominant discourse about organisations and management. What is striking about such formulations is just how thoroughly people disappear from view. For example, I recently made a contribution to a programme aimed at developing the strategy competence of senior managers at a major international corporation. I listened to the session just before I was due to talk. The session took the form of a report back by small groups on their discussion of a number of case studies of strategic success and failure in other large companies. The conversation ran entirely in terms of abstract entities. *Toyota* was said to have decided to enter the Chinese market and an intense discussion followed on why *Toyota* had done this, what *China* expected in return and whether it had been the 'right' strategy or not. The whole discussion was purely speculative, since none of the discussants, including the presenter, had any involvement with Toyota and few if any had actually been to China. When a particular decision looked puzzling, discussants looked for rational reasons for Toyota having made it and, if they could find none, they concluded that it had been a mistake. No one ever suggested that we might need to understand the figuration of power relations amongst senior groups of managers at Toyota, or that the special interests and private agendas of senior managers and their Chinese counterparts might have had something to do with the decisions. It took only a few minutes discussion at the start of my session for participants to see just how abstract their discussion had been and how totally absent human beings had been.

Second-order abstracting is a major activity in organisations today. It is also a major aspect of organisational research and management education. Economic, industrial, and organisational trends are abstractions. Strategy discussions are abstraction. Vision and mission statements are not only abstract generalisations but also idealisations of those abstractions. Targets set for public sector organisations, or any other organisation for that matter, are abstractions. However, to label as second-order abstractions so many of the activities that take up peoples' time in any organisation is not to denigrate or dismiss such activities. Scott (1998) makes the point strongly that large-scale change and improvement does require second-order abstraction; but he also insists that the state simplification, or abstraction, taken on its own cannot accomplish change or improvement. The second-order abstraction must be interpreted in terms of local contingent situations in the everyday, practical activities of people in local situations if they are to have the potential for beneficial effect. Many organisations create climates of fear which suppress local interaction. We have a tendency to become so immersed in the abstractions of models and plans that we collapse the practical art of local interaction into a stereotypical activity called 'implementation' and, as a result, we lose sight of what is happening until it is too late. It is not difficult to see the strength of this point in modern corporations. For example, major banks do have systems of regulation and control which should prevent rogue traders taking financial positions which jeopardise the whole organisation. However, these regulations can easily be re-interpreted, ignored or circumvented as we see repeatedly. To think that it is enough to set up an abstract system is to be in constant danger of unpleasant surprises. What is called for, then, is a renewed attention to everyday forms of experience and how particular first- and second-order abstractions are being taken up in ways which might be helpful but also in ways which might be harmful. Shifting the focus to local interaction will open up the possibility of reflecting on the usefulness or otherwise of the abstracting activity we now so blindly undertake in completely taken-for-granted ways.

The interaction of immersing and abstracting activities

Although I have been drawing a conceptual distinction between the activities of immersing and abstracting, in life they can never be separated: they are paradoxically related in that there is no meaning without abstraction and nothing for meaning to be about without immersion. Without second-order abstraction there could be no modern states, modern organisations or modern science and without immersion and accompanying first-order abstraction there would be no means to perpetually construct societies, organisations and sciences. Second-order abstractions, especially those claiming to accord with science, are very powerful rhetorical ploys in the modern world and can certainly be used as techniques of domination, but they do also create greater 'visibility' from a distance and so make some forms of improvement possible. The ability to express and utilise second-order abstractions, which reflect powerful modern ideologies of control and improvement, is of major importance in the inclusion–exclusion dynamics of modern organisations. Second-order abstracting as described above is an activity that people engage in together in ordinary local interaction: scientists, administrators, managers, policy makers, and analysts are interacting daily in their own local communities to produce standards, measures, models, forecasts, targets, plans and monitoring reports. Second-order abstracting is itself one pattern of local interaction, one way of immersing in local interaction as suggested above. Also, those engaging in the activity of abstracting are not simply adopting a distanced, analytical attitude – they are also deeply immersed in their worlds of abstraction. Richard Dawkins, the popularising scientist of evolution, provides a dramatic example in his latest books and documentary films in which he displays enormous passion for the scientific abstraction of evolutionary theory and righteous anger at those who contest it. Scientists are immersed in their science and the ideology of that science. They are also immersed in the politics of funding their work. In fact abstractions are not only emerging in local interaction in one group, but they come to have meaning in how they are taken up in the local interactions of other groups. Abstractions, by their very nature as generalisations and simplifications, can only be reflected in conduct through the ways in which people are interpreting them in their own contingent, local interactions. They have to be particularised or functionalised. So, a chief executive who, after the local interaction of discussion with colleagues, announces a new vision will discover what this means in how others take it up, or not, in many other local interactions.

16.6 Reasoning, measuring, forecasting and modelling in strategic management

Previous sections of this chapter have argued that all reasoning requires phenomena to be simplified into generalised categories and stereotypes. This was described as first-order abstracting. Second-order abstracting then focuses on measuring and manipulating these first-order abstractions in the form of modelling and forecasting as the basis of technically rational decision-making. In reviewing how the processes of organising and strategising are thought about in the dominant discourse, Chapter 7 pointed to the way in which the process of technical rationality was increasingly problematised. In the early days of theorising about organisations and strategy, the emphasis was very much on analytical reasoning applied to quantitative data in order to deduce optimal actions. Strategising was thought about primarily in terms of identifying simple cause-and-effect links so as to choose actions with a high probability of producing optimal performance. The earliest critiques of technical rationality pointed to how the ideal of analytical, reductionist, linear, instrumental reasoning was impossible to apply in practice because of the costs involved and because of the limited capacity of the human brain. It was argued that the strategy process in practice was a form of bounded rationality. Even this notion of bounded rationality was found to be an idealisation of reason, because in practice any reasoning process is highly conditioned by the interpretive frameworks in terms of which people have no option but to think about the situations in which they have to choose actions. As a result of their interpretive frameworks, people would inevitably ignore some features of the situation and reach biased views about the situation, often leading them to inertia and drift. Then, psychodynamic perspectives point to the role of unconscious, irrational processes in determining what people do and how this can obstruct rationality. The limitations of objective reasoning processes were even further stressed by those who argued that people together enact: that is, actively select and create their world of experience. Social constructionists argued that people create the world of their experience in language. Postmodernism takes this problematising of objective reasoning a step further in arguing that there are as many views of the world as there are people and therefore there is no grand narrative, no theory that can claim to be fundamental in any sense. Taken to its extreme this leads to a view in which there is no reality out there, only our stories, and one story is as good as another.

The theory of complex responsive processes continues with this critique of the strategy process as one of technical rationality, but stops short of postmodernism in arguing for a way of understanding that does, in a sense, offer a grand narrative and makes fundamental claims about human relating. It argues that all human relating is fundamentally conversational and that conversation is, and always was, the conversation of gestures. It argues that all human relating is, and always was, power relating and it argues that the basis of patterns of power relations is ideological. It argues that all human experience has a narrative structure and that the criteria for the choices people make within the ongoing narrative of experience are fundamentally based on the evaluative criteria of ideology. In making these claims, the theory of complex responsive process remains firmly within modernism, just as what I have been calling the dominant discourse does. The theory of complex responsive processes problematises human reason much as the debate in the dominant discourse does, even taking this problematisation a step further in emphasising the fundamentally uncertain and perpetually constructed nature of human futures and in emphasising the fundamental interdependence of human agents.

However, no matter how problematic, the human capacity for reasoning remains of great importance and has enormous consequences. The previous chapters in this part have not mentioned reasoning processes much, simply because these chapters have been concerned with understanding the basic nature of human agency and human action of which reasoning is only one aspect. In their communicative interaction, their power relating and their ideologically based choosing, people employ their capacity to reason and in fact reflect in a reasoned manner on their very processes of reasoning. After all, despite not mentioning reason, all of the previous chapters in this part have been exercises in reasoning about human interaction in a structured and rational manner. Complex responsive processes of reasoning, therefore, remain of fundamental importance no matter how problematic they might be. What the theory of complex responsive processes seeks to provide is a rigorously reasoned, unashamedly theoretical but hopefully useful way of thinking about human processes of thinking which must include human processes of reasoning. Instead of simply taking rationality for granted, the invitation is to reflect on the manner in which we are reasoning in any specific situation.

Just as the theory of complex responsive processes is not some kind of justification or prescription for abandoning reason (the head!) in favour of muddling through or in favour of emotion (the body!), so it is also not a justification or prescription for abandoning any attempt to measure important aspects of organisational life or to abandon any attempt to forecast anything. Instead, it offers a way of thinking about the activities of measuring and forecasting by providing a perspective from which one can ask whether particular measurements and particular attempts to forecast make any sense in a particular situation. For example, take the widely accepted approach to making investment decisions having long-term consequences. When I talk to managers about unpredictable long-term futures, someone will often say that, since managers must make investment decisions with very long-term consequences, they must be able to predict. And clearly managers do this. But are the predictions worth anything and are they actually the basis of their investment decisions?

Prediction and investment decisions

The normal technique for making long-term investment decisions is to undertake a discounted cash-flow analysis. This involves modelling the future by measuring the costs and the outcomes of the investment in financial terms and forecasting these variables over a long time period, typically 25 years. It is also usual to specify a number of different scenarios and to calculate the return on the investment for each scenario. This is supposed to enable managers to compare the outcomes of different investment options in different possible situations, so enabling them to choose the one most likely to produce a desired outcome. Consider what happened at a meeting of top executives I was consulting to. They arrived at a meeting at which they were going to put forward a recommendation on a particular large investment proposal which would have consequences for many years to come. As they entered the room, the financial analysts handed them a piece of paper which listed twelve scenarios, each based on different assumptions about costs, prices and volumes of product. The rates of return varied across the scenarios from a large negative to a large positive return. The executives started to question the financial analysts, asking why one rate of return was higher or lower than another. The analysts rapidly encountered difficulties in giving satisfactory replies, because there were so many different assumptions in the various scenarios that they could not remember them all. Tempers were becoming frayed and then the chief executive laughingly intervened and said, 'Don't get upset – the one thing we all know for sure is that none of these scenarios will ever happen!'

What is happening here? A group of very competent and intelligent executives are going through a procedure in what looks like a highly rational manner, based on what looks like objective data, but in fact they all know that the future is unknowable. They are apparently going to make a decision on the basis of information that they all agree is completely unreliable. They all agree that they cannot forecast in this detail over this time period. Further discussion revealed that there had been a number of informal conversations between the directors in small groups of two or three. They had all already agreed that they would support the investment proposal even though they had not seen any of the forecasts. On what did they base their agreement? They had agreed that if they did not make the investment they would not be 'in the game' in that particular market. They had argued that if they did not make the investment then a rival would, and this could make the rival more powerful in the market to the point where that rival might even acquire them. They formed the judgement that, although they could not know what would happen, it would nevertheless be better to make the investment than not to. This seems to me to be an entirely reasonable argument and they thought so too. However, they were not proposing to discuss the real reasons for the investment in public because they did not sound rational and objective enough. They needed the cash-flow forecasts in order to present a case to the non-executive directors on their board. In other words, the apparently rational analysis was to be used as a rhetorical ploy to persuade others to accept the judgement of the executive directors and, of course, the non-executives knew this but also needed to have a rational case so that they could not be blamed if things went wrong.

The theory of complex responsive processes, therefore, offers managers a way of thinking about what they are doing. It is not possible to make long-term investment decisions on the basis of forecasts because the long-term future is unknowable. It is because of the inherent uncertainty of organisational life that commercial enterprises have the opportunity to earn a profit. In capitalist, market economies, profit is the reward for bearing uncertainty. Uncertainty is unique and unknowable compared with risk, which can be assessed in terms of probability and so insured against. An organisation bearing risk is rewarded with an insurance premium. An organisation bearing uncertainty is rewarded with profit. To earn a profit, managers must make judgements and undertake investments whose outcome they cannot know in advance. In such situations the use of discounted cash flow analyses can only ever be a rhetorical ploy. Knowing this, managers can at least thoroughly explore the real reasons they have for making an investment even if they find they have to present the public case in some other way.

The complex responsive processes perspective, therefore, is a useful one in understanding just when one can forecast, over what time period, and just what measurements make sense for just what purpose in particular situations.

I would like to make one other point about prediction. While a forecast is a quantitative statement, a prediction could take a qualitative form. Chapter 14 presented Mead's explanation of human consciousness in which a person is conscious because he or she has the capacity to take the attitude of the other, including the attitude of the generalised other. In other words, through a life history in a community with a history, each person can predict to some extent how others might respond to his or her next action. As we interact in ordinary ways with each other every day, we are always expecting some response, which is a form of predicting. Our action is always future oriented. At the same time, however, we do not know what the responses will be – we know that our predictions in ordinary social life are going to be far from perfect. For this reason, effective people remain alert to the differences between their predictions and the responses they evoke so that they are able to continually adjust their actions. In other words, alert people are those who are aware of the predictably unpredictable nature of the responses they are likely to evoke. So just knowing that the future is not knowable is not a recipe for despair but a realisation that is essential to effective conduct.

In the investment decision example given above I referred to the decision technique as a model and the next section looks in more detail at the use of the second-order abstractions of models from the complex responsive processes perspective.

Modelling

Second-order and critical systems thinkers (*see* Chapter 9) adopt what is essentially a qualitative modelling approach to their work. The immediate concern of the systems practitioner is with some *problem issue or situation* about which some *group of people* feel that they need to *make decisions* and take actions in order to bring about some improvement. The practitioner aims to *intervene* in this situation in order to identify how this issue or situation *should* be formulated, how the decision *should* be taken and how it *should* be implemented. The purpose is to specify some kind of procedure that the group *should* follow in order to improve the situation, recognising that it will probably be impossible to optimise the decision outcome. Improvement is understood as securing some desired or intended outcomes. The unquestioned assumption is that problem formulation/analysis, decision making and implementation are separate activities. They may overlap, they may circle around many iterations, but conceptually they are separate. The assumption is that thought is apart from action.

The practitioner operating from the complex responsive processes perspective does so on the basis that thinking and talking are action. What is of interest is the conversational process in which a group of people are coming to feel that there is some kind of issue or situation of concern, even though as yet they do not know what it is. The perspective is, then, not what people should be doing but what they actually are doing as the practitioner joins them. Here the practitioner joins a group of people as a participant in their conversations, seeking to understand something of the organising themes that are emerging in these conversations.

The systems practitioner prepares for an intervention by gathering data and interviewing those involved or affected by the situation in order to formulate some kind of view of what is going on. The systems practitioner has various techniques for doing this, such as preparing a 'rich picture' of the situation or summaries of evaluations of the situation made by various participants (*see* Chapter 9). This information is prepared as some kind of presentation or feedback to those who will participate in the intervention and it is the basis on which the practitioner advises on who the appropriate group of participants should be.

From a complex responsive processes perspective, the practitioner does not join a group with the intention of structuring or shaping the situation or the conversations in which an issue is emerging. The practitioner has no intention of creating the right conditions for better conversations or identifying the right people to be involved in them. There is no intention to design anything, improve it, or make it right or more creative. Instead, the intention is the same as that of other participants – namely, to understand what they are all doing together, what they are talking about and why. So, for example, Shaw (2002) explains how she asks people how they came to be involved in the current conversation, because their stories begin to indicate what they are actually doing in the living present. In participating in this storytelling she draws attention in certain directions rather than others by emphasising certain moments rather than others and using certain forms of expression rather than others. In so doing she is drawing attention to how these stories create meaning, changing in emphasis as people go on thinking and speaking about them. People identify with each other's stories and so sustain their relationships. This process does not simply reaffirm existing ideas but enlivens the senses of participants, stirring them from the habit of attending to experiences in familiar ways to awaken a fresh appreciation of their experience.

For Shaw (2002), there is no intention to prepare for the work to be done at some later point because in their already conversing, the work is under way in what she calls 'gatherings'. Instead of selecting a key group of influencers, formal or informal, to initiate change, she pays attention to the way in which influence is spontaneously arising in webs of relationships in particular contexts, reflected in people gathering together in some way. Gatherings are provoked by the urgent need to make sense of some dimly perceived issues, making it inevitable that their conversation will be characterised by a vague sense of why they are there. Instead of a clear formulation of an enquiry and special invitations to a representative sample of stakeholders, Shaw seeks ways to connect people so that gatherings will arise spontaneously because of some interest in common. Such gatherings are not representative, fair or consultative but, rather, they are active. The point is to work with the potential for change, finding ways of convening forums that tap people's interests, enthusiasms or frustrations and which demand an intensive interaction to create meaningful forms of activity that 'move things on'. These discussions have an 'everyday quality' – they are branching, meandering, associative and engaging. They are similar to the modes people value and recognise in many informal kinds of conversation. They include formulating and making reference to proposals, analysis and frameworks. They involve speculation, anecdotes and personal revelation. They are characterised by feeling and bodily sensations that all are resonating and responded to in different ways. It is a very active, searching, exploratory form of communication in which the way the future is under perpetual construction is more than usually evident.

The systems practitioner designs some kind of intervention event such as a meeting, workshop or learning event in which participants explore the nature of the issue/situation and possible responses to it. The systems practitioner has a collection of methodologies, methods, tools and techniques to draw upon in designing the intervention events. For example, there are various heuristics, procedures and *models* developed by systems thinkers for application to ambiguous problem situations characterised by power differences and ideological features. The methods and techniques aim to surface multiple evaluations of the situation in what is a pluralistic approach. All of these methodologies, techniques and so on are systemic. This means that they focus attention on some *whole* or system and the interconnections that produce the system. The implicit assumption is that it is only by affecting the whole that improvement can be assured. This is because complex interconnections could overcome attempts at partial improvement. The systems practitioner is seeking to assist people to draw boundaries around the problem situation, identifying the whole system of which it is an aspect. They recognise the difficulties of doing this in complex situations and so advocate the drawing of multiple boundaries and the exploration of ethical and power implications of doing so. Each model or system identified is recognised as only a partial view of the whole, one that depends upon the particular paradigm of those drawing the boundary.

Systems practitioners think of themselves as facilitators who structure, shape and guide workshops and other intervention events using the methodologies of systems thinkers. They keep it rational, to the point and following the agenda. For example, they present lists of questions to workshop participants asking them to evaluate their current situation and how they plan to do things differently. They support workshop participants in looking at where they want to go. Such information may then be used to design subsequent learning events. They give exercises to particip-ants in learning events, such as imagining that they have just climbed out of a time capsule five years into the future.

In relation to the group faced with the problem situation, the stance of the systems practitioner is one of involvement in that the work is done with the people involved. The systems practitioner joins the group but always does so in a particu-lar manner – namely, as the bringer of systematic sets of conceptual paradigms, a system of methodologies, a plurality of methods, techniques, heuristics, lists of questions and models. The systems thinker analyses the situation in order to select appropriate paradigms and methodologies for the situation in accordance with some kind of meta-paradigm or meta-methodology. In other words, the systems thinker sets some kind of agenda.

In the stages leading up to these events, and in the events themselves, then, systems practitioners see themselves as participating with those whom they are advising in the formulation and exploration of the problem situation. However, in an important sense they are all taking the stance of the objective observer of the situation simply because they analyse the situation, design the intervention events and select the appropriate models. The participants also then take this objective position in applying the *models* to their situation.

From the complex responsive processes perspective, Shaw argues that meetings which are carefully orchestrated and over-specified in advance increase the likelihood of people reconstructing the familiar. Outcomes, procedures for working together, agendas, roles to be taken up by those present, forms of contribution and prepared presentations, all conspire to reduce the experience of uncertainty as the experience of acting into the known is engineered. She argues that under-specification increases the experience of diversity and multiplicity, disturbing routine responses and increasing the potential for novelty. For Shaw, facilitating means participating as fully and responsively as possible, voicing one's opinions, associations and ideas along with everyone else. In doing this she is sensing the move towards and away from agreement, of shifts in power difference, the development and collapse of tensions, the variations in engagement, the different qualities of silence, the rhetorical ploys, the repetition of familiar turns of phrase or image, the glimpsing and losing of possibility, the ebb and flow of feeling tone, the dance of mutual constraint. She tries to participate in the conversation in a way that helps to hold open the interplay of sense making rather longer than would occur in her absence, to hold open the experience of not knowing. In doing this she is resisting the enormous pressure for closure.

Notice the difference between the systems and complex responsive processes accounts of practice. The systems practitioner arrives at the situation with a set of methodologies, models, techniques and so on, to shape the discussion. There is a design and something of an agenda. From the complex responsive processes perspective the practitioner's methodology is the ordinary, everyday conversational process that is already under way – there are no formal models. The practitioner does not set any agenda at all but seeks to understand the shifting thematic patterning of the processes of interaction as the basis on which to contribute to it, just as all the other participants are doing. There is little emphasis on facilitating in the sense of structuring, summarising, writing bullet points on flipcharts, calling for feedback or model building. Instead, by responding to what others are saying, by linking themes, the practitioner is helping to articulate emerging themes and in so doing is influencing the further patterning of the conversation. It is these shifts in communicative patterning, the widening and deepening of communication, which constitute organisational change.

This means that, unlike the systems practitioner, the practitioner from a complex responsive processes perspective is not concerned with understanding *the* organisation as a whole system, but is concerned with the detail of the local interactions between people, the interplay of their intentions, in the living present; and in this local interaction, it is of great importance to understand the articulations people give of of the unity of experience in terms of imaginative constructs of 'whole', idealised organisations.

In systemic practice, those working in the intervention make decisions and take actions to improve the situation. For the complex responsive processes practitioner, the action and the work have been going on all the time and in this work decisions and actions are continually emerging or being blocked.

Systems practitioners are well aware of the highly complex, ill-structured nature of the situations that groups in organisations face. Their response is pluralism, which means employing combinations of given paradigms, methodologies, methods and models. Instead of proposing a single, or even a few consistent hypotheses, they encourage those they work with to explore many hypotheses, selecting particular models according to what the culture allows. From the complex responsive processes perspective, one is sceptical of this notion of pluralism – that is, identifying and selecting different paradigms for evaluation. Instead, the practice is concerned with what is emerging, and since what is emerging is individual and collective identities, one is sceptical about the possibility of simply switching paradigms as systemic practice suggests. In the kind of practice I am describing the focus of attention is on emerging themes and there is no notion of anyone drawing boundaries around a system.

The use of qualitative models related to whole organisations focuses attention at the macro level, the population-wide patterns, in the belief that this can be affected directly. The complex responsive processes approach focuses attention on the micro on the basis that population-wide patterns cannot be directly operated on because they emerge in local interaction. The models can help to articulate the population-wide patterns and so provoke conversation but cannot provide a direct intervention tool.

Quantitative modelling

In a very general sense, the previous chapters of this part have outlined a model. This is a model of local interaction between members of a group of people in which they form desires and intentions concerning their own local interactions and concerning the generalisations and idealisations of the population-wide patterns that emerge in their local interactions. This is their experience, and they often talk and feel about this experience in terms of a unity expressed as an imaginatively constructed 'whole' directed to the future, although they may usually not be all that aware of the imaginatively constructed nature of this unity of experience. Any theory can be thought of as a model in this kind of way. However, the term 'model' is also used in a much more restricted sense as an analytical, often mathematical, construct of a system, sometimes incorporating empirical measurements of some kind. Such models are sometimes used by managers and policy makers as aids to decision-making. How would one understand such models and their use from a complex responsive processes perspective?

The formal mathematical modeller usually makes a distinction between a group of decision-makers, the problem situation that they are facing, and the alternative strategies they might deploy to deal with the problem situation, just as the qualitative modellers described in the last section do. The decision-makers tend to be thought of as acting within or upon the situation and in order to assist them to make an appropriate decision, the modeller constructs a model of the situation to enable them to explore the possible consequences of alterative decisions they could take in order to better achieve their objectives. They are conversing in ways patterned by activities of second-order abstracting.

The model, therefore, focuses on the situation and the alternative ways of dealing with it, while the group of decision-makers slip unnoticed into the background. It is implicitly assumed that the individual decision-makers act according to rationalist causality (*see* Chapter 3), rather than the assumption made in the theory of complex responsive process of transformative causality in human action. Abstracting from the experience of the decision-makers themselves, as happens in the use of the model, is perfectly understandable because a formal mathematical model could not capture the micro-detail of the conversational, ideological and power-relating interactions between people that the theory of complex responsive processes focuses on. The first point to notice, then, is how formal mathematical modelling necessarily abstracts from direct human experience and constructs a set of formal, abstract relationships relating to the whole situation. The situation is normally understood as a system at the macro level, and traditional systems models average away any micro diversity and so implicitly assume formative causality (*see* Chapter 3) in which the system model unfolds the hypothesis of the modeller. Second-order systems thinkers referred to in the last section do recognise that the decision-makers are not separate from the situation and so the model of the situation is widened to incorporate the decision-makers themselves. However, they are then observing themselves observing the situation and we get into infinite regress. There are two problems with a great many formal mathematical models. First, by modelling at a macro level, they average away diversity and, second, they separate decision-makers and situation.

From a complex responsive processes perspective, the situation is not a given that can be modelled apart from the decision-makers, although temporarily thinking this might be instructive. Instead, the situation is the history of the decision-makers and their processes. This history has produced particular configurations of resources (e.g. a particular configuration of transport facilities) and particular patterns of habits that we call 'culture' or 'social structure'. In the living present, as a group of decision-makers are acting, their actions are simultaneously enabled and constrained by these resource configurations and cultural patterns. In their acting they are continually re-enacting, but in subtly different ways, the configurations and patterns and so potentially transforming them. In this way there is no split causality, because both the situation and the decision-makers are thought of according to transformative causality. The situation is part of the decision-makers and vice versa. The decision-makers are co-creating or enacting the situation. They may or they may not construct and use models but, if they do, the models are tools and the important point is just how those tools are employed in the complex responsive processes of making decisions.

A few system models (*see* the section on Allen's work in Chapter 11) do partially take account of human diversity and so produce models based on a form of transformative causality (*see* Chapter 12). However, there is still the split causality of rationalist decision-makers in the background and the transformative causality of the model itself. Furthermore, since it reflects transformative causality, this kind of model now evolves unpredictably – it takes on a life of its own. Since the model cannot capture all of the details of the situation, it and the situation it is modelling will evolve in completely different ways. The model's micro diversity could amplify in one way, while the situation's micro diversity could amplify in different ways. It follows that the decision-makers could not use their models in the rational calculating manner that might have been hoped for in the traditional models.

However, they could learn a lot about the dynamics of the situation, about the uncertainty and unpredictability of it, even though they could not directly calculate decisions from it. This immediately undermines the rational causality being assumed about the decision-makers. I would then argue that the decision-makers making the decisions also need to be understood in terms of transformative causality because they are an integral part of the situation. This is what the theory of complex responsive processes seeks to do. From this perspective, models are understood as tools, amongst other tools, used in the communicative processes of decision-making.

How might people be using these tools? Decision-makers are confronted by many possible futures and so seek to develop some idea of the possible consequences of the actions they choose. A macro-model of the situation, particularly one incorporating some degree of diversity, provides a tool for exploring possible consequences in terms of generalisations. In complex responsive processes terms one can think of these as models of social objects, including idealisations thereof. Any problem situation needs to be understood in terms of its wider social contexts – in terms of the generalisations of social objects and cult values, including technology and resources. A model of relationships between such generalisations could give useful insights even though it can never capture how the actual particularisations of these generalisations will be made. For example, Chapter 11 described Allen's model of police targeting suspects and the unintended consequences this can have. This insight could lead to very different conversations about targets.

16.7 Summary

To summarise, organisations exist to enable joint action and people can only act jointly through their relationships with each other. People relate to each other through complex responsive processes that can be understood in terms of interacting propositional and narrative themes. The themes take many forms. They may be ideological themes. They may take the form of intentions, expressions of emotion, descriptions and so on. Simultaneous interaction between many themes taking different forms constitutes the conversational life of an organisation and the strategic narratives that emerge from them. The process of relating through conversation constrains that relating and so establishes power relations. Conversation and power relations are simply different words for the same phenomenon: namely, that of relating between people. An organisation is processes of relating where relating is the conversational life of organisational members in which they form patterns of power relations and make ideologically based choices. Conversational life cannot develop according to an overall blueprint since no one has the power to determine what others will talk about all the time. Conversation is thus local interaction, which includes the use of maps and models as tools, continuously producing emergent population-wide patterns as strategy narratives.

Further reading

Ideas in this chapter are further developed by Fonseca (2001), Streatfield (2001). Further developments can be found in Stacey and Griffin (2005), Griffin and Stacey (2005), Stacey (2005), Stacey and Griffin (2006), Shaw and Stacey (2006), Stacey and Griffin (2008), and Mowles, Stacey and Griffin (2008).

Questions to aid further reflection

1. What do you understand by the term 'second-order abstraction'?
2. What do you think of those who advocate storytelling as a useful form of intervention in organisations?
3. What stories do you have to tell of shadow conversations in your organisation?
4. What role, if any, do you think humour plays in organisational life?
5. What activities in your organisation lead you to believe that unconscious processes might be at play and how might they affect strategy?

Chapter 17

Complex responsive processes of strategising

Acting locally on the basis of global goals, visions, expectations and intentions for the 'whole' organisation over the 'long-term future'

This chapter invites you to draw on your own experience to reflect on and consider the implications of:

- Articulating and acting upon goals, visions, expectations and intentions for the 'whole' organisation over the 'long-term future'.

- Thinking about the role of second-order abstraction in strategising activities in organisations.

- The roles that manager and leaders play in organisational strategy.

- Organisational resources as patterns of trust and as a basis of power relations.

- The meaning of technology in human interaction.

- Markets as patterns of relationships and as ideology.

- The role of strategic planning.

- How organisational strategy can be understood as continually iterated and potentially transformed identity narratives.

This chapter seeks to develop an understanding of what people in organisations are actually doing in their strategising activities and addresses aspects of organisation and strategy, such as resource bases and competitive advantage, which feature prominently in most discussions on strategy but have hardly been referred to in the chapters of Part 3 so far. The reference to these aspects has been sparse or absent, not because they are unimportant but because the main concern has been with thinking about the fundamentals of human interaction in a manner that differs from the dominant discourse, as a basis for thinking more specifically about strategy. Moving in thought to a different way of understanding human interaction leads to different ways of thinking about markets, resources, technology, performance, improvement, and strategising and it is to that different understanding that this chapter now turns. This chapter continues to explore issues raised in Chapter 16 in seeking to understand the ordinary, everyday local activities of strategising in organisations. It is important to read this chapter, I think, for the same reasons as the last chapter – because it attempts to bring together the ideas about human agency explored in previous chapters in Part 3 to present a way of understanding strategic management from a complex responsive processes perspective.

17.1 Introduction

The last chapter explored how our reflection on and thinking about our experience of organisational life takes the form of narratives, and also of abstract maps and models to which the labels of 'strategy' and 'strategising' may be attached. I now want to move on more specifically to how we might understand what strategy is and what it means to strategise from the perspective of complex responsive processes.

Chapter 16 pointed out how the functioning of the modern state depends crucially on the ability of relatively small groups of people to exert, from a central position, some degree of control over the activities of very large numbers of other people. This exercise of control by a few who take up institutional roles at the apex of a centralised hierarchy is inevitably carried out some distance away from the contingent local situations in which the many controlled are operating. Those powerful people attempting to control from a central position, therefore, have to rely on generalisations and simplifications across many local situations and whole populations where those simplifications abstract from the detail of local interaction. If the state is to function effectively, those at the top of a centralised management structure have no option but to rely on these abstract simplifications in order to pursue institutional purposes through exerting some degree of control over the behaviour of people by enforcing generalised rules of conduct which protect productive activity, enable the raising of revenues in a reasonably efficient and acceptable manner, and make it possible to account for expenditure and improve services. However, this means that the few powerful have to think and formulate their policies in terms of stereotypical global categories; they have to act on the basis of standards and measures; they have to operate according to global maps and models. As described in Chapter 16, these are the activities of second-order abstracting.

The points made in the above paragraph about the governance of the modern state apply just as much to modern organisations of every kind. I would argue that they too cannot function efficiently without leaders and managers in some kind of centralised hierarchy, who formulate, apply, and even enforce policies which amount to second-order abstractions that people make particular in some way in their many, many local interactions. Those at the top of modern organisational hierarchies are distant from those performing the business of the organisation and find that they can only operate in terms of highly abstract maps and models of their own and other organisations. Just as in the case of the modern state, so in the case of modern organisations these abstract maps and models do change behaviour across whole populations. However, this necessary drawing away from actual experience in local situations also exacts a price. People actually respond to the unavoidably abstract gestures of their leaders and managers in ways that reflect the dynamic variety of their many, many local situations. Of particular importance, as far as both the modern state and modern organisations are concerned, is the fact that abstract control from the centre will be interpreted differently in many local situations, which will generate conflict, outright opposition and the subtle practice of the arts of resistance. The abstract policies and strategies of those at the centre will therefore never work perfectly and will always be characterised by unexpected and unintended developments which will provoke further changes in policies and strategies. The point of major importance is that we cannot understand corporate governance, policy making and strategic management simply by focusing attention on the global abstractions articulated by leaders and managers, which is what the dominant discourse does. In addition, and at the same time, we need to be sensitive to the local responses to those global abstractions in which they derive their meaning and it has been the purpose of Chapters 13, 14 and 15, in particular, to explore explanations of the nature of these local responses.

According to the theory of complex responsive processes, therefore, strategic management is the governance of organisations on the basis of global second-order abstractions as gestures made by leaders and managers which evoke many, many local responses constituting the ordinary politics of everyday life. From a complex responsive processes perspective, the word *strategy* refers to the sometimes articulated, generalised, thematic patterns of governance which people are taking up and making particular in their many, many local interactions across a whole population over long time periods. Furthermore, changes in strategic generalisations emerge in the local particularising activities of people in a population, and leaders and managers becoming aware of this evolution may articulate these changes in the further development of their abstract maps and models. When people belonging to a small group interact with each other locally in ways that affect larger populations over long time periods we can classify this interaction as that of *strategising*. Strategising is thus a category of local interaction to which we apply a particular label to aid our own thinking. Strategising can only take the same form as any other kind of local interaction we may want to identify so that what distinguishes strategising from any other form of local interaction is the extent of the responses evoked over space and time and sometimes the object of attention of those interacting, such as abstract maps and models. Strategy as population-wide patterns of governance emerges in the interplay of many local interactions just as any other population-wide pattern does.

Realised organisational strategies are be understood, not as the result of implementation carried out by managers, but as patterns of joint activity which emerge across the populations of people constituting organisations in their many, many local interactions in which they are making particular to their situation the abstract maps and models articulated by the more powerful. Strategy as realised patterns of joint activity emerges through the many, many local interactions between members of organisations and between them and members of other organisations where those local interactions are fundamentally conversational in nature, characterised by relations of power sustained by ideologies which also form the basis of the choices people make and the intentions and plans they form, including desires, intentions and plans for the emerging population-wide patterns of strategy. Similarly, desired strategy cannot be understood simply as the choices of leaders, but must be understood as desires and intentions people develop for emerging population-wide patterns and the articulations they make of these desires, all in their ongoing local interaction with each other. Leaders are even more involved in this local, ordinary politics of organisational life than anyone else, and their actions are usually more influential than those of others involved. One of the most powerful ways in which they exert this influence is to make present to others abstract articulations of desired strategies, desired futures, in the form of goals, visions and missions, for example. In other words, they choose articulations of desired strategies. However, such choices will only have any impact if they resonate with the desires of others and are taken up in the many local interactions across the organisation. Furthermore, even if their desires are enthusiastically taken up, leaders cannot choose realised strategy because that can only emerge in the interplay of many, many intentions across many, many other organisations.

According to the theory of complex responsive processes, therefore, activities of strategising are essentially the local activities of ordinary daily politics in which people are formulating abstractions, and making them particular by negotiating choices, intentions, and responses to 'outcomes' which are often surprising and unwanted by anyone. Central to any understanding of processes of strategising, therefore, is the emerging patterns of power relations and the reflected dynamics of inclusion and exclusion. Power relations are sustained and changed through ideology. Power and ideology therefore lie at the centre of all process of strategising and are always reflected in the population-wide patterns of governance we call strategy. The formulations of the second-order abstractions of strategy to be found in the dominant discourse are then understood as important ways of expressing ideologies and engaging in power relations. The next section explores how we might understand strategic choice theory as a form of second-order abstracting.

17.2 Strategic choice theory as second-order abstraction

From a complex responsive processes perspective, the 'whole organisation' is not a thing but an imaginative construct which expresses some felt unity of the experience of people engaged in working together. This imaginative construct is not a thing but a dynamic, ongoing process arising in social interaction, and such activity has the inevitable effect of including some and excluding others in the ongoing dynamics of power relations. This imaginative construct of the whole organisation quite clearly involves abstracting, because it is a generalisation, a stereotype, a simplified category of thought, and it is further abstraction to think of processes of including and excluding as the drawing of boundaries around the abstraction called an 'organisation'. In thinking and talking in this way, we are necessarily drawing away from our experience of actual organisations in all their variety and from actual processes of including and excluding. The variety of the ongoing experience of a particular organisation is averaged away and any differences between it and other organisations are simplified in the imaginative construct. The theory of complex responsive processes seeks to explain how people express such imaginative constructs, understood as first- and second-order abstractions, in their ongoing local interactions in which those very constructs emerge and evolve. Over the course of history, many of the imaginative constructs of 'wholes' which emerge in ongoing local interaction have come to be idealised – they have become cult values or ideologies which people functionalise in their local interactions.

In experience, then, organisations can be understood to be patterns of interaction emerging across a population which are experienced and sometimes articulated as abstractions and idealised 'wholes' in the imaginations of many, many people in their ongoing local interactions with each other as they work together. People acting jointly in an organisation are always interacting locally and they are doing so on the basis of imaginative abstract global generalisations and idealisations. People find themselves immersed, deeply involved, in their organisational experience, and at the same time they have the capacity to reflect upon the generalisations and idealisations that are forming and being formed by their local interactions. In the modern world, such reflection inevitably involves the second-order abstraction of maps and models in a very widespread way.

Strategic choice theory, however, is not based on a notion of the 'whole' as imaginative construct. It is based on a notion of the 'whole' organisation as either a system ('thing') with a boundary that actually exists or as a useful hypothesis according to which an organisation is thought about 'as if' it were a system or thing with a boundary. This way of conceptualising the 'whole' reifies the abstraction of a 'whole' organisation as category or stereotype – in fact, anthropomorphises it, and sometimes even claims that it is alive. Whole organisations are thought of as agents independent of the people who are actually acting. Indeed, actual people are rendered invisible in this process of what amounts to second-order abstracting in which first-order abstractions, stereotypical whole organisations, now interact with each other in abstract models of industries and markets. This move in thought does make it possible to talk in much simpler ways about the strategic actions which groups of people in each organisation are taking or might take in the future, and it makes it possible to measure generalised activities as well as and carry out highly sophisticated forms of analysis. These second-order abstractions do affect what people do, but the danger is that our attention is so exclusively focused on abstractions that we are no longer even aware that they are abstractions and so we become blind to what we as people are actually doing. If we are to understand what actually happens, then we must be able to understand not just the abstraction of organisation and the further abstraction of 'its direction' but also the lived experience of people immersed in daily organisational life in which they are particularising these abstractions.

Strategic choice theory is based on the idea that leaders and managers can choose both the articulation of imaginative constructs – that is, abstract generalised themes of organisational governance – and also, to some extent at least, the outcomes produced by people acting upon these generalised themes, a possibility denied by the theory of complex responsive processes. Strategic management prescriptions based on strategic choice theory call for the analysis of the *environment*, which includes the *industry* and the *markets*, of the organisation, as well as its *resources*, such as human resources, skills and competences. However, just as the *organisation* is an abstraction, so are the *environment*, the *industry*, the *markets* and the *resources*. They are all standardised categories within which differences are averaged out. As such, their characteristics, such as size, can be measured and proxy measures can even be developed for their qualities, such as customer satisfaction. The measurement of abstract standardised categories can be analysed using mathematical and statistical techniques to yield trends, such as rising costs, or relationships between one abstraction and another, such as market shares. All of this is clearly abstracted from the actual lived experience of those doing the work of the organisation since they do not encounter trends, shares, markets or industries but rather they encounter other people who are buying or selling.

According to strategic-choice theory leaders and managers should, in the context of the analyses just described, specify *goals, aims, objectives and targets* for the organisation in terms of *measured indices* of, for example, profit, value of sales, and numbers of people using a particular service. All these highlighted terms are also standardised simplifications in which flows of money are categorised into various costs, revenues, and expenditures. Again, these are all clearly abstractions from what is being achieved, even from what it is possible to achieve, in the many, many local situations in which the activities of organisation are performed. Having selected the goals to be achieved by their organisation, the process of abstraction continues in the form of articulating *plans* for intentional actions to be taken to achieve goals, such as investing in technologies to lower costs and so increase volumes sold. These are also all abstractions from the actual actions of, say, installing new equipment by a particular group of people, at a particular time, in a particular place.

All the prescribed steps in strategic-choice theory are therefore abstract operations on abstract simplifications and standardised categories. Looking at these activities from a complex responsive process perspective, we could understand them all as formulations or articulations of generalised patterns of interaction emerging across a population. They can also be described in other ways, with essentially the same meaning as social objects, or as articulations of the organisational habitus, or as attempts to define the rules of the organisational game people are invested in. As I have repeatedly said, these generalised simplifications only have any effect in the way they are made specific in the many, many contingent situations in which people find that they have to act. Actual conduct in organisations makes particular the generalised abstractions which are goals and plans, taking account of the variety of these particular situations which makes it unlikely that things will simply go to plan so as to achieve goals. The plans themselves are the simplifying and generalising activities of abstraction. Subsequent monitoring process will all be conducted in terms of these abstractions.

To talk in this way about strategic management conducted according to the prescriptions of strategic choice theory as activities of abstracting is by no means to dismiss them as somehow misguided or unnecessary. They do affect what people do in their local interactions but the problem is that they very frequently prompt behaviour which negates the original purpose to produce unexpected and unwanted outcomes. When performance targets are set and linked to rewards, for example, people generally meet them. When the UK government sets target for hospital waiting times, staff at the hospitals demonstrate achievement of the targets, some of which is genuine and some of which is not. In either event, the abstract global targets are actually taken up in many, many local interactions, and it is quite possible that this will result in genuine improvement. However, since the improvement arises in many, many local interactions, it may well be accompanied by all kinds of unintended consequences. Focusing attention on explicit strategic management as activities of abstraction provokes a different way of thinking about them, because they are now understood to be inseparable from the local interactions they may or may not evoke. Those local interactions of the ordinary politics of everyday life are just as much processes of strategic management as the abstract analysis and the abstract manipulation of goals and plans. Indeed, the abstract analyses themselves take place in local interaction so that analysis, measuring, target setting, action plan choices are all aspects of the ordinary politics of daily organisational life.

The role of strategic planning

In the literature on organisations, and in the way managers in organisations talk, strategic planning means deciding on some kind of population-wide outcome for some long-term period ahead: say, five years. Once formulated, the plan is then implemented. The assumption is that it is possible to design population-wide patterns well before they are realised and this in turn implies that it is possible to predict the outcomes of action taken now to a degree useful enough to enable a choice now between one action and another. Local interaction is then understood as the process of implementing the plan or design. The plan or design is the 'thought' and the implementation is the 'action'. This is the essence of the planning and design schools of strategic management in the literature, it is how managers think and talk in most organisations, and it is what governments have imported from business as the basis of centralised, managerialist forms of public sector governance.

As we have seen in Part 1, a number of writers and practitioners have been critical of this approach for some time and emphasised processes of learning in the formation of strategy. Senge, a key writer in this tradition, claims that organisations develop according to a limited number of general archetypes and that systems thinking allows managers to identify leverage points (thought) in organisations and then operate (action) on them to shift from a dysfunctional archetype. So, here too we get the idea that population-wide patterns can be identified beforehand and changed directly through operating at leverage points. Local interaction then becomes working in teams to learn and so shift individual mental models and global archetypes. In both the planning and the learning approaches the focus of attention is on the population-wide and long term, the macro level, and it is thought possible to operate directly on the population-wide in some way so as to actualise prior intention regarding the population-wide patterns. Local interaction in both cases is simply implementation.

A complex responsive processes perspective emphasises the unpredictability of long-term, population-wide patterns, holding that any design or plan for these patterns – that is, for the organisation as a 'whole' – can only achieve what they claim to achieve with regard to short-term, repetitive and thus reasonably predictable activity. Even then, any plans, designs, visions, or descriptions of archetypes are simply articulations of population-wide generalisations, and as such they are abstractions.

Strategic plans are second-order abstractions taking the form of maps and models. Furthermore, from a complex responsive processes perspective these abstractions can be thought of as articulations of social objects and cult values or as descriptions of the desired organisational game and the desired rules it is proposed that the game should be played by. As social objects and rules of the game, however, these articulations have to be made particular in each specific, contingent situation which leads to explorative conflict that must be negotiated. Rules are interpreted and re-interpreted in specific circumstance so, for example, rules about what should appear on the balance sheets of banks are re-interpreted by individual banks to exclude items they decide to define as 'off balance sheet'. So, even with regard to the short term and the rather repetitive, it is problematic to think of planning activities as straightforward determinants of what happens. Central to the complex responsive processes perspective is the notion of emergence according to which population-wide patterns continually emerge in local interaction, and this means that they are not the consequence of any overall plan or design but of the interplay between local plans and designs. There may well be articulations of desires for realised population-wide patterns in the form of global plans and designs, but they cannot function as the cause of the population-wide pattern because such desires and articulations are simply gestures and what actually happens will also depend upon the processes of particularisation: that is, on the interplay of many, many intentions.

So, in these circumstances any claims that strategic planning and organisational leverage activities actually cause what happens are highly problematic. If this is so, then what roles do strategic plans, visions and missions actually play? The following are possibilities:

- Instead of being causes of what happens, plans and designs may well amount to fantasies whose main function is to serve as social defences against anxiety. The problem with such defences is that they might blinker people and, if taken seriously, could easily get in the way of more improvisational, spontaneous behaviour. Such activities might then largely be a distracting waste of time which could be discontinued with the benefits far outweighing any drawbacks.

- However, if the articulation of population-wide patterns and desires for them are understood as gestures in ongoing processes of local interaction, they may serve provocative, or even inspirational, purposes in generating further conversation. Instead of being planned, however, the population-wide patterns will emerge in those further conversations in the many, many local interactions that they take place in and this is especially true for population-wide patterns displaying any form of novelty. Those engaged in such local interactions do have intentions and plans for their own local interaction and desires for the population-wide pattern, but the actual population-wide patterns emerge in the interplay between all of their intentions/plans and desires. Since the interplay cannot be planned, neither can the population-wide pattern. Instead, the local interaction takes on the form of improvisational acting with a high degree of spontaneity or, alternatively, of stuck repetition. Such improvisational/spontaneous acting cannot be said to be planning, although it does not mean that there is no intention on the part of those engaging in such activity. However, since they are responses to plans, the plans as gestures also play a part, they do affect behaviour but not as simply as is sometimes supposed.

- The processes of formulating long-term strategic plans may themselves form a particular organisational game in which people are unreflectively preoccupied. Strategic planning may well be an important game, people may be invested in this game, because of the interests being sustained or threatened. Strategic planning will normally have the characteristics of organisational rituals which sustain official ideologies, so conferring legitimacy to existing patterns of power relations. The ostensible aim is to create a desired future and, even if this is the aim, there are other undisclosed aims to do with ideology and power. These ritualistic, ideological and legitimising functions are not be dismissed – they are important aspects of organisational life.

- Strategic plan documents may also serve a purpose as rhetorical artefacts. They may be used in the ordinary daily politics of organisational life to persuade others to agree to certain actions. They may be used as a form of insurance if actions produce bad outcomes. So, plans must be presented to banks as part of the process of raising loans. All involved know that the plans are unlikely to be achieved, but if there is a default on the loan the lenders can claim that they followed rational procedures. Plans may be used as reporting devices to show compliance with some decree of a higher authority. Shareholders require information and plans serve this purpose too. As publications they can be important forms of public relations and even propaganda.

The perspective I am suggesting, therefore, requires us to think much more carefully about what we think we are doing when we articulate long-term plans for whole populations and believe that we can thereby change those whole population. This is a widespread belief reflected in culture-change programmes, quality assurance, total quality management, business process re-engineering and many other such global change programmes. A complex responsive processes view turns the dominant discourse on its head. Instead of change occurring as the result of the plan, change programme, or vision of leaders or dominant coalitions, change emerges in many local interactions in which leaders and the most powerful are very influential participants, but participants nonetheless. Instead of being the straightforward cause of change, the activities of planning, forming visions and so on serve many other purposes. They may perform the function of social defences against anxiety. They may be rhetorical tools or ploys in the political processes in which strategies emerge. They may be public relations tools directed at audiences both internal and external to the organisations. They may even be propaganda and spin. They may serve the purpose of avoiding being blamed if things go wrong – people can always point to the rational approaches they used to choose their actions, claiming that it is not their fault if things went wrong.

To summarise: the theory of complex responsive process argues against thinking that strategic planning causes what happens to an organisation, because what happens to an organisation depends upon the interplay of actions taken by members of the organisation and members of many, many other organisations. However, the theory of complex responsive processes does not lead to a prescription for abandoning strategic planning. The theory is a way of thinking about what people actually do and, since people in organisations actually do plan strategically, the theory invites reflection on why they are doing so and what this activity achieves. Moving to a perspective which does not take planning for granted invites a deeper reflection on what people actually find themselves doing. This opens up greater choices about whether in some circumstances they should plan and in others not; and what form the planning should take given what they are trying to achieve with it. Instead of naively taking planning to be 'practical' and invitations to reflect as 'impractical', the theory of complex responsive processes leads to a view in which, although unfamiliar, there is nothing so practical as repeated examination of what we are doing and why we are doing it.

I now want to reflect on some of the key abstractions on which strategic-choice theory is based and consider just what it is that they are abstracting from.

Resources: finance, human competences and technology

Strategic-choice theory draws on classical micro economics to define resources as the raw materials, equipment and fixed assets, technologies, and human capabilities that organisations use to produce the products and services that justify their continuing existence. As has already been stated, the organisation and each of its resources are simplified categories abstracted away from the actual daily experience of doing organisational work. The sections that follow describe what experience is being abstracted from by each category of resources from the perspective of complex responsive processes. The purpose is to indicate a different way of thinking about resources which does not focus entirely on the abstraction. First, consider financial resources, since this is the resource that enables people in an organisation to acquire most other forms of resource.

Financial resources

From a classical economic perspective money serves a number of purposes:

- It is a medium for the exchange of goods and services, so providing a more efficient alternative to bartering;
- It functions as a measure of revenues and expenditures: that is, as a unit of account;
- It is a store of value and so functions as an asset that can be used to settle liabilities.

Originally, money took the form of some valuable but easily transportable commodity, but even from the earliest days it was not simply a commodity like all others, because it could only serve its three purposes if it was trusted by people to reliably serve these purposes. Money, therefore, was always implicated in social arrangements of particular kinds, expressed in institutional forms which, for example, provided assurance of the gold content of any coins used for exchange. So, even as commodities like gold and silver, money was always a social phenomenon. This becomes even more evident as exchange comes to be carried out using notes which promise to pay the bearer certain sums of commodity money. Paper money was of course far more convenient than transporting bulky commodities, but its use depends even more on relationships of trust between people. Banks emerged as trusted institutional providers of paper money backed by the gold in their vaults. This institutional arrangement made it possible for banks to print more promissory notes than the gold in their vaults because, provided that they continued to trust it, people would not all demand payment of their notes at the same time. If trusting relationships were breached, there would be a run on the bank and it could collapse, bringing wider social consequences.

Other institutional forms, therefore, evolved as central banks to support and control the banks. Eventually the connection between gold and paper promises to pay became more and more tenuous, so the commodity backing was dropped altogether. Basically, then, the modern monetary system consists of a number of complex networks of financial institutions of various types. All of these institutions have both assets and liabilities. One category is generally referred to as the *commercial banks* and its assets take the form of the loans it makes to organisations and individuals. Its assets are the liabilities of others. The commercial banks also have liabilities, and these are the sums it owes to other organisations and individuals who have deposited money with it and which it promises to repay when those organisations and individuals demand it. Modern money consists of these bank liabilities and it only has value, it can only perform its three functions, if people trust the bank's ability to honour its liabilities. Modern banks, of course, carry out much more complex operations than those just outlined and they are highly interconnected across the globe. Any significant collapse in one major bank, which is of course the destruction of its liabilities and therefore the destruction of money, would soon spread to others and, if taken to its conclusion, would lead to the total destruction of money and therefore the collapse of economic activity around the world.

The point I am trying to make is this. There is a strong tendency to talk about money as a thing. This had some basis in reality many centuries ago when money was a commodity, but in modern times money is no more and no less than the liabilities of certain institutions to organisations and individuals. From the perspective of the latter, money is an asset, an expectation of being paid, constituted by the liabilities of banks. Furthermore, the liabilities of the banks, their abilities to pay, depend upon the reliability of their assets: that is, the promises of others to pay them; and, of course, these promises to pay are the liabilities of other organisations and individuals, the very ones whose assets are the promises to pay of the banks. The fundamental reality of modern financial resources, therefore, is that of population-wide patterns of tightly coupled relationships between very large numbers of individuals and organisations in which each promises to pay others and expects to be paid by others and the ability of each depends upon the ability to pay of the others – circular patterns of relationships which depend entirely in qualities of trust, in turn based on belief in the ability and willingness of others to carry out their obligations. And what makes it all quite strange is that the fulfilment of a promise to pay is itself simply a promise to pay. It all works in terms of promises of promises, recorded and manipulated by computers, having no physical reality at all. The only reality in this important game is the ongoing construction of trust.

According to the theory of complex responsive processes, these population-wide patterns of expectation and trust, which are our financial resources, all emerge in many, many local interactions. We can see this in the population-wide pattern of interaction which came to be known in 2007 as 'the credit crunch'. In the United States in the years leading up to 2007, large number of banks had made subprime loans to borrowers with poor or no credit histories, colloquially known as 'Ninja' (no income, no jobs or assets) loans. So, across the United States in many, many local interactions, individual bank branches were making loans to particular individuals at particular times and, as the widespread pattern began to emerge, it was labelled 'Ninja'. In other local interactions, other financial institutions were 'repackaging' these loans into a great array of often sophisticated and difficult-to-understand financial securities and derivatives and then selling them on to other financial institutions. It became possible to make huge profits from re-packaging and passing on the risk to others in the belief that this was a high-profit but very low-risk activity. Incentives were provided for executives to sell as many products as possible, bonuses often being tied to targets set for numbers of deals without concern for quality. However, while one section of a financial institution might be passing on the risk to others, another part of the same institution might well be buying repackaged financial products from other financial institutions. Furthermore, at any one time a financial institution was holding a stock of its own re-packaged securities waiting to be passed on to others. So, if any setback was experienced, if the game of musical chairs suddenly stopped, institutions would be left holding their own dodgy products as well, perhaps, as holding the dodgy products of others. Any setback would rapidly affect all institutions holding any of the high-risk assets, including those manufacturing them who had not yet passed them on, because each depended upon the others. The 'credit crunch', emerged in the interplay of local responsive intentions to yield patterns that no one chose or wanted.

In complex responsive processes terms, financial resource is, therefore, a social object in that it describes a general tendency on the part of large numbers of people to act in broadly similar ways in relation to what are called 'financial assets and liabilities'. This social object, or tendency to act, is reflected in a whole set of financial institutions such as banks, central banks, government financial departments with their policies, and regulatory institutions with their monitoring functions. Financial resources feature in many ways in most social acts. In modern societies most people understand how to gain access to money, and how to deal with banks and other financial institutions. Those who have access to substantial financial resources are treated in very different ways from those who have little access. The social object of money conveys meaning that is far more than simply access to resources. Another, perhaps the most important, aspect of money from a complex responsive processes point of view is its role in the figuration of power relations. Since we all need money to live and carry out any enterprise we are interested in, those who have control over money are needed by those who do not. Such need is the basis of power relations with the power balance tilted substantially towards those who have most access to financial resources.

Who controls money is a reflection of a community's history and its institutional arrangements. Hundreds of years ago in Western Europe and North America, the acquisition of wealth frequently occurred through the exercise of violence, including force-backed demands for tributes and tax payments, through the patronage and protection of those who had access to force, and through the laws of inheritance, which enabled the passing of wealth from one generation to the next. As Elias, has shown, the development of Western society involved the gradual monopolisation of force by the state, bringing with it the monopolisation of authority to demand tax payments. Control over money came to depend more and more on institutional arrangements according to which some people were given the legitimate role of authorising the use of money by others. More recently, changing tax regimes have weakened, to some extent, the inheritance of wealth from one generation by the next. For people in modern societies, therefore, control over the allocation of money resources has come to be vested in organisations and, more specifically, in legitimately appointed roles in a hierarchy of managers who have authority to allocate money to others and who are held accountable for its use by those in the other organisations, such as banks and investment funds, who provide it.

The most important point about financial resources, from a complex responsive processes point of view, is the institutional arrangements, the procedures and routines, for legitimising the allocation of these resources and the monitoring of how they are used. These routines and procedures establish figurations of power relations and generate a considerable volume of organisational conversation. The ordinary, everyday activities of strategising involve conversations in which those who want to pursue a project must persuade those with authority to allocate resources to them. In other words, financial resources are distributed in the ordinary politics of everyday organisational life. The more ostensibly objective and credible the case that applicants make for resources, and, even more important, the more impressive their track record of the previous use of resources, the more likely they are to be allocated resources. Resource-allocation activities may, therefore, have the appearance of technical rationality, indeed it is of great importance that it should have such an appearance, but the resource-allocation activities themselves are highly political. They are important in sustaining and changing the pattern of power relations and, therefore, reflect ideologies that are often undiscussable. What the money can be used for and how it can be used reflect the norms and values that have evolved in the organisation and in the wider society. The allocation procedures themselves reflect ideologies to do with surveillance and control.

What the previous paragraphs have described is the ongoing ordinary experience of financial resource as the experience of political interaction between people in local situations from which emerge trust, mistrust and so population-wide patterns of financial resource. However, an important aspect of this local interaction is the articulation and belief in abstractions. The notion of 'financial resource' is itself a simplified category that abstracts from the complex patterning of trust and mistrust which 'it' actually consists of. The institutions which set monetary policies and the regulations financial institutions should follow are themselves abstractions. Talking about the 'money supply' is a metaphor of something physical and is an abstraction. The regulations that financial institutions and other organisations and individuals are required to follow are all simplifications and so abstractions. Monetary and fiscal policies are developed in highly abstract conversations about abstract notions of whole economies and flows of money, taxes and government expenditures. These abstractions are of the greatest importance in developing a generalised way of understanding the complex ongoing network of relationships and the patterns that emerge from them. Thinking requires abstraction, and so thinking about financial resources necessarily involves thinking and talking in terms of abstraction. From such abstract conversation there emerge policies and regulations as generalisations to be taken up in many, many local interactions. To recognise the abstract nature of policies and regulations is to realise that, as generalisations, they will have to be made specific in many, many local situations which policy makers and regulators cannot control. Policy making and regulation then come to be understood as ongoing, never-ending processes of interaction.

Financial resources and resource allocation, then, are not primarily based on rational analysis reflecting choices made about the resource base required to secure competitive advantage. Of course, concern with an appropriate resource base is a factor in the allocation conversation, but the rational language of competitive advantage is more often likely to be the rhetoric used to justify allocation decisions that are actually being made on the basis of experience-based judgements and the sustaining and changing of power relations.

Consider now how we would think about human resources as an abstract category from a complex responsive processes perspective.

Human resources and competences

It is revealing to track the change in the name of the organisational function which deals with people. Before the middle of the twentieth century, many organisations had what they called 'staff departments' whose role was the usually somewhat benevolent one of administering the benefits the organisation provided for employees. The ideal was to represent employee concerns in some way in order to head off conflict and resultant strikes. In the second half of the twentieth century the name of these departments was changed to that of 'Personnel Departments', which signalled a more formal approach to negotiating the terms and conditions of employment and attending to the growing legal frameworks governing employment matters. The ideal became one to do with ensuring that the organisation complied with the law on employment matters and negotiated effectively with unions. The profile of this Personnel function was certainly higher than the old staff departments, but directors of Personnel rarely had seats on the organisation's board of directors; it was a service department, a cost centre, rather than a department central to the organisations' activities. Then in the 1980s another name change occurred, this time to the Human Resource function. This signalled a shift in the ideal function from one supposedly focused mainly on employees to one which saw employees as a resource that the organisation used to achieve its aims. A much more instrumental approach was thus signalled and at the same time increasing legislation covering all aspects of the treatment of employees including laws to do with equality aimed against discrimination meant that the Human Resource function became primarily concerned with protecting the organisation against employees who could bring expensive laws suits. These developments occurred during the move to investment capitalism in the 1980s in which the supreme stakeholder was the shareholder and the role of leaders and managers was to maximise shareholder returns. In this process employees were much lower down the order of stakeholders and regarded much more instrumentally as resources to be used to maximise profits. Perhaps this is why Human Resource Directors still do not often sit on the board of directors.

What happened then was a process of increasing abstraction from the actual experience of people interacting with each other locally to get their work done. The benefit of this abstraction and the enormous increase in policies and procedures governing every aspect of organisational life is that a high degree of control from the centre becomes possible, making it possible to protect the organisation to a much greater extent from lawsuits. However, in covering over the actual experience of local interaction, the focus on abstraction increases the practice of resistance, often creates enormous frustration and can seriously lower work motivation and morale. Indeed, regarding human persons as a resource, as a means to the objective of an inanimate thing, is clearly unethical, because surely persons are ends in themselves.

In performing its functions of recruiting human resources matched to the organisation's needs, human resource functions have increasingly developed a focus on identifying necessary skills and competences in a clear way and defining steps to go through in order to acquire them either through recruitment or training and development. What has happened, therefore, is the abstraction of skills and competences from the fuzzier, more nebulous and improvisational nature of actual skills and competences exercised by expert workers in local contingent situations. As a result, the actual experience of skill is covered over by an abstract category called 'skill'. The complex responsive processes perspective refocuses attention from what members of an organisation should be doing according to the abstract category of competence to what they are already, and always have been, doing which has to do with experience of relating and managing in relationship with others in local situations. This is a reflexive activity requiring each of us to pay more attention to our own part in what is happening around us in which we develop reflective self-knowledge in taking our own experience seriously. This is not to dismiss the usefulness of the abstract categories of skills and competences, but to understand that those abstractions acquire their meaning and exercise their effects for good and bad in many, many local interactions.

Furthermore, when attention is broadened from the abstract categories of skill and competence to encompass the wider context in which they emerge and evolve, we come to see that the skills and competences required for the reflection and reflexivity of broadening attention are difficult to develop and just as difficult to sustain. They are competences that do not usually feature in the skill sets prescribed for managers. Examples of the necessary skills are: the capacity for self-reflection and owning one's part in what is happening; skill in facilitating fluid conversation; ability to articulate what is emerging in conversations; and sensitivity to group dynamics. These skills become essential to notions of leadership and the role of top executives because their greater power renders their impact on others all the greater. Furthermore, these skills are not easily taught, perhaps they cannot be taught, in an abstract way. They are acquired in the experience of exercising them. It is striking how absent they are in recruitment specifications and in training and development programmes. Finally, the excessive focus on abstract skills and competences formulated in procedures diverts people from the spontaneous exercise of expert skill in doing their work and can thus actually reduce flexibility and performance.

Next, consider technological resources.

Technology

From the perspective of strategic choice theory, an organisation's technology consists, first, of the physical objects of tools, although this term is now often used to denote procedures or analytical frameworks prescribed for use by managers to manage more effectively. Second, the term 'technology' encompasses the ways people use tools – that is, the techniques, skills and competences employed by the organisation's human resources to carry out the work of the organisation more effectively and efficiently. Technology is thus an important source of competitive advantage, and investment in its design and acquisition is an important strategy. The approaches of strategic choice theory focus attention on technology as an abstract category to be analysed rationally and incorporated in strategic plans, which are also second-order abstractions. The discussion is in terms of the abstract notions of organisation, resources, technologies and strategic plans, and they are abstractions from the experience of tools, techniques and skills in the local interactive experience of people in which they carry out their organisational work.

In the experience of local interaction, tools and other physical objects in nature are not just objects we operate with and upon, because they have meaning for us, including highly emotional significance. The key point here has to do with *meaning*. We respond emotionally and intellectually to the *meaning* that physical objects such as computers, assembly lines, cars, clothes, jewellery, our own bodies, mountains and lakes, have for us. Mead makes the profoundly important point that meaning cannot be located in a physical object (*see* Chapter 13). Physical objects have no meaning because meaning cannot be 'had'; it is continually emerging in iterated gestures and responses where meaning is evoked in the response. For Mead, meaning is the social act and the social act is meaning. In this way of thinking, meaning arises in interacting and it does not exist anywhere, even as the vocal act of the word, let alone in a physical object. So, it follows that a physical object such as a tool can only be meaningful insofar as it is somehow taken up in our interactions with each other. Meaning arises as the particularising of the social object in specific situations. Take a car as an example. The car in itself, as a physical object, has no meaning and can therefore arouse no emotion in those using it. However, a car is not simply a physical object but also, at the same time, a social object, that is, a generalised tendency to act which is common to a number of people. This generalised tendency could take the form of respecting those who own big cars, for example. What is evoking the response of respect here is not the physical object of the big car but the social object of 'big car'. Such social objects can be idealised so that 'big car' becomes a cult value.

Mead's notion of social objects provides a way of understanding technology from the perspective of complex responsive processes (Johannessen and Stacey, 2005). First, the social object of technology must be distinguished from technology as physical object. Some of the tools involved in a technology can be understood as physical objects designed and constructed by people to purposefully accomplish their activities. As such, technology is to be found in nature as other physical objects are. However, techniques for using tools – that is, people's knowledge, skills, practices and methods of tool use – always involve complex social acts. Accordingly, technology is a social object to be found only in experience. Technology in the form of physical objects is also, in use, immediately a social object – that is, generalised tendencies for large numbers of people to act in fairly similar ways in using the physical objects of technology. In their particularisation these generalised tendencies evolve further as small differences are amplified – the causality is transformative. Technology is then understood not simply as physical objects to be found in nature, but, at the same time, as social objects to be found in our experience of complex social acts. This gives us an understanding of technology as being perpetually iterated in the particularising of the generalised tendencies to act in the present. As with other social objects, technologies can also be idealised and so form cult values. For example, technology and progress become conflated as cult values offering to people's imaginations a future free of poverty, disease and inequality. Widespread dissemination of technology then also becomes a cult value which suppresses the harmful consequences of technology.

An example of technology as social object is provided by internet and email technologies. The tools are computers, servers and software programs and these are physical objects. Their mere existence creates tendencies for large numbers of people to communicate with each other through email and accessing databases. This is the generalised tendency to act in similar ways as social objects. These generalised tendencies are iterated in each present as rather repetitive, habitual techniques. In their continual iteration, technologies are particularised in specific situations. We send emails to each other and conduct transactions over the internet, for example, with banks. Such particularisation is inevitably a conflictual process in that techniques are adapted to the demands of particular situations with their specific understanding of the past and expectations of the future. For example, as the use of email spreads in organisations, conflicts arise as to the purposes it can be used for. People start using emails for personal purposes and this often conflicts with business requirements, leading to policies specifying what uses are to be allowed or prohibited. The possibility of technological transformation arises in this particularising as techniques are spontaneously adapted to variations in specific situations and then potentially amplified. For example, the internet has become a means of transacting payments. Then there is the development of fraud, illegal and immoral uses, viruses and ways of dealing with them. Technology as social object exists only insofar as it is taken up, or particularised, in the ordinary, everyday local interactions between people. This technology of electronic communication is also idealised, and its widespread availability becomes a cult value offering a future of access to communication for all and so greater democracy. Another cult value around this technology is that of control to be achieved by increasing electronic surveillance.

Thinking about technology in this way focuses attention not only on the physical objects of tools but also on the complex responsive processes of relating in which the generalised/idealised social object called technology is particularised. This brings to the fore questions of power, control and identity. Consider some examples.

Reading and writing is a technology that is essential to scientific progress and the development of tools and techniques. However, reading and writing are also social objects. Abram (1996) points out how reading and writing have led to the replacement of the sensuous, embodied style of consciousness found in oral cultures with a more detached, abstract mode of thinking. When concepts such as 'virtue' and 'justice' are recorded in writing, they acquire an autonomy and permanence independent of ordinary experience. Abstraction becomes a way of thinking and speaking as well as of writing. Donaldson (2005) argues that reading and writing not only eclipse nature but also tend to eclipse local, bodily human interaction in the present. Drawing on Elias (2000), she suggests that a new technology (including writing and printing) can be understood as an unplanned process that transforms the society which has produced it. Drawing on Ong (2002), Donaldson points to how literacy and printing have influenced human patterns of relating. The technology of writing fosters logic and abstraction. Writing also sets up the conditions for objectivity. It fosters precision and distanced forms of communication between people. Writing led to a shift from 'hearing dominance' to 'sight dominance' and print continued the trend. The abstract, objective thinking fostered by writing and reading has also been idealised to become cult values of rationality and objectivity.

Modern technologies of information and communication are other examples of social objects that profoundly affect the pattern of our interactions and even the conceptions we have of ourselves. The development of computers has been accompanied by the development of cognitivist psychology in which mind has come to be thought of as an information-processing device rather like a computer. The mind has come to be thought of and modelled as a map, again reflecting technology. The development of the camera obscura some 250 years ago was accompanied by a view of mind as an internal world that made representations of objects in outside reality. As social object, technology shapes our thinking in many areas apparently unconnected with that technology itself. Technology provides metaphors for our thinking about everything around us. So we think of organisations as machines or as ships to be steered by their leaders. The social objects of technology, therefore, affect how we experience ourselves, our identities, and they of course impact on patterns of social relations. Through the cult values they give rise to, they become embedded in our ideologies. One only has to think of the technology of fast foods and that of contraception to see what enormous shifts in social relations accompany the evolution of technology.

The point, then, is that technology is not simply a resource to be analysed and chosen in order to achieve some organisational objective or to produce success, as it is in strategic choice theory. This is to understand technology as physical object. From a complex responsive processes perspective, technology is far more importantly also a social object. Technology has an impact on the local interactions of strategising persons and hence on the emergent population-wide patterns of strategy. This impact takes place in the particularising of the generalisations/idealisations of technology as social object in specific situations; and it is in these activities of particularising the abstract strategies of technology that technology continues to evolve. Thinking about technology in these more complex ways has the potential to widen and deepen conversational interaction in organisations.

A complex responsive processes perspective on resources of all kinds recognises the fundamentally relational and social nature of resources and regards processes of abstracting from this complex experience to think in general ways about what is emerging from this experience as abstract categories of tools, techniques, skills and competences. While thinking in these abstract terms plays a major role in choosing strategic actions, it frequently succumbs to the tendency to collapse into reification, so that technologies and techniques are thought of as existing things. This focuses attention simply on abstractions and so covers over the local interactive experience in which technology as meaning emerges. Much the same can be said about the abstract category we call *markets*.

Markets

In the dominant discourse on organisations and strategy, reflecting its origins in economics, markets are usually talked about in terms of the 'forces' of demand and supply, as well as the 'consumer' preferences 'driving' demand and the product features required to meet customer 'needs'. The concern is with industry 'structures' and market 'positions'. The forces, drivers, structures and positions are usually quantified to provide information for the analytical techniques to be used in making strategic decisions. As with the dominant discourse on resources, the concern is with the macro level of the 'whole' and with choosing success factors for the 'whole'. This is certainly the terms in which most managers in organisations still talk.

Enough has been said in previous paragraphs to see that all of the terms in inverted commas are the simplified, standardised, averaged categories of abstractions and how the markets and industries are models composed of the abstract categories and, as such, constitute second-order abstractions. The analyses of markets and industries as the basis for choosing strategies are thus highly abstract activities.

The abstractions described in the last paragraph are abstractions from the experience of local activities in which people exchange goods and services with each other. There are in actuality no 'forces' or 'drivers', no 'consumers and customers' with generalised 'needs', only specific people in specific place at specific times engaged in activities of exchange for all sorts of individual, contingent reasons. People are engaged in patterns of relationship which can be understood as social objects, or games, in which all more or less understand the roles they play as they enact their investment in and preoccupation with market games. Markets are social phenomena and, as we know, they have come to be idealised or demonised, taking the form of cult values. The actual experience of markets is in the local interactions in which the generalisations and idealisations of cult values, social objects, are made specific. In the dominant discourse on strategy, the cult values and social objects of markets are articulated as generalised categories and models of second-order abstraction, and these articulations are taken up in the local interactions of exchange between people. What the abstractions mean and the effect they have all arise in local interaction.

Again, this recognition of the importance of local interaction is in no way to deny the usefulness of thinking and talking in abstract terms, because if decisions are to be made at a distance from local interactions of work, as they must in modern organisations, then they cannot be made on the basis of every contingency – they can only be made on the basis of abstractions and subsequent attempts to control from a distance depend up on them too. What the theory of complex responsive processes seeks to draw attention to is the manner in which these concepts abstract from the ordinary experience of managers as they engage daily with their 'markets'. The theory seeks to do this by pointing to how managers and everyone else in an organisation take up the abstraction called the 'market' in their local interactions with actual *people* in other organisations or households. Managers, marketers, salespeople and purchasers are always meeting people in other organisations and engaging them in conversation, in local interaction, just as they do in any other organisational activity. The theory of complex responsive processes therefore seeks to widen the focus of attention to include the local interactions in which abstractions are utilised.

Mead used the market as one of his examples of a social object. Markets can be understood as the generalisation, the social object of market, which is constantly being made particular in many, many local interactions. The dominant discourse is primarily concerned with the generalisation, with measuring *it* and articulating trends in *its* movement, while the complex responsive processes view is concerned with just how organisational members are making such generalisations particular in their ordinary, everyday local interactions with people in other organisations. As they engage in the social activity of market, large numbers of people are acting in largely similar ways in which the actions of purchasing and selling, of all the players in the market, are implicated in the actions of all of them.

The activity of the market is thus conversational in nature and such activity also immediately constitutes figurations of power. Such power figurations are sustained by ideologies. Indeed, the notion of 'the market system' is itself an ideology, a cult value. While this is the experience which we should be aware of it nevertheless remains useful to think in terms of second-order abstractions.

Next, consider the kind of abstraction involved in the theory of the learning organisation.

17.3 The learning organisation as second-order abstraction

The theory of strategic management as process of learning is no less abstract than that of strategic choice. Just as with strategic choice theory, the theory of organisational learning processes is also cast in terms of the abstract notion of 'the organisation'. To get some idea of the particular abstractions involved in learning organisation theory, we can consider each of the learning disciplines identified by Senge (*see* Chapter 5):

- *systems thinking.* This is thinking in terms of a model of organisations, industries and societies consisting of categories of managers, customers, suppliers and so on. It is therefore clearly a second-order abstraction (*see* Chapter 16) which abstracts from the ongoing temporal, responsive and improvisational nature of local interaction.

- *personal mastery.* The person dealt with in this concept is an average, standardised person understood from the humanistic theory of psychology in which individuals possess selves which they can in a way choose to change. The person here is an abstract stereotype or category acting according to a model that is also necessarily abstract in that it draws away from the experience of interaction, reflecting the great difficulty people have in controlling their behaviour and acting on self-interest and greed.

- *mental models.* According to this notion, persons possess minds that process information into the form of mental models, which is clearly a second-order abstraction. In this theory of mind as system it is assumed that people are able to engineer changes in their own mental models and that this is what learning is. These models of mind draw away from the experience of local interaction in which people are preoccupied with social games that they enact without forming representing models.

- *shared vision.* According to this notion it is the role of leaders to develop a persuasive view of what an organisation could be in the future and persuade others to follow it. Such a vision is a cult value, because it presents a future shorn of all obstacles to its achievement. In actual experience we always encounter obstacles to realising our desires, not least because they do not coincide with the desires of others.

- *team learning.* Here the notion of a team is a generalised category of cooperation, an abstraction from the messy local interaction of ongoing conflict and negotiation.

The model of the learning organisation is, therefore, as much an abstraction as the models of strategic choice. Again, this should not be taken to mean that there is no point to thinking and talking in this abstract way. It too is part of the attempt to govern from a distance. But to focus on the abstraction and ignore what it is abstracting from is to operate on a highly inadequate basis.

Knowledge and organisations

Closely linked to the theory of learning organisations is the approach to knowledge management (*see* Chapter 5), which calls for steps to measure 'intellectual capital' on the grounds that what is measured can be managed. The aim of measuring intellectual capital is that of managing its contribution to shareholder value. The notion of intellectual capital is clearly an abstraction as are the models of knowledge underlying it and the proposals of ways to measure it. The theory of complex responsive processes is based on the argument that meaning, and therefore knowledge, arises in the local, detailed, ordinary communicative interaction of people in organisations in the living present. Knowledge creation is an evolutionary process of reproduction and potential transformation at the same time. In other words, knowledge is neither stored nor shared because it is not an 'it' at all but a process. Knowledge cannot be grasped, owned by anyone or traded in any market, and its creation is a process of communicating and power relating that is both stimulating and anxiety provoking at the same time. If one takes a view of knowledge creation along these lines, it is impossible to manage knowledge. The whole notion that an organisation can own 'intellectual capital' – that is, can own the attitudes, competence and intellectual agility of individuals – is quite consistent with the abstract models of knowledge in organisations, but it abstracts from the complex relational processes in local interactions in which we experience the evolution of knowledge. It may serve some purpose to talk in abstract terms about knowledge, but our attention really needs to be directed to the wider processes we actually experience if we are not to undertake knowledge management actions which are almost entirely fictions.

A central feature of the systemic theory of knowledge creation in organisations (*see* Chapter 5) is the split it makes between tacit and explicit knowledge. Tacit knowledge is assumed to arise in individual minds and this is thought to create a problem for organisations. The assumption is that humans are reluctant to share their individual tacit knowledge with others. To the extent that they do, it is in informal exchanges, and systemic views tend to express a profound mistrust of these informal exchanges. This leads to the major emphasis on the conversion of individual tacit knowledge into explicit form and the storing of that explicit knowledge in systems. The categories of tacit and explicit are obviously standardised categories abstracted from experience, and the models of knowledge management based on them are also clearly second-order abstractions. The complex responsive processes perspective, on the other hand, holds that tacit and explicit knowing are facets of the same communicative process and, therefore, that it makes no sense to talk about them separately or to believe that one is converted into the other. Furthermore, knowledge is not simply located in individual minds, nor is it stored in any straightforward sense. Instead, knowledge is continuously replicated and potentially transformed in the communicative interaction between people. Knowledge is not understood to be 'property' at all but active relational processes between human persons and a reflection of human identity, which cannot be captured, stored or owned. Now this form of reasoning which I have presented is also an abstraction, but is so as a way of thinking about actual relationships in specific situations rather than as the foundations of the further abstraction of a model. It is a way of thinking about the interactional processes in which conversation may indeed centre on a model but, in retaining sight of relational processes, it offers a wider perspective on such models.

If one starts from the basic assumption that the origins of knowledge are located in tacit form in the heads of individuals, it is a natural step to advocate that organisations pay particular attention to hiring and retaining a professional elite. From the perspective of complex responsive processes it is not particularly clear that simply hiring and retaining individual professionals has very much to do with knowledge creation. If knowledge arises in communicative interaction, then what matters is the process of relating that individual professionals engage in, not simply how clever or competent they are as individuals.

Systemic views of knowledge creation and management also present prescriptions concerned with spreading knowledge around an organisation. If knowledge is created in individual heads, and if human nature is such that individuals selfishly seek to keep it to themselves, then it becomes a prime management task to design structures, systems and behaviours to overcome these selfish tendencies and spread knowledge around the organisation. However, if knowledge is not a thing but a process of making meaning, where meaning is continuously reproduced and potentially transformed in the action of communicative relating between human bodies, then one cannot speak of sharing it, or of spreading it around an organisation. Any concern with 'improving' knowledge-creating capacity becomes a concern with the qualities and the dynamics of human relating in the living present. Attention is then focused on the power relations being sustained and shifted in communicative interaction and on the ideologies unconsciously making patterns of power relations feel natural.

Closely linked to prescriptions for hiring and retaining of professionals are those for training and developing people. Again, these prescriptions reflect the underlying assumption that knowledge is stored in individual heads. The aim of training and development is, then, to increase the competence, skill and knowledge of the individual, including the capacity to work as a member of a team. The emphasis is placed on managing not just the activities of training and development but the quality of the learning process itself. The view of knowing as process counters the widespread tendency to focus attention on knowledge as artefact or systems tool. Instead of focusing attention on the tool, the perspective I am suggesting focuses attention on how the tools are used. The tools are used in wider processes of communicative interaction in which particular ways of talking are 'in' and others are 'out'. A concern with the knowledge creation process would, therefore, involve an exploration of this dynamic as it manifests in local situations in the living present. What kind of exclusion is operating? What impact does this have in terms of obstructing or encouraging the emergence of new knowledge? Such questions soon lead to reflection on the manner in which ideologically based power relations are being sustained and challenged. What impact does this have on communicative interaction and the emergence of knowledge? A concern with the knowledge-creating process also involves an exploration of the identity-threatening and anxiety-provoking aspects of the process, so focusing attention on these and other aspects of the conversational life of an organisation and its transformative potential.

17.4 Institutions and legitimate structures of authority

The dominant discourse on organisations often proceeds in terms of the second-order abstractions of markets, cultures, social forces and social structures where these abstractions are generally reified so that we slip into the habit of regarding organisations, cultures, societies, forces and structures as things with an independent existence outside our interaction with each other, even following their own laws. We may even anthropomorphise them and come to think of them as organisms with their own lives quite apart from our own. However, on careful consideration, it becomes clear that what we are referring to when we use these terms is nothing more than widespread, enduring and repetitive patterns of interaction with each other that we call routines or habits. When we reify or anthropomorphise these routines and habits, we tend to think of them as external powers causing our interactions. The perspective of complex responsive processes avoids such anthropomorphising and reifying and does not regard routines and habits as causal powers with regard to our interactions. Instead, we come to see that global routines and habits emerge in our local interactions and continue to be sustained as they are iterated from present to present in those local interactions. Social forces, social structures, routines and habits can all be understood as generalisations that are particularised over and over again in each specific situation we find ourselves in. In other words, they are social objects, generalised tendencies to act. Furthermore, these generalisations are often idealised and come to form the cult values we repeatedly have to functionalise in our interaction. Routines and habits do not have any separate existence, and to analyse them as such is to engage in second-order abstractions. In our experience, however, routines and habits are the actions of people and it as actions of emotional, creative and destructive, spontaneous and stuck people that they need to be understood.

This way of understanding routines and habits focuses attention on the inevitably conflictual nature of particularising the general and the idealised. If people simply apply some generalisation or idealisation in an absolutely rigid way, then there need be no conflict but particularising them in specific, unique situations means making choices. Since different individuals and different groupings of them will be making different interpretations of the situation, they will be pressing for different choices to be made. Which of those conflicting choices is actually made will be the result of negotiation and this immediately raises the matter of power. The particular choices made will reflect the figurations of power – the choices of individuals and groups will prevail when the power ratio is titled in their favour. Power figurations emerge in the interaction between people, and like all other organising themes there is a strong tendency for them to become habitual, generalised and even idealised. From a complex responsive processes perspective one understands institutionalised instruments, or technologies, of power to be just such generalised/idealised/habitual figurations of power relations. They too are iterated and particularised in each present and it is in such particularisation that they evolve. They are not to be found as things or forces outside our experience of interaction but only in that experience.

Local interactions form and are formed by population-wide patterns of power relations expressed in the identity-creating dynamics of inclusion and exclusion which are always reflections of ideologies. Ideology is constituted in the paradoxical interplay of people acting on desires, norms and values as restrictions, compulsions and voluntary commitments to choices of action. It is these complex responsive processes of relating that constitute the game in which we are all daily immersed. But this activity of immersing in the game is by no means mindless. The activity of immersing is in fact a highly skilled performance, and some of the skills take the form of thinking and reflecting in terms of both the first-order abstracting of categories of experience from our interaction with each other and the second-order form of abstracting in which we construct maps, models, system designs and plans of those categories to increase our ability to control from a distance. In this way we take up and continue to evolve in our local interactions the generalised and idealised narratives and propositions of our history and a feature of great significance in this activity is the formation of institutions and legitimate patterns of authority. From a complex responsive processes perspective such institutions and legitimate 'structures' of authority are not primarily the realisations of rational designs and plans to achieve clearly defined objectives but, rather, the articulations of actual or desired population-wide power figurations and ideologies, very much to do with identity, that are emerging in many local interactions. It is in these highly complex, responsive processes of interaction that we jointly carry out our tasks in organisations.

For example, Chapter 2 described the evolution of university-based business schools. This did not happen as the result of a central decision to set up a population-wide network of business schools to provide an education that would produce more efficient managers upon whom profitability and continuing economic growth depended. Instead, business schools began to appear as an expression of the ideologies of wealthy industrialists who believed that managers should be ethically responsible stewards of society's resources. As institutions they were expressions of the search for legitimacy and acceptable identity on the part of a new class of functionaries called 'managers'. The continuing evolution of business schools expressed changing ideologies, power figurations and identities, recently reflecting and shaping investment capitalism, for example. In the UK there are now central government policies with the rational aim of re-focusing universities and business schools on training people to meet the needs of the economy, and such policies are affecting how universities are governed. It is by no means clear that, however, this is having the intended effect of producing more efficient managers; many are concerned at the decline in educational standards which economic instrumentalist approaches are producing, while others cynically claim that the response of the universities to such policies is simply a public relations façade behind which business continues as usual. Chapter 2 also mentioned the emergence of powerful independent management consultancies in the USA which later spread across Europe and then the rest of the world. Here again there was no central intention to create an industry of independent management consultants. The opportunity for independent management consultancies was opened up by the Glass-Steagall Act passed by Congress in 1933 and the potential for rapid growth in consulting activities was also create by government policies requiring due diligence and other reports.

Yet another example of the impact of institution formation is provided by the development of institutions that legitimise the proposition that there is global warming caused by human activity, in turn providing the legitimisation of pressure on governments to take action to control carbon dioxide emissions. Booker (2009) begins the story of how the issue of global warming became such a powerful political issue with the work of a team of scientists at the University of California's Scripps Institution of Oceanography who had been recording the amount of carbon dioxide in the Earth's atmosphere for 30 years. These measurements showed that the volume of carbon dioxide had increased from 316 parts per million parts (ppm) of atmosphere in 1959 to 340ppm by 1980 and they were projecting a further rise to a level above 400ppm within decades. They argued that this increase was too much for the plants and oceans to absorb and that was why global temperatures were rising. Members of the Scripps Institution had been engaged in the debate that had been taking place over decades in the institutionalised scientific community about whether global warming was occurring and, if so, whether it was caused by man-made increases in carbon dioxide levels. In many local interactions various views about global warming were emerging. Maurice Strong had heard one of these scientists lecture on global warming and this was later to influence him when he became the first Chairman of the UN Conference on the Human Environment in 1972 which led to the UN Environment Program (UNEP) with Strong as its first director. He believed that the problems of humanity were due to selfish materialism, and one example of this was how humans were destroying the climate on which they depended. What was happening here can be understood as the institutionalisation of a particular ideology and a particular issue. In 1979 UNEP and the World Meteorological Organisation (WMO) organised the first World Climate Conference in Vienna which called for the prevention of man-made climate change. This was followed by many other conferences with the 15th meeting in Copenhagen in December 2009 attended by all of the world's major political figures. In 1988 the UN established an Intergovernmental Panel on Climate Change (IPPC) and by 2009 this had become the accepted authority on climate change providing the basis for the world's most powerful figures accepting that the science on climate change was settled. However, many were claiming that the IPCC blocked the work of scientists who disagreed with the man-made climate-change hypothesis. Any who disagree are now known as 'climate change deniers' and 'flat-earthers'. There have been scandals about attempts to distort data and exaggerate claims in the reports of the IPCC. The scientific hypothesis has, therefore, emerged as a very powerful ideology which is having a major impact on government policies around the world and this has been made possible by the founding of institutions such as the IPCC. The received scientific wisdom and its policy implications are, however, generating considerable conflict amongst nations as they negotiate measures to control carbon dioxide emissions that will not harm their economies. In fact, it has generated major new businesses – for example, the trade in carbon emission credits and the development of wind electricity industry. What we see here is the emergence of major change strategies across the globe in many, many local interactions in which the generalisations and idealisations we call 'institutions' are being made particular.

The point I am making is this. It is easy from the emphasis I have been placing on how population-wide patterns emerge in local interaction to conclude that any attempt to design institutions or intentionally formulate and promulgate policies and procedures is futile or at least flawed. Such a conclusion, however, simply shifts the focus of attention from one pole, autonomous design, to the other pole, emerging pattern, and the consequence of doing this is that we still have an inadequate explanation of what we are doing in our experience of organisational life. Quite clearly, central authorities do develop and enforce central policies and institutions are designed. However, to understand the effect of such activities we need to see how they only ever have any impact insofar as they are taken up in many, many local interactions and the impact depends on just how they are taken up. So, policies and institutions emerge in the local interactions of policy makers who articulate the patterns that are emerging in the form of policies, laws and institutional arrangements, the effects of which emerge in the local interactions of the many, many people affected by those policies, laws and institutions. The policies, laws and institutions all take the form of generalisations, frequently second-order abstractions, and also idealisations and what effect they have depends upon the particularising in local interaction in which the policies, laws and institutions will evolve further.

Furthermore, as we can see quite clearly in the above example of the institutional framework of action against global warming, institutions and the ideologies they embody play a major part in the ongoing evolution of organisations and societies. Organisational life is both sustained and changed in the ongoing interplay between generalised/idealised institutions and the legitimacy they provide, on the one hand, and the particularising effect of local interactions. The ordinary politics of daily life encompass both the population-wide and the local, both the general and the particular, at the same time.

We can understand policies and procedures to be generalised rules which people are supposed to follow. However, what it means to follow a rule is far from simple. Taylor (1995) argues that following a rule is a social practice. What people do mostly flows from a usually inarticulate understanding of the situation they are acting in. This inarticulate understanding is the social control which earlier chapters of this book have referred to as *social object*, *habitus* and *game*. A rule only has a meaning, people only know how to follow it, because of this inarticulate, bodily, background understanding. Since no rule can deal with all specific local situations, following a rule effectively also requires a skilled performance in how to interpret the rule in those specific circumstance and negotiate its acceptance by others.

The wider understanding of plans, rules and institutions all as social phenomena reflecting patterns of power and identity, described in this and the previous section, suggest another way in which we might understand strategy and that is as an identity narrative.

17.5 Strategy as identity narrative

Chapter 2 proposed a wider definition of the primary concern of strategy as having to do with how and what an organisation becomes whatever it becomes. This wider definition regards strategy as fundamentally a matter of identity. Identity answers the questions 'who are we?' and 'what are we doing together?' The identity that an organisation comes to express and how it comes to express it can be thought about in terms of the dominant discourse described in the above paragraph. Or the matter of identity can be thought about in the terms suggested in Chapter 12 as the interplay of many, many intentions of individuals and groupings within and between organisations. This interplay of many intentions always occurs in local interactions between people from which emerge population-wide patterns of relationships between people called 'organisations' which define their collective and individual identities. Strategy can then be understood as the evolution of the iterated and potentially transformed patterns of identity emerging in local interaction. Chapters 13 and 15 have explored in some detail how we might understand local interaction as conversational processes forming and being formed by ideologically based figurations of power relations and ideologically based choices and intentions. Chapter 14 explored the paradoxical links between local interaction and population-wide patterns where the latter are thought of as social objects, cult values and imaginative 'wholes'.

Every organisation is a population of persons cooperating and competing with each other in performing some joint activity in order to accomplish some purpose, and such accomplishment always involves cooperating and competing with other persons in other organisational populations. The accomplishment of purposeful joint activity is possible only because all involved communicate with each other, and my argument is that such communication takes the form of local conversational interaction with its characteristics of power relations and ideologically based choices. All organisational activity, therefore, can be understood as conversational interaction, and this includes the activities of strategising.

Take the typical strategy away-day, for example. A typical strategy away-day takes the form of a small number of the most powerful executives of an organisation staying together at some venue away from their offices. The occasion may begin in the evening with a dinner and much informal conversation, patterned primarily as narrative – the executives tell stories of a successful development here, a concern there, and a failure elsewhere. They are certainly interacting locally and their informal conversations are themselves creating narratives that are surely strategising activities in that the stories told may well have an impact on what the executives attend to when they return to the office. The next day they assemble in a meeting room and the chief executive goes through a PowerPoint® presentation giving the key results for the past year. He takes the major turn, others may occasionally take a turn but only to ask for clarification, and the formal, presentational conversation is patterned mainly through propositional themes. However, the conversation soon shifts to narrative mode as the executives begin to discuss how and why the particular results presented came about and what this reflects about their strategy: that is, about their intentions for the future of the organisation. They may start talking about whether they are on track or not in strategic terms and telling stories of what has been happening to justify their positions.

When they start talking about strategy, they are actually taking up a population-wide, generalised narrative that emerged at last year's away-day and was conveyed to others in the organisation. This strategy was in fact a narrative describing what activities would be continued, how some might be changed and how new ones might be developed. It was a story about purpose. Indeed it was an identity story, one articulating some kind of answer to the questions: who are we? Who are we striving to be? What are we doing together? What do we want to be doing together? People in many, many local interactions across the organisational population have already taken up that narrative and, in many of these, the narrative will have undergone some subtle, and some not so subtle, changes. It is this evolving narrative that is now taken up by the powerful executives in the conversations at their away-day meeting and in their conversations the narrative also continues to evolve. How it does so depends upon their conversational processes, the turn-taking and turn-making patterns, the figurations of power this reflects, the ideological themes supporting these figurations and the rhetorical ploys people are employing in their talking together.

17.6 Summary

This chapter has explored how one might think, from a complex responsive processes perspective, about central concerns of organisational strategists to do with technologies, resources, markets, performance and improvement. The central argument regarding all of these matters is as follows. The dominant discourse approaches all of these matters from a macro perspective and seeks to identify means of operating directly at the macro level on the 'whole' organisation – this is an activity of second-order abstracting. The complex responsive processes perspective is one in which such a 'whole' is an imaginative construct, a felt sense of unity of experience; and what the imaginative construct amounts to is generalisations and idealisations of population-wide patterns of joint activity. These patterns emerge in local interactions in which the generalisations and idealisations are taken up and made particular and functional. It follows that operating directly on the 'whole' amounts simply to articulating generalisations and idealisations, which may or may not be useful, but what happens will happen through the many local responses to them. The perspective of complex responsive process, therefore, takes the form of first-order abstraction, indeed all thought does, but it seeks to avoid second-order abstraction by avoiding reasoning to do with forces, structures, maps and models and focusing on narrative patterns of experience instead. However, narratives of experience include the use people make of the second-order subtractions of the dominant discourse.

Further reading

Ideas in this chapter are further developed by Fonseca (2001), Streatfield (2001). Further developments can be found in Stacey and Griffin (2005), Griffin and Stacey (2005), Stacey (2005), Stacey and Griffin (2006), Shaw and Stacey (2006), Stacey and Griffin (2008), and Mowles, Stacey and Griffin (2008). Taylor (1995) provides an insightful account of what it means to follow a rule. Tobin (2005), Taylor (2005), Williams (2006) and Mowles (2009) write about the experience of leadership from the perspective of complex responsive processes. Alvesson and Sveningsson (2003a) provide an insightful critique of modern concepts of leadership.

Questions to aid further reflection

1. What reasons would you have for claiming that the dominant discourse about strategic management either does or does not focus attention almost exclusively on second-order abstractions.

2. In what way, if at all, does it make sense to think of strategy as fundamentally a narrative of identity?

3. How would you describe the actual activities of strategising that human agents engage in?

4. If strategy emerges in the interplay of local intentions, how would you think about organisational performance and improvement?

5. What are the strategic implications of thinking about technology as social object?

6. What are the implications of thinking about markets not in terms of abstract forces but as patterns of relationships between people?

7. What is the nature of managing knowledge and measuring intellectual capital?

8. If the future is unpredictable how would you thinking about activities of planning in organisations?

Chapter 18

Complex responsive processes
Implications for thinking about organisational dynamics and strategy

This chapter invites you to draw on your own experience to reflect on and consider the implications of:

- The move from a systemic to a responsive processes way of thinking about human interaction.

- The move from understanding individual persons as autonomous to thinking about them as interdependent.

- The move to understanding people as participants in processes of interaction in which it is not possible to take an external position.

- The move from a dual theory of causality to a paradoxical theory of causality.

- Strategy and change from the perspective of complex responsive processes.

- Thinking about control, performance and improvement from a complex responsive processes perspective.

- Thinking about organisational and management research and its contribution to strategising processes.

The purpose of this final chapter is to compare the theory described in Part 3 of this book with the theories reviewed in Part 1 and in so doing point to some implications for thinking about organisational dynamics and strategy.

18.1 Introduction

In Chapter 2 I suggested that this book would be dealing with the following questions. How do populations of interdependent people who constitute organisations, and populations of such organisations, change and evolve over time? How have these populations come to be what they are and how will they become whatever they become? How does one explain the dynamics of evolving organisations? What do strategy, strategic direction and strategic thinking mean? How does a strategy come into being and how is it manifested? I also suggested that the way one answers these questions depends upon the frame of reference from which one approaches them. In Part 1 I reviewed a number of different systemic frames of reference and how they deal with these questions. In this chapter I want to consider how the theory of organisations as complex responsive processes, explored in Part 3 of this book, deals with the above questions and in so doing compare this theory with systemic perspectives. The chapter then goes on to consider how the theory of complex responsive processes refocuses attention in thinking about organisations and their strategies, about control, performance and improvement and about management research. First, however, I give a brief summary of the theory described in Chapters 12 to 17.

18.2 Key features of the complex responsive processes perspective

Chapters 12 to 17 have outlined the basis of a complex responsive processes theory of organisations. From this perspective, organisations are iterated patterns of interaction between people. They take the form of social objects – that is, generalised tendencies on the part of large numbers of people, to act in similar ways in similar situations. When people describe an organisation, they describe who its members are collectively, what they stand for, and what they do. In other words, they articulate generalisations about collective activity, or population-wide patterns. Furthermore, there is a powerful tendency to idealise these generalisations about collective identity, so providing a felt sense of the unity of experience taking the form of an imaginative 'whole' which members co-construct. Such an imaginative 'whole' is fundamentally ideological in nature and people tend to describe it in terms of cult values. Organisations, then, are generalised patterns of interaction between human persons, idealised by them as imaginative 'wholes' which provide powerful experiences of 'we' identity to them. Strategising is the activity of members making sense of and exploring their desires and intentions for the evolution of their 'we' identities, of the imaginative wholes, which actually emerge, as patterns of activity across an organisational population, in the interplay of their intentions in local interactions. This desired strategy can only be articulated and thought about in terms of some form of abstraction from the detail of actual experience. Strategising is conversation conducted in the first-order abstractions of stereotypes and categories which can take the form of narrative or of propositions. First-order abstractions of this kind can be used to elaborate on and intensify our actual experience of our local interactions. Or those first-order abstractions can become the building block of maps and models. This is second-order abstraction in that it moves even further away from the actual experience of local interaction. The move to second-order abstraction is the basis of any form of centralised control from a distance and is thus essential for the governance of modern organisations. Population-wide patterns are presented in standardised general ways that simplify local interaction by averaging out differences. However, realised strategy is the population-wide patterns of relationships and activities that emerge in the local interplay of intentions in specific contingent situations as people take up the narratives and models of strategy. In both desired and realised forms, strategy is basically expressed as narratives of identity, the first being generalised and idealised abstractions from experience while the latter is contingent, local experience displaying unexpected change.

Local interaction is then central to understanding organisations and strategising activities because it is in this local activity that there emerges the population-wide patterns of organisation and strategy both desired and realised. The theory stresses the following inextricably intertwined aspects of human local interaction:

- Interaction is always communicative and communication always takes place in the medium of symbols in the conversation of gestures. Symbols are always social acts – that is, the gesture of one body responding to its own gesture by taking the attitude of others and of the generalised/idealised other, while being responded to by others. Meaning emerges in such communicative interaction. Particularly important are the vocal symbols of language, and ordinary, everyday conversation is a particularly important form of communicative interaction in the medium of language. Feelings and other forms of bodily communication are, however, always involved.

- Interaction between human persons is always power relating because in relating to each other people are always simultaneously constraining and enabling each other's actions. Power relations are felt as the dynamics of inclusion and exclusion.

- In the activity of their conversational and power relating, people are always making choices on the basis of evaluative criteria which constitute ideology.

- As experience, the patterning of conversation, power relating and ideologically based choosing simultaneously forms and is formed by themes taking a predominantly narrative form.

- Patterns are articulated and acted upon as first- and second-order abstractions taken up by people in their experience of being immersed in their organisational game.

- The identities of persons in both their collective and individual aspects arise in interaction.

The term 'complex responsive processes of relating', therefore, always encompasses communicative interaction, power relating and ideologically based choices and it is in such responsive processes of relating, including deliberate intention and design, that human beings create meaning and accomplish sophisticated joint action of any kind. The key feature of all human groups, organisations, institutions and societies is this joint action. Joint action is possible only because complex responsive processes of relating produce emergent, coherent, meaningful patterns of interaction both locally and population-wide at the same time and because human beings are capable of articulating these patterns in the form of first- and second-order abstractions which they take up in their local interactions.

The theory postulates that these coherent, meaningful patterns of interaction take the form of narrative and propositional themes that organise and are simultaneously organised by people interacting with each other. In other words, interaction is self-organising in that meaningful patterns emerge in local interactions between people in the living present, in the absence of any prior design, blueprint or plan for population-wide patterns. Self-organisation, understood as local interaction, means that human agents are choosing, intending, their next actions in response to others, where those choices reflect their own local organising principles, based on a life history in a community with a history. This is self-organising in the sense that human agents always have the potential for spontaneity and do not simply follow centrally determined rules of conduct – they take up centrally determined rules of conduct in their local interactions in ways that adapt the rules to local contingencies. People do design and they do use blueprints and plans but these are all tools they use in their communicative interaction with each other and what happens depends upon the interplay of intentions, plans and choices. People have desires for their imaginatively constructed 'wholes' but what happens does so because of the interplay of their desires. There are no designs, blueprints or plans for interaction itself, for the interplay of intentions, and the tools emerge in the interaction between people. Although interaction is always local, the emergent patterns of meaning may be very widespread due to the fact that people do not interact in one local situation only. Local interaction produces the emergent population-wide patterns of social objects as such objects are made particular. A particular understanding of experience follows. Experience is the direct interaction between human bodies and the joint action accomplished in that interaction. Experience is participation in direct interaction, not participation in some abstract system.

The thematic patterning of communicative interaction has many continuously intertwining, inseparable aspects. These aspects are formal and informal, conscious and unconscious, legitimate and shadow themes organising and being organised by the experience of interaction. Furthermore, interaction is always evolving as the past is iterated in the living present in which the future is perpetually constructed. Other important aspects of interaction, therefore, are continuity and the spontaneity of the transformation of organising themes at the same time. In other words, in the continual iteration of the living present, thematic patterns are reproduced as habits, norms, routines and customs. Social structures, cultures, organisations, institutions and societies, therefore, are not things but perpetually reproduced thematic patterns of relating between people, taking habitual forms. People are immersed in the game of ongoing local interaction but they also have the capacity for abstracting from that experience in the first-order form of categories and stereotypes, importantly expressed in narrative, and in the second-order form of generalised maps and models which average out local differences.

Change, or evolution, in the rather repetitive patterns of experience is possible only because in their iteration they are never reproduced exactly. This is because of the diversity of the people interacting, the imperfection of reproduction (memory) of past habitual interaction, and the inherent spontaneity or human capacity to choose responses, at least to some extent. Since human interaction is nonlinear, its iteration has the capacity to amplify small differences caused by spontaneity and imperfect reproduction into major qualitative changes in population-wide patterns of relating. It is in this manner that human interaction evolves in novel ways.

The theory of complex responsive processes, therefore, reflects a theory of transformative causality. This means that the causality of human interaction is not a dual one as in systems thinking. In systems thinking there is, on the one hand, formative unfolding of that which is already enfolded (the known) in the system of which people are parts through, say, design or some pre-given motivation such as a vision. On the other hand, there is rationalist individual choice. Instead, in responsive processes thinking, human interaction is perpetually constructing the future as the known-unknown: that is, as continuity and potential transformation at the same time. This is a fundamentally paradoxical theory of causality.

Furthermore, what is being perpetually constructed as continuity and potential transformation is human identity: that is, human meaning. Human identity has two inseparably interwoven aspects, namely, individual and collective, that which Elias called 'I' and 'we' identities. From a complex responsive process perspective, *an organisation is evolving identity*. In talking about organisations, the normal practice is to focus almost exclusively on collective or 'we' identities. The complex responsive process perspective, however, encourages us not to lose sight of the fact that 'I' identities are inseparable from 'we' identities. For example, General Electric (GE) is recognised as perhaps the world's largest corporation, which provides a wide range of products and services. It presents itself to, and is recognised by, many of us as a competitive company that operates with integrity and values its people. In other words, GE is a recognisable collective identity and, as such, is a key aspect of the identities of the people who work there. They take pride in telling people that they work for GE and experience a real sense of loss if their part of GE is sold to another corporation. This view of identity makes sense of the trauma individuals experience when they are ejected from an organisation or when their organisation is dissolved or merged with another. What is threatened is far greater than economic well-being; it is the very identities of people that are threatened.

This immediately leads us to the definition of strategy implicit in the theory of complex responsive processes. Strategy is the evolving narrative pattern of organisational identity. It is the evolving pattern of what an organisation is. An organisation is what it is because of a history of relating and it will become what it becomes in the local communicative interaction and power relating between people in the living present. If we want to understand strategy, then we need to understand the evolving complex responsive processes of relating between people who constitute an organisation in their local interaction.

Box 18.1 summarises key points about the dynamics of complex responsive processes.

18.3 How the theory of complex responsive processes answers the four key questions

Four questions were posed in Chapter 2 and used to explore important features of a number of theories of organisation. These questions relate to:

1. How the theory in question understands the nature of interaction.

2. What views the theory takes on human action.

3. The methodological position that the theory adopts.

4. The manner in which it deals with paradox.

This section will examine how the complex responsive processes theory of organisation deals with these questions and how this differs from other theories.

Box 18.1	Complex responsive processes: main points on organisational dynamics

- Organisations are complex responsive processes of relating between people. Since relating immediately constrains, it immediately establishes power relations between people.
- Complex responsive processes are patterned as propositional and narrative themes that organise the experience of relating and, thus, power relations.
- These themes take many forms. Of great importance are the official ideological themes that determine what it is legitimate to talk about in an organisation and the unofficial ideologies which may be supporting or subverting official ideologies.
- Conversational patterns may take stable forms of repetition in which people are stuck. They may also take more fluid forms, analogous to the dynamics of the edge of chaos.
- Change occurs in novel ways through the presence of sufficient diversity in organising themes. This is expressed in fluid conversation in which shadow themes test the legitimate.
- The evolution of fluid conversation and the emergence of creative new directions are radically unpredictable.
- Fluid conversation is made more possible when people are able to live with anxiety.
- The choices people make are fundamentally based on ideology.
- Population-wide patterns emerge in local interaction.
- There is no guarantee of success.

The nature of human interaction

Strategic choice theory is built on a systemic notion of interaction in which organisations adapt to their environments in a self-regulating, negative-feedback (cybernetic) manner so as to achieve their goals. The dynamics, or pattern of movement over time, are those of movement to states of stable equilibrium. Prediction is not seen as problematic. The analysis is primarily at the macro level of the organisation in which cause and effect are related to each other in a linear manner. Micro diversity receives little attention and interaction is assumed to be uniform and harmonious.

Learning organisation theory also adopts a systemic perspective on human interaction, but one that takes account of positive as well as negative feedback. From the systems dynamics perspective the dynamic is that of non-equilibrium in which unexpected outcomes appear. However, this theory holds that when managers understand the positive and negative feedback structure of the whole system they will be able to identify leverage points through which they can control it. This theory does not explore the implications of radical unpredictability. Here, too, the analysis is at the macro level of the organisation but this time connections between cause and effect take nonlinear forms in which the connections might be distant over time and space. Again, little attention is paid to micro diversity and successful interaction is still assumed to be harmonious, although this theory does recognise obstacles to the achievement of such harmony.

The third theory reviewed, psychodynamics, also takes a systemic perspective on interaction, this time open systems theory. Here the focus is on regulation at permeable boundaries between system and environment and between subsystems of the system. The dynamics of human open systems are somewhat turbulent and the importation of primitive human behaviour disrupts organisational learning. This possibility requires careful management of boundaries and radical unpredictability does not feature as an important characteristic. This theory sees the purpose of management as intervention aimed at enabling equilibrium adaptation to the organisation's environment. The analysis here is at a far more micro level than is the case with strategic choice and the learning organisation, taking account of the behaviour of members of an organisation, particularly the unconscious causes of that behaviour. Micro diversity is recognised and success is a state of adaptation to reality.

These three approaches to organisations are, therefore, based on a systemic theory of interaction. This means that interaction between people is assumed to create a whole, a system, of which they are parts and so subjected in some way to the purpose of the whole. Later developments in second-order systems thinking all continue on the basis of a theory of systemic interaction. Various strands of systems thinking may differ according to whether they view systems as reality itself or mental constructs of reality, but they continue to take a systemic perspective on interaction. This also applies to more recent developments in organisational theory to do with knowledge management. However, although still couched in systems terms, second-order systems thinking and the theorising on knowledge creation in communities of practice do depart from the dominant discourse in providing a much richer picture of the complexities of social interaction, emphasising matters such as power, politics and ideology. Social constructionist views of organisational processes are less couched in terms of systems and stress to co-creation of social realties in conversation, so presenting a further challenge to the dominant discourse. Critical management studies (labour process theory) move on from the dominant discourse in even more radical ways by abandoning the concept of system as far as organisations are concerned and emphasising actual process of power relations and ideology.

A number of writers have been moving to a systemic perspective on human action drawn from chaos and complexity theory. Attention is drawn to the dynamics of the edge of chaos and the self-organising, emergent properties of the system. Attention is also drawn to the possibility of unpredictability, but this is often not seen as essential or requiring further exploration. The analysis tends to be at the macro level of the organisation as a whole, although some do focus upon micro diversity to some extent. Most writers apply complexity theory to organisations within the systemic theory of interaction.

The complex responsive processes perspective described in Chapters 12 to 17 is built upon a completely different theory of interaction or process (*see* Chapters 9 and 12). It regards interaction between people as iterated processes of communication and power relating. There is no notion here of a system, and what people are producing in their interaction is further patterns of interaction in which they imaginatively construct 'wholes', unities of experience, which they tend to idealise. Such imaginative 'wholes' are understood as ideologies rather than systems. The theory of complex responsive processes, therefore, represents a move from a spatial metaphor of inside and outside to temporal processes of continual reproduction and potential transformation. Complex responsive processes are fundamentally conversational in nature, forming and being formed by power relations and ideologically based choices. The analysis focuses at a micro level and concentrates on the paradoxical dynamics of stable instability in which local interaction produces emergent population-wide patterns in relating and these could take novel forms through the amplification of diversity and human spontaneity. This perspective emphasises the importance of diversity and deviance as essential to the internal capacity to change spontaneously. In this evolving, potentially creative process, unpredictability is central, inviting further exploration of how people act into the unknown.

The comparison that I have made above between organisational theories suggests a move from one theory of interaction to another so that uncertainty and unpredictability, and their relationship with diversity and creativity, are increasingly taken into account.

Human psychology

Strategic choice theory takes a cognitivist view of human nature. Here, mind is understood to be a property of the individual brain. The brain/mind processes symbolic information, forming representations and models of a pre-given reality. Humans then act on the basis of their mental models. The individual is primary in that knowing and acting do not depend fundamentally on relationships between individuals. Individuals form groups and being part of a group may then affect individual behaviour. This theory places great emphasis on the importance of the intentions formed and expressed by autonomous individuals. Emotion is often seen as a dangerous disruption of rational choice capacity and power is understood as an attribute of an individual, often in terms of official authority. Creativity is an attribute of an individual.

Learning organisation theories employs the same theory of human nature. However, they also combine this with notions from humanistic psychology in which the central motivation for action is the urge individuals have to actualise themselves, finding their true selves as it were. Again, individuals form groups and these groups affect their behaviour. Leadership is a competence possessed by individuals and intention is a characteristic of individuals. Emotions of a positive kind are emphasised. Power as an attribute of charismatic individuals comes to the fore. Creativity is in the end seen as an attribute of an individual, although a role is also ascribed to cohesive teamwork. Humanistic psychology also immediately focuses attention on the individual, but in a way rather different from cognitivism. The central tenet here is the belief that the human individual is fundamentally motivated by self-realisation, or self-actualisation. Human knowing and acting, and therefore human learning, are driven by the need to find the self. Others, in the form of community, are very important to emotional well-being but it is not postulated that the group or the community actually forms the individual. In fact, the self-actualising individual has to find his or her true self despite group pressures to conform.

Psychoanalytic perspectives on organisations combine open systems theory with a view of human nature derived from psychoanalysis. The fundamental motivation for human behaviour here is the mental ideas of inherited animal instincts called the drives. Aggressive and libidinal drives blindly seek satisfaction but encounter social prohibition. Individual mental processes are structured by this encounter with the social. Individuals form groups but considerable account is taken of the impact group processes have on individual behaviour, particularly those that are unconscious. The theory focuses on how regression to primitive behaviour can destroy rational thinking and learning. An important insight into the nature of the relationship between individual and group is that about leadership. Individuals may be sucked into leadership positions by unconscious dynamics of the group. Leadership is no longer simply a competence of the individual. Emotion and power play a much more important role in understanding the development of an organisation than they do in the theories of strategic choice and the learning organisation. The impact of emotions of a negative kind and of individual and group fantasy life is taken into account, as are the negative aspects of power. Creativity is an individual attribute arising in the ability to hold anxiety and engage in play.

Second-order systems thinking does not depart in any radical way from the individualist psychologies of the dominant discourse. Many of those developing the knowledge management perspective on organisations, as well as those understanding organisations as communities of practice, adopt a constructivist view of psychology. Here, individuals are thought of as selecting or enacting the world into which they act. In this way, interacting individuals co-create their worlds. However, the individual still remains primary, although much more importance is attached to social interaction. A clear move away from individualist psychology is made by social constructionist approaches which move from the pole of the individual to the pole of the social. Critical management studies probably imply a psychology in which individual actions are formed by economic and political structures.

The writers reviewed in Chapter 11 import a theory of interaction drawn from chaos and complexity theory into their theory of organisations. They combine this with the same cognitivist, constructivist and humanistic views of human nature as those found in strategic choice, learning organisation theory, as well as knowledge management and communities of practice perspectives. The individual, therefore, remains central, and as a result these writers do not go further, in my view, than the other systemic theories reviewed in Part 1. More attention may be paid to the creative aspects of instability but, for most, the same views on control are retained and creativity continues to be regarded as an attribute of an individual. Individuals, according to this theory, are essentially cybernetic entities who can take the position of objective observer of an external reality.

The complex responsive processes theory of organisations makes a radical departure from systemic thinking when it comes to human psychology. While the systemic theories reviewed in Part 1 combine a theory of interaction with a theory of human psychology, the complex responsive processes perspective is a theory of human psychology that is also a theory of interaction. There is no split between psychology and sociology. While systemic theories distinguish between individual and group as different levels of analysis, the complex responsive processes perspective is one in which the individual is the singular of interdependent people while the group is the plural of interdependent people.

The fundamental proposition is that individuals and groups form and are formed by each other simultaneously. Individual minds are not seen purely as a process of brain computation, nor are they seen as motivated by primitive drives formed in the mind by the clash with the social. From a complex responsive processes perspective, the fundamental motivator of human behaviour is the urge to relate. From this perspective, there can be no human individual outside of relationship. Mind is silent, private conversation structured by, and always resonating and changing with, vocal, public conversation in groups. This theory moves away from the notion of the autonomous individual containing a mind as an internal world to the notion of interdependent people, to social selves. Power relations and the ideologies supporting them, as well as emotions and fantasies, are all central to this theoretical perspective. Intention is no longer an attribute of an individual. Instead, it emerges in conversational relationship to be articulated by an individual. Leadership is no longer simply an individual competence but a form of relationship. Creativity arises in patterns of relationship in which there is sufficient deviance and subversion.

Methodological position

The methodological position adopted by strategic choice and learning organisation theorists is that of the objective observer who stands outside the organisational system and observes it as a pre-given reality. The purpose is to manipulate and control the system. When the writers reviewed in Chapter 11 take chaos and complexity theory into theorising about organisations, they mostly adopt the same methodological position as that of the dominant discourse. The manager is implicitly ascribed the same role and prescriptions are made as to how the manager may control, direct or at least disturb or perturb the system.

Those adopting psychoanalytic perspectives move some way from this position in that they adopt methodologies analogous to the clinical. They advocate action research in which the researcher participates with members of an organisation and uses his or her feelings as information. However, some notion of objective observation is retained. The researcher, and the manager, takes a position at the boundary of the system in order to avoid being sucked into unconscious group processes (Stapley, 1996).

Those who take second-order, soft and critical systems perspectives, as well as some of those who talk of communities of practice and knowledge management, adopt a reflexive and participative methodological position. They display great awareness of the co-constructed nature of knowledge and many actively look for multiple perspectives on any situation. Many move from the position of the objective observer to methodologies of participative enquiry (Reason, 1988) where researchers understand themselves to be participants in processes of enquiry. This is a reflexive methodology (Steier, 1991) in which organisations are understood to be social constructions (Gergen, 1982). However, while seeking to deal with the fact that humans are both observers and participants in their own action, many of the writers in the traditions just referred to continue to do so from a systemic perspective. They still understand human interaction as producing a system. This inevitably leads to a methodological dualism in which people move from the participant position to the observer position and back again. Critical systems thinking develops this kind of dualism into a whole system of methodologies.

The complex responsive processes perspective seeks to sustain a methodological position in which people are both participants and observers at the same time. This has implications for how the role of the manager is understood. Neither researcher nor manager can step outside the conversational processes that are the organisation simply because their work requires them to talk to others. What they say affects what they hear and what they hear affects what they say. From this perspective, then, a manager cannot stand outside organisational processes and control, direct, shape, influence, condition or perturb them in an intentional way. All such intentions are gestures made to others in an organisation and what happens depends on the ongoing responses. The methodology for understanding complex responsive processes is essentially reflexive.

This perspective on the nature of management leads to a completely different understanding of the dynamics of stable instability. The writers reviewed in Chapter 11 tend to equate the dynamics of the edge of chaos with crises. They tend to see the manager as one who stands outside the system and pushes, or nudges, it into instability, disturbance and crisis. One prescription is to place people under more stress so that they will be motivated to change and so 'unleash the power of self-organisation'. The notion of the edge of chaos used in a complex responsive processes perspective is completely different. The analogue of this dynamic is fluid conversation. People can only engage in this when the pattern of their relationships provides good enough capacity for living with the anxiety of facing the unknown. Crisis and stress are not relational qualities that contain anxiety, rather they increase it. The edge of chaos, from the perspective I am suggesting, is safe enough, exciting enough patterns of relationships, not terrifyingly stressful ones.

Paradox

Paradox is not central to the theories of strategic choice, learning organisations, knowledge management and communities of practice or the importation of chaos and complexity theory into organisational thinking through cognitivist and constructivist perspectives on psychology. Contradiction, tension and dilemmas are recognised but they are seen as resolvable. It is indeed the purpose of management, according to these theories, to resolve them. The reason is that all of these theories are fundamentally systemic and it is of the essence of systems thinking to eliminate paradox in dualistic thinking. Those challenging the dominant discourse in the form of second order systems thinking, communities of practice and social constructionism usually do not rely in a fundamental way on paradox.

Paradox plays a much more important role in psychoanalytic theories and is seen as fundamental to human life. The theory of complex responsive processes places even more emphasis on paradox in that the individual and the group are paradoxically formed by and forming each other at the same time. Particularly important is the emphasis placed on the paradox of predictability and unpredictability at the same time. Paradox, of course, cannot be resolved or harmonised, only endlessly transformed.

In this section I have compared the answers to the four key questions given by various *systemic* theories of organisation with those provided by complex responsive *processes* theory. I suggest that the move from systems to responsive processes leads to a radically different understanding of organisational evolution. It is radical in that it abandons the assumptions of the autonomous individual and the position of the objective observer, without moving to the social pole but retaining a paradoxical view in which individuals form the social while being formed by it at the same time. It replaces the split between individual and social and assumes the simultaneous social construction of group and individual identities and the methodological position of reflexivity in both individual and social terms. Another move is away from thinking of oneself as manager in terms of the objective designer, towards thinking of oneself as an active participant in complex processes of relating to other people in all its aspects, both good and bad. In the following sections of this chapter, I want to explore how this theoretical shift focuses the attention of practitioners and researchers on factors that are, in some respects, very different from most other theories.

18.4 Refocusing attention: strategy and change

Strategic choice, learning organisation and knowledge management theories take the methodological position of the objective observer where the manager stands outside the organisation understood as a system and thinks in terms of controlling it. These theories, therefore, immediately have an application to do with the intentional control of the system by the observing manager. It is then a natural step to formulate general prescriptions for the application of control. The prescriptions take the form of tools and techniques of analysis and monitoring. Furthermore, some test of the validity of the tools and techniques is required. This is provided by pointing to case studies and anecdotes of how organisations that use particular tools and techniques, or have particular attributes, are successful while those that do not use, or possess, them fail. It seems to me that psychoanalytic perspectives on organisations hold the position of the objective observer much less firmly. The concern with application then becomes less central and the focus shifts more to understanding what is happening in an organisation. Rather than straightforward prescriptions, those working from a psychoanalytic perspective provide hypotheses for joint discussion with members of an organisation in specific, rather than general, cases. Much the same can be said of those approaches which challenge the dominant discourse in one way or another: namely, second-order systems thinking, social constructionism, communities of practice and critical management studies.

A theory of organisations as complex responsive processes of relating joins other challengers of the dominant discourse by firmly making a methodological move away from the notion of the manager as objective observer. Managers are understood to be participants in the complex responsive processes of interaction with others, with the possibility of engaging in emergent enquiry into what they are doing and what steps they should take next. They also have the possibility of enquiring into the nature of their own complex responsive processes of relating. This is what it means to be reflexive. However, this theory provides an explanation of what managers are doing, rather than prescribing what they should be doing, and it is quite common for managers to avoid taking the possibilities for inquiring into what they are doing and who they are. The question then becomes why they are not taking up the possibility of reflection. The whole purpose of the theoretical shift I have been suggesting is to focus attention on processes that managers are held to be engaging in but which dominant theories either do not focus upon or tend to do so in a prescriptive way. The purpose is not to apply or prescribe but to refocus attention. When people focus their attention differently, they are highly likely to take different kinds of actions. However, a theory that focuses attention on contingent local interaction and emergent population-wide patterns can hardly yield general prescriptions on how that local interaction should proceed and what should emerge from it. The theory would be proposing to do the opposite of what it is explaining. Instead, the theory of complex responsive processes invites recognition of the uniqueness and non-repeatability of experience and, at the same time, its iterated repetitive quality.

If you focus your attention according to strategic choice, learning organisation and knowledge management theories, the lack of application and prescription implied by complex responsive processes theory is highly unsatisfactory. The tendency is to dismiss it as useless, as not practical, for this reason. However, if you take the perspective of complex responsive processes theory, rather than trying to make it fit into some other theory, you might come to value what it does, namely refocuses attention. I have found that even if managers accept this, they immediately ask for examples of where people have refocused attention in the way suggested and whether they were then successful. Again, this is approaching the theory of complex responsive processes from the frame of reference of the other theories. One of the main properties of the dynamics of stable instability is the escalation of small changes into qualitatively different patterns. Patterns of stable instability may be similar to each other but they are never repeated in the same way. They are paradoxically unique and repetitive at important levels of detail. Organisations characterised by the dynamics of stable instability will therefore all be unique in some important way so that giving examples of success in one organisation to managers in another is likely to be spurious. Perhaps this is why the track record of identifying attributes of successful organisation is so poor. Instead of looking for understanding in other people's experience one might look for it in one's own experience.

Consistent with the nature of the theory I am talking about, therefore, I will not be providing applications or prescriptions. What I will be trying to point to is how the theory shifts the focus of attention. First, consider how attention is focused on the quality of participation.

Focusing attention on the quality of participation

Whenever I talk to managers about the complex responsive processes perspective, they immediately ask what it says that 'you' need to do to bring about the success of an organisation. When I ask who this 'you' is, they usually say that they mean the top executives of an organisation. The main issue here is how one is thinking about what the top executives of an organisation are doing. From the dominant systemic perspective they are implicitly thought of first as standing outside the organisation understood as a system and operating on it in some way, and then as participating in the system as parts of it. From the complex responsive processes perspective, top executives are thought of as participating with other members in evolving processes of communicating and power relating. The meaning of participation is completely different in the two perspectives. In the systemic perspective, participation means participating in an abstract 'whole' or system and in the complex responsive processes perspective it means participating in direct interaction with other people. In the former case, participation creates a 'whole' outside of the direct experience of interaction; in the latter case, participation means creating further interaction, including the imaginatively creative acts of creating a felt sense of unity in experience.

Strategic choice theory holds that the top executives can form organisation-wide intentions for an organisation's future evolution. It also holds that if they then appropriately motivate other members of their organisation, those members will move according to the intention that top executives have ascribed to the system. In the language of complex responsive processes theory, when top executives articulate an organisation-wide intention, they are engaging in the activities of second-order abstraction which they communicate as gestures to other members of an organisations. However, while top executives can and do make intentional gestures of an abstract kind to all members of an organisation, they cannot determine the responses to those gestures throughout the organisation. They may try to forestall responses of a deviant kind by appropriate motivation, which is also a gesture in abstract form, and handle unexpected responses from others by making further, organisation-wide, intentional gestures. However, all of these gestures will also evoke response that those at the top cannot determine so they inevitably find themselves caught in ongoing process of trying to control the responses their gestures evoke and never fully succeeding. In strategic choice theory, there is no recognition of this ongoing process and no attention is paid to the fundamental uncertain nature of organisational life and the inevitability of the unexpected.

Learning organisation theory does take account of unexpected response to the organisation-wide, abstract intentional gestures of top executives. However, it holds that they can intentionally operate at leverage points so as to get the responses they want, more or less. Creativity here is the intentional change of mental models by individuals. From psychoanalytic perspectives, top executives can choose task and role definitions and design structures that will hold disruptive unconscious processes at bay. Those employing complexity theory in what I have called an orthodox way point to unpredictability of responses and to their self-organising and emergent nature. However, they hold that top executives can choose simple rules or intentionally create crises that will move their organisation to a dynamic in which it can be successful.

In second-order systems thinking, researchers, consultants and managers evaluate a problem situation, invite the 'right' participants to engage with it, encourage them to interact, trigger their enthusiasm and present them with the selected systems models that they think are appropriate to the problem situation. In the communities of practice perspective, someone formulates a design for learning.

In all these cases, the top executives are making choices about how they are to operate on the system as a whole and it is being assumed that they can determine the responses that their gestures call forth. In effect, this assumes that there is a special category of person in an organisation who alone has free will and choice, or agency, with all the others reduced to automata. Even members of that special category then have to become a part in the system they have designed, implying that they are only free while they are designing the system.

From the complex responsive processes perspective, no manager can stand outside an organisation and choose how it is to operate. Instead, all managers are active participants with each other in the interactive processes that are the organisation. Top executives can and do form organisation-wide intentions about their organisation. They can and do identify leverage points. They can and do design structures to contain unconscious processes and sometimes they do set simple rules and intentionally cause crises. They can and do prepare designs for learning and they do try to identify the 'right' people. They can and do select and recommend systems models that they think are relevant to particular problem situations. However, all of these intentions and designs emerge as abstractions in the conversations top executives have with each other and with other people. Furthermore, top executives can never design the responses to these gestures. Small changes may escalate and people will engage in local conversations and power relations, often organised by shadow themes, from which unexpected responses may well emerge. Attention is then focused on the thematic patterning of interaction, such as the pattern of power relations, the patterns of inclusion and exclusion, the ideological themes sustaining them and the feelings of anxiety and shame aroused by shifts in patterns of identity.

I am suggesting, then, that in moving from the position of manager as objective observer of a system to that of manager as participant in emergent enquiry, attention is focused on the unexpected and complex patterning of the responses of organisational members to managers' intentions. Intention and design are understood as emergent and problematic processes and attention is focused on the interplay of intentions. The emphasis shifts from the manager focusing on how to make a choice to focusing on the quality of participation in local conversations from which such choices and the responses to them emerge. It becomes a personal matter of reflecting together on the quality of participation.

Focusing attention on the quality of conversational life

In organisations, relationships between people are organised in conversation that forms and is formed by the power relations between them. Conversational relating is organised by themes of an ideological nature that justify the patterns of power relations. Intentions emerge as do other themes organising the experience of relating, as do the responses these intentions call forth. New themes emerge as people struggle to understand each other and as their conversations are cross-fertilised through conversations with people in other communities and disciplines. Organisations change when the themes that organise conversation and power relations change. Learning is change in these themes. Knowledge is language and meaning emerges as themes interact to form conversation.

Attention is thus focused on the conversational life of an organisation as the changing, evolving, local communicative interaction and power relating, sometimes patterned as intention and design using abstract communicative tools such as systems models. The quality of that conversational life is thus paramount. Increasingly, those challenging the dominant discourse (*see* Chapter 9) are focusing on conversations, story and narrative. However, even amongst these challengers, there is sometimes a tendency to seek to design special forms of conversation known as dialogue and special forums such as communities of practice. From the complex responsive processes perspective the emphasis is on ordinary, everyday conversation. The key role of managers is their participation in those conversations and their facilitation of different ways of conversing. A key implication of this way of understanding life in organisations has to do with being sensitive to the themes that are organising conversational relating. Another is awareness of the rhetorical ploys that are being used to block the emergence of new conversational themes. From this perspective, effective managers are those who notice the repetitive themes that block fluid conversation and participate in such a way as to assist in shifting those themes. They may do this, for example, by repeatedly asking why people are saying what they are saying. Effective managers will seek opportunities to talk to people in other communities and bring themes from those conversations into the conversational life of their own organisation. They will be particularly concerned with trying to understand the covert politics and unconscious group processes they are caught up in and how those might be trapping conversation in repetitive themes. They will also pay attention to the power relations and the ideological basis of those power relations and of the choices people make as expressed in conversations.

Focusing attention on the quality of anxiety and how it is lived with

A theory of organisation as complex responsive processes focuses attention on the importance of fluid conversation in which people are able to search for new meaning. Anxiety is an inevitable companion of shifts in themes that organise the experience of relating because such shifts create uncertainty, particularly uncertainty around individual and collective identities. Themes organising the experience of relating are not only expressed in the vocal, public conversations between people, they also resonate with and change the silent, private conversations that are individual minds. Change in organisations is also, at the same time, deeply personal change for individual members. New ways of talking publicly are reflected in new ways of individuals making sense of themselves. Such shifts unsettle the very way in which people experience themselves. It is because of these deeply personal reasons that shifting patterns of conversation give rise to anxiety, but without this there can be no emergence of creative new themes.

When one thinks in this way, the manner in which people live with anxiety is crucial to organisational change and innovation. When managers focus attention on this matter they begin to pay attention to what it is about particular work, at a particular time, in a particular place, that gives rise to anxiety. They pay attention to the nature of this anxiety. They ask what makes it possible to live with the anxiety so that it is also experienced as the excitement required to enable people to continue struggling with the search for new meaning. What are we doing that enables us, or disables us, from living with the anxiety that change generates? Central to this possibility is sufficient trust between those engaging in difficult conversations. Attention is then focused on what, in a particular organisation, at a particular time, is promoting or destroying trust.

What will be seriously questioned from the perspective of complex responsive processes is prescriptions that have to do with setting stretching targets and placing people under stress in the belief that this will move them to try harder. What this may do is simply make them feel more anxious and so less likely to develop the kind of conversational life that makes creativity possible.

Focusing attention on the quality of diversity

One of the most distinctive aspects of a theory of complex responsive processes is the way in which it focuses attention on diversity. The other theories reviewed in this book tend to focus attention on consensus and where they do raise the matter of diversity they tend to deal with it in an abstract and idealised manner (*see* Chapter 8). Strategic choice theory focuses attention on the importance of members of an organisation sharing the same commitment to its policies and its chosen strategic direction. Learning organisation theory focuses attention on the importance of people in an organisation being committed to the same vision and working together harmoniously in cohesive teams. Psychoanalytic perspectives focus attention on the importance of people understanding the nature of boundaries and having shared understandings of their roles and tasks. Many of those who import complexity theory into their theorising about organisations in systemic ways stress the importance of people sharing a few simple rules, although some have laid great emphasis on diversity (*see* Chapter 11). The theory I am suggesting takes a paradoxical perspective.

The paradox is this. If members of an organisation have nothing in common at all, then obviously any kind of joint action will be impossible. However, if they conform too much then the emergence of new forms of behaviour is blocked. Organisations display the internal capacity to change spontaneously only when they are characterised by diversity. This focuses attention on the importance of deviance and eccentricity. It focuses attention on the importance of unofficial ideologies that undermine current power relations. Such unofficial ideologies are expressed in conversations organised by shadow themes. A condition for creativity is, therefore, some degree of subversive activity with the inevitable tension this brings between shadow and legitimate themes organising the experience of relating. Diversity is inseparable from conflict.

It is difficult to get one's mind around what this means. It does not make much sense to me to move from noting the importance of deviance to thinking that managers, in their legitimate roles, should promote deviance. It would then not be deviance. It makes little sense to advocate harnessing shadow conversational themes in order intentionally to generate creativity. The shadow so harnessed is no longer the shadow. It makes little sense to say that managers should take steps to unleash self-organisation. This implies that it is not going on already, when the whole point of the theory of complexity is that it is explaining how things already are. It also makes little sense to me to respond to the recognition of diversity by prescribing 'respect' for diversity. I think that this is a form of disengagement in which everyone politely ignores the differences while claiming to respect them. I think this is a defensive manoeuvre that blocks the explorative conflict provoked by diversity, which is how some new understanding might emerge.

For me, the implication of recognising the importance of deviance has to do with people making sense of their own engagement with others in the shadow conversations that express deviance. It means paying attention to how what they are doing may be collusively sustaining the legitimate themes organising experience, so making change impossible. It means developing a greater sensitivity to the unconscious way in which together people create categories of what is 'in' and what is 'out' and the effect that this has on people and organisations. These dynamics of power relating, inclusion–exclusion and shame are central to the complex responsive processes perspective.

Focusing attention on unpredictability and paradox

Perhaps the most radical implication of complex responsive processes theory is the severe limits to certainty and predictability that it points to. This is a major departure from other theories of organisation, which either virtually ignore or at least downplay the radical unpredictability of the long-term evolution of organisations. What does paying attention to such unpredictability imply?

First, for me, it means thinking about how to cope with not knowing and the potential for feelings of incompetence and shame that this arouses. Managers in organisations often find themselves in situations in which they must act without knowing what the outcome of their actions will be over long time periods. They must act because failure to act will also have unpredictable long-term outcomes. Furthermore, managers can and do act, often very creatively, when they do not know what the long-term outcomes of their actions will be – when they do not really know what they are doing.

These situations are made much more difficult, I think, when management is understood from perspectives that lead people to believe that long-term predictability is possible if one is well informed and competent enough. When the inevitable surprise comes then this view leads to a search for whom to blame. The perspective that predictability is possible leads to the view that the surprise must be due to ignorance, incompetence or some form of bad behaviour in that people did not do what they were supposed to do. In my experience, this judgement is frequently completely unjustified in that very intelligent managers do the best they can and still the surprises come. When you take the complex responsive processes perspective, surprise is part of the internal dynamic of the processes themselves. Surprise is inevitable no matter how well informed, competent and well behaved everyone is. Surprise is inseparable from creativity. I believe that thinking in this way is itself a way of living with the anxiety of not knowing. It is quite natural not to know and this does not have to incapacitate one. It is possible to carry on working together even in the condition of not knowing. Emergent meaning, often of a new and creative kind, is produced in conversational processes characterised by 'not knowing'.

This way of thinking encourages one to pay more attention to what one actually does as one holds the position of not knowing long enough for the new to emerge. One implication of this position has to do with the criteria used to judge a quality action. The systemic theories reviewed in Part 1 implicitly assume that the criterion for selecting a quality action is its outcome. Quality actions are those that produce desired outcomes. However, in an unpredictable world, the outcomes of an action cannot be known in advance. It is necessary to act and then deal with the consequences. This does not make action impossible or futile. It simply means that people select actions on the basis of other criteria for quality. For example, in a highly uncertain world a quality action is one that keeps options open for as long as possible. A quality action is one which creates a position from which further actions are possible. That is why the option of doing nothing is such a poor response to uncertainty. If the response to uncertainty is to stay at home, the options opened up by journeying forth will never be available. Another criterion for a quality action is that it should enable errors to be detected faster than do other options. Finally, the most important criteria for quality actions are moral and ethical in nature. An action may be taken without the actor knowing its outcome simply because the action is judged to be good in itself. One is not absolved of responsibility simply because one does not know the outcome. Even if I do not know how my action will turn out, I am still responsible and will have to deal with the outcome as best I can. In the end, quality action is ideologically based.

Just as the unpredictability arising in complex interactions imposes limits on what it is possible to know about outcomes of actions, so the complexity of the interactions itself imposes limits on how much of it can be understood. Managers often cannot know the long-term outcomes of their actions and they usually cannot understand the full nature of the complex responsive processes of organising. However, this does not disable action either because the process is one in which local interaction produces an emergent population-wide pattern. It is not necessary to understand the 'whole' in order to act; it is simply necessary to act on the basis of one's own local understanding, which will always include one's perceptions and feelings about social objects and cult values. This is a very different notion from that in, say, learning organisation theory where understanding the whole system is essential to learning. Unlike systemic theories of any kind, one is not seeking the whole or trying to be comprehensive.

The focus on long-term unpredictability has implications for the meaning of control. As it is normally understood in other theories of organisation, control is a cybernetic process. It is an activity that ensures the achievement of chosen outcomes. In highly complex processes with emergent and unpredictable long-term outcomes, this form of control is impossible. This does not mean that there is no control, however. It simply means that control has to be understood in a different way. Control then takes the form of constraint. As I have often pointed out in previous chapters, all acts of relating impose constraint on all of those relating. Control takes the form of relating itself, that is, mutual constraint. Control is understood as social processes of power relations, ideology and socialised self-control.

Notions of complexity, long-term unpredictability and control as constraint have implications for many activities that are currently taken for granted by managers. If these notions are taken seriously, they lead to a number of questions. For example: why do people prepare long-term forecasts if it is impossible to make useful long-term forecasts? Why do they adopt investment appraisal methods that require detailed quantitative forecasts over long time periods? Complexity theory suggests that it is impossible to make such forecasts so why do people carry on doing so? If organisations are not simply cybernetic systems, why is so much effort expended on cybernetic systems of quality control? One important implication of a complex responsive processes theory of organising may have to do with putting a stop to many initiatives and abandoning control systems and procedures that are not fulfilling the purposes they are supposed to fulfil. The savings in time, resources and human stress might be considerable.

The theory of complex responsive processes particularly focuses attention on the paradoxical nature of organisational life:

- Organising is at the same time intentional and emergent in the interplay of intentions. Intention emerges in local, self-organising processes of conversation while at the same time organising that conversation.
- Conversational patterns in an organisation enable what is being done and at the same time constrain what is done as power relating.
- The performance of complicated tasks requires that they be divided up but at the same time they have to be integrated.
- The same processes of local interaction and emergent population-wide pattern creatively produce new forms while at the same time destroying others. New conversational themes and power relations emerge while older ones are destroyed.
- Themes organising the experience of relating in conversation are both stable and unstable at the same time. They are in control and not in control at the same time.

- The emergence of new themes organising the experience of relating is both predictable and unpredictable at the same time.
- Managers operate in a state of knowing and not knowing at the same time.
- Complex responsive processes organise both conformity and deviance at the same time.

Managing is then a process of continually rearranging the paradoxes of organisational life.

18.5 Refocusing attention: control, performance and improvement

In Chapter 2, I suggested that strategic management is concerned with the phenomena of populations of interacting people undertaking some kind of collective activity in groups in which they interact with people in other groups, including the large groups called 'organisations'. The key question relates to the nature of the processes through which these populations of interacting people evolve over long time periods. I have argued that it is too simple to suggest that they evolve in directions chosen separately by groups of senior executives within each of them. The interaction between them simply makes this impossible. Nor can change in any one group or organisation of people be chosen by groups of other people called 'senior executives'. The complex interactions between groupings of people within and across organisations make this impossible too. I am not arguing that senior executives cannot, do not, or should not make choices. They can, they do, and they should. What I am arguing is that these choices are gestures in an ongoing conversation of gestures evoking responses in the interplay of intentions out of which the evolution of organisations emerges.

What I have been pointing to is a theory of emergent strategy. Strategies emerge, intentions emerge, in the ongoing conversational life of an organisation and in the ongoing conversations between people in different organisations. Strategic management is the process of actively participating in the conversations around important emerging issues. Actual strategic direction is not set in advance but understood in hindsight as it is emerging or after it has emerged. This is because, if small changes can escalate to have enormous consequences, then the distinction between what is strategic and what is, say, tactical becomes very problematic. The distinction can only be identified after the event. Complex responsive processes theory therefore leads to a different conceptualisation of strategy, strategic management and control.

Control

In the systemic theories of organisation reviewed in Part 1, the role of the manager is always thought to be that of formulating the purpose (visions, aims, goals, objectives, performance targets) of the organisation and controlling its movement into the future so as to achieve its purpose. It is recognised that this is difficult and cannot be perfectly achieved, but it is thought that managers nevertheless need to be in control as much as possible, designing and using systems for this purpose. To be 'in control' means to more or less control the movement into the future of the whole organisational system through some kind of monitoring of its progress. Control means ensuring that movement into the future realises or unfolds a future state already enfolded in the present or past as the intention or desire of top managers, or of the democratic intention or desire of organisational members. Control requires organisational members to conform and sustain consensus. The implicit view is that without such control there would be anarchy. Control is ensured through conscious, formal, legitimate decisions based on the assumed possibility of reasonably useful predictions of the future. Some opposites of being 'in control' are taking piecemeal decisions, reacting, not knowing and conflicting. In systemic theories of organisation, effective managers remove the characteristics of 'not in control' so as to avoid 'drifting' or anarchy.

For a long time now, management research has frequently pointed to the messiness of actual decision-making processes in organisations. Chapter 7 referred to Lindblom (1959) who talked about organisational decision making as 'muddling through', whereas March and Olsen (1972) referred to it as 'garbage can' decision making and Mintzberg and Waters (1985) pointed to *both* deliberate *and* emergent strategies in the sense that strategy is sometimes the former and sometimes the latter. It is rare for management theorists, or practitioners for that matter, to think of organisational control in paradoxical terms. Streatfield (2001) explores his own experience of control as a manager at various hierarchical levels in organisations and comes to think about control in paradoxical terms:

> My experience is that of communicatively interacting with others at all times in the known and the unknown at the same time. I would certainly not label what my colleagues and I were doing as 'muddling' or as an inferior kind of 'garbage can' decision making. I have been arguing for a way of thinking about the dynamics of human relating and joint action, that is, the dynamics of organizations, which is essentially paradoxical. This is the paradoxical dynamic of being 'in control' and 'not in control' at the same time. The apparently messy processes of communicative interaction I have been describing are not some second best but, rather, the only way we know of living with paradox. The very dynamics of organizational life call for the kind of complex responsive processes of relating that I have been describing. It is in these processes that the dynamic is created. The processes only appear to be messy and less than competent from the perspective of mainstream thinking about management. From the complex responsive process way of thinking, management skills and competencies lie in how effectively managers participate in those processes. They provide a way of thinking about what competent managers actually do to live effectively in the paradox of organizing. And what they actually do is continue to interact communicatively, especially in the medium of conversation, in spite of not knowing and not being simply 'in control'. (p. 128)

Streatfield argues that instead of collapsing to either the 'in control' or the 'not in control' pole, we can make more sense of the activities of the manager if we understand that organisational life requires living with paradox. Managers are 'in control' and 'not in control' at the same time and they display the courage to continue participating in the making of meaning in paradox. The essential function of managers cannot be to control the paradoxical movement of continuity and transformation, of the known–unknown, because it is impossible for any participant to be in control of it. But this does not simply mean that managers are not in control. Instead, managers are simultaneously 'in control' and 'not in control' in the sense that they intend their next gestures, which are simultaneously evoked by previous responses. There is coherence, which emerges as continuity and potential transformation of identity in the perpetual construction of the future. The distinguishing feature of management is not control but courage to carry on creatively despite not knowing and not being in control, with all the anxiety that this brings.

The central notion of systemic thinking, that of the manager being 'in control', is therefore much more problematic than is usually assumed because managers are both 'in control' and 'not in control' at the same time. The key question then becomes how managers operate effectively and maintain reasonably orderly states of affairs if they are not simply 'in control'. From the perspective of complex responsive processes, it is transiently stable patterns of meaning arising in local interaction that maintain a sense of order and therefore a sense of control as managers go about their daily activities. Intentional goal-oriented acts emerge in the local conversations of managers and those conversations function as patterning, meaning-making processes. These communicative interactions constitute the way in which managers, individually and collectively, maintain their sense of self and their defences against anxiety. An organisation is local processes of interaction in which intention and meaning emerge and anxiety is lived with. These interconnected processes across an organisation generate collective emergent outcomes that cannot be traced back to specific actions. Processes of decision-making, change and performance achievement emerge in the local negotiation of patterns of meaning in which each individual struggles, in participation with others, to maintain a sense of self in an uncertain world.

Streatfield is making it clear that when one understands that organisations are emergent processes of communicative interaction and power relating, one does not conclude that things just happen. Instead, he points to how what happens is due to the detail of what managers as interacting individuals are doing, particularly in their ordinary, everyday conversations with each other. Emphasising the emergent nature of social interaction in no way lessens the accountability and responsibility of the interacting individuals. On the contrary, one can no longer blame a system for what is happening, because what happens is due to the detail of how each of us is interacting with others. Each of us has to take ethical responsibility for what we do despite not knowing or being in control of the outcomes of our actions.

Performance and improvement

A central concern of the dominant discourse on strategy, for practitioners and researchers alike, is with securing at least acceptable organisational performance and with continually improving that performance. The dominant discourse overwhelmingly focuses attention at the macro level on the 'whole' organisation. The concern is with identifying the causes of successful performance and the causes of improvement in order to identify strategies and interventions that will operate on the 'whole' so as to secure success and bring about improvement. The problem is that despite many decades of practice and research, which have produced huge libraries of prescriptions and descriptive writings, the identification of how to consistently secure successful performance eludes us. Yet organisations continue to function – some disappear, others appear – and taken together it all more or less works. Over the past two decades public sector organisations have been subjected to enormous pressure to improve performance. In terms of performance targets there has been some patchy improvement in some sectors but how to secure widespread public sector improvement continues to elude us. And yet it all more or less works.

The theory of complex responsive processes seeks to provide a way of understanding why this is happening and in the course of doing so problematises the way of thinking underlying the dominant discourse. It does so by arguing that generalised/idealised population-wide patterns, imaginatively constructed as 'wholes', emerge in myriad local interactions in which they are made particular and functional. This suggests that the reason why the means of operating directly on the 'whole' to secure performance and make improvements has eluded us is that it is impossible in the first place. Improvement in performance of a 'whole' can only emerge in myriad local interactions.

This in no way amounts to a dismissal of the concern with performance and improvement or to a dismissal of any abstract generalised/idealised statements or policies regarding performance and improvement. Instead it directs attention to the particularising, locally interactive processes in which such generalisations and idealisations are taken up. Performance and improvement are not simply given but, like strategy, are under perpetual construction in the meaning-making activities of local interaction.

18.6 Refocusing attention: research

The difficulty of providing traditional scientific evidence in an uncertain world calls for a different approach to research method.

Research on an evidence base

In Chapter 8 I reviewed the literature on an evidence base for the success of the prescriptions described in Part 1 of this book and concluded that there is no comprehensive, reliable scientific evidence base to support them. I want to argue now that the analysis of human interaction in organisations as complex responsive processes, to be found in previous chapters of this Part 3, provides the reasons for this failure to establish an evidence base. The very notion of empirical evidence in the traditional scientific method is based on a particular understanding of causality as efficient causality having the structure of 'if x . . . then y'. Thus, in Newton's laws of motion there is a cause, force applied to an object, and an effect, movement of the object. The relationship between the cause and the effect is linear – that is, proportional – so that *if*, in a vacuum, the force is doubled *then* the object moves twice as far. Such causal relationships are ahistorical; they are generalisations which apply at all times in all places. In other words, time and context are irrelevant. Empirical evidence is then provided by an accumulation of measurements and, if they fail to falsify the prediction, the causal connection is taken to be a law of nature. However, in research on organisations and their management, indeed in research on all human action, the empirical evidence provided usually takes the form of identifying a statistical association between one thing and another, say, between winning a prize for TQM systems and higher profitability. But a statistical association does not 'prove' a causal link. Perhaps prizes are won because higher profits make it possible for organisations to fund expensive TQM systems, not the other way around. Chapter 10 in Part 2 of this book provides a brief summary of the development since the 1950s of what have come to be called the 'complexity sciences' where relationships between variables are nonlinear rather than linear so that the relationships are historical and therefore time and context dependent – in fact, events are in some important sense unique and repetitive at the same time – the fractal quality of regular irregularity. This makes the standard method of accumulating evidence highly problematic, because that standard method is based on the assumption of simply repetitive events. Evidence is accumulated by observing repetitions in traditional science but rather different notions of evidence need to be developed for the complexity sciences.

All of the research into an evidence base, summarised in Chapter 8, looked for links between a management action and some successful outcome and most also made the assumption that relationships are linear. In studies of the learning organisation, nonlinear causality was assumed but then collapsed into linear relationships between a leverage point and an outcome. In the end all the research into an evidence base implied linear causality. However, if we develop explanations of organisational life that are informed by the complexity sciences, as Part 3 of this book does, then evidence would have to be based on nonlinear, that is, non-proportional, relationships between variables, where time and context are extremely important in understanding the relationship between one variable and another. Any evidence provided will then depend on the time period selected and the place in which the events are occurring as well as other aspects of context. It follows that any relationship anyone identifies between a management action and an outcome could have far more to do with a particular time period and place where the sample is selected than anything else. Evidence will always be very temporary and highly contested, particularly when other difficulties are added. Defining what performance, success and improvement all mean is very difficult and always reflects the ideology of the definer.

In a linear world of equilibrium and predictability the sparse research into an evidence base for management prescriptions and the confused findings it produces would be a sign of incompetence; it would not make much sense. But if organisations are actually patterns of nonlinear interaction between people; if small changes could produce widespread major consequences; if local interaction produces emergent global pattern; then it will not be possible to provide a reliable evidence base. In such a world it makes no sense to conduct studies looking for simple causal relationships between an action and an outcome. The chapters of Part 3 present arguments that human action is nonlinear, that time and place matter a great deal, and that since this precludes simple evidence bases we do need to rethink the nature of organisations and the roles of managers and leaders in them.

Method of researching organisations and management

The complex responsive processes way of understanding life in organisations has implications for appropriate methods of research in management and leadership. The emphasis on participation in local interactions raises fundamental questions about objectivity in social research and focuses our attention much more clearly on the subjective nature of experience in organisations. The method of research then becomes that of making sense of one's own experience. The method is that of taking one's experience seriously with the aim of reflexively exploring the complex responsive processes of human relating. Experience is the experience of local interaction and this immediately suggests that organisations need to be understood in terms of the experience of their members and others with whom those members interact. From the perspective of complex responsive processes, the appropriate method for understanding, for researching into, organisations is itself complex responsive processes. Research itself is also complex responsive processes and the research method becomes reflection on ordinary, everyday experience. Experience is felt, meaningful engagement in relating to others and to oneself as we do whatever we come together to do. Experience refers to interdependence, to the social, as the fundamental human reality. Since such interaction between living bodies is patterned primarily as narrative themes, taking one's experience seriously is the activity of articulating and reflecting upon these themes. In other words, the method is that of giving an account, telling the story, of what I think and feel that I and others are doing in our interaction with each other in particular contexts over particular periods of time and what sense we are together making of the much wider emergent patterns across populations. Since what I and we are doing is inseparable from who I am and who we are, a meaningful narrative is also always expressing, that is, iterating or co-creating, individual and collective identities. Taking one's experience seriously, through articulating the narrative themes organising the experience of being together, is an essentially reflexive activity and in its fullest sense this is a simultaneously individual and social process, including the social patterns that are much wider than our own immediate interaction.

It is the explicitly reflexive nature of the narrative that distinguishes it as a research method from the literary story. The research narrative is explicit and ordinary, as opposed to the poetic license of the literary story, which has the potential for drawing attention to the epic nature of human experience or simply describing imaginative fantasy. The narrative as research method is reflexive in an individual sense insofar as the narrator is making explicit the way of thinking that he or she is reflecting in the construction of the story. In other words, the reflexive personal narrative is explaining why it has the particular focus it has and how the narrator's past experience is shaping the selection of events and their interpretation. The narrator is making explicit, as far as possible, the assumptions being made and the ideology being reflected, in explicating the particular meaning being put forward in the narrative. At the same time, the narrative as research method is no less import-antly reflexive in a social sense. Social reflexivity requires the narrator to explicitly locate his or her way of thinking about the story being told in the traditions of thought of his or her society, differentiating between these traditions in a critically aware manner. In other words, the narrator as researcher engages intensively with literature relevant to his or her particular narrative accounts and makes explicit the ideological underpinnings and power relation implications. The literary story leaves interpretation of meaning largely to the reader while the narrative method of research rigorously sets out the writer's interpretations and assumptions.

There are three important questions which must be addressed by any research method and these relate to ideology, ethics and validity or legitimacy. The ideology of the complex responsive processes research method will be addressed below. The use of narratives of personal experience of interaction with others raises important ethical questions. The first matter has to do with writing about people one is interacting with and the related issue of disclosing confidential material. In a more conventional approach, involving say interviews, the ethical approach is usually to inform those one is writing about of what one is doing and then show them what one has written, concealing identities as appropriate. However, a researcher writing about his or her own personal experience of his everyday work activities can hardly keep informing people that he might possibly write about what they are doing together. The best that can be done is to inform colleagues in general about what one is doing and then write about the experience in a way that does not reveal their identities but still presents a 'reliable' account of what is going on. Other than this, there is no general ethical rule to guide the researcher in the traditional sense of thought before action. Consistent with the complex responsive processes approach, the ethics of what one does as a researcher, as with what one does in all other situations, is contingent upon the situation and the emerging and ongoing negotiation with those with whom one is interacting. The second ethical matter has to do with inviting people to undertake a form of research that can carry with it considerable risks. The risks are potentially hostile responses from others one is writing about and the threats that what is written might present to existing power relations and one's own job security. Here again, there can be no general ethical rule, only the contingent negotiation of how to proceed in particular situations so that the research work does not create undue risks for the researcher. Finally, there is the matter of validity or legitimacy. Clearly, there can be no objective validity for the obvious reason that the research is an interpretation, a subjective reflection on personal experience. However, it is not any arbitrary account in that it must make sense to others, resonate with the experience of others and be persuasive to them. Furthermore, it must be justifiable in terms of a wider tradition of thought that the community being addressed finds persuasive, or at least plausible. The value of this kind of research, we would claim, is that it presents accounts of what people actually experience in their organisational practice with all its uncertainty, emotion and messiness, rather than highly rational, decontextualised accounts and their hindsight view.

The reflexive, reflective approach I have been describing as a research method is much more than 'simply research'. It is also an indication of how leader-managers might conceive of themselves as 'researchers' using this method to explore who they are and what they are doing together as well as who they wish to become and what they would like to do together. The approach is not simply research because at the same time it is the exploration of the fundamental questions of strategy – the strategic exploration of identity.

If one takes the view that knowledge emerges and evolves in a *history* of social interaction, rather than being developed by an autonomous individual, then one attaches central importance to research as a participative, social process. Research on organisations is then done by participating in a community of researchers who are together exploring the meaning they are making of their experience. This inevitably involves conflict as people explore their differences and, indeed, this conflict is essential for the movement of thought. Research proceeds by researchers engaging in argument around difference, feeling themselves compelled to justify the perspective they take in its difference from other perspectives. Research, from this perspective, is not an activity which is separate from practice, because the reflective practitioner is, on the view so far presented, inevitably also a researcher in that both are engaged in reflecting upon their own experience. It follows that research is closely linked to the iteration and possible transformation of identity. This is because identity is the answer to the questions: who am I? Who are we? What am I doing? What are we doing? What is going on? How do we now go on together? Effective research is potentially transformative of identity and is therefore bound to expose vulnerability and raise existential anxiety with all the emotion this brings with it.

What I have been saying has focused attention on research as an activity of the researcher making sense of his or her own experience of local interactions. However, researchers can and do focus on interactions of others at a distance, often concerned with population-wide patterns and second-order abstractions from them. I am not trying to suggest that this is an invalid or inferior form of research. Clearly, it is not, just as macro policy is not rendered invalid or inferior to local interaction. What is being suggested, though, is that even when concerned with the second order abstractions of population-wide patterns, the activities of the researcher are, nevertheless, reflexive engagement in the local interactions of some research community.

The status of knowledge on organisation and management

In Chapter 8 I argued that organisation and management studies do not constitute a science in anything like the same way as the natural sciences, despite frequent claims that they do. The reason they cannot be sciences in the natural science sense is that the propositions and prescriptions of management and organisations studies are not backed up by anything like the rigorous evidence base demanded by a strict view of what a science is. In the last section of this chapter, I gave reasons for claiming that there never can be an evidence base for management and organisational prescriptions. However, if this is the case then what status does knowledge about organisations and their management have? Are the propositions and prescriptions simply rhetoric? Are they mainly social defences against the anxiety of not knowing and not being in control (*see* Chapter 6)? Is knowledge about organisations and their management better described as philosophy, hermeneutics, phenomenology, judgement or, intuition? Or is it simply magical-mythical, even quasi-religious thinking? Is organisation largely unconscious habitus, and management simply mindless immersion in the game? Or as I have been arguing in this chapter so far, is managing both immersing in the game and at the same time potentially a form of reflection, of reflexive knowing? Is it narrative rather than propositional knowledge? These questions have given rise to a very large literature stretching back a long time.

One way of dealing with these questions, adopted by a number of authors (for example Chia and Holt, 2009), is to draw on Aristotle's distinctions between:

- *episteme* which is the abstract, generalisable, universal knowledge that can be written and recorded. This is theoretical knowledge which does not necessarily have any practical impact;
- *techne* which is the knowledge associated with making something, possessed by a competent expert. This knowledge is the source of purposeful interventions to

change and shape the world. *Techne* is a form of *poiesis*, productive knowledge which produces outcomes;

- *phronesis* which is associated with *praxis* rather than poiesis where praxis is the conduct of one's life as a citizen of the *polis* or state. Phronesis is activity that is an end in itself and may leave no outcome – it refers to the striving of a person. Praxis draws the self into action in which it is absorbed and is inseparable from the person. It is not so much a form of knowing as a resourcefulness of mind in responding to unique situations. It is not consciously acquired but arises in action to realise itself. It is the act of immersed action and is purposive arising from internalised tendencies brought about by socialisation. When acting purposively one cannot do other than what one is doing while acting purposefully is acting according to a choice. Phronesis is an internalised disposition to act;

- *métis* which is a form of unreflective, practical knowing which combines intuition and a sense of opportunism, a cunning way of knowing. It is an internalised mindless coping.

Some writers, such as Chia and Holt (2009) take knowledge of organisational and management to be mainly of the *phronesis* and métis kinds, while most in the dominant discourse implicitly view it as *episteme* and/or *techne*. The theory of complex responsive processes seeks to understand how knowledge about organisations and management is created in the ordinary politics of everyday organisational life in which they negotiate what to do next, and in the course of which they co-create knowledge in all the forms listed above which serve the purposes of rhetoric, defences against anxiety, rational choices, propaganda and many more.

18.7 Rethinking the roles of leaders and managers

In refocusing attention on different aspects of strategy, change, control, performance, improvement and management research, the theory of complex responsive processes inevitably leads to a major rethinking of the roles of managers and leaders in organisations.

From a complex responsive processes perspective, leaders and managers are particularly influential players in the organisational game of strategic management, the game being that of the ordinary politics of everyday life in organisations. Leaders are even more involved in this local, ordinary politics of organisational life than anyone else and their actions are usually more influential than those of others involved. One of the most powerful ways in which they exert this influence is to make present to others abstract articulations of desired strategies, desired futures, in the form of goals, visions and missions, for example. In other words, they choose articulations of desired strategies. Such political activities include planning, goal setting, envisioning and all the other activities which command the attention of the dominant discourse. However, these activities are now understood as activities of second-order abstraction (*see* Chapter 16) in which leaders and managers design procedures, plans, visions, maps and models aimed at making local interactions legible from the centre. However, this activity is essentially one of simplification, and what happens depends just as much on how the simplifications are taken up in local interaction, which continues to remain illegible from the centre. The result is highly limited but very important forms of control from the centre. In carrying out these activities leaders and managers, now understood as much the same activities, they are participating with everyone else in important processes of identity formation; they are actors in the emerging identity narrative of their organisation. Fundamentally, leading and managing are social interactions of mutual recognition.

In their participation in the process of conversation, power relating and ideologically based intentions, managers and leaders are gesturing and responding to each other according to their own historically evolved capacity to respond. They are enabled to respond in certain ways and constrained from responding in others by that capacity, which has emerged from their histories of interacting with others in which social objects have become aspects of their very selves. Some agents will have developed wider-ranging capacities for taking the attitude of others and of the social object than others. Some will have evolved capacities that enable them to respond more effectively and more successfully than others do. In organisational terms, some members will have more knowledge and more understanding than others and so the power ratio will be tilted toward them. Some agents interact with more agents than others. Some are able to stand back and understand something of the larger processes in which they are participating, which does not mean that they are stepping outside those processes and understanding them from the perspective of the objective observer. Instead they are reflecting, as participants, on the nature of what is happening in the situations in which they are participating. They are in effect researching their own experiences. Managers and leaders can usefully be thought of as organisational researchers.

Managers and leaders occupy powerful roles at the top of legitimate organisational hierarchies which involve allocating resources and in so doing they both enable and constrain other members of the organisation. They design sets of procedures and hierarchical reporting structures but always in local interactions in which they are responding to what has just been happening. They legitimise some actions and not others. They gesture to very large numbers of others. They make statements about visions and missions. They make decisions and take actions that greatly affect a great many others. What they cannot do, however, is programme the responses those others will make. They cannot control the interplay of intentions. The powerful may identify what kind of responses they would like by making statements about values and required cultures and behaviours. They may try to motivate others to adopt all of this. They may have desires and dreams. However, people will still only be able to respond according to their own local capacities to respond and the most powerful will find that they have to respond to the responses that they have evoked and provoked.

From a complex responsive processes perspective, no one can determine the dynamic of interaction within an organisation because that dynamic depends upon what others both within that organisation and in other organisations are doing. In other words, an individual, or a group of individuals, powerful or otherwise, can make gestures of great importance, but the responses called forth will occur in local situations in the living present and from these there will emerge the population-wide patterns of strategic activity that perpetually constructs an organisation's future. Instead of taking it for granted that powerful chief executives actually individually change organisations directly through their intended actions, the complex responsive processes perspective focuses attention on the communicative processes in which the mere presence of, the images of and the fantasies about leaders all affect local processes of communicative interaction in the living present from which emerge the population-wide patterns that are organisations. Emergence, then, has very little, if anything at all, to do with chance. No one can shape, influence or condition emergence. Those who emerge as leaders are those who display a greater spontaneity and have a greater ability to deal with the ongoing purpose or task for which others are interacting. The leader is an individual who is able to enter into the attitudes of others, so enhancing connection and interaction between group members. This notion of a leader does not simply locate leadership in the individual by ascribing leadership purely to the personal attributes of the leader. This is because the leader is actually constructed in the recognition of others. It does not matter what leadership attributes one has if no one recognises them. And, of course, one cannot be a leader if one does not recognise the recognition of others and so recognise them. Leaders, therefore, emerge in complex responsive processes of mutual recognition.

Managing and leading are inevitably and intimately connected to ethics. For the dominant discourse, the ethics of leadership is a matter of explicating the rules or qualities of the harmonious organisational whole and of individuals conforming to it. As a result, people experience themselves as the victims of the systems they think they have created. The theory of complex responsive processes of relating provides an alternative way of thinking about leadership and ethics in which the ethics of action are processes of perpetual negotiation that depend upon personal desires, aims and aspirations as well as natural contingencies. What each of us does matters even though we cannot know what the outcome of our actions will be and because we cannot know we are morally required to give account of our actions to others. This applies no less to managers and leaders than to the rest of us. Instead of leading us to feel hopeless, victimised or rebellious, this perception encourages us to pay attention to what we are doing and to believe that this is effective in some way, even though we cannot know how. Managing and leading are exercises in the courage to go on participating creatively despite not knowing.

There are strong tendencies for a group to idealise the leader, who thereby becomes a cult leader – that is, leader of a group of people directly enacting idealised values, cult values, to which they are subtly pressured to conform. This blocks the functionalising of the ideals, which is what an organisation needs in order to come alive in the present. However, leaders often do not recognise this process of idealisation and are often not prepared for the denigration which will inevitably follow. Leaders are often not aware of the powerful roles they come to play in the fantasy lives of others. Followers project their dependence needs, reflecting core conflict in their lives, on to leaders and displace their own ideals, wishes and desires on to them too. Leaders do this just as others do, the difference being that they project their inner conflicts on to a much larger real-world stage that includes their followers. Leaders and followers join each other in scenarios that are the basis of imagined, desired and feared relationships between them. Rather than the myth of the heroic, well-balanced hero of the dominant discourse, we come to recognise what we experience of leaders who do not function very well and quite often they are definitely dysfunctional. Such dysfunctional leadership has not attracted very much attention in most of the management literature, but it occurs frequently and it is therefore a matter of importance to understand something about it. Functional leaders assist in the containment of anxiety and thus help to create the possibility of learning, but dysfunctional, neurotic leaders may well become caught up, and drive others to become caught up, in neurotic defences that will block such learning.

18.8 Summary

Systemic theories of organisation see strategy as the usually rational choice or intention of some or all of the members of an organisation and the intentional overcoming of obstacles to the implementation of such choices. The psychoanalytic approach pays particular attention to how irrational processes might interfere with this choice or intention. Intention is understood as the choice, or design, made by autonomous individuals, usually taking the position of the independent observer. The criteria for the choice focus on desired, predetermined outcomes.

The complex responsive processes perspective makes a substantial move in a number of ways. First, it directs attention to how intention emerges in local interaction taking the form of ordinary conversation between people. This replaces the notion that intention is the expression of an autonomous individual who reflects and makes choices in the light of expected outcomes, as it were, after consulting with others. So, the first move is to focus on how intention emerges rather than on what it is. The second move is to focus attention on how the irremovable interdependence of people involves the interplay of intentions and it is from this interplay that organisations evolve. The third move is to focus attention on diversity and how the amplification of differences is the process of change. Novel intention initially emerges in the tension between legitimate and shadow themes organising the experience of being together: that is, in ordinary conversations at the margins of the organisation. The fourth move is to understand the role of the abstract maps and models of strategy in a different way – namely, as generalised gestures that will evoke many local responses and as social objects that will be made particular in many, many local situations. The result is that the interplay of intentions and deliberate designs produces emergent patterns, many of which are unexpected and often unwanted. We come to in a different way the contributions that processes of reasoning and modelling can make to thinking about strategy from a complex responsive processes point of view. The fifth move is to think differently about management leadership as a fundamentally social process of mutual recognition. Managers and leaders participate in very influential ways in the interplay of intentions in which strategies emerge but they cannot determine what will emerge.

Further reading

Further material on research methods can be found in Stacey and Griffin (2005); Steier (1991); Alvesson and Skoldberg, K. (2000); and Denzin and Lincoln (2005). Streatfield (2001) is useful to read on the question of control. Stacey (2005, 2009) and Mowles (2007;

2008a and b) give a more detailed discussion of some of the key topics in this chapter. Donaldson (2005) writes about the technology of writing. Sarra (2006) discuses the emotional experience of performance management in the health sector. Williams (2006) discusses the experience of leading public sector organisations in a performance management regime. Alvesson and Sveningsson (2003b) write about the drawbacks of modern concepts of leadership. Norman (2006) describes the experience of clinical risk assessment in the health sector. Williams (2005) discusses narrative methodology. Mowles (2008c, 2010a, 2010b) looks at questions of evidence, practice and the contribution to practice of the complex responsive processes perspective.

Questions to aid further reflection

1. Does taking a complex responsive processes perspective amount to a call for a new kind of organisation?

2. Does the emphasis on widening and deepening conversation, on relationships, mean that people should bring to awareness what they think is going on between them? In other words does it lead to a prescription for managers to spend time discussing their own group dynamics and bringing everything out into the open?

3. Does the emphasis on ordinary conversation lead to the need to develop good conversations?

4. Does the emphasis on relationships amount to a prescription for managers to develop good relationships and pay more attention to the greater good?

5. Are organisations real and can they have an identity?

6. What happens to the emphasis placed on the 'task' by many other perspectives, if one takes the perspective of complex responsive processes?

7. What is wrong with thinking in systems terms?

8. Is emergence a matter of fate?

9. What are the applications of complex responsive processes theory and what is practical about it? Is it blindingly obvious?

10. How does intention feature in the theory of complex responsive processes?

11. Does the theory of complex responsive processes amount to an ideology inviting the formation of a cult?

12. What role does modelling play in strategising?

13. What are the implications for research method and how do they differ from other ways of doing qualitative research?

References

A

Abernathy, W. J. and Hayes, R. (1980), 'Managing our Way to Economic Decline', *Harvard Business Review*, July–August, 67–77.

Abraham, F. D. (1995), *Chaos Theory in Psychology*, Westport, CT: Praeger.

Abram, D. (1996), *The Spell of the Sensuous*, New York: Vintage Books.

Ackoff, R. L. (1981), *Creating the Corporate Future*, New York: Wiley.

Ackoff, R. L. (1994), *The Democratic Organization*, New York: Oxford University Press.

Akhavein, J. D., Berger, A. N. and Humphrey, D. B. (1997), 'The Effects of Megamergers on Efficiency and Prices: Evidence from a bank profit function', *Review of Industrial Organization*, 12(1), 95–139.

Aldrich, H. (1979), *Organizations and Environments*, Englewood Cliffs, NJ: Prentice-Hall.

Alexander, S. (1920), *Space, Time and Deity* (Two Volumes), London: Macmillan.

Allen, P. M. (1998a), 'Evolving complexity in social science', in Altman, G. and Koch, W. A. (eds), *Systems: New Paradigms for the Human Sciences*, New York: Walter de Gruyter.

Allen, P. M. (1998b), 'Modelling complex economic evolution', in Schweitzer, F. and Silverberg, G. (eds), *Selbstorganisation*, Berlin: Duncker & Humblot.

Allen, P. M., Strathern, M. and Baldwin, J. S. (2005), 'Complexity of social economic systems: the inevitability of uncertainty and surprise', in McDaniel Jr., R. R. and Driebe, D. J. (eds), *Uncertainty and Surprise in Complex Systems: Questions on Working with the Unexpected*, Heidelberg: Springer.

Allen, P. M., Strathern, M. and Baldwin, J. S. (2006), 'Evolutionary drive: new understandings of change in socio-economic systems', *Emergence: Complexity and Organization*, vol. 8, no. 2.

Alvesson, M. and Skoldberg, K. (2000), *Reflexive Methodology: New Vistas for Qualitative research*, London: Sage.

Alvesson, M. and Karreman, D. (2000a), 'Taking the linguistic turn in organizational research: Challenges, responses, consequences', *Journal of Applied Behavioral Science*, 36, 2, pp. 136–59.

Alvesson, M. and Karreman, D. (2000b), 'Varieties of discourse: On the study of organizations through discourse analysis', *Human Relations*, 53, 9, pp. 1125–49.

Alvesson, M. and Skoldberg, K. (2000), *Reflexive Methodology: New Vistas for Qualitative Research*, Sage: London.

Alvesson, M. and Karreman, D. (2001), 'Odd Couple: Making Sense of the Curious Concept of Knowledge Management', *Journal of Management Studies*, 38, 7, 995–1018.

Alvesson, M. and Sveningsson, S. (2003a), 'Good Visions, Bad Micro-management and Ugly Ambiguity: Contradictions of (Non-)Leadership in a Knowledge-intensive Organization', *Organization Studies*, 24, 6, 961–88.

Alvesson, M. and Sveningsson, S. (2003b), 'Managers Doing Leadership: The Extra-Ordinarization of the Mundane', *Human Relations*, 56, 12, 1435–69.

Ameriks, K. (ed.) (2002), *The Cambridge Companion to German Idealism*, Cambridge: Cambridge University Press.

Amihud, Y. and Miller, G. (1998), *Bank Mergers & Acquisitions*, Amsterdam: Kluwer Academic Publishers.

Andersen, E. S., Grude, K. V. and Haug, T. (1995), *Goal Directed Project Management: Effective Techniques and Strategies*, 2nd edition, London: Kogan Page.

Anderson, C. and McMillan, E. (2003), 'Of Ants and men: self organized Teams in Human and Insect Organizations', *Emergence*, 5(2), 29–41.

Anderson, P. (1999), 'Application of Complexity Theory to Organization Science', *Organization Science*, 10(3), 216–32.

Anderson, P. W., Arrow, K. J. and Pines, D. (1988), *The Economy as an Evolving Complex System*, Menlo Park, CA: Addison-Wesley.

Andrade, G., Mitchell, M. L. and Stafford, E. (2001), 'New Evidence and Perspectives on Mergers', *Harvard Business School Working Paper*, no. 01–070.

Andre, P., Kooli, M. and L'Her, J. (2004), 'The Long-Run Performance of Mergers and Acquisitions: Evidence from the Canadian stock market', *Financial Management*, 33(4), 15–25.

Andrews, K. R. ([1971] 1987), *The Concept of Corporate Strategy*, Homewood, IL: Irwin.

Ansoff, H. I. (1991), 'Critique of Henry Mintzberg's "The Design School: Reconsidering the Basic Premises of Strategic Management" ', *Strategic Management Journal*, 12, 171–95.

Ansoff, I. (1965), *Corporate Strategy*, New York: McGraw-Hill.

Ansoff, I. (1990), *Implanting Corporate Strategy*, Hemel Hempstead: Prentice Hall.

Aram, E. (2001), 'The experience of complexity: learning as the potential transformation of identity', unpublished PhD thesis, University of Hertfordshire, UK.

Argyris, C. (1990), *Overcoming Organizational Defenses: Facilitating Organizational Learning*, Boston: Allyn & Bacon.

Argyris, C. and Schön, D. (1978), *Organizational Learning: A Theory of Action Perspective*, Reading, MA: Addison-Wesley.

Armstrong, J. S. (1982), 'The value of formal planning for strategic decisions: Review of empirical research', *Strategic Management Journal*, 3(3), 197–211.

Ashby, W. R. (1945), 'The effect of controls on stability', *Natura*, vol. 155, pp. 242–3.

Ashby, W. R. (1952), *Design for a Brain*, New York: Wiley.

Ashby, W. R. (1956), *Introduction to Cybernetics*, New York: Wiley.

Ashforth, B. E. and Mael, F. (1989), 'Social identity theory and the organization', *Academy of Management Review*, 14, 20–39.

Ashmos, D. P., Duchon, D., McDaniel, R. R. and Huonker, J. W. (2002), 'What a Mess! Participation as a Simple Managerial rule to "Complexify" Organizations', *Journal of Management Studies*, 39(2), 189–206.

Axelrod, R. and Cohen, M. D. (1999), *Harnessing Complexity: Organizational Implications of a Scientific Frontier*, New York: The Free Press.

B

Bacharach, S. B. and Lawler, E. J. (1980), *Power and Politics in Organizations*, San Francisco: Jossey-Bass.

Baddeley, A. (1990), *Human Memory: Theory and Practice*, Hove, Sussex: Lawrence Erlbaum Associates.

Baets, W. (1999), *A Collection of Essays on Complexity and Management*, London: World Scientific Publishing Co.

Bales, R. F. (1970), *Personality and Interpersonal Behavior*, New York: Holt.

Balogon, J., Huff, A. S. and Johnson, P. (2003), 'Three responses to the methodological challenges of studying strategizing', *Journal of Management Studies*, vol. 40, no. 1, pp. 198–224.

Barnard, C. I. (1948), *Organization and Management: Selected Papers*, Cambridge, MA: Harvard University Press.

Barney, J. B. (1991), 'Firm resources and sustained competitive advantage', *Journal of Management*, vol. 17, no. 1, pp. 99–120.

Barr, P. S., Stimpert, J. L. and Huff, A. S. (1992), 'Cognitive change, strategic action and organizational renewal', *Strategic Management Journal*, vol. 13, Special Issue, Summer, pp. 15–36.

Bateman, A., Brown, D. and Pedder, J. (2000), *Introduction to Psychotherapy: An Outline of Psychodynamic Principles and Practice*, 3rd edition, London: Routledge.

Bateson, G. (1972), *Steps to an Ecology of Mind*, New York: Ballantine Books.

Baumol, W. J. and Benhabib, J. (1989), 'Chaos: significance, mechanism and economic applications', *Journal of Economic Perspectives*, Winter, vol. 3, no. 1, pp. 77–105.

Beer, S. ([1959] 1967), *Cybernetics and Management*, London: English Universities Press.

Beer, S. (1966), *Decision and Control: The Meaning of Operational Research and Management Cybernetics*, London: Wiley.

Beer, S. (1979), *The Heart of the Enterprise*, Chichester: Wiley.

Beer, S. (1981), *The Brain of the Firm*, Chichester: Wiley.

Beinhocker, E. D. (2006), *The origin of Wealth: Evolution, Complexity and the Radical Remaking of Economics*, Harvard: Harvard Business School Press.

Belbin, R. M. (1981), *Management Teams: Why They Succeed or Fail*, Oxford: Heinemann.

Bertalanffy, L. von (1968), *General Systems Theory: Foundations, Development, Applications*, New York: George Braziller.

Bhaktin, M. M. (1986), *Speech Genres and Other Late Essays*, Austin, Texas: University of Texas Press.

Billing, S. (2008), 'The role of propaganda in managing organizational change: ethics, conflict and compromise in consulting', in Stacey, R. and Griffin, D. (eds), *Complexity and the experience of values, conflict and compromise in organizations*, London: Routledge.

Bion, W. (1961), *Experiences in Groups and Other Papers*, London: Tavistock.

BMA (2004), 'Briefing: measuring performance in the national health service'. Available online at: http://www.bma.org.uk.ap.nsf/content/measureper.

Boden, D. (1994), *The Business of Talk: Organizations in Action*, Cambridge: Polity Press.

Boden, M. A. (ed.) (1996), *The Philosophy of Artificial Life*, Oxford: Oxford University Press.

Bogner, W. C. and Thomas, H. (1993), 'The role of competitive groups in strategic formulation: a dynamic integration of two competing models', *Journal of Management Studies*, vol. 30, no. 1, pp. 51–67.

Bohm, D. (1965), *The Special Theory of Relativity*, New York: W. A. Benjamin.

Bohm, D. (1983), *Wholeness and the Implicate Order*, New York: Harper & Row.

Bohm, D. and Peat, F. D. (1989), *Science, Order and Creativity*, London: Routledge.

Boisot, M. (2000), 'Is There a Complexity Beyond the Reach of Strategy?', *Emergence, Complexity & Organization*, 2(1), 114–34.

Boje, D. M. (1991), 'The storytelling organization: a study of performance in an office supply firm', *Administrative Science Quarterly*, 36, 106–26.

Boje, D. M. (1994), 'Organizational storytelling: the struggle of pre-modern, modern and postmodern organizational learning discourses', *Management Learning*, 25(3), 433–62.

Boje, D. M. (1995), 'Stories of the storytelling organization: a postmodern analysis of Disney as Tamara-Land', *Academy of Management Journal*, 38(4), 997–1055.

Bolman, L. and Deal, T. (1997), *Reframing Organizations*, 2nd edition, San Francisco: Jossey-Bass.

Booker, C. (2009), *The Real Global Warming Disaster*, London: Continuum.

Borgatta, E. F., Couch, A. S. and Bales, R. F. (1954), 'Some findings relevant to the great man theory of leadership', *American Sociology Review*, vol. 19, pp. 755–9.

Boulding, K. E. (1956), 'General systems theory: the skeleton of science', *Management Science*, vol. 2, pp. 97–108.

Bourdieu, P. (1998), *Practical reason: On the Theory of Action*, Cambridge: Polity Press.

Boyne, A. G. and Walker, R. M. (2002), 'Total Quality Management and Performance: An Evaluation of the Evidence and Lessons for Research on Public Organizations', *Public Performance and Management Review*, 26(2), 111–30.

Braverman, H. (1974), *Labor and Monopoly Capitalism*, New York: Monthly Review Press.

Brews, P. J. and Hunt, M. R. (1999), 'Learning to plan and planning to learn: resolving the planning school/learning school debate', *Strategic Management Journal*, 20(10), 889–913.

Briggs, J. and Peat, F. (1989), *The Turbulent Mirror*, New York: Harper & Row.

Broad, C. D. (1925), *The Mind and its Place in Nature*, London: Routledge and Kegan Paul.

Brown, J. K., Sands, S. S. and Thompson, G. C. (1969), 'Long-Range Planning in the USA: N.I.C.B. Survey', *Long Range Planning*, March, 44–51.

Brown, J. S. (1991), 'Research that reinvents the corporation', *Harvard Business Review*, vol. 69, January–February, pp. 102–11.

Brown, J. S. and Duguid, P. (1991), 'Organizational learning and communities-of-practice: toward a unified view of working, learning and innovation', *Organization Science*, vol. 2, no. 1, pp. 40–56.

Brown, J. S. and Duguid, P. (2001), 'Knowledge and organization: a social practice perspective', *Organization Science*, vol. 12, no. 2, pp. 198–215.

Brown, S. L. and Eisenhardt, K. (1998), *Competing on the Edge: Strategy as Structured Chaos*, Boston, MA: Harvard Business School Press.

Brundin, E. (2002), *Emotions in Motion: The Strategic Leader in a Radical Change Process*, JIBS Dissertation Series No. 12, Jonkoping International Business School.

Brundin, E. and Melin, L. (2003), 'Unfolding the dynamics of emotions in strategizing: how emotion drives or counteracts change activities', *EGOS Colloquium 2003*.

Bruner, J. S. (1986), *Actual Minds, Possible Worlds*, Cambridge, MA: Harvard University Press.

Bruner, J. S. (1990), *Acts of Meaning*, Cambridge, MA: Harvard University Press.

Burawoy, M. (1979), *Manufacturing Consent*, Chicago: Chicago University Press.

Burgelman, R. A. (1991), 'Intraorganizational ecology of strategy making and organizational adaptation: theory and field research', *Organization Science*, vol. 2, no. 3, pp. 239–62.

Burgelman, R. A. and Grove, A. S. (2007), 'Let Chaos Reign, then Rein in Chaos – Repeatedly: Managing Strategic Dynamics for Corporate Longevity', Stanford University Graduate School of Business Research, Paper No. 1954, 28, 965–79.

Burke, R. (1999), *Project Management: Planning and Control Techniques*, 3rd edition, New York: Wiley.

Burke, W. W. (2008/1982), *Organization change: The Theory and Practice*, Thousand islands, CA: Sage Publications Inc.

Burkitt, I. (1991), *Social Selves: Theories of the Social Formation of Personality*, London: Sage.

Burton-Jones, A. (1999), *Knowledge Capitalism: Business, Work and Learning in the New Economy*, Oxford: Oxford University Press.

C

Callon, M. and Latour, B. (1981), 'Unscrewing the big Leviathan: how actors macrostructure reality and how sociologists help them to do so', in Knorr-Cetina, K. and Cicourel, V. (eds), *Advances in Social Theory and Methodology: Toward an Integration of Micro- and Macro-Sociologies*, Boston, MA: Routledge & Kegan Paul.

Campbell, A. and Tawady, K. (1990), *Mission and Business Philosophy: Winning Employee Commitment*, Oxford: Heinemann.

Campbell-Hunt, C. (2000), 'What have we learned about generic competitive strategy? A meta analysis', *Strategic Management Journal*, 21(2), 127–54.

Campbell-Hunt, C. (2007), 'Complexity in practice', *Human Relations*, 60(5), 793–823.

Carlisle, Y. and McMillan, E. (2006), 'Innovation in Organizations from a Complex Adaptive Systems Perspective', *Emergence, Complexity & Organization*, 8(1), 2–9.

Cartwright, S. and Cooper, C. L. (1996), *Managing Mergers, Acquisitions and Strategic Alliances: Integrating People and Cultures*, London: Butterworth-Heinemann.

Casti, J. (1994), *Complexification: Explaining a Paradoxical World through the Science of Surprise*, London: HarperCollins.

Caudron, S. (1998), 'Diversity', *Watch*, 29(2), 91–4.

Chakravarthy, B. S. and Doz, Y. (1992), 'Strategy process research: focusing on corporate self-renewal', *Strategic Management Journal*, vol. 13, Special Issue, pp. 5–15.

Chandler, A. D. (1962), *Strategy and Structure: Chapter in the History of Industrial Enterprise*, Cambridge, MA: MIT Press.

Checkland, P. B. (1981), *Systems Thinking, Systems Practice*, Chichester: Wiley.

Checkland, P. B. (1983), 'OR and the systems movement: mapping and conflicts', *Journal of the Operational Research Society*, vol. 34, p. 661.

Checkland, P. B. and Holwell, S. (1998), *Information, Systems and Information Systems*, Chichester: Wiley.

Checkland, P. B. and Scholes, P. (1990), *Soft Systems Methodology in Action*, Chichester: Wiley.

Chia, R. and Holt, R. (2006), 'Strategy as Practical coping: A Heideggerian Perspective', *Organization Studies*, 27(5), 635–55.

Chia, R. C. H. and Holt, R. (2009), *Strategy without Design: the silent efficacy of indirect action*, Cambridge: Cambridge University Press.

Child, J. (1972), 'Organisational structure, environment and performance: the role of strategic choice', *Sociology*, vol. 6, no. 1, pp. 1–21.

Child, J. (1984), *Organisation*, London: Harper & Row.

Churchman, C. West (1968), *The Systems Approach*, New York: Delacorte Press.

Churchman, C. West (1970), *The Systems Approach and its Enemies*, New York: Basic Books.

Coase, R. (1937), 'The nature of the firm', *Economica*, 4, 386–405.

Cohen, J. and Stewart, I. (1994), *The Collapse of Chaos: Discovering Simplicity in a Complex World*, New York: Viking.

Cohen, M. D., March, J. G. and Ohlsen, J. P. (1972), 'A garbage can model of organizational choice', *Administrative Science Quarterly*, vol. 17, pp. 1–25.

Coleman, H. J. (1999), 'What Enables Self-Organizing Behavior in Business', *Emergence*, 1(1), 33–48.

Collingridge, D. (1980), *The Social Control of Technology*, Buckingham: Open University Press.

Collins, E. B. and Holton, E. F. (2004), 'The effectiveness of managerial leadership development programs: A meta-analysis of studies from 1982 to 2001', *Strategic Management Journal*, 15(2), 217–48.

Collins, J. (2001), *Good to Great*, New York: Harper Business.

Cooperrider, D. and Srivastva, S. (1987), 'Appreciative inquiry in organizational life', *Research in Organizational Change and Development*, 1, 129–69.

Coopey, J. (1995), 'The learning organization: power, politics and ideology', *Management Learning*, vol. 29, no. 3, pp. 193–214.

Coser, L. A. (1956), *The Functions of Social Conflict*, New York: The Free Press.

Coser, L. A. (1967), *Continuities in the study of social conflict*, New York: Free Press.

Crawley, J. (1992), *Constructive Conflict Management*, London: Nicholas Brealey Publishing.

Crook, T. R., Ketchen, D. J., Combs, J. G. and Todd, S. Y. (2008), *Strategic Management Journal*, 29(11), 1141–54.

Cyert, R. M. and March, J. G. (1963), *A Behavioral Theory of the Firm*, Englewood Cliffs, NJ: Prentice-Hall.

D

D'Aveni, R. (1995), *Hypercompetitive Rivalries*, New York: Free Press.

Dalal, F. (1998), *Taking the Group Seriously: Towards a Post-Foulkesian Group Analytic Theory*, London: Jessica Kingsley.

Dalton, D. R., Daily, C. M., Ellstrand, A. E. and Johnson, J. L. (1998), 'Meta-analytic reviews of board composition, leadership structure, and financial performance', *Strategic Management Journal*, 19(3), 269–90.

Damasio, A. R. (1994), *Descartes' Error: Emotion, Reason and the Human Brain*, London: Picador.

Damasio, A. R. (1999), *The Feeling of What Happens: Body and emotion in the making of consciousness*, London: Heinemann.

Davenport, T. H. and Prusak, L. (1998), *Working Knowledge: How Organizations Manage What they Know*, Cambridge, MA: Harvard University Press.

Davies, P. (1987), *The Cosmic Blueprint*, London: William Heinemann.

Davies, P. (2004), 'Star cross'd', *Guardian Unlimited*, 20 November. Available online at: http://society.guardian.co.uk/nhsperformance/comment/0,8146,1362727,00.html.

Deal, T. T. A. and Kennedy, A. A. (1988), *Corporate Culture: The Rites and Rituals of Corporate Life*, Harmondsworth, Middlesex: Penguin.

Deetz, S. and White, W. J. (1999), 'Relational Responsibility or Dialogic Ethics: A questioning of McNamee and Gergen', in McNamee, S. and Gergen, K. J. (1999), *Relational Responsibility: Research for sustainable dialogue*, Thousand Oaks, CA: Sage.

De Geuss, A. (1988), 'Planning as Learning', *Harvard Business Review*, March–April, 70–4.

Delmar, F. and Shane, S. (2003), 'Does business planning facilitate the development of new ventures?', *Strategic Management Journal*, 24(12), 1165–85.

Denzin, N. K. and Lincoln, Y. (2005), *The Sage Handbook of Qualititave Research*, London: Sage.

Department of Health (2000), *The NHS Plan*, London: The Stationery Office.

Dewey, J. (1934), *A Common Faith*, New Haven, CT: Yale University Press.

de Waal, F. (2006), *Primates and Philosophers: how morality evolved*, Princeton: Princeton University Press.

de Wit, B. and Meyer, R. (2005), *Strategy Synthesis: Resolving Strategy Paradoxes to Create Competitive Advantage*, London: Thomson Learning.

De Rond, M. and Thietart, R. A. (2007), 'Choice, Chance, and inevitability in strategy', *Strategic Management Journal*, 28, 535–51.

Dickerson, A., Gibson, H. D. and Tsakalotos, E. (1997), 'The Impact of Acquisitions on Company Performance: Evidence from a large panel of UK firms', *Oxford Economic Papers*, 49(3), 344–61.

DiMaggio, P. J. and Powell, W. W. (1991), 'Introduction', in Powell, W. W. and DiMaggio, P. J. (eds), *New Institutionalism in Organizational Analysis*, Chicago: Chicago University Press, pp. 1–38.

Dixon, M. (ed.) (2000), *Project Management Body of Knowledge*, 4th edition, Peterborough, UK: Association for Project Management.

Donaldson, A. (2005), 'Writing in organizational life: how a technology simultaneously forms and is formed by human interaction', in Stacey, R. (ed.), *Experiencing Emergence in Organizations: Local Interaction and the Emergence of Global Pattern*, London: Routledge.

Dopson, S. (2001), 'Applying an Eliasian Approach to Organizational Analysis', *Organization*, 8, 3, 515–35.

Dougherty, D. (1992), 'A practice-centered model organizational renewal through product innovation', *Strategic Management Journal*, vol. 13, Special Issue, Summer, pp. 77–92.

Downs, A., Durant, R. and Carr, A. N. (2003), 'Emergent Strategy Development for Organizations', *Emergence*, 5(2), 5–28.

Drabæk, I. (2008), 'Compromising as processes of moving forward in organizations', in Stacey, R. and Griffin, D. (eds), *Complexity and the experience of values, conflict and compromise in organizations*, London: Routledge.

Dugdale, R. (2002), *Pursuing Perfection in the Bradford Health Community*, Bradford Community National Health Service Trust.

Duncan, R. (1972), 'Characteristics of organizational environments and perceived uncertainty', *Administrative Science Quarterly*, vol. 17, pp. 313–27.

Dunphy, D. C. (1968), 'Phases, roles and myths in self analytic groups', *Journal of Applied Behavioural Science*, vol. 4, pp. 195–226.

E

Easterby-Smith, M. and Araujo, L. (1999), 'Organizational learning: current debates and opportunities', in Easterby-Smith, M., Burgoyne, J. and Araujo, L. (eds), *Organizational Learning and the Learning Organization*, London: Sage.

Edelenbos, J., Gerrits, L. and Gils, M. (2008), 'The Coevolutionary Relation Between Dutch Mainport Policies and the Development of the Seaport Rotterdam', *Emergence, Complexity & Organization*, 10(2), 49–61.

Edelmann, R. J. (1993), *Interpersonal Conflicts at Work*, Leicester: The British Psychological Society.

Eisenhardt, K. M. (1989), 'Making fast strategic decisions in high-velocity environments', *Academy of Management Journal*, 32(3), 543–76.

Elgar, A. (1975), 'Industrial Organizations: a processual perspective', in McKinlay, J. B. (ed.), *Processing People: Cases in Organizational Behaviour*, New York: Holt, Reinhart & Winston.

Elias, N. ([1939] 2000), *The Civilizing Process*, Oxford: Blackwell.

Elias, N. (1970), *What is Sociology?* New York: Columbia University Press.

Elias, N. (1978), *What is Sociology?* London: Hutchinson.

Elias, N. (1987), *Involvement and Detachment*, Oxford: Blackwell.

Elias, N. (1989), *The Symbol Theory*, London: Sage Publications.

Elias, N. (1991), *The Society of Individuals*, Oxford: Blackwell.

Elias, N. (1998), *On Civilization, Power, and Knowledge*, Chicago, IL: University of Chicago Press.

Elias, N. and Scotson, J. ([1965] 1994), *The Established and the Outsiders*, London: Sage.

Ellemers, N. (1993), 'The influence of socio-structural variables on identity management strategies', in Stroebe, V. and Hewstone, M. (eds), *European Review of Social Psychology*, vol. 4, pp. 27–58, New York: Wiley.

Eskildson, L. (2006), 'TQM's Role in Corporate Success: Analyzing the Evidence', *National Productivity Review*, 14(4), 25–38.

Etzioni, A. (1961), *Complex Organizations*, New York: Holt, Rinehart & Winston.

Ezzamel, M., Willmott, H. and Worthington, F. (2001), 'Power, Control and Resistance in "The Factory that Time Forgot" ', *Journal of Management Studies*, 38(8), 1054–79.

F

Fayol, H. ([1916] 1948), *Industrial and General Administration*, London: Pitman.

Festinger, L., Schachter, S. and Back, K. (1950), *Social Pressures in Informal Groups: A Study of a Housing Project*, New York: Harper & Row.

Fiedler, F. E. (1967), *A Theory of Leadership Effectiveness*, New York: McGraw-Hill.

Fiske, S. T. and Taylor, S. E. (1991), *Social cognition*, New York: McGraw-Hill.

Flood, R. L. (1990), 'Liberating systems theory: towards critical systems thinking', *Human Relations*, vol. 43, pp. 49–75.

Flood, R. L. (1999), *Rethinking the Fifth Discipline: Learning within the Unknowable*, London: Routledge.

Floyd, S. W. and Wooldridge, B. (1992), 'Middle management involvement in strategy and its association with strategic type: a research note', *Strategic Management Journal*, vol. 13, Special Issue, Summer, pp. 153–68.

Foerster, H. von (1984), 'On constructing reality', in Foerster, H. von (ed.), *Observing Systems*, Seaside, CA: Intersystems.

Fonseca, J. (2001), *Complexity and Innovation in Organizations*, London: Routledge.

Forrester, J. (1958), 'Industrial dynamics: a major breakthrough for decisionmaking', *Harvard Business Review*, vol. 36, no. 4, pp. 37–66.

Forrester, J. (1961), *Industrial Dynamics*, Cambridge, MA: MIT Press.

Forrester, J. (1969), *The Principles of Systems*, Cambridge, MA: Wright-Allen Press.

Foulkes, S. H. (1948), *Introduction to Group Analytic Psychotherapy*, London: William Heinemann Medical Books.

Foulkes, S. H. (1964), *Therapeutic Group Analysis*, London: George Allen & Unwin.

Frankfurt, H. (1971), 'Freedom of the will and the concept of a person', *Journal of Philosophy*, vol. 67, no. 1, pp. 5–20.

Friis, P. (2004), 'The relevance of theatre and improvisation to consulting for organisational change', unpublished thesis, University of Hertfordshire.

Friis, P. and Larsen, H. (2006), 'Theater and social change', in Shaw, P. and Stacey, R. (eds), *Experiencing risk, spontaneity and improvisation in organizational change: working live*, London: Routledge.

Fulmer, R. M. and Rue, L. W. (1973), *The practice and profitability of Long Range Planning*, Oxford: The Planning Executives Institute.

G

Gabriel, Y. (1998), 'Same old story or changing stories? Folkloric, modern and postmodern mutations', in Grant, D., Keenoy, T. and Oswick, C. (eds), *Discourse and Organisation*, London: Sage.

Galbraith, J. R. and Kazanian, R. K. (1986), *Strategy Implementation: Structure, Systems and Process*, St Paul, MN: West.

Gallese, V. (2001), 'The "shared manifold" hypothesis: from mirror neurons to empathy', in Thompson, E. (ed.), *Between Ourselves: Second-Person Issues in the Study of Consciousness*, Thorverton, UK: Imprint Academic.

Gardner, H. (1985), *The Mind's New Science: A History of the Cognitive Revolution*, New York: Basic Books.

Garfinkel, H. (1967), *Studies in Ethnomethodology*, Englewood Cliffs, NJ: Prentice-Hall.

Garud, R. and Van de Ven, A. H. (1992), 'An empirical evaluation of the internal corporate venturing process', *Strategic Management Journal*, vol. 13, Special Issue, Summer, pp. 93–110.

Garven, D. A. (1993), 'Building a learning organization', *Harvard Business Review*, July–August.

Gell-Mann, M. (1994), *The Quark and the Jaguar*, New York: Freeman.

Gergen, K. J. (1982), *Toward Transformation in Social Knowledge*, New York: Springer.

Gergen, K. J. (1985), 'The social constructionist movement in modern psychology', *American Psychologist*, vol. 40, pp. 266–75.

Gergen, K. J. (1991), *The Saturated Self: Dilemmas of Identity in Contemporary Life*, New York: Basic Books.

Gergen, K. J. (1999), *An Invitation to Social Construction*, Thousand Oaks, CA: Sage.

Gershenson, C. and Heylighen, F. (2003), 'When can we call a system self-organizing?', in Banzhaf, W., Christaller, T., Dittrich, P., Kim, J. T. and Ziegler, J. (eds), *Advances in Artificial Life*, Proceedings of the 7th European Conference, ECAL 2003, Dortmund.

Giddens, A. (1976), *New Rules of Sociological Method*, London: Hutchinson.

Giddens, A. (1979), *Central Problems in Social Theory*, London: Macmillan.

Giddens, A. (1984), *The Constitution of Society: Outline of the Theory of Structuration*, Cambridge: Polity Press.

Gilbert, J. A. and Ivancevich, J. M. (2000), 'Valuing diversity: a tale of two organizations', *Academy of Management Executive*, vol. 14, no. 1, pp. 93–105.

Gilbert, J. A., Stead, B. A. and Ivancevich, J. M. (1999), 'Diversity Management: A New Organizational Paradigm', *Journal of Business Ethics*, 21(1), 61–76.

Gilmore, F. F. and Brandenburg, R. G. (1962), 'Anatomy of Corporate Planning', *Harvard Business Review*, Nov–Dec, 61–9.

Ginsberg, A. and Venkatraman, N. (1992), 'Investing in new information technology: the role of competitive posture and issue diagnosis', *Strategic Management Journal*, vol. 13, Special Issue, Summer, pp. 37–54.

Glasl, F. (1999), *Confronting Conflict*, Gloucestershire: Hawthorn Press.

Gleick, J. (1988), *Chaos: The Making of a New Science*, London: William Heinemann.

Goffman, E. (1981), *Forms of Talk*, Philadelphia, PA: University of Pennsylvania Press.

Goldsmith, W. and Clutterbuck, D. (1984), *The Winning Streak*, London: Weidenfeld & Nicholson.

Goldstein, J. (1994), *The Unshackled Organization: Facing the Challenge of Unpredictability through Spontaneous Reorganization*, Portland, OR: Productivity Press.

Goldstein, J. (1999), 'Emergence as a Construct: History and Issues', *Emergence*, 1(1), 49–72.

Goldstein, J. (2000), 'Emergence: A Construct Amid a Thicket of Conceptual Snares', *Emergence*, 2(1), 5–22.

Goldstein, J. A., Hazy, J. K. and Silberstang, J. (2008), 'Complexity and Social Entrepreneurship: A Fortuitous Meeting', *Emergence, Complexity & Organization*, 10(3), 3, vi–x.

Goodwin, B. (1994), *How the Leopard Changed its Spots*, London: Weidenfeld & Nicolson.

Goodwin, R. M. (1951), 'Econometrics in business-style analysis', in Hansen, A. H. (ed.), *Business Cycles and National Income*, New York: W. W. Norton.

Goold, M. and Campbell, A. (1987), *Strategies and Styles*, Oxford: Blackwell.

Goold, M. and Quinn, J. J. (1990), *Strategic Control: Milestones for Long Term Performance*, London: Hutchinson.

Gould, L., Stapley, L. and Stein, M. (eds) (2001), *The Systems Psychodynamics of Organizations: Integrating the Group Relations Approach, Psychoanalytic and Open Systems Perspectives*, New York: Karnac.

Grace, M. (2003), 'Origins of Leadership: the Etymology of Leadership', *Selected Proceedings from 2003 Conference of the International Leadership Association*, 1–15.

Grant, R. M. (2003), 'Strategic Planning in a turbulent environment: evidence from the oil majors', *Strategic Management Journal*, 24(6), 491–517.

Grant, D., Keenoy, T. and Oswick, C. (eds) (1998), *Discourse and Organisation*, London: Sage.

Greenley, G. E. (1986), 'Does Strategic Planning Improve Performance?', *Long Range Planning*, 19(2), 101–9.

Greiner, L. E. (1972), 'Evolution and revolution as organizations grow', *Harvard Business Review*, vol. 50, July–August, pp. 37–46.

Greiner, L. E. and Schein, V. E. (1988), *Power and Organization Development: Mobilizing Power to Implement Change*, Reading, MA: Addison-Wesley.

Griffin, D. (2002), *The Emergence of Leadership: Linking Self-Organization and Ethics*, London: Routledge.

Griffin, D. and Stacey, R. (eds) (2005), *Complexity and the Experience of Leading Organizations*, London: Routledge.

Griffin, D., Shaw, P. and Stacey, R. (1998), 'Speaking of complexity in management theory and practice', *Organization*, vol. 5, no. 3, pp. 295–310.

Grimshaw, J. M. and Eccles, M. (2004), 'Is evidence-based implementation of evidence-based care possible?', *Medical Journal of Australia*, 180, 50–51.

Grint, K. (2005), 'Problems, problems, problems: the social construction of leadership', *Human Relations*, 58(11), 1467–94.

Grol, R. and Wensing, M. (2004), 'What drives change? Barriers to and incentives for achieving evidence-based practice', *Medical Journal of Australia*, 180: 57–60.

Groot, N. (2005), 'Senior Executives and the Emergence of Local Responsibilities in Large Organizations: a complexity approach to potentially better results', Unpublished PhD thesis: University of Hertfordshire.

Guba, E. G. (2005), 'Paradigmatic controversies, contradictions, and emerging confluences', in Denzin, N. K. and Lincoln, Y. S. (eds), *Handbook of Qualitative Research*, 3rd edition, Thousand Oaks, CA: Sage.

Guba, E. G. and Lincoln, Y. S. (1995), 'Competing paradigms in qualitative research', in Denzin, N. K. and Lincoln, Y. S. (eds), *Handbook of Qualitative Research*, Thousand Oaks, CA: Sage.

H

Hamel, G. and Prahalad, C. K. (1989), 'Strategic intent', *Harvard Business Review*, vol. 67, May–June, pp. 63–76.

Hamel, G. and Prahalad, C. K. (1990), 'The core competence of the corporation', *Harvard Business Review*, vol. 68, no. 3, pp. 79–81.

Hamel, G. and Prahalad, C. K. (1994), *Competing for the Future*, Boston, MA: Harvard Business School Press.

Hannan, M. T. and Freeman, J. (1989), *Organizational Ecology*, Cambridge, MA: Harvard University Press.

Hardwick, C. T. and Landuyt, B. F. (1961), *Administrative Strategy*, New York: Simmons-Boardman.

Haspeslagh, P. C. (1982), 'Portfolio planning: uses and limits', *Harvard Business Review*, Jan–Feb, 58–73.

Hayes, N. (1994), *Foundations of Psychology*, London: Routledge.

Haynes, P. (2003), *Managing Complexity in the Public Services*, Maidenhead Berkshire: Open University Press (McGraw-Hill Education).

Healthcare Commission (2005), *Acute and Specialist Trust Overview, Healthcare Perform-ance Ratings*. Available online at: http://ratings2005.healthcarecimmission.org.uk/trust/overview/acute_overview.asp.

Hegel, G. W. F. (1807), *The Phenomenology of the Spirit*, Bamberg: Joseph Anton Goebhardt, translated by A. V. Miller, Oxford: Oxford University Press.

Henderson, B. D. (1970), *The Product Portfolio*, Boston, MA: Boston Consulting Group.

Hendricks, K. B. and Singhal, V. (1997), 'Does Implementing an Effective TQM Program Actually Improve Operating Performance? Empirical Evidence from Firms That Have won Quality Awards', *Management Science*, 43(9), 1258–74.

Hendricks, K. B. and Singhal, V. (2000), 'Firm characteristics, total quality management and financial performance', *Journal of Operations Management*, 238, 1–17.

Hendricks, K. B. and Singhal, V. (2001), 'The Long run Stock Price Performance of Firms with Effective TQM Programs', *Management Science*, 47(3), 359–68.

Heron, J. and Reason, P. (1997), 'A Participatory inquiry paradigm', *Qualitative Inquiry*, 2(1), 41–56.

Hersey, P. and Blanchard, K. (1988), *Organizational Behavior*, Englewood Cliffs, NJ: Prentice-Hall.

Herzberg, F. (1966), *Work and the Nature of Man*, Cleveland, OH: World.

Hirschhorn, L. (1990), *The Workplace Within: Psychodynamics of Organizational Life*, Cambridge, MA: MIT Press.

Hodge, B. and Coronado, G. (2007), 'Understanding Change in Organizations in a Far-from-Equilibrium World', *Emergence, Complexity & Organization*, 9(3), 3–15.

Hodgson, G. M. (2000), 'The Concept of Emergence in Social Science: Its History and Importance', *Emergence*, 2(4), 66–77.

Hofer, C. W. and Schendel, D. (1978), *Strategy Evaluation: Analytical Concepts*, St Paul, MN: West.

Hogg, M. A. and Abrams, D. (1999), 'Social identity and social cognition: Historical back-ground and current trends', in Abrams, D. and Hogg, A. (eds), *Social identity and social cognition*, pp. 1–25, Oxford: Blackwell.

Hogg, M. A., Terry, D. J. and White, K. M. (1995), 'A tale of two theories: a critical com-parison of identity theory with social identity theory', *Social Psychology Quarterly*, 58, 255–69.

Holland, J. (1998), *Emergence from Chaos to Order*, New York: Oxford University Press.

Holmes, J. and Stube, M. (2003), *Power and Politeness in the Workplace: A Sociolinguistic Analysis of Talk at Work*, London: Pearson Education.

Hosking, D. M. and McNamee, S. (eds) (2006), *The Social Construction of Organization*, Liber & Copenhagen Business School Press.

Huff, J. O., Huff, A. S. and Thomas, H. (1992), 'Strategic renewal and the interaction of stress and inertia', *Strategic Management Journal*, vol. 13, Special Issue, Summer, pp. 55–76.

Hurst, D. (1995), *Crisis and Renewal: Meeting the Challenge of Organizational Change*, Boston, MA: Harvard Business School Press.

Hurst, D. K. (1986), 'Why strategic management is bankrupt', *Organizational Dynamics*, vol. 12, Autumn, pp. 4–77.

Hurst, E. G. (1982), 'Controlling strategic plans', in Lorange, D. (ed.), *Implementation of Strategic Planning*, Englewood Cliffs, NJ: Prentice-Hall.

Huselid, M. A., Jackson, S. E. and Schuler, R. S. (1997), 'Technical and strategic human resource management effectiveness as determinants of firm performance', *Academy of Management Journal*, 40(1), 171–88.

Hussey, D. E. (1991), 'Implementing strategy through management education and training', in Hussey, D. E. (ed.), *International Review of Strategic Management*, vol. 2, no. 1.

I

Ingham, H., Kran, I. and Lovestam, A. (2007), 'Mergers and Profitability: A Managerial success Story?', *Journal of Management Studies*, 29(2), 195–208.

Isaacs, W. (1999), *Dialogue and the Art of Thinking Together*, New York: Doubleday.

Isenhart, M. W. and Spangle, M. (2000), *Collaborative Approaches to Resolving Conflict*, London: Sage.

Iterson, A. van, Mastenbroek, W., Newton, T. and Smith, D. (eds) (2002), *The Civilized Organization: Norbert Elias and the Future of Organization Studies*, Amsterdam: John Benjamins Publishing Company.

J

Jackall, R. (1988), 'Moral mazes: the world of corporate managers', in Handel, M. J. (ed.), *The Sociology of Organizations: Classic, Contemporary and Critical Readings*, Oxford: Oxford University Press.

Jackson, M. C. (2000), *Systems Approaches to Management*, New York: Kluwer.

Jacques, E. (1955), 'Social systems as a defence against persecutory and defensive anxiety', in Klein, M., Heinmann, P. and Money-Kyrle, P. (eds), *New Directions in Psychoanalysis*, London: Tavistock. (Also published in Gibbard, G. S., Hartman, J. J. and Mann, R. D. (1974), *Analysis of Groups*, San Francisco: Jossey-Bass.)

James, W. (1902), *The Varieties of Religious Experience*, Cambridge, MA: Harvard University Press.

Jarzabkowski, P. (2003), 'Strategic practices: an activity theory perspective on continuity and change', *Journal of Management Studies*, vol. 40, no. 1, pp. 23–55.

Jefferson, G. (1978), 'Sequential aspects of storytelling in conversation', in Shenkein, J. (ed.), *Studies in the Organization of Conversational Interaction*, New York: Academic Press.

Joas, H. (2000), *The Genesis of Values*, Cambridge: Polity Press.

Johannessen, S. and Stacey, R. (2005), 'Technology as social object', in Stacey, R. (ed.), *Experiencing Emergence in Organizations: Local Interaction and the Emergence of Global Pattern*, London: Routledge.

Johnson, G. (1987), *Strategic Change and Management Process*, Oxford: Blackwell.

Johnson, G., Melin, L. and Whittington, R. (2003), ' "Guest editors" introduction: micro strategy and strategizing: towards an activity-based view', *Journal of Management Studies*, vol. 40, no. 1, pp. 3–22.

Johnson, G., Scholes, K. and Whittington, R. (2005), *Exploring Corporate Strategy*, 7th edition, Harlow: Pearson Education.

K

Kandola, R. S. and Fullerton, J. (1994), *Managing the Mosaic: Diversity in Action (Developing Strategies)*, Chartered Institute of Personnel and Development.

Kant, I. (1790), *Critique of Judgement*, trans. W. S. Pluhar, Indianapolis: Hackett (1987).

Kast, F. E. and Rosenzweig, J. E. (1985), *Organization and Management – A Systems and Contingent Approach*, New York: McGraw-Hill.

Kauffman, S. A. (1995), *At Home in the Universe*, New York: Oxford University Press.

Kellert, S. H. (1993), *In the Wake of Chaos*, Chicago, IL: University of Chicago Press.

Kelly, S. and Allison, A. (1999), *The Complexity Advantage: How the Science of Complexity can Help your Business Achieve Peak Performance*, New York: McGraw-Hill.

Kelsey, D. (1988), 'The economics of chaos or the chaos of economies', *Oxford Economic Papers*, vol. 40, pp. 1–31.

Ketovi, M. and Castener, X. (2004), 'Strategic planning as an integrative device', *Administrative Science Quarterly*, vol. 49, pp. 337–65.

Kets de Vries, M. F. (1989), *Prisoners of Leadership*, New York: Wiley.

Khurana, R. (2007), *From Higher Aims to Hired Hands: The Social Transformation of Business Schools and the Unfulfilled Promise of Management as a Profession*, Princeton, NJ: Princeton University Press.

Kiel, L. D. (1994), *Managing Chaos and Complexity in Government*, San Francisco, CA: Jossey-Bass.

Kiersey, D. and Bates, M. (1978), *Please Understand Me: Character and Temperament Types*, Del Mar, CA: Prometheus Nemesis Books.

King, D. R., Dalton, D. R., Daily, C. M. and Covin, J. G. (2003), 'Meta-analyses of post-acquisition performance: indications of unidentified moderators', *Strategic Management Journal*, 25(2), 187–200.

Klein, M. (1975), *The Writings of Melanie Klein*, London: Hogarth Press.

Kleiner, A. and Roth, G. (1997), 'How to make experience your best teacher', *Harvard Business Review*, vol. 68, September–October, pp. 112–22.

Knights, D. and Willmott, H. (2007), *Introducing Organizational Behaviour Management*, London: Cengage Learning.

Kolb, D. M. and Bartunek, J. M. (1992), *Hidden Conflicts in Organisations*, Newbury Park, CA: Sage.

Kono, T. (1983), 'Long Range Planning-Japan U.S.A.–A Comparative Study', in Hussey, D. (ed.), *The Truth about Corporate Planning*, Oxford: Pergamon Press, 153–73.

Korte, R. F. (2007), 'A review of social identity theory with implications for training and development', *Journal of European Industrial Training*, vol. 31, no. 3, pp. 166–80.

Kudla, R. J. (1980), 'The effects of strategic planning on common stock returns', *The Academy of Management Journal*, 23(1), 5–20.

L

Lacey, P. (2006), 'The Experience of Power, Blame and Responsibility in the Health Sector', in Stacey, R. and Griffin, D. (eds), *Complexity and the Experience of Managing in the Public Sector*, London: Routledge.

Langley, A. (1999), 'Strategies for theorizing from process data', *Academy of Management Review*, vol. 24, no. 4, pp. 691–710.

Langton, C. G. (1996), 'Artificial life', in Boden, M. A. (ed.), *The Philosophy of Artificial Life*, Oxford: Oxford University Press.

Lannemann, J. W. (1999), 'On being relational in an accountable way: The question of agency and power', in McNamee, S. and Gergen, K. J. (eds), *Relational Responsibility: Resources for sustainable dialogue*, Thousand Oaks, CA: Sage.

Larsen, H. (2005), 'The experience of change in the profession of clinical psychology in the UK', unpublished thesis, University of Hertfordshire.

Latour, B. and Woolgar, S. (1979), *Laboratory Life: The Social Construction of Scientific Facts*, Beverly Hills, CA: Sage.

Lave, J. and Wenger, E. (1991), *Situated Learning: Legitimate Peripheral Participation*, New York: Cambridge University Press.

Lawrence, P. R. and Lorsch, J. W. (1967), *Organization and Environment*, Cambridge, MA: Harvard University Press.

Learned, E. P., Christensen, C. R., Andrews, K. R. and Guth, W. D. (1965), *Business Policy: Text and Cases*, Homewood, IL: Irwin.

Leonard, D. and Strauss, S. (1997), 'Putting your company's whole brain to work', *Harvard Business Review*, vol. 67, July–August, pp. 111–21.

Levy, D. (1994), 'Chaos theory and strategy: theory, application, and managerial implications', *Strategic Management Journal*, vol. 15, pp. 167–78.

Levy, S. (1992), *Artificial Life*, New York: First Vintage Books.

Lewes, G. H. (1875), *Problems of Life and Mind*, vol. 2, London: Tribuner.

Lewin, R. and Regine, B. (2000), *The Soul at Work*, London: Orion Business Books.

Lewis, D. S., French, E. and Steane, P. A. (1997), 'Culture of conflict', *Leadership and Organisational Development Journal*, vol. 18, no. 6, pp. 275–82.

Lichtenstein, B. B., Uhl-Bien, M. R., Seers, A., Orton, J. D. and Schreiber, C. (2006), 'Complexity Leadership Theory: An Interactive Perspective On Leading in Complex Adaptive Systems', *Emergence, Complexity & Organization*, 8(4), 22–12.

Likert, R. (1961), *New Patterns of Management*, New York: McGraw-Hill.

Lincoln, Y. S. and Guba, E. G. (1985), *Naturalistic inquiry*, Beverly Hills, CA: Sage Publications Inc.

Lindblom, L. (1959), 'The science of muddling through', *Public Administration Review*, vol. 19, pp. 79–88.

Lissack, M. and Roos, J. (1999), *The Next Common Sense: Mastering Corporate Complexity through Coherence*, London: Nicholas Brealey.

Lock, D. (2003), *Project Management*, 8th edition, Aldershot: Gower.

Lohr, K. N. (ed.) (2001), *Crossing the Quality Chasm*, Washington, DC: Institute of Medicine.

Luhmann, N. (1984), *Social Systems*, Stanford, CA: Stanford University Press.

M

MacIntosh, R. and MacLean, D. (1999), 'Conditioned Emergence: A dissipative structures approach to transformation', *Strategic Management Journal*, 20, 4: 297–316.

Mackey, A. (2008), 'The effect of CEOs on firm performance', *Strategic Management Journal*, 29(12), 1357–67.

Maitlis, S. and Lawrence, B. (2003), 'Orchestral manoeuvres in the dark: understanding failure in organizational strategizing', *Journal of Management Studies*, vol. 40, no. 1, pp. 109–39.

March, J. G. and Olsen, J. P. (1972), 'A garbage can model of organizational choice', *Administrative Science Quarterly*, vol. 17, no. 1.

March, J. G. and Simon, H. A. (1958), *Organizations*, New York: Wiley.

Marion, R. (1999), *The Edge of Organization: Chaos and Complexity Theories of Formal Social Systems*, Thousand Oaks, CA: Sage.

Marquis, J. P., Lim, N., Scott, L. M., Harrell, M. C. and Kavanagh, J. (2009), 'Managing Diversity in Corporate America: An Exploratory Analysis', Occasional Paper, Rang Corporation.

Maslow, A. (1954), *Motivation and Personality*, New York: Harper & Row.

Mastenbroek, W. F. G. (1987 [1993]), *Conflict Management and Organisational Development*, Chichester: John Wiley & Son Ltd.

Maturana, H. R. and Varela, F. J. (1987), *The Tree of Knowledge: The Biological Roots of Human Understanding*, Boston, MA: Shambala.

Mayo, E. (1945), *The Social Problems of an Industrial Civilization*, Cambridge, MA: Harvard University Press.

Mayr, E. (1988), *Toward a New Philosophy of Biology: Observations of an Evolutionist*, Cambridge, Mass: Harvard University Press.

McCleod, J. (1996), 'Qualitative research methods in counselling psychology', in Woolfe, R. and Dyden, W. (eds), *Handbook of Counselling Psychology*, London: Sage.

McCulloch, W. S. and Pitts, W. (1943), 'A logical calculus of ideas imminent in nervous activity', *Bulletin of Mathematical Biophysics*, vol. 5, pp. 115–33.

McGill, I. and Beaty, L. (2001), *Action Learning*, revised 2nd edition, London: Kogan.

McKelvey, B. (2003), 'From Fields to Science: Can Organization Studies make the Transition?', in Westwood, R. and Clegg, S., *Point/Counterpoint: Central Debates in Organization Theory*, Oxford: Blackwell.

McKenna, C. D. (2006), *The World's Newest Profession: Management consulting in the twentieth century*, Cambridge: Cambridge University Press.

McKinsey, J. O. (1932), 'Adjusting Policies to Meet Changing Conditions', *American Management Association General Management Series*, AM116, New York.

McNamee, S. and Gergen, K. J. (1999), *Relational Responsibility: Resources for sustainable dialogue*, Thousand Oaks, CA: Sage.

Mead, G. H. (1908), 'The philosophical basis for ethics', *International Journal of Ethics*, vol. 18, pp. 311–23.

Mead, G. H. (1923), 'Scientific method and the moral sciences', *International Journal of Ethics*, vol. 33, pp. 229–47.

Mead, G. H. (1932), *The Philosophy of the Present*, Chicago: University of Chicago Press.

Mead, G. H. (1934), *Mind, Self, and Society: From the Standpoint of a Social Behaviourist*, Chicago: University of Chicago Press.

Mead, G. H. (1938), *The Philosophy of the Act*, Chicago: University of Chicago Press.

Meek, J. W., De Ladurantey, J. and Newell, W. (2007), 'Complex systems, governance and policy administration consequences', *Emergence, Complexity & Organization*, 9(1–2), 24–36.

Menzies Lyth, I. (1975), 'A case study in the functioning of social systems as a defence against anxiety', in Coleman, A. and Bexton, W. H. (eds), *Group Relations Reader*, Sausalito, CA: GREX.

Mezrich, B. (2009), *The Accidental Billionaire: Sex, Money, Betrayal and the Founding of Facebook*, London: William Heinemann.

Midgley, G. (2000), *Systemic Intervention: Philosophy, Methodology, and Practice*, New York: Kluwer.

Miller, C. C. and Cardinal, L. B. (1994), 'Strategic Planning and firm performance: a synthesis of more than two decades of research', *The Academy of Management Journal*, 37(6), 1649–61.

Miller, D. and Friesen, P. H. (1980), 'Momentum and revolution in organizational adaptation', *Academy of Management Journal*, vol. 23, pp. 591–614.

Miller, E. J. (1977), 'Organisational development and industrial democracy: a current case-study', in Cooper, C. (ed.), *Organisational Development in the UK and USA: A Joint Evaluation*, London: Macmillan.

Miller, E. J. (1983), *Work and Creativity*, Occasional Papers, London: Tavistock.

Miller, E. J. (1993), *From Dependency to Autonomy: Studies in Organization and Change*, London: Free Association Books.

Miller, E. J. and Rice, A. K. (1967), *Systems of Organization: The Control of Task and Sentient Boundaries*, London: Tavistock.

Mingers, J. (1995), *Self-Producing Systems: Implications and Applications of Autopoiesis*, New York: Plenum Press.

Mintzberg, H. (1973), *The Nature of Managerial Work*, New York: Harper & Row.

Mintzberg, H. (1983), *Power in and around Organizations*, Englewood Cliffs, NJ: Prentice-Hall.

Mintzberg, H. (1987), 'Crafting strategy', *Harvard Business Review*, vol. 65, no. 4, July–August, pp. 66–75.

Mintzberg, H. (1989), *Mintzberg on Management: Inside Our Strange World or Organizations*, New York: The Free Press.

Mintzberg, H. (1990), 'The Design School: Reconsidering the Basic Premises of Strategic Management', *Strategic Management Journal*, 11, 171–95.

Mintzberg, H. (1991), 'Learning 1, Planning 0 Reply to Igor Ansoff', *Strategic Management Journal*, 12, 463–6.

Mintzberg, H. (1994), *The Rise and Fall of Strategic Planning*, Hemel Hempstead: Prentice Hall.

Mintzberg, H. (1998), 'The manager's job', in Mintzberg, H. and Quinn, J. B. (eds), *Readings in the Strategy Process*, Upper Saddle River, NJ: Simon & Schuster.

Mintzberg, H. (2007), *Tracking Strategies: Towards a General Theory*, Oxford: Oxford University Press.

Mintzberg, H. and Waters, J. A. (1985), 'Of strategies deliberate and emergent', *Strategic Management Journal*, vol. 6, pp. 257–72.

Mintzberg, H., Ahlstrand, B. and Lampel, J. (1998), *Strategy Safari*, Harlow: Pearson Education.

Mintzberg, H., Théorêt, A. and Raisinghani, D. (1976), 'The structure of the unstructured decision making process', *Administrative Science Quarterly*, vol. 21, no. 2, pp. 246–75.

Mitleton-Kelly, E. (2006), 'Co-evolutionary Integration: The Co-Creation of a New Organizational Form Following a Merger and Acquisition', *Emergence, Complexity & Organization*, 8(2).

Moore, D. G. (1959), 'Managerial Strategies', in Warner, W. L. and Martin, N. H. (eds), *Industrial Man*, New York: Harper & Rowe, 219–26.

Morgan, C. L. (1896), *Habit and Instinct*, London/New York: Edward Arnold.

Morgan, C. L. (1927), *Emergent Evolution*, 2nd edition, London: Williams and Norgate.

Morgan, C. L. (1933), *The Emergence of Novelty*, London: Williams and Norgate.

Morgan, G. (1997), *Images of Organization*, 2nd edition, Thousand Oaks, CA: Sage.

Morrill, C. (1991), 'Conflict management, honour, and organizational change', *American Journal of Sociology*, vol. 97, pp. 585–622.

Mowles, C. (2007), 'Promises of transformation: Just how different are development INGOs?', *Journal of International Development*, vol. 19 (3), 401–12.

Mowles, C. (2008a), 'Values in international development organisations: Negotiating non-negotiables', *Development in Practice*, vol. 18 (1), 5–16.

Mowles, C. (2008b), 'Finding room for values in required ways of working: values, power, conflict and compromise in aid agencies', in Stacey, R. and Griffin, D. (eds), *Complexity and the experience of values, conflict and compromise in organizations*, London: Routledge.

Mowles, C. (2008c), 'What Practical Contribution Can Insights from the Complexity Sciences Make to the Theory and Practice of Development Management?', *Journal of International Development, Special Issue*: 20, 6, 804–820.

Mowles, C. (2009), 'Consultancy as Temporary Leadership: Negotiating Power in Everyday Practice', *International Journal of Learning and Change*, vol. 3, no. 3, 281–93.

Mowles, C. (2010a), 'Successful or not? Evidence, emergence and development management', *Development in Practice*.

Mowles, C. (2010b), 'The Practice of Complexity: Review, Change and Service Improvement in an NHS Department', *Journal of Health Organisation and Management*, vol. 24, Issue 1.

Mowles, C., Stacey, R. and Griffin, D. (2008), 'What contribution can insights from the complexity sciences make to the theory and practice of development management?', in Chia, R. (ed.), *In the Realms of Organization: essays for Robert Cooper*, London: Routledge.

N

Nelson, R. R. and Winter, S. G. (1982), *An Evolutionary Theory of Economic Change*, Cambridge, MA: Harvard University Press.

Newbert, S. L. (2006), 'Empirical research on the resource-based view of the firm: an assessment and suggestions for further research', *Strategic Management Journal*, 28(2), 121–46.

Newman, W. H. (1951), *Administrative Action: The Techniques of Organization and Management*, Englewood-Cliffs, NJ: Prentice-Hall.

Newton, T. (1999), 'Power, Subjectivity and British Organisational Psychology: The Relevance of the Work of Norbert Elias', *Sociology*, 33, 2, 411–40.

Newton, T. (2001), 'Organization: the Relevance and Limitations of Elias', *Organization*, 8, 3, 467–95.

Nicolis, G. and Prigogine, I. (1989), *Exploring Complexity: An Introduction*, New York: W. H. Freeman.

Nonaka, I. (1988a), 'Creating organizational order out of chaos: self renewal in Japanese firms', *California Management Review*, Spring, pp. 57–73.

Nonaka, I. (1988b), 'Toward middle-up-down management: accelerating information creation', *Sloan Management Review*, vol. 29, no. 3, pp. 9–18.

Nonaka, I. (1991), 'The knowledge-creating company', *Harvard Business Review*, vol. 69, November–December, pp. 96–104.

Nonaka, I. and Takeuchi, H. (1995), *The Knowledge-Creating Company: How Japanese Companies Create the Dynamics of Innovation*, Oxford: Oxford University Press.

Norman, K. (2006), 'The Experience of Clinical Risk Assessment in the Health Sector', in Stacey, R. and Griffin, D. (eds), *Complexity and the Experience of Managing in the Public Sector*, London: Routledge.

O

Oberholzer, A. and Roberts, V. Z. (1995), *The Unconscious at Work: Individual and Organizational Stress in the Human Services*, London: Routledge.

Ong, W. J. (2002), *Orality and Literacy*, London and New York: Routledge.

O'Regan, N. and Ghobadian, A. (2007), 'Formal strategic planning: annual raindance or wheel of success?', *Strategic Change*, 16(1–2), 11–22.

Owen, H. (1992), *Open Space Technology: A User's Guide*, Potomac, MD: Abbott Publishing.

P

Pascale, R. T. and Athos, A. (1981), *The Art of Japanese Management*, New York: Simon & Schuster.

Pascale, R. T., Millemann, M. and Gioja, L. (2000), *Surfing the Edge of Chaos: The Laws of Nature and the New Laws of Business*, New York: Crown Business.

Pearce, J. A., Freeman, E. and Robinson, R. B. (1987), 'The tenuous link between formal planning and financial performance', *The Academy of Management Journal*, 12(4), 658–67.

Pedersen, J. S. and Dobbin, F. (2006), 'In search of identity and legitimation: bridging organization culture and neoinstitutionalism', *American Behavioral Scientist*, 49(7), 897–907.

Perrow, C. (1972), *Complex Organizations*, London: Scott Foresman.

Peters, E. E. (1991), *Chaos and Order in the Capital Markets: A New View of Cycles, Prices and Market Volatility*, New York: Wiley.

Peters, T. J. and Waterman, R. H. (1982), *In Search of Excellence*, New York: Harper & Row.

Pettigrew, A. M. (1977), 'Strategy formulation as a political process', *International Studies of Management and Organization*, vol. 7, no. 2, pp. 78–87.

Pettigrew, A. M. (1992), 'The character and significance of strategy process research', *Strategic Management Journal*, vol. 13, pp. 5–16.

Petzinger, T. (1999), *The New Pioneers: The Men and Women Who Are Transforming the Workplace and Marketplace*, New York: Simon & Schuster.

Pfeffer, J. (1981), *Power in Organizations*, Cambridge, MA: Ballinger.

Pfeffer, J. and Sutton, R. (2006), *Hard Facts, Dangerous Half-Truths and Total Nonsense: Profiting from Evidence-Based Management*, Boston: Harvard Business School Press.

Phelan, S. (1999), 'A note on the correspondence between complexity and systems theory', *Systemic Practice and Action Research*, vol. 12, no. 3, pp. 237–46.

Philips, A. W. (1950), 'Mechanical models in economic dynamics', *Econometrica*, vol. 17, pp. 283–305.

Pinto, J. K. (ed.) (1998), *Project Management Handbook*, San Francisco: Jossey-Bass.

Polanyi, M. (1958), *Personal Knowledge*, Chicago: University of Chicago Press.

Polanyi, M. (1960), *The Tacit Dimension*, London: Routledge & Kegan Paul.

Polanyi, M. and Prosch, H. (1975), *Meaning*, Chicago: University of Chicago Press.

Porter, M. (1980), *Competitive Strategy: Techniques for Analyzing Industries and Competitors*, New York: The Free Press.

Porter, M. (1985), *Competitive Advantage: Creating and Sustaining Superior Performance*, New York: The Free Press.

Porter, M. (1987), 'From competitive advantage to corporate strategy', *Harvard Business Review*, vol. 63, May–June, pp. 43–59.

Prigogine, I. (1997), *The End of Certainty: Time, Chaos and the New Laws of Nature*, New York: The Free Press.

Prigogine, I. and Stengers, I. (1984), *Order Out of Chaos: Man's New Dialogue with Nature*, New York: Bantam Books.

Q

Quinn, J. B. (1978), 'Strategic change: logical incrementalism', *Sloan Management Review*, vol. 1, no. 20, Fall, pp. 7–21.

Quinn, J. B. (1980), *Strategic Change: Logical Incrementalism*, Homewood, IL: Richard D. Irwin.

Quinn, J. B., Anderson, P. and Finkelstein, S. (1996), 'Managing professional intellect: making the most of the best', *Harvard Business Review*, March–April, pp. 71–80.

R

Rajagopalan, N. and Finkelstein, S. (1992), 'Effects of strategic orientation and environmental change on senior management reward systems', *Strategic Management Journal*, vol. 13, Special Issue, Summer, pp. 127–42.

Ralls, J. G. and Webb, K. A. (1999), *The Nature of Chaos in Business: Using Complexity to Foster Successful Alliances and Acquisitions*, Houston, TX: Gulf Publishing.

Rapoport, A. (1974), *Conflict in Man-made Environment*, Harmondsworth: Penguin Books Ltd.

Rapoport, A. (1976), Creating Shareholder Value: The new standard for bussiness performance, Simon & Schuster.

Ray, T. S. (1992), 'An approach to the synthesis of life', in Langton, G. C., Taylor, C., Doyne Farmer, J. and Rasmussen, S. (eds), *Artificial Life II*, Santa Fé Institute, Studies in the Sciences of Complexity, vol. 10, Reading, MA: Addison-Wesley.

Reason, P. (1988), *Human Inquiry in Action: Developments in New Paradigm Research*, London: Sage.

Reason, P. and Heron, J. (1995), 'Co-operative inquiry', in Smith, J. A., Harré, R. and Van Langenhove, L. (eds), *Rethinking Methods in Psychology*, London: Sage.

Regner, P. (2003), 'Strategy creation in the periphery: inductive versus deductive strategy making', *Journal of Management Studies*, vol. 40, no. 1, pp. 57–82.

Regner, R. K. and Huff, A. S. (1993), 'Strategic groups: a cognitive perspective', *Strategic Management Journal*, vol. 14, pp. 103–24.

Reilly, E. W. (1955), 'Planning the Strategy of the Business', *Advanced Management*, Dec, 8–12.

Reynolds, C. W. (1987), 'Flocks, herds and schools: a distributed behaviour model', Proceedings of Siggraph '87, *Computer Graphics*, vol. 21, no. 4, pp. 25–34.

Richard, O., Barnett, T., Dwyer, S. and Chadwick (2004), 'Cultural Diversity in Management, Firm Performance, and the Moderating role of Entrepreneurial Orientation dimensions', *Academy of Management Journal*, 47(2), 255–66.

Richardson, G. P. (1991), *Feedback Thought in Social Science and Systems Theory*, Philadelphia, PA: University of Pennsylvania Press.

Robertson, D. A. and Caldart, A. A. (2008), 'Natural Science Models in Management: Opportunities and Challenges', *Emergence, Complexity & Organization*, 10(2), 49–61.

Robinson, G. and Dechant, K. (1997), 'Building a business case for diversity', *Academy of Management Executive*, 11(3), 21–31.

Rousseau, D. M. (2006), 'Is there such a thing as "evidence-based management"?', *Academy of Management Review*, 31(2), 256–69.

Rousseau, D. M., Manning, J. and Denyer, D. (2008), 'Evidence in Management and Organizational Science: Assembling the Field's Full Weight of Scientific Knowledge through Synthesis', *Annals of the Academy of Management*, 2, 475–515.

Rowe, A. J., Mason, R. O., Dickel, K. E. and Snyder, N. H. (1989), *Strategic Management and Business Policy: A Methodological Approach*, Reading, MA: Addison-Wesley.

Rue, L. W. and Fulmer, R. W. (1973), 'Is long range planning profitable?', *Proceedings of the Academy of Management*, 66–73.

Rumelt, R. D. (1974), *Strategy, Structure and Economic Performance*, Boston, MA: Harvard Business School Press.

Rumelt, R., Schendel, D. and Teece, D. J. (1994), 'Fundamental issues in strategy', in Rumelt, R., Schendel, D. and Teece, D. J. (eds), *Fundamental Issues in Strategy*, Cambridge, MA: Harvard Business School Press.

Rush, J. C., White, R. E. and Hurst, D. C. (1989), 'Top management teams and organizational renewal', *Strategic Management Journal*, vol. 10, pp. 87–105.

Rycroft, R. W. and Kash, D. E. (1999), *The Complexity Challenge: Technological Innovation for the 21st Century*, New York: Pinter.

S

Sacks, H. (1992), *Lectures on Conversation*, ed. G. Jefferson, Oxford: Blackwell.

Salvato, C. (2003), 'The role of micro-strategies in the engineering of form evolution', *Journal of Management Studies*, vol. 40, no. 1, pp. 83–108.

Samra-Fredericks, D. (2003), 'Strategizing as lived experience and strategists' everyday efforts to shape strategic direction', *Journal of Management Studies*, vol. 40, no. 1, pp. 141–74.

Sanders, T. I. (1998), *Strategic Thinking and the New Science: Planning in the Midst of Chaos, Complexity, and Change*, New York: The Free Press.

Sarbin, T. R. (1986), 'The narrative as a root metaphor for psychology', in Sarbin, T. R. (ed.), *Narrative Psychology: The Storied Nature of Human Conduct*, New York: Praeger.

Sarra, N. (2005), 'Organizational development in the National Health Service', in Stacey, R. and Griffin, D. (eds), *A Complexity Perspective on Researching Organizations: Taking Experience Seriously*, London: Routledge.

Sarra, N. (2006), 'The Emotional Experience of Performance Management in the Health Sector: The corridor', in Stacey, R. and Griffin, D. (eds), *Complexity and the Experience of Managing in the Public Sector*, London: Routledge.

Schein, E. H. (1988), *Process Consultation. Vol. II: Lessons for Managers and Consultants*, Reading, MA: Addison-Wesley.

Schendel, D. (1992), 'Introduction to the summer 1992 special issue on "strategy process" research', *Strategic Management Journal*, vol. 13, Special Issue, Summer, pp. 1–4.

Schenkman, L. and Le Baron, B. (1989), 'Nonlinear dynamics and stock returns', *Journal of Business*, vol. 62, no. 3.

Schermerhorn, R., Hunt, J. G. and Osborn, R. N. (1991), *Managing Organizational Behaviour*, New York: Wiley.

Schreiber, C. and Carley, K. M. (2006), 'Leadership Style as an Enabler of Organizational Complex Functioning', *Emergence, Complexity & Organization*, 8(4), 61–76.

Schwenk, C. and Thomas, H. (1983), 'Formulating the mess: the role of decision and problem formulation', *Omega: The International Journal of Management Science*, vol. 11, no. 3, pp. 239–52.

Scott, J. C. (1990), *Domination and the Arts of Resistance: Hidden Transcripts*, New Haven: Yale University Press.

Scott, J. C. (1998), *Seeing Like a State: How Certain Schemes to Improve the Human Condition Have Failed*, New Haven: Yale University Press.

Scott, W. (2001), *Institutions and Organizations*, Thousand Oaks, CA: Sage.

Seddon, J. (2008), *Systems Thinking in the Public Sector: the failure of the reform regime and a manifesto for a better way*, Axminster: Triachy Press.

Selznick, P. (1957), *Leadership in Administration: A Sociological Interpretation*, Evanston, IL: Row Peterson.

Senge, P. M. (1990), *The Fifth Discipline: The Art and Practice of the Learning Organization*, New York: Doubleday.

Senge, P. M., Scharmer, C. O., Jaworski, J. and Flowers, B. S. (2005), *Presence: Exploring Profound Change in People, Organizations and Society*, London: Nicholas Brealey Publishing.

Sewell, G. and Wilkinson, B. (1992), 'Empowerment or emasculation? Shopfloor surveillance in a Total Quality Management Organisation', in Blyton, P. and Turnbull, P. (eds), *Re-assessing Human Resource Management*, London: Sage.

Shannon, C. and Weaver, W. (1949), *The Mathematical Theory of Communication*, Urbana, IL: University of Illinois Press.

Shapiro, E. R. and Carr, Wesley, A. (1991), *Lost in Familiar Places*, New Haven, CT: Yale University Press.

Shaw, P. (2002), *Changing the Conversation: Organizational Change From a Complexity Perspective*, London: Routledge.

Shaw, P. and Stacey, R. (2006), *The Experience of Risk, Spontaneity and Improvization in Organizational Change: Working Live*, London: Routledge.

Shegloff, E. A. (1991), 'Reflections on talk and social structure', in Boden, D. and Zimmerman, D. H. (eds), *Talk and Social Structure*, Cambridge: Polity Press.

Shelton, C. D. and Darling, J. D. (2004), 'From chaos to order: exploring new frontiers in conflict management', *Organisational Development Journal*, vol. 22, no. 3, pp. 22–41.

Shotter, J. (1983), ' "Duality of structures" and "intentionality" in an ecological psychology', *Journal for the Theory of Social Behavior*, vol. 13, pp. 19–43.

Shotter, J. (1993), *Conversational Realities: Constructing Life Through Language*, Thousand Oaks, CA: Sage.

Shotter, J. and Katz, A. M. (1997), 'Articulating a practice from within the practice itself: establishing formative dialogues to the use of a "social poetics" ', *Concepts and Transformations*, vol. 2, pp. 71–95.

Short, J. C., Ketchen, D. J., Palmer, T. B. and Hult, G. T. (2006), 'Firm, strategic group, and industry influences on performance', *Strategic Management Journal*, 28(2), 147–67.

Simon, H. A. (1952), 'On the Application of Servomechanism Theory in the Study of Production Control', *Econometrica*, 20(2), 467–82.

Simon, H. A. (1960), *The New Science of Management Decision*, Englewood Cliffs, NJ: Prentice Hall.

Simon, H. A. (1969), *The Sciences of the Artificial*, Cambridge, MA: MIT Press. (See in particular Chapter 5, 'The sciences of design: creating the artificial'.)

Skjorshammer, M. (2001), 'Conflict management in a hospital', *Journal of Management in Medicine*, vol. 15, no. 2, pp. 156–66.

Smith, D. (2001), *Norbert Elias and Modern Social Theory*, London: Sage.

Soeters, J. and Iterson, A. van (2002), 'Blame and praise gossip in organizations', in Iterson, A. van, Mastenbroek, W., Newton, T. and Smith, D. (eds), *The Civilized Organization: Norbert Elias and the Future of Organizational Studies*, Amsterdam: John Benjamins, pp. 25–40.

Soltani, E. and Pei-Chun Lai (2007), 'Approaches to quality management in the UK: survey evidence and implications', *Benchmarking: An International Journal*, 14(4), 429–54.

Sommer, S. C., Loch, C. H. and Dong, J. (2009), 'Managing Complexity and Unforeseeable Uncertainty in Startup Companies: An empirical Study', *Organization Science*, 20(1), 118–133.

Springett, N. (1998), 'Producing strategy in the 1990s: the rhetorical dynamics of strategic conversation', Complexity and Management Centre Working Paper no. 21, University of Hertfordshire.

Stacey, R. (2001), *Complex Responsive Processes in Organizations: Learning and Knowledge Creation*, London: Routledge.

Stacey, R. (2003), *Complexity and Group Processes: A Radically Social Understanding of Individuals*, London: Brunner-Routledge.

Stacey, R. (ed.) (2005), *Experiencing Emergence in Organizations: Local Interaction and the Emergence of Global Pattern*, London: Routledge.

Stacey, R. (2009), *Complexity and organizational reality: the need to re-think management after the collapse of investment capitalism*, London: Routledge.

Stacey, R. and Griffin, D. (eds) (2005), *A complexity perspective on researching organizations: taking Experience Seriously*, London: Routledge.

Stacey, R. and Griffin, D. (eds) (2006), *Complexity and the Experience of Managing in the Public Sector*, London: Routledge.

Stacey, R. and Griffin, D. (eds) (2008), *Complexity and the Experience of Values, Conflict and Compromise in Organizations*, London: Routledge.

Stacey, R., Griffin, J. D. and Shaw, P. (2000), *Complexity and Management: Fad or Radical Challenge to Systems Thinking?* London: Routledge.

Stapley, L. F. (1996), *The Personality of the Organisation: A Psychodynamic Explanation of Culture and Change*, London: Free Association Books.

Steier, F. (1991), *Research and Reflexivity*, Thousand Oaks, CA: Sage.

Stewart, I. (1989), *Does God Play Dice? The Mathematics of Chaos*, Oxford: Blackwell.

Stickland, F. (1998), *The Dynamics of Change: Insights into Organizational Transition from the Natural World*, London: Routledge.

Streatfield, P. (2001), *The Paradox of Control in Organizations*, London: Routledge.

Sun Tzu (1971), *The Art of War* (S. B. Confitt, translator), New York: Oxford University Press.

Surie, G. and Hazy, J. K. (2006), 'Generative Leadership: Nurturing Innovation in Complex Systems', *Emergence, Complexity & Organization*, 8(4), 13–26.

Sveiby, K. E. (1997), *The New Organizational Wealth: Managing and Measuring Knowledge-Based Assets*, San Francisco, CA: Berrett & Koehler.

Sword, L. D. (2007), 'Complexity science conflict analysis of power and protest', *Emergence, Complexity & Organization*, 9(3), 47–61.

T

Tajfel, H. (1972), 'Social categorization' (English manuscript of 'la categorisation sociale'), in Moscovici, S. (ed.), *Introduction à la Psycologie Sociale* (Vol. I, pp. 272–302), Paris: Larousse.

Tajfel, H. and Turner, J. C. (1979), 'An integrative theory of intergroup conflict', in Austin, W. G. and Worchel, S. (eds), *The social psychology of intergroup relations*, (pp. 3–7). Monterey, CA: Brooks-Cole.

Taylor, C. (1995), *Philosophical Arguments*, Cambridge, MA: Harvard University Press.

Taylor, C. (2007), *A Secular Age*, Cambridge, MA: The Belknap Press of Harvard University Press.

Taylor, F. ([1911] 1967), *Scientific Management*, New York: Harper Brothers.

Taylor, J. (2005), 'Leadership and cult values: moving from the idealized to the experienced', in Griffin, D. and Stacey, R. (eds), *Complexity and the Experience of Leading Organizations*, London: Routledge.

Taylor, W. A. and Wright, G. H. (2002), 'A longitudinal study of TQM implementation: factors influencing success and failure', *Omega*, 3(2), 97–111.

Thietart, R. A. and Forgues, B. (1995), 'Chaos theory and organisation', *Organisation Science*, vol. 6, no. 1, pp. 19–31.

Thomas, D. A. and Ely, R. J. (1996), 'Making differences matter: a new paradigm for managing diversity', *Harvard Business Review*, pp. 79–90.

Thompson, J. D. and Tuden, A. (1959), 'Strategies, structures and processes of organisational decisions', in Thompson, J. D. *et al.* (eds), *Comparative Studies in Administration*, Pittsburgh, PA: University of Pittsburgh Press.

Tichy, G. (2001), 'What Do We Know about Success and Failure of Mergers?', *Journal of Industry, Competition and Trade*, 1(4), 347–94.

Tilles, S. (1963), 'How to Evaluate Corporate Strategy', *Harvard Business Review*, July–Aug, 111–20.

Tobin, J. (2005), 'The role of leader and the paradox of detached involvement', in Griffin, D. and Stacey, R. (eds), *Complexity and the Experience of Leading Organizations*, London: Routledge.

Tolbert, P. S. and Zucker, L. G. (1996), 'The institutionalization of institutional theory', in Clegg, S. R., Hardy, C. and Nord, W. R. (eds), *A Handbook of Organization Studies*, London: Sage.

Townley, B. (1994), *Reframing Human Resource Management: Power, ethics and the subject at Work*, London: Sage.

Traylen, H. (1994), 'Confronting hidden agendas: co-operative inquiry with health visitors', in Reason, P. (ed.), *Participation in Human Inquiry*, Sage: London.

Trist, E. L. and Bamforth, K. W. (1951), 'Some social and psychological consequences of the long wall method of coal getting', *Human Relations*, vol. 5, pp. 6–24.

Truss, C. (2001), 'Complexities and Controversies in Linking HRM with Organizational Outcomes', *Journal of Management Studies*, 38(8), 1121–49.

Tsoukas, H. (1996), 'The firm as a Distributed Knowledge System: A Constructionist Approach', *Strategic Management Journal*, 17(Winter Special Issue), pp. 11–25.

Tsoukas, H. T. (1997), 'Forms of knowledge and forms of life in organised contexts', in Chia, R. (ed.), *In the Realms of Organisation: essays for Robert Cooper*, London: Routledge.

Turner, J. R. (1999), *The Handbook of Project-Based Management*, 2nd edition, New York: McGraw-Hill.

Turner, J. R., Grude, K. V. and Thurloway, L. (1996), *The Project Manager as Change Agent: Leadership, Influence and Negotiation*, New York: McGraw-Hill.

Turquet, P. (1974), 'Leadership: the individual and the group', in Gibbard, G. S., Hartman, J. J. and Mann, R. D. (eds), *Analysis of Groups*, San Francisco, CA: Jossey-Bass.

Tushman, M. L. and Romanelli, E. (1985), 'A metamorphosis model of convergence and reorientation', in Straw, B. and Cummings, E. (eds), *Research in Organizational Behavior*, vol. 7, Greenwich, CT: Jai Press.

Tustin, A. (1953), *The Mechanism of Economic Systems*, Cambridge, MA: Harvard University Press.

Twomey, D. F. (2006), 'Designed Emergence as a Path to Enterprise Sustainability', *Emergence, Complexity & Organization*, 8(3), 12–23.

V

Van de Ven, A. (1992), 'Suggestions for studying strategy process: a research note', *Strategic Management Journal*, vol. 13, Special Issue, Summer, pp. 169–91.

Van de Ven, A. H. and Johnson, P. E. (2006), 'Knowledge for Theory and Practice', *Academy of Management Review*, vol. 31, no. 4, 802–21.

van Iterson, A., Mastenbroek, W. and Soeters, J. (2001), 'Civilizing and Informalizing: Organizations in an Eliasian Context', *Organization*, 8, 3, 497–514.

van Knippenberg, A. and Ellemers, N. (1993), 'Strategies in intergroup relations', in Hogg, M. A. and Abrams, D. (eds), *Group motivation: Social psychological perspectives*, pp. 17–23, London: Harvester Wheatsheaf.

Varela, F. J., Thompson, E. and Rosch, E. (1995), *The Embodied Mind: Cognitive Science and Human Experience*, Cambridge, MA: MIT Press.

Volberda, H. W. and Elfring, T. (eds) (2001), *Rethinking Strategy*, London: Sage.

von Glasersveld, E. (1991), 'Knowing without metaphysics: Aspects of the radical constructivist position', in Steier, F. (ed.), *Research and Reflexivity*, London: Sage.

Vroom, V. H. and Yetton, P. W. (1973), *Leadership and Decision Making*, Pittsburgh, PA: University of Pittsburgh Press.

Vygotsky, L. S. (1978), *Mind in Society: The Development of Higher Psychological Processes*, Cambridge, MA: Harvard University Press.

W

Waldrop, M. M. (1992), *Complexity: The Emerging Science at the Edge of Chaos*, Englewood Cliffs, NJ: Simon & Schuster.

Webster, G. and Goodwin, B. (1996), *Form and Transformation: Generative and Relational Principles in Biology*, Cambridge: Cambridge University Press.

Weick, K. ([1969] 1979), *The Social Psychology of Organizing*, New York: McGraw-Hill.

Weick, K. (1995), *Sensemaking in Organizations*, Thousand Oaks, CA: Sage.

Wenger, E. (1998), *Communities of Practice: Learning, Meaning and Identity*, New York: Cambridge University Press.

Wernerfelt, B. (1984), 'A resource-based view of the firm', *Strategic Management Journal*, vol. 5, no. 2, pp. 171–80.

Westphal, J. D. and Frederickson, J. W. (2001), 'Who directs strategic change? Director experience, the selection of new CEOs, and change in corporate strategy', *Strategic Management Journal*, 22(12), 1113–37.

Wheatley, M. J. (1999), *Leadership and the New Science*, revised edition, San Francisco: Berrett & Koehler.

Wheeler, W. (1926), 'Emergent Evolution of the Social', in Brightman, E. (ed.), *Proceedings of the Sixth International Congress of Philosophy*, New York, 33–46.

Whitehead, A. N. (1926), *Science and the Modern World*, Cambridge: Cambridge University Press.

Whitehead, A. N. (1978), *Process and Reality*, New York: The Free Press.

Whittington, R. (2001), *What is Strategy – and Does it Matter?* London: Thomson Learning.

Whittington, R. (2002a), 'The work of strategizing and organizing: for practice perspective', *Strategic Organization*, vol. 1, no. 1, pp. 119–27.

Whittington, R. (2002b), 'Practice perspectives on strategy: unifying and developing a field', *Academy of Management Conference Proceedings*, Denver.

Wiener, N. (1948), *Cybernetics: or Control and Communication in the Animal and the Machine*, Cambridge, MA: MIT Press.

Williams, R. (2005a), 'Belief, truth and justification: issues of methodology, discourse and the validity of personal narratives', in Stacey, R. and Griffin, D. (eds), *A Complexity Perspective on Researching Organizations: Taking Experience Seriously*, London: Routledge.

Williams, R. (2005b), 'Leadership, power and problems of relating in processes of organizational change', in Griffin, D. and Stacey, R. (eds), *Complexity and the Experience of Leading Organizations*, London: Routledge.

Williams, R. (2005c), 'Experiencing national education policies in local interaction', in Stacey, R. (ed.), *Experiencing Emergence in Organizations: local interaction and the emergence of global pattern*, London: Routledge.

Williams, R. (2006), 'The Experience of Leading Public Sector Organizations in a Performance Management Regime', in Stacey, R. and Griffin, D. (eds), *Complexity and the Experience of Managing in the Public Sector*, London: Routledge.

Williamson, O. E. (1975), *Markets and Hierarchies: Analysis and anti-Trust Implications – A Study in the Economics of Internal Organization*, London: Macmillan.

Willmott, H. (1993), 'Strength is Ignorance; Slavery is Freedom: Managing Culture in Modern Organizations', *Journal of Management Studies*, 30, 4, 1–38.

Willmott, H. (2003), 'Renewing *Strength*: Corporate Culture Revisited', *Management*, 6, 3, 73–87.

Wiltbank, R., Dew, N., Read S. and Sarasvaty, S. D. (2006), 'What to do Next? The Case for Non-Predictive Strategy', *Strategic Management Journal*, 27, 981–98.

Winnicott, D. W. (1965), *The Maturational Processes and the Facilitating Environment*, London: Hogarth Press.

Winnicott, D. W. (1971), *Playing and Reality*, London: Tavistock. (Reprinted in 1993 by Routledge.)

Wolfram, S. (1986), *Theory and applications of cellular automata*, Singapore: World Scientific.

Wood, D. R. and LaForge, R. L. (1979), 'The impact of comprehensive planning on financial performace', *The Academy of Management Journal*, 22(3), 516–31.

Wood, R. (2000), *Managing Complexity: How Businesses Can Prosper in the Connected Economy*, London: Profile Books.

Wright, P., Pringle, C. and Kroll, M. (1992), *Strategic Management: Text and Cases*, Needham Heights, MA: Allyn & Bacon.

Z

Zimmerman, B. J. (1992), 'The inherent drive towards chaos', in Lorange, P., Chakravarty, B., Van de Ven, A. and Roos, J. (eds), *Implementing Strategic Processes: Change, Learning and Cooperation*, London: Blackwell.

Zucker, L. (1977), 'The role of institutionalisation in cultural persistence', *American Journal of Sociology*, 42, 726–43.

Index

Abernathy, W.J. 12
abiguity in narrative 417
Abram, D. 450
Abrams, D. 215
abstracting in strategy processes 414–15
  immersing, interaction with 422
acceptability of long-term strategic plans 74–5
Ackoff, R.L. 203, 208
administration
  science of 8
agency theory 12
agents in complex adaptive systems 244
  conflicting constraints on 352
  homogeneous 248–50
  and human action 317, 319
  rules of interaction 257
aggressive leaders 140
Akhavein, J.D. 182
Alexander, S. 254
Allen, P.M. 121, 242, 243, 253, 268, 269–71, 285,
    313, 315
Alvesson, M. 175
Amihud, Y. 182
analogies in complex adaptive systems 316–18
  and organisations 319
Anderson, C. 279
Anderson, P. 279
Anderson, P.W. 240
Andrade, G. 182
Andre, P. 183
Andrews, K.R. 13, 43, 72
anecdotal evidence 176
Ansoff, H.I. 185
Ansoff, I. 13, 43, 72
anticipatory regulators 69
anxiety 131, 132, 394
  and conversation 345–6
  of managers, quality of 479
appearance, knowledge of 51
Apple 265–7

Aram, E. 394
Araujo, L. 119
Argyris, C. 107–9, 116, 119, 123
Armstrong, J.S. 177
Ashby, W.R. 55, 67
Ashforth, B.E. 215
Ashmos, D.P. 281
Athos, A. 12, 83
attitude of generalised other 355–7
authoritarian use of power 114–15
autonomous individual 53–4, 57
autopoietic systems 106, 221–2

Bacharach, S.B. 115
Bacon, F. 48
Bain & Company 10
Bales, R.F. 138
Bamforth, K.W. 128–9
bank mergers, success of 182
banks 443–4
Barnard, C.I. 13
Barney, J.B. 72
Barr, P.S. 157
basic assumption behaviour 345, 395
Bateson, G. 107, 116, 186, 202
Baumol, W.J. 240
Beer, S. 55
Beinhocker, E.D. 278–9
Benhabib, J. 240
Bertalanffy, L. von 55, 127
Bhaktin, M.M. 407
Bion, W. 131, 133, 136, 143, 345
Blanchard, K. 84
blockages in dialogue 111–12
Boden, D. 338, 339
Bogner, W.C. 43
Bohm, D. 111
Boids simulation 248–9, 312–13
Boisot, M. 281
Boje, D.M. 416

Booker, C. 457–8
Borgatta, E.F. 138
Boston Consulting Group 10, 77
Boulding, K.E. 55
boundaries in communities of practice 218
boundary judgements 208, 210
bounded rationality 149–52
  bureaucracy and dominant coalitions
    151–2
Bourdieu, P. 412–13, 417
Boyne, A.G. 181
Brandenberg R.G. 13
Braverman, H. 223
Brews, P.J. 177
Broad, C.D. 254
broken Guitar 308
Brown, J.K. 11
Brown, J.S. 116, 119–20, 163, 217, 416
Brown, S.L. 274–5
Brundin, E. 165, 166, 169
Bruner, J.S. 214, 416–17
Burawoy, M. 223
bureaucracy and dominant coalitions 151–2
Burgelman, R.A. 178, 281
Burke, R. 188
Burton-Jones, A. 116
business planning on innovation 177–8
Business Process Re-engineering (BPR) 181,
    182
butterfly effect 239

Caldart, A.A. 279
Campbell, A. 83
Campbell-Hunt, C. 177, 279
Cardinal, L.B. 177
Carley, K.M. 283
Carlisle, Y. 279
Carr, W.A. 137
Cartwright, S. 183
case studies 176
Caudron, S. 192
causal duality in critical systems thinking 211
causality
  circular 70
  in complexity 252–3
  formative 52
  if-then 49, 52, 57
  in learning organisations 113–14
  nature of 34–5
  rational 57
  teleological 53
  transformative 252–3

Centre for Quality of Care Research (Netherlands)
    180
Chakravarthy, B.S. 43, 157, 161, 163
Chandler, A.D. 13, 43, 77
change
  in conversation 343–4
  cultural, in long-term plans 78–9
  in responsive processes theory 467–8
chaos, edge of 274
chaos theory 237
  and industry 263–4
  and responsive processes theory 311–12
Checkland, P.B. 203, 205–8
Chia, R.C.H. 186, 201, 221, 222–3, 490–1
Child, J. 156
choice and freedom 50
Chomsky, n. 80
Christensen, C.R. 13
Churchman, C.W. 203, 204–5, 206, 208
circular causality 70
classical approach 44
classification of schools of strategic thinking 43–4
Clausewitz, K. von 6
Clinton, Hilary 308
Club of Rome 12
Clutterbuck, D. 179
Coase, R. 212
cognitive frames of reference 157–9
cognitive psychology 80–1
cognitive school 43, 44
cognitive science 80–1
cognitivism 55
  and open systems theory 143
cognitivist psychology 103–10
Cohen, M.D. 152–3, 167
Coleman, H/J/ 279
collegial use of power 115
Collingridge, D. 153
Collins, Dan 309
Collins, E.B. 178
Collins, J. 178
commitment in critical systems thinking 211
communication
  as conversation of gestures 353, 354–61
  sender-receiver model 80–1
  as social act 331–7
communicative interaction 330
communities of practice 217–20
  abstractions 219
community of practice, managers as 7–8
competitive advantage of technology 446–7
competitive interaction 265

complex adaptive systems 244–53
  and analogies 316–18
  and chaos 312
  environmental information in 255–6
  fitness landscapes in 246–8
  inherent patterning capacity 245–6
  nonlinear models in 256
  organisational interpretations 313–14
  organisations as 278–9
  simulating populations
    of homogeneous agents 248–9, 312–18
    of interacting heterogeneous agents 248–9,
      314–15
  studies of 245
complex responsive processes theory see responsive
    processes theory
complex systems
  industries as 263–71
    and chaos theory 263–4
    fitness landscapes for 264–8
  in learning organisations 101–2
  methodology 286
  organisations as 271–84
    Beinhocker on 278–9
    Brown and Eisenhardt on 274–5
    Lewin and Regine on 276–7
    Morgan on 272–3
    Nonaka on 273
    Pascale on 277–8
    Sanders on 273–4
    Thietart and Forgues on 271–2
    Wheatley on 275–6
  pressure points in 102
complexity
  interpretations of 253–9
    Gell-Mann on 255–6
    Goodwin on 258
    Holland on 256–7
    Kauffman on 257–8
    Langton on 255
    Prigogine on 258
  and organisations 15, 18
computer industry, growth and development 264–5
computer simulations 9
configuration school 43
conflict 191–2
  negotiation of 357–8
congruence in long-term plans 76
conscious organisations 409–10
consciousness 332–3
constitutive ideas 50
constructionism 32

constructivist psychology 105–6, 201
consultants 137
contingency view of strategy 156
control and control systems
  in long-term plans 77–8
  managers in 483–5
controlling leaders 140
conversation 330
  and anxiety 345–6
  dynamics of 344–6
  emergence of themes 403–11
  kinds 339
  leadership 346–7
  as local interaction 366
  by managers, quality of 478–9
  in organisations 337–44
    intention 341
    rhetoric 341–3
    strategy and change 343–4
    thematic patterning 339–41
    turn-taking/turn-making 337–9
  participation in 338–9
  as strategy 330
conversation of gestures 331–7
  consciousness 332–3
  generalised other 335
  human communication as 353, 354–61
  language 333–4
  by leaders 368
  processes of self 335–7
  and sender-receiver model 334–5
  as significant symbols 332
Cooper, C.L. 183
Cooperrider, D. 214
Coopey, J. 120
Copernicus 48
Coronado, G. 279
corporate planning 11, 12
corporate strategy 11
Coser, L.A. 191
cost-accounting systems 9
counteracting forces in chaos 271–2
creativity 187
'credit crunch' (2007) 444–5
critical systems 59
critical systems thinking 208–12
  boundary judgements in 208, 210
  holism 209
  multiple realities in 209
  participation in 209
  systemic intervention in 208–9
critical theory 194–5

Crook, T.R. 178
cult values 359, 376–8
    narrative form of 411
    technology as 450
cultural change in long-term plans 78–9
cultural school 43, 44
cultural strand 206–7
cybernetic systems 55, 56, 58
    and causality 70–2
    in strategic choice theory 66–72
        equilibrium 66–7
        goal-seeking adaptation 68
        and human action 67–8
        negative feedback 66–8
        regulators 68–70
cybernetic systems theory 9
Cyert, R.M. 151, 156

Dalal, F. 391
Damasio, A.R. 332
D'Aveni, R. 88
Davenport, T.H. 116
Dawkins, R. 422
De Geuss, A. 179
de Rond, M. 220–1
de Waal, F. 332
Deal, T.T.A. 390
Dean, Howard 307
Dechant, K. 192
decision making
    responsive processes perspectives on 394–6
    in soft systems methodology 207
    techniques 10
    see also strategy processes
Deetz, S. 215
defence routines in organisations 109
deliberately emergent strategy processes 158
Delmar, F. 177
dependence in groups 133–4
Descartes, R. 48, 49
descriptive schools 43, 44
    cognitive school 43, 44
    cultural school 43, 44
    entrepreneurial school 43, 44
    environmental school 43, 44
    learning school 43, 44
    power school 43, 44
design school of strategy 43, 44, 184–5
desires 378–9
detached leaders 140
detatched participation 338
determinism 235

Dewey, J. 362, 378–9
dialogue 111–12
    in relational co-constructionism 214
dichotomy 35
Dickerson, A. 183
Dimaggio, P.J. 157, 213
dissipative structures 240–3
    and complex adaptive systems 312
distribution chains
    in learning organisation 101
diversity
    and managers, quality of 479–80
    in organisations 192–3, 268
dliemmas 35
Dobbin, F. 212
dominant coalitions 151–2
Donaldson, A. 450
Dopson, S. 387
double-loop learning 108–9
Downs, A. 279
Doz, Y. 43, 157, 161, 163
duality 35–6
    of relative and realist knowledge 50–1
    in systems thinking (Kant) 54, 298
Duguid, P. 119–20, 163, 217, 416
Dunphy, D.C. 139
dynamic equilibrium 67
dynamic phenonema 28–9
    degrees of detail 29–30
    idealism 32
    interaction 30–1
    paradoxical phenonema 29
    realism 31
    relativism 32

Easterby-Smith, M. 119
Eccles, M. 180
Edelenvos, J. 281
education
    for management 8–12
    models of management 8
efficiency in scientific management 58
efficient causality 301
Eisenhardt, K.M. 274–5
Elias, N. 194, 254, 316, 366, 390, 407, 412, 417, 450
    on conversation 336, 338
    on gossip 392–3
    on norms 379
    on power 387–9, 395
    on responsive processes 298–9, 300–10
    on social order 301–3

Ellemers, N. 215
Ely, R.J. 193
emancipation in critical systems thinking 211, 212
emergence
    in complex adaptive systems 244–5, 253, 279, 281
    conflicting constraints on 352
    conversation as 330
    in dissipative structures 242
    and intention 309–10
    of novelty 267
    and social order 302
    in strategic decision making 153, 158
        and intention 184–7
emotional conflict 191
enactment in learning organisations 106–7
    and representation 118–19
entrepreneurial school of strategy 43, 44, 184
environmental school 43, 44
error, search for 153–4
error-controlled regulators 69
Eskildson, L. 181
ethics and leadership 384–7
Etzioni, A. 83
European Foundation for Quality Management 181
evolution approach 44
exclusion, dynamics of 390–2
    emotional aspects 393
    shame and panic in 393–4
experience
    in learning organisations 123
    narrative patterning of 411–15
    in open systems theory 145
    role of narrative and storytelling 415–17
    second-order abstracting 418–22
    in strategic choice theory 94
experience curves in long-term plans 76–7
expert behaviour 108
explicit knowledge 116–18, 454
explorative conflict 358
Ezzamel, M. 182

Facebook
    development of 304–7
    and national politics 307–8
failure work 190
Fayol, H. 56, 57
    management activities 57
feasibility oflong-term strategic plans 75
feedback
    in learning organisations 102–3
        lags in 101–2

limits to growth 103
    see also negative feedback
Festinger, L. 85
Fiedler, F.E. 84
fight/flight in groups 134
finance, teaching of 12
financial performance and long-term strategic plans 74
financial resources
    complex responsive processes theory on 446
    for long-term strategic plans 75
    as social object 445
    in strategic choice theory 443–7
Finkelstein, S. 161
firms
    analysis of 177–8
    and TQM 181
first-order desires 378
fishing industry 270–1
Fiske, S.T. 215
fitness landscapes 246–8
    industries exploration of 264–8
Flood, R.L. 203, 204, 208
Floyd, S.W. 161
Foerster, H. von 201
Fonseca, J. 407
forecasting as second-order abstracting 423
foresight 353–4
Forgues, B. 271–2
formal organisations 409
formative causality 52, 301
    in learning organisations 107
    and self-organisation 252
    systems in 187
Forrester, J. 55, 100, 101
Foulkes, S.H. 336, 344, 347
fractal chaos 238, 311
frames of reference, rhetoric as 342
Frankfurt, H. 378
Frederickson, J.W. 177
Freeman, J. 185
Friesen, P.H. 157
Friis, P. 363
Fullerton, J. 194
Fulmer, R.M. 11

Gabriel, Y. 416
Galbraith, J.R. 78
Gallese, V. 332
game, preoccupation in 412–13
garbage-can decision making 152–3, 167
Gardner, H. 55, 80
Garfinkel, H. 337

Garud, R. 155
Garven, D.A. 116
Gate Gourmet 303–4
Gell-Mann, M. 244, 255–6, 257, 258
general systems 55
general systems theory 127, 129
    and organisational psychodynamics 130
generalised articulations of activity as strategy 352
generalised other 335, 354
    attitude of 355–7
generalising in human communication 354–61, 362
Gergen, K.J. 32, 213, 214, 215, 411, 473
Gershenson, C. 279
Ghobadian, A. 177
Giddens, A. 168–9
Gilbert, J.A. 192, 193
Gilmore, F.F. 13
Ginsberg, A. 157
Glasl, F. 191
Gleick, J. 237, 239
global warming 457–8
goal-seeking adaptation to environment 68
Goffman, E. 337
Goldsmith, W. 179
Goldstein, J. 253, 254, 279
'good enough holding' 345
Goodwin, B. 51, 253, 255, 258
Goodwin, R.M. 55, 100
Goold, M. 177
gossip 392–3
governance 436
Graham, Alexander 308
Grant, D. 416
Grant, R.M. 177
Greenley, G.E. 177
Greiner, L.E. 115, 157, 159–60
Griffin, D. 54, 123, 254, 275, 276, 278, 283, 286,
    298, 386
Grimshaw, J.M. 180
Grint, K. 215
Grol, R. 180
Groot, N. 357–8
group think 110
groups
    and the individual 33–4
    and infantile mechanisms 133–5
    relevance of 84–5
    in strategic choice theory 84–5
    as systems 53
Grove, A.S. 178, 281
Guba, E.G. 175
Guth, W.D. 13

habitus 412
Hamel, G. 86–7
Hannan, M.T. 185
Hardwick, CC.T. 13
Harvard Business School 13
Haspeslagh, P.C. 11
Hayes, N. 12, 215
Haynes, P. 279
Hazy, J.K. 282
healthcare, and ideology 382–4
Hegel, G.W.F. 36, 187, 298
    on responsive processes thinking 299–300
Henderson, B.D. 77
Hendricks, K.B. 181
Heron, J. 175
Hersey, P. 84
Hertzberg, F. 82
Hertzberg, H. 81
heterogeneous agents, simulating populations of
    248–9
heterogeneous complex adaptive agents 252
Hewlett-Packard 182
hidden transcripts 407–9
high-dimensional chaos 237
histrionic leaders 140
Hodge, B. 279
Hodgson, G.M. 253, 254
Hofer, C.W. 73, 76
Hogg, M.A. 215
holism 209
Holland, J. 244–5, 255, 256–7, 258
Holmes, J. 413
Holt, R. 186, 201, 221, 222–3, 490–1
Holton, E.F. 178
Holwell, S. 207
homeostasis in systems 55
homogeneous agents, simulating populations of 248–9
Hosking, D.M. 214
Huff, A.S. 43
Huff, J.O. 157
human communication as conversation of gestures
    353, 354–61
human nature
    and choice 91–2
    in complex systems 285
    and learning organisations 121–2, 469
    in open systems theory 142–4
    in responsive processes theory 470–1
    and strategic choice theory 91–2, 469
    and systems 316–17
human psychology 471–3
    and paradox 474–5

Human Relations School of scientific management 57
human resource management (HRM) 182
and diversity 193
evolution of roles 447
for long-term strategic plans 75, 78
in strategic choice theory 447–8
human systems 54–6
humanistic psychology 81–4
in learning organisations 110–14
methodology of 473
Hume, David 49
Hunt, M.R. 177
Huselid, N.A. 182
Hussey, D.E. 78
hypercompetition 89

'I-me' dialectic 335–6
IBM 265–7
idealism 32
identity in communities of practice 217
identity narrative, strategy as 459–61
ideology 382
and healthcare 382–4
in institutions 456–7
legitimate themes in 404
and power 387–9
if-then causality 49, 52, 57
in cybernetic systems 68
in strategy without design 220
imaginative constructs 362–3
IMD (Switzerland) 11
IMEDE (Switzerland) 11
IMI (Switzerland) 11
immersing in strategy processes 413–14
abstracting activities, interaction with 422
implementation science 10–181
improvement
in critical systems thinking 211, 212
managers and 485–6
inclusion, dynamics of 390–2
emotional aspects 393
shame and panic in 393–4
individual
and the group 33–4
relationship to organisations 83
industries as complex systems 263–71
and chaos theory 263–4
evolution of 268–71
fitness landscapes for 264–8
infantile mechanisms 131–3
groups and 133–5
informal organisations 409

information systems in long-term plans 77–8
Ingham, H. 183
inherent patterning capacity 245–6
innovation
business planning on 177–8
trial-and-error 155
INSEAD (France) 11
institutional theory 212–13
institutions as social objects 456–9
instrumental conflict 191
Intel 265
intentions
conversation as 330, 341
and emergence 184–7, 309–10
interplay of 302
inter-group conflict 192
inter-organisational conflict 192
interacting heterogeneous agents, simulating populations of 248–9
interaction 30–1, 235
in complex adaptive systems 245–6
in complex systems 284–5
in learning organisations, nature of 120–1
in open systems theory 141–2
within organisms 51–2
rules of in complex adaptive systems 257
in strategic choice theory 90–1
between systems 30
interaction models 16–17
interactive planning 203–4
interpersonal conflict 191
intersubjective themes in conversation 340
intrapersonal conflict 191
investment capitalism 13
investment decisions, strategy of 424–6
involved participation 338
Isaacs, W. 111, 120
iteration 320
Ivancevich, J.M. 193

Jackson, M.C. 203, 208–11
Jacques, E. 137
James, W. 378
Jarzabkowski, P. 165, 168, 169
Jefferson, G. 337
Joas, H. 336, 378, 379
Johannesen, S. 449
John Laing 11, 12
Johnson, Boris 308
Johnson, G. 157, 162
Johnson, P.E. 175
joint action in relational co-constructionism 214

joint enterprise in communities of practice 217
joint stock companies 7

Kandola, R.S. 194
Kant, E. 32, 89, 103, 201, 205, 206, 235, 252, 297–9
  autonomous individual 53–4, 57
  on ethics 385
  formative causality 52
  key concepts 54
  noumenal 50
  phenomenal 50
  self-organising systems 50–3
Karreman, D. 175
Katz, A.M. 342
Kauffman, S.A. 52, 244, 246, 248, 253, 257–8
Kazanian, R.K. 78
Kelsey, D. 240
Kennedy, A.A. 390
Kerry, John 307
Kets de Vries, M.F. 139–40
Khurana, R. 7, 9
King, D.R. 183
Klein, M. 131, 132, 143
Kleiner, A. 116
Knights, D. 213, 223
knowledge creation 273, 454–5
knowledge management 116–18, 454–5
Kono, T. 11
Korte, R.F. 215
Kudla, R.J. 176
K.Weick, 105, 106–7, 119, 157, 186

labour process theory 187, 223–4
LaForge, R.L. 176
Landuyt, B.F. 13
Langley, A. 163
Langton, C.G. 244, 255, 258
language 333–4
Lannemann, J.W. 215
Larsen, H. 363
last day of drinking on the tube 308–9
Lave, J. 120, 217
Lawler, E.J. 115
Lawrence, B. 165, 169
Lawrence, P.R. 129
leaders/leadership 13
  in complex systems 281–2
  and conversation 346–7
  in dominant coalitions 367–8
  ethics and 384–7
  neurotic forms 139–41

  in open systems 138–9
  role of 369–71
  roles of 491–4
  in strategic choice theory 84–5
Learned, E.P. 13
learning organisations 59
  blockages in dialogue 111–12
  causality 113–14
  constructivist psychology in 105–6
  defined 119
  dialogue in 111–12
  enactment in 106–7
  evidence on 178–9
  humanistic psychology in 110–14
  knowledge management in 116–18, 454–5
  and organisational learning 119–20
  personal mastery in 103–5
  as second-order abstraction 453–5
  single- and double-loop learning 107–10
  system dynamics 100–3
    feedback processes 102–3
    nonllinearity 100–1
    principles 101–2
    production and distribution chains 101
  team learning 110–14
    shared models in 110–12
  and vested interests 114–16
learning process 80–1
learning school 43, 44
legitimate themes 403–9
Leibnitz, G.W. 48, 49
Leonard, D. 116
Levy, D. 263–4
Lewes, G. 253
Lewin, R. 276–7, 280
libido 131
Lichtenstein, B.B. 281
life cycle theory of time 159–60
Likert, R. 58
Lincoln, Y.S. 175
Lindblom, L. 152, 153, 484
linear programming 9
linear relationships and causality 34–5
living systems 283–4
local interactions 217
  between agents 352
  central role of 466
  conversation as 366
  links to population-wide social patterns 353, 361–9
    imaginative constructs 362–3
    spontaneity 363

local interactions (*continued*)
  in markets 452
  strategic planning in 440
  strategising in 436
  and technology 449, 451
Locke, J. 49
logical analysis 207
logical incrementalism 154–5
  in strategic choice theory 89
London Business School 11
long-term predictions 274
long-term strategic plans
  complex responsive processes theory on 440–1
  evaluating 74–7
    acceptability 74–5
    criteria for 73
    feasibility 75
    suitability or fit 75–7
  formulating 72–3
  implementing 74–7
  impossibility of 264
  plans and planning 72
  prediction 73
Lorsch, J.W. 129
low-dimensional chaos 238

McCain, John 307, 308
McCleod, J. 417
McCulloch, W.S. 55, 80
MacIntosh, R. 280
McKenna, C.D. 10
Mackey, A. 177
McKinsey Consultancy 13, 14
MacLean, D. 280
McMillan, E. 279
McNamee, S. 214, 215
macro view of strategy processes 166–8
Mael, F. 215
Maitlis, S. 165, 169
management
  education for 8–12
  evidence-based 179–80
  as particularising 365
  as science 7, 56
management science 10, 56–8
  evidence for 174–84
  statistical analysis in 175–6
managerial cognition, as process 157, 159
managerial interpretation, as process 157
managers
  anxiety, quality of 479
  as community of practice 7–8

control by 483–5
frames of reference of 157–9
improvement by 485–6
participation by 476–8
reflection, need for 475–6
in role of scientist 57, 59
roles of 491–4
training 9–10
unpredictability and paradox 480–3
March, J.G. 151, 156, 484
Marion, R. 264–8, 285
markets
  negative feedback in 67
  and resource-based view of strategy 86–7
  in strategic choice theory 451–3
Marquis, J.P. 192
Maslow, A. 81, 83
masochistic leaders 141
Mastenbroek, W.F.G. 191
mathematical chaos theory 237–40, 311
Maturana, H.R. 32, 105, 221
Mayo, E. 57
Mayr, E. 254
MBAs, standardisation of 10
Mead, G.H. 194, 298, 310, 318, 320, 425, 449
  on communicative interaction 330, 331–3, 335–7
    and population-wide strategies 353, 354, 357, 358, 360–1, 364–6
  on cult values 376–7, 378
  on ethics 386
  on labour process theory 223–4
meaning in communities of practice 217
Meek, J. 279, 281
Melin, L. 165, 169
mental models 453
Menzies Lyth, I. 137
mergers and acquisitions 182–3
Mezrich, B. 304
micro view of strategy processes 168–70
microcomputers, growth and development 264–5
Microsoft 265, 266
MICS 264
Midgley, G. 203, 208
Miller, C.C. 177
Miller, D. 43, 157
Miller, E.J. 58, 135, 136
Miller, G. 182
Miller E.J. 135, 136
Mingers, J. 208
Mintzberg, H. 43, 44, 88, 99, 149, 157–8, 167, 177, 184–6, 413, 484
Mitleton-Kelly, E. 279

modelling 426–9
  quantitative 430–1
  as second-order abstracting 423
Moore, D.G. 13
moral practice 204
morbido 131
Morgan, C.L. 254
Morgan, G. 272–3
morphological field 258
motivation in organisations 82–3
motivational factors in scientific management 57
Motorola 265
muddling through 152–3
multiple realities in critical systems thinking 209
mutual engagement 217

narcissistic leaders 141
narrative, features of 416–17
narrative patterning
  of conversation 403–11
  of experience 411–15
    role of storytelling 415–17
negative feedback
  in chaos theory 238
  in open systems theory 128–9
  in strategic choice theory 66–8
    equilibrium 66–7
    and human action 67–8
    stability and instability 67
negotiation conflict 191
negotiation of conflict 357–8
Nelson, R.R. 43, 163
network analysis 9
neurotic forms of leadership 139–41
Newbert, S.L. 178
Newman, W.H. 13
Newton, T. 48, 389–90
NHS
  and ideology 382–4
  public and hidden transcripts in 408
  responsive processes on 358–9
  second-order abstracting 419–22
Nicolis, G. 240, 242
Nonaka, I. 116, 117, 118, 120, 273
nonlinearity
  and false information 269
  in learning organisations 100–1
  in organisations 35
norms 379
  and values 381–2
noumenal reality (Kant) 50
novelty 52–3, 187, 245–267

Obama, Barack 307–8
Olsen, J.P. 484
oneness in groups 134
Ong, W.J. 450
open systems theory 127–30
  boundary in 127, 135–6
  conflicting subsystems 129–30
  experience in 145
  human beings, nature of 142–4
  infantile mechanisms 131–3
    groups and 133–5
  interaction, nature of 141–2
  leadership in 138–9
    neurotic forms 139–41
  methodology in 144
  negative feedback in 128–9
  paradox 144
  psychosocial subsystems 128
  technical subsystems 128–9
  unconscious processes 130–1, 135–8
O'Regan, N. 177
organisational learning 119–20
  defined 119
  methodology and 122
  vested interests on 114–16
organisational psychodynamics
  main points 130, 135
  and responsive processes theory 469–70, 471–2
organisational science
  evidence for 174–84
  statistical analysis in 175–6
organisational strategies 436–7
organisational structure, long-term 77
organisations
  as complex systems 271–84
  conscious and unconscious 409–10
  conversation in 337–44
    intention 341
    rhetoric 341–3
    strategy and change 343–4
    thematic patterning 339–41
    turn-taking/turn-making 337–9
  defence routines in 109
  formal and informal 409
  as goal-seeking systems 68
  management of 9
  as patterns of interaction 357
  relationship to individual 83
  as social objects 364–6
  as systems 35, 53
organised anarchy 115–16, 152–3
organising themes in conversation 340

pairing in groups 134
panic 394
paradox
  in complex systems 286
  and human psychology 474–5
  and learning organisations 122–3
  managers and 480–3
  nature of 35–6
  in open systems theory 144
  in strategic choice theory 93
  in strategy processes 413–15
paradoxical phenonema 29
paranoid leaders 140
participation 205
  in communities of practice 218
  in conversation 338–9, 347
  by managers 476–8
particularising in human communication 354–61,
  362
Pascale, R.T. 12, 83, 277–8, 280
passive-aggressive leaders 140
Pearce, J.A. 177
Pedersen, J.S. 212
Pei-Chun Lai 181
performance appraisal as cybernetic system
  58
period two attractor 237
Perrow, C. 158
personal mastery 103–5, 453
persuasion, rhetoric as 342
Peters, E.E. 240
Peters, T.J. 12, 14, 43, 72, 81–2, 178–9
Pettigrew, A.M. 43
Pfeffer, J. 79, 158, 179
Phelan, S. 204
phenomena in strategic choice theory
  89–90
phenomenal reality (Kant) 50
Philips, A.W. 55, 100
Pitts, W. 55, 80
planning school of strategy 43, 44, 184–5
pluralism in critical systems thinking 211
point attractors 237
Polanyi, M. M. 116, 118, 119, 254
polarised conflict 358
policy, origins 6
political behaviour and long-term plans 79
population-wide social patterns
  links to local interactions 353, 361–9
    imaginative constructs 362–3
    spontaneity 363
  strategic planning in 440

populations of organisations 28
  dynamic phenonema 28–9
    degrees of detail 29–30
  interactions 30–1
  paradoxical phenonema 29
Porter, M. 43, 72, 73, 76
positioning school of strategy 43, 44, 184, 185
positive feedback 238
potential transformation in conversation
  344–5
Powell, W.W. 157, 213
power
  authoritarian use of 114–15
  collegial use of 115
  and conversation 345
  and decision making 394–6
  and ideology 387–9
  in relational co-constructionism 215, 216–17
power/dependency conflict 191
power differentials 387–8, 391–2
power law 267, 275
power school 43, 44
power vacuums 115–16
Prahalad, C.K. 86–7
prediction 425–6
preoccupation in the game 412–13
prescriptive schools 43, 44
  design school 43, 44
  planning school 43, 44
  positioning school 43, 44
presencing in dialogue 112
pressure groups and long-term strategic plans
  74–5
pressure points in complex systems 102
Prigogine, I. 253, 255, 258, 268, 320
  on dissipative structures 240, 242–3
process approach 44
process vs content in strategic choice theory 88
processes of self 335–7
product life cycle in long-term plans 76
product portfolio in long-term plans 77
production chains
  in learning organisation 101
Prosch, H. 118, 119
Prusak, L. 116
psychosocial subsystems 128
public organisations, TQM in 181
public transcripts 407–9
purposive development 52

quality management as cybernetic system 58
quantitative modelling 430–1

queuing theory 9
Quinn, J.B. 116, 154–5, 158
Quinn, J.J. 177

Rajagopalan, N. 161
Rapoport, A. 191
rational causality 301
rational objectivity 48–50
rational processes
    bounded rationality 149–52
    error, search for 153–4
    trial-and-error action 152–5
rationalist causality 57, 267
rationality, defined 150
Ray,T.S. 249, 251, 369
realism 31
realist knowledge 50
    contradiction with relative knowledge 50–1
realistic conflict 191
reality
    nature of 49
    noumenal and phenomenal 50
    as sensation 50
reason 49
Reason, P. 33, 175, 473
reasoning as first-order abstracting 422
reductionism 235
reflection 402
reflexivity 33
Regine, B. 276–7, 280
Regner, P. 164–5
Regner, R.K. 43
regulative ideas 50
regulators in cybernetic systems 68–70
    complexity of 69
reification in communities of practice 218
Reilly, E.W. 13
relational co-construction 213–15
relational-responsive form of understanding
        342
relative knowledge 50
    contradiction with realist knowledge 50–1
relativism 32
repetition in conversation 344
representation vs enactment 118–19
requisite variety, law of 70, 72, 88
research 486–91
    evidence base for 486–7
    methods 487–90
    status of knowledge 490–1
resource-based view of strategic choice 86–7
    evidence on 178

resources in strategic choice theory 443–51
    financial resources 443–7
    human resources 447–8
    technology 448–51
responsive processes theory 299–310
    analogies in 316–18
    and chaos theory 311–12
    and complex adaptive systems 312–18
    conversation in 330
    on decision making 394–6
    Elias on 300–10
    entities in 321–2
    Hegel on 299–300
    iteration in 320
    and modelling 426–9
    NHS example 358–9
    norms, values and ideology 381–2
    and organisational dynamics 469
    and organisations 401
    and quantitative modelling 431
    and reasoning 422, 423–4
    research on 486–91
    on strategic management 436
    strategy in 352
    and systemic processes 320–3
    and technical rationality 423
    and time 318–20
    on 'whole' organisation 437–8
reward systems as cybernetic system 58
Reynolds, C.W. 248, 312
rhetoric 341–3
    ploys 342
Rice, A.K. 58, 135, 136
Richard, O. 192
Robertson, D.A. 279
Robinson, G. 192
role conflict 191
Romanelli, E. 157
Roth, G. 116
Rousseau, D.M. 179
Rue, L.W. 11
rules in complex adaptive systems 257
Rumelt, R. 163

Sacks, H. 337, 338–9
Salvato, C. 163–4, 169
Samra-Fredericks, D. 166, 169, 342
Sanders, T.I. 273–4, 280
Sarbin, T.R. 417
scepticism 32, 49
Schein, E.H. 83
Schein, V.E. 115

Schendel, D. 73, 76, 161–2
Schermerhorn, R. 191
Scholes, P. 203, 207
Schön, D. 107–8, 116, 119
Schreiber, C. 283
scientific management 56–8
Scientific Revolution 48–50
Scotson, J. 390, 392
Scott, J.C. 222, 408, 414, 417, 419, 421
Scott, W. 213
second-order abstraction 418–22
   and human psychology 472–3
   methodology of 473–4
   and the modern state 419–22
   in strategic choice theory 437–53
      markets 451–3
      resources 443–51
      role of strategic planning 440–3
   on strategic management 436
second-order desires 378
second-order systems thinking 201–12
   Churchman on 204–5
   and critical systems thinking 208–12
   defined 201
   interactive planning 203–4
   learning levels 202
   and soft systems methodology 205–8
second-ordering principle 257
Seddon, J. 190
self-organisation 223
   and causality 252
   in complex adaptive systems 244–5
   in complex systems 273, 276, 279, 280–1, 366
   in dissipative structures 241
   and social order 302
self-organising systems 50–3
self-regulation in systems 55
Selznick, P. 13, 43
sender-receiver model of communication 80–1
   and conversation of gestures 334–5
Senge, P.M. 99, 102, 111, 112, 116, 120, 188, 440, 453
Severin, Eduardo 304–8
Sewell, G. 223
shadow themes 403–9
shame 393–4
Shane, S. 177
Shannon, C. 55, 81
Shapiro, E.R. 137
shared repertoire in communities of practice 217
shared vision 453
Shaw, P. 343, 427–8

Shegloff, E.A. 337
Short, J.C. 177
Shotter, J. 107, 166, 214, 215, 341–2, 411
Simon, H.A. 80, 100, 151
simple rules of interaction 264, 274, 283–4
Singhal, V. 181
single-loop learning 107–8
Siz Sigma 181
Skoldberg, K. 175
Smith, Adam 221
Smith, D. 393
smoking, and attitude of generalised other 355–6
social act, communication as 331–7
social conflict 191
social constructionism 32, 33
social constructionist approaches 212–17
   institutional theory 212–13
   organisational fields 213
   relational co-construction 213–15
   social identity theory 215–17
social control 360–1
social identity theory 215–17
social objects 358–60
   as cult value 359
   key points 361
   markets as 452
   narrative form of 411
   organisations as 364–6
   reading and writing as 450
   technology as 449
   as tendency to act 360, 365
social participation 217
social practice 217
social structure in conversation 344–345
society as system 53
soft systems 59
soft systems methodology (SSM) 205–8
   interventions 207
   phases 206
   strands 206–7
Soltani, E. 181
Sommer, S.C. 281
spontaneity 363
Springett, N. 342
Srivastva, S. 214
stability in scientific management 58
stable instability 236, 238, 243
Stacey, R. 52, 53, 254, 277, 300, 449
stakeholders 74–5
Stapley, L.F. 345, 473
Steier, F. 33, 473
Stengers, I. 240, 242

Stewart, I. 237
storytelling 415–17
strange attractors 238, 311
strategic choice theory
  cognitive psychology 80–1
  cybernetic systems 66–72
  evidence base for 176–8
  experience 94
  and human nature 91–2, 469
  humanistic psychology 81–4
  and imaginative constructs 438–9
  interactions 90–1
  interactive planning in 203–4
  leadership 84–5
  and limitations of choice 87–8
  long-term strategy see long-term strategic plans
  and measurement 439
  methodology of 93, 473
  and paradox 93
  phenomena 89–90
  process vs content 88
  resource-based view 86–7
  as second-order abstraction 437–53
    markets 451–3
    resources 443–51
    role of strategic planning 440–3
  uncertainty 87–8
  on 'whole' organisation 438
strategic decision making 152–3, 154–5
  investment decisions 424–6
strategic logic to long-term plans 75–6
strategic management 12, 453
strategic planning, role of 440–3
strategising 436
strategy
  conversation as 330
    and change 343–4
  as generalised articulations of activity 352
  as identity narrative 459–61
  origins 6
  as patterns of joint activity 436–7
  as 'whole' 401–2
  without design 220–3
strategy processes
  activity-based view of 162–6
  cognitive frames of reference in 157–9
  contingency view of 156
  as deliberately emergent 158
  growth phases 160
  interpretive view of 157
  paradoxical nature of 413–15
  rational processes in 149–55

review of 161–2
systemic thinking about 166–70
  macro view 166–8
  micro view 168–70
and time 159–61
Strauss, S. 116
Streatfield, P. 484–5
Strong, M. 458
Stube, M. 413
substantive conflict 191
subsystems in open systems theory
  conflicting 129–30
  infantile mechanisms 131–3
  psychosocial 128
  technical 128–9
suitability of long-term strategic plans 75–7
Summers, Larry 306
Sun Tzu 6
Surie, G. 282
surveys 176
Sutton, R. 179
Sveiby, K.E. 116
Sword, L.D. 281
SWOT analysis 76
system dynamics in learning organisation 100–3
  feedback processes 102–3
  nonllinearity 100–1
  principles 101–2
  production and distribution chains 101
System of System Methodologies (SOSM) 210
systemic intervention in critical systems thinking 208–9
systems 187–91
  different meanings of 187–90
  and human nature 316–17
  as management tool 190–1
  as 'wholes' 401
systems analysis 9
systems dynamics 55, 56
systems theory 9
systems thinking 58–9, 453
  dualistic (Kant) 54
  and human systems 54–6
  in organisations 56–8
  second-order 201–12
systemtic approach 44
systemtic processes
  entities in 321–2
  and responsive processes 320–3

tacit knowledge 116–18, 454
Tajfel, H. 215

Takeuchi, H. 116, 118, 120, 273
task systems 136–7
Tawady, K. 83
Taylor, C. 417, 459
Taylor, F. 56, 57
Taylor, J. 386
Taylor, S.E. 215
Taylor, W.A. 181
team learning 110–14, 453
    shared models in 110–12
teamwork in scientific management 57
technical rationality 154, 157, 423
technical subsystems 128–9
technology in strategic choice theory 448–51
teleological causality 53
tendency to act, attitude as 355
Terry, D.J. 215
thematic patterning of conversation .339–41, 467
themes
    dynamics of 410–11
    emergence of in conversations 403–11
    legitimate and shadow 403–9
        deviance example 406–7
        equal opportunities example 403–6
        innovation example 407
        public and hidden transcripts 407–9
Thietart, R.A. 220–1, 271–2
Thomas, D.A. 193
Thomas, H. 43
Thompson, J.D. 156
Tichy, G. 183
Tilles, S. 13
time
    and responsive processes thinking 318–20
    in strategy processes 159–61
Tolbert, P.S. 157
Total Quality Management (TQM) 181
Total Systems Intervention (TSI) 210
Townley, B. 223
transformation
    in conversation 344–5
    in learning 113
transformative causality 252–3, 467–8
    modelling in 431
    and responsive processes 300, 301, 317
trial-and-error action 151, 152–5
    innovation processes 155
    logical incrementalism 154–5
Trist, E.L. 128–9, 135
Truss, C. 182
Tsoukas, H. 118, 415
Tuden, A. 156

turn-taking/turn-making in conversation 337–9
Turner, J.C. 215
Turquet, P. 134
Tushman, M.L. 157
Tustin, A. 55, 100
Twomey, D.F. 279

uncertainty
    in nature 236
    in strategic choice theory 87–8
    in strategic decision making 153
unconscious organisations 409–10
unconscious processes 130–1, 135–8
    in organisational psychodynamics 135
unpredictability 220–3
    managers and 480–3
unstable stability 236

value chain analysis 76
value work 190
values 379–81
    and norms 381–2
Van de Ven, A.H. 155, 163, 175
van Iverson, A. 390
van Knippenberg, A. 215
Varela, F.J. 32, 105, 221
Veblen, T. 254
Venkatraman, N. 157
vested interests on organisational learning
        114–16
    authoritarian use of power 114–15
    collegial use of power 115
    power vacuums 115–16
Vroom, V.H. 84
Vygotsky, L.S. 165, 214

Walker, R.M. 181
Waterman, R.H. 12, 14, 43, 72, 81–2, 178–9
Waters, J.A. 43, 99, 149, 484
Weaver, W. 55, 81
Webster, G. 51
Wenger, E. 7, 120, 217, 218–19
Wensing, M. 180
Wernerfelt, B. 86
Westphal, J.D. 177
Wheatley, M.J. 275–6, 280
Wheeler, W. 254
White, K.M. 215
White, W.J. 215
Whitehead, A.N. 254, 320
Whittington, R. 44, 162–3, 165, 168, 169
'wholes' as systems 401, 470

Wiener, N. 55, 66
Wilkinson, B. 223
Williamson, O.E. 212
Willmott, H. 213, 223
Wiltbank, R. 220
Winklevoss, T. & C. 305, 306
Winnicott, D.W. 143
Winter, S.G. 43, 163
Wolfram, S. 16

Wood, D.R. 176
Wooldridge, B. 161
Wright, G.H. 181

Yetton, P.W. 84

Zucker, L. 213
Zucker, L.G. 157
Zuckerberg, Mark 304–8